DEPARTMENT OF CORRECTIONS

STATE OF KANSAS

ILLINOIS CORRECTIONAL INDUSTRIES

NEVADA CORRECTIONS

THE GREAT SEAL OF THE STATE OF NEVADA

ARKANSAS DEPARTMENT OF CORRECTION

HONOR INTEGRITY PUBLIC SERVICE

ACCREDITED ACA

AMERICAN CORRECTIONAL ASSOCIATION

ALABAMA DEPT. OF CORRECTIONS

ALABAMA GREAT SEAL

STATE OF NEBRASKA

CORRECTIONAL SERVICES

ILLINOIS SERVING JUSTICE

SEAL OF THE STATE OF ILLINOIS

SERVING ILLINOIS CORRECTIONS

NEW HAMPSHIRE DEPARTMENT OF CORRECTIONS

STATE OF VERMONT DEPARTMENT OF CORRECTIONS

VERMONT

WEST VIRGINIA STATE OF WEST VIRGINIA MONTANI SEMPER LIBERI DIVISION OF CORRECTIONS

JUNE 20 1863

WISCONSIN DEPARTMENT OF CORRECTIONS

Corrections
in the 21st Century

eighth edition

Frank Schmalleger, PhD
Distinguished Professor Emeritus
University of North Carolina at Pembroke

John Ortiz Smykla, PhD
Director and Professor
Florida Atlantic University

CORRECTIONS IN THE 21ST CENTURY, EIGHTH EDITION

Published by McGraw-Hill Education, 2 Penn Plaza, New York, NY 10121. Copyright © 2017 by McGraw-Hill Education. All rights reserved. Printed in the United States of America. Previous editions © 2015, 2013, and 2011. No part of this publication may be reproduced or distributed in any form or by any means, or stored in a database or retrieval system, without the prior written consent of McGraw-Hill Education, including, but not limited to, in any network or other electronic storage or transmission, or broadcast for distance learning.

Some ancillaries, including electronic and print components, may not be available to customers outside the United States.

This book is printed on acid-free paper.

1 2 3 4 5 6 7 8 9 LWI 21 20 19 18 17 16

ISBN 978-1-259-82401-2
MHID 1-259-82401-2

Chief Product Officer, SVP Products & Markets: *G. Scott Virkler*
Vice President, General Manager, Products & Markets: *Michael Ryan*
Vice President, Content Design & Delivery: *Kimberly Meriwether David*
Managing Director: *David Patterson*
Brand Manager: *Penina Braffman*
Product Developer: *Jamie Laferrera*
Marketing Manager: *Meredith Leo*
Director, Content Design & Delivery: *Terri Schiesl*
Program Manager: *Jennifer Shekleton*
Content Project Managers: *Heather Ervolino, Katie Klochan*
Buyer: *Susan K. Culbertson*
Content Licensing Specialists: *Lori Slattery (Text)*
Cover Image: Source: Adapted from "Mass Incarceration: The Whole Pie 2016", Prison Policy Initiative, http://www.prisonpolicy.org/reports/pie2016.html; Corrections Professionalism logo © Jonathon Smykla
Compositor: *SPi Global*
Printer: *LSC Communications*

All credits appearing on page or at the end of the book are considered to be an extension of the copyright page.

Library of Congress Cataloging-in-Publication Data

Names: Schmalleger, Frank, author. | Smykla, John Ortiz, author.
Title: Corrections in the 21st century / Frank Schmalleger, PhD,
   Distinguished Professor Emeritus, University of North Carolina at
   Pembroke, John Ortiz Smykla, PhD, Distinguished University Professor,
   University of West Florida.
Description: Eighth edition. | New York, NY : McGraw-Hill Education, [2016]
Identifiers: LCCN 2016025410 | ISBN 9781259824012 (alk. paper)
Subjects: LCSH: Corrections—United States. | Corrections—Vocational
   guidance—United States.
Classification: LCC HV9471 .S36 2016 | DDC 364.6023/73--dc23 LC record
available at https://lccn.loc.gov/2016025410

mheducation.com/highered

dedication }

For my granddaughters, Ava and Malia

—Frank Schmalleger

For my wife, Evelyn, my granddaughter, Harper Grace, and my grandson, Holden Fate

—John Smykla

Expanded Contents

PART 2 COMMUNITY CORRECTIONS 69

- New QR codes that direct students to videos and podcasts to extend the ideas discussed in the chapter.
- Data revision on jails: occupancy, number of public versus private, and size, location, and budgets.
- Updated material on California's Realignment.
- Updated discussion of promising approaches to reentry well suited to the jail setting.
- Revised research on jail industry programs making headlines around the country.

Chapter 7

- New web-based videos featuring the authors have been added to the chapter. They are entitled *Prison Industries* and *Prison Overcrowding*.
- New and significantly shortened chapter merging Chapters 7 and 13.
- New chapter-opening story.
- Updated coverage of the effect of cuts in corrections budgets on personnel, salaries, benefits, overtime, programs, facilities, and services and how states are turning to evidence-based practices, the federal Second Chance Act, drug courts, veterans courts, reentry courts, technology, and assistance from professional associations and advocacy groups for guidance on the effective use of the funds they have.
- Latest data on characteristics of adults under jurisdiction of state and federal prisons.
- Revised discussion of how the movement in EBC and the economic downturn have caused a decline in state prison populations.
- New QR codes that direct students to videos and podcasts to extend the ideas discussed in the chapter.
- New research on states with the most expensive prisoners.
- Updated data on the cost of state and federal incarceration.
- Updated discussion of states' use of Justice Reinvestment.
- Expanded coverage of inmates' use of cell phones in prison, including new policies to curb their use and new federal legislation making it a felony for inmates to possess them or a wireless device.
- Expanded coverage of the use of security technology to recognize, track, and detect prison offenders and officers and added discussion of the overuse of "virtual visiting."

- Introduction of the Solitary Confinement Study and Reform Act of 2015 to reform the practice of solitary confinement in the U.S. federal prison system.
- New end-of-chapter review material.

Chapter 8

- New web-based videos featuring the authors have been added to the chapter. They are entitled *Parole and Reentry* and *Parole: The Good and the Bad.*
- New chapter-opening story.
- Chapter significantly shortened.
- Updated material in response to the economic crisis on how states are handling technical violations of the formerly incarcerated.
- New exhibit summarizing Second Chance Act offender reentry demonstration projects.
- New coverage of the principles and programs for successful reentry from corrections scholars Jeremy Travis, Ed Latessa, and Elizabeth Gaynes.
- Expanded coverage on the needs of prisoners returning to their communities, "ban the box," and the Second Chance Act.
- New coverage of the National Institute of Corrections tool for structured decision making to serve as an aid in determining parole prognosis (potential risk of parole violation).
- New research on reentry problems for black women.
- New QR codes that direct students to videos and podcasts to extend the ideas discussed in the chapter.
- New exhibit and discussion of the signs that as mandatory minimum sentences and three-strikes laws are rolled back, parole boards might reemerge with more power.
- Revised and expanded analysis of the important topic of what works for parole supervision.
- Latest data on characteristics of adults on parole are included.
- Updated and expanded coverage on the question, "Can parolees vote?"
- New material on reentry court evaluations noting the randomized study being conducted for the U.S. District Court for the Northern District of Florida, the only one of its kind in the United States.

Chapter 9

- New web-based videos featuring the authors have been added to the chapter. They are entitled *Staff Subculture* and *Prisoner Radicalization*.
- New chapter-opening story on the Pew Charitable Trusts reporting on the shortage of qualified correctional officers across the country.
- New exhibit detailing correctional officer pay in various jurisdictions and showing that many COs can earn substantially more than their base pay through overtime work.
- Revised and expanded section on correctional officer stress to include discussion of the Desert Waters Correctional Outreach organization.
- New section on "Fraternization with Inmates," using the case of Joyce Mitchell (from New York) as an illustration.

Chapter 10

- Revised chapter-opening story.
- Updated data reported under the federal Survey of Sexual Victimization in correctional facilities.
- New web-based videos featuring the authors have been added to the chapter. They are entitled *Inmate Subculture* and *Inmate Roles*.
- Updated data on imprisoned women and the growth of women's imprisonment.
- New figure showing the increase in women's incarceration.
- "Gender-responsiveness" added and defined as a key term.

Chapter 11

- Discussion of a new U.S. Supreme Court case, *Holt* v. *Hobbs* (2015), involving an inmate's claims for permitted religious practice.
- A new web-based video featuring the authors has been added to the chapter. It is entitled *Prisoner Rights*.
- Discussion of an older case, that of *Sostre* v. *McGinnis* (1964), to illustrate the historical "hands-off" approach characteristic of federal courts prior to the 1970s.
- New photos added to enhance the visual appeal of the chapter.

Chapter 12

- New chapter-opening story.
- Significantly shortened chapter.
- Updated coverage on how states are addressing the health care needs of special-needs inmates.
- Latest data on the prevalence of HIV in prison.

- New career profile of Jose Ortiz-Cruz, Programs Coordinator for the Charlotte County Sheriff's Office, Punta Gorda, Florida.
- Key findings from the American Correctional Association's survey of inmate mental health care.
- Latest data on the characteristics of older inmates (the "silver tsunami" of aging prisoners) and new discussion of why states are not using their compassionate, medical, or geriatric prisoner release laws.
- New QR codes that direct students to videos and podcasts to extend the ideas discussed in the chapter.

ORGANIZATION

The Eighth Edition of *Corrections in the 21st Century* has been shortened to better reflect aspects of the correctional process. Chapters are grouped into four parts, each of which is described in detail in the following paragraphs.

Part One, "Introduction to Corrections," provides an understanding of corrections by explaining the problem of mass incarceration and the goals underlying the correctional enterprise and by describing the how and why of criminal punishments. Part One identifies professionalism as the key to managing correctional personnel, facilities, and populations successfully. Standard-setting organizations such as the American Correctional Association, the American Jail Association, the American Probation and Parole Association, and the National Commission on Correctional Health Care are identified, and the importance of professional ethics for correctional occupations and correctional administrators is emphasized.

Part Two, "Community Corrections," explains what happens to most convicted offenders, including diversion (the suspension of formal criminal proceedings before conviction in exchange for the defendant's participation in treatment), probation, and intermediate sanctions.

Part Three, "Institutional Corrections," provides a detailed description of jails, prisons, and parole. The reentry challenges facing inmates released from prisons are explained. Education, vocational preparation, and drug treatment programs that are intended to prevent reoffending also are explored.

Part Four, "The Prison World" provides an overview of life inside prison from the points of view of both inmates and staff. Part Four also describes the responsibilities and challenges surrounding the staff role. Chapter 12 focuses attention on special correctional populations, including inmates who are elderly, have HIV/AIDS, are substance abusers, and are mentally and physically challenged. We have chosen to integrate our coverage of women in corrections—including information about the important NIC report titled "Gender Responsive Strategies: Research, Practice, and Guiding Principles for Women Offenders"—throughout the body of the text rather than isolating it in Chapter 12.

PEDAGOGICAL AIDS

Working together, the authors and editor have developed a learning system designed to help students excel in the corrections course. In addition to the many changes already mentioned, we have included a wealth of new photographs to make the book even more inviting and relevant.

To this same end, our real-world chapter-opening vignettes give the material a fresh flavor intended to motivate students to read on; our photo captions, which raise thought-provoking questions, actively engage students in the learning process. Carefully updated tables and figures highlight and amplify the text coverage. And chapter outlines, objectives, and reviews, plus marginal definitions and an end-of-book glossary, all help students master the material.

The Schmalleger/Smykla learning system goes well beyond these essential tools, however. As mentioned, *Corrections in the 21st Century* offers a unique emphasis on corrections professionalism, an emphasis that has prompted us to create a number of innovative learning tools that focus on the real world of corrections:

- A concentration on *Evidence-Based Corrections*—What actually works in correctional settings? that is, what correctional programs are effective in reducing recidivism and in preventing future crimes? Evidence-based corrections is an exciting new development in the corrections field, and a number of agencies, institutions, and organizations now emphasize the use of scientific evidence. Evidence-based policy, which builds on evidence-based corrections, is an approach that helps people make well-informed decisions about policies and programs by putting the best available evidence from research at the heart of policy development and implementation.
- *Career Profiles*—enlightening minibiographies of corrections professionals, such as a parole officer, a victims' advocate, a corrections officer, a youth counselor, and a substance abuse manager.
- *Economic Realities and Corrections*–boxes throughout the text to recognize budgetary constraints affecting correctional agencies nationwide, highlighting innovative evidence-based practices demonstrating "what works."
- *Ethics and Professionalism*—boxes that highlight ethical codes and critical concerns

from America's premier corrections-related professional associations. Included are features from the American Correctional Association, the American Jail Association, the American Probation and Parole Association, International Association of Community Corrections, the International Association of Correctional Training Personnel, National Association of Pretrial Services Agencies, and others. Included in each Ethics and Professionalism box are author-created Ethical Dilemmas, which present students with ethical questions from the corrections field and guide them to an insightful resolution. Ethical Dilemmas are supplemented with web-based resources maintained by the authors and specifically selected to help students navigate particular ethics-related issues.

- CrimeSolutions.Gov - boxes that use the National Institute of Justice's research to rate the effectiveness of programs and practices in achieving criminal justice related outcomes in order to inform practitioners and policy makers about what works, what doesn't, and what's promising in criminal justice.

In addition to the features we have developed to further our goal of creating a uniquely practical, professionally oriented text, we also have included end-of-chapter review material to help students master the concepts and principles developed in the chapter:

- *Chapter Summary*—a valuable learning tool organized into sections that mirror the chapter-opening objectives exactly; the summary restates all of the chapter's most critical points.
- *Key Terms*—a comprehensive list of the terms defined in the margins of the chapter, complete with page references to make it easy for students to go back and review further.
- *Questions for Review*—objective study questions (exactly mirroring the chapter-opening objectives and summary) that allow students to test their knowledge and prepare for exams.
- *Thinking Critically About Corrections*—broad-based questions that challenge students to think critically about chapter concepts and issues.
- *On-the-Job Decision Making*—unique experiential exercises that enable students to apply what they have learned in the chapter to the daily work of correctional personnel.
- *QR Codes*—unique machine-readable codes in every chapter directing students to videos and podcasts that extend the ideas discussed in the chapter, providing a truly interactive learning experience.

McGraw-Hill Connect®
Learn Without Limits

Connect is a teaching and learning platform that is proven to deliver better results for students and instructors.

Connect empowers students by continually adapting to deliver precisely what they need, when they need it, and how they need it, so your class time is more engaging and effective.

73% of instructors who use **Connect** require it; instructor satisfaction **increases** by 28% when **Connect** is required.

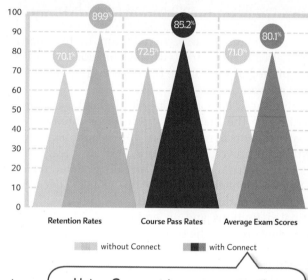

Connect's Impact on Retention Rates, Pass Rates, and Average Exam Scores

Using **Connect** improves retention rates by **19.8%**, passing rates by **12.7%**, and exam scores by **9.1%**.

Analytics

Connect Insight®

Connect Insight is Connect's new one-of-a-kind visual analytics dashboard that provides at-a-glance information regarding student performance, which is immediately actionable. By presenting assignment, assessment, and topical performance results together with a time metric that is easily visible for aggregate or individual results, Connect Insight gives the user the ability to take a just-in-time approach to teaching and learning, which was never before available. Connect Insight presents data that helps instructors improve class performance in a way that is efficient and effective.

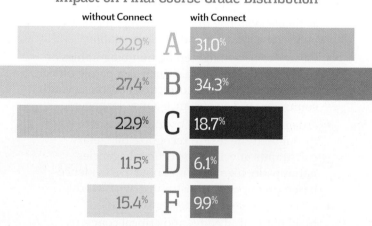

Impact on Final Course Grade Distribution

Adaptive

THE **ADAPTIVE** **READING EXPERIENCE** DESIGNED TO TRANSFORM THE WAY STUDENTS READ

More students earn **A's** and **B's** when they use McGraw-Hill Education **Adaptive** products.

SmartBook®

Proven to help students improve grades and study more efficiently, SmartBook contains the same content within the print book, but actively tailors that content to the needs of the individual. SmartBook's adaptive technology provides precise, personalized instruction on what the student should do next, guiding the student to master and remember key concepts, targeting gaps in knowledge and offering customized feedback, and driving the student toward comprehension and retention of the subject matter. Available on tablets, SmartBook puts learning at the student's fingertips—anywhere, anytime.

Over **8 billion questions** have been answered, making McGraw-Hill Education products more intelligent, reliable, and precise.

www.mheducation.com

connect®

The Eighth Edition of *Corrections in the 21th Century* is now available online with Connect, McGraw-Hill Education's integrated assignment and assessment platform. Connect also offers SmartBook for the new edition, which is the first adaptive reading experience proven to improve grades and help students study more effectively. All of the title's website and ancillary content is also available through Connect, including:

- A full Test Bank of multiple choice questions that test students on central concepts and ideas in each chapter.
- An Instructor's Manual for each chapter with full chapter outlines, sample test questions, and discussion topics.
- Lecture Slides for instructor use in class.
- Web-based instructional videos featuring the authors, and emphasizing key concepts.

IN APPRECIATION

Writing a textbook requires a great deal of help and support. We gratefully acknowledge the contributions of the following individuals who helped in the development of this textbook.

Steve Abrams, Ret.
California Department of Corrections and
   Rehabilitation
Santa Rosa, California

Stanley E. Adelman
University of Arkansas School of Law
Little Rock, Arkansas
University of Tulsa College of Law
Tulsa, Oklahoma

Colleen Andrews
Ozarks Technical Community College
Springfield, Missouri

Cassandra Atkin-Plunk
Florida Atlantic University
Boca Raton, Florida

John Augustine
Triton College
River Grove, Illinois

Tom Austin, Ret.
Shippensburg University
Shippensburg, Pennsylvania

Ken Barnes
Arizona Western College
Yuma, Arizona

Jeri Barnett
Virginia Western Community College
Roanoke, Virginia

Rose Johnson Bigler
Curry College
Milton, Massachusetts

Kathy J. Black-Dennis
University of Louisville
Louisville, Kentucky

Robert Bohm, Ret.
University of Central Florida
Orlando, Florida

Paul Bowdre
SUNY Canton
Canton, New York

David A. Bowers Jr.
University of South Alabama
Mobile, Alabama

Greg Brown
Westwood College of Technology
Denver, Colorado

David C. Cannon
Henry Ford College
Dearborn, Michigan

David E. Carter
Southern Oregon University
Ashland, Oregon

Jason Clark-Miller
Tarrant County College
Fort Worth, Texas

Lonnie DePriest
Albany Technical College
Albany, Georgia

Kenneth L. Done
Coahoma Community College
Clarksdale, Mississippi

Vicky Dorworth
Montgomery College
Rockville, Maryland

Carrie L. Dunson
Central Missouri State University
Warrensburg, Missouri

Michael Earll
Western Technical College
La Crosse, Wisconsin

Hilary Estes
Southern Illinois University, Carbondale
Carbondale, Illinois

Robert Figlestahler
Eastern Kentucky University
Richmond, Kentucky

Lynn Fortney, Ret.
EBSCO Subscription Services
Birmingham, Alabama

Harold A. Frossard
Moraine Valley Community College
Palos Hills, Illinois

Michelle Furlow
Moraine Valley Community College
Palos Hills, Illinois

Don Drennon
Gala Federal Bureau of Prisons
Atlanta, Georgia

Donna Hale Ret.
Shippensburg University
Shippensburg, Pennsylvania

Homer C. Hawkins
Michigan State University
East Lansing, Michigan

Nancy L. Hogan
Ferris State University
Big Rapids, Michigan

Ronald G. Iacovetta
Wichita State University
Wichita, Kansas

Connie Ireland
California State University, Long Beach
Long Beach, California

James L. Jengeleski. Ret.
Shippensburg University
Shippensburg, Pennyslvania

Brad Johnson
Atlanta, Georgia

Kathrine Johnson
University of West Florida
Ft. Walton Beach, Florida

John Calvin Jones
North Carolina A&T State University
Greensboro, North Carolina

Kay King
Johnson County Community College
Overland Park, Kansas

Mike Klemp-North
Ferris State University
Big Rapids, Michigan

Julius Koefoed Kirkwood
Community College
Cedar Rapids, Iowa

Michael Kwan
Salt Lake Community College
Taylorsville, Utah

James Lasley
California State University, Fullerton
Fullerton, California

Walter B. Lewis
St. Louis Community College at Meramec
Kirkwood, Missouri

Shelley Listwan
Kent State University
Kent, Ohio

Jess Maghan
Forum for Comparative Correction
Chester, Connecticut

Preston S. Marks
Keiser University

Laurie A. Michelman
Cayuga Community College
Auburn, New York

Rosie Miller
Coahoma Community College
Clarksdale, Mississippi

Alvin Mitchell
Delgado Community College
New Orleans, Louisiana

Etta Morgan
Pennsylvania State University
Capital College, Pennsylvania

Kathleen Nicolaides
University of North Carolina, Charlotte
Charlotte, North Carolina

Sarah Nordin
Solano Community College
Suisun City, California

Michael F. Perna
Broome Community College
Binghamton, New York

Terry L. Pippin
College of Southern Nevada
Henderson, Nevada

Lisa Pitts
Washburn University
Topeka, Kansas

Scott Plutchak
University of Alabama at Birmingham
Birmingham, Alabama

Bobby B. Polk
Metropolitan Community College
Omaha, Nebraska

Wayne D. Posner
East Los Angeles College
Monterey Park, California

Melissa L. Ricketts
Shippensburg University
Shippensburg, Pennsylvania

Barbara R. Russo
Wayne Community College
Goldsboro, North Carolina

John Sloan
University of Alabama at Birmingham
Birmingham, Alabama

Larry E. Spencer
Alabama State University
Montgomery, Alabama

Anthony C. Trevelino
Camden County College
Blackwood, New Jersey

Sheryl Van Horne
Radford University
Radford, Virginia

Shela R. Van Ness
University of Tennessee at Chattanooga
Chattanooga, Tennessee

Gennaro F. Vito
University of Louisville
Louisville, Kentucky

Brenda Vos
University of North Florida
Jacksonville, Florida

Kiesha Warren-Gordon
Ball State University
Muncie, Indiana

Anthony White
Illinois Central College
East Peoria, Illinois

Earl White
Illinois Central College
Peoria, Illinois

Ed Whittle
Florida Metropolitan University at
   Tampa College
Tampa, Florida

Beth Wiersma
University of Nebraska at Kearney
Kearney, Nebraska

Robert R. Wiggins
Cedarville College
Cedarville, Ohio

Jeffrey Zack
Fayetteville Technical Community College
Fayetteville, North Carolina

Kristen M. Zgoba
Rutgers University
Piscataway, New Jersey

Dawn Zobel
Federal Bureau of Prisons
Alderson, West Virginia

Finally, we want to acknowledge the special debt that we owe to the McGraw-Hill team, including brand manager Penina Braffman for keeping the project on track; marketing manager Meredith Leo for seeing value in this textbook; the developmental editing team at ansrsource for their attention to the many day-to-day details that a project like this entails; project manager Heather Ervolino; buyer Susan K. Culbertson; full-service project manager Suresh Rajamoni; content licensing specialist Lori Slattery; photo researcher LouAnn Wilson; copy editor Sue Nodine; and indexer Judy Lyon Davis. The professional vision, guidance, and support of these dedicated professionals helped bring this project to fruition. A hearty "thank you" to all.

Frank Schmalleger

John Smykla

Introduction to Corrections

Part One develops an understanding of corrections by examining the purposes of corrections and by describing the forces molding contemporary corrections.

Today, crime rates are falling but the number of people under correctional supervision (on probation or parole or in jail or prison) has only started to decline from historical highs. Get-tough-on-crime attitudes, the War on Drugs, and the reduction in the use of discretionary parole releases explain what some have seen as the overuse of imprisonment in the past two decades. The current period of mass incarceration is the result.

Professionalism is the key to effectively managing correctional populations—and that is especially true today in today's mass incarceration era. Standard-setting organizations such as the American Correctional Association, the American Jail Association, the American Probation and Parole Association, and the National Commission on Correctional Health Care offer detailed sets of written principles for correctional occupations and correctional administrators.

Nevertheless, professional credentialing in corrections is relatively new.

The professional nature of corrections is also seen in the way sanctions are developed. From a time when theory and practice advocated indeterminate sentences to the legislatively mandated determinate sentences of today, correctional decision makers have had to use their knowledge of human behavior, philosophy, and law to construct sanctions that are fair and just. The correctional goals of retribution, just deserts, deterrence, incapacitation, rehabilitation, and restoration have produced the sanctions of probation, intermediate sanctions, jail, prison, parole, and capital punishment.

Part One also discusses evidence-based corrections (EBC) or the use of social scientific techniques to determine the most workable and cost-effective programs and initiatives. Choosing the best programs means understanding the political, social, economic, human, and moral consequences of crime control. For that reason, corrections is a field in which complex decision making requires the skills of trained professional staff and administrators.

© Photo by Scott Olson/Getty Images

[1]

CORRECTIONS
An Overview

CHAPTER OBJECTIVES

After completing this chapter you should be able to do the following:

1. Describe the corrections explosion of the past 40 years, including the recent leveling off of correctional populations.

2. Describe how crime is measured in the United States, and list the kinds of crimes that cause people to enter correctional programs and institutions.

3. List and describe the various components of the criminal justice system, including the major components of the corrections subsystem.

> *The growth in incarceration rates in the United States over the past 40 years is historically unprecedented and internationally unique.*
>
> —National Research Council, 2014

In 2015, a drone dropped a package of heroin, marijuana, and tobacco into the prison yard at Ohio's Mansfield Correctional Institution, leading to a fight between as many as 75 inmates who struggled over the drugs. The drone, which was captured on security cameras, flew off and disappeared—leaving investigators few clues about where it originated.[1]

Drone-delivered contraband is just one of the many issues facing correctional administrators today. In a typical year, for example, inmates across the country file around 175,000 fraudulent income tax returns, claiming refunds totaling more than $2.5 billion.[2]

Similarly, prisoners' use of outlawed cell phones to make calls from inside of correctional institutions has grown exponentially as the number of phones in general circulation has expanded. Recently, for example, California correctional officers seized nearly 6,000 banned cell phones from the state's prisoners, while officials with Maryland's Department of Public Safety and Correctional Services confiscated over 3,600 cell phones in the past three years.[3]

A remote-controlled drone. How do drones illustrate some of the problems that prison administrators face today?
© Doxieone Photography/Getty Images RF

Drug-dropping drones, illicit cell phone usage, fraudulent tax return filing, and similar other outlawed[4] activities that occur behind prison bars illustrate the close connection that inmates retain to the outside society, and raise the question, "Do prisons really make us safe?"[5] What about other corrections programs, such as probation, parole, jails, alternative sentencing programs, and institutions for juvenile offenders? If they make our society a safer place in which to live, then the recent and rapid growth in correctional populations that took place over the past 30 years—and which is discussed in the next section of this chapter—is understandable. If they don't contribute much to safety and security, however, then we must look elsewhere to understand why such rapid growth occurred.

The Guardian, "Drone's Heroin Delivery to Ohio Prison Yard Prompts Fights Among Inmates" http://www.theguardian.com/us-news/2015/aug/04/drone-drug-delivery-ohio-prison-fight-heroin-marijuana-tobacco

THE CORRECTIONS EXPLOSION: WHERE DO WE GO NOW?

`CO1-1`

One amazing fact stands out from all the contemporary information about corrections: While serious **crime** in the United States consistently declined throughout much of the 1990s, and while such declines continued into the first decades of the 21st century, the number of people under correctional supervision in this country—not just the number of convicted offenders sent to **prison**—continued to climb, and only started to level off after 2010. Crime rates are approximately 20 percent lower today than they were in 1980. In fact, they are near their lowest level in 25 years.

Please read the National Research Council's 2014 report, The Growth of Incarceration in the United States: Exploring Causes and Consequences, at http://www.nap.edu/read/18613/chapter/1#ii, or scan this code with the QR app on your smartphone or digital device to view it.

crime

A violation of a criminal law.

prison

A state or federal confinement facility that has custodial authority over adults sentenced to confinement.

mass incarceration

The overuse of correctional facilities, particularly prisons, in the United States—as determined by historical and cross-cultural standards. We live in an era of mass incarceration.

But the number of people on probation is up almost 300 percent since 1980, the nation's prison population has increased by more than 400 percent, and the number of persons on parole more than doubled. Between 1980 and 2014, the federal imprisonment rate increased 500 percent, from 11 inmates for every 100,000 U.S. residents to 68. During the same period, annual spending on the federal prison system rose 600 percent, from $970 million to more than $6.7 billion in inflation-adjusted dollars. Prison expenditures grew from 14 percent of the Justice Department's total outlays to 23 percent.[6] States, like the federal government, recorded sharp increases in incarceration and corrections costs over the past three decades. However, between 2007 and 2015, some states made research-driven policy changes to control prison growth, reduce recidivism, and contain costs. While the federal imprisonment rate continued to rise during that period, the state rate declined slightly. Numbers like these show that we live in an era of **mass incarceration**, and the provision of correctional services of all kinds has become a major strain on governments at all levels. Exhibit 1–1 illustrates trends in national prison populations.

The question is, Why? Why did the correctional population increase so dramatically in the face of declining crime rates? And why is the United States now in the midst of an era of mass incarceration? The answer to these questions, like the answers to most societal enigmas, is far from simple, and it has a number of dimensions.

First, it is important to recognize that get-tough-on-crime laws, such as the three-strikes (and two-strikes) laws that were enacted in many states in the mid-1990s, fueled rapid increases in prison populations. The conservative attitudes that gave birth to those laws are still with us, and most of the increase in state prison populations has come from imprisoning more people for violent crimes for longer periods of time.[7] At the federal level, the Violent Crime Control and Law Enforcement Act of 1994 encouraged

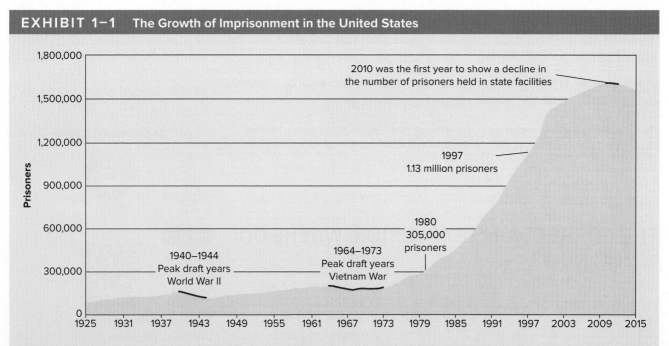

EXHIBIT 1–1   The Growth of Imprisonment in the United States

2010 was the first year to show a decline in the number of prisoners held in state facilities

1997
1.13 million prisoners

1980
305,000 prisoners

1940–1944
Peak draft years
World War II

1964–1973
Peak draft years
Vietnam War

Source: Bureau of Justice Statistics, *Crime and Justice Atlas 2000* (Washington, DC: Bureau of Justice Statistics, 2001), pp. 42–43; and Danielle Kaeble, Lauren Glaze, Anastasios Tsoutis in *Correctional Populations in the United States, 2014* (Washington, DC: Bureau of Justice Statistics, 2015).

EXHIBIT 1-2	Number of State Prisoners by Offense, 2014		
Type of Offense	**All**	**Male**	**Female**
Violent offenses	704,800	670,900	34,000
Property offenses	255,600	229,500	26,000
Drug offenses	208,000	186,000	22,000
Public-order offenses	146,300	137,900	8,400

Source: Adapted from E. Ann Carson, *Prisoners in 2014* (Washington, DC: Bureau of Justice Statistics, 2015).

Note: Detail may not sum to total due to rounding.

longer prison sentences for more crimes and led to the adoption of harsher sentencing regimes throughout the nation.[8]

A second reason correctional populations have rapidly increased can be found in the nation's War on Drugs. The War on Drugs led to the arrest and conviction of many offenders, resulting in larger correctional populations in nearly every jurisdiction (especially within the federal correctional system). A 2015 report by the congressional Colson Task Force on Federal Corrections, for example, found that "The biggest driver of growth" in the federal prison population was "federally sentenced drug offenders, almost all of whom were convicted of drug trafficking." Many drug offenders—especially traffickers—are sentenced to lengthy prison terms, further increasing the number of people behind bars, and many such offenders have multiple convictions, including use (or possession) of a firearm during a drug transaction.[9] In Exhibit 1–2, compare the total number of individuals incarcerated for drug offenses with, for example, the total incarcerated for property offenses. Although they account for a large portion of the nation's correctional population, drug arrests do not figure into the FBI's calculations of the nation's rate of serious crimes. Hence, the War on Drugs goes a long way toward explaining the growth in correctional populations even while the rate of "serious crime" in the United States appeared to be declining.

Third, parole authorities, fearing civil liability and public outcry, became increasingly reluctant to release inmates. This contributed to a further expansion of prison populations.

Fourth, as some observers have noted, the corrections boom created its own growth dynamic.[10] As ever increasing numbers of people are placed on probation, the likelihood of probation violations increases. Prison sentences for more violators result in larger prison populations. When inmates are released from prison, they swell the numbers of those on parole, leading to a larger number of parole violations, which in turn fuels further prison growth. Statistics show that the number of criminals being sent to prison for at least the second time has increased steadily, accounting for approximately 35 percent of the total number of admissions.[11]

One 2015 analysis of the dramatic increase in imprisonment, found that it "was not driven by a centralized national-level strategy for dealing with crime and was not based on a coherent body of empirical knowledge demonstrating that prisons improved public safety."[12] Instead, said the report, "it was the product of layers of legislative decisions, primarily enacted at the state level, to charge and imprison more offenders, increase sentences, limit prison releases, and expand" prison capacity. These decisions led to a new era in which prisons became primary weapons in the nation's war on crime.

U.S. correctional populations have grown dramatically over the past 30 years, as this image of inmates living in a modified gymnasium at the Mule Creek State Prison in Ione, California, illustrates. What factors led to a substantial increase in the use of imprisonment in this country beginning in the 1980s?

© Justin Sullivan/Getty Images

Historical Roots of the Corrections Explosion

Seen historically, the growth of correctional populations may be merely the continuation of a long-term trend. A look at historical data shows that correctional populations continued to increase through widely divergent political eras and economic conditions. Census reports show an almost relentless increase in the rate of imprisonment over the past 160 years. In 1850, for example, only 29 people were imprisoned in this country for every 100,000 persons in the population.[13] By 1890, the rate had risen to 131 per 100,000. The rate grew slowly until 1980, when the rate of imprisonment in the United States stood at 153 per 100,000. At that point, a major shift toward imprisonment began. While crime rates rose sharply in the middle to late 1980s, the rate of imprisonment rose far more dramatically. Today, the rate of imprisonment in this country is around 612 per 100,000 persons—close to an all-time high.[14] Exhibit 1–3 illustrates changes in the rate of imprisonment over the past 160 years. Probation statistics—first available in 1935—show an even more amazing rate of growth. Although only 59,530 offenders were placed on probation throughout the United States in 1935, around 3.9 million people are on probation today.[15] Finally, it is worth noting that although prison populations finally started to decrease a few years ago, much of that decrease was due to initiatives such as California's realignment strategy (discussed elsewhere in this text), which repositioned sentenced inmates from state facilities to those at the county level—thus lowering the "official" rate of imprisonment, but not necessarily resulting in a decline in the number of people held behind bars.

Turning the Corner

While get-tough-on-crime attitudes continue to persist in American society today, they have largely been trumped by the economic realities brought on by the Great Recession of the early 21st century. State budgets have been hard pressed to continue funding prison expansion, and the number of

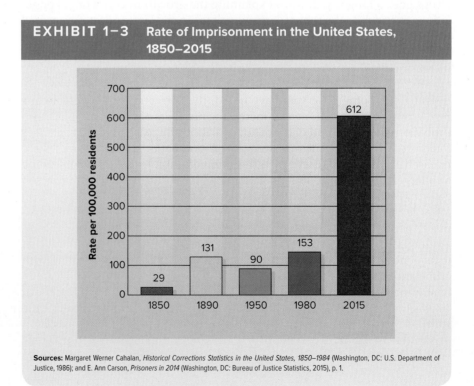

EXHIBIT 1–3 **Rate of Imprisonment in the United States, 1850–2015**

Sources: Margaret Werner Cahalan, *Historical Corrections Statistics in the United States, 1850–1984* (Washington, DC: U.S. Department of Justice, 1986); and E. Ann Carson, *Prisoners in 2014* (Washington, DC: Bureau of Justice Statistics, 2015), p. 1.

people behind bars began to show a slow decline beginning around 2010. Alternatives to imprisonment, most of which will be discussed in coming chapters, are many and include probation, fines, and community service—to which convicted offenders are being sentenced in increasing numbers. In order to reduce correctional expenditures even further, some states are using forms of early release from prison, shortening time served, reducing the period of probation or parole supervision, and shifting the responsibility of supervising convicted offenders to county-level governments (and away from state responsibility). We will examine these innovations at various places throughout this text, especially in a number of Economic Realities and Corrections boxes that are found in different chapters.

As states grappled with the economic realities of reduced revenues and constrained budgets, it became increasingly important to get the most "bang for the buck," so to speak, out of correctional programs. Moreover, responsible legislators and other policymakers are beginning to realize that spending policies of the past will not work in the future. Recently, in her presidential address to the Academy of Criminal Justice Sciences, Melissa Hickman Barlow outlined a plan for the implementation of **sustainable justice**. Barlow defined sustainable justice as "criminal laws and criminal justice institutions, policies, and practices that achieve justice in the present without compromising the ability of future generations to have the benefits of a just society."[16] Barlow's call for affordable justice, based on principles and operating practices that can be carried into the future without bankrupting generations yet to come, represents an important turning point in our nation's approach to corrections and other justice institutions.

As we will see in the next chapter, the evidence-based movement in corrections, which seeks to evaluate programs and services to see which are the most effective relative to their costs, plays a widening role in correctional administration today—and should contribute much to the call for sustainable justice.

Correctional Employment

Growing correctional populations and increasing budgets have led to a dramatically expanding correctional workforce and enhanced employment opportunities within the field. In 2015, for example, the Texas Department of Criminal Justice offered a $4,000 recruiting bonus for new correctional officers. It required a one-year commitment to work in a state corrections facility after hiring.[17]

sustainable justice

Criminal laws and criminal justice institutions, policies, and practices that achieve justice in the present without compromising the ability of future generations to have the benefits of a just society.

Scan this code with the QR app to hear Sentencing Project Director, Marc Mauer, discuss reducing prison populations in Texas in the face of budget constraints. The transcript of the interview can be read here: http://www.texastribune.org/texas-legislature/82nd-legislative-session/marc-mauer-the-tt-interview/

EXHIBIT 1-4	**Careers in Corrections**

Academic teacher	Field administrator	Psychologist
Activity therapy administrator	Fugitive apprehension officer	Recreation coordinator
Business manager	Human services counselor	Social worker
Case manager	Job placement officer	Statistician
Chaplain	Mental health clinician	Substance abuse counselor
Chemical dependency manager	Parole caseworker	Unit leader
Children's services counselor	Parole officer	Victim advocate
Classification officer	Presentence investigator	Vocational instructor
Clinical social worker	Probation officer	Warden/superintendent
Correctional officer	Program officer	Youth services coordinator
Dietary officer	Program specialist	Youth supervisor
Drug court coordinator	Programmer/analyst	

According to historical reports, persons employed in the corrections field totaled approximately 27,000 in 1950.[18] By 1975, the number had risen to about 75,000. Estimates published by the National Institute of Corrections (NIC) in 2014 show that a total of 761,355 government employees throughout the United States worked in corrections, with a total monthly payroll exceeding $3 billion.[19] NIC also found that the average hourly and annual wage for correctional officers and jailers was $20.94 and $43,550, respectively; for correctional first-line supervisors wages were $29.31 and $60,970, respectively; and for probation officers, it was $25.18 and $52,380, respectively.[20] Exhibit 1–4 shows some of the employment possibilities in corrections.

New prisons mean jobs and can contribute greatly to the health of local economies. Some economically disadvantaged towns—from Tupper Lake, in the Adirondack Mountains of upstate New York, to Edgefield, South Carolina—cashed in on the prison boom, having successfully competed to become sites for new prisons. Until recently, the competition for new prison facilities was reminiscent of the efforts states made years ago to attract new automobile factories and other industries.

CRIME AND CORRECTIONS

The crimes that bring people into the American correctional system include felonies, misdemeanors, and minor law violations that are sometimes called *infractions.*

Felonies are serious crimes. Murder, rape, aggravated assault, robbery, burglary, and arson are felonies in all jurisdictions within the United States, although the names for these crimes may differ from state to state. A general way to think about felonies is to remember that a **felony** is a serious crime whose commission can result in confinement in a state or federal correctional institution for more than a year.

In some states, a felony conviction can result in the loss of certain civil privileges. A few states make conviction of a felony and the resulting incarceration grounds for uncontested divorce. Others prohibit convicted felony offenders from running for public office or owning a firearm, and some exclude them from professions such as medicine, law, and police work.

Huge differences in the treatment of specific crimes exist among states. Some crimes classified as felonies in one part of the country may be misdemeanors in another. In still other states, they may not even be crimes at all! Such is the case with some drug law violations and with social order offenses such as homosexual acts, prostitution, and gambling.

Misdemeanors, which compose the second major crime category, are relatively minor violations of the criminal law. They include crimes such as petty theft (the theft of items of little worth), simple assault (in which the victim suffers no serious injury and in which none was intended), breaking and entering, the possession of burglary tools, disorderly conduct, disturbing the peace, filing a false crime report, and writing bad checks (although the amount for which the check is written may determine the classification of this offense). In general, misdemeanors can be thought of as any crime punishable by a year or less in confinement.

Within felony and misdemeanor categories, most states distinguish among degrees, or levels, of seriousness. Texas law, for example, establishes five felony classes and three classes of misdemeanor—intended to guide judges in assessing the seriousness of particular criminal acts. The Texas penal code then specifies categories into which given offenses fall.

felony

A serious criminal offense; specifically, one punishable by death or by incarceration in a prison facility for more than a year.

misdemeanor

A relatively minor violation of the criminal law, such as petty theft or simple assault, punishable by confinement for one year or less.

A third category of crime is the **infraction**. The term, which is not used in all jurisdictions, refers to minor violations of the law that are less serious than misdemeanors. Infractions may include such violations of the law as jaywalking, spitting on the sidewalk, littering, and certain traffic violations, including the failure to wear a seat belt. People committing infractions are typically ticketed—that is, given citations—and released, usually upon a promise to appear later in court. Court appearances may be waived upon payment of a fine, which is often mailed in.

infraction

A minor violation of state statute or local ordinance punishable by a fine or other penalty, or by a specified, usually very short term of incarceration.

Measuring Crime

CO1-2

Two important sources of information on crime for correctional professionals are the FBI's Uniform Crime Reporting Program (UCR) and the Bureau of Justice Statistics' National Crime Victimization Survey (NCVS). Corrections professionals closely analyze these data to forecast the numbers and

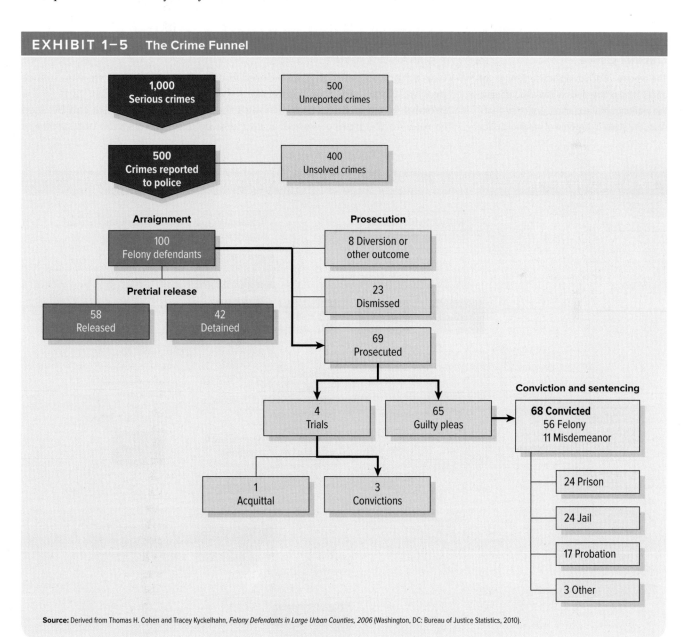

EXHIBIT 1–5 The Crime Funnel

Source: Derived from Thomas H. Cohen and Tracey Kyckelhahn, *Felony Defendants in Large Urban Counties, 2006* (Washington, DC: Bureau of Justice Statistics, 2010).

correctional clients

Prison inmates, probationers, parolees, offenders assigned to alternative sentencing programs, and those held in jails.

types of **correctional clients** to expect in the future. The forecasts can be used to project the need for different types of detention and rehabilitation services and facilities.

The Crime Funnel

Not all crimes are reported, and not everyone who commits a reported crime is arrested, so relatively few offenders enter the criminal justice system. Of those who do, some are not prosecuted (perhaps because the evidence against them is insufficient), others plead guilty to lesser crimes, and others are found not guilty. Some who are convicted are diverted from further processing by the system or may be fined or ordered to counseling. Hence, the proportion of criminal offenders who eventually enter the correctional system is small, as Exhibit 1–5 shows.[21]

criminal justice

The process of achieving justice through the application of the criminal law and through the workings of the criminal justice system. Also, the study of the field of criminal justice.

CO1-3 # CORRECTIONS AND THE CRIMINAL JUSTICE SYSTEM

Corrections is generally considered the final stage in the criminal justice process. Some aspects of corrections, however, come into play early in the process. Keep in mind that although the term **criminal justice** can be used to refer to the justice *process,* it can also be used to describe our *system* of

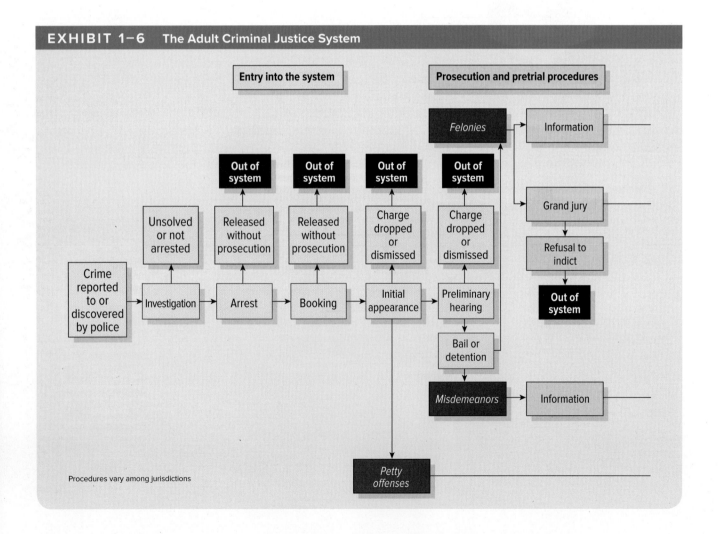

EXHIBIT 1–6   The Adult Criminal Justice System

Entry into the system

Prosecution and pretrial procedures

Procedures vary among jurisdictions

justice. Criminal justice agencies, taken as a whole, are said to compose the **criminal justice system**.

The components of the criminal justice system are (1) police, (2) courts, and (3) corrections. Each component, because it contains a variety of organizations and agencies, can be termed a *subsystem*. The subsystem of corrections, for example, includes prisons, agencies of probation and parole, jails, and a variety of alternative programs.

The *process* of criminal justice involves the activities of the agencies that make up the criminal justice system. The process of criminal justice begins when a crime is discovered or reported.

Court decisions based on the due process guarantees of the U.S. Constitution require that specific steps be taken in the justice process. Although the exact nature of those steps varies among jurisdictions, the description that follows portrays the most common sequence of events in response to serious criminal behavior. Exhibit 1–6, which diagrams the American criminal justice system, indicates the relationship among the stages in the criminal justice processing of adult offenders.

criminal justice system

The collection of all the agencies that perform criminal justice functions, whether these are operations or administration or technical support. The basic divisions of the criminal justice system are police, courts, and corrections.

Entering the Correctional System

The criminal justice system does not respond to all crime because most crimes are not discovered or reported to the police.[22] Law enforcement

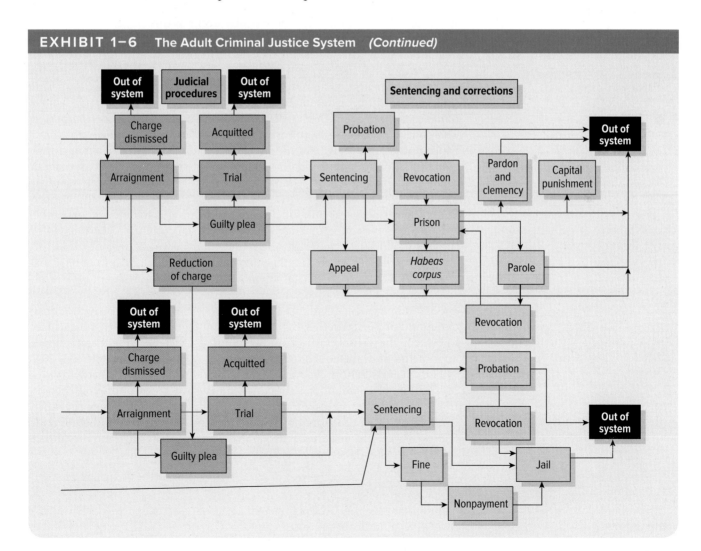

EXHIBIT 1–6 The Adult Criminal Justice System *(Continued)*

agencies learn about crimes from the reports of citizens, through discovery by a police officer in the field, or through investigative and intelligence work. Once a law enforcement agency knows of a crime, the agency must identify and arrest a suspect before the case can proceed. Sometimes a suspect is found at the scene; other times, however, identifying a suspect requires an extensive investigation. Often no one is identified or apprehended—the crime goes unsolved. If an offender is arrested, booked, and jailed to await an initial court appearance, the intake, custody, confinement, and supervision aspects of corrections first come into play at this stage of the criminal justice process.

Prosecution and Pretrial Procedure

After an arrest, law enforcement agencies present information about the case and about the accused to the prosecutor, who decides whether to file formal charges with the court. If no charges are filed, the accused must be released. The prosecutor can also drop charges after filing them. Such a choice is called *nolle prosequi;* and when it happens, a case is said to be "nolled" or "nollied."

A suspect charged with a crime must be taken before a judge or magistrate without unnecessary delay. At the initial appearance, the judge or magistrate informs the accused of the charges and decides whether there is probable cause to detain him or her. Often, defense counsel is also assigned then. If the offense charged is not very serious, the determination of guilt and the assessment of a penalty may also occur at this stage.

In some jurisdictions, a pretrial-release decision is made at the initial appearance, but this decision may occur at other hearings or at another time during the process. Pretrial release on bail was traditionally intended to ensure appearance at trial. However, many jurisdictions today permit pretrial detention of defendants accused of serious offenses and deemed dangerous, to prevent them from committing crimes in the pretrial period. The court may decide to release the accused on his or her own recognizance, into the custody of a third party, on the promise of satisfying certain conditions, or after posting a financial bond. Conditions of release may be reviewed at any later time while charges are still pending.

In many jurisdictions, the initial appearance may be followed by a preliminary hearing. The main function of this hearing is to determine whether there is probable cause to believe that the accused committed a crime within the jurisdiction of the court. If the judge or magistrate does not find probable cause, the case is dismissed. However, if the judge finds probable cause for such a belief, or if the accused waives the right to a preliminary hearing, the case may be bound over to a grand jury.

A grand jury hears evidence against the accused, presented by the prosecutor, and decides whether there is sufficient evidence to cause the accused to be brought to trial. If the grand jury finds sufficient evidence, it submits an indictment to the court.

Not all jurisdictions use grand juries. Some require, instead, that the prosecutor submit an information (a formal written accusation) to the court. In most jurisdictions, misdemeanor cases and some felony cases proceed by the issuance of an information. Some jurisdictions require indictments in felony cases. However, the accused may choose to waive a grand jury indictment and, instead, accept service of an information for the crime.

Judicial Procedures

adjudication

The process by which a court arrives at a final decision in a case.

Adjudication is the process by which a court arrives at a decision in a case. The adjudication process involves a number of steps. The first is

arraignment. Once an indictment or information is filed with the trial court, the accused is scheduled for arraignment. If the accused has been detained without bail, corrections personnel take him or her to the arraignment. At the arraignment, the accused is informed of the charges, advised of the rights of criminal defendants, and asked to enter a plea to the charges.

If the accused pleads guilty or pleads *nolo contendere* (accepts a penalty without admitting guilt), the judge may accept or reject the plea. If the plea is accepted, no trial is held and the offender is sentenced at this proceeding or at a later date. The plea may be rejected if, for example, the judge believes that the accused has been coerced. If this occurs, the case may proceed to trial. Sometimes, as the result of negotiations between the prosecutor and the defendant, the defendant enters a guilty plea in expectation of reduced charges or a light sentence. *Nolo contendere* pleas are often entered by those who fear a later civil action and who therefore do not want to admit guilt.

If the accused pleads not guilty or not guilty by reason of insanity, a date is set for trial. A person accused of a serious crime is guaranteed a trial by jury. However, the accused may ask for a bench trial, in which the judge, rather than a jury, serves as the finder of fact. In both instances, the prosecution and defense present evidence by questioning witnesses, and the judge decides issues of law. The trial results in acquittal or conviction of the original charges or of lesser included offenses. A defendant may be convicted at trial only if the government's evidence proves beyond a reasonable doubt that the defendant is guilty, or if the defendant knowingly and voluntarily pleads guilty to the charges.

Sentencing and Sanctions

After a guilty verdict or guilty plea, sentence is imposed. In most cases, the judge decides on the sentence, but in some states, the sentence is decided by the jury, particularly for capital offenses, such as murder.

To arrive at an appropriate sentence, a court may hold a sentencing hearing to consider evidence of aggravating or mitigating circumstances. In assessing the circumstances surrounding a criminal act, courts often rely on presentence investigations by probation agencies or other designated authorities. Courts may also consider victim impact statements.

The sentencing choices available to judges and juries frequently include one or more of the following:

- the death penalty;
- incarceration in a prison, a jail, or another confinement facility;
- community service;
- probation, in which the convicted person is not confined but is subject to certain conditions and restrictions;
- fines, primarily as penalties for minor offenses; and
- restitution, which requires the offender to provide financial compensation to the victim.

In many states, *mandatory minimum* sentencing laws require that persons convicted of certain offenses serve a minimum prison term, which the judge must impose and which may not be reduced by a parole board or by "good-time" deductions.

After the trial, a defendant may request appellate review of the conviction to see whether there was some serious error that affected the

arraignment

An appearance in court prior to trial in a criminal proceeding.

nolo contendere

A plea of "no contest." A no-contest plea may be used by a defendant who does not wish to contest conviction. Because the plea does not admit guilt, however, it cannot provide the basis for later civil suits.

Jodi Arias on the witness stand in 2013. She was convicted of killing her lover, Travis Alexander. He had been shot in the face, stabbed 29 times, and had his throat slashed. Arias was sentenced to spend the rest of her life in prison, and is currently housed in the Arizona State Prison Complex–Perryville. What happens to defendants after they enter the correctional system?
© AP Photo/Ross D. Franklin, Pool

defendant's right to a fair trial. In some states, the defendant may also appeal the sentence.

At least one appeal of a conviction is a matter of right. Any further appeal (to a state supreme court or in the case of federal court convictions, to the U.S. Supreme Court) is *discretionary,* which means that the higher court may or may not choose to hear the further appeal. After losing all their available *direct* appeals (also known as *exhaustion of state remedies*), state prisoners may also seek to have their convictions reviewed *collaterally* in the federal courts via a writ of *habeas corpus.* In states that have the death penalty, appeals of death sentences are usually automatic, and extensive federal *habeas corpus* review often takes place before the sentence of death is actually carried out.

The Correctional Subsystem

After conviction and sentencing, most offenders enter the correctional subsystem. Before we proceed with our discussion, it is best to define the term *corrections.* As with most words, a variety of definitions can be found.

In 1967, for example, the President's Commission on Law Enforcement and Administration of Justice wrote that *corrections* means "America's prisons, jails, juvenile training schools, and probation and parole machinery." It is "that part of the criminal justice system," said the commission, "that the public sees least of and knows least about."[23]

Years later, in 1975, the National Advisory Commission on Criminal Justice Standards and Goals said in its lengthy volume on corrections, "*Corrections* is defined here as the community's official reactions to the convicted offender, whether adult or juvenile."[24] The commission noted that "this is a broad definition and it suffers . . . from several shortcomings."

We can distinguish between institutional corrections and noninstitutional corrections. A report by the Bureau of Justice Statistics (BJS) says that **institutional corrections** "involves the confinement and rehabilitation of adults and juveniles convicted of offenses against the law and the confinement of persons suspected of a crime awaiting trial and adjudication."[25] BJS goes on to say that

institutional corrections

That aspect of the correctional enterprise that involves the incarceration and rehabilitation of adults and juveniles convicted of offenses against the law, and the confinement of persons suspected of a crime awaiting trial and adjudication.

correctional institutions are prisons, reformatories, jails, houses of correction, penitentiaries, correctional farms, workhouses, reception centers, diagnostic centers, industrial schools, training schools, detention centers, and a variety of other types of institutions for the confinement and correction of convicted adults or juveniles who are adjudicated delinquent or in need of supervision. [The term] also includes facilities for the detention of adults and juveniles accused of a crime and awaiting trial or hearing.

According to BJS, **noninstitutional corrections**, which is sometimes called **community corrections**, includes "pardon, probation, and parole activities, correctional administration not directly connectable to institutions, and miscellaneous [activities] not directly related to institutional care."

As all these definitions show, in its broadest sense, the term *corrections* encompasses each of the following components, as well as the process of interaction among them:

- the *purpose* and *goals* of the correctional enterprise;
- jails, prisons, correctional institutions, and other *facilities*;
- probation, parole, and alternative and diversionary *programs*;
- federal, state, local, and international correctional offices and *agencies*;
- counseling, educational, health care, nutrition, and many other *services*;
- correctional *clients*;
- corrections *volunteers*;
- corrections *professionals*;
- fiscal appropriations and *funding*;
- various aspects of criminal and civil *law*;
- formal and informal *procedures*;
- effective and responsible *management*;
- community *expectations* regarding correctional practices; and
- the machinery of *capital punishment*.

When we use the word *corrections*, we include all of these elements. Fourteen elements, however, make for an unwieldy definition. Hence, for purposes of discussion, we will say that **corrections** refers to all the various aspects of the pretrial and postconviction management of individuals accused or convicted of crimes. Central to this perspective is the recognition that corrections—although it involves a variety of programs, services, facilities, and personnel—is essentially a management activity. Rather than stress the role of institutions or agencies, this definition emphasizes the human dimension of correctional activity—especially the efforts of the corrections professionals who undertake the day-to-day tasks. Like any other managed activity, corrections has goals and purposes. Exhibit 1–7 details the role of corrections as identified by the American Correctional Association (ACA).

Police arrest a drug dealer. While marijuana and some other previously illicit drugs are freely available in many states today—especially to those who are sick—not all drugs have been decriminalized. What role does the criminal justice system play in the maintenance of social order?
© moodboard/Getty Images

noninstitutional corrections (also *community corrections*)

That aspect of the correctional enterprise that includes pardon, probation, and parole activities, correctional administration not directly connectable to institutions, and miscellaneous activities not directly related to institutional care.

corrections

All the various aspects of the pretrial and postconviction management of individuals accused or convicted of crimes.

EXHIBIT 1-7   **American Correctional Association**

Public Correctional Policy on the Role of Corrections

The overall role of corrections is to enhance public safety and social order. Adult and juvenile correctional systems should:

- implement court-ordered sanctions and provide supervision of those accused of unlawful behavior prior to and after adjudication in a safe and humane manner;
- offer the widest range of correctional programs that are based on exemplary practices, supported by research and promote pro-social behavior;
- provide gender- and culturally-responsive programs and services for preadjudicated and adjudicated offenders that will enhance successful reentry to the community and that are administered within the least restrictive environment consistent with public, staff and offender safety;
- address the needs of victims of crime;
- routinely review correctional programs and reentry services to ensure that they are addressing the needs of offenders, victims, and the community; and
- collaborate with other professions to improve and strengthen correctional services and to support the reduction of crime and recidivism.

Source: Copyright © American Correctional Association. Reprinted with permission.

REVIEW AND APPLICATIONS

SUMMARY

1 Although crime rates are at their lowest level in more than 20 years, correctional populations have been increasing because of get-tough-on-crime attitudes, the nation's War on Drugs, and the increasing reluctance of parole authorities, fearing civil liability and public outcry, to release inmates. Consequently, we are now witnessing an era of mass incarceration. At the same time, growth in correctional populations and in spending on prisons and jails has led to a dramatically expanding correctional workforce and to enhanced employment opportunities within the field.

2 Two important sources of crime statistics are the FBI's Uniform Crime Reporting Program and the National Crime Victimization Survey, published by the Bureau of Justice Statistics. The crimes that bring people into the American correctional system include felonies, which are relatively serious criminal offenses; misdemeanors, which are less serious crimes; and infractions, which are minor law violations.

3 The main components of the criminal justice system are police, courts, and corrections. Each can be considered a subsystem of the criminal justice system. The major components of the corrections subsystem are jails, probation, parole, and prisons. Jails and prisons are examples of institutional corrections, while probation and parole are forms of noninstitutional corrections.

KEY TERMS

crime, p. 4

prison, p. 4

mass incarceration, p. 4

sustainable justice, p. 7

felony, p. 8

misdemeanor, p. 8

infraction, p. 9

correctional clients, p. 10

criminal justice, p. 10

criminal justice system, p. 11

adjudication, p. 12

arraignment, p. 13

nolo contendere, p. 13

institutional corrections, p. 14

noninstitutional corrections, p. 15

community corrections, p. 15

corrections, p. 15

QUESTIONS FOR REVIEW

1 Why have correctional populations in the United States dramatically increased over the past few decades? How does the rise in correctional populations compare with changes in crime rates over time?

2 What are the kinds of crimes that cause offenders to enter correctional institutions? To enter other kinds of correctional programs?

3 What are the major components of the criminal justice system? What aspects of the corrections subsystem can you identify?

THINKING CRITICALLY ABOUT CORRECTIONS

Vision

Dianne Carter, former president of the National Academy of Corrections, once said, "Too often in corrections, only worker skills are targeted for training, and the organization misses a significant opportunity to communicate its vision and mission."[26] Do you agree or disagree with this statement? Why?

ON-THE-JOB DECISION MAKING

Training

Today is the first day of your job as a correctional officer. A severe statewide shortage of officers required you to begin work immediately before training, which you are scheduled to attend in three months. When you arrive at the facility, you are ushered into a meeting with the warden. He welcomes you and gives you a brief pep talk. He asks if you have any concerns. You tell him, "Well, I feel a little uneasy. I haven't gone through the academy yet." "Don't worry," he says, "all our new recruits get on-the-job experience before a slot in the academy opens up. You'll do fine!" He shakes your hand and leads you to the door. After you leave the warden's office, you are given a set of keys and a can of mace. The shift supervisor, a sergeant, gives you a brief tour of the prison. Then he tells you that as you learn your job, you will spend most of your time with another officer, though pairing up will not always be possible.

The officer you are assigned to accompany is Harold Gates. At first, you follow Officer Gates across the compound, getting more familiar with the layout of the facility. Then you spend an uneventful afternoon working with Officer Gates in the yard. At 4:30, Officer Gates instructs you to make sure that all inmates have left the classroom building in preparation for a "count." As you enter the building, you encounter a group of six inmates heading toward the door. Before you can move to the side, one of the inmates walks within an inch of you and stares at you. The others crowd in behind him. You can't move. You are pinned to the door by the men. The man directly in front of you is huge—over 6 feet tall and about 280 pounds. His legs look like tree trunks, and his arms are held away from his body by their sheer bulk. You're staring at a chest that could easily pass as a brick wall. With a snarl he growls, "What do you want?"

1. How do you respond? Would you feel more confident responding to a situation like this if you had had some training?

2. If you tell the inmates that it's time for a count and to move along, what will you do next? Will you ask anyone for guidance in similar future situations or just chalk up the encounter to a learning experience? To whom might you talk about it?

3. Suppose you are a manager or supervisor at this facility. How would you handle the training of new recruits?

Leadership

You are a correctional officer at the McClellan Correctional Facility. You and your coworkers have been following, with high interest, the events at Brownley, another correctional facility located approximately 35 miles away. Prisoner rioting at Brownley during the past four days has left 4 correctional officers and 19 prisoners seriously hurt. It now appears, though, that while tensions remain high, the riot has been contained and the prisoners at Brownley are settling back down. The uneasy truce, however, mandates resolution of the issues that led to the riot in the first place.

The main issue leading to the riot was the prisoners' claims of mistreatment at the hands of certain members of the Brownley correctional staff. State correctional administrators have determined that an essential first step in preventing future riots is replacement of certain members of the correctional staff at Brownley. You are called to your supervisor's office, where she informs you that you are being reassigned temporarily to Brownley, with a possibility that the reassignment may become permanent.

This news does not make you happy. The logistical impact alone is irritating because it will mean a significant commute each day. More important, though, is that you will be leaving a cohesive team of skilled and dedicated correctional officers with whom you have developed a close bond. You trust each other, and you trust your leaders. There's no telling what you will encounter at Brownley.

Your worst fears are realized when you report for your first shift and your new sergeant takes you aside. "We can't let them win on this," he says. "You know the drill. Stay on 'em hard, and don't cut 'em any slack. We need to let them know from the get-go that things haven't changed—we're still in charge, whether they like it or not, and we ain't gonna take any guff from the likes of them!"

It is immediately apparent to you that your sergeant has a strong "us-against-them" perspective. Your experience tells you that such an attitude at the leadership level likely induces similar, often stronger attitudes at the correctional officer level, and your common sense tells you that this is probably the root of the problem at Brownley.

1. How do you respond to your new sergeant?

2. If you elect to keep this information to yourself, how will you establish yourself with the Brownley inmates as a CO who does not subscribe to the other CO's practices without appearing weak or exploitable?

3. If you elect to bring this information to the attention of someone higher up in the supervisory chain, how will you deal with potential adverse reactions from your new coworkers?

CORRECTIONS TODAY

Evidence-Based Corrections and Professionalism

© Jeff Greenberg/Photo Edit

CHAPTER OBJECTIVES

After completing this chapter you should be able to do the following:

1 Define evidence-based corrections, and explain the important role that it plays in corrections professionalism today.

2 Explain the importance of professionalism in the corrections field, and describe the characteristics of a true professional.

3 Understand what is meant by social diversity, and explain why issues of race, gender, and ethnicity are important in corrections today.

> *The use of evidence-based practices in corrections and public policy is now considered the gold standard for policy and program development.*
>
> —Richard Tewksbury and Jill Levenson, "When Evidence Is Ignored: Residential Restrictions for Sex Offenders."
>
> —*Corrections Today*, December 1, 2007, p. 34

In late 2015, the *Washington Post* reported on the consequences of California's Proposition 47—a voter-approved measure intended to put an end to the mass incarceration era in California.[1] The proposition was meant to save the state money by keeping low-level offenders out of prison and by releasing some nonviolent offenders who were already behind bars. Specifically, the measure permits offenders who are currently serving felony prison sentences for certain nonviolent crimes to apply to have their sentences reduced to misdemeanors—meaning they would likely be released and placed on probation.

A newly released state prisoner being fitted with donated clothing. California's Proposition 47 has led to the release of thousands of inmates who had been imprisoned for nonviolent offenses. Did the Proposition meet its intended goals?
© Jim West image BROKER/Newscom

The *Post,* however, found what it called "unintended effects" of changes in the law brought about by Proposition 47. Less than a year after its passage, 4,300 state prisoners had seen their sentences lowered and had been released. Financial savings were considerable, but police chiefs across the state began reporting that their officers had to deal with many of those released offenders "again and again." The term "frequent flier" came to be applied to offenders who knew how to lawfully use the provisions of Proposition 47 to stay out of prison, while continuing to violate the law. One Riverside, California, criminal, for example, was arrested for stealing appliances on 13 different occasions over the course of three months, only to be charged with a misdemeanor and be quickly released each time.

The *Post* also found that a year after Proposition 47 passed, robberies were up by 23 percent in San Francisco, property thefts had risen 11 percent in Los Angeles, and certain other categories of crime were up 36 percent in La Mirada, and 68 percent in Desert Hot Springs. While the *Post* said that it was too early to tell whether passage of Proposition 47 had led to these crime increases, it did say that there had not been enough evidence for voters to know which way to vote on the issues—nor to assess the likely consequences of the proposition's passage. Finally, a year later, Magnus Lofstrom, senior fellow with the Public Policy Institute of California, said that he was waiting for additional statistics on crime rates before assessing the impact of Proposition 47. Lofstrom noted, "It is important to recognize that it might have an impact on crime, it might very well put some upward pressure on crime rates."[2]

Evidence-Based Corrections

CO2-1 # EVIDENCE-BASED CORRECTIONS (EBC)

Many would say that California voters would have been well served by the availability of evidence depicting the likely consequences for the state if Proposition 47 was enacted. The scientific study of corrections, and of correctional policies and programs, is referred to as **evidence-based corrections (EBC)**. The evidence-based model uses empirical data to determine what works in correctional settings—that is, which correctional programs are effective at meeting correctional goals, such as reducing recidivism and preventing future crimes. EBC is a hallmark of contemporary corrections and is regarded as the gold standard by which correctional programs and services are evaluated today. EBC uses ongoing, critical reviews of research literature to identify credible scientific evidence and involves rigorous quality assurance to ensure that evidence-based practices are replicated with fidelity and that new practices are evaluated to determine their effectiveness.

The National Institute of Corrections says that evidence-based practice **(EBP)** (1) implies that there is a definable outcome(s), (2) works to identify the best available strategy or program, (3) uses measurable program features and, measurable outcomes, and (4) is defined according to practical realities (i.e. public safety, recidivism, victim satisfaction, etc.) rather than immeasurable moral or value-oriented standards or beliefs.[3]

EBP, a closely related concept, refers to the implementation of programs that have been studied and found to be effective. Although EBC and EBP are different sides of the same coin, EBC is primarily concerned with study and evaluation, while EBP focuses on the practical use of programs that have been found to be effective.

One important component of EBC is **cost-benefit analysis**, which seeks to assess the effectiveness of correctional approaches relative to their costs. While EBC is a theme of this text, another theme is economic realities in corrections. As you will see, the two themes go hand in hand.

The History of EBC

The evidence-based model began to be used in this country in 1992 when it was first applied to the medical sciences. Soon, the value of EBP was recognized in many fields, including education, psychology, psychiatry, sociology, and criminal justice.

In the mid-1990s, two separate efforts were made to identify crime and justice-related programs that were effective and to assess the methodological quality of each of the studies.[4] The first effort was undertaken in 1996, when the Center for the Study and Prevention of Violence (CSPV) at the Institute of Behavioral Science, University of Colorado–Boulder, developed the Blueprints for Violence Prevention program. The program, which remains well known today, identified 10 model programs for delinquency prevention and intervention that met strict scientific standards of program effectiveness. That same year, Congress mandated a "comprehensive evaluation of the effectiveness of Department of Justice grants to assist state and local law enforcement communities in preventing crime." The result was a highly visible effort to identify EBPs in criminal justice. The evaluations were undertaken by faculty members at the University of Maryland, who reviewed research studies carried out in various settings nationwide. The Maryland study was one of the first large-scale efforts to "score" the criminal

Visit https://www.youtube.com/watch?v=1legHJ16Ums to watch a video about correctional officers on the front line of evidence-based corrections, or scan this code with the QR app on your smartphone or digital device to view it.

evidence-based corrections (EBC)

The application of social scientific techniques to the study of correctional practices, programs, and procedures for the purpose of increasing effectiveness and enhancing the efficient use of available resources.

evidence-based practice (EBP)

The implementation of programs that have been studied and found to be effective.

cost-benefit analysis

A systematic process used to calculate the costs of a program relative to its benefits. Programs showing the largest benefit per unit of expenditure are seen as the most effective.

Susan Turner, director of the Center for Evidence-Based Corrections at the University of California, Irvine. Turner is shown at the Orange County (California) jail. What is evidence-based corrections?

Photo by Steve Zylius/UC Irvine Communications

justice studies that it reviewed based on the strength of the scientific methods that they employed.

Only a year later, in what many say was the official beginning of the evidence-based movement in corrections, came the 1997 publication of a lengthy report to the U.S. Congress, entitled *Preventing Crime: What Works, What Doesn't, What's Promising.*[5] The report, known as a meta-analysis because it assessed more than 500 previously completed studies of various crime prevention programs, looked at the effectiveness of correctional programs in seven different settings: families, police, community, place security, labor markets, schools, and the criminal justice system. Researchers discovered that a number of the evaluated programs could be declared successful. Successful efforts became known as *what works* programs—defined as those that are reasonably certain to reduce recidivism. Other programs were found likely to fail to reduce recidivism and were listed in the category of what does not work. Finally, some programs, which fell into a middle ground, were termed *promising*.

It was not long before other universities focused on EBPs, and in 2005 the University of California–Irvine announced the creation of its Center for Evidence-Based Corrections. The center, which continues to thrive today, seeks "to put science before politics when managing state correctional populations," and to help "corrections officials make policy decisions based on scientific evidence."[6] Similarly, the Center for Advancing Correctional Excellence at George Mason University, another well-known institution of higher learning, espouses an evidence-based model.

EBC has become worldwide in scope. Australia's famed Griffith University, for example, runs the Global Centre of Evidence-Based Corrections and Sentencing, and other major universities around the world have similar programs or are developing them.

Today, the federal government, through the National Institute of Justice, identifies and showcases successful EBPs via its Crime Solutions website (crimesolutions.gov). The site lists hundreds of programs that have been evaluated by expert reviewers who rate them as "effective," "promising," or as having "no effects" (Exhibit 2–1).

What Is Evidence?

In any discussion of EBC (also known as *evidence-based penology*), it is important to remember that the word *evidence* refers to scientific evidence, not to criminal evidence. Corrections professionals who adhere to an evidence-based philosophy acknowledge the problem-solving potential of social science research methods, read correctional publications and journals, and keep abreast of the latest findings in their field. They also work to implement the most successful evidence-based programs of relevance to their programs or jurisdictions.

How EBP Is Utilized in Corrections

Law enforcement and correctional agencies are always seeking the best methods to deter individuals from committing crimes or to prevent them from reoffending. When crimes are committed, law enforcement professionals apprehend the perpetrators and correctional professionals process, monitor, and rehabilitate those individuals throughout their confinement.

In order to reduce recidivism, an ever-increasing number of correctional programs and agencies at both the federal and state level are instituting EBP as the standard for all policies and procedures. Instead of using procedures that may work in one situation but not in another, EBP provides guidelines

EXHIBIT 2−1   Evidence-based Corrections in Action: Sample Program Evaluation at CrimeSolutions.Gov.

SOURCE: National Institute of Justice, https://www.crimesolutions.gov/PracticeDetails.aspx?ID=52 (accessed January 15, 2016).

that determine the most effective strategy for a given locale based on the results of research.

Recently, for example, the state of West Virginia formed the Justice Center for Evidence-Based Practice (JCEBP) whose job it is to use the best available evidence for informed decision making in justice agencies throughout the state. Similarly, the Pennsylvania Commission on Crime and Delinquency (PCCD) created the Resource Center for Evidence-Based Prevention and Intervention Programs and Practices to help increase the use of EBPs

Graduates from a corrections academy celebrate at the completion of their studies. What are the components of corrections professionalism?

© AP Photo/Mary Altaffer

throughout Pennsylvania's justice-related agencies. Finally, Colorado's Department of Public Safety has created a statewide Evidence-Based Practices Implementation for Capacity (EPIC) program intended to enhance the capabilities of the state's justice system within existing budgetary limits.

The federal Bureau of Justice Assistance (BJA) notes that the state-level programs described here "all represent a shift from reliance solely on outside experts to having internal subject matter experts and a state driven commitment to utilizing evidence-based practices and programs."[7] BJA believes that "as policymakers around the country continue to see and understand the potential for using EBPP's to decrease crime, victimization, and criminal justice expenditures, other states may soon adopt similar programs." With the sobering budget realities of the coming years, the work of state-level centers for EBPs provide a blueprint for not only continuing the success of state programs, but also for protecting the investments of time and energy that have already gone into changing the way that the criminal justice system uses resources, sees research and evaluation, and reacts to new and innovative ways of protecting the public.

The Reach of Evidence-Based Studies in Corrections

Some evidence-based studies focus on particular programs and practices, while others are more far-reaching. An example of the former is a 2011 study conducted by the Minnesota Department of Corrections, which found that prison visitation has a significant impact on recidivism, with "frequent and recent visits" being closely associated with a decreased risk of recidivism. A surprising finding from the study was that "any visit reduced the risk of recidivism by 13 percent for felony reconvictions. . . ."[8]

One recent, and some would say surprising, large-scale evidence-based assessment of the effectiveness of imprisonment, in general, concluded that "there is little evidence that prisons reduce recidivism and at least some evidence to suggest that they have a criminogenic effect." The study authors noted that "the policy implications of this finding are significant, for it means that beyond crime saved through incapacitation, the use of custodial sanctions may have the unanticipated consequence of making society less safe."[9]

If the findings of this study are validated by further investigation, then it would seem that the wider use of community corrections, reentry programs, and sentences that divert offenders from prison will serve the rehabilitative goals of society better than imprisonment and will likely lead to a reduction in corrections-related budgets.

Visit http://justicestudies.com//qrcodes/ebcp. pdf or scan this code with the QR app on your smartphone or digital device and read *Evidence-Based Correctional Practices*, a paper that introduces some important concepts in the field of evidence-based corrections.

Corrections Professionalism

CO2-2

PROFESSIONALISM IN CORRECTIONS

Only a few decades ago, some writers bemoaned the fact that the field of corrections had not achieved professional status. Happily, much has changed over the past half century. By 1987, Bob Barrington, who was then the executive director of the International Association of Correctional Officers, was able to proclaim, in a discussion about prisons, that "correctional facilities . . . run smoothly and efficiently for one basic reason: the professional and forward-thinking attitudes and actions of the correctional officers employed."[10]

Writers on American criminal justice have said that the hallmark of a true profession is "a shared set of principles and customs that transcend self-interest and speak to the essential nature of the particular calling or trade."[11] This description recognizes the selfless and ethical nature of professional work. Hence, "professionals have a sense of commitment to their professions that is usually not present among those in occupational groups."[12] Work within a profession is viewed more as a "calling" than as a mere way of earning a living. "Professionals have a love for their work that is above that of employment merely to receive a paycheck."[13]

Although it is important to keep formal definitions in mind, for our purposes, we will define a **profession** as an occupation granted high social status by virtue of the personal integrity of its members. We can summarize the *attitude* of a true professional by noting that it is characterized by the following:

- a spirit of public service and interest in the public good;
- the fair application of reason and the use of intellect to solve problems;
- self-regulation through a set of internal guidelines by which professionals hold *themselves* accountable for their actions;
- continual self-appraisal and self-examination;
- an inner sense of professionalism (i.e., honor, self-discipline, commitment, personal integrity, and self-direction);
- adherence to the recognized ethical principles of one's profession (see the Ethics and Professionalism box in this chapter); and
- a commitment to lifelong learning and lifelong betterment within the profession.

Most professional occupations have developed practices that foster professionalism among their members.

profession

An occupation granted high social status by virtue of the personal integrity of its members.

Offices of the American Correctional Association (ACA) in Alexandria, Virginia. The ACA is a leading proponent of professionalism in corrections. What does corrections professionalism entail?

Courtesy of American Correctional Association

Standards and Training

Historically, professional corrections organizations and their leaders have recognized the importance of training. It was not until the late 1970s, however, that the American Correctional Association (ACA) Commission on Accreditation established the first training standards. The commission did the following:

- specified standards for given positions within corrections;
- identified essential training topics;
- set specific numbers of hours for preservice (120) and annual in-service training (40); and
- specified basic administrative policy support requirements for training programs.[14]

Following ACA's lead, virtually every state now requires at least 120 hours of preservice training for correctional officers working in institutional settings; many states require more. Probation and parole officers are required to undergo similar training in most jurisdictions, and correctional officers working in jails are similarly trained.

Through training, new members of a profession learn the core values and ideals, the basic knowledge, and the accepted practices central to the profession. Setting training standards ensures that the education is uniform. Standards also mandate the teaching of specialized knowledge. Standards supplement training by doing the following:

- setting minimum requirements for entry into the profession;
- detailing expectations for those involved in the everyday life of correctional work; and
- establishing basic requirements for facilities, programs, and practices.

From the point of view of corrections professionals, training is a matter of personal responsibility. A lifelong commitment to a career ensures that those who think of themselves as professionals will seek the training needed to enhance their job performance.

Basic Skills and Knowledge

In 1990, the Professional Education Council of the American Correctional Association developed a model entry test for correctional officers. The test was intended to increase professionalism in the field and to provide a standard criminal justice curriculum.[15]

The council suggested that the test could act "as a quality control measure for such education, much as does the bar exam for attorneys." The standard entry test was designed to "reveal the applicant's understanding of the structure, purpose, and method of the police, prosecution, courts, institutions, probation, parole, community service, and extramural programs." It was also designed to "test for knowledge of various kinds of corrections programs, the role of punitive sanctions and incapacitation, and perspective on past experience and current trends."

More recently, Mark S. Fleisher of Illinois State University identified four core traits essential to effective work in corrections.[16] The traits are as follows:

- **Accountability.** "Correctional work demands precision, timeliness, accountability and strong ethics." Students may drift into patterns of irresponsibility during their college years. Once they become correctional officers, however, they need to take their work seriously.
- **Strong writing skill.** Because correctional officers must complete a huge amount of paperwork, they need to be able to write well. They should also be familiar with the "vocabulary of corrections."

Ethics and Professionalism

American Correctional Association Code of Ethics

1. Members shall respect and protect the civil and legal rights of all individuals.
2. Members shall treat every professional situation with concern for the welfare of the individuals involved and with no intent to gain personally.
3. Members shall maintain relationships with colleagues to promote mutual respect within the profession and improve the quality of service.
4. Members shall make public criticism of their colleagues or their agencies only when warranted, verifiable, and constructive.
5. Members shall respect the importance of all disciplines within the criminal justice system and work to improve cooperation with each segment.
6. Members shall honor the public's right to information and share information with the public to the extent permitted by law subject to individuals' right to privacy.
7. Members shall respect and protect the right of the public to be safeguarded from criminal activity.
8. Members shall refrain from using their positions to secure personal privileges or advantages.
9. Members shall refrain from allowing personal interest to impair objectivity in the performance of duty while acting in an official capacity.
10. Members shall refrain from entering into any formal or informal activity or agreement that presents a conflict of interest or is inconsistent with the conscientious performance of duties.
11. Members shall refrain from accepting any gifts, services, or favors that are or appear to be improper or imply an obligation inconsistent with the free and objective exercise of professional duties.
12. Members shall clearly differentiate between personal views/statements and views/statements/positions made on behalf of the agency or Association.
13. Members shall report to appropriate authorities any corrupt or unethical behaviors for which there is sufficient evidence to justify review.
14. Members shall refrain from discriminating against any individual because of race, gender, creed, national origin, religious affiliation, age, disability, or any other type of prohibited discrimination.
15. Members shall preserve the integrity of private information; they shall refrain from seeking information on individuals beyond that which is necessary to implement responsibilities and perform their duties; members shall refrain from revealing nonpublic information unless expressly authorized to do so.
16. Members shall make all appointments, promotions, and dismissals in accordance with established civil service rules, applicable contract agreements, and individual merit, rather than furtherance of personal interests.
17. Members shall respect, promote, and contribute to a work-place that is safe, healthy, and free of harassment in any form.

Adopted by the Board of Governors and Delegate Assembly in August 1994.

Source: Copyright © American Correctional Association. Reprinted with permission.

Ethical Dilemma 2–1: In light of tight state budgets and overcrowded prisons, should governors use their authority to provide early release for some inmates? If so, under what circumstances? For more information, go to Ethical Dilemma 2–1 at www.justicestudies.com/ethics08.

Ethical Dilemma 2–2: You are the warden of the only medium security prison in your state. Your nephew is sentenced to serve 10 years in your institution. Using the ACA Code of Ethics as a guide, determine what ethical issues you will face. For more information, go to Ethical Dilemma 2–2 at www.justicestudies.com/ethics08.

Ethical Dilemma 2–3: One of your fellow correctional officers accepts candy and snacks from one of the inmates. She doesn't ask for the snacks, nor does she do any favors for the inmate. Should you report this activity? Will you report it? Using the ACA Code of Ethics, determine the ethical issues, if any, involved in this behavior. For more information, go to Ethical Dilemma 2–3 at www.justicestudies.com/ethics08.

Ethical Dilemmas for every chapter are available online.

- **Effective presentational skills.** "A correctional career requires strong verbal skills and an ability to organize presentations." Effective verbal skills help officers interact with their peers, inmates, and superiors.
- **A logical mind and the ability to solve problems.** Such skills are essential to success in corrections because problems arise daily. Being able to solve them is a sign of an effective officer.

Photo © Rhianna Johnson

Rhianna Johnson

Education Director, Larch Corrections Center, Yacolt, Washington

Rhianna Johnson is the Education Director at Larch Corrections Center, a minimum security male prison camp in Washington State. The facility houses approximately 480 inmates who are less than four years from their release dates. The Education Department at Larch Corrections Center operates through a partnership between Clark College and Washington Department of Corrections. It provides classes in vocational programs, GED, and other skills. All Washington State prison facilities provide educational programming for inmates.

Mrs. Johnson worked in higher education as an instructor, advisor, and manager for several years before moving into corrections education. With a master's degree in sociology, she was interested in issues related to criminology, social equity, and inmate reentry. She decided to take her experience supporting students on a college campus into the prison setting in order to prepare offenders for career and personal goals. Working in a prison, she says, was somewhat of an adjustment. "At times, it is challenging because of the political disagreements associated with educating inmates," she adds. Mrs. Johnson thoroughly enjoys working with inmates and challenging stereotypes. She supervises faculty who agree that teaching in a prison setting is highly rewarding.

> "The challenges of educating inmates lead to huge personal rewards."

CO2-3 SOCIAL DIVERSITY IN CORRECTIONS

The corrections profession faces a number of social issues that are of special concern to Americans today. Contemporary issues include questions about the purposes and appropriateness of punishment in general and the acceptability of capital punishment in particular; the usefulness of alternative or nontraditional sanctions; the privatization of correctional facilities; and the rights and overall treatment of prisoners. At the forefront of today's issues are those involving concerns about gender, race, ethnicity, and other forms of social diversity.

While a number of these issues are discussed in later chapters, this brief section provides definitions of some of the terms that will be discussed and suggests some structure for what is to follow.

Some terms, such as *race,* are not easy to define. Historical definitions of race have highlighted some supposed biological traits, such as skin color, hair type, or shape of the skull and face. Eighteenth-century European physical anthropologists distinguished between white, black, and Asian (or "yellow") races. The notion of race, however, is now generally recognized as a social construct and is not seen as an objective biological fact. Moreover, racial distinctions have blurred throughout American society, which has long been characterized as a melting pot. Nonetheless, when asked, the majority of Americans today still identify themselves as members of a particular racial group.

To say that race is a social construct means that racial distinctions are culturally defined. It does *not* mean, however, that such distinctions are without consequences. On the contrary, great social significance is often attached to biological or other indicators of race, and race plays a crucial role in social relations. *Racism,* which is also socially constructed, can be the result. **Racism** has been defined as social practices that explicitly or implicitly attribute merits or allocate value to members of racially categorized groups solely because of their race.[20] In the field of corrections, as in other social endeavors, racism (rather than race itself) is the real issue because it can lead to forms of racial discrimination, including inequities in hiring and promotion for those working in

racism

Social practices that explicitly or implicitly attribute merits or allocate value to individuals solely because of their race.

corrections, and to unfairness in the handling of inmates or other correctional clients because of their race.

Considerable overlap exists between the concept of race and that of *ethnicity*. In contemporary usage, both terms imply the notion of lineage, or biological and regional as well as cultural background and inheritance. Of the two, however, ethnicity is most closely associated with cultural heritage. Members of an ethnic group generally share a common racial, national, religious, linguistic, and cultural origin. Hence, from an ethnic perspective, a person might identify himself or herself as Hungarian, even though he or she has never lived in Hungary, does not speak Hungarian, and knows little of the history of the Hungarian nation. Ethnic differences can lead to serious consequences as prison gangs built around ethnicity demonstrate.

At first blush, the term *gender* seems more straightforward than race or ethnicity because it relates to differences between the sexes. In fact, many critical issues that concern correctional administrators today reflect a rapid increase in the number of women entering correctional service.

For many years, corrections was a male-dominated profession. Although the correctional process has always involved some women, historically most women in the profession have attended to the needs of the small number of females held in confinement. It wasn't until the 1970s that women began to enter the corrections professions in significant numbers. Many went to work in facilities that housed males, where they soon found themselves confronting *gender bias* from an entrenched macho culture.

Today, women working in correctional facilities largely have been accepted, as evidenced by the fact their proportion is more than double the proportion of female law enforcement officers: Thirty-five percent of correctional officers in the United States are women, while only 13 percent of police officers are female. As Exhibit 2–3 shows, however, women working in corrections tend to be concentrated in the lower ranks and are underrepresented in supervisory positions. According to the National Center for Women in Policing,

Colette Peters, Oregon Director of Corrections. In recent years, the number of women working in corrections has increased significantly. Do you think that gender bias exists within the correctional career field today?

Reprint with permission of State Corrections Director Colette Peters

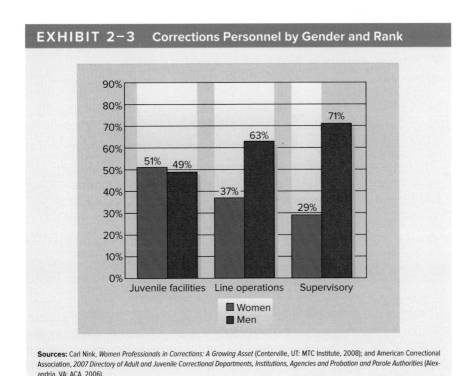

EXHIBIT 2–3   Corrections Personnel by Gender and Rank

Juvenile facilities: Women 51%, Men 49%
Line operations: Women 37%, Men 63%
Supervisory: Women 29%, Men 71%

Sources: Carl Nink, *Women Professionals in Corrections: A Growing Asset* (Centerville, UT: MTC Institute, 2008); and American Correctional Association, *2007 Directory of Adult and Juvenile Correctional Departments, Institutions, Agencies and Probation and Parole Authorities* (Alexandria, VA: ACA, 2006).

women of color hold 12.9 percent of corrections positions, 9.7 percent of top command positions, and 9.1 percent of supervisory positions.[21]

Race, ethnicity, and gender are all aspects of social diversity—although diversity in society extends to many other areas as well, such as economics, religion, education, intellectual ability, and politics. Keep in mind, as you read through this textbook, that in the field of corrections diversity issues can be described from four perspectives: (1) as they impact individual correctional clients; (2) as they determine correctional populations and trends; (3) as they affect the lives and interests of those working in the field of corrections; and (4) as they change the structure and functioning of correctional institutions, facilities, and programs.

REVIEW AND APPLICATIONS

SUMMARY

1 Professionalism in corrections is important because it can win the respect and admiration of others outside of the field. Moreover, professionals are regarded as trusted participants in any field of endeavor. This chapter also discussed seven aspects of a professional attitude.

2 Evidence-based corrections is the application of social scientific techniques to the study of everyday corrections procedures for the purpose of increasing effectiveness and enhancing the efficient use of available resources. When discussing evidence-based corrections, it is important to remember that the word *evidence* refers to scientific, not criminal, evidence.

3 Social diversity encompasses differences of race, gender, and ethnicity and is important in corrections today because it impacts individual correctional clients, influences correctional populations and trends, affects the lives and interests of those working in the field of corrections, and may help determine the structure and functioning of correctional institutions, facilities, and programs.

KEY TERMS

evidence-based corrections (EBC), p. 21

evidence-based practice (EBP), p. 21

cost-benefit analysis, p. 21

profession, p. 25

corrections professional, p. 28

professional associations, p. 28

certification, p. 28

racism, p. 30

QUESTIONS FOR REVIEW

1 Explain the importance of professionalism in corrections and list the seven characteristics of a professional attitude.

2 What is evidence-based corrections? What role does it play in corrections professionalism today?

3 What is meant by the term *social diversity*, and why is the issue of social diversity important in corrections today?

THINKING CRITICALLY ABOUT CORRECTIONS

Professionalism

Harold Williamson, a writer in the corrections field, has noted, "Higher levels of professionalization require greater amounts of training and usually involve increased specialization when compared to lesser professionalized activity. Higher levels of professionalization also involve the learning of more abstract knowledge and information."[22] Do you agree? Why or why not?

ON-THE-JOB DECISION MAKING

Evidence-Based Decisions

You are a captain in charge of programs at a large state correctional facility. The programs that you oversee offer a variety of opportunity to inmates, including jobs training, general education, and psychological counseling. The programs under your area of responsibility have names such as "Alcoholics and Narcotics Anonymous," "Anger Management," "Arts on the Inside," "Batterers Intervention," "Bible Study," "Developing Adults with Necessary Skills (DAWNS)," "Employability Skills Class," "First Step," "General Equivalency Classes," "Prison Fatherhood," "Learn to Read," "Meditation on the Inside," "A New Leash on Life," "Residential Substance Abuse Treatment (RSAT)," "Self-Esteem Class," "SISTA/NIA-HIV Awareness," "Vocational Training," "Yoga 4 Change," "Thinking 4 a Change," and "WorkNet Solutions."

Unfortunately, the state legislature has decided to cut prison budgets, and prison programs are targeted for substantial cost reductions. This means that you will have to decide which programs to keep, and which to reduce in size, or eliminate entirely.

Your boss, the prison warden, has asked you to draft a written plan that identifies the programs whose funding will be reduced. You have begun to think about what you will write into the plan, keeping in mind the needs of the inmates in your facility. You think about their personal and psychological well-being, and recognize that counseling programs are important, but you also know that job skills training programs provide a valuable opportunity for success upon release.

As you continue your internal dialogue, you remember what you learned in a class that you took at the local college. The class, entitled "Introduction to Corrections," taught you that the best decisions are usually evidence-based—that is, made on the basis of scientific findings that demonstrate what is most effective at achieving the goals that you've set. As you continue thinking, a number of questions arise. They are:

1. What are the most important programs in the institution over which I have control?
2. Which are likely to meet their goals?
3. Where can I find evidence-based studies that will help me make the best decisions?

How will you answer those questions?

Official White House Photo by Pete Souza

SENTENCING

To Punish or to Reform?

CHAPTER OBJECTIVES

After completing this chapter you should be able to do the following:

1 Describe the central purpose of criminal punishment.

2 Name the seven goals of criminal sentencing.

3 List and explain the sentencing options in general use today.

4 Describe the characteristics of persons on death row today.

5 Summarize the research on victim race and capital punishment.

6 Summarize the changes in the public's attitudes toward capital punishment.

7 Discuss the changes in the application of capital punishment as a result of *Furman* v. *Georgia* and *Gregg* v. *Georgia*.

8 Explain the death penalty appeals process.

9 Summarize Liebman's findings on the frequency of errors in capital punishment cases.

10 Explain the Supreme Court's reasoning for banning the execution of persons with mental retardation and juveniles.

11 Discuss federal and state sentencing trends and reforms.

12 Integrate the four principles related to fairness in sentencing for a hypothetical offense and offender.

> *When and if the will to roll back mass incarceration and to create just, fair, and effective sentencing systems becomes manifest, the way forward is clear.*
>
> —Michael Tonry, Professor of Law and Public Policy, University of Minnesota Law School.

On July 16, 2015, President Barack Obama became the first sitting president to visit a federal prison when he traveled to the El Reno Federal Correctional Institution outside Oklahoma City, where he met with six inmates serving time for drug offenses. President Obama invited VICE Media to film the event for the documentary *Fixing the System*.

President Obama told the media that the nation needs to reconsider policies that contribute to a huge spike in the number of people behind bars. "There are people who need to be in prison. . . . And I don't have tolerance for violent criminals." But the president argued it is time to change laws that impose lengthy mandatory sentences on nonviolent drug offenders, who are disproportionately black and Latino.[1]

President Obama and Shane Smith, cofounder and CEO of VICE Media, met one-on-one to discuss the president's visit. Here is one excerpt:

Shane Smith: There are more federal incarcerations for drug offenses than there are for homicide, aggravated assault, kidnapping, robbery, weapons, immigration, arson, sex offenses, extortion, bribery, etcetera, etcetera, combined.* How did that happen?

President Obama: I think there was a lot of fear. The War on Drugs, the crack epidemic, it became, I think, a bipartisan cause to get tough on crime. Incarceration became an easy, simple recipe in the minds of a lot of folks. Nobody ever lost an election because they were too tough on crime. And so nobody stepped back and asked, is it really appropriate for somebody who's engaged in a serious but nonviolent drug offense to get more time than a rapist? What's been interesting is that violent crime rates have consistently declined, and the costs of incarceration obviously have skyrocketed.

This chapter discusses sentencing and sentences. **Sentencing** is a court's imposition of a penalty on a convicted offender. A **sentence** is the penalty imposed.

This chapter introduces you to the goals of sentencing, sentencing options and types of sentencing, sentencing trends and reforms, and issues in fair sentencing.

Visit https://www.youtube.com/watch?v=HgIANRLcNv0 or scan this code with the QR app on your smartphone or digital device and watch the trailer of *Fixing the System,* President Barak Obama's visit to the El Reno Federal Correctional Institution to talk with federal prison inmates about their offenses and rehabilitation and interview with Shane Smith, cofounder and CEO of VICE Media. If you were President Obama what would you tell the American public about mass incarceration? If you were Mr. Smith, what questions would you have asked President Obama?

sentencing

The imposition of a criminal sanction by a sentencing authority, such as a judge.

sentence

The penalty a court imposes on a person convicted of a crime.

Sentencing Goals

CO3-1

SENTENCING: PHILOSOPHY AND GOALS

Philosophy of Criminal Sentencing

Philosophers have long debated *why* a wrongful act should be punished. Many social scientists suggest that criminal punishment maintains and defends the **social order.** By threatening potential law violators and by making the lives of violators uncomfortable, they say, punishments reduce the likelihood of future or continued criminal behavior.

social order

The smooth functioning of social institutions, the existence of positive and productive relations among individual members of society, and the orderly functioning of society as a whole.

revenge

Punishment as vengeance; an emotional response to real or imagined injury or insult.

retribution

A sentencing goal that involves retaliation against a criminal perpetrator.

`CO3-2`

just deserts

Punishment deserved. A just deserts perspective on criminal sentencing holds that criminal offenders are morally blameworthy and are therefore *deserving* of punishment.

Still, one might ask, instead of punishing offenders, why not offer them psychological treatment or educate them so that they are less prone to future law violation? The answer to this question is far from clear. Although criminal sentencing today has a variety of goals, and educational and treatment programs are more common now in corrections, punishment still takes center stage in society's view.

The Goals of Sentencing

Sentencing has a variety of purposes. As shown in Exhibit 3–1, the goals of sentencing are (1) revenge, (2) retribution, (3) just deserts (or the fact of deserving punishment), (4) deterrence, (5) incapacitation, (6) rehabilitation or reformation, and (7) restoration.

Revenge One of the earliest goals of criminal sentencing was revenge. **Revenge** can be described as both an emotion and as an act in response to victimization. Victims sometimes feel as though an injury or insult requires punishment in return. When they act on that feeling, they have taken revenge.

While we think of vengeance as a primitive need, it continues to play a role in contemporary societies. For example, following the November 2015 terrorist attack in Paris, which claimed 129 lives, French President François Hollande announced his intention of finding his inner-Robespierre and employing the guillotine to execute ISIS-linked terrorists. Similarly, had the terrorists who perpetrated the 9/11 attacks been captured (instead of dying in the suicide attacks), there can be little doubt that many Americans would have sought revenge on the perpetrators through our justice system—as was done with Zacarias Moussaoui, the "twelfth highjacker," who was in jail at the time of the 9/11 attacks.

Retribution **Retribution** involves the payment of a debt to both the victim and society and, thus, atonement for a person's offense. Historically, retribution was couched in terms of "getting even," and it has sometimes been explained as "an eye for an eye, and a tooth for a tooth." *Retribution* literally means "paying back" the offender for what he or she has done. Retribution is predicated on the notion that victims are *entitled* to reprisal.

Because social order suffers when a crime occurs, society is also a victim. Hence, retribution, in a very fundamental way, expresses society's disapproval of criminal behavior and demands the payment of a debt to society. It is not always easy to determine just how much punishment is enough to ensure the debt is paid.

A crowded city street. Many social scientists say that criminal punishments help maintain social order. What would a society without order be like?

© glowimages/Getty Images RF

Just Deserts Retribution is supported by many sentencing schemes today—although the concept is now often couched in terms of **just deserts** even though there is a difference between retribution and just deserts. The concept of just deserts de-emphasizes the emotional component of revenge by

EXHIBIT 3-1 Goals of Criminal Sentencing

Goal	Rationale
Revenge	Punishment is equated with vengeance and involves an emotional response to criminal victimization.
Retribution	Punishment involves a "settling of scores" for both society and the victim.
	Victims are entitled to "get even."
Just deserts	Offenders are morally blameworthy and deserving of punishment.
	Punishment restores the moral balance disrupted by crime.
Deterrence	Punishment will prevent future wrongdoing by the offender and by others.
	Punishment must outweigh the benefits gained by wrongdoing.
Incapacitation	Some wrongdoers cannot be changed and need to be segregated from society.
	Society has the responsibility to protect law-abiding citizens from those whose behavior cannot be controlled.
Rehabilitation or Reformation	Society needs to help offenders learn how to behave appropriately.
	Without learning acceptable behavior patterns, offenders will not be able to behave appropriately.
Restoration	Crime is primarily an offense against human relationships and secondarily a violation of a law.
	All those who suffered because of a crime should be restored to their previous sense of well-being.

claiming that criminal acts are *deserving* of punishment, that offenders are *morally blameworthy,* and that they must be punished. In this way, just deserts restores the moral balance to a society wronged by crime.

Andrew von Hirsch, who identified the rationales underlying criminal punishment, says that when someone "infringes the rights of others . . . he deserves blame [and that is why] the sanctioning authority is entitled to choose a response that expresses moral disapproval: namely, punishment."[2] Hence, from a just deserts point of view, justice *requires* that punishments be imposed on criminal law violators.

Of all the purposes of punishment that are discussed here, only retribution and just deserts are past oriented. That is, they examine what has already occurred (the crime) in an effort to determine the appropriate sentencing response.

Deterrence A third goal of criminal sentencing is deterrence. **Deterrence** is the discouragement or prevention of crimes similar to the one for which an offender is being sentenced. Unlike retribution and just deserts, deterrence is future oriented in that it seeks to prevent crimes from occurring. Two forms of deterrence can be identified: specific and general.

Specific deterrence is the deterrence of the individual being punished from committing additional crimes. Long ago, specific deterrence was achieved through corporal punishments that maimed offenders in ways that precluded their ability to commit similar crimes in the future. Spies had their eyes gouged out and their tongues removed, rapists were castrated,

deterrence

The discouragement or prevention of crimes through the fear of punishment.

specific deterrence

The deterrence of the individual being punished from additional crimes.

thieves had their fingers or hands cut off, and so on. Even today, in some countries that follow a strict Islamic code, the hands of habitual thieves are cut off as a form of corporal punishment.

general deterrence

The use of the example of individual punishment to dissuade others from committing crimes.

General deterrence occurs when the punishment of an individual serves as an example to others who might be thinking of committing a crime—thereby dissuading them from their planned course of action. The **pleasure-pain principle,** which is central to modern discussions of general deterrence, holds that actions are motivated primarily by the desire to experience pleasure and avoid pain. According to this principle, the threat of loss to anyone convicted of a crime should outweigh the potential pleasure to be gained by committing the crime.

pleasure-pain principle

The idea that actions are motivated primarily by a desire to experience pleasure and avoid pain.

For punishment to be effective as a deterrent, it must be relatively certain, swiftly applied, and sufficiently severe. *Certainty, swiftness,* and *severity* of punishment are not always easy to achieve. Although it may not be easy for all offenders to get away with crime, the likelihood that any individual offender will be arrested, successfully prosecuted, and then punished is far smaller than deterrence advocates would like it to be. When an arrest does occur, an offender is typically released on bail, and, because of an overcrowded court system, the trial, if any, may not happen until a year or so later.

incapacitation

The use of imprisonment or other means to reduce an offender's capability to commit future offenses.

Incapacitation Proponents of **incapacitation** advocate that offenders should be prevented from committing further crimes either by their (temporary or permanent) removal from society or by some other method that restricts their physical ability to reoffend. Prison is synonymous with incapacitation because as long as the criminal is incarcerated, he or she cannot commit crimes against the rest of us. The belief is the pain or suffering imposed on an offender through incapacitation is justified because it reduces or prevents the further harm that would have been caused to the rest of society by the future crimes of that offender. The concern is with the victim, or potential victim. The rights of the offender merit little consideration.

Incapacitation in the form of imprisonment is considered to be a strategy that "works" because, for the duration of their prison sentence, offenders are restricted from committing crimes within the community. However prisoners commit crimes in prison against staff and other inmates, and there is evidence that some inmates can continue to commit crime. For example, Sheikh Omar Abdel Rahman, the blind sheikh who is serving a life sentence in New York for conspiring to bomb a number of New York landmarks, was accused of sending messages from prison through visiting attorneys to members of Gama'a al-Islamiyya, Egypt's largest militant group. Other inmates use smuggled-in cell phones to threaten victims and witnesses and commit credit card fraud.

truth in sentencing (TIS)

The sentencing principle that requires an offender to serve a substantial portion of the sentence and reduces the discrepancy between the sentence imposed and actual time spent in prison.

Pursuant to the goal of incapacitation, offenders are not rehabilitated. Criminals are incarcerated not to teach them the consequences of their actions, but to bring them under such an environment where they are not able to engage in crime. Incarceration incapacitates the prisoner by physically removing her or him from the society in which the crimes were committed. **Truth-in-sentencing** and **three-strikes laws** are examples of incapacitation. The most cited example of the severity of the three-strikes law is the case of Jerry Williams, who, in 1995, was sentenced to life imprisonment in California without parole for stealing a piece of pizza.

three-strikes laws

Three-strikes laws impose mandatory prison sentences, generally a life sentence, on those convicted of an offense if they have been previously convicted of two prior serious criminal offenses.

The most severe and permanent form of incapacitation is capital punishment. What is indisputable is that once put to death, an individual is incapable of committing further offenses. Capital punishment is, therefore, undeniably "effective" in terms of its incapacitative function.

Rehabilitation or Reformation The goal of **rehabilitation** or **reformation** is to change criminal lifestyles into law-abiding ones. Rehabilitation has been accomplished when an offender's criminal patterns of thought and behavior have been replaced by allegiance to society's values. Rehabilitation focuses on medical and psychological treatments and on social skills training, all designed to "correct" the problems that led the individual to crime.

A subgoal of rehabilitation is **reintegration** of the offender with the community. Reintegrating the offender with the community means making the offender a productive member of society—one who contributes to the general well-being of the whole.

Rehabilitation, which became the focus of American corrections beginning in the late 1800s, led to implementation of indeterminate sentencing practices (soon to be discussed), probation, parole, and a separate system of juvenile justice. During the 1970s, however, rehabilitation came under harsh criticism. As American society experienced disruptions brought about by economic change, the decline of traditional institutions, and fallout from the war in Vietnam, conservatives blamed the rehabilitative ideal for being too liberal, and liberals condemned it for providing an unfair basis for coercive action against disenfranchised social groups.[3] About the same time, an influential and widely read study by Robert Martinson, which evaluated rehabilitation programs nationwide, reported that few, if any, produced real changes in offender attitudes.[4] Dubbed the "nothing works doctrine," Martinson's critique of rehabilitation as a correctional goal led some states to abandon rehabilitation altogether or to de-emphasize it in favor of the goals of retribution and incapacitation. In other states, attempts at rehabilitation continued but were often muted.

Today, in the face of a difficult economy, many state governments and private organizations are reembracing rehabilitation, emphasizing the cost savings that can result from lowering prison populations and successfully reintegrating past offenders into society. According to Francis T. Cullen and Paul Gendreau, it is time to give the rehabilitative ideal a second chance. They call for *reaffirming rehabilitation*. "Many [rehabilitative] programs fail to work," say Cullen and Gendreau, "because they either are ill-conceived (not based on sound criminological theory) and/or have no therapeutic integrity (are not implemented as designed)." "We would not be surprised,"

rehabilitation (also *reformation*)

The changing of criminal lifestyles into law-abiding ones by "correcting" the behavior of offenders through treatment, education, and training.

reintegration

The process of making the offender a productive member of the community.

As a goal of sentencing, incapacitation restrains offenders from committing more crimes by isolating them from society. Does this threat of social isolation encourage law-abiding behavior?

© Design Pics/Kristy-Anne Glubiish RF

RELIABLE RESEARCH. REAL RESULTS.

Enter your keyword(s)   Search Site   Advanced Search

EVIDENCE-BASED CORRECTIONS
Reduced Probation Caseload in Evidence-Based Setting (Iowa)

The Reduced Probation Caseload in Evidence-Based Setting (Iowa) program aims to intensify the probation experience by reducing the caseloads of probation officers dealing with certain offenders—typically, the more high-risk probationers. In conjunction with the use of other evidence-based tools and risk assessment techniques, the reduction in caseloads aims to reduce probationers' recidivism in high-risk cases by providing more hands-on monitoring and greater scrutiny of their rehabilitative efforts and treatment progress.

The principal evidence-based practices that the program relies on are officer training to identify probationers' static and dynamic risks factors to determine the appropriate level of supervision based on likelihood of re-offense. (Static risk factors are features of the offender's history that predict recidivism but are not amenable to change—e.g., age and prior offenses. Dynamic risk factors are changeable factors such as substance abuse and negative peer associations.) In evidence-based settings, resources are concentrated on high-risk offenders, including treating and monitoring dynamic factors, such as illegal drug use. This allows for only the highest risk offenders to be placed on the reduced probation caseloads, making best use of correctional resources in a risk-needs-responsivity (RNR) framework. The RNR model has three core principles:

1. *Risk principle:* The level of services should be matched to the level of the offender. High-risk offenders should receive more intensive services; low-risk offenders should receive minimal services.

2. *Need principle:* Target criminogenic needs with services—that is, target those factors that are associated with criminal behavior. Such factors might include substance abuse, pro-criminal attitudes, criminal associates, and the like. Do not target other, non-criminogenic factors (such as emotional distress, self-esteem issues) unless they act as a barrier to changing criminogenic factors.

3. *Responsivity principle:* The ability and learning style of the offender should determine the style and mode of intervention. Research has shown the general effectiveness of using social learning and cognitive—behavioral style interventions.

The program is rated Effective. Participants in the treatment group were arrested less often than the control group. At the maximum 36-month follow-up, the treatment significantly reduced the likelihood of recidivism by 47 percent for property and violent crime and 20 percent for all offenses. However, there was no difference between treatment and control groups on revocation rates.

Source: Adapted from https://www.crimesolutions.gov/ProgramDetails.aspx?ID=259.

---

they write, "if young children turned out to be illiterate if their teachers were untrained, had no standardized curriculum, and met the children once a week for half an hour."[5] Until recently, contend Cullen and Gendreau, many correctional treatment programs were in such a state.

Other writers hold that continued efforts at rehabilitation are mandatory for any civilized society as a moral obligation, not merely as an effort to save money. "In order to neutralize the desocializing potential of prisons," says Edgardo Rotman, "a civilized society is forced into rehabilitative undertakings. These become an essential ingredient of its correctional system taken as a whole. A correctional system" with no "interest in treatment," says Rotman, "means . . . de-humanization and regression."[6]

Restoration Over the past few decades, a new goal of criminal sentencing, known as **restoration,** has developed. **Restorative justice** is based on the belief that criminal sentencing should involve restoration and justice for all involved in or affected by crime.

Advocates of restorative justice (or, as some agencies refer to it, *community justice* or *reparative justice*) believe that crime is committed not just against the state but also against victims and the community. Restorative

restoration

The process of returning to their previous condition all those involved in or affected by crime—including victims, offenders, and society.

restorative justice

A systematic response to wrongdoing that emphasizes healing the wounds of victims, offenders, and communities caused or revealed by crime.

40

justice is especially concerned with repairing the harm to the victim and the community. Harm is repaired through negotiation, mediation, and empowerment rather than through retribution, deterrence, and punishment. A restorative justice perspective allows judges and juries to consider **victim-impact statements** in their sentencing decisions. These are descriptions of the harm and suffering that a crime has caused victims and their survivors. Also among the efforts being introduced on behalf of victims and their survivors are victim assistance and victim compensation programs.

victim-impact statement

A description of the harm and suffering that a crime has caused victims and survivors.

Advocates of restorative justice believe not only that the victim should be restored by the justice process but also that the offender and society should participate in the restoration process. To this end, efforts at restoration emphasize the successful reintegration of offenders into the community as well as victims' rights and needs. Another aspect of involving offenders in restoration is having them actively address the harm they have caused. The system strives to accomplish this by holding them directly accountable and by helping them become productive, law-abiding members of their community.[7] Restorative justice programs try to personalize crime by showing offenders the consequences of their behavior.

Restorative justice is based on the premise that because crime occurs in the context of the community, the community should be involved in addressing it. Particular restorative justice or community justice programs might use any of the following: (1) victim–offender mediation, (2) victim–offender reconciliation, (3) victim-impact panels, (4) restorative justice panels, (5) community reparative boards, (6) community-based courts, (7) family group conferences, (8) circle sentencing, (9) court diversion programs, and (10) peer mediation.

Restorative justice seeks to restore the health of the community, repair the harm done, meet victims' needs, and require the offender to contribute to those repairs. Thus, the criminal act is condemned, offenders are held accountable, offenders and victims are involved as participants, and repentant offenders are encouraged to earn their way back into the good graces of society.

SENTENCING OPTIONS AND TYPES OF SENTENCES

CO3-3

Legislatures establish the types of sentences that can be imposed. The U.S. Congress and the 50 state legislatures decide what is against the law and define crimes and their punishments in the jurisdictions in which they have control. Chapter 1 taught you the stages of criminal justice processing of adult offenders. Chapters 4 through 8 detail the types of state sentencing options that are frequently used. For example, Chapter 4 discusses probation goals, history, characteristics of probationers, how it is organized and administered, private probation, what probation officers do, issues of caseload size and technology, and probation revocation hearings. Similar detail is covered in subsequent chapters for intermediate sanctions (Chapter 5), jails (Chapter 6), prisons (Chapter 7), and parole (Chapter 8).

One sentence that is becoming less frequently used across the United States is capital punishment. The trends in capital punishment today are these: Death sentences are down, executions are down, and public support for capital punishment is falling. For these reasons, we have chosen not to devote a complete chapter to a sentencing option that is waning. Instead, we will highlight the major themes of capital punishment in this chapter after progressing through a brief introduction of the sentences that

EXHIBIT 3–2   Types of Sentences

capital punishment Lawful imposition of the death penalty.

community service A sentence to serve a specified number of hours working in unpaid positions with nonprofit or tax supported agencies.

consecutive sentences Sentences served one after the other.

concurrent sentences Sentences served together.

day fine A financial penalty scaled both to the defendant's ability to pay and the seriousness of the crime.

deferred sentence A sentence that is postponed for a specific period to allow the court to evaluate the conduct of the offender during the deferred period (usually community supervision). If the defendant successfully completes the court order, the charges are normally dismissed and do not remain on the defendants' record.

determinate sentence (also fixed sentence) A sentence of a fixed term of incarceration, which can be reduced by good time (days or months prison authorities deduct from a sentence for good behavior and other reasons).

fine A financial penalty used as a criminal sanction.

flat sentences Those that specify a given amount of time to be served in custody and allow little or no variation from the time specified.

habitual offender statute A law that (1) allows a person's criminal history to be considered at sentencing or (2) makes it possible for a person convicted of a given offense and previously convicted of another specified offense to receive a more severe penalty than that for the current offense alone.

indeterminate sentence A sentence in which a judge specifies a maximum length and a minimum length, and an administrative agency, generally a parole board, determines the actual time of release.

intensive supervision probation (ISP) Control of offenders in the community under strict conditions, by means of frequent reporting to a probation officer whose caseload is generally limited to 30 offenders.

intermediate sanctions New punishment options developed to fill the gap between traditional probation and traditional jail or prison sentences and to better match the severity of punishment to the seriousness of the crime.

jail Locally operated correctional facilities that that confine people before or after conviction.

life sentence (also life imprisonment and life without parole [LWOP]) A sentence condemning a convicted offender to spend the rest of her or his life in prison.

mandatory minimum sentencing Sentences required by statute for those convicted of a particular crime or a particular crime with special circumstances, such as robbery with a firearm or selling drugs to a minor within 1,000 feet of a school, or for those with a particular type of criminal history.

mandatory sentences Those that are required by law under certain circumstances—such as conviction of a specified crime or of a series of offenses of a specified type.

maximum sentence The maximum amount of time a convicted person can be held in custody.

minimum sentence The minimum amount of time a convicted person can be held in custody.

parole The conditional release of a prisoner, prior to completion of the imposed sentence, under the supervision of a parole officer.

presumptive sentence The expected sentence; sentences presumed to be appropriate and judges are expected to follow unless they document reasons for departing from the guidelines.

prison A state or federal confinement facility that has custodial authority over adults sentenced to confinement.

probation The conditional release of a convicted offender into the community, under the supervision of a probation officer. It is conditional because it can be revoked if certain conditions are not met.

restitution Payments made by a criminal offender to his or her victim (or to the court, which then turns them over to the victim) as compensation for the harm caused by the offense.

sentencing commission A group assigned to create a schedule of sentences that reflect the gravity of the offenses committed and the prior record of the criminal offender.

sentencing enhancements Legislatively approved provisions that mandate longer prison terms for specific criminal offenses committed under certain circumstances (such as a murder committed because of the victim's race or a drug sale near a school) or because of an offender's past criminal record.

suspended sentence A legal term for a judge's delaying of a defendant's serving of a sentence after they have been convicted or found guilty in order to allow the defendant to perform a period of community supervision. If the defendant does not break the law during the probationary period, the sentence is normally eliminated. However, unlike a deferred sentence, a suspended sentence remains on a defendant's criminal record permanently.

straight (also flat) sentence A fixed sentence with no maximum or minimum associated with it.

three-strikes laws Statutes that impose mandatory prison sentences, generally a life sentence, on those convicted of an offense if they have been previously convicted of two prior serious criminal offenses.

truth in sentencing (TIS) The sentencing principle that requires an offender to serve a substantial portion of the sentence (usually 85 percent) and reduces the discrepancy between the sentence imposed and actual time spent in prison.

are more frequently given by the courts and the corrections system. Unlike capital punishment, probation, intermediate sanctions, jail, prison, and parole are not on the cutting table. They are being transformed through evidence-based practices. They require more discussion and understanding as we prepare for criminal sentencing in the second half of the 21st century.

Exhibit 3–2 is a guide to the sentencing options and sanctions in use across the United States. Our intent here is to review briefly the sequence of sentencing options after conviction, recognizing that they are discussed in more depth in the chapters that follow, and to allow sufficient coverage of capital punishment.

Probation

The sentencing options that may be available to judges and juries begin with probation and end with capital punishment. If a defendant is sentenced to probation, she or he is on conditional release into the community and under the supervision of a probation officer. It is conditional because it can be revoked if certain conditions are not met. On January 1, 2015, about 1 in 63 adults was on probation. And even though more adults are on probation than in jail and prison, the majority of the $60 billion corrections budget is given to jails and prisons, causing problems with high probation caseloads, case investigations, and supervision, as you will learn.

Many jurisdictions have a variety of offenders on probation (e.g., property offenders, domestic abusers, felony and misdemeanor offenders, and sex offenders). It all boils down to the capacity of the individual jurisdiction, what the community will tolerate, state statutes, resource availability, etc. How well someone does on probation depends on how well the offender's needs are assessed, how well they are supervised, and what resources the agency has available to assist in its supervision and rehabilitation. The motivation of the offender is also a factor that has to be considered. Assessing a probationer's risk and needs and providing the right treatment at the right level is an evidence-based practice that contributes to successful probation outcomes and is discussed in more depth later.

Intermediate Sanctions

Probation can either stand alone as a criminal sanction or be combined with any of the intermediate sanctions discussed in Chapter 5. As you will learn, intermediate sanctions have been developed to fill the gap between traditional probation and traditional jail or prison sentences and to better match the severity of punishment to the seriousness of the crime. Among the more frequently used intermediate sanctions are *intensive supervision probation* (ISP), *community service,* and *fines.* ISP is control of offenders in the community under strict conditions, by means of frequent reporting to a probation officer whose caseload is generally limited to 30 offenders. Community service is a sentence to serve a specified number of hours working in unpaid positions with nonprofit or tax-supported agencies. And a fine is a financial penalty used as a criminal sanction. Community service and fines are seldom, if ever, used as stand-alone criminal sanctions in the United States as they are in Western Europe. In the United States, they are added as conditions of probation.

Jail and Prison

Moving further into the stages of criminal justice processing, you often hear the terms *jail* and *prison* used interchangeably. However there are big differences between the two. Whether a person is confined in jail or prison says something important about the crime committed and the stages of criminal justice processing. The major difference between jail and prison is the length of the individual's sentence. Jails are used to hold people who have been recently arrested or people who are charged with a crime and unable to post bail. It can also house people who are given short sentences, generally one year or less.

By contrast, a prison is designed for long-term confinement. The majority of convicted criminals serve their sentences in a prison. Under closer scrutiny, however, the distinction between jail and prison in terms of the length of an offender's sentence blurs. Because of overcrowding in state and federal prisons, almost 82,000 prisoners serving sentences longer than one year were held in local jails on January 1, 2015, a slight decline of 5 percent from the year before.[8] Louisiana houses more than 50 percent of its state prisoners in local jails.

You will also learn that who runs the facility is important. Jails are locally run. Except for six states that run combined jail/prison systems (Alaska, Connecticut, Delaware, Hawaii, Rhode Island, and Vermont), jails are local correctional facilities, paid for mostly by local tax dollars (although most receive some state funding) and, in most counties, administered by locally elected sheriffs. Prisons, on the other hand, are state facilities, supported by state taxpayers (most prisons also receive some type of federal funding) and administered by wardens who are appointed by the governor.

In spite of their differences, however, most jails and prisons face the same challenges: overcrowding, high recidivism rates, large numbers of offenders who are mentally ill, and overrepresentation of minorities. On January 1, 2015, 1 in 106 adults was in jail or prison: 744,592 persons were confined in our nation's jails, and 1,561,500 were held in state and federal prisons.

Parole

Persons leaving jail or prison are often continued under some type of community supervision (sometimes known as parole). However, across the past 30 years, almost one-third of the states and the federal government eliminated parole for reasons you will learn about in Chapter 8. Many argue that sentencing policies and practices—mandatory minimum sentences, truth-in-sentencing statutes, three-strikes laws, life without parole, punitive sentencing guidelines, and the movement to abolish parole—fueled the mass incarceration in the United States that we see today. Policy makers, politicians from both sides of the aisle, and scholars are calling for the return of some positive features of the indeterminate sentencing system, including parole. We share some of that sentencing reform vision with you later in this chapter.

Parole, like probation, faces challenges. The biggest is offender reentry. Almost 2,000 persons leave prison every day. Their job prospects are dim, their chances of finding a place to live are bleak, and their health is poor. Is it any wonder that two-thirds are rearrested within three years and one-half are reincarcerated?

To change this cycle of failure, the U.S. Congress and state and local governments are creating opportunities to provide employment assistance, substance abuse treatment, housing, family programming, mentoring, victim support, and other services that can make a person's transition from prison or jail safer and more successful. Three major initiatives include the Second Chance Act, the "ban the box" movement, and reentry court—opportunities unknown a decade ago—which are discussed in more detail in Chapter 8.

- The national Second Chance Act supports state, local, and tribal governments and nonprofit organizations in their work with grants to reduce recidivism and improve outcomes for people returning from state and federal prisons and local jails.
- The "ban the box" movement encourages local, state, and federal governments to remove barriers to qualified workers with criminal

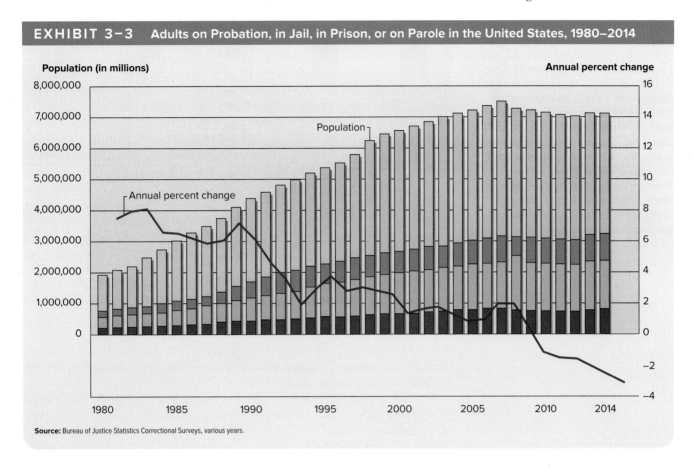

EXHIBIT 3–3 Adults on Probation, in Jail, in Prison, or on Parole in the United States, 1980–2014

Source: Bureau of Justice Statistics Correctional Surveys, various years.

records by prohibiting employers from requiring disclosure of past convictions on *initial* job applications. Employers can ask about criminal backgrounds and run background checks after determining that an applicant meets minimum job qualifications.

- Reentry courts are specialized courts (much like drug courts) that manage the return to the community of offenders released from jail or prison to the community using the authority of the court to apply graduated sanctions and positive reinforcement and to marshal resources to support the individual's reintegration.

Exhibit 3–3 displays these recent trends in correctional punishment.

Capital Punishment

Capital punishment was once common throughout the world and imposed for many crimes, including murder, rape, stealing, witchcraft, piracy, desertion, sodomy, adultery, concealing the birth or death of an infant, aiding runaway slaves, counterfeiting, and forgery. Criminals were boiled, burned, roasted on spits, drawn and quartered, broken on wheels, disemboweled, torn apart by animals, gibbeted (hung from a post with a projecting arm and left to die), bludgeoned (beaten to death with sticks, clubs, or rocks), or pressed (crushed under a board and stones).

Capital punishment began changing in the 18th century during the Enlightenment. This philosophical movement led to many new theories on crime and punishment. One of these theories proposed that punishment

capital punishment

Lawful imposition of the death penalty.

Capital Punishment

On September 30, 1283, Dafydd ap Gruffydd, the last native prince of Wales, was condemned to die for plotting the death of King Edward I. On October 3, 1283, Dafydd was dragged through the streets behind a horse, hanged and then revived, disemboweled (his stomach was cut open, and his intestines were removed and thrown into a fire as he watched), beheaded, and then drawn and quartered. Drawing-and-quartering was officially abolished as a method of execution in Britain in 1870. Why did penalties involving torture disappear?
© Corbis

should fit the crime. Penalties involving torture began to disappear, and the use of the death penalty diminished.

By 1950, as prosperity followed World War II, public sentiment for capital punishment faded. The number of executions dropped. Support for capital punishment was at its lowest in 1966 (42 percent), and constitutional challenges were starting to surface. The watershed case in capital punishment took place in 1972 when the Court decided *Furman* v. *Georgia.*[9] The Court held that Georgia's death penalty statute, which gave the sentencing authority (judge or trial jury) complete sentencing discretion without any guidance as to how to exercise that discretion, could result in arbitrary sentencing and was therefore in violation of the Eighth Amendment's ban against cruel and unusual punishment.

Four years later, in *Gregg* v. *Georgia,* the Supreme Court upheld guided discretionary capital statutes, opining that "such standards do provide guidance to the sentencing authority and thereby reduce the likelihood that it will impose a sentence that fairly can be called capricious and arbitrary." Almost 45 years later, the trends in capital punishment are these: Death sentences are at an historic low, executions reached a 25-year low, and since 1973, 156 persons have been **exonerated** and freed from death row.

Capital Punishment Around the World In 2014 Amnesty International documented 607 executions in 22 countries, but the total did not include figures from China, which executes more people than the rest of the world combined. The five countries that reported the most executions in 2014 were China (1,000s), Iran (289 officially and at least 454 more that were not acknowledged), Saudi Arabia (at least 90), Iraq (at least 61), and the United States (35).[10]

On January 1, 2015, the majority of countries (140) had abolished the death penalty in law or in practice.[11] Fifty-eight countries still retain it.

States With and Without Capital Punishment At midyear 2015, 20 states and the District of Columbia had abolished the death penalty. Thirty states, the U.S. military, and the federal government still retain it (see Exhibit 3–4).

exonerate

To clear of blame and release from death row.

Visit http://www.deathpenaltyinfo.org/documents/FactSheet.pdf or scan this code with the QR app on your smartphone or digital device. There, you will find information on the number of persons executed since 1976, the race of victims and defendants executed and recent studies on race, death row exonerations, characteristics of persons on death row, executions by state and region, number of death sentences since 1998, and other facts about capital punishment.

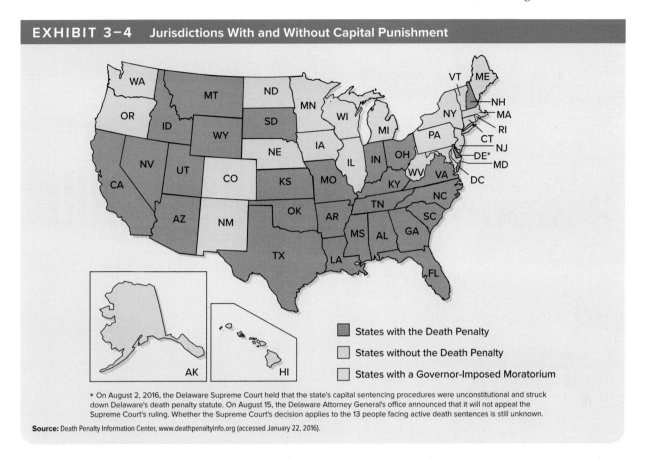

EXHIBIT 3–4 Jurisdictions With and Without Capital Punishment

- States with the Death Penalty
- States without the Death Penalty
- States with a Governor-Imposed Moratorium

* On August 2, 2016, the Delaware Supreme Court held that the state's capital sentencing procedures were unconstitutional and struck down Delaware's death penalty statute. On August 15, the Delaware Attorney General's office announced that it will not appeal the Supreme Court's ruling. Whether the Supreme Court's decision applies to the 13 people facing active death sentences is still unknown.

Source: Death Penalty Information Center, www.deathpenaltyinfo.org (accessed January 22, 2016).

The first person executed after *Gregg* v. *Georgia* was Gary Gilmore, who gave up his right to appeal and was executed by firing squad on January 17, 1977, by the state of Utah. Since then, 1,422 have been executed. See Exhibit 3–5 for the number of executions from 1976 through 2015 in the United States and around the world.

Today in the United States, what constitutes a **capital crime**—a crime that is punishable by death—is defined by law. This definition varies among jurisdictions. In Delaware, for example, first-degree murder with at least one

capital crime

A crime for which the death penalty may but need not necessarily be imposed.

On May 2, 2013, Maryland governor Martin O'Malley signed legislation that abolished capital punishment and replaced it with the sentence of life in prison without the possibility of parole. Do you think the eight states that abolished capital punishment since 2007 (New York and New Jersey in 2007; New Mexico in 2009; Illinois in 2011; Connecticut in 2012; Maryland in 2013; Nebraska in 2015; and Delaware in 2016) will be the "bellwether" of the American death penalty?

© AP Photo/Patrick Semansky

EXHIBIT 3–5   People Executed, 1976–2015

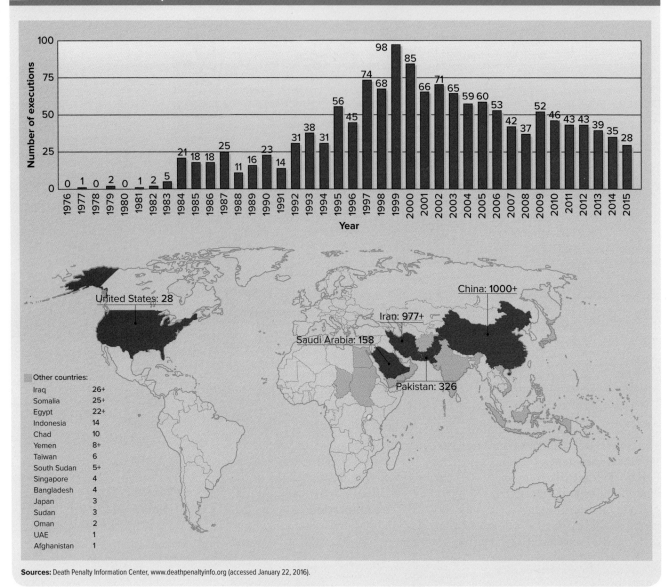

Sources: Death Penalty Information Center, www.deathpenaltyinfo.org (accessed January 22, 2016).

statutory aggravating circumstance is a capital crime. In Nevada, first-degree murder with at least 1 of 15 aggravating circumstances is a capital crime. In Texas, criminal homicide with one of nine aggravating circumstances is a capital offense.[12]

CO3-4   **Characteristics of Persons on Death Row**   At year end 2015, 2,984 persons were awaiting execution, a decrease of almost 300 from one decade earlier. At the time of Gary Gilmore's execution on January 17, 1977, there were 423 people on death row. Ten years later, the number was 1,984. After more than 20 years of continued increase in the number of people sentenced to die in the United States, the number on death row peaked in 2000 to 3,593 and has been decreasing ever since.

Today, U.S. juries are imposing fewer death sentences than they did on average during the 1990s. In the 1990s, an average of almost 300 people were sentenced to death each year. In the first decade of the 20th century,

Few issues generate more public controversy than that of the death penalty. In some states there are movements to end the death penalty, but in others, the move is to speed up death row appeals and complete the sentence of execution. Do demonstrations such as these influence the public policy implemented by state legislatures?
Left: © Alex Wong/Getty Images; Right: © Jack Kurtz/The Image Works

the average was almost 135 per year. Since 2011, the average has dropped to 74 per year. Almost 50 percent of the nation's death row population is in three states: California (746), Florida (400), and Texas (265). Exhibit 3–6 shows additional characteristics of inmates under sentence of death.

Victim Race and Capital Punishment Defendant–victim racial combinations have been the subject of considerable debate.[13] Recognizing that whites and minorities are murder victims in approximately equal numbers, why is it that more than 75 percent of the victims in cases resulting in executions since 1977 have been white? Does it imply that white victims are

CO3-5

EXHIBIT 3–6 Characteristics of Prisoners Under Sentence of Death, January 1, 2016

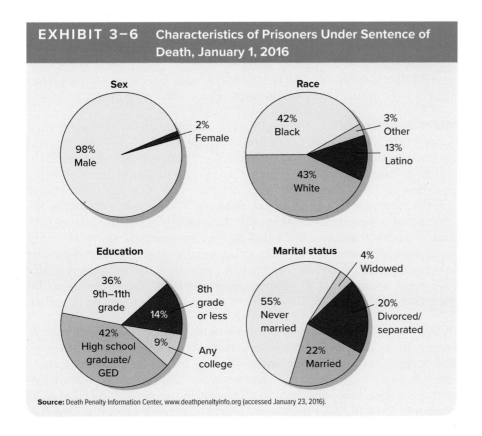

Sex
- 98% Male
- 2% Female

Race
- 42% Black
- 43% White
- 3% Other
- 13% Latino

Education
- 36% 9th–11th grade
- 8th grade or less
- 14%
- 42% High school graduate/GED
- 9%
- Any college

Marital status
- 55% Never married
- 4% Widowed
- 20% Divorced/separated
- 22% Married

Source: Death Penalty Information Center, www.deathpenaltyinfo.org (accessed January 23, 2016).

Reporters observe the execution chair in which Gary Gilmore sat when facing a Utah firing squad on January 17, 1977. Upper right on the chair back are the bullet holes. Draped over the back of the chair is the corduroy material hood that Gilmore wore during the execution. On March 15, 2004, Utah repealed its use of the firing squad, leaving lethal injection as the only option. Should condemned inmates be permitted to choose the method of their execution if, when they were sentenced to die, state law allowed the choice?

© Bettmann/Corbis

considered more important by the criminal justice system? Some have argued that blacks and Hispanics are more likely than whites to be sentenced to death and executed because they are more likely to be arrested on facts that can support a capital charge and because whites are more likely to negotiate plea bargains that spare their lives. Others disagree, citing consistent patterns of racial bias.[14] Since the General Accounting Office first studied the issue of interracial murders and sentencing in 1990 and reported that race of the victim influences the likelihood of being charged with capital murder or receiving the death penalty, many scholars have found the same pattern. For example:

- Jurors in Washington state are three times more likely to recommend a death sentence for a black defendant than for a white defendant in a similar case.
- In Louisiana, the odds of a death sentence were 97 percent higher for those whose victim was white than for those whose victim was black.
- A study in California found that those who killed whites were more than three times more likely to be sentenced to death than those who killed blacks and more than four times more likely than those who killed Latinos.
- In 96 percent of states where there have been reviews of race and the death penalty, there was a pattern of either race-of-victim or race-of-defendant discrimination, or both.

The public also believes that decision making in homicide cases is not influenced by the same factors in all cases. According to the 2015 American Values Survey by the Public Religion Research Institute, 53 percent of all Americans agreed with the statement, "A black person is more likely than a white person to receive the death penalty for the same crime," while 45 percent disagreed.

Methods of Execution Five methods of execution are used in the United States: (1) lethal injection, (2) electrocution, (3) lethal gas, (4) hanging, and (5) firing squad. All states and the federal government use lethal injection as their primary method of execution. States use a variety of protocols using one, two, or three drugs. The three-drug protocol uses an anesthetic or sedative, typically follpancuronium, followed by bromide to paralyze the inmate and potassium chloride to stop the inmate's heart. The one- or two-drug protocols typically use a lethal dose of an anesthetic or sedative and avoid the controversy of the short-acting sedative wearing off and leading to consciousness of the inmate. Another problem is that manufacturers of anesthetics are refusing to provide departments of corrections drugs for executions, which also explains, in part, the reason executions have stalled.

CO3-6 **Public Opinion and Capital Punishment** Support for capital punishment in the United States dropped by 2 percentage points from 2014 to 2015, and opposition rose to its highest levels since before the Supreme Court's ruling in *Furman* v. *Georgia*.[15] In October 2015, Gallup reported that 61 percent of the American public said they favor the death penalty, down from 63 percent in 2014 and near the 40-year low of 60 percent support recorded in

2013. Support was 19 points below the 80 percent who told Gallup in 1994 that they supported capital punishment. More than one-third (37 percent) said they opposed the death penalty, the most in 43 years and 21 points above levels reported in the mid-1990s. Support for capital punishment is higher in the states that have it—64 percent versus 54 percent elsewhere. In a wider gap, persons in death penalty states divide about evenly in their preference for capital punishment versus life without the possibility of parole (LWOP). However, in states without capital punishment, LWOP is preferred by a 20-point margin.[16] The poll results are consistent with other signs of declining support for the death penalty: eight states have abolished the death penalty since 2007, and death sentences are at their lowest level since capital punishment was reinstated. Even with historic lows in death sentencing, the poll reports the highest percentage of Americans to say the death penalty is imposed too often (27 percent). There are many arguments favoring capital punishment and many arguments opposing it. Some of the arguments—pro and con—are summarized in Exhibit 3–7. Where do you stand?

EXHIBIT 3–7   Arguments Favoring and Opposing the Death Penalty

PRO

- It deters people from crime through fear of punishment; it exerts a positive moral influence by stigmatizing crimes of murder and manslaughter.
- It is a just punishment for murder; it fulfills the "just deserts" principle of a fitting punishment; life in prison is not a tough enough punishment for a capital crime.
- It is constitutionally appropriate; the Eighth Amendment prohibits cruel and unusual punishment, yet the Fifth Amendment implies that, with due process of law, one may be deprived of life, liberty, or property.
- It reduces time spent on death row to reduce costs of capital punishment and the attendant costs of postconviction appeals, investigations, and searches for new evidence and witnesses.
- It protects society from the most serious and feared offenders; it prevents the reoccurrence of violence.
- It is more humane than life imprisonment because it is quick; making the prisoner suffer by remaining in prison for the rest of his or her life is more torturous and inhumane than execution.
- It is almost impossible for an innocent person to be executed; the slow execution rate results from the process of appeals, from sentencing to execution.

CON

- It does not deter crime; no evidence exists that the death penalty is more effective than other punishments.
- It violates human rights; it is a barbaric remnant of an uncivilized society; it is immoral in principle; and it ensures the execution of some innocent people.
- It falls disproportionately on racial minorities; those who murdered whites are more likely to be sentenced to death than are those who murdered blacks.
- It costs too much; $2 million to $5 million are poured into each execution while other criminal justice components such as police, courts, and community corrections lack funding.
- It boosts the murder rate; this is known as the *brutalizing effect;* the state is a role model, and when the state carries out an execution, it shows that killing is a way to solve problems.
- Not everyone wants vengeance; many people favor alternative sentences such as life without parole.
- It is arbitrary and unfair; offenders who commit similar crimes under similar circumstances receive widely differing sentences; race, social and economic status, location of crime, and pure chance influence sentencing.

CO3-7

The Courts and Capital Punishment When the Supreme Court ruled in *Furman* v. *Georgia* in 1972, it also voided 40 death penalty statutes and committed the death sentences of all 629 death row inmates around the United States, and suspended the death penalty because existing statutes were no longer valid. It is important to note that the Court majority did *not* rule that the death penalty itself was unconstitutional but that only the way in which it was administered at that time.

States responded to the *Furman* decision by rewriting their capital punishment statutes to limit discretion and avoid arbitrary and inconsistent results. The new death penalty laws took two forms. Some states imposed a **mandatory death penalty** for certain crimes, and others permitted **guided discretion**, which sets standards for judges and juries to use when deciding whether to impose the death penalty.

In 1976, the U.S. Supreme Court rejected mandatory capital punishment statutes but approved guided discretion statutes in *Gregg* v. *Georgia*. In its ruling, the Court approved automatic appellate review, a proportionality review whereby state appellate courts compare a sentence with those of similar cases, and a **bifurcated trial**, or special two-part trial. The first part of a bifurcated trial, the *guilt phase,* decides the issue of guilt. If the defendant is found guilty, the second part of the trial, the *penalty phase,* takes place. The penalty phase includes presentation of facts that mitigate or aggravate the circumstances of the crime. **Mitigating circumstances** are factors that may reduce the culpability of the offender (make the defendant less deserving of the death penalty). **Aggravating circumstances** are factors that may increase the offender's culpability (make the defendant more deserving of death).

In 2002, the U.S. Supreme Court handed down another decision that shaped capital sentencing. In *Ring* v. *Arizona,*[17] the Court held that only juries, not judges, can determine the presence of "aggravating factors" to be weighed in the capital sentencing process. Although judges may still reduce sentences, the Court held that a defendant may not receive a penalty that exceeds the maximum penalty that he or she would have received if punished according to the facts in the jury verdict.

mandatory death penalty

A death sentence that the legislature has required to be imposed upon people convicted of certain offenses.

guided discretion

Decision making bounded by general guidelines, rules, or laws.

bifurcated trial

Two separate hearings for different issues in a trial, one for guilt and the other for punishment.

mitigating circumstances

Factors that, although not justifying or excusing an action, may reduce the culpability of the offender.

aggravating circumstances

Factors that may increase the culpability of the offender.

CO3-8

Appealing the Death Penalty Capital punishment cases may pass through as many as 10 courts across three stages: trial and direct review, state postconviction appeals, and federal *habeas corpus* appeals (see Exhibit 3–8).

In stage one, trial and direct review, a death sentence is imposed. The laws of all states require that legal issues about the trial and sentence automatically be appealed to the state appellate courts. Alabama and Ohio have two rounds of appeals in the direct review process; this means that the legal issues may be heard first in the state court of criminal appeals (court 1) before reaching the state supreme court (court 2). These courts evaluate the trial for legal or constitutional errors and determine whether the death sentence is consistent with sentences imposed in similar cases. State appellate courts seldom overturn a conviction or change a death sentence. The defendant then petitions the U.S. Supreme Court (court 3) to grant a petition for a writ of *certiorari*—a written order to the lower court whose decision is being appealed to send the records of the case forward for review. Stage one, direct review, consumes about five years—half of the time required for the entire appeals process. Nationally, the rate of **serious error** (error that substantially undermines the reliability of the guilt finding or death sentence imposed at trial) discovered on direct review is 41 percent.

If the defendant's direct appeals are unsuccessful and the Supreme Court denies review, stage two—state postconviction appeals—begins. At this point, many death row inmates allege ineffective or incompetent trial

serious error

Error that substantially undermines the reliability of the guilt finding or death sentence imposed at trial.

EXHIBIT 3-8   The Capital Criminal Process: Trial Through State and Federal Postconvictions

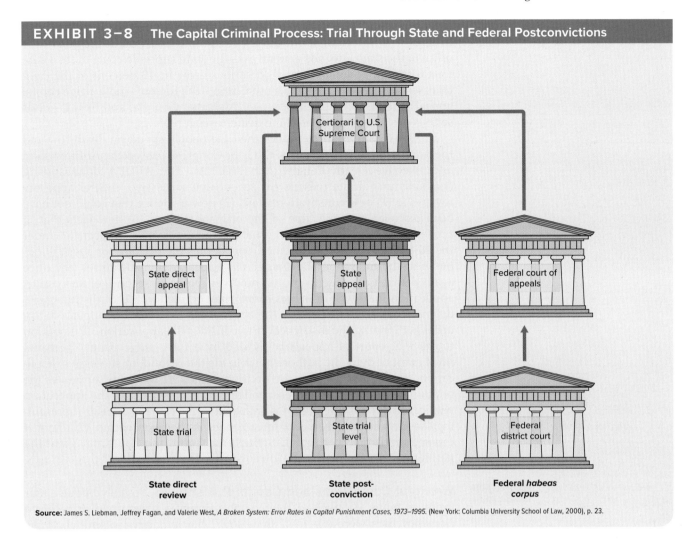

| State direct review | State post-conviction | Federal *habeas corpus* |

Source: James S. Liebman, Jeffrey Fagan, and Valerie West, *A Broken System: Error Rates in Capital Punishment Cases, 1973–1995.* (New York: Columbia University School of Law, 2000), p. 23.

counsel, and new counsel is appointed. The new counsel petitions the trial court (court 4) with newly discovered evidence; questions about the fairness of the trial; and allegations of jury bias, tainted evidence, incompetence of defense counsel, and prosecutorial or police misconduct. If the trial court denies the appeals, they may be filed with the state's appellate courts (either directly to the state supreme court or, if there exists a dual level of appellate review as in Alabama and Ohio, through a petition first to the state court of criminal appeals (court 5) followed by a petition to the state supreme court (court 6). Most often, the state appellate courts deny the petition. Defendant's counsel then petitions the U.S. Supreme Court (court 7). If the U.S. Supreme Court denies the petition for a writ of *certiorari,* stage two ends and stage three begins. The rate of serious error found on state postconviction appeals is 10 percent.

In stage three, the federal *habeas corpus* stage, a defendant files a petition in U.S. district court (court 8) in the state in which the defendant was convicted and is incarcerated and alleging violations of constitutional rights. Such rights include the right to due process (Fourteenth Amendment), prohibition against cruel and unusual punishment (Eighth Amendment), and effective assistance of counsel (Sixth Amendment). If the district court denies the petition, defense counsel submits it to the U.S. court of appeals (court 9) for the circuit representing the jurisdiction. If the court of appeals denies the petition, defense counsel asks the U.S. Supreme Court (court 10) to grant a writ of *certiorari*. If the U.S. Supreme Court denies *certiorari*, the office of the state attorney general asks the state supreme court to set a date for execution. Federal courts find serious error in 40 percent of the capital cases they review. The Eleventh Circuit—the nation's most active capital appeals circuit with jurisdiction over Alabama, Georgia, and Florida—finds serious error in 50 percent of the death cases it reviews.

In 1996, in an effort to reduce the time people spend on death row and the number of federal appeals, the U.S. Congress passed the Antiterrorism and Effective Death Penalty Act (AEDPA). The AEDPA defines filing deadlines and limits reasons for second, or successive, federal appellate reviews to (1) new constitutional law, (2) new evidence that could not have been discovered at the time of the original trial, or (3) new facts that, if proven, would be sufficient to establish the applicant's innocence. Under the AEDPA, if the U.S. Supreme Court denies the petition for a writ of *certiorari* in the final federal *habeas corpus* appeal, defense counsel may once again petition the federal courts; however, before a second, or successive, application for a writ of *habeas corpus* may be filed in a U.S. district court, defense counsel must petition the appropriate U.S. court of appeals for an order authorizing the district court to consider the application. The petition to the U.S. court of appeals is decided by a three-judge panel; the panel must grant or deny the authorization to file the second, or successive, application within 30 days after the petition is filed. If the panel approves the petition, the district court must render a decision regarding the application within 180 days. If the motion is appealed to the court of appeals representing the jurisdiction, the court must render its decision within 120 days. If the petition is filed with the U.S. Supreme Court, the Court may grant the petition for *certiorari* or let the lower court's decision stand.

CO3-9 **Wrongful Convictions and Capital Punishment** Possibly because four times as many people had their death sentences overturned or received clemency than were executed since 1977, the Judiciary Committee of the U.S. Senate asked Columbia law professor James Liebman to calculate the frequency of error in capital cases.[18] Liebman and his colleagues studied what happened when 4,578 capital cases were appealed. Their conclusion

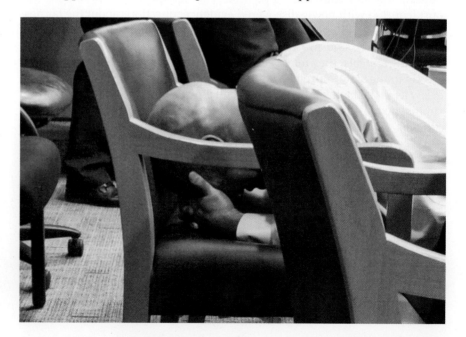

On December 21, 2012, former Florida death row inmate Seth Penalver was aquitted of all charges and freed from Florida's death row 13 years after being sentenced to death. At the time of his exoneration, Penalver was the 24th person released from death row in Florida, the most of any state. Since 1983, 156 persons have been released from death row, and news of their innocence has set off a new debate over capital punishment in the United States. How has the Liebman report shaped the debate?

© Sun-Sentinel/ZUMAPRESS.com/Alamy

is powerful: The overall rate of prejudicial error in the U.S. capital punishment system is 68 percent. More than two of every three capital judgments reviewed by the courts were found to be seriously flawed. Ten states (Alabama, Arizona, California, Georgia, Indiana, Maryland, Mississippi, Montana, Oklahoma, and Wyoming) have overall error rates of 75 percent or higher. Almost 1,000 of the cases sent back for retrial ended in sentences less than death, and 87 ended in *not guilty* verdicts.

Liebman and his colleagues found two types of serious error. The first is incompetent defense lawyering (accounting for one-third of all state postconviction appeals). A review of death penalty cases in Pennsylvania spanning three decades found that lawyers who handle such cases—typically at taxpayers' expense because the defendants are indigent—are often overworked and underpaid and present only the barest defense.[19] These lawyers neglect basic steps, including interviewing defendants, seeking witnesses, and investigating a defendant's background.

The second is prosecutorial suppression of evidence that the defendant is innocent or does not deserve the death penalty (accounting for almost 20 percent). When the errors were corrected through the stages already discussed, 8 of 10 people on retrial were found to deserve a sentence less than death and 7 percent were found innocent of the capital crime. Exhibit 3–9 shows that for every 100 death sentences imposed, 41 were turned back at the trial and direct review phase because of serious error. Of the 59 that passed to the state postconviction stage, 10 percent—6 of the original 100—were turned back due to serious flaws. Of the 53 that passed to the next stage of federal *habeas corpus,* 40 percent—an additional 21 of the original 100—were turned back because of serious error. Together, 68 of the original 100 were thrown out after 9 to 10 years had passed because of serious flaws. Of the 68 individuals whose death sentences were overturned for serious error, 82 percent (56) were found on retrial not to deserve the death penalty, including 5 who were found innocent of the offense. Each one had spent an average of nine years and two months on death row.

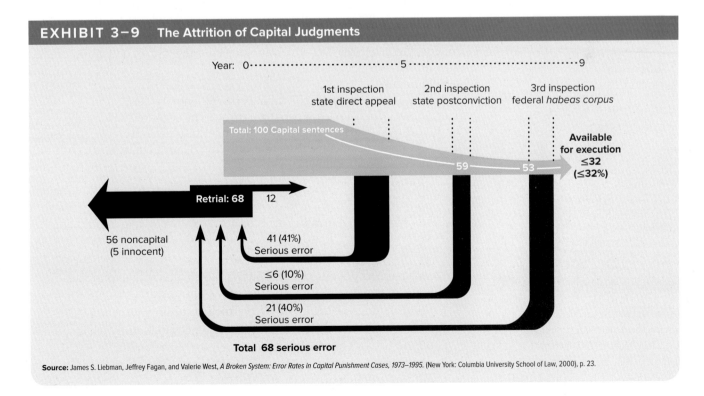

EXHIBIT 3–9   The Attrition of Capital Judgments

Source: James S. Liebman, Jeffrey Fagan, and Valerie West, *A Broken System: Error Rates in Capital Punishment Cases, 1973–1995.* (New York: Columbia University School of Law, 2000), p. 23.

What if a death sentence is imposed today in the United States? What could the defendant, relative, lawyer, or judge expect? Liebman and his colleagues answer this way: "The capital conviction or sentence will probably be overturned due to serious error. It'll take 9 or 10 years to find out, given how many other capital cases being reviewed for likely error are lined up ahead of this one. If the judgment is overturned, a lesser conviction or sentence will probably be imposed."[20]

If death sentences are not reliable and persons are wrongfully convicted and sentenced, the error has serious consequences for the wrongly convicted, for the family of the victim whose search for justice is incomplete, for the family of the person wrongly convicted in terms of the prolonged and distorted grief they suffer, for subsequent victims of the real offender still at large, and for the public in terms of lost confidence in the criminal justice system. The actual perpetrators remain in society to commit additional crimes, and many death row exonerees remain under a cloud of police suspicion because law enforcement failed to find the true offender.

Another consequence of wrongful convictions not often discussed is the cost of serious errors. On January 25, 2005, a federal jury in Chicago found two FBI agents liable for framing Steve Manning, former Chicago police officer and awarded Manning $6.5 million.[21] Eddie Lowery received a $7.5 million settlement along with apologies from officials in Riley County, Kansas, where he was arrested in 1981 for the rape of an elderly woman. He served 10 years in prison and registered as a sex offender after he was paroled. In 2003, the original rape kit was sent for DNA testing. It showed that Lowery couldn't have committed the rape. Illinois death row inmate Dennis Williams received $13 million from Cook County (Chicago) after he was exonerated.

Today, 30 states, the District of Columbia, and the federal government have passed laws that compensate people wrongfully convicted. Texas, a state best known as the leader in capital punishment, now has another distinction: It is the most generous in compensating those who were wrongfully convicted. Between 1992 and 2013, Texas paid more than $65 million to 89 wrongfully convicted people.[22] Nobody knows the exact amount that has been paid out nationally, but it is reasonable to believe that prejudicial error is costly. It includes money lost on education, health and human services, community protection, and economic growth and development.

How can we reduce serious capital error? Liebman identifies two options. The first is to end the death penalty entirely. The second is to curb the scope of the death penalty to reach only the small number of offenses on which there is broad social consensus that only the death penalty will serve. The reforms he suggests follow:[23]

1. Require proof beyond any doubt that the defendant committed the capital crime.
2. Require that aggravating factors substantially outweigh mitigating ones before a death sentence may be imposed.
3. Bar the death penalty for people with extenuating circumstances.
4. Make life imprisonment without parole an alternative to the death penalty and clearly inform juries of the option.
5. Abolish judge overrides of jury verdicts imposing life sentences.
6. Use comparative review of murder sentences to identify what counts as the "worst of the worst."
7. Base charging decisions in potentially capital cases on full and informed deliberations.

Visit http://www.law.virginia.edu/html/news/2009_spr/garrett.htm or scan this code with the QR app on your smartphone or digital device and watch the podcast of University of Virginia Law School Professor Brandon Garrett explain his research on why some people are induced to confess. How does this information relate to ideas discussed in this chapter?

8. Make all police and prosecution evidence bearing on guilt versus innocence and on aggravation versus mitigation available to the jury at trial.

9. Insulate capital sentencing and appellate judges from political pressure.

10. Identify, appoint, and compensate capital defense counsel in ways that attract an adequate number of well-qualified lawyers to do the work.

Another option that Ohio and a few other states are considering is to create a statewide commission to replace local prosecutors in making the decision as to when to seek the death penalty. James Brogan, a retired appeals court judge from Dayton, told the Ohio Supreme Court that "As [Ohio Supreme Court] Justice Paul Pfeifer said, it's a lottery whether or not you get the death penalty depending on where you live."[24] In Tennessee, county prosecutors submit murder cases to a statewide commission, which has the ultimate authority to decide whether a death sentence should be pursued.

Today 10 states require videotaping of at least some interrogations such as those in crimes that carry the death penalty, and seven state supreme courts have required or strongly encouraged recording.[25]

Banning the Execution of Persons with Mental Retardation and Juveniles On June 19, 2002, the U.S. Supreme Court held in *Atkins* v. *Virginia* that execution of offenders with mental retardation is cruel and unusual punishment prohibited by the Eighth Amendment. The Court argued that a national consensus has developed against executing this group of people. At that time, 12 states banned executions altogether. However, beginning in 1988, Arizona, Arkansas, Colorado, Connecticut, Florida, Georgia, Indiana, Kansas, Kentucky, Maryland, Missouri, Nebraska, New Mexico, New York, North Carolina, South Dakota, Tennessee, Washington, and the federal government passed statutes banning the execution of offenders with mental retardation. The Court argued that it was not so much the number of states that had passed similar statutes but the consistency of the direction of change. In the words of the Court, "Given the well-known fact that anti-crime legislation is far more popular than legislation providing protections for persons guilty of violent crime, the large number of states prohibiting the execution of people with mental retardation (and the complete absence of states passing legislation reinstating the power to conduct such executions) provides powerful evidence that today our society views these offenders as categorically less culpable than the average criminal. The evidence carries even greater force when it is noted that the legislatures that have addressed the issue have voted overwhelmingly in favor of the prohibition."[26] However, the Court left the definition of mental retardation up to individual states, and some states, like Florida, set a rigid IQ threshold of 70 to determine whether or not a person suffers from mental retardation and would not allow other evidence showing substantial limitations in intellectual functions of reasoning or problem-solving, limitations in adaptive behavior or "street smarts," or evidence of the condition before age 18.

But on May 27, 2014, the U.S. Supreme Court ruled in *Hall* v. *Florida* that Florida's strict IQ cut-off for determining a person's eligibility for the death penalty was unconstitutional. The majority of justices said that Florida must take into account that intellectual disability is a *condition,* not a number, and that Florida cannot ignore the standard error of measurement in all IQ tests. The Court pointed to the American Medical Association's finding that IQ scores have a standard error of approximately five points. The IQ score of Freddie Lee Hall, the Florida death row inmate whose case was before the Court, was 71,

CO3-10

Visit https://www.oyez.org/cases/2013/12-10882 or scan this code with the QR app on your smartphone or digital device and listen to the U.S. Supreme Court's opinion announcement in *Hall* v. *Florida* on May 27, 2014. The Court ruled that Florida's strict IQ cutoff for determining a person's eligibility for the death penalty was unconstitutional. The majority of justices said that Florida must take into account that intellectual disability is a condition, not a number, and that Florida cannot ignore the standard error of measurement in all IQ tests. How does this information relate to ideas discussed in this chapter?

one point above the Florida cut-off of 70. Viewing Hall's IQ using the standard error of measurement, the Justices said that Hall's IQ range is between 66 and 76, and they reversed the judgment of the Florida Supreme Court.

Three years later, on March 2, 2005, the U.S. Supreme Court, by a narrow 5–4 vote in *Roper* v. *Simmons,*[27] said it was unconstitutional and in violation of the Eighth Amendment's ban on cruel and unusual punishment to execute people for crimes they committed before turning age 18. The Court's ruling vacated the death sentences of 72 people on death rows across the United States. The offenders wound up with life sentences, many without parole.

In deciding *Roper* v. *Simmons,* the justices reasoned several things. First, they said that the trend toward banning capital punishment for juveniles reflected "evolving standards of decency that mark the progress of a maturing society."

Second, the justices cited scientific literature from the American Academy of Child and Adolescent Psychiatry, the American Medical Association, and the American Psychological Association showing that adolescents lack mature judgment, are less aware of the consequences of their decisions and actions, are more vulnerable than adults to peer pressure, and have a greater tendency toward impulsiveness and lesser reasoning skills, regardless of how big they are or how tough they talk.

And third, the justices cited overseas legal practices and pointed out that the death penalty for juvenile offenders has become a uniquely American practice. The justices said that the United States' practice of executing juvenile criminals was out of line with other developed countries.

CO3-11 SENTENCING TRENDS AND REFORMS

There is growing momentum for sentencing reform in the United States. The reforms have been evolving in a direction emphasizing being smart on crime and evidence-based approaches to public safety. Bipartisan support at federal, state, and local levels has shaped new sentencing and reentry policies and addressed the runaway expenditures incurred over the past four decades. The American Correctional Association's policy on sentencing is shown in Exhibit 3–10.

President Obama signing the Fair Sentencing Act of 2010
© Jewel Samad/AFP/Getty

EXHIBIT 3–10 **American Correctional Association**

Public Correctional Policy on Sentencing

The American Correctional Association actively promotes the development of sentencing policies that should:

- be based on the principle of proportionality. The sentence imposed should be commensurate with the seriousness of the crime and the harm done;
- be impartial with regard to race, ethnicity, and economic status as to the discretion exercised in sentencing;
- include a broad range of options for custody, supervision, and rehabilitation of offenders;
- be purpose-driven. Policies must be based on clearly articulated purposes. They should be grounded in knowledge of the relative effectiveness of the various sanctions imposed in attempts to achieve these purposes;
- encourage the evaluation of sentencing policy on an ongoing basis. The various sanctions should be monitored to determine their relative effectiveness based on the purpose(s) they are intended to have. Likewise, monitoring should take place to ensure that the sanctions are not applied based on race, ethnicity, or economic status;
- recognize that the criminal sentence must be based on multiple criteria, including the harm done to the victim, past criminal history, the need to protect the public, and the opportunity to provide programs for offenders as a means of reducing the risk for future crime;
- provide the framework to guide and control discretion according to established criteria and within appropriate limits and allow for recognition of individual needs;
- have as a major purpose restorative justice—righting the harm done to the victim and the community. The restorative focus should be both process and substantively oriented. The victim or his or her representative should be included in the "justice" process. The sentencing procedure should address the needs of the victim, including his or her need to be heard and, as much as possible, to be and feel restored to whole again;
- promote the use of community-based programs whenever consistent with public safety; and
- be linked to the resources needed to implement the policy. The consequential cost of various sanctions should be assessed. Sentencing policy should not be enacted without the benefit of a fiscal-impact analysis. Resource allocations should be linked to sentencing policy so as to ensure adequate funding of all sanctions, including total confinement and the broad range of intermediate sanction and communitybased programs needed to implement those policies.

Source: Copyright © American Correctional Association. Reprinted with permission.

At the federal level, the Fair Sentencing Act of 2010 reduced the disparity in sentencing between crack and powder cocaine offenses; the Second Chance Act of 2008 funds some $70 million in reentry services annually across the United States; and in 2005, the U.S. Supreme Court's decision in *Booker* made federal sentencing guidelines advisory, thereby giving federal judges a greater degree of sentencing discretion.

Today, one of the most powerful voices for reforming the federal prison system is the Charles Colson Task Force on Federal Corrections. (Colson was special counsel to President Richard Nixon from 1969 to 1973. He pled guilty to obstruction of justice for his role in Watergate and served seven months in federal prison. He later went on to found the Prison Fellowship, the world's largest prison ministry. Congress created the Charles Colson Task Force on Federal Corrections in 2014 as a nine-person, bipartisan, blue ribbon panel charged with developing practical, data-driven policy recommendations to enhance public safety by creating a more just and efficient federal corrections system.)

On January 26, 2016, following 12 months of interviews, data analysis, and other research, the panel published a 132-page consensus-based report

Visit http://colsontaskforce.org/uncategorized/transforming-prisons-restoring-lives-final-recommendations-charles-colson-task-force-federal-corrections/ or scan this code with the QR app on your smartphone or digital device and watch the podcast of the Charles Colson Task Force on Federal Corrections deliver its final report. How does this information relate to ideas discussed in this chapter?

that *"the federal prison population should be reduced by 60,000 people over the coming years and thereby achieve a savings of over $5 billion, allowing for reinvestment in programs proven to reduce crime. And furthermore, in line with one of the themes of this book, these reforms and savings can be achieved through evidence-based policies that protect public safety"* (emphasis added).[28]

The panel found that punitive mandatory minimum sentences for drug crimes represent "the primary driver" of prison overcrowding. The report recommended that mandatory minimum sentences be reserved for the most violent offenders. The report also said that almost 80 percent of federal inmates convicted of drug crimes had no prior criminal history. The panel urged Congress to create a path for prisoners who have served more than 15 years to apply for shorter sentences by giving judges a "second look" at their cases. The report also urges more oversight and resources for the Federal Bureau of Prisons—and for programs that return inmates to their communities and foster bonds with their families.

The panel made six recommendations. Space does not allow us to comment on each one. We refer the reader to the adjacent QR code and suggest watching the podcast of the panel's presentation.

The Panel Delivering its report,
January 26, 2016.
© Matthew Johnson for the Urban Institute

Recommendation 1: At sentencing, the federal system should reserve prison beds for those convicted of the most serious federal crimes.

Recommendation 2: In prison, the federal Bureau of Prisons should promote a culture of safety and rehabilitation and ensure that programming is allocated in accordance with individual risk and needs.

Recommendation 3: Throughout the prison term, correctional policies should incentivize participation in risk-reduction programming.

Recommendation 4: Prior to and following release, the federal correctional system should ensure successful reintegration by using evidence-based practices in supervision and support.

Recommendation 5: The federal criminal justice system should enhance performance and accountability through better coordination across agencies and increased transparency.

Recommendation 6: Congress should reinvest savings to support the expansion of necessary programs, supervision, and treatment.

Panel members praised state lawmakers in Georgia, South Carolina, Texas, Utah, and other states who reexamined their own state's expensive taste for incarceration and embraced a more diversified, evidence-based approach that delivers better public safety at less cost by requiring more offender risk and needs assessment, supporting prisoner reentry into the community, and increasing their reliance on data-driven criminal justice policy development using evidence-based practices. What we present here is a snapshot of some of those state sentencing and corrections reforms and trends.[29]

In 2013, 35 states passed 85 bills to change some aspect of how their criminal justice system addresses sentencing and corrections in five areas: reduce prison populations and costs, expand or strengthen community-based sanctions, implement risk and needs assessment, support the reentry of offenders into the community, and make better informed criminal justice policy using evidence-based practices.

Reducing Prison Populations and Costs

Legislators in several states became more aware of the questionable benefits as well as the fiscal and social costs of many of the hallmarks of the tough-on-crime era and repealed or narrowed mandatory sentencing, reclassified offenses, altered sentencing presumptions, or expanded access to early release. For example, state legislatures in Colorado, Georgia, Hawaii, Illinois, Indiana, Kansas, and Oregon repealed, limited, or suspended mandatory minimum penalties if certain conditions are present in the case. Colorado, Connecticut, Indiana, Maryland, Oregon, South Dakota, Vermont, and Washington reclassified low-level crimes from felonies to misdemeanors. Colorado, Maryland, Oregon, and South Dakota also made probation the presumptive sentence for some offenses that previously allowed for prison. Maryland also repealed capital punishment, substituting LWOP. Following Alaska, Colorado, and Washington's lead in legalizing marijuana for personal use, a number of states and local jurisdictions also eliminated criminal penalties for possessing small amounts of marijuana and replaced them with civil fines.

In addition to these sentencing reforms, several states implemented mechanisms for the safe and early release of offenders already in custody. Louisiana expanded the availability of good-time credits from 250 to 360 days for prisoners who complete education, job skills training, and therapeutic programs. Other states (New Hampshire, North Dakota, and West Virginia) advanced parole eligibility dates for certain nonviolent offenders.

Expand and Strengthen Community Corrections

In addition to passing legislation to reduce the level of incarceration, states also passed sentencing reforms that expand and strengthen community-based responses to crime. Arkansas and New Jersey are among six states that increased options for defendants to be diverted from criminal processing if they stay crime free for a specific period of time and complete a community-based program. Charges are usually dropped for defendants who complete the program. Illinois and Vermont passed legislation expanding the use of home detention as an alternative to incarceration. Louisiana, Oregon, Texas, and West Virginia expanded the pool of offenders, especially low-level drug offenders, eligible for substance abuse probation programs. Michigan and Missouri passed legislation establishing mental health and veterans courts. Other states expanded the use of drug courts (Chapter 5) and reentry courts (Chapter 8). Legislators in Kansas, South Dakota, and West Virginia recognized that revocations from community-based sentences for technical (not new crime) violations account for a significant number of admissions to prison and adopted laws that give judges (and probation officers if the offender waives her or his right to appear before judge) a range of sentencing options to match the severity of the penalty to the type and scope of the offense. For example, in Kansas, the court may continue or modify the conditions of community supervision. With each subsequent violation, the court may (1) order the defendant be jailed for no more than six days per month for up to three months (imposed only in two- or three-day consecutive periods such as weekends to maintain employment and family ties), (2) order the defendant jailed for 120 days, (3) send the defendant to state prison for 180 days, and (4) revoke community supervision and order the original sentence be served.

And finally, Colorado, Idaho, and a few other states passed laws that award offenders who are consistently compliant with court orders early discharge and possibly an offense downgrade to reduce the consequences that stem from a felony conviction.

Implement Risk and Needs Assessment

Legislators also recognize that risk and needs assessments are proven evidence-based practices that can reduce levels of incarceration. Oklahoma, Texas, and other states are using validated risk assessment at the pretrial stage, at sentencing, and before a person leaves prison in order to structure supervision in accordance with supervision results and focus resources on moderate- and high-risk offenders.

Support Prisoner Reentry

Earlier we discussed briefly the roadblocks that offenders face when leaving jail or prison. Legislators now recognize that supporting the transition from jail or prison back to the community can reduce recidivism and the collateral consequences that result from a criminal conviction and improve public safety and that, in the long run, it is cheaper than incarceration. States like Indiana and Utah took steps to expand options for sealing or expunging criminal records. Nevada reduced the waiting period from seven to five years before a person may petition the court to seal his or her records. Utah added felony drug possession to the list of offenses that may be expunged. Other states passed laws that clarify and strengthen record-sealing policies. Colorado now requires probation officers to advise offenders of their right to have their criminal record sealed at the final supervision meeting. North Carolina now prohibits employers and educational institutions from *requiring* the disclosure of expunged records of arrest, charges, or convictions. In North Carolina, a person with an expunged criminal record is not required to disclose any prior arrest, charges, or convictions. And Texas law now mandates that court clerks are prohibited from disclosing expunged criminal records.

To increase the chances of successful offender reentry, 12 states and many local communities require employers to defer any inquiry about a job applicant's past convictions until after her or his application has progressed to a first or second interview, the initiative known as "ban the box" discussed earlier. Georgia gives judges in drug and mental health courts the discretion to fully or partially restore driving privileges. Louisiana now mandates that having a criminal record does not disqualify someone from adopting a child. And Rhode Island gives "certificates of recovery and reentry" to offenders with the purpose of helping prospective landlords and employers make more informed decisions about applicants with criminal records.

Laws were also passed to strengthen "in-jail and in-prison" programming. Nebraska legislators commissioned a program to strengthen family-based reentry planning in order to lower recidivism and enhance family economic stability. California now provides that an inmate leaving county jail cannot be terminated from state Medicaid because of incarceration. Maine allows offenders with unpaid fines to cover the balance by performing community service. And the West Virginia commissioner of corrections was charged with appointing directors of housing and employment to develop and strengthen housing and employment opportunities for persons released from custody.

Make Better Informed Criminal Justice Policy Using Evidence-Based Practices

Several states created independent bodies to increase their reliance on data-driven policy development. Mississippi established a task force to (1) examine disparities in sentencing, drug court, intensive supervision, other alternatives to incarceration and the number of persons incarcerated under mandatory minimum sentencing and (2) issue findings and make recommendations designed to prevent, deter, and reduce crime and violence, reduce recidivism, improve cost-effectiveness, and ensure that justice is achieved at every step in criminal justice processing. And Montana established a statewide reentry task force designed to develop and implement reentry programs for high-risk inmates within one year of release from prison.

Other state legislatures now require cost and benefit analysis of specific criminal justice interventions. The public and legislators are asking what else might be done to achieve public safety goals if incarceration is failing to have a positive impact on persons who are released from jail or prison. Oregon and Vermont, and a handful of other states, now require fiscal impact statements for all bills that either modify or create new sentencing or corrections policies.

In summary of these sentencing trends and reforms, we see the direction the American public and their legislators are crafting for the second half of the 21st century. States are reexamining the ways they respond to offenders at every stage of criminal justice processing. The pendulum has swung from tough-on-crime policies to what is *effective* in terms of cost and outcomes. Evidence-based, data-driven practices, and reliance on the support of external groups of experts and stakeholders are being used to reduce prison populations, strengthen community-based punishments, balance budgets, and improve public safety. A state map of legislation most representative of the five broad areas of reform in sentencing and corrections is shown in Exhibit 3–11.

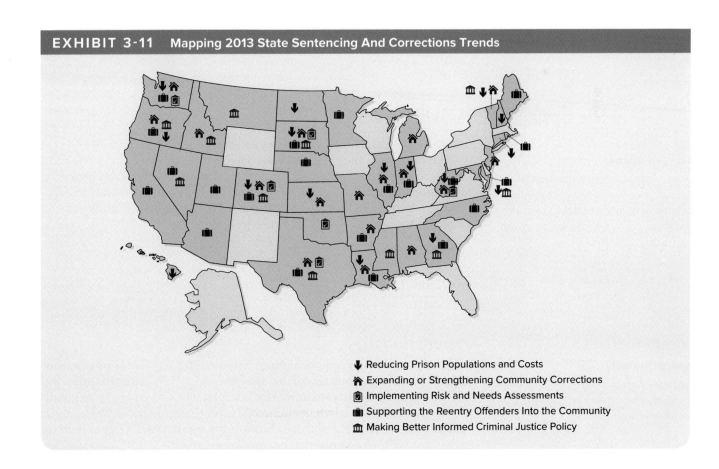

EXHIBIT 3-11   Mapping 2013 State Sentencing And Corrections Trends

⬇ Reducing Prison Populations and Costs
🏠 Expanding or Strengthening Community Corrections
🗒 Implementing Risk and Needs Assessments
💼 Supporting the Reentry Offenders Into the Community
🏛 Making Better Informed Criminal Justice Policy

In the face of challenging economic conditions a number of states have recently moved to maximize the return on money that they spend on corrections—including jails, prisons, and probation and parole. The Washington, D.C.-based Sentencing Project identified five areas that have seen recent legislative action by states wanting to save money while at the same time controlling crime and ensuring public safety. Areas identified by the project, along with related initiatives include:

- *Relaxed mandatory minimums:* In 2012, California voters approved a change in the state's three-strikes law to keep certain offenders from being imprisoned for life following the commission of a third felony. Other states have enacted sentencing reforms to limit the use of incarceration for selected offenders.

- *Sentence modifications and decriminalization:* A few states, like Alaska, Colorado, and Washington, have decriminalized the possession of small amounts of marijuana for personal use, and others have decreased the sentence to be served for other drug offenses. Some have increased the amount of time by which inmates can reduce their sentences for good behavior. One state—Georgia—has created a system of "accountability courts," which are designed to substitute treatment for imprisonment as a sanction for drug-involved offenders. Still others have raised the dollar amount needed to charge a theft crime as a felony, and have implemented a sentencing structure for such offenses that more closely ties punishment to the value of property stolen.

- *Probation and parole reform:* A number of states, including Delaware, Georgia, and Missouri, have enacted legislation to limit the use of imprisonment for technical violations of parole, and have expanded the use of incarceration alternatives, such as home confinement. Some states, most notably Louisiana, have recently expanded parole eligibility for certain crimes and have provided for the possibility of parole for some offenders sentenced to life in prison.

- *Capital punishment changes:* Since 2007, eight states eliminated the death penalty as a sentencing option, substituting life without parole in its place. While life in prison is expensive, it can cost more to prosecute and defend (using public funds) a capital case, than it does to house an inmate sentenced to life in prison.

- *Reforms affecting juvenile justice:* A number of states, including California, Louisiana, and Pennsylvania, have legislatively authorized changes in the handling of individuals who had been sentenced to life without parole as juveniles. Such changes include eliminating life without parole for juveniles who committed offenses other than homicide, and making it possible for those who received such sentences as juveniles to petition the court for a resentencing hearing. Similarly, Colorado has limited the authority of juvenile court judges to transfer cases to adult criminal court.

While many states have sought to curb expenditures in almost all budgetary areas, not all states relaxed their sentencing practices. Massachusetts, for example, recently increased mandatory minimum sentences for certain repeat offenders.

Source: Nicole D. Porter, *The State of Sentencing 2012* (Washington, DC: The Sentencing Project, 2013).

CO3-12

ISSUES IN SENTENCING

fair sentencing

Sentencing practices that incorporate fairness for both victims and offenders. *Fairness* is said to be achieved by implementing principles of proportionality, equity, individualization, and parsimony.

Many sentencing reforms have been an attempt to reduce disparity in sentencing and make the process fairer. The term **fair sentencing,** or *fairness in sentencing,* has become popular in recent years. Although fair sentencing today often refers to fairness for *victims,* many suggest that any truly fair sentencing scheme must incorporate fairness for both victims and offenders. These are the issues related to fairness in sentencing:

- proportionality
- equity
- individualization
- parsimony

Proportionality

proportionality

The sentencing principle that the severity of punishment should match the seriousness of the crime for which the sentence is imposed.

Proportionality is the sentencing principle that the severity of punishment should match the seriousness of the crime for which the sentence is imposed. This does not mean that sentences for comparable crimes should be identical, but rather that there must be good reasons for substantial variations in sentences and that the seriousness of the crime must have an upper limit on the severity of the sentence that may be imposed for it.

Equity

Equity is the sentencing principle that similar crimes and similar criminals should be treated alike. Sentencing should be guided by established, regularly applied standards or guidelines, thereby making the process more transparent, the procedures fairer, and judges more accountable. Requiring judges to sentence regularly with applicable standards or to explain why not gives offenders the basis on which to appeal decisions they believe to be unjust.

Individualization

Fairness in sentencing was also addressed by the blue ribbon Colson Task Force on Corrections mentioned earlier. The panel concluded that sentencing decisions and correctional interventions should be **individualized**. The unique circumstances and attributes of each case and each person entering the criminal justice system should inform the sentence and the rehabilitation programs, treatment, and services provided.

Parsimony

Sentences should be the least necessary in a given situation to attain its end. That is to say that sentences should be no more severe, disruptive, or harmful to an offender's ability to live a law-abiding life than is minimally necessary. Two-and-one-half centuries ago, Cesare Beccaria, founder of the Classical School of Criminology, said that imposition of a sentence more severe than is necessary is "superfluous and for that reason tyrannical."[30] Such sentences are wasteful expenditures of capital and serve no good purpose.

equity
The sentencing principle that similar crimes and similar criminals should be treated alike and sentences should be guided by established, regularly applied standards or guidelines.

individualization
The sentencing principle that the unique circumstances and attributes of each case and each person entering the criminal justice system should inform the sentence and the rehabilitation programs, treatment, and services provided.

parsimony
Sentences should be the least necessary in a given situation to attain its end. Imposition of a sentence more severe than is necessary is harmful.

REVIEW AND APPLICATIONS

SUMMARY

1 The central purpose of criminal punishment is to maintain social order.

2 The goals of criminal sentencing today are (1) revenge, (2) retribution, (3) just deserts, (4) deterrence, (5) incapacitation, (6) rehabilitation or reformation, and (7) restoration.

3 Sentencing options in use today include probation, intermediate sanctions, jail and prison, parole, and capital punishment.

4 Today, 2,984 prisoners are on death row, a decrease of almost 300 from one decade earlier. Almost 50 percent of the nation's death row population is in three states: California (746), Florida (400), and Texas (265). Ninety-eight percent of all prisoners on death row are male, 58 percent are minority, 51 percent have a high school diploma (or GED) or higher, and 55 percent never married.

5 In 1990, the General Accounting Office reported that race of the victim influences the likelihood of being charged with capital murder or receiving the death penalty. In 96 percent of states where there have been reviews of victim race and the death penalty, there was a pattern of either race-of-victim or race-of-defendant discrimination, or both. The public also perceives that decision making in homicide cases is not influenced by the same factors in all cases. Fifty-three percent of all Americans agree with the statement, "A black person is more likely than a white person to receive the death penalty for the same crime," while 45 percent disagreed.

6 In October 2015, Gallup reported that 61 percent of the American public said they favor the death penalty, down from 63 percent in 2014 and near the 40-year low of 60 percent support recorded in 2013. More than one-third (37 percent) said they opposed the death penalty, the most in 43 years and 21 points above levels reported in the mid-1990s. Support for capital punishment is higher in the states that have it—64 percent versus 54 percent elsewhere. The poll reports the highest percentage of Americans say the death penalty is imposed too often (27 percent).

7 In 1976, the U.S. Supreme Court rejected mandatory capital punishment statutes but approved guided discretion statutes in *Gregg* v. *Georgia.* The Court approved automatic appellate review, a proportionality review, and a bifurcated trial. The penalty phase includes presentation of facts that mitigate or aggravate the circumstances of the crime.

8 Death penalty cases may pass through as many as 10 courts and across three stages: trial and direct review, state post-conviction appeals, and federal *habeas corpus* appeals.

9 Liebman found that the frequency of errors in capital punishment cases is 68 percent. More than two of every three capital judgments reviewed by the courts were found to be seriously flawed. Ten states (Alabama, Arizona, California, Georgia, Indiana, Maryland, Mississippi, Montana, Oklahoma, and Wyoming) had overall error rates of 75 percent or higher. Almost 1,000 of the cases sent back for retrial ended in sentences less than death, and 87 ended in not guilty verdicts.

10 In 2002, the Court held in *Atkins* v. *Virginia* that execution of offenders with mental retardation is cruel and unusual punishment prohibited by the Eighth Amendment because a national consensus has decided against executing these offenders. In 2005, the Court held in *Roper* v. *Simmons* that execution of persons for crimes they committed before turning age 18 was also unconstitutional and in violation of the Eighth Amendment. The Court's reasoning in both cases was similar: The large number of states banning the execution of people with mental retardation and of persons who committed capital crimes before turning age 18 provided evidence that our society views offenders with mental retardation and juveniles as categorically less culpable than the average criminal.

11 At the federal level, the U.S. Supreme Court's decision in *Booker* made federal sentencing guidelines advisory; the Second Chance Act of 2008 funds millions of dollars in reentry services annually across the United States; and in 2010, the Fair Sentencing Act reduced the disparity in sentencing between crack and powder cocaine offenses. Elsewhere in the federal system, the Charles Colson Task Force on Federal Corrections recommended that (1) the federal prison population should be reduced by 60,000 people over the coming years and achieve a savings of more than $5 billion for reinvestment in evidence-based programs proven to reduce crime; (2) mandatory minimum sentences should be reserved for the most violent offenders; and (3) Congress should create a path for prisoners who have served more than 15 years to apply for shorter sentences by giving judges a "second look" at their cases. The panel made six additional recommendations. At the state level, 35 states passed 85 bills to reduce prison populations and costs, expand or strengthen community-based sanctions, implement risk and needs assessment, support the reentry of offenders into the community, and make better informed criminal justice policy using evidence-based practices.

12 Application of the four principles of fairness in sentencing using a hypothetical offense and offender scenario will vary.

KEY TERMS

sentencing, p. 35	truth in sentencing (TIS), p. 38	guided discretion, p. 52
sentence, p. 35	three-strikes laws, p. 38	bifurcated trial, p. 52
social order, p. 35	rehabilitation, p. 39	mitigating circumstances, p. 52
revenge, p. 36	reintegration, p. 39	aggravating circumstances, p. 52
retribution, p. 36	restoration, p. 40	serious error, p. 52
just deserts, p. 36	restorative justice, p. 40	fair sentencing, p. 64
deterrence, p. 37	victim-impact statement, p. 41	proportionality, p. 64
specific deterrence, p. 37	capital punishment, p. 45	equity, p. 65
general deterrence, p. 38	exonerate, p. 46	individualization, p. 65
pleasure-pain principle, p. 38	capital crime, p. 47	parsimony, p. 65
incapacitation, p. 38	mandatory death penalty, p. 52	

QUESTIONS FOR REVIEW

1 What is the central purpose of criminal punishment.

2 What are the seven goals of criminal sentencing?

3 What are the major sentencing options in wide use in the United States today?

4 What are the characteristics of persons on death row today?

5 Summarize the research on victim race and capital punishment.

6 Summarize the changes in the public's attitudes toward capital punishment.

7 What changes were made in the application of capital punishment as a result of *Furman* v. *Georgia* and *Gregg* v. *Georgia?*

8 Explain the death penalty appeals process.

9 Assess the importance of Liebman's findings on the frequency of error in capital punishment cases.

10 Argue for and against the Supreme Court's reasoning for banning the execution of persons with mental retardation and juveniles.

11 Defend the need for federal and state sentencing trends and options.

12 Justify the four principles of fairness in sentencing.

THINKING CRITICALLY ABOUT CORRECTIONS

Rehabilitation

Edgardo Rotman says, in *Beyond Punishment,* "Rehabilitation . . . can be defined tentatively and broadly as a right to an opportunity to return to (or remain in) society with an improved chance of being a useful citizen and staying out of prison."[31] Do you agree that offenders have a right to rehabilitation? Why or why not?

Murder Rates and the Death Penalty

According to the Death Penalty Information Center, death penalty states record higher murder rates than non-death-penalty states. On January 1, 2014, the average murder rate among death penalty states was 4.7 per 100,000 population; for non-death-penalty states, the rate was 3.9. The South executes the largest percentage of offenders who are convicted of a capital crime (81 percent) and records the highest murder rate (5.5 murders per 100,000 people); the Northeast executes the fewest (0.2 percent) and records the lowest murder rate, 3.3. What conclusions might you draw from these data? How might we prevent geographical unfairness?

Federal Corrections

The 10-member Colson Task Force on Federal Corrections is composed of Republican and Democrat federal and state congressional leaders, a federal judge, a U.S. attorney, a state warden, a professor, and representatives from local agencies. The members crossed political lines to issue a consensus-based report calling for the federal Bureau of Prisons to reduce its population by 60,000 inmates and reserve mandatory minimums for violent offenders only, and it urged Congress to create a path for prisoners who have served more than 15 years to apply for shorter sentences by asking their judges to give their cases a second look. How would you defend these reforms to persons who advocate for tough-on-crime approaches?

ON-THE-JOB DECISION MAKING

Recidivism

You have spent the past six years as a counselor at a minimum-security state correctional facility. Your effectiveness has earned you a strong reputation throughout the Department of Corrections as a specialist in prerelease counseling, a program designed to prepare inmates for their return to society upon parole or completion of their sentence.

Lately, a series of highly publicized violent crimes has been committed by former inmates of the state's super–maximum-security facility. All were released recently upon completion of their sentences, and all had moved almost directly from their cell back to the criminal lifestyle that originally landed them in prison.

Hard-line correctional officers insist that because those incarcerated in the "supermax" are the worst of the worst, they cannot be trusted to behave during prerelease counseling. The safety risks such inmates represent, they say, make leaving them in their cells until the law requires they be set free the only sensible course of action. What happens after that, in the hard-liners' opinions, is both the decision and responsibility of the former inmate.

Reformers insist that immediate recidivism is the likely outcome of releasing inmates directly from a harsh, totally controlled lockdown environment. They call for significant transitional counseling as essential for helping inmates adjust to free society and for defusing their angry urge to make society pay for the harsh life from which they are being released.

Both the governor and the commissioner of corrections face daily media demands to explain what the administration is going to do about this problem. In particular, the governor is under the gun because his opponent in the upcoming and hotly contested gubernatorial race has seized on this as an issue that demonstrates "this governor's inability, or unwillingness, to take the tough steps necessary to protect the good citizens of our state."

You have been asked to speak at a meeting to develop potential courses of action to address this problem. The meeting will be chaired by the corrections commissioner, and various wardens, assistant wardens, and senior correctional specialists from throughout the state will attend. It is likely but not yet confirmed that the governor will also attend. Think about the federal and state trends in sentencing and corrections discussed in this chapter.

1. What issues will you address?
2. How might you resolve the conflict between the need to protect counselors and staff from the often violent behavior of supermax inmates and the need to provide this critical prerelease counseling to these troubled inmates?
3. How would you respond to hard-line corrections officers who contend that what happens after release is not their problem?

Community Corrections

Part Two examines probation and intermediate sanctions.

Probation is the conditional release of convicted offenders under community supervision. The degree of supervision depends on an offender's risk level. Some offenders pose no risk to the community. For them, checking in monthly at an automated probation kiosk may be all that is necessary. On the other hand, high-risk offenders require intensive face-to-face supervision and sometimes random drug testing, community service, and home confinement with remote-location monitoring.

Sanctions more punitive than probation but not as restrictive as incarceration are called *intermediate sanctions.* Drug court, economic sanctions, community service, day reporting centers, remote-location monitoring, residential centers, and boot camps are some intermediate sanctions.

Today, the current probation and parole workforce of 50,000 investigates and supervises more than 5 million adults under probation, parole, and intermediate sanctions. These officers are faced with enormous case investigation and supervision challenges that include increasing caseloads without new resources, deciding on what information to include in a presentence report, figuring out how to structure the report so it is read, and incorporating novel forms of technology into their day-to-day jobs.

Whether supervision is low level or intense, many probationers will violate its technical conditions. Others will commit new crimes. Tightening the offender's supervision without resorting to using an already overburdened system of incarceration is a challenge that probation officers face. The decision to revoke probation and incarcerate the offender is influenced by legal, social, political, and economic issues.

© Marmaduke St. John/Alamy Stock Photo RF

© McGraw-Hill Education/Mark Dierker, photographer

PROBATION

How Most Offenders Are Punished

CHAPTER OBJECTIVES

After completing this chapter you should be able to do the following:

1 Define *probation* and know its goals.

2 Explain the reasons for using probation.

3 Describe some of the characteristics of adults on probation.

4 Explain the different ways that probation is administered.

5 Describe the measures used to evaluate probation.

6 Describe the investigation and supervision functions of probation officers.

7 Explain revocation hearings.

> *We won't get true public safety and protection for crime victims until we invest in community corrections—because most offenders are not behind bars, but living as our neighbors.*
>
> —Anne Seymour, national crime victim advocate

In 2015, Molly Shattuck, mother of three and 38 years of age, made headlines when she became the oldest NFL cheerleader in history winning a spot on the Baltimore Ravens football squad on her first tryout. She cheered for the Ravens for two seasons until she was 41.[1]

In November 2014, though, Shattuck hit rock bottom. She was arrested on charges of third-degree rape, unlawful sexual contact, and giving alcohol to minors; a plea deal later reduced the charge to a less serious rape offense. Police said she performed oral sex on the friend of her son (both minors) over Labor Day weekend at a Bethany Beach, Delaware, summer home. Over the summer of 2014, Shattuck and the boy exchanged sexualized texts and e-mails and occasionally met in parked cars.

Judge E. Scott Bradley sentenced the mother of three to the maximum 15-year prison term for fourth-degree rape but suspended the prison time to two years of probation. She must also report to a violation of probation center every other weekend, starting in September 2015, and complete 48 weekends there. The judge also ordered Shattuck to pay $10,650 in restitution to the victim's family. Shattuck must register in Delaware as a sex offender, and except for her own three children, she cannot have contact with people younger than 18. What condition do you think would persuade a judge to sentence a mother and socialite to probation for performing oral sex on a minor?

In August 2015, Molly Shattuck, former NFL Baltimore Ravens cheerleader, was sentenced to two years probation for raping a 15-year old boy at a vacation home in Delaware. The boy was a friend of Shattuck's son and was the same age. In addition to two years' probation, she was ordered to report to a probation center for 48 weekends and pay $10,650 in restitution to the boy's family. Shattuck is now a registered sex offender in Delaware: https://sexoffender.dsp.delaware.gov. How would you weigh the competing interests in this case to arrive at the sentence given to Shattuck?

© Algerina Perma/Baltimore Sun/TNS via Getty Images

PROBATION

CO4-1

Probation is the most frequently used form of criminal punishment (see Exhibit 4–1). It is a way to keep the offender at home in the community, avoid incarceration, and carry out sanctions imposed by the court or the probation agency. **Probation** is the conditional release of a convicted offender into the community under the supervision of a probation officer (PO). It is conditional because if the probationer violates the conditions of her or his probation, the judge may either set more restrictive conditions of probation, or revoke probation and sentence the defendant to prison. Later in this chapter, we discuss the impact that revoking even a small percentage of the probation population can have on the prison population.

probation

The conditional release of a convicted offender into the community, under the supervision of a probation officer. It is conditional because it can be revoked if certain conditions are not met.

Reasons for and Goals of Probation

CO4-2

Probation is used for at least four reasons. First, probation permits the offender to remain in the community for reintegration purposes. Offender reintegration is more likely to occur if social and family ties are not broken by incarceration.

EXHIBIT 4–1   Adults on Probation, on Parole, in Jail, or in Prison

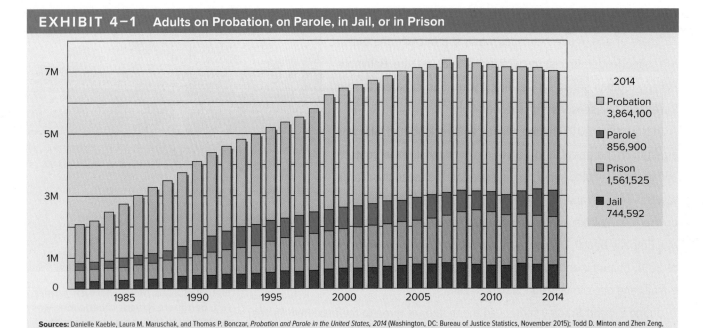

2014

☐ Probation
3,864,100

■ Parole
856,900

☐ Prison
1,561,525

■ Jail
744,592

Sources: Danielle Kaeble, Laura M. Maruschak, and Thomas P. Bonczar, *Probation and Parole in the United States, 2014* (Washington, DC: Bureau of Justice Statistics, November 2015); Todd D. Minton and Zhen Zeng, *Jail Inmates at Mid-year 2014* (Washington, DC: Bureau of Justice Statistics, June 2015); E. Ann Carson, *Prisoners in 2014* (Washington, DC: Bureau of Justice Statistics, September 2015); and Pew Center on the States, *The High Cost of Corrections in America* (Washington, DC: Pew Center on the States, June 2012).

Probation

Second, probation avoids prison institutionalization and the stigma of incarceration. Prison institutionalization is the process of learning and adopting the norms and culture of institutional living. Living in the artificial environment of an institution does not teach prisoners how to live in the free world. Probationers do not experience prison institutionalization, nor do they have to worry about the negative effects of being treated like a prisoner, which decrease even further their ability to function as a law-abiding citizen when released.

The third reason for probation is that it is less expensive than incarceration, more humanitarian, and at least as effective as incarceration in reducing future criminal activity.

The final reason for probation is that it is fair and appropriate sentencing for offenders whose crimes do not merit incarceration. Furthermore, probation is the base from which more severe punishments can be built. Not all crimes deserve incarceration, nor do all crimes deserve probation. Probation is preferred when the offender poses no threat to community safety, when community correctional resources are available, and when probation does not unduly deprecate the seriousness of the offense. Assessment tools that determine the risk and needs of each offender and statutory sentencing guidelines help identify which offenders deserve community-based punishment and which deserve institutional punishment.

Most probation programs share five goals:

1. Protect the community by preparing the presentence report (PSR) to assist judges in sentencing and supervising offenders. The PSR indicates the degree of risk an offender poses to the community. (We will return to the PSR later in this chapter.)

2. Carry out sanctions imposed by the court. POs accomplish this by educating offenders about the orders of the court, supervising offenders, and removing them from the community when they violate the conditions of their probation.

Probation officials across the country increasingly have to do more with less. They oversee agencies that are responsible for record numbers of people under community supervision. Today, 1 in 52 adults in the United States is on probation or parole. Although their budgets are being cut, probation departments are expected to improve the success rates of the increasing numbers of individuals they supervise and to reduce crime in the community by preventing reoffending. These high expectations and the intense public scrutiny that follows a high-profile failure require that probation officials revisit their agency's goals, processes, and measures for success.

The core mission of a probation department is to reduce probationer recidivism. Reviewing a growing body of knowledge and experience, experts point to four evidence-based practices that are essential to probation agencies' success in achieving this mission, especially during tough fiscal times. Based on current best practices, probation departments should

1. Effectively assess probationers' criminogenic risk and need as well as their strengths (also known as "protective factors");

2. Employ smart, tailored supervision strategies;

3. Use incentives and graduated sanctions to respond promptly to probationers' behaviors; and

4. Implement performance-driven personnel management practices that promote and reward recidivism reduction.

From 2005 to 2008, researchers at the Council of State Governments worked with leaders from Travis County (Austin, Texas) to design and integrate each of the four core practices into the department's everyday processes. In spite of the economic recession that started in 2008, when researchers returned to Travis County in 2011 to examine the long-term impact of the department's transformation, they found that implementing the four practices of recidivism reduction is not only possible but also can yield dramatic and positive improvements for the involved agency, the community, and probationers.

• Felony probation revocations declined by 20 percent.

• Felony technical revocations fell by 48 percent—the largest reduction in the five most populous counties in Texas, and nearly 10 times the statewide reduction of 5 percent.

• The decreased number of technical revocations averted $4.8 million in state incarceration costs.

• Reductions in motions to revoke probation averted close to $400,000 in local jail costs in one year (based on costs of $24 per day per person).

• The one-year rearrest rate for probationers fell by 17 percent compared with that of similar probationers before the departmental overhaul.

• Rearrest rates for low-risk offenders declined by 77 percent.

Source: Tony Fabelo, Geraldine Nagy, and Seth Prins, *A Ten-Step Guide to Transforming Probation Departments to Reduce Recidivism* (New York: Council of State Governments Justice Center, 2011); Danielle Kaeble, Laura M. Maruschak, and Thomas P. Bonczar, *Probation and Parole in the United States, 2014* (Washington, DC: U.S. Department of Justice, Bureau of Justice Statistics, November 2015).

3. Conduct a risk–needs assessment to identify the level of supervision and the services probationers need.

4. Support crime victims by collecting information that describes the losses, suffering, and trauma experienced by a crime victim or by the victim's survivors. This information is reported to the court in a written document called the *victim-impact statement.* The judge considers it when sentencing the offender. The information is particularly valuable for sentences that include restitution.

5. Coordinate and promote the use of community resources. POs refer offenders to community agencies and programs that serve the offenders' needs. Such programs include drug and alcohol treatment, job training, vocational education, anger management, and life skills training.

Not all probation agencies achieve these objectives in the same way. A probation department's orientation is a function of many things, including department philosophy, leadership, the community served, and the offenders supervised. Some departments lean more toward treating the offender; others lean more toward offender control. It is likely that the majority of probation departments do both, depending on the need and the situation. The American Probation and Parole Association (APPA) policy on probation is found in Exhibit 4–2. What are the beliefs upon which probation is premised?

EXHIBIT 4-2	American Probation and Parole Association Position Statement on Probation

Probation

Purpose

The purpose of probation is to assist in reducing the incidence and impact of crime by probationers in the community. The core services of probation are to provide investigation and reports to the court, to help develop appropriate court dispositions for adult offenders and juvenile delinquents, and to supervise those persons placed on probation. Probation departments in fulfilling their purpose may also provide a broad range of services including, but not limited to, crime and delinquency prevention, victim restitution programs and intern/volunteer programs.

Position

The mission of probation is to protect the public interest and safety by reducing the incidence and impact of crime by probationers. This role is accomplished by:

- assisting the courts in decision making through the probation report and in the enforcement of court orders;
- providing services and programs that afford opportunities for offenders to become more law-abiding;
- providing and cooperating in programs and activities for the prevention of crime and delinquency; and
- furthering the administration of fair and individualized justice.

Probation is premised upon the following beliefs:

Society has a right to be protected from persons who cause its members harm, regardless of the reasons for such harm.   It is the right of every citizen to be free from fear of harm to person and property. Belief in the necessity of law to an orderly society demands commitment to support it. Probation accepts this responsibility and views itself as an instrument for both control and treatment appropriate to some, but not all offenders. The wise use of authority derived from law adds strength and stability to its efforts.

Offenders have rights deserving of protection.   Freedom and democracy require fair and individualized due process of law in adjudicating and sentencing the offender.

Victims of crime have rights deserving of protection. In its humanitarian tradition, probation recognizes that prosecution of the offender is but a part of the responsibility of the criminal justice system. The victim of criminal activity may suffer loss of property, emotional problems, or physical disability. Probation thus commits itself to advocacy for the needs and interests of crime victims.

Human beings are capable of change.   Belief in the individual's capability for behavioral change leads probation practitioners to a commitment to the reintegration of the offender into the community. The possibility for constructive change of behavior is based on the recognition and acceptance of the principal of individual responsibility. Much of probation practice focuses on identifying and making available those services and programs that will best afford offenders an opportunity to become responsible, law-abiding citizens.

Not all offenders have the same capacity or willingness to benefit from measures designed to produce law-abiding citizens.   Probation practitioners recognize the variations among individuals. The present offense, the degree of risk to the community and the potential for change can be assessed only in the context of the offender's individual history and experience.

Intervention in an offender's life should be the minimal amount needed to protect society and promote law-abiding behavior.   Probation subscribes to the principle of intervening in an offender's life only to the extent necessary. Where further intervention appears unwarranted, criminal justice system involvement should be terminated. Where needed intervention can best be provided by an agency outside the system, the offender should be diverted from the system to that agency.

Punishment.   Probation philosophy does not accept the concept of retributive punishment. Punishment as a corrective measure is supported and used in those instances in which it is felt that aversive measures may positively alter the offender's behavior when other measures may not. Even corrective punishment, however, should be used cautiously and judiciously in view of its highly unpredictable impact. It can be recognized that a conditional sentence in the community is, in and of itself, a punishment. It is less harsh and drastic than a prison term but more controlling and punitive than release without supervision.

Incarceration may be destructive and should be imposed only when necessary.   Probation practitioners acknowledge society's right to protect itself and support the incarceration of offenders whose behavior constitutes a danger to the public through rejection of social or court mandates. Incarceration can also be an appropriate element of a probation program to emphasize the consequences of criminal behavior and thus effect constructive behavioral change. However, institutions should be humane and required to adhere to the highest standards.

Where public safety is not compromised, society and most offenders are best served through community correctional programs.   Most offenders should be provided services within the community in which they are expected to demonstrate acceptable behavior. Community correctional programs generally are cost-effective and they allow offenders to remain with their families while paying taxes and, where applicable, restitution to victims.

Source: Reprinted with permission of American Probation and Parole Association.

History of Probation

Probation in America developed during the 19th century. What started as a charitable and volunteer movement took almost 125 years to become available to adults in every state across the country.

Probation Begins in America In 1841, when 57-year-old John Augustus, a wealthy Boston shoemaker, became interested in the operation of the courts, the practice of probation began to emerge. Augustus was particularly sensitive to the problems of persons charged with violating Boston's vice or temperance laws. He was a member of the Washington Total Abstinence Society, an organization devoted to the promotion of temperance. By posting bail in selected cases, he had the offenders released to his care and supervision, and so began the work of the nation's first PO, an unpaid volunteer.

By the time of his death in 1859, Augustus had won probation for almost 2,000 adults and several thousand children. Several aspects of his probation system are still in use. Augustus investigated the age, character, and work habits of each offender. He identified persons he thought redeemable and "whose hearts were not fully depraved, but gave promise of better things." He made probation recommendations to the court. He developed conditions of probation and helped offenders with employment, education, and housing. And he supervised offenders during their probation, which lasted, on the average, about 30 days.

After Augustus's death in 1859, unpaid volunteers continued his work. In 1878, the Massachusetts legislature passed the first statute authorizing probation and provided for the first paid PO.[2] The second state to pass a probation statute was Vermont, in 1898. As more and more states passed laws authorizing probation, it became a national institution. On March 4, 1925, President Calvin Coolidge signed the National Probation Act. The act authorized each federal district court to appoint one salaried PO with an annual income of $2,600.[3] By 1925, probation was available for juveniles in every state; by 1956, it was available for adults in every state.

John Augustus (1785–1859) was a Boston shoemaker who invented probation in 1841 and became the first "unofficial" PO. He is called the founder of probation. Which aspects of Augustus's probation system are still in use today?

Courtesy of American Probation & Parole Association

CO4-3 ## Characteristics of Adults on Probation

For the seventh consecutive year, U.S. adults under community supervision declined in 2014. At 2014 yearend 3,864,100 were on probation, down by about 45,300 offenders from yearend 2013.[4] In 2014, the average length of stay on probation was 21.9 months.[5]

Exhibit 4–3 shows that the majority of adults on probation are in regular caseloads, they have one face-to-face contact with their POs per month, and the cost of their supervision is $3.07 per day. By contrast, offenders who pose a higher risk of reoffending or who might otherwise be incarcerated are placed in intensive supervision caseloads. Each caseload averages 29 offenders with seven face-to-face contacts with their POs per month, and costing approximately $8.96 per day. Without probation, it can cost as much as $100 per day to incarcerate an offender. Probation is cost-effective, providing it can protect the community by matching the level of supervision with the level of risk an offender poses.

Exhibit 4–4 presents selected characteristics of the 3.9 million adults on probation at yearend 2014. Most characteristics of adult probationers have remained stable for the past 15 years. Males made up three-quarters (75 percent) of the adult probation population. More than half (54 percent) of probationers were white non-Hispanic, and nearly one-third (30 percent) were black non-Hispanic. Nearly three-quarters (73 percent) were on active status, and about 1 in 5 (19 percent) were being supervised for a violent offense. Fifty-six percent of probationers were being supervised for a felony offense in 2014 compared to 52 percent in 2000.

Recently, researchers at the Department of Justice (DOJ) learned from hour-long interviews with active probationers that 9 percent of male probationers and 28 percent of female probationers had been physically or sexually abused before their sentence and before age 18.[6] (Prevalence estimates of child abuse in the general population are 5 to 8 percent for males and 12 to 17 percent for females.) Abused probationers told DOJ researchers that the abuser was either a family member or someone they knew intimately. Researchers are just beginning to study the link between child abuse and offending.

At yearend 2014, 1,568 adults were on probation for every 100,000 persons age 18 and older in the United States, down from 1,602 per 100,000 at yearend 2010. The largest adult probation populations are in Georgia

EXHIBIT 4-3 | Probation Statistics

Case Type*	Average Caseload per Officer	Average Number of Face-to-Face Contacts Between Probationer and Officer per Month	Average Cost per Day per Probationer
Regular	139	1	$3.07
Intensive	29	7	8.97
Electronic	6	3	8.71
Special	45	4	4.27

*Regular supervision: Supervision of a probationer according to normal/average number of visits, contacts, or reports with a probation officer. **Intensive supervision:** Supervision of a probationer that includes a greater number of visits, contacts, or reports to or from a probation officer than exists under regular supervision. Offenders who pose a higher risk of reoffending or who might otherwise be incarcerated are candidates for placement under intensive supervision. **Electronic supervision:** Supervision of a probationer that includes the use of an electronic monitoring device such as an ankle bracelet, pager, or voice verification telephone that assists probation officers in ascertaining an offender's whereabouts. **Special supervision:** Supervision of a probationer that includes special programming such as boot camp, substance abuse treatment programs, sex offender treatment, or other programs or services. More about intensive, electronic, and special supervision programming is discussed in Chapter 5.

Source: Adapted from Camille Graham Camp and George W. Camp, *The Corrections Yearbook, 2000,* pp. 170, 172, 176, 177, and 187. Copyright © 2000 Criminal Justice Institute; and Pew Center on the States, *One in 31: The Long Reach of American Corrections* (New York: Pew Charitable Trusts, March 2009).

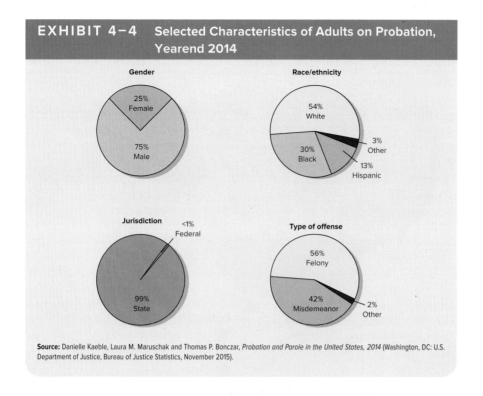

EXHIBIT 4–4 Selected Characteristics of Adults on Probation, Yearend 2014

Gender
- 25% Female
- 75% Male

Race/ethnicity
- 54% White
- 3% Other
- 13% Hispanic
- 30% Black

Jurisdiction
- <1% Federal
- 99% State

Type of offense
- 56% Felony
- 42% Misdemeanor
- 2% Other

Source: Danielle Kaeble, Laura M. Maruschak and Thomas P. Bonczar, *Probation and Parole in the United States, 2014* (Washington, DC: U.S. Department of Justice, Bureau of Justice Statistics, November 2015).

(471,067) and Texas (388,101). The smallest adult probation populations are in New Hampshire (3,910) and Wyoming (5,196). Only 22,668 persons were on federal probation at yearend 2011.

The three states that use probation the most are Georgia (6,161 per 100,000 adult population), Idaho (2,761), and Rhode Island (2,793). The three states that use probation least are New Hampshire (368 per 100,000 adult population), Nevada (548), and West Virginia (488).

Who Administers Probation?

As probation spread throughout the United States in the late 19th and early 20th centuries, its organization and administration depended on local and state customs and politics. Currently, probation in the 50 states is administered by more than 2,000 separate agencies, reflecting the decentralized and fragmented character of contemporary corrections. The agencies have a great deal of common ground, but because they developed in different contexts, they also have a lot of differences in goals, policies, funding, staffing, salaries, budgets, and operation.

The agencies that administer probation, as with the rest of the criminal justice system, have steadily shifted the costs of probation to those accused and convicted of breaking the law. The Department of Justice's March 2015 report on practices in Ferguson, Missouri, highlights the overreliance on court fines as a primary source of revenue for the city.[7] Offender fees are popular because the criminal justice system has exploded. Reforming the criminal justice system and de-escalating mass incarceration—topics once taboo in legislative halls across the country—are now commonplace themes of discussion. The Brennan Center for Justice at the New York University School of Law estimates the fiscal costs of corrections at more than $80 *billion* annually.[8] In most states, corrections is the third-largest category of spending, behind education and health care. In 2007, only five states spent more on corrections than higher education. In 2013, that number increased

CO4-4

Visit http://www.npr.org/player/v2/mediaPlayer. html?action=1&t=1&islist=false&id=3121585 16&m=313996804 or scan this code with the QR app on your smartphone or digital device and read about the explosion of fees charged to criminal defendants across the United States. How does this information relate to ideas discussed in this chapter?

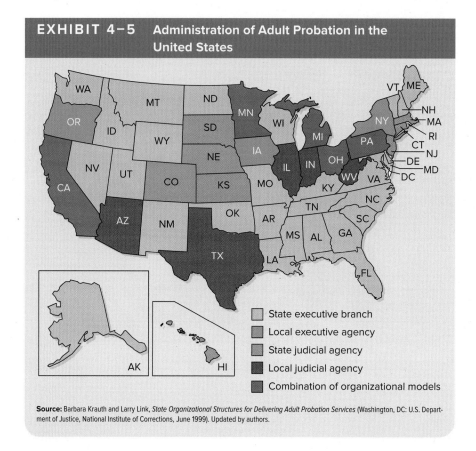

EXHIBIT 4–5   Administration of Adult Probation in the United States

State executive branch
Local executive agency
State judicial agency
Local judicial agency
Combination of organizational models

Source: Barbara Krauth and Larry Link, *State Organizational Structures for Delivering Adult Probation Services* (Washington, DC: U.S. Department of Justice, National Institute of Corrections, June 1999). Updated by authors.

to 11 states. It is not surprising, then, that 44 states charge individuals for using probation services—anywhere from $80 to $100 per month.[9] Probationers can also be charged for the special conditions of their probation such as wearing an electric monitor, which can cost as much as an additional $300 a month. Missouri charges probationers and parolees $60 a month. In Colorado, it's $50 a month. Hawaii charges felony probationers $150 a month. New Mexico law allows probation authorities to collect up to $185 a month from felony probationers. Iowa charges probationers and parolees a one-time enrollment fee of $250. Michigan imposes a fee on a sliding scale of up to 5 percent of monthly income, not to exceed a monthly total fee of $135.

Most states waive or reduce fees for probationers and parolees who are indigent. In Florida, for example, an offender who qualifies for the services of a public defender at trial is presumed to be low income and will be required to pay a fee of $50 a month, which is less than half the amount charged for others on regular probation. In Pennsylvania, offenders who have poverty-level income, are students, or are collecting welfare are entitled to a reduction or a waiver of a $25 monthly supervision fee imposed on those who can afford to pay.

Probation is commonly considered a part of the correctional system, although it is technically a function of the court system. Exhibit 4–5 gives a state-by-state breakdown of how probation is administered.[10]

Privatizing Probation There is also movement toward privatization in community corrections, including offender assessment, drug testing and treatment, electronic monitoring, halfway house management, and probation field services. There is no census on the number of persons who are under private community supervision. However, at least 1,000 courts in several states allow private companies to oversee probation for minor offenses, collecting outstanding debts and court costs and, oftentimes, adding their own fees for services such as ankle monitors and late payment.

In most states, the impetus for privatizing community supervision was similar: Staffing and resources were not keeping pace with increasing caseloads. Community supervision officials believed they had exhausted the use of interns and volunteers, and obtaining funding for new staff was not possible. States partnered with the private sector to monitor the low-risk offender population, a group who generally has few needs, whose past records reflect little or no violence, and who successfully completes probation about 90 percent of the time.

The most often cited rationale for charging probation fees is to offset burgeoning correctional budgets, even though the practice has had mixed results. The second most cited justification is based on the theory that forcing offenders to pay for their community supervision "teaches them a lesson" that is grounded in rehabilitation and/or deterrence.

However, the debate over privatizing community supervision has its critics. Opponents argue that since society has chosen to punish individuals, it should be prepared to pay the cost of punishment. To ask the offender to pay the cost of her/his probation is unjust because it is like punishing them again by charging them for a multitude of services. Opponents also point to the burden on most families when probation fees take away groceries, mortgage and rent, child care, and utilities.

Consider the situation in Georgia. In 2003, Georgia passed SB 474 that transferred supervision of 25,000 convicted misdemeanants from the state Department of Corrections to individual counties and permitted each county to contract with a for-profit probation agency to supervise these misdemeanants. Today, approximately 40 private probation agencies are registered in Georgia; they employ 850 POs and serve 640 courts. In Georgia, every person who cannot pay his or her misdemeanor fine on the day of court is placed on probation under the supervision of a private, for-profit company until he or she pays the fine. For example, assume you are ordered to pay $200 for a traffic fine. If you have enough money to pay it on the day you go to court, you can avoid probation. If you cannot, you must pay your fine and a monthly supervision fee in the range of $35–$44 to a private company in weekly or biweekly installments over a period of three months to a year. By the time your probation is over, you may have paid more than two or three times the amount that the judge had ordered. In Americus, Georgia, one high school student convicted of violating the terms of his learner's permit served seven months on probation and paid $505 in court fines and probation fees. Had he been able to pay the fine the day he was sentenced, he would have paid only $155.

Does Probation Work?

The most common question asked about probation is, "Does it work?" In other words, do persons granted probation refrain from further crime?

A probation officer involves an offender's family to help with rehabilitation. POs also refer offenders to community agencies to help them overcome the problem that led to their offending behavior. What obstacles might a PO face in making referrals to a community agency and involving the family in offender rehabilitation?
© McGraw-Hill Education/Aaron Roeth, photographer

Visit https://www.youtube.com/ watch?v=015mdURr2Dw or scan this code with the QR app on your smartphone or digital device and watch the Human Rights Watch documentary about private probation. How does this information relate to ideas discussed in this chapter?

CO4-5

recidivism

The repetition of criminal behavior; generally defined as *rearrest*. It is the primary outcome measure for probation as it is for all corrections programs.

Recidivism—generally defined as *rearrest*—continues to be the primary outcome measure for probation, as it is for all corrections programs. And if recidivism is the only measure of probation's effectiveness, the reality is that more than 35 percent of probationers fail to successfully complete their period of probation.[11] However, probation is a collection of strategies, some control oriented, some treatment oriented. How these different strategies are measured answers the question "Does probation work?"

Today, the push for evidence-based corrections highlights the importance of using scientific research to study correctional policy. Although the body of scientific evidence to make informed decisions about whether probation strategies reduce criminal activity is not large, we know from sophisticated evaluations in Florida, Maryland, and Washington that control-focused strategies (for example, intensive supervision and remote location monitoring) alone do not reduce criminal activity. However, when control-focused strategies are combined with treatment strategies, there is scientific evidence that probation achieves, on average, a statistically significant 8 to 22 percent reduction in the recidivism rates of program participants compared with a treatment-as-usual group.[12] Still others suggest that if probation agencies adhere to the seven principles of effective rehabilitation—(1) target criminogenic needs (*criminogenic needs* are characteristics, traits, problems, or issues of an individual that directly relate to the individual's likelihood to commit another crime, such as low levels of educational and employment performance, or substance abuse); (2) provide intensive services to high-risk rather than low-risk offenders; (3) match styles of service delivery to offender responsivity; (4) adhere to the principles of social and behavioral learning; (5) emphasize positive reinforcers rather than negative ones; (6) develop offender coping skills; and (7) employ staff supportive of offender rehabilitation—criminal activity can be reduced by as much as 50 percent.[13]

We also know that recidivism rates vary from place to place, depending on the seriousness of offenses; population characteristics; average length of probation; and the amount and quality of intervention, surveillance, and enforcement. James Gondles Jr., executive director of the American Correctional Association, argues that, by the time offenders reach probation, other institutions of social control have failed. If the offending behavior could have been controlled, families, neighborhoods, schools, and other social institutions would have controlled it. Offending behavior is not easy to correct and for that reason, Gondles believes that probation systems across the United States need help.

> [Probation officers] are often held accountable for the failures of other elements of the criminal justice community. Therefore, all of us in corrections must help them by doing our own jobs better, to escape the perception that they are ineffective. We must work together to ensure that all elements of the criminal justice system receive adequate funding and that all elements of the criminal justice system work closer together to provide offenders with the services they require.[14]

The APPA, representing U.S. POs nationwide, argues that recidivism rates measure just one probation task while ignoring others. The APPA has urged its member agencies to collect data on other outcomes, such as the following:

- amount of restitution collected;
- number of offenders employed;
- amounts of fines and fees collected;
- hours of community service performed;
- number of treatment sessions attended;

© Clarissa Grissette

Clarissa Grissette

U.S Probation Officer, U.S. District Court, Middle District of Florida, Tampa, Florida

Clarissa Grissette is a U.S. probation supervision officer for the U.S. District Court, Middle District of Florida, in Tampa. Clarissa supervises offenders, using evidenced-based practices, who have committed federal crimes. She helps offenders reintegrate back into society by providing them with resources based on their needs. She uses evidence-based tools such as the "post-conviction risk assessment" that evaluates offenders' personal needs and the "substance abuse subtle screening inventory" to evaluate whether they need substance abuse treatment.

Clarissa earned her bachelor's degree in criminology and criminal justice from Florida Atlantic University (FAU) in 2009. She interned with the Broward County Sheriff's Office and worked closely with the homicide unit. During her internship, she participated in police ride-alongs, observed autopsies, completed summary reports, and organized case files.

Prior to federal appointment, she worked as a state probation officer for the Florida Department of Corrections for five years, and in January 2015, she was promoted to a drug offender probation officer and intensively monitored offenders with substance abuse and mental health problems. During her time as an officer with the Florida Department of Corrections, she received her master's degree in criminology and criminal justice from FAU in 2014, which helped her obtain her current position as a federal officer.

Grissette has a genuine desire to help offenders reintegrate back into the community while motivating them to exercise prosocial behaviors and engage in prosocial activities. Her passion for offender success placed her in a perfect occupation that she dedicates her life into perfecting. She believes everyone deserves a second chance, sometimes even a third. Her position requires exceptional communication skills, organization, patience, love for people, and commitment. She is under the direction of Chief Joe Collins, who instilled in her that "People can do amazing things when challenged and supported." The point is to have students realize the need to be positive and respectful around everyone they encounter.

As a PO, Clarissa conducts prerelease home visits and interviews family members to determine if the environment is suitable for an inmate once he/she is released from federal custody. Once a probationer is released, she evaluates the totality of their circumstances and prior criminal history and creates a case plan tailored to their needs to ensure they are given the tools/resources to successfully complete supervision.

Clarissa recalls that, "The Criminal Justice and Criminology graduate program at Florida Atlantic University literally changed my life! It was one of the best decisions I could have made. The program was very rigorous and intense, but I learned so much, which prepared me for the job I currently have. Dr. Santos and Dr. Schiff were two professors that will forever remain highlighted in my life. Some of the courses I completed under their instruction challenged me and developed me professionally."

Clarissa wants students to know that during the application process for her to become a federal probation officer, her neighbors, former professors, and previous employers were interviewed. She had to sign release forms to have her credit and medical history (including counseling) checked. Her previous coworkers were interviewed, and she had to complete a writing test and a sentencing scoring sheet. Once hired, an updated background check is completed every five years.

> *"People can do amazing things when challenged and supported."*

- percentage of financial obligations collected;
- rate of enrollment in school;
- number of days of employment;
- educational attainment; and
- number of days drug free.

Advocates of measures other than recidivism tell us that probation should be measured by what offenders do while they are in probation programs, not by what they do after they leave.

Visit https://www.youtube.com/ watch?v=wVHEx7bJZnU or scan this code with the QR app on your smartphone or digital device and watch the podcast of Durham, North Carolina, probation officer Allison Stahl discuss her job, why she chose corrections, and what makes her job rewarding. How does this information relate to ideas discussed in this chapter?

Case investigation

The first major role of probation officers, consisting of interviewing the defendant and preparing the presentence report (PSR).

CO4-6 WHAT PROBATION OFFICERS DO

POs have two important roles: case investigation and client supervision.

Case Investigation

Case Investigation includes the preparation of a PSR, which the judge uses in sentencing an offender. The PSR is prepared by the probation department of a court; it provides a social and personal history as well as an evaluation of a defendant as an aid to the court in determining a sentence. In some states, for example, Missouri, the report is called a *sentence assessment report*.[15] As the centerpiece of Missouri's sentencing guidelines, it sets forth the recommended sentence options and the appropriate correctional resources available both in the community and in prison.

Purposes of the Presentence Report The PSR has two main purposes. First, and most important, the PSR assists the court in reaching a fair sentencing decision. The specific content areas of the PSR vary from jurisdiction to jurisdiction, but common areas include (1) information regarding the current offense; (2) the offender's past adult and juvenile criminal record; (3) family history and background; and (4) personal data about education, health, employment, and substance abuse history. In addition, some state statutes dictate content areas such as victim-impact statements. It is not uncommon for jurisdictions to include a sentencing

A PO interviews a defendant in preparation of the presentence report (PSR). Case investigation is the first major role of a PO. The PSR provides a social and personal history as well as an evaluation of the defendant as an aid to the court in determining a sentence. What questions should a PO ask the defendant?

© Mark Harvey/Alamy

recommendation in the PSR. However, sentencing reforms are limiting judicial sentencing discretion, so the PSR recommendation is much less important than it once was.

The second purpose of the PSR is to outline a treatment plan for the offender. During the investigation, in addition to determining the degree of risk the offender poses to the community, the PO identifies treatment needs so that the offender can receive appropriate services (counseling, treatment, education, community service, restitution, employment, and some form of supervision) during probation or in jail or prison.

Creating a Presentence Report The PSR starts with an interview between the PO and the defendant. The interview follows a structured format for obtaining information on the offense and the offender.

In the PSR, the PO estimates the offender's degree of risk to the community and need factors (sociological, psychological, and economic) that impact criminal behavior. They administer a comprehensive risk and needs assessment that differentiates between the high-risk offenders, who need multiple face-to-face contacts, drug tests, and other surveillance checks each week, and the low- or reduced-risk offenders who require minimal surveillance to be successful.

The PO summarizes the information gathered and, in most jurisdictions, makes a sentence recommendation. If the sentence recommended is incarceration, in most jurisdictions the length must be within guidelines set by statute (see Chapter 3). However, if the sentence recommended is probation or some other intermediate sanction (see Chapter 5), few jurisdictions have guidelines for sentence length. Only recently have some states (e.g., Delaware, Minnesota, North Carolina, and Pennsylvania) begun to design sentencing guidelines for nonprison sentences such as probation. Copies of the PSR are filed with the court and made available to the judge, the prosecutor, and the defense attorney. Exhibit 4–6 is an example of a short-form federal PSR. Space does not allow us to include everything. Not shown here is the officer's summary of the defendant's pretrial adjustment, substance abuse history, education and vocational skills, employment record, financial condition, and necessary monthly living expenses.

Disclosure of Presentence Reports One of the most important questions about the PSR is whether the defendant has a constitutional right to see it and challenge the statements contained in it. Some judges and POs oppose disclosure for several reasons. First, they fear that persons having knowledge about the offender will refuse to give information if the defendant knows they have given information about him or her. Second, they believe that, if the defendant challenges information in the PSR, court proceedings may be unduly delayed. Third, opponents believe that to give the defendant some kinds of information, such as psychological reports, might be harmful to that defendant. And fourth, they argue the PSR is a private and confidential court document.

On the other hand, advocates of disclosure argue that fundamental fairness and due process demand that convicted persons should have access to the information in the PSR on which their sentence is based so they can correct inaccuracies. However, the U.S. Supreme Court has held, in *Williams* v. *Oklahoma* (1959), that unless disclosure is required by state law or court decisions, there is no denial of due process of law when a court considers a PSR without disclosing its contents to the defendant or giving the defendant an opportunity to rebut it.

United States Probation and Pretrial Services

Charter for Excellence.

We, the members of Probation and Pretrial Services of the United States Courts, are a national system with shared professional identity, goals, and values. We facilitate the fair administration of justice and provide continuity of services throughout the judicial process. We are outcome driven and strive to make our communities safer and to make a positive difference in the lives of those we serve. We achieve success through interdependence, collaboration, and local innovation. We are committed to excellence as a system and to the principles embodied in this Charter.

We are a unique *profession*.

Our profession is distinguished by the unique combination of:

A multidimensional knowledge base in law and human behavior;

A mix of skills in investigation, communication, and analysis;

A capacity to provide services and interventions from pretrial release through post-conviction supervision;

A position of impartiality within the criminal justice system; and

A responsibility to positively impact the community and the lives of victims, defendants, and offenders.

These *goals* matter most.

Our system strives to achieve the organizational goals of:

Upholding the constitutional principles of the presumption of innocence and the right against excessive bail for pretrial defendants by appropriately balancing community safety and risk of nonappearance with protection of individual liberties;

Providing objective investigations and reports with verified information and recommendations to assist the court in making fair pretrial release, sentencing, and supervision decisions;

Ensuring defendant and offender compliance with court-ordered conditions through community-based supervision and partnerships;

Protecting the community through the use of controlling and correctional strategies designed to assess and manage risk;

Facilitating long-term, positive changes in defendants and offenders through proactive interventions; and

Promoting fair, impartial, and just treatment of defendants and offenders throughout all phases of the system.

We stand by these *values*.

Our values are mission-critical:

Act with integrity.

Demonstrate commitment to and passion for our mission.

Be effective stewards of public resources.

Treat everyone with dignity and respect.

Promote fairness in process and excellence in service to the courts and the community.

Work together to foster a collegial environment.

Be responsible and accountable.

Ethical Dilemma 4–1: Does gender or celebrity status play a role in who gets probation? For more information, go to Ethical Dilemma 4–1 at www.justicestudies.com/ethics08.

Ethical Dilemma 4–2: Should probation officers be advocates for sentencing reform? Why or why not? What are the issues? For more information, go to Ethical Dilemma 4–2 at www.justicestudies.com/ethics08.

Ethical Dilemmas for every chapter are available online.

The trend today is toward limited disclosure of information to the defendant's attorney. The American Bar Association favors disclosure of the factual contents and conclusions of the PSR (not the sources of confidential information) and the defendant's opportunity to rebut them.[16] Federal courts require that the PSR be disclosed to the defendant, his or her counsel, and to the attorney for the government, except in three instances: when disclosure might disrupt rehabilitation of the defendant, when information disclosed in the PSR was obtained on the promise of confidentiality, and when disclosure might result in harm to the defendant or any other person.

Supervision

The second major role of probation officers is client supervision. Probation **supervision** has three main elements: resource mediation, surveillance, and enforcement. *Resource mediation* means providing offenders access to a wide variety of services, such as job development, substance abuse treatment, counseling, and education. *Surveillance* means monitoring the activities of probationers through office meetings, home and work visits, drug and alcohol testing, and contact with family, friends, and employers. *Enforcement* means making probationers accountable for their behavior and making sure they understand the consequences of violating the conditions of probation. Client supervision that uses prosocial modeling and reinforcement, problem solving and cognitive techniques, such as the STARR training program for federal community supervision officers discussed in the adjacent QR code, are core skills for reducing recidivism in probation supervision.

Building a relationship with the offender and developing rapport are also important. Scholars and practitioners tell us that probation officers must be aware of the cultural differences between themselves and their probationers and understand that diversity if they are to build rapport and help change offending behavior. Recall from our earlier discussion that the majority of probationers are male and almost half are members of minority groups. Slightly more than half of the POs are female, and three-fourths of all POs are white. The demographic differences between POs and probationers raise questions on how POs can build rapport across gender, race, and ethnicity. Without rapport, experts believe there is more likelihood that probationers will miss scheduled appointments, not follow through on referrals, violate the conditions of probation, reoffend, and end up back in the system. Experts suggest five strategies to build rapport between the probationer and PO.[17]

1. Sincerity is one thing that allows probationers to forgive POs who violate a cultural norm such as saying the wrong thing.
2. High service energy sends a message to probationers that the PO is in their corner. The probationers may think that less service energy has something to do with ethnic differences.
3. Knowledge of the probationers' culture increases empathy in the cross-cultural counseling relationship. For example, if the probationer speaks English as a second language, it would be helpful in building rapport for the officer to learn key words and phrases in the probationer's native language.
4. A nonjudgmental attitude increases the officer's credibility.
5. Helping probationers with needed resources facilitates rapport building and officer credibility. The United States Probation and Pretrial Services Charter for Excellence (similar to a code of ethics) shown in the accompanying Ethics and Professionalism box reinforces these rapport-building strategies.

supervision

The second major role of probation officers, consisting of resource mediation, surveillance, and enforcement.

Visit https://www.crimesolutions.gov/ProgramDetails.aspx?ID=236 or scan this code with the QR app on your smartphone or digital device and learn about STARR (Staff Training Aimed at Reducing Rearrest), a training program for federal community supervision officers that the National Institute of Justice's CrimeSolutions.gov rates as a "promising" evidence-based practice. How does this information relate to ideas discussed in this chapter?

Olmsted County (Rochester, Minnesota) PO Bernie Sizer (right), tests Kevin Rood for alcohol during a visit to Rood's apartment. Case supervision is the second major role of a PO. What are the three main elements of case supervision?

© AP Photo/Ann Heisenfelt

| EXHIBIT 4-6 | Sample Presentence Report |

IN THE UNITED STATES DISTRICT COURT
FOR THE NORTHERN DISTRICT OF ALABAMA

UNITED STATES OF AMERICA	)	
	)	PRESENTENCE
	)	REPORT
v.	)	
EDDIE PALMER	)	Docket No. CR 16-H-248-S

Prepared For: Honorable Casandra Phillips
                   U.S. District Judge

Prepared By: Noelle Koval
                   U.S. Probation Officer
                   Birmingham, AL (205)555-0923

Offense: Count One: Possession With Intent to Distribute a Schedule II Controlled Substance (Cocaine Base), not less than 10 Years and not more than Life and/or $4,000,000 Fine. With Enhancement, Mandatory Life and/or $8,000,000 Fine.

Release Status: Released on $25,000 unsecured bond on 8/26/16
                              Remanded to custody on 12/14/16

Identifying Data

Date of Birth:	1/9/80
Age:	37
Race:	B
Sex:	M

Charge(s) and Conviction(s)

Eddie Palmer was indicted on two counts by the September 2016 Grand Jury for the Northern District of Alabama. Count One charged that on June 12, 2016, the defendant unlawfully possessed with intent to distribute approximately 500 grams of a mixture or substance containing a detectable amount of cocaine, Schedule II controlled substances, in violation of 21 USC § 841(a)(1). Count Two charged that on June 12, 2016, the defendant carried a firearm during the commission of a drug trafficking crime in violation of 18 USC § 924(c)(1). The October 2016 Grand Jury returned a superseding indictment in which the defendant was charged in two counts. Count One charges that on June 12, 2016, the defendant intentionally possessed with intent to distribute approximately 100 grams of a mixture or substance containing a detectable amount of cocaine base and approximately 240 grains of a mixture or substance containing a detectable amount of cocaine, Schedule II controlled substances, in violation of 21 USC § 841(a)(1). Count Two charges that on June 12, 2016, the defendant carried a firearm during the commission of a drug trafficking crime in violation of 18 USC § 924(c)(1). On December 14, 2016, Palmer pled guilty to Count One, and Count Two was dismissed on motion of the government. Sentencing was continued generally to a later date.

Caseload The average PO in the United States supervises approximately 139 offenders.[18] Such large caseloads do not allow probation officers time for adequate resource mediation, surveillance, or enforcement. A number of jurisdictions are experimenting with Probation Automated Management (PAM). The PAM kiosk is similar to an ATM and allows low-risk probationers to report in 24 hours a day, seven days a week, with their fingerprints as biometric identifiers. The fingerprints are compared to the ones collected when the offender first began probation. Some kiosks also take a digital face photo.

Once a match is established, the offender can interact with the kiosk by pressing buttons on the touch screen. Data are entered to verify address and employment status and to respond to questions asked by the PO. Advocates

EXHIBIT 4–6	Sample Presentence Report (*continued*)

SENTENCING RECOMMENDATION
UNITED STATES DISTRICT COURT
FOR THE NORTHERN DISTRICT OF ALABAMA

UNITED STATES V. EDDIE PALMER   **DOCKET NO. CR 16-H-248-S**

TOTAL OFFENSE LEVEL: 29

CRIMINAL HISTORY CATEGORY: III

	Statutory Provision	Guideline Provisions	Recommended Sentence
CUSTODY:	Mandatory Life	Mandatory Life	Life
PROBATION:	N/A	N/A	N/A
SUPERVISED RELEASE:	Not Less Than 10 Years	10 Years	10 Years
FINE:	$8,000,000	$15,000 to $8,000,000	$15,000
RESTITUTION:	N/A	N/A	N/A

Justification

The sentence of life is mandatory. Supervised release must be 10 years. A $15,000 fine is recommended because it is incumbent upon the defendant to demonstrate that he does not have the financial ability to pay a fine. He and his attorney have not cooperated in providing information, and it appears that he does have the ability to pay the minimum fine based on his purported monthly income from trafficking in illegal drugs.

Voluntary Surrender

The defendant is in custody.

Respectfully Submitted,

Noelle Koval

Noelle Koval
U.S. Probation Officer

of probation kiosks argue that they save scarce jail beds for those offenders posing a serious risk to the community and that POs can devote more of their face-to-face time with serious offenders. Most departments that use probation kiosks still require the offender to report face-to-face, perhaps once a month.

What is the ideal caseload for probation and parole? The issue has been discussed for as long as there have been professionals in the field. Because probation and parole are pluralistic, highly decentralized, and engaged in by hundreds of departments at the federal, state, county, and municipal levels across the United States, in the early 1990s the APPA adopted the position that a workload model that focused on the amount of time that is required to supervise a particular case up to standards was a sounder, more defensible method of determining the number of staff to supervise an agency's caseload. Yet legislators and policymakers continued to ask, "What is the ideal caseload size?"

Recognizing the need for straightforward caseload standards, in 2006 the APPA consulted experienced practitioners and researchers. It found that with the emergence in the 1990s of the body of research on correctional treatment effectiveness known as evidence-based practices, a robust set of effective strategies of correctional treatment could guide the development of caseload standards. The key is to use evidence-based practices. The APPA believes that "community corrections agencies need to stop wasting time

At the entrance to the Olmsted County jail in Rochester, Minnesota, first- and second-time offenders convicted of drunk driving are required to appear before the automated kiosk once a month and check in by handprint to answer questions about their progress. Probation kiosks are used to supervise low-risk offenders who do not require face-to-face contact with a PO. What advantages and disadvantages do you see in this approach?

© AP Photo/Ann Heisenfelt

on what does not work or what may even do 'harm' and focus their resources on what does work and does do 'good' in terms of public safety."[19]

Based on current best practices, APPA recommends that probation departments should:

1. effectively assess probationers' criminogenic risks and needs, as well as assess their strengths;
2. employ smart and tailored supervision strategies;
3. use incentives and graduated sanctions to respond promptly to probationers' behaviors; and
4. implement performance-driven personnel management practices that promote and reward recidivism reduction.

The number of cases that can be supervised by a probation or parole officer based on the type of case and level of supervision is shown in Exhibit 4–7. APPA made the caseload size recommendations flexible by stating them in terms of cases-to-staff ratios so agencies that use a team approach can use the recommendations, and framed them as numbers not to be exceeded. Framing the recommendations helps reduce the chance that better staffed agencies will not be forced to allow caseloads to increase.

Regardless of their level of supervision, all probationers are subject to "general" conditions of supervision. These include reporting to a PO as directed, paying court-ordered monies, working, obeying all laws, and being "of general good behavior." Exhibit 4–8 presents, as an example, the general conditions for all probationers in Georgia. The court may also order "special conditions" that relate directly to the offender's particular crime or history. For example, a person convicted of cybercrime may be subject to the special conditions shown in Exhibit 4–9.

Technology and Supervision There is also a wide variety of technological tools to help POs in client supervision that only a few years ago did not exist. Computer programs can track fine and probation payments, alert POs when their clients are behind on payments, and help them track whether

EXHIBIT 4-7	Adult and Juvenile Caseload Standards

ADULT STANDARDS

Case Type	Cases-to-Staff Ratio
Intensive	20:1
Moderate to high risk	50:1
Low risk	200:1
Administrative	No limit? 1,000?

JUVENILE STANDARDS

Case Type	Cases-to-Staff Ratio
Intensive	15:1
Moderate to high risk	30:1
Low risk	100:1
Administrative	Not recommended

Source: American Probation and Parole Association, *Caseload Standards for Probation and Parole* (Lexington, KY: APPA, September, 2006). Reprinted with permission of APPA.

EXHIBIT 4-8 | State of Georgia General Conditions of Probation

The court shall determine the terms and conditions of probation and may provide that the probationer shall:

1. avoid injurious and vicious habits;

2. avoid persons or places of disreputable or harmful character;

3. report to the probation supervisor as directed;

4. permit the supervisor to visit him at his home or elsewhere;

5. work faithfully at suitable employment insofar as may be possible;

6. remain within a specified location;

7. make reparation or restitution to any aggrieved person for the damage or loss caused by his offense, in an amount to be determined by the court. Unless otherwise provided by law, no reparation or restitution to any aggrieved person for the damage or loss caused by his offense shall be made if the amount is in dispute unless the same has been adjudicated;

8. make reparation or restitution as reimbursement to a municipality or county for the payment for medical care furnished the person while incarcerated pursuant to the provisions of Article 3 of Chapter 4 of this title. No reparation or restitution to a local governmental unit for the provision of medical care shall be made if the amount is in dispute unless the same has been adjudicated;

9. repay the costs incurred by any municipality or county for wrongful actions by an inmate covered under the provisions of paragraph (1) of subsection (a) of Code Section 42-4–71;

10. support his legal dependents to the best of his ability;

11. violate no local, state, or federal laws and be of general good behavior; and

12. if permitted to move or travel to another state, agree to waive extradition from any jurisdiction where he may be found and not contest any effort by any jurisdiction to return him to this state.

Source: Georgia Department of Corrections, Probation Division, General Conditions of Probation, Code Section 42-8–35.

probationers have satisfied the conditions of their sentences. Kiosk reporting, secure remote alcohol detection, voice verification, facial recognition, and radio-frequency identification chips that are designed to fit under the skin and can be read in a manner similar to a bar code at the grocery store are electronic tools that have the potential to enhance community supervision.

Another technological innovation, one of the more interesting strategies for managing the three elements of probation supervision, is mapping technology or geographic information systems (GIS). Mapping has helped law enforcement locate hot spots of crime. Police departments used to map with pins on a "point map." Today, mapping is done electronically and affords complex and instant analyses. Probation departments use mapping as a tool for the management of offenders in the community. Mapping helps ensure that probation and parole officers are dispersed in areas with high concentrations of offenders.

For example, the Wisconsin Department of Corrections found through mapping that "if you have an area with a drug usage problem, we would bring drug programming to that area. Really, our experience was we got better attendance and better completion rates with that."[20] The Center for Alternative Sentencing and Employment in New York uses mapping to monitor employment rates in areas where ex-offenders will reside and, with the assistance of community agencies, helps them find a job link upon leaving prison.

EXHIBIT 4-9	Specific Probation Conditions for Computer Crime

(A = Internet Access Permitted; B = Limited or 0 Access to Internet)	A	B
You shall consent to your probation officer and/or probation service representative conducting periodic unannounced examinations of your computer(s) equipment which may include retrieval and copying of all memory from hardware/software to ensure compliance with this condition and/or removal of such equipment for the purpose of conducting a more thorough inspection; and consent at the direction of your probation officer to having installed on your computer(s), at your expense, any hardware or software systems to monitor your computer use or prevent access to particular materials. You hereby consent to the periodic inspection of any such installed hardware or software to insure it is functioning properly.	X	X
You shall not possess encryption or steganography software.	X	X
You shall provide your probation officer accurate information about your entire computer system and software; all passwords used by you; and your Internet Service Provider(s).	X	X
You shall possess only computer hardware or software approved by your probation officer. You shall obtain written permission from your probation officer prior to obtaining any additional computer hardware or software or Internet Service Provider(s).	X	X
You shall refrain from using a computer in any manner that relates to the activity in which you were engaged in committing the instant offense or violation behavior.	X	X
You shall provide truthful information concerning your identity in all Internet or e-mail communications and not visit any "chat rooms" or similar Internet locations/sites where minors are known to frequent.	X	
You shall maintain a daily log of all addresses you access via any personal computer (or other computer used by you), other than for authorized employment, and make this log available to your probation officer.	X	
You shall not create or assist directly or indirectly in the creation of any electronic bulletin board, Internet Service Provider, or any other public or private network without the prior written consent of your probation officer. Any approval shall be subject to any conditions set by the U.S. Probation Office of the Court with respect to that approval.	X	X
You shall not possess or use a computer with access to any "on-line" computer service at any location (including employment or education) without prior written approval of the U.S. Probation Office of the Court. This includes any Internet Service Provider, bulletin board system, or any other public or private computer network. Any approval shall be subject to any conditions set by the U.S. Probation Office or the Court with respect to that approval.		X
You shall not purchase, possess, or receive a personal computer which utilizes a modem, and/or an external mode.		X
You will have an occupational condition that you can not be employed directly or indirectly where you are an installer, programmer, or "trouble shooter" for computer equipment.	X	X

Source: Arthur L. Bowker and Gregory B. Thompson, "Computer Crime in the 21st Century and Its Effects on the Probation Officer," *Federal Probation*, vol. 65, no. 2 (September 2001), p. 21.

CO4-7 Revocation of Probation

revocation hearing

A due process hearing that must be conducted to determine whether the conditions of probation have been violated before probation can be revoked and the offender removed from the community.

revocation

The formal termination of an offender's conditional freedom.

If the offender willfully violates the conditions of his or her probation, a **revocation hearing** is usually the next step. A revocation hearing is a due process hearing that must be conducted by the court or probation authority to determine whether the conditions of probation (or parole as we will see in Chapter 8) have been violated before probation can be revoked and the offender removed from the community. **Revocation** is the formal termination of an offender's conditional freedom.

Revocation is a serious matter for four reasons. First, the offender might lose his or her freedom to remain in the community. Second, the handling of probation violators by supervision agencies and courts consumes a significant portion of the court's time, energy, and resources. One jurisdiction estimated that, in addition to the equivalent of more than two full-time POs, the various stages of the probation violation process consume the

A supervision officer interviews a crime victim. Case investigation is one of a supervision officer's most important tasks. What questions would you ask a crime victim as part of the investigation?
© sturti/Getty Images RF

equivalent of a full-time judge, prosecutor, and courtroom staff.[21] Third, the cost of keeping an offender under probation supervision is much lower than that required for care and treatment in prison or jail. For example, we saw in Exhibit 4–3 that the per day cost of probation ranges from $3.07 to $8.97, depending on the level of supervision and risk an offender poses, but more than $100 per day to incarcerate an offender.[22] And fourth, imprisoning offenders who otherwise would have been placed on probation may force their families to go on welfare or make greater demands on community resources.

But the question is which sanction to use—jail or a community-based sanction? While the public and criminal justice practitioners often view community-based punishments such as those discussed in Chapter 5 as substantially less onerous than incarceration, Wood and May and others have shown that offenders do not hold the same views.[23] Many offenders—particularly those with prior prison experience—would choose to serve a year of incarceration rather than serve any amount of a community-based sanction in order to avoid incarceration. Recently, Wodahl, Boman, and Garland looked at more than 800 probation violations committed by adult felony offenders under intensive supervision probation in Wyoming and found no evidence to suggest that jail sanctions were any more effective than community-based sanctions. They write, "The imposition of a jail sanction for offender noncompliance as opposed to a community-based sanction did not affect the number of days until the next violation, the number of subsequent violations, or the overall likelihood of completing supervision. Furthermore, the number of times an offender went to jail, the number of days spent in jail, or the timing of the jail sanction did not influence offender outcomes."[24]

Findings like these, along with the financial, social, and potentially criminogenic effects of jail, call into question the use of jail as a means of punishing persons for violating probation.

Recently, in an effort to increase the rate of success of probationers, a judge in Hawaii took a group of "high-risk" probationers, gave them "warning hearings," and told them that while the rules of probation were not changing, the old rules would now be strictly enforced.[25] Those who violate the conditions of probation would be arrested. Probationers who fail a morning drug test would be arrested immediately, appear in court within hours, and have the terms of their probation modified to include a short jail stay (usually over a weekend in order to promote ongoing employment). The judge also assured those who needed drug treatment, mental health therapy, or other social services that they would get the treatment they needed and were expected to attend and complete the program. Hawaii's program that requires random drug tests of probationers and, for those who fail, an immediate short stint (typically two days) in jail with no exceptions has been copied in at least 18 states. All sites report the same results: drastic reductions in illicit-drug and/or alcohol use, reoffending, revocation, and time behind bars.[26] Hawaii's HOPE probationers are longtime criminally active drug users with an average of 17 prior arrests. According to an independent study funded by the National Institute of Justice, when compared to offenders on standard probation, offenders on HOPE Probation were 55 percent less likely to be arrested for a new crime, 72 percent less likely to use drugs, 61 percent less likely to skip appointments with their supervisory officers, and 53 percent less likely to have their probation revoked. That suggests to the researchers that more than mere deterrence is at work; HOPE clients seem to be gaining the ability to control their own behavior. The National Institute of Justice views HOPE as a promising evidence-based practice. See crimesolutions.gov.

Violations That Trigger Revocation   Revocation is triggered in one of two ways. Either offenders willfully violate the *technical* conditions of their probation, or they commit *new offenses.*

A **technical violation** is failure to comply with conditions of probation. It is not a criminal act; most revocations are the result of technical violations. According to the National Institute of Corrections (NIC), the most likely reason for revocation of probation (and parole) is a technical violation.[27] The most commonly committed technical violations are positive urinalysis, failure to participate in treatment, **absconding** (fleeing without permission of the jurisdiction in which the offender is required to stay), and failure to report to the PO. Most POs do not ask the court to revoke probation for an occasional technical violation. They understand that technical violations are supervision issues and best handled by program or treatment referrals. One analyst in the NIC report commented, "If our jails and prisons are filled with offenders who are merely noncompliant, there will be no room for the dangerous offender."[28] To ensure compliance, POs can tighten the offender's supervision with a reprimand, increase reporting requirements, limit travel or other privileges, increase drug/alcohol testing, make treatment/education referrals, restructure payments (for probationers who demonstrate an inability to pay in accordance with the court-established payment plan), or extend the terms of probation.

A **new offense violation** is the arrest and prosecution for the commission of a new crime. Depending upon the seriousness of the new offense, the court may, in response to a violation of probation (or parole, see Chapter 8) based on a new offense, impose a sentence of incarceration upon revocation of probation, *plus* any new sentence of incarceration that may be imposed for the new offense. The two sentences may be imposed to run concurrently or consecutively (see Chapter 3). In the case of parole, a new offense violation may trigger return to prison to serve out the unexpired sentence *plus* the sentence for the new offense. The point to remember is that a substantial percentage of the prison population each year is composed of probation (and parole) violators.

Revocation Hearings   Revocation hearings usually begin with a violation report prepared by the PO. They are governed by the 1973 U.S. Supreme Court decision known as *Gagnon* v. *Scarpelli.* In this case, the Court said that

technical violation

A failure to comply with the conditions of probation.

absconding

Fleeing without permission of the jurisdiction in which the offender is required to stay.

new offense violation

The arrest and prosecution for the commission of a new crime.

Visit http://www.oyez.org/cases/1970-1979/1972/1972_71_1225 or scan this code with the QR app on your smartphone or digital device and listen to the oral arguments before the United States Supreme Court in *Gagnon* v. *Scarpelli* on Tuesday, January 9, 1973, and decided May 14, 1973. How does this information relate to ideas discussed in this chapter?

there was no difference between probation and parole revocation because both of them resulted in loss of liberty. The Court extended the same rights to probationers that it had granted to parolees a year earlier in *Morrissey v. Brewer*. The Court ruled that probation cannot be revoked without observing the following elements of due process:

1. written notice of the charge;
2. disclosure of the evidence to the probationer;
3. the opportunity to be heard in person and present evidence as well as witnesses;
4. the right to confront and cross-examine witnesses;
5. the right to judgment by a detached and neutral hearing body;
6. a written statement of the reasons for revoking probation; and
7. the right to counsel under "special circumstances" depending on the offender's competence, case complexity, and mitigating circumstances.

REVIEW AND APPLICATIONS

SUMMARY

1 *Probation* is the conditional release of a convicted offender into the community under the supervision of a PO. Most probation programs are designed to (1) protect the community by assisting judges in sentencing and supervising offenders, (2) carry out sanctions imposed by the court, (3) help offenders change, (4) support crime victims, and (5) coordinate and promote the use of community resources.

2 Probation is used for four reasons: (1) It permits offenders to remain in the community for reintegration purposes, (2) it avoids institutionalization and the stigma of incarceration, (3) it is less expensive than incarceration and more humanitarian, and (4) it is appropriate for offenders whose crimes do not necessarily merit incarceration.

3 At yearend 2014 federal, state, and local probation agencies supervised almost 3.9 million adult U.S. resident, with misdemeanor convictions accounting for 42 percent. Twenty-five percent of all probationers were women, and 54 percent of probationers were white.

4 In 29 states, a state or local agency delivers adult probation services. In three states, adult probation services are delivered exclusively through county or multicounty agencies in the executive branch. In eight states, the judicial branch of government is responsible for adult probation services. In five states, local agencies in the judicial branch deliver adult probation services. And in five states, adult probation services are delivered through some combination of state executive branch, local executive agencies, or local agencies in either the judicial or the executive branch.

5 Corrections professionals urge evaluators to collect data on outcomes other than recidivism, such as amount of restitution collected, number of offenders employed, amounts of fines and fees collected, hours of community service, number of treatment sessions completed, percentage of financial obligations collected, rate of enrollment in school, number of days employed, educational attainment, and number of days drug free.

6 Case investigation and client supervision are the two major roles of POs. Investigation includes the preparation of a presentence report (PSR), which the judge uses in sentencing an offender. Supervision includes the functions of resource mediation, surveillance, and enforcement.

7 A *revocation hearing* is a due process hearing that must be conducted to determine whether the conditions of probation have been violated before probation can be revoked and the offender is removed from the community. Probation can be revoked when offenders fail to comply with the technical conditions of probation or commit new crimes.

KEY TERMS

probation, p. 71

recidivism, p. 80

investigation, p. 82

supervision, p. 85

revocation hearing, p. 90

revocation, p. 90

technical violation, p. 92

absconding, p. 92

new offense violation, p. 92

QUESTIONS FOR REVIEW

1 Explain probation and its goals.

2 Defend the reasons for using probation.

3 Construct a profile of the characteristics of adults on probation.

4 Summarize the different ways that probation is administered.

5 Evaluate the measures of probation.

6 Distinguish between the investigation and supervision functions of probation and provide an example of each.

7 Summarize what occurs at a revocation hearing.

THINKING CRITICALLY ABOUT CORRECTIONS

Privatizing Probation

With at least 1,000 courts in several states allowing private companies to oversee probation for minor offenses, collecting outstanding debts and court costs, and oftentimes adding their own fees for services such as ankle monitors and late payment, how can government continue to privatize probation and avoid a charge similar to the one brought by the U.S. Department of Justice's Civil Rights Division against the municipal court in Ferguson, Missouri, that it handles most charges *not* with the primary goal of administering justice or protecting the rights of the accused, but of maximizing revenue?

Probation Effectiveness

Recidivism is one current measure of probation effectiveness. Others include the amount of restitution collected, the number of offenders employed, the amounts of fines and fees collected, the number of hours of community service performed, the number of treatment sessions completed, the percentage of financial obligations collected, the rate of school enrollment, the level of educational attainment, the number of days employed, and the number of days drug free.

1. How important to you, as a taxpayer, is recidivism as a measure of program success?

2. Do you believe probation officers can really keep offenders from committing new crimes or violating the conditions of their probation?

3. If you were a probation officer today, by which outcome measures would you want to be judged? Why?

4. If recidivism is used as a measure of probation's effectiveness, how should it be defined?

ON-THE-JOB DECISION MAKING

Responding to Program Violations

The new diversion program in your county was developed to help first-time misdemeanor drug offenders avoid incarceration and seek help in controlling their dependency. Your job as the new diversion officer is to set the conditions of the diversion program and then monitor and enforce compliance. One of your first clients fails the required weekly drug test. Think about Wodahl, Boman, and Garland's research on the effectiveness of jail and community-based sanctions and argue in favor of jail or a community-based sanction.

Probation and Recidivism

At a recent staff meeting, the chief PO reported that the department's recidivism rate exceeded the national average by 5 percent. The chief asks what can be done about it. You say, "Look at other measures besides recidivism." The chief asks you to explain. What do you say?

INTERMEDIATE SANCTIONS

Between Probation and Incarceration

© Larry French/AP Photo for NADCP

CHAPTER OBJECTIVES

After completing this chapter you should be able to do the following:

1. Define *intermediate sanctions* and describe their purpose.

2. Describe how intensive supervision probation works.

3. Explain what drug courts are.

4. Explain how day fines differ from traditional fines.

5. Describe what a sentence to community service entails.

6. Explain what day reporting centers are.

7. Describe how remote-location monitoring works.

8. Explain what residential reentry centers are.

9. Identify the major features of boot camps.

10. Define *community corrections*.

11. Explain what community corrections acts are.

> *The use of intermediate sanctions is a cost-effective way to keep low-level offenders, such as drug and/or alcohol offenders, in the community, allowing them to avoid the criminogenic effects imprisonment may have.*
>
> —Michael Tonry, professor of law and public policy, University of Minnesota Law School

After spending one year in South Africa's Kgosi Mampuru II prison on a five-year sentence for culpable homicide in the killing of his girlfriend, Reeva Steenkamp, former Olympic athlete Oscar Pistorius, nicknamed the "Blade Runner" because he ran on special carbon-fiber prostheses, was released from a South African prison in October 2015 and placed under house arrest and correctional supervision for four years.[1] South Africa's correctional services act allows convicted criminals who have served at least one-sixth of their sentence to serve the remainder under house arrest. The conditions governing Pistorius's home confinement include community service, employment, psychotherapy, ban from alcohol use and firearms, drug testing, and restrictions on his movement. (As this book goes to press, the Supreme Court of Appeal of South Africa overturned the culpable homicide verdict, convicted Pistorius of murder, and sentenced him to six years imprisonment.) Other persons on house arrest may also be required to wear an electronic bracelet (known as remote-location monitoring and described later in this chapter). More than 125,000 people were supervised with the devices in 2015, up from 53,000 in 2005. Do you think house arrest with remote-location monitoring, one of the **intermediate sanctions** discussed in this chapter, is a viable option in controlling offender behavior?

© Hugo Philpott/UPI/Newscom

Visit http://www.cnn.com/2015/10/19/africa/south-africa-oscar-pistorius-released-house-arrest/ or scan this code with the QR app on your smartphone or digital device and listen to the CNN broadcast of Oscar Pistorius's release from prison. How does this information relate to ideas discussed in this chapter?

intermediate sanctions **CO5-1**

New punishment options developed to fill the gap between traditional probation and traditional jail or prison sentences and to better match the severity of punishment to the seriousness of the crime.

Intermediate Sanctions

INTERMEDIATE SANCTIONS

Sanctions less restrictive than prison but more restrictive than probation are not new. Variations of intermediate sanctions like many of those discussed later in this chapter (restitution, fines, and community service) were used as sentences in ancient Israel, Greece, and Rome. Other intermediate sanctions—such as drug court, remote-location monitoring, boot camps, and day fines—started in the 1980s as a way to respond to an increasing number of convicted offenders and widescale prison overcrowding. Prior to this, sentencing options were limited to incarceration or probation. However, there was growing sentiment that some crimes were too severe to be punished by placing the offender on probation, but those same crimes were not severe enough to warrant incarceration. Therefore, states started to develop a series of intermediate sanctions that fell somewhere between probation and incarceration. What is new today is the

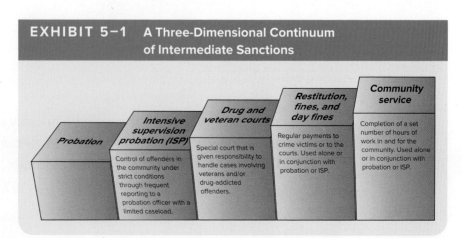

EXHIBIT 5–1   A Three-Dimensional Continuum of Intermediate Sanctions

Probation

Intensive supervision probation (ISP)
Control of offenders in the community under strict conditions through frequent reporting to a probation officer with a limited caseload.

Drug and veteran courts
Special court that is given responsibility to handle cases involving veterans and/or drug-addicted offenders.

Restitution, fines, and day fines
Regular payments to crime victims or to the courts. Used alone or in conjunction with probation or ISP.

Community service
Completion of a set number of hours of work in and for the community. Used alone or in conjunction with probation or ISP.

effort to bring all these sanctions together into a comprehensive sentencing system like the one suggested in Exhibit 5–1, which provides judges an expanded menu of corrections options. Relatively less intrusive interventions proportional to the severity of a violation and the risk of the offender are to the left in Exhibit 5–1; more intrusive ones are to the right. Exhibit 5–1 is also multidimensional, creating depth for each step on the continuum. For example, if an offender on intensive supervision probation (ISP) fails to report as scheduled (whether to an ISP officer or via an automated probation machine as described in Chapter 4) and is relatively low risk, it may be appropriate to require more frequent reporting for a period of time within ISP than to move to the next higher level of intervention.

Intermediate sanctions are most often used for offenders considered non-violent and low risk. They usually require the offender to lead a productive life in the community by working (finding work if unemployed) or learning new job skills; to perform unpaid community service; to pay restitution to victims; to enroll in a treatment or educational program; or sometimes to do all of these.

Intermediate sanctions are sometimes referred to as *alternatives to incarceration.* They may be used at initial sentencing, after an offender has made progress in compliance and treatment, or as a way to reduce the correctional population.

Value of Intermediate Sanctions

Since January 1, 2002, the nation's jail and prison population has continued to exceed 2 million inmates, placing a heavy economic burden on taxpayers. That burden includes the cost of building, maintaining, and operating prisons and jails as well as the loss of offenders' contributions and the cost of caring for the destabilized families left behind. In addition, overcrowded jails and prisons are hard to manage and staff, and they invite disorder. The fiscal crisis that began in December 2007 is moving many governors and legislators to think "outside the cell" and turn to intermediate sanctions as a way to keep low-level offenders out of prison and in their communities.

Professional associations too are calling for greater use of intermediate sanctions. The American Jail Association, for example, believes that intermediate sanctions—not prison—should be the backbone of the corrections systems (see Exhibit 5–2). This kind of thinking enables criminal justice

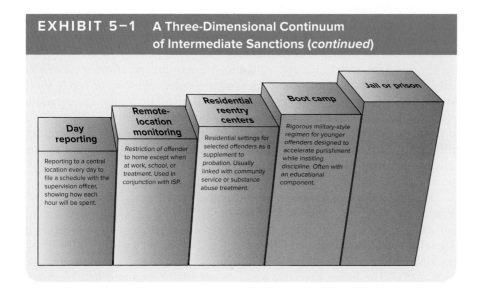

EXHIBIT 5–1 A Three-Dimensional Continuum of Intermediate Sanctions (*continued*)

Day reporting

Reporting to a central location every day to file a schedule with the supervision officer, showing how each hour will be spent.

Remote-location monitoring

Restriction of offender to home except when at work, school, or treatment. Used in conjunction with ISP.

Residential reentry centers

Residential settings for selected offenders as a supplement to probation. Usually linked with community service or substance abuse treatment.

Boot camp

Rigorous military-style regimen for younger offenders designed to accelerate punishment while instilling discipline. Often with an educational component.

Jail or prison

| EXHIBIT 5–2 | American Jail Association Resolution |

Intermediate Punishments

WHEREAS, the American Jail Association (AJA) recognizes the detrimental impact that crowding places on local jails; and

WHEREAS, many of those who are incarcerated in jails do not pose a known danger to themselves or to society;

THEREFORE BE IT RESOLVED THAT AJA supports the expansion of intermediate punishments in states and localities throughout America for offenders who do not pose a known danger to public safety. AJA believes that intermediate punishments address real concerns of constituents.

Source: Copyright © American Jail Association. Reprinted with permission.

officials to give nonviolent offenders intermediate sanctions, thereby teaching them accountability for their actions and heightening their chances for success in the community while reserving expensive prison and jail space for violent offenders. Advocacy of intermediate sanctions by professional organizations such as the American Jail Association, the American Correctional Association, the American Probation and Parole Association, and the International Community Corrections Association can significantly advance career opportunities.

Finally, numerous national and statewide polls tapping public attitudes about preferences for intermediate sanctions with treatment over incarceration give policymakers and legislators breathing room on moves to reduce prison populations during this time of budget crises in states. The public supports intermediate sanctions with treatment over incarceration for low-level drug offenders, and they favor sentencing nonviolent offenders to community service or probation instead of imprisonment.[2] "When the public is made aware of the possible range of punishments, and given information about how and with whom they are used, they support alternatives to incarceration."[3] Surveys sponsored by the Pew Center on the states found that a majority of 1,200 registered voters believe that too many people are in prison, a fifth of prisoners could be released without posing a threat to public safety, and there are more effective, less expensive alternatives to prison for nonviolent offenders and that expanding those alternatives is the best way to reduce the crime rate. Furthermore, they supported the "justice reinvestment" concept of using money saved from cutting back on prison expenditures for intermediate sanctions.[4]

Intermediate sanctions are valuable for a number of reasons. First, they provide a means for offenders who are not dangerous to repay their victims and their communities. Second, intermediate sanctions promote rehabilitation—which most citizens want, but most prisons and jails find difficult to provide—and the reintegration of the offender into the community. And third, once the programs are in place, they can do these things at a comparatively low cost. Compare the lower costs of intermediate sanctions with jail and those for prison in Exhibit 5–3.

Do some judges go too far in crafting innovative intermediate sanctions? You be the judge. In Cleveland, Ohio, Judge Pinkey Carr sentenced a man for threatening a police officer to stand outside a police station wearing a sign that read, "I apologize to Officer Simone and all police officers for being an idiot calling 911 threatening to kill you. I'm sorry and it will never happen again." The judge gave the sign her personal touch and hand-lettered

EXHIBIT 5-3	Average Annual Cost of Correctional Options per Participant	
Prison		$27,200
Jail		24,000
Intensive supervision (surveillance and treatment)		8,200
Drug court		7,000
Intensive supervision (surveillance only)		4,300
Day reporting center		3,900
Mental health courts		3,100
Inpatient intensive drug treatment		1,600
Electronic monitoring (parole and parole)		1,100
Outpatient nonintensive drug treatment		900

Sources: Vera Institute of Justice, *The Potential of Community Corrections to Improve Safety and Reduce Incarceration* (New York: Vera Institute of Justice, July 2013); West Huddleston and Douglas B. Marlowe, *Painting the Current Picture: A National Report on Drug Courts and Other Problem-Solving Court Programs in the United States* (Alexandria, VA: National Drug Court Institute, July 2011); "Benefit-Cost Results, Adult Criminal Justice," Washington State Institute for Public Policy, www.wsipp.wa.gov/BenefitCost?topicId=2 (accessed November 20, 2015); Niyi Awofeso, "Measuring and Evaluating Quality of Health Care Services in Prisons and Jails," *American Jails*, vol. 22, no. 3 (July 2008), pp. 35–38.

the sign herself. It may be funny, but is it legal and does it have a rehabilitative purpose? George Washington University law professor Jonathan Turley argues that "stunt" sentences rarely have anything to do with legal justice and are better suited to courtroom reality shows. However in 2004's *United States* v. *Gementera,* the Ninth Circuit ruled that the district court judge who sentenced a mail thief to wear a sign that read, "I stole mail; this is my punishment," imposed the punishment for the stated and legitimate statutory purpose of rehabilitation and to a lesser extent for general deterrence and for protection of the public.

Varieties of Intermediate Sanctions

The specific varieties of intermediate sanctions discussed in the following subsections include intensive supervision probation, drug and veterans courts, fines, community service, day reporting centers, remote-location monitoring (formerly known as *house arrest* and *electronic monitoring (EM)*), residential reentry centers, and boot camps.

Intensive Supervision Probation Probation with frequent contact between offender and probation officer, strict enforcement of conditions, random drug and alcohol testing, and other requirements is known as **intensive supervision probation (ISP)**.

As a technique for increasing control over offenders in the community, ISP has gained wide popularity. It allows offenders to live at home but under more severe and more punitive restrictions than those of conventional probation. The primary purpose of such program restrictions and surveillance is to protect the community and deter the offender from breaking the law or violating the conditions of release. Requirements of ISP usually include performing community service, attending school or treatment programs, working or looking for employment, meeting with a probation officer (or team of officers) as often as five times a week, and submitting to curfews, employment checks, and tests for drug and alcohol use. Because of the frequency of contact, subjection to unannounced drug tests, and rigorous enforcement of restitution, community service, and other conditions, ISP is thought more appropriate for higher-risk offenders.

CO5-2

intensive supervision probation (ISP)

Control of offenders in the community under strict conditions by means of frequent reporting to a probation officer whose caseload is generally limited to 30 offenders.

An ISP officer explains court-ordered sanctions to a probationer. Frequent face-to-face contact is a condition of ISP. What other controls are used to monitor offenders on ISP?

© McGraw-Hill Education/Aaron Roeth Photography

ISP was initially the most popular intermediate sanction. It emerged in the 1960s as an effort to improve offender rehabilitation by reducing probation and parole caseloads from 100 or more to 30. However, researchers soon discovered that small caseloads led to enhanced supervision and control (and more violations) but not necessarily to enhanced treatment.[5] It wasn't until ISP combined supervision and control with treatment components and skill development programs and reinforced clearly identified behaviors that it became effective.[6]

Evidence-based research on ISP has produced two main findings. First, restraining offenders in the community by increasing surveillance and control over their activities does *not* reduce their criminal activities.[7] Offenders sentenced to surveillance-oriented ISP programs commit new crimes at about the same rate as comparable offenders receiving different sentences. Also, technical violation and revocation rates are typically higher for ISP surveillance-oriented programs because more frequent contact makes misconduct more likely to be discovered. Early proponents of surveillance-oriented ISP programs argued that ISP would reduce recidivism rates, rehabilitate offenders, and save money and prison resources. However, most evaluations suggest that the combination of high revocation rates and the cost of processing revocations makes savings unlikely.[8]

On the other hand, scientific analysis of 10 treatment-oriented ISP programs indicates, on average, a statistically significant 21.9 percent reduction in the recidivism rates of program participants compared with a treatment-as-usual group[9]—what some call "extremely successful."[10] Two ISP programs that the U.S. Department of Justice says have strong evidence indicating that they achieve their intended outcomes are the Reduced Probation Caseload programs in Iowa and Oklahoma. In Iowa, ISP significantly reduced the likelihood of recidivism by 47 percent for property and violent crime and 20 percent for all offenses. In Oklahoma, the results showed that the treatment group was arrested less often than the control group. At the maximum 1½-year follow-up, the treatment group had a significantly lower probability of recidivism than the control group with a roughly 30 percent lower recidivism rate.[11] According to the editors of the *Criminal Justice Newsletter*, "The lesson from this research is that it is the treatment—not the intensive monitoring—that results in recidivism reduction."[12] Rearrests are reduced when offenders receive treatment in addition to the increased surveillance and control of ISP programs.

CO5-3 **Drug Courts** Can you cure addiction by locking it up? Some say it doesn't cure it but makes it worse. Enter drug court, a recent innovation within the American criminal justice system.

Drug court is a special court that is given responsibility to handle cases involving drug-addicted offenders.[13]

Drug courts vary across jurisdictions and no drug court is exactly the same as the next, but there are two general types: deferred prosecution programs (pretrial diversion or "preplea") and postplea. People who enter a deferred prosecution program are diverted into the drug court system *before* being convicted, are not required to plead guilty, and are prosecuted only if they fail to complete the program.

Postplea programs require participants to plead guilty to the charges against them and have their sentences deferred or suspended while they

drug court

A special court that is given responsibility to treat, sanction, and reward drug offenders with punishment more restrictive than regular probation but less severe than incarceration.

are in the program. The sentence will be waived or reduced, and often the offense will be expunged from their record if they complete the program. The case will be returned to court, and the people will face sentencing on their previously entered guilty plea if they fail to satisfy the program requirements. The majority (58 percent) of adult drug courts follow a post-plea model.

Drug court is a new intermediate sanction that uses the power of the court to treat, sanction, and reward drug offenders with punishment more restrictive than regular probation but less severe than incarceration. In 1989, troubled by the devastating impact of drugs and drug-related crime on Dade County (Florida) neighborhoods and the criminal justice system, Miami judge Herbert M. Klein developed the nation's first drug court. The number of drug courts has grown from 1 in 1989 to almost 2,500 today.[14]

In addition to the adult drug court that most of us are familiar with, new forms of drug courts are emerging.[15] The different types today include:

1. Veterans Treatment Court uses veterans as mentors to help other veterans engage in treatment and counseling to address their unique needs. Since the first veterans court was established in Buffalo, New York, in 2008, 264 veterans courts now operate in 37 states and serve an estimated 13,200 veterans who otherwise would be incarcerated.[16]

2. DWI Court, a postconviction court, is dedicated to changing the behavior of alcohol-dependent repeat offenders arrested for DWI.

3. Family Drug Court targets parental substance abuse in juvenile abuse, neglect, and dependency cases.

4. Federal Reentry Court is a postadjudication court that provides a blend of treatment and sanction alternatives to address behavior, rehabilitation, and community reentry for nonviolent, substance-abusing federal offenders.

5. Juvenile Drug Court handles selected delinquency cases and in some instances, status offenders who are identified as having problems with alcohol and/or other drugs.

6. Reentry Drug Court facilitates the reintegration of drug-involved offenders into communities upon their release from local or state correctional facilities.

7. Tribal Healing to Wellness Court is a component of the tribal justice system that incorporates and adapts a wellness concept to meet the specific substance abuse needs of each tribal community.

8. The Back on TRAC clinical justice model targets college students whose excessive use of substances has continued despite higher education's best efforts at education, prevention, or treatment and has ultimately created serious consequences for themselves or others.

In comparison with the aims of other types of courts, those of the drug court are nonadversarial, much less punitive, and more healing and

Judge Sarah Smith congratulates drug court participant Bronco Anderson in her Tulsa, Oklahoma, courtroom for completing phase one and moving to phase two of the drug court program. Drug courts treat, sanction, and reward drug offenders with punishment more restrictive than regular probation but less severe than incarceration. What are the key components of drug court?
© AP Photo/John Clanton

EXHIBIT 5-4   Ten Key Components of Drug Courts

1. Drug courts integrate alcohol and other drug treatment services with justice system case processing.
2. Using a nonadversarial approach, prosecution and defense counsel promote public safety while protecting participants' due process rights.
3. Eligible participants are identified early and promptly placed in the drug court program.
4. Drug courts provide access to a continuum of alcohol, drug, and other related treatment and rehabilitation services.
5. Abstinence is monitored by frequent alcohol and other drug testing.
6. A coordinated strategy governs drug court responses to participants' compliance.
7. Ongoing judicial interaction with each drug court participant is essential.
8. Monitoring and evaluation measure the achievement of program goals and gauge effectiveness.
9. Continuing interdisciplinary education promotes effective drug court planning, implementation, and operations.
10. Forging partnerships among drug courts, public agencies, and community-based organizations generates local support and enhances drug court program effectiveness.

Source: National Association of Drug Court Professionals, *Defining Drug Courts: The Key Components* (Alexandria, VA: Author, 2004).

Visit https://www.youtube.com/watch?v=EJi1ud GWxrM or scan this code with the QR app on your smartphone or digital device and watch Dr. Doug Marlowe, Chief of Science, Law and Policy with the National Association of Drug Court Professionals, discuss best practices in adult drug courts. How does this information relate to ideas discussed in this chapter?

restorative in nature. The key components of drug courts are shown in Exhibit 5–4. The "key components" are hypothesized to include a multidisciplinary team approach, an ongoing schedule of judicial status hearings, weekly drug testing, sanctions and incentives, and a regimen of substance abuse treatment. Successful completion of the treatment program results in dismissal of the charges, reduced or set-aside sentences, lesser penalties, or a combination of these.

Compared to the small number of scientific studies examining the effectiveness of other intermediate sanctions on reducing criminal activity, a relatively large number of evidence-based studies have examined the effectiveness of drug courts. A number of analyses and evaluations have been conducted examining the effectiveness of drug courts, and they generally conclude that drug courts can reduce recidivism by an average of 8 to 14 percent. Furthermore, the reductions in recidivism were shown to last at least three years, and in one study, the effects lasted an astounding 14 years.[17] The most influential components of the drug treatment court model are the role of judicial status hearings, drug treatment, and the drug treatment judge.

Drug courts are also cost-effective. Evaluations of drug courts nationwide find that they save taxpayers money compared to probation and/or incarceration due to reductions in arrests, case processing, jail occupancy, and victimization costs. The Washington State Institute for Public Policy estimated the annual cost of drug court participation to be $4,300 per person compared to $23,000 per year for incarceration.[18]

Despite the successes of drug courts during the past 20 years, they remain available to less than 10 percent of drug addicted offenders. Although every state has at least one drug court, only a handful of states—like New Jersey and New York—have one in every county.[19] Advocates say the main reason for their scarcity is a lack of money. The National Association of Drug Court Professionals says that $1.5 billion in federal money—along with matching money from states—could treat all who need it. An approximate number of drug courts in each state is shown in Exhibit 5–5.

EXHIBIT 5–5 Drug Courts in the United States

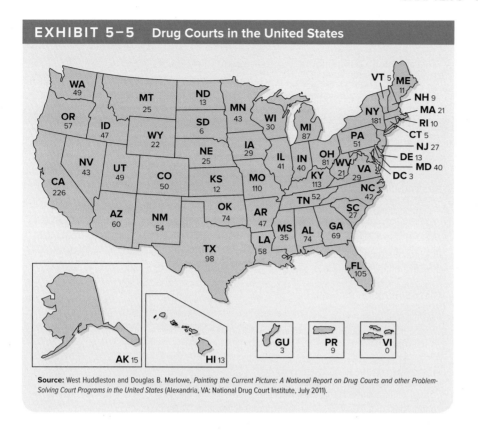

Source: West Huddleston and Douglas B. Marlowe, *Painting the Current Picture: A National Report on Drug Courts and other Problem-Solving Court Programs in the United States* (Alexandria, VA: National Drug Court Institute, July 2011).

Fines A **fine** is a financial sanction requiring a convicted person to pay a specified sum of money. The fine is one of the oldest forms of punishment. It is, in practice, the criminal justice tool for punishing minor misdemeanors, traffic offenses, ordinance violations, and corporations. In the United States, fines are rarely regarded as a tough criminal sanction. They are not taken seriously for at least four reasons. First, judicial, legislative, and prosecutorial attitudes restrict the use of fines to traffic offenses, minor misdemeanors, and ordinance violations. Second, a judge seldom has enough reliable information on an offender's personal wealth to impose a just fine. Third, mechanisms for collecting fines are often ineffective. Far too often, the responsibility for collecting fines has been left to probation officers, who are already overburdened and have no interest in fine collection. As a result, fines are seldom paid. Fourth, many believe that fines work a hardship on the poor while affluent offenders feel no sting. Five notable corporate fines are shown in Exhibit 5–6.

A **day fine** is a financial penalty based on the seriousness of the crime and the defendant's ability to pay. It is called a *day fine* because it is based on the offender's daily income. Day fines, also called *structured fines,* have been common in some northern and western European countries for many years. They were introduced in Sweden in the 1920s and were quickly incorporated into the penal codes of other Scandinavian countries. West Germany adopted day fines as a sentencing option in the early 1970s. Today, Sweden and Germany have made day fines the preferred punishment for most criminal cases, including those involving serious crimes. In Germany, for example, day fines are the only punishment for three-quarters of all offenders convicted of property crimes and two-thirds of offenders convicted of assaults.[20] In most Scandinavian countries, day fines are used for punishing traffic offenses. For example, the day fine of an heir to a family-owned

fine

A financial penalty used as a criminal sanction.

day fine

A financial penalty scaled both to the defendant's ability to pay and the seriousness of the crime.

EXHIBIT 5-6 | **Notable Fines and Penalties Charged to Corporations**

Big Tobacco: $206 billion

In what was then the largest civil settlement in U.S. history, 46 states reached a $206 billion settlement with the tobacco industry over health care costs related to smoking in November 1998.

J.P. Morgan Chase: $13 billion

J.P. Morgan Chase reached a deal to pay $13 billion to end a number of civil investigations into its sale of mortgage securities prior to the financial crisis.

BP: $4 billion

BP Exploration and Production pled guilty to manslaughter charges and agreed to pay a record $4 billion in government penalties in response to the 2010 Deepwater Horizon explosion and oil spill. The oil company also agreed to a $525 million settlement to resolve civil charges with the Securities and Exchange Commission for lying to investors about how much oil flowed into the Gulf during the spill.

GlaxoSmithKline: $3 billion

In what could be the largest health care fraud settlement in the United States, drug maker GlaxoSmithKline pled guilty to criminal charges it illegally marketed the drug Paxil for treating depression in patients under age 18, which the drug had not been approved for.

HSBC: $1.9 Billion

HSBC Holdings agreed to pay $1.9 billion in fees and penalties to resolve charges that the London-based bank's weak oversight of transactions helped Latin American drug cartels launder billions of dollars. The bank also violated U.S. sanctions against Cuba, Iran, Libya, Sudan, and Burma, by conducting transactions for customers in those countries.

Day Fines

sausage business in Finland was caught driving 50 miles per hour (mph) in a 25-mph zone and fined $217,000. With Finnish tax records showing his wealth at $8 million, he was given a world-record speeding fine. His fine more than doubles the existing records of a $96,000 fine given in 2002 to Annssi Vanjoki, a Nokia vice president, for driving his Harley-Davidson 17 miles above the speed limit on a Helsinki street; a $31,200 fine given in 2001 to Pekka Ala-Pietila, Nokia president, for driving through a red light; a $71,000 fine given in 2000 to Jaakko Rysola, dot-com millionaire, for zigzagging through Helsinki in his Ferrari; and a $122,974 fine given in 2009 to the heir of a Norwegian shipping family for drunk driving. If Tiger Woods's 2014 car crash had happened in any of these countries, he would have paid a day fine of more than $300,000 rather than a fixed fine of $164 because he makes roughly $10 million each month.[21]

The planning process for introducing day fines is unique for each jurisdiction, depending on its organizational structure, traditions, personalities, and legal culture. Once a system for imposing day fines is put in place, the next step is to develop a structured process for setting fines. This structured process is the feature that distinguishes day fines from traditional fines. The process usually has two parts: (1) a unit scale that ranks offenses by severity and (2) a valuation scale for determining the dollar amount per unit for a given offender.

The first step in setting a day fine is to determine the number of fine units to be imposed. A portion of the unit scale used in a Staten Island, New York, day fine experiment is shown in Exhibit 5–7. The number of units ranges from a low of 5 to a high of 120 for the most serious misdemeanors handled by the court. For example, the presumptive number of units for the

EXHIBIT 5-7 Example of a Day Fine Unit Scale

Staten Island Day Fine Unit Scale (Selected Offense Categories)

Penal Law Charge*	Type of Offense**	Number of Day Fine Units		
		Discount	PRESUMPTIVE	Premium
120.00 AM	Assault 3: Range of 20–95 DF			
	A. Substantial Injury	81	**95**	109
	Stranger-to-stranger; or where victim is known to assailant, he/she is weaker, vulnerable			
	B. Minor Injury	59	**70**	81
	Stranger-to-stranger; or where victim is known to assailant, he/she is weaker, vulnerable; or altercations involving use of a weapon			
	C. Substantial Injury	38	**45**	52
	Altercations among acquaintances; brawls			
	D. Minor Injury	17	**20**	23
	Altercations among acquaintances; brawls			
110/120.00 BM	Attempted Assault 3: Range of 15–45 DF			
	A. Substantial Injury	38	**45**	52
	Stranger-to-stranger; or where victim is known to assailant, he/she is weaker, vulnerable			
	B. Minor Injury	30	**35**	40
	Stranger-to-stranger; or where victim is known to assailant, he/she is weaker, vulnerable; or altercations involving use of a weapon			
	C. Substantial Injury	17	**20**	23
	Altercations among acquaintances; brawls			
	D. Minor Injury	13	**15**	17
	Altercations among acquaintances; brawls			

* AM = Class A Misdemeanor; BM = Class B Misdemeanor.
** DF = Day Fines.
Source: Adapted from Bureau of Justice Assistance, *How to Use Structured Fines (Day Fines) as an Intermediate Sanction* (Washington, DC: Bureau of Justice Assistance, 1996), p. 59.

offense of assault with minor injury and aggravating factors is 70; the range is from 59 to 81 units. The presumptive number is the starting point. Negotiation and consideration of individual circumstances may raise or lower the number. There is no magic in the unit scale established. What is important is to establish a scale broad enough to cover the full range of offenses handled by the courts that will use structured fines.

Once the unit scale is established, the second step is to create a valuation table. The purpose of the valuation table is to establish the dollar amount of each fine. A portion of the valuation table used in the Staten Island experiment is shown in Exhibit 5–8. Net daily incomes run down the left side, and numbers of dependents run across the top. Net daily income is the offender's income (after-tax wages, welfare allowance, unemployment compensation, etc.) divided by the number of days in a payment period. Staten Island planners also adjusted the net daily income downward to account for subsistence needs, family responsibilities, and incomes below the poverty line.

Suppose a defendant convicted of assault, with minor injury and aggravating factors, has a net daily income of $15 and supports four people, including herself. Find the row for her net daily income. Move across the row to the column for the number of dependents. The figure there is the value of one structured fine unit for that defendant. Multiply the number of fine units to be imposed (70) by the value of a single fine unit (3.38). The product, $236.60, is the amount of the day fine to be imposed.

EXHIBIT 5-8	Example of a Day Fine Valuation Table

Staten Island, New York, Valuation Table Dollar Value of One Day Fine Unit, by Net Daily Income and Number of Dependents

Net Daily Income ($)	Number of Dependents (Including Self)							
	1	2	3	4	5	6	7	8
3		1.05	0.83	0.68	0.53	0.45	0.37	0.30
4	1.70	1.40	1.10	0.90	0.70	0.60	0.50	0.40
5	2.13	1.75	1.38	1.13	0.88	0.75	0.62	0.50
6	2.55	2.10	1.65	1.35	1.05	0.90	0.75	0.60
7	2.98	2.45	1.93	1.58	1.23	1.05	0.87	0.70
8	3.40	2.80	2.20	1.80	1.40	1.20	1.00	0.80
9	3.83	3.15	2.48	2.03	1.58	1.35	1.12	0.90
10	4.25	3.50	2.75	2.25	1.75	1.50	1.25	1.00
11	4.68	3.85	3.03	2.47	1.93	1.65	1.37	1.10
12	5.10	4.20	3.30	2.70	2.10	1.80	1.50	1.20
13	5.53	4.55	3.58	2.93	2.28	1.95	1.62	1.30
14	7.85	4.90	3.85	3.15	2.45	2.10	1.75	1.40
15	8.42	5.25	4.13	3.38	2.63	2.25	1.87	1.50

Source: Adapted from Bureau of Justice Assistance, *How to Use Structured Fines (Day Fines) as an Intermediate Sanction* (Washington, DC: Bureau of Justice Assistance, 1996), p. 64.

Even though day fines have been tried experimentally in some areas of the United States including Arizona, Connecticut, Iowa, New York, and Oregon, there has been little evidence-based research on the effectiveness of fines in reducing recidivism rates. The Washington State Institute for Public Policy wrote that day fine programs need additional research and development before we can conclude that they do or do not work (i.e., reduce crime outcomes).[22] However, because the use of fines could reduce the costs of courts and corrections and because day fines address problems of inequality, fines are a promising intermediate sanction. At present, most Western justice systems, except the United States, rely heavily on financial penalties. In the 21st century, U.S. jurisdictions are likely to continue their experiments with monetary penalties and to assign them greater importance.

CO5-5

community service

A sentence to serve a specified number of hours working in unpaid positions with nonprofit or tax-supported agencies.

Community Service **Community service** is a sentence to serve a specified number of hours working in unpaid positions with nonprofit or tax-supported agencies. Community service is punishment that takes away an offender's time and energy and is sometimes called a "fine of time."

Community service as a criminal sanction began in the United States in 1966 in Alameda County, California. Municipal judges there devised a community service sentencing program for indigent women who violated traffic and parking laws. Too poor to pay fines, these women were likely to be sentenced to jail. But putting them behind bars imposed a hardship on their families. Community service orders (CSOs) increased sentencing options, punished the offenders, lightened the suffering of innocent families, avoided the cost of imprisonment, and provided valuable services to the community. As Alameda judges gained experience with the new sentencing option, they broadened the program to include male offenders, juveniles, and persons convicted of crimes more serious than traffic or parking violations.

The Alameda County community service program received international attention. England and Wales developed pilot projects in the 1970s, using community service as a midlevel sanction between probation and prison and as an alternative to prison sentences up to six months. By 1975, community service had become a central feature of English sentencing. The approach swept throughout Europe, Australia, New Zealand, and Canada.

However, what had begun as an American innovation atrophied in the United States.[23] Today in this country, community service is seldom used as a separate sentence. Instead, it may be one of many conditions of a probation sentence as in the case of Vitalii Sediuk. Nor is it viewed as an alternative to imprisonment in the United States, as it is in other countries. Generally speaking, in the United States, public officials do not consider any sanction other than imprisonment punitive enough. Substituting community service for short prison sentences is not accepted. This is unfortunate because community service is a burdensome penalty that meets with widespread public approval,[24] is inexpensive to administer, and produces public value. Also, it can be scaled to the seriousness of the crime. Proponents of community service include the American Correctional Association (see Exhibit 5–9).

Community service can be an intermediate sanction by itself or be used with other penalties and requirements, including substance abuse treatment, restitution, or probation. In the federal courts, community service is not a sentence, but a special condition of probation or supervised release set forth in the presentence report. Offenders sentenced to community service are usually assigned to work for government or private nonprofit agencies. They restore historic buildings; maintain parks and construct campsites; clean roadways and county fairgrounds; remove snow from around public buildings; perform land and river reclamation; and renovate schools and nursing homes. The service options are limited only by the imagination of the sentencing judge and the availability of personnel to ensure that the offender fulfills the terms of the sentence. To become and remain a tough criminal sanction, community service must have credible and efficient enforcement mechanisms.

By the late 1980s, some form of community service sanction was in use in all 50 states. When Congress passed the Comprehensive Crime Control Act and Criminal Fine Enforcement Act of 1984, it mandated that felons who receive a sentence (except for class A or B felony—the most serious) must be ordered to pay a fine, make restitution, and/or work in community service. The Bureau of Justice Statistics estimates conservatively that 6 percent of all felons in the United States are sentenced to perform community service, often in conjunction with other sanctions.[25]

States like Washington, Georgia, and Texas are making extensive use of community service. At least one-third of Washington's convicted felons receive sentences that include community service. Washington State sentencing guidelines permit substitution of community service for incarceration at a rate of 8 hours of work for 1 day of incarceration, with a limit of 30 days. Most jurisdictions recognize 240 hours as the upper limit for community service. Washington State also is breaking new ground in sentencing reform with the idea of *interchangeable sentences* for nonviolent or not very violent crimes against strangers. The actual sentence depends on the

Vitalii Sediuk was convicted of misdemeanor battery and pled no contest. He was sentenced to 36 months of probation; fined $220; ordered to stay 500 yards away from red carpets, Hollywood premiers, and award shows; and given 20 days of community service cleaning up Griffin Park in Los Angeles for punching Brad Pitt as the actor signed autographs for his fans at the premier of Maleficent. At the time of the Pitt attack, Sediuk was already on probation for crashing the stage at the Grammy Awards as Adele was presented with an award by Jennifer Lopez and Pitbull. What do you think? Is community service "fluff," or can it be fashioned as a serious criminal sanction?

© David Buchan/Getty Images

EXHIBIT 5-9   American Correctional Association

Public Correctional Policy on Community Service and Restorative Justice

Introduction:

Establishing a sense of community is an important part of the rehabilitation process of offenders. Whether within an institution or as part of community corrections, it is beneficial to promote community service for offenders to assist their reentry into society and to promote the positive restoration within the community of the harm that criminal activity has caused.

Policy Statement:

The American Correctional Association supports community service for offenders and urges its use as consistent with correctional management principles and public safety objectives.

While promoting community service, justice systems and institutions must consider factors that contribute to the success of the effort for the offender and the public.

Therefore, when developing criteria for successful community service efforts, criminal justice and rehabilitative programs must:

A. Enhance public safety;

B. Integrate the offender into the community;

C. Contribute to principles of restorative justice;

D. Gain public support for programs and promoting acceptance of offenders;

E. Enhance the self-esteem of offenders by using their time, talents and skills to benefit themselves and others;

F. Provide value to government, the community and nonprofit organizations;

G. Provide valuable, transferable skills to offenders;

H. Balance community service with other responsibilities including family and work, and the availability of transportation;

I. Restore public confidence in offenders; and

J. Maintain public confidence in the justice system.

Source: Copyright © American Correctional Association. Reprinted with permission.

Visit www.corrections.com/news/article/30116-inside-nic-a-discussion-with-community-services-division-chief-jim-cosby or scan this code with the QR app on your smartphone or digital device and read the interview with Jim Cosby, Community Services Division Chief with the National Institute of Corrections and learn about his philosophy of community service. How does this information relate to ideas discussed in this chapter?

CO5-6

day reporting center (DRC)

A nonresidential facility to which an offender reports every day or several days a week for supervision and treatment.

offender and the purposes to be served. For those with little or no income, community service may substitute for a fine.

There is no evidence-based corrections literature examining the effectiveness of community service on reducing criminal activity. What we find instead are descriptions of community service programs in use across the United States. Before it can be concluded that community service does or does not reduce criminal activity, strong research designs are needed. Until then, the jury is still out on community service.

Day Reporting Centers   **Day reporting centers (DRCs)** are nonresidential facilities that are used as a form of intermediate sanction for offenders as a condition of probation or for offenders released from prison. DRCs have three primary goals: (1) enhance supervision and surveillance of offenders, (2) provide treatment directly or through collaboration with community treatment programs, and (3) reduce jail and prison crowding. DRCs differ in their implementation and the clients they serve but generally require offenders to attend the facility for multiple hours each week for supervision and other programming such as counseling, educational courses, employment training, and referrals for additional services. Offenders are typically ordered to attend a DRC for three months and report to the center every weekday.

Corey Fleetion

Manager of the Escambia County Work Release Program, Pensacola, Florida

Corey Fleetion is the manager of the Escambia County Work Release Program in Pensacola, Florida. He has been employed with the Department of Community Corrections for 20 years. During this period, he has worked in various positions within the department—probation assistant, probation officer, senior probation officer, work release program coordinator/supervisor—and is currently work release program manager. He has worked in pretrial release (PTR), Community Confinement Program (CCP), and the Work Release Program (WRP) and has monitored caseloads of felony and misdemeanor clients as well as inmates on global positioning (GPS)/electronic monitoring system. He was very instrumental in identifying, interviewing, and referring potential inmates in the jail to the Escambia County Drug Court Program. He also assisted circuit and county courts in the first appearance by presenting criminal NCIC/FCIC history. His everyday responsibilities include supervising probation and corrections officers, conducting field visits of inmates and attending violation of probation hearings. Maintaining current policy and procedures for the WRP is vital to ensure that it runs smoothly and effectively.

Fleetion is actively involved in numerous professional and community organizations. He has served more than 15 years with the Florida Council on Crime and Delinquency, serving as vice president, president, and many terms as secretary and treasurer. He is a committee member of the Supervisory Advisory Board of the Florida State Employees Credit Union. As a member of the Workforce Escarosa Youth Development Council, he provides positive input to enhance the opportunities for job training and placement for youth in his community. He also serves as the financial officer of Kingdom Builders Christian Ministries.

Fleetion graduated as class Valedictorian of Coosa County High School in Rockford, Alabama. He continued his education by attending and graduating from the University of Montevallo, Montevallo, Alabama. While a student there, he received an academic scholarship (Talented Minority Undergraduate), and in 1991, he received his bachelor's degree with a major in social work and minor in psychology. He attended the University of Tennessee in Knoxville, Tennessee in 1988 and continued postgraduate education at the University of West Florida in Pensacola, Florida.

His advice to others is to be aware and learn from your surroundings. Trust yourself and your abilities. There are no short cuts to maturity. He believes that every obstacle is an opportunity and one must never underestimate the value of her or his work as a leader. As you stay in tune with your effects of your leadership, you must always use wisdom, enjoy what you are doing, and have a sense of purpose in fulfilling your destiny.

> "... every obstacle is an opportunity and one must never underestimate the value of her or his work as a leader."

DRCs typically offer numerous services to address offenders' problems, and they strictly supervise offenders in a setting that is more secure than probation but less inhibiting than incarceration. DRCs differ from other intermediate sanctions by a marked concentration on rehabilitation. Staff members assess the offender's needs and offer her or him various types of in-house treatment and referral programs, including substance abuse treatment, education, vocational training, and psychological services. DRCs have an aura of rigor that appeals to those wanting punishment and control of offenders, and it appeals to those advocating more access to treatment for offenders. While DRCs differ in the type of offenders they serve, they all have three common threads: frequent reporting, significant programming to assist offenders, and offender accountability.

DRCs first developed in Great Britain in 1972. British officials noted that many offenders were imprisoned not because they posed a risk to the public but because they lacked basic skills to survive lawfully. Frequently, such offenders were dependent on drugs and alcohol. In 1986, the Hampden County Sheriff's Department in Springfield, Massachusetts, established the first DRC in the United States. Ten years later, a National Institute of Justice survey (NIJ) identified 114 DRCs in 22 states.[26] In addition to the number of DRCs operated by public entities, the private sector also operates DRCs. For example, The GEO Group Inc., the world's leading provider of institutional and community reentry services, operates 71 DRCs around the United States.

DRCs provide rehabilitation for offenders through intensive programming, while retaining a punishment component by maintaining a highly structured environment. DRCs commonly require offenders to obey a curfew, perform community service, and undergo drug testing. Participants check in at the center in person daily or several times a week and telephone periodically. They are responsible for following a full-time schedule that includes a combination of work, school, and substance abuse or mental health treatment. Most programs require a daily schedule of each participant's activities. Some are highly intensive, with 10 or more supervision contacts per day, and a few include 24-hour remote-location or other electronic monitoring (EM). Some centers refer clients to service agencies; others provide services directly. Some focus on monitoring; others emphasize support. Some, like the DRC in Kern County, California, require offenders to pass through phases. Phase I, "intensive supervision," requires participants to check in seven days a week and drug test once a week. Phase II, "intermediate supervision," requires participants to check in five days per week and drug test twice per month. Phase III, "regular supervision," requires participants to check in three days per week and drug test once per month. The aftercare phase requires participants to check in once a month with no

GEO Reentry Services, a private provider of community reentry services with headquarters in Boca Raton, Florida, operates DRCs in California, Colorado, Kansas, Illinois, Louisiana, Kentucky, Pennsylvania, New Jersey, Virginia, and North Carolina. One of the services offered at the centers is cognitive skills and behavioral restructuring courses that help offenders identify and change the antisocial beliefs, thoughts, and values that contribute to criminal behavior. Through the use of modeling, role-playing, and reinforcement, cognitive-behavioral interventions assist offenders in developing the positive thinking, judgment, and decision-making skills that promote prosocial behavior. What do we know about DRCs' effectiveness in reducing criminal activity?

Courtesy of BI Incorporated

drug testing requirements. All participants are given a breathalyzer test each time they report to the DRC.

There have been few evaluations of DRCs. Most of the early evaluations were favorable, but they were based on impressions, not the kind of strong methodological designs that further the evidence-based literature that we emphasize throughout this book. Two recent studies come close, but they offer contradictory results. In 2009, researchers at Rutgers University tracked offenders released from New Jersey prisons in 2004 and found that offenders who were paroled to a DRC upon release from prison were less likely to be reconvicted and reincarcerated when compared to individuals who maxed-out their prison sentences without any form of community supervisions, individuals who were paroled but did not have any community program involvement, or individuals who were paroled to a hallway back program (hallway back programs [HWBs] are residential facilities that serve as an alternative sanction to parole revocation or as a special condition of parole release).[27] Even though the findings suggest promise for DCRs, the researchers did not randomly assign subjects to max-out, out on parole, DRC, or HWB groups. Hence, the potential for selection bias raises questions about research validity. But we should also say that random assignment, which is the gold standard of research, is not always logistically or morally possible. Public safety concerns require legislatures, judges, and paroling authorities to consider offender and offense characteristics when making release decisions.

Four years later, other researchers from Rutgers and the University of Nevada-Reno used the gold standard of research—namely, random assignment—and assigned offenders released from New Jersey prisons in 2007 to either a DRC or an intensive community supervision program and found that parolees assigned to a DRC fared no better and, in some instances, significantly worse than parolees assigned to intensive community supervision.[28] During the three-month study period and the 15-month postcompletion period, DRC participants were more likely to be arrested for a new offense, less likely to be employed, more likely to be reconvicted of a new offense, and more likely to fail drug testing. The researchers concluded that DRCs should not be used as an alternative to incarceration. However, their conclusion spurred a counterargument: Perhaps the designs of the programs used in the 2007 DRC study sites were not of sufficient quality; perhaps the sample size was too small to reach a measurable effect; perhaps the programs targeted the wrong offenders; perhaps the duration of the program (also known as "dosage") wasn't long enough. More DRCs that adhere to program fidelity, use validated tools that identify the right offenders, offer the right amount of treatment, and are assessed using scientific principles are needed before we can decide if DRCs are effective, promising, or have no effects. What we know about the effectiveness of DRCs today is this: the jury is still out.

A probation officer sets up an exclusion zone in red for an offender who is territory-restricted. What are the pros and cons of remote location monitoring as a probationary strategy?
Reprinted with permission of Corey Fleetion

Remote-Location Monitoring Technologies that probation and parole officers use to monitor remotely the physical location of an offender are known as **remote-location monitoring**. There is no exact accounting on the number of persons under remote-location monitoring. An *Associated Press* investigation published in July 2013 estimated the number at 100,000. In September, 2016, researchers with the PEW Charitable Trusts estimated more than 125,000 people were under remote-location monitoring supervision, up from 53,000 in 2005.

CO5-7

remote-location monitoring

Technologies, including Global Positioning System (GPS) devices and EM, that probation and parole officers use to monitor remotely the physical location of an offender.

Initially, remote-location monitoring targeted only the traditional clients of house arrest: low-risk probationers, such as those convicted of DUI. More recently, however, it has expanded to include people awaiting trial or sentencing, offenders on probation and parole, and juvenile offenders. Furthermore, whereas electronic house arrest initially gained acceptance as a response to property crimes, advances in remote-location monitoring allow pretrial officers and probation and parole officers to set up exclusion zones (such as schools, parks, and homes) for offenders who are territory-restricted (e.g., stalkers and child molesters).

In theory, remote-location monitoring satisfies three correctional goals. First, it incapacitates the offender by restricting him or her to a single location. Second, remote-location monitoring is punitive because it forces the offender to stay home when not at work, school, counseling, or community service. And third, it contributes to rehabilitation by allowing the offender to remain with his or her family and continue employment, education, or vocational training.

Remote-location monitoring uses technological systems such as EM, global positioning systems (GPSs), voice verification, and other tracking systems to verify a person's physical location, either periodically or continuously, 24 hours a day. Some GPS ankle bracelets are microphone-equipped. They have the same features as a cellular phone and can record the offender's private conversations without their knowledge and without a court warrant, which raises civil liberty issues.

Major benefits of remote-location monitoring are the offender avoids incarceration, continues to contribute to the support of his or her family, and pays taxes; plus, the cost is significantly less than incarceration. The average cost of incarcerating a state or federal inmate has been estimated to range from $36 to $123 per day depending upon the level of security.[29] In contrast, the daily cost of remote-location monitoring is between $3 and $5, and GPS monitoring is between $5 and $11.[30] Moreover, many courts order program participants to pay all or part of the costs. All states except Hawaii and the District of Columbia require offenders to pay a fee for remote-location monitoring in order to reduce the burden on taxpayers and, in some cases, to actually make money from it.[31]

As stated earlier, from 2005 through January 1, 2016, the use of electronic monitoring grew by 140 percent (from around 53,000 to more than 125,000 today).[32] But the practice can also be abused. In 2014, a Richland County, South Carolina, unemployed construction worker, who lives on a monthly $900 disability check, was arrested for failure to use his turn signal at an intersection.[33] His license was initially suspended for a DUI and his arrest record included charges for domestic violence and disorderly conduct. As a condition of his $2,100 bail, the judge ordered him to wear an ankle monitor. In Richland County, any person ordered to wear the ankle monitor as a condition of bail must lease the bracelet from Offender Management Services (OMS), which charges the offender $9.25 per day, plus a $179.50 set-up fee. By August 2015, the unemployed construction worker paid more than $2,500 to OMS. Realizing he had run out of money and gone broke, he turned himself in. When he appeared in court, he was informed that his case had actually been dismissed two months earlier, but he was never informed—even though he continued to pay for the electronic monitor. Thus, while remote location monitoring constitutes a promising form of punishment, it should not be used to invade an offender's privacy, stigmatize the individual, or cause him or her financial hardship.

It is easy to find evaluations of remote-location monitoring that show positive results. For example, a review of the performance of 17,000 participants in the federal home confinement program found that 89 percent

Visit www.npr.org/2014/05/19/312158516/increasing-court-fees-punish-the-poor or scan this code with the QR app on your smartphone or digital device and listen to National Public Radio's Joseph Shapiro's report, "As Court Fees Rise, the Poor Are Paying the Price." How does this information relate to ideas discussed in this chapter?

successfully completed the program.[34] And when researchers with the Center for Criminology and Public Policy Research at Florida State University compared the experiences of more than 5,000 medium- and high-risk offenders who were monitored electronically to more than 266,000 offenders not placed on monitoring during a six-year period, they found that EM reduced the risk of failure by 31 percent.[35]

However, when researchers examine the body of literature on remote-location monitoring more closely, they find two things. First, the methods used in these studies do not meet the threshold of scientific rigor. Very few employ the gold standard of research—randomly assign subjects to remote-location monitoring programs (the experimental group) and others to programs-as-usual (the control group). And even if randomization is employed, most studies do not focus on the different kinds of remote-location monitoring, meaning what type of monitoring was used, how did it operate, how reliable was the equipment (down time, location failures, errors, tampering), and ways in which remote-location monitoring is linked to other forms of community supervision and treatment. Without scientific rigor, it is questionable whether the available research can be a guide for policymakers on important questions, beginning with "is remote-location monitoring effective?"

And second, the studies focus only on whether remote-location monitoring suppresses an individual's criminal behavior rather than changes it. The positive results noted above in the study of federal home confinement and GPS monitoring in Florida may simply be the result of the extra surveillance offered by remote-location monitoring. The majority of studies on remote-location monitoring do not examine the therapeutic aspects of correctional programs that are known to reduce criminal activity. Changes in an offender's cognitive skills of thinking, reasoning, empathy, and problem solving are seldom subject to the same evaluation that control and surveillance are. After reviewing thousands of studies on correctional interventions, management policies, and treatment and rehabilitation programs, Dr. Doris MacKenzie, professor of criminology and criminal justice at the University of Maryland and former scientist with the U.S. Department of Justice, wrote, "Restraining offenders in the community by increasing surveillance and control over their activities does not reduce their criminal activities."[36] ". . . effective correctional programs must focus on changing the individual."[37] Unless remote-location monitoring is coupled with other wraparound services such as employment readiness, cognitive behavioral therapy, and substance abuse treatment, and without measuring its effectiveness on reducing criminal activity, reporting only on control and surveillance leads to the conclusion that remote-location monitoring does not work.

Residential Reentry Centers A **residential reentry center (RRC)** is a medium-security correctional setting that resident offenders are permitted to leave regularly—unaccompanied by staff—for work, educational or vocational programs, or treatment in the community but require them to return to a locked facility each evening. The objectives of RRCs are community protection and offender reintegration. Community protection is achieved by screening offenders; setting curfews; administering drug or polygraph tests; confirming that when residents leave the center they go directly to work, school, or treatment; and providing a medium-security correctional setting. Reintegration is achieved by giving residents opportunities to learn and use legitimate skills, thereby reducing their reliance on criminal behavior. Staff members determine the obstacles to each resident's reintegration; plan a program to overcome those obstacles; and provide a supportive environment to help the resident test, use, and refine the skills needed.

CO5-8

residential reentry center (RRC)

A medium-security correctional setting that resident offenders are permitted to leave regularly—unaccompanied by staff—for work, education or vocational programs, or treatment in the community but require them to return to a locked facility each evening.

Initially, such centers were called *halfway houses* and were for offenders who either were about to be released from an institution or were in the first stages of return to the community. However, as the number of halfway houses grew and new client groups (divertees, pretrial releasees, and probationers) were added, the umbrella term *residential reentry center* was adopted. Some RRCs specialize in a type of client or treatment—for example, in drug and alcohol abuse, violent and sex offenders, women, abused women, or prerelease federal prisoners. Some are public and some private.

Unfortunately, it is not possible to know how many RRCs there are today, or how many offenders they serve. One difficulty in estimating the number of offenders that RRCs serve is that many residents are already counted in the publications of persons under correctional supervision in jail and prison and on probation and parole published annually by the U.S. Department of Justice, Bureau of Justice Statistics.

The federal Bureau of Prisons (BOP) has the largest number of inmates (9,446) in more than 200 RRCs nationwide representing almost 4.8 percent of the BOP's total population.[38] Almost 80 percent of eligible federal prisoners are released through RRCs where they spend, on average, three to four months before being released into the community. Federal RRCs hold inmates accountable by conducting in-house counts throughout the day at scheduled and random intervals. RRC staff assists inmates in obtaining employment through a network of local employers, employment job fairs, and training classes in résumé writing, interview techniques, etc. Ordinarily, offenders are expected to be employed 40 hours/week within 15 calendar days after their arrival at the RRC. During their stay, offenders are required to pay a subsistence fee to help defray the cost of their confinement; this charge is normally 25 percent of their gross income. RRCs offer drug testing and substance abuse programs. Based upon the inmate's needs and substance abuse history, they may be referred for substance abuse treatment by contracted treatment providers. And RRCs provide offenders an opportunity to access medical and mental health care and treatment. The intent is to assist the offender in maintaining continuity of medical and mental health care and treatment.

The benefits of RRCs are many. RRCs benefit offenders by providing them with the basic necessities of food, clothing, and shelter while they find housing and employment. RRCs also offer residents emotional support to deal with the pressures of readjustment and help them obtain community services. Benefits to the community include a moderately secure correctional setting in which residents' behavior is monitored and controlled, as well as an expectation that opportunities for offenders to get on their feet will reduce postrelease adjustment problems and criminal behavior. For the criminal justice system, an RRC offers a low-cost housing alternative to incarceration of nonviolent offenders. An RRC can control offenders in the community at less cost than building and operating more secure facilities. It may also serve as an enhancement to probation and an option for dealing with probation and parole violators.

There has not been much research on the effectiveness of RRCs compared to other intermediate sanctions discussed in this chapter. The state of Colorado conducted a statewide study of recidivism of halfway house clients and analyzed information on all offenders ($n = 3,054$) who terminated from 25 halfway houses.[39] The study tracked cases for 24 months. It reported that 69 percent had no arrest within 24 months. Of the 31 percent who recidivated within 24 months, the majority of cases were drug or alcohol related. Only 3.4 percent were for violent offenses. High-risk, prior criminal history, young age, and lack of postrelease supervision predicted future offending. The report recommended that intensive treatment, therapeutic community models, and multidisciplinary approaches to deal with drug and alcohol addiction should be replicated across the state. The report also called for specific aftercare services to enhance offenders' likelihood of success, maximize public safety, and reduce recidivism.

Recently a study of Ohio's 38 RRCs found that RRCs were most effective with parole violators and higher-risk and proposed using more RRCs as ways to cut prison costs in Ohio.[40] Furthermore, the most effective RRC programs provided the greatest number of services targeting criminogenic needs, offered cognitive behavioral treatment, and engaged in role playing and practicing of newly learned skills.

The absence of an adequate body of scientifically rigorous evaluations of RRCs and the current focus on control and suppression instead of individual-level behavioral changes in thinking, reasoning, and problem solving that are known to reduce a person's propensity to commit crime means we cannot say that RRCs reduce criminal activity. Nor can we say that RRCs are ineffective. We can only say that the impact of RRCs is unknown until an adequate body of scientifically rigorous literature becomes available.

CO5-9

Boot Camps In 1983, in an effort to alleviate prison crowding and reduce recidivism, the departments of corrections in Oklahoma and Georgia opened the first adult prison programs modeled after military boot camps. Since then, boot camp (sometimes referred to as *shock incarceration, intensive confinement centers* [ICCs], or *work ethic camps*) has become an increasingly popular intermediate sanction.

Boot camp is a short institutional term of confinement, usually followed by probation, that includes a physical regimen designed to develop self-discipline, respect for authority, responsibility, and a sense of accomplishment. According to the NIJ, four characteristics distinguish boot camps from other correctional programs:

boot camp

A short institutional term of confinement that includes a physical regimen designed to develop self-discipline, respect for authority, responsibility, and a sense of accomplishment.

1. military drill and ceremony,
2. a rigorous daily schedule of hard labor and physical training,
3. separation of boot camp participants from the general prison population, and
4. the idea that boot camps are an alternative to long-term confinement.

However, as you will learn, the use of correctional boot camps is on the decline, and the evidence-based literature reports that the average boot camp has no effect on recidivism.[41] The Federal Bureau of Prisons ended its boot camps in 2005 and most states shifted their camps toward what they call more "evidence-based" rehabilitative models.

However, that hasn't stopped some sheriffs from implementing them. David A. Clarke Jr., sheriff of Milwaukee County, Wisconsin, calls his boot camp a "Discipline, Order, Training and Structure" program.[42] Eligibility criteria include low-level offenders who are in physical shape and don't present serious behavioral problems. Inmates wear uniforms, rise early, participate in rigorous physical training by drill instructors (former war veterans from Iraq and Afghanistan), be required to say "yes, sir" and "no, sir," and take classes on job readiness, anger management, and building positive relationships with friends and spouses. Sheriff Clarke is unmoved by those who say such programs do not work. He believes that inmates need to have discipline instilled before other reform efforts at education and job training can work.

Critics have raised questions about using boot camps as a correctional tool. They note that correctional boot camp programs are built on a model of military basic training that the military itself has found lacking and in some cases has revised. Critics also argue that the military model was designed to

The military-style training and drill that characterize boot camps are frequently supplemented with substance abuse education and vocational training. What aftercare programs might contribute to the effectiveness of boot camp strategies?
© AP Photo/Don Ryan

produce a cohesive fighting unit and that after military boot camp there is further specialized training and career planning. That is not a goal of corrections. One analyst wrote, "If an offender can't read [or] write and is drug-involved, sending him to a 90-day boot camp that does not address his job or literacy needs will only have a short-term effect, if any, on his behavior."[43]

Although boot camps are promoted as a means of reducing recidivism rates, there is no evidence that they significantly reduce recidivism or promote socially desirable activities. A multisite evaluation of boot camps in Texas, South Carolina, and Florida showed no significant differences in reoffending rates among the different groups of offenders.[44] Research on Oklahoma's boot camp program revealed that even when the researchers controlled for type of offense, age, and race on recidivism, boot camp graduates recidivated more frequently than either traditionally incarcerated inmates or probationers.[45] Research published on a county-based boot camp in Florida shows similar results. The likelihood of an offender being rearrested was unaffected by his or her being sent to boot camp. Eighty-one percent of the boot camp graduates were rearrested, averaging 271 days before rearrest. Seventy-three percent of the comparison group was rearrested, averaging 290 days before rearrest.[46]

Some researchers have reported that boot camp graduates have higher self-esteem, have better attitudes toward family, are less likely to see themselves as victims of circumstances, and are more likely to feel in control of their future.[47] However, with limited exceptions, these positive changes didn't translate into reduced recidivism. Research into what boot camp participants say they'll do is less conclusive than research into what they've actually done.

Also disappointing is that the recidivism rates of boot camp graduates are very similar to those of other parolees.[48] One-third to one-half of boot camp participants fail to complete their programs and are sent to prison as a result. In most programs, close surveillance of graduates after release leads to technical violation and revocation rates that are higher than those of comparable offenders in less intensive programs.

Governors, legislatures, and correctional administrators nationwide are coping with budget cutbacks while being under pressure to deliver ever better public safety outcomes.

The governor of Georgia signed legislation to reduce the number of low-level drug possession offenders in prison and expand the use of intermediate sanctions including drug courts, which help treat addicts and hold offenders accountable in the community.

The governor of Pennsylvania signed a law directing low-level nonviolent offenders into community supervision, saving the state $250 million through 2018.

The governor of Texas scrapped plans to build three new prisons, saving his state $2 billion and reinvesting it in treating offenders with mental health and addiction problems.

Why are states pursuing intermediate sanctions that before the economic recession of 2007 would have been called liberal policies on crime and punishment? The first reason is that the economic recession has forced governors, legislators, and correctional administrators to take a hard look at the amount of money being spent on the prison system. Huge prison spending is now viewed as running counter to fiscal conservatism.

Twenty years ago the United States spent $7 billion on its prison population of 970,000 inmates. Today, states are spending between $60 to $80 billion on a prison population of almost 1.4 million inmates. As budgets have tightened, other important functions of government have been squeezed to pay for the escalation in prison spending.

At the same time, many liberals and conservatives have come to recognize that prison is ineffective in rehabilitating offenders. Half of prisoners released are expected to be back in prison within three years. Many have come to see prison as a poor method of achieving prisoner reform. Therefore, the fiscal crisis that began in December 2007 is moving many governors and legislators to think "outside the cell" and turn to intermediate sanctions as a way to keep low-level offenders out of prison and in their communities. Is the public buying it? According to a national public opinion survey conducted in January 2012 and similar surveys in Georgia, Missouri, and Oregon, the answer is a resounding "yes." Three key takeaways from that national survey are these:

1. American voters believe too many people are in prison and the nation spends too much on imprisonment.
2. Voters overwhelmingly support a variety of policy changes that shift non-violent offenders from prison to more effective, less expensive intermediate sanctions like those discussed in this chapter.
3. Support for intermediate sanctions is strong across political parties, regions, age, gender, and racial/ethnic groups.

Specifically, 84 percent of respondents believe that some of the money that we are spending on locking up low-risk, nonviolent inmates should be shifted to strengthening intermediate sanctions. Sixty-nine percent agree that there are more effective, less expensive intermediate sanctions to prison for nonviolent offenders and expanding those alternatives is the best way to reduce the crime rate. And four of five people want to send fewer low-risk, nonviolent offenders to prison and reinvest in intermediate sanctions.

We are seeing significant pieces of legislation favoring intermediate sanctions for nonviolent offenders. Over the past several decades, legislatures passed "tough-on-crime" measures that increased penalties, prison sentences, and skyrocketed the cost of penal incarceration—key reasons why with less than 5 percent of the world's population, the U.S. has almost 25 percent of the world's prisoners.

Without question, voters want a strong public safety system in which criminals are held accountable and illegal activities have consequences. Voters also believe that these goals can be reached while reducing the size and cost of the prison system. Intermediate sanctions can help.

Boot camps are also promoted as a means of reducing prison crowding and corrections costs. However, a number of researchers have found that most boot camps have not reduced prison crowding because the programs are designed for offenders who would otherwise be on probation, not those who would otherwise have received prison terms.[49] MacKenzie and her colleagues found in a multisite evaluation of boot camps that only two of the five boot camp programs examined appeared to save prison beds. The remaining three boot camp programs appeared to increase the need for prison beds.[50] Crowding can be reduced only if boot camp participants are selected from inmates already incarcerated and only if their participation substantially reduces their overall sentence lengths.

The body of evidence-based corrections literature tells us this about correctional boot camps:

1. There is an adequate body of scientifically rigorous research examining correctional boot camps.
2. The military atmosphere of correctional boot camps does not bring about individual-level changes in thinking, reasoning, and problem solving.

3. An aftercare component to correctional boot camp *may* reduce recidivism, but there is little information about the *type* of aftercare that programs provide. Are individual-level changes the result of drug treatment, employment, or something else? We do not know.

4. To date, it is impossible to say why the recidivism of some correctional boot camp participants is lower than the comparison group.

5. If the goal of correctional boot camp is to reduce recidivism, then there is little reason to continue its use.

COMMUNITY CORRECTIONS

In Chapter 1, you learned that the correctional system can be either institutional or noninstitutional. The intermediate sanctions discussed in this chapter, probation (Chapter 4), and parole (Chapter 8) are examples of correctional activities not directly related to institutional care.

There is no consensus in the field of criminal justice on the definition of **community corrections**. Sometimes the term refers to noninstitutional programs. Sometimes it refers to programs administered by local government rather than the state. Other times, it indicates citizen involvement.

We define *community corrections* as a philosophy of correctional treatment that embraces (1) decentralization of authority from state to local levels; (2) citizen participation in program planning, design, implementation, and evaluation; (3) redefinition of the population of offenders for whom incarceration is most appropriate; and (4) emphasis on rehabilitation through community programs.

Today, all of the major components of the criminal justice system have alliances with the community. The field is experiencing many changes, including the following:

- *community policing*—a law enforcement strategy to get residents involved in making their neighborhoods safer by focusing on crime prevention, nonemergency services, public accountability, and decentralized decision making that includes the public;

- *community-based prosecution*—a prosecution strategy that uses a combination of criminal and civil tactics and the legal expertise, resources, and clout of the prosecuting attorney's office to find innovative solutions to a neighborhood's specific problems;

- *community-based defender services*—a defender strategy that provides continuity in representation of indigent defendants and helps defendants with personal and family problems that can lead to legal troubles; and

- *community courts*—a judicial strategy of hearing a criminal case in the community that is most affected by the case and including that community in case disposition.

The American Correctional Association's support of community corrections is shown in Exhibit 5–10.

Community Corrections Acts

This spirit of correctional collaboration and community partnership has led 36 states to pass **community corrections acts (CCAs)** (Exhibit 5–11). CCAs are state laws that give economic grants to local communities to establish community corrections goals and policies and to develop and operate community corrections programs. Under a typical CCA, the state provides local

community corrections

A philosophy of correctional treatment that embraces (1) decentralization of authority, (2) citizen participation, (3) redefinition of the population of offenders for whom incarceration is most appropriate, and (4) emphasis on rehabilitation through community programs.

community corrections acts (CCAs)

State laws that give economic grants to local communities to establish community corrections goals and policies and to develop and operate community corrections programs.

| EXHIBIT 5-10 | American Correctional Association |

Public Correctional Policy on Community Corrections

Introduction:

Community corrections programs are an integral component of a graduated system of sanctions and services. They enable offenders to work and pay taxes, make restitution, meet court obligations, maintain family ties, and develop and/or maintain critical support systems with the community. To be successful, community corrections programs must promote public safety and a continuum of care that responds to the needs of victims, offenders, and the community. These programs should include a collaborative comprehensive planning process for the development of effective policies and services.

Policy Statement:

Community corrections programs include residential and nonresidential programs. Most community corrections programs require offenders to participate in certain activities or special programs that are specifically directed toward reducing their risk to the community. Those responsible for community corrections programs, services, and supervision should:

A. seek statutory authority and adequate funding, both public and private, for community programs and services as part of a comprehensive corrections strategy;

B. develop and ensure access to a wide array of residential and nonresidential services that address the identifiable needs of victims, offenders and the community;

C. inform the public about the benefits of community programs and services; the criteria used to select individuals for these programs; and the requirements for successful completion;

D. recognize that public acceptance of community corrections is enhanced by the provision of victim services, community service and conciliation programs;

E. mobilize the participation of a well-informed constituency, including citizen advisory boards and broad-based coalitions, to address community corrections issues;

F. participate in collaborative, comprehensive planning efforts which provide a framework to assess community needs and develop a systemwide plan for services; and

G. ensure the integrity and accountability of community programs by establishing a reliable system for monitoring and measuring performance and outcomes in accordance with accepted standards of professional practices and sound evaluation methodology.

Source: Copyright © American Correctional Association. Reprinted with permission.

agencies the funds to create or expand intermediate sanctions for certain offenders in the community, and in return, the state benefits by avoiding the costs of incarceration. The funding usually supports a spectrum of community-based punishments, including traditional probation supervision to ISP, day reporting centers, RRCs, and other specialized programs and services such as drug courts. These programs usually range from a few hundred dollars to more than $7,000 per offender per year—far less than the annual cost of housing a state prisoner.

Minnesota was one of the first states to enact a CCA. The Minnesota Community Corrections Act of 1973 provides funding to counties or groups of counties to develop community-based sanctions and programs. Funding is awarded based on local population, and counties must submit a comprehensive plan every two years indicating how the money will be spent.

The success of Minnesota's CCA can be seen in Minnesota's incarceration rate, second lowest in the United States today. Compare Minnesota, a CCA state, with its Wisconsin neighbor that is a non-CCA state. Both states have similar crime rates and populations. However, because Minnesota uses community punishments more than incarceration, its incarceration

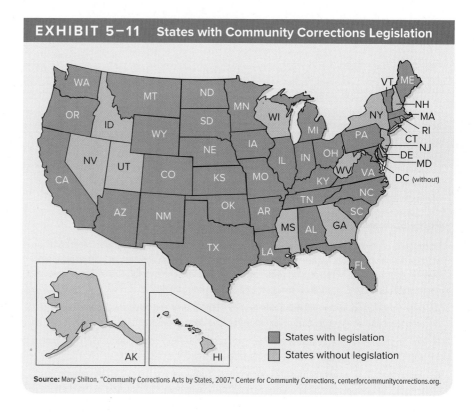

EXHIBIT 5–11   States with Community Corrections Legislation

■ States with legislation
□ States without legislation

Source: Mary Shilton, "Community Corrections Acts by States, 2007," Center for Community Corrections, centerforcommunitycorrections.org.

rate (189 prisoners per 100,000 adult population) is one-half of Wisconsin's (370 prisoners per 100,000 adult population).[51] If Minnesota incarcerated at the same level as Wisconsin, taxpayers would need to add 24 prisons and increase the state prison budget by $419.5 million annually (and that does not include the cost of actual prison construction).[52]

Simply having correctional programs in a community does not mean that a community corrections program exists. Consistent goals and consistent approaches to achieving those goals are the backbone of successful community corrections. Community corrections legislation can help accomplish that consistency.

Will the U.S. public support using intermediate sanctions like those discussed in this chapter to respond to nonserious crime? The answer is that a majority will. The National Council on Crime and Delinquency (NCCD) commissioned Zogby International to conduct a national public opinion poll about U.S. voter attitudes toward intermediate sanctions for nonserious offenders.[53] Poll results show that a majority of U.S. adults believes that offenders who commit nonserious crimes do not need incarceration; almost 8 in 10 believe that the appropriate sentence for nonserious offenders are the intermediate sanctions discussed in this chapter; almost 8 in 10 believe intermediate sanctions do not decrease public safety; half believe intermediate sanctions save money; and almost half believe that intermediate sanctions are more effective at reducing recidivism than prison or jail time. NCCD estimates that over $7 billion can be saved if 80 percent of nonviolent, nonserious offenders are sentenced to alternatives instead of incarceration. A savings of this magnitude in the current economic crisis would reduce the economic burden on institutional corrections and fund community corrections and intermediate sanctions that are more appropriate for nonserious, nonviolent offenders.

Ethics and Professionalism

International Community Corrections Association Code of Ethics

Preamble

The International Community Corrections Association, as a private, non-profit, membership organization, acts as a world unifying body and public advocate for the causes and concerns of community-based residential services in the fields of criminal and juvenile justice, substance abuse, mental health, and mental retardation. As such, it expects of its members compassion, belief in the dignity and worth of human beings, respect for individual differences and a commitment to quality care for its clients. It requires of its members the professional background, research, and expertise necessary to ensure performance of effective quality services delivered with integrity and competence. ICCA affirms its primary goal is the successful reintegration of the client into the community.

Basic Precepts

A. General conduct

1. We are committed to contributing time and professional expertise to activities that promote respect for the utility, integrity, and competence of those in the field of community-based residential services.
2. We will not condone dishonesty, fraud, deceit, or misrepresentation.
3. We will distinguish clearly between statements and actions made as private individuals and as representatives of agencies or organizations and IHHA.
4. We will conduct our daily relationships in a dignified, courteous, and professional manner and will not exploit our professional relationships for personal gain.
5. We will work for change and improvement as part of the human service system within the framework of existing policy, procedures, and tradition, respecting all elements of the system and interacting with each in a spirit of cooperation.
6. We will uphold and advocate for the values, knowledge, and need for community-based residential services.
7. We will be committed to the development of sound policies and programs to maintain the quality and effectiveness of or services.

B. Ethical responsibilities to clients

1. We do not practice nor condone any form of discrimination on the basis of race, color, sex, age, religion, national origin, mental or physical handicap or any other preference or personal characteristic, condition or status.
2. We will serve clients with the maximum application of professional skill, competence, and dedication to help them assume responsibility for themselves.

3. Exploitation of relationships with clients will not be condoneds.
4. We will uphold clients' rights to a relationship of mutual trust, privacy, and confidentiality and to responsible use of information.
5. Adherence to standards essential to the health and safety, as well as to the well being of clients, is fundamental to the quality of life and will be a primary concern.
6. We will assist clients to achieve self-fulfillment and maximum potential within the limits of the equal rights of others and the client's legitimate desires and interests.
7. Toward those whose behavior is unacceptable, we will determine our course between empathy and allowing the client the freedom to take responsibility for his actions.
8. Our goal will be to provide clients with the opportunity for change and self-regulation and the achievement of their maximum potential.

C. Ethical responsibilities to colleagues

1. Respecting the training and performance of colleagues and other professionals, we will extend the cooperation necessary to enhance effective quality services to all.
2. We will respect differences of opinion and practice of colleagues and other professionals, expressing criticism in verbal or written communications in a responsible, appropriate, and constructive manner.
3. We will extend to colleagues of other professions the same respect and cooperation that is extended to members of the International Halfway House Association.

D. Ethical responsibilities to employers and contractors

1. We will adhere responsibly to commitments made to our employers and contractors.
2. We will work to improve agencies' and contractors' policies and procedures and the efficiency, effectiveness, and quality of services.
3. We pledge integrity in contracting for the provision of client services, procurement of grants, and purchase of service contracts from any source.
4. We affirm the obligation of contracting agencies to negotiate fairly for the provision of client services and to avoid any practice resulting in unfair advantage to one party over another.

E. Ethical responsibilities to the community

1. We recognize our responsibility to the client without disregarding our responsibility to the community.
2. Believing in man's ability to overcome his problems within the community, we will remain committed to helping clients to return to their communities as productive citizens.

Source: Reprinted by permission of the International Community Corrections Association.

REVIEW AND APPLICATIONS

SUMMARY

1 *Intermediate sanctions* is the term given to the range of new sentencing options developed to fill the gap between traditional probation and traditional jail or prison sentences, better match the severity of punishment to the seriousness of the crime, reduce institutional crowding, and control correctional costs. Punishments typically identified as intermediate sanctions include intensive supervision probation (ISP), drug courts, fines, community service, day reporting centers, remote-location monitoring, residential reentry centers, and boot camps.

2 *Intensive supervision probation* (ISP) is control of offenders in the community through strict enforcement of conditions and frequent reporting to a probation officer with a reduced caseload. ISP programs exist in all 50 states. They may be state or county programs and may be administered by parole, probation, or prison departments.

3 *Drug courts* are special courts that are given responsibility to handle cases involving drug-addicted offenders.

4 A *day fine* is a financial punishment scaled to the seriousness of the offense and the offender's ability to pay. A traditional fine is based on a fixed amount, without regard to the offender's ability to pay.

5 *Community service* is a sentence to serve a specified number of hours working in unpaid positions with nonprofit or tax-supported agencies. Research suggests that, for offenders who do not present unacceptable risks of future violent crimes, community service costs much less than prison, has comparable recidivism rates, and presents negligible risks of violence by those who would otherwise be confined.

6 A *day reporting center* (DRC) is a nonresidential facility to which an offender reports each day to file a daily schedule with a supervision officer, showing how each hour will be spent. DRCs aim to provide strict surveillance over offenders and, depending on their resources, provide treatment services, refer offenders to community social service agencies, or arrange to have community agencies offer services on site.

7 *Remote-location monitoring* refers to technologies that probation and parole officers use to monitor remotely the physical location of an offender. For example, home-based electronic monitoring (EM) is often used by officers to monitor remotely offenders who are restricted to their homes.

8 *Residential reentry centers* (RRCs) are medium-security correctional settings that resident offenders are permitted to leave regularly—unaccompanied by staff—for work, educational or vocational programs, or treatment in the community but require them to return to a locked facility each evening.

9 *Boot camp* is a short institutional term, usually followed by probation, that includes a physical regimen designed to develop self-discipline, respect for authority, responsibility, and a sense of accomplishment.

10 *Community corrections* is a philosophy of correctional treatment that embraces decentralization of authority from state to local levels; citizen participation in program planning, design, implementation, and evaluation; redefinition of the population of offenders for whom incarceration is most appropriate; and emphasis on rehabilitation through community programs.

11 *Community corrections acts (CCAs)* are state laws that give economic grants to local communities to establish community corrections goals and policies and to develop and operate community corrections programs. CCAs decentralize services and engage communities in the process of reintegrating offenders by transferring correctional responsibility from the state to the community and by providing financial incentives for communities to manage more of their own correctional cases.

KEY TERMS

intermediate sanctions, p. 96

intensive supervision probation (ISP), p. 99

drug court, p. 100

fine, p. 103

day fine, p. 103

community service, p. 106

day reporting center (DRC), p. 108

remote-location monitoring, p. 111

residential reentry center (RRC), p. 113

boot camp, p. 115

community corrections, p. 118

community corrections acts (CCAs), p. 118

QUESTIONS FOR REVIEW

1 Explain intermediate sanctions and describe their purpose.

2 Differentiate between intensive supervision probation and regular probation.

3 Distinguish between drug courts and other types of courts.

4 Explain the principles behind day fines.

5 Why is community service sometimes called a "fine of time"?

6 What are the features of a day reporting center?

7 For which offenders do you believe remote-location monitoring is most beneficial?

8 What criteria would you use to assess the effectiveness of residential reentry centers?

9 What would you predict about the future of boot camps from the literature?

10 Discuss the importance of community involvement in community corrections.

11 How do community corrections acts implement the philosophy of community corrections?

THINKING CRITICALLY ABOUT CORRECTIONS

Fines

Summarizing the results of a national survey of judges' attitudes toward fines, researchers noted that "at present, judges do not regard the fine alone as a meaningful alternative to incarceration or probation."[54] What could you tell such judges to convince them that day fines, or structured fines, are a viable sentencing option?

Day Reporting Centers

The evidence is mixed on whether day reporting centers have any impact on reducing criminal activity. Recognizing that it takes time, money, and talent to build an adequate body of scientifically rigorous research, explain to a group of legislators why they should not pull the plug on day reporting centers quite yet. What will you tell them is lacking in the literature before they can make an informed policy decision?

ON-THE-JOB DECISION MAKING

Why Community Service?

Your state legislature recently passed a bill authorizing community service, in addition to other penalties, for all but the most serious Class A felonies. Part of the bill requires each probation department to send one or more probation officers to a workshop to prepare for implementing the bill. The chief

probation officer designates you. Before the workshop, you are asked to consider this issue in advance. How can you link community service to the harm caused by the offense? Why is it that apologies and restitution are always linked to the harm, but community service is rarely so connected? How can your agency avoid assigning hours of labor arbitrarily (oftentimes defined in terms of personal preference or convenience; for example, the offender likes working with children or lives near a particular service agency, such as a food bank) and instead make sure that community service labor is linked to the identified harm of the crime and make amends to the victim and/or affected community? What will you say?

Are Drug Courts Working?

Imagine that you are Herbert M. Klein, founder of the nation's first drug court in Miami, Florida, in 1989. Experience tells you that drug courts provide closer, more comprehensive supervision and much more frequent drug testing and monitoring than other forms of community supervision. Yet some researchers are finding that there is no difference in arrest rates between drug court offenders and comparison group members, and if there is, it's difficult to say why. The media ask you to respond. What do you say? You might consider searching the links on the home page of the National Association of Drug Court Professionals at www.nadcp.org/ for additional information.)

Institutional Corrections

Part Three examines jail, prison, and parole. These three correctional components account for almost 3.2 million offenders daily.

How much have jail inmates and facilities changed since the country's first jail officially opened in Philadelphia in 1773? As you will learn, many of today's jails are large and some are quickly adapting high technology and new architectural designs to their purposes. As you will learn, the jail population has remained steady for the past few years and is significantly lower than its peak in 2008. Concerns are still being raised over jail services for women offenders, the overrepresentation of minorities and the mentally ill, pay-to-stay jail programs, privatization, reentry, and jail standards.

Prisons also first developed in Pennsylvania. In 1790, a wing of the Walnut Street Jail was devoted to long-term incarceration and served as a model for the world's first prison, the Eastern State Penitentiary, in 1829. The architecture of jails and prisons changed over the years from linear to podular. Prisoner supervision approaches also changed from indirect to direct. On January 1, 2015, the Federal Bureau of Prisons and 18 states exceeded the maximum measure of their prison facilities' capacity. Is privatization the answer? In prisons, too, minorities are overrepresented and the majority of women in prison are women of color.

Each day, almost 2,000 people will leave prison. How prepared are they to reenter society? Did they receive the educational and vocational preparation and drug treatment they need to minimize their likelihood of reoffending? Unfortunately, probably not. Prisons simply do not have the resources to rehabilitate all inmates under their care. The federal Second Chance Act, passed by Congress in 2008, helps offenders make successful transitions from prison or jail back to the community by providing employment assistance, substance abuse treatment, housing, family programming, mentoring, victim support, and other services to reduce reoffending and violating probation and parole.

$576,000 a day.[2] However, there are alternatives to money bail that are just as effective, as this chapter will show.[3]

The Eighth Amendment of the U.S. Constitution provides that bail not be excessive for people accused of offenses:

> Excessive bail shall not be required, nor excessive fines imposed, nor cruel and unusual punishments inflicted.

Bail is "excessive" when it is set at a figure higher than an amount reasonably likely to ensure the defendant's presence at the trial. You learned in Chapter 1 that a person's bail can be decided at several stages of the pretrial process (arrest, initial appearance, preliminary hearing, and arraignment). The pretrial process a person goes through and the type of bail available depends on the state and jurisdiction in which she or he is arrested.

A person may be released after their arrest in several ways as they await their court date. The release options that require money to get out of jail pretrial are:

- **Cash bond.** Pay the full bail amount.
- **Deposit bond.** Pay a percentage of the bail amount, usually 10 percent.
- **Property bond.** Submit a deed that allows the court to place a lien on a property.
- **Bail bond.** Pay a nonrefundable fee, usually 10 percent of the bail amount, to a for-profit bail bonding company that enters into an agreement with the court that, in the event the person misses a court appearance, the company would owe the court the full amount of the monetary bail.

The release options that do not involve money up front to get out of jail pretrial are:

- **Release on recognizance.** A promise to return to court.
- **Conditional release.** Release under specific conditions.
- **Release to pretrial services.** Conditions set by a supervising pretrial service agency.
- **Unsecured bond.** The person will be liable for a fee if he or she misses the court hearing.

Concerns over Money for Bail

Until the 1990s, release on recognizance was the most common type of pretrial release. By 2006, however, its use had declined by one-third and the use of financial pretrial release through commercial bail bonding companies increased proportionally.

The judicial system predominantly depends on monetary bail under the assumption that it protects public safety and ensures that the released individual returns to court. However, the practice of paying money for bail is under considerable scrutiny. Research shows that people held in jail pretrial end up with more restrictive sentencing outcomes than people who are free pending trial. Compared to low-risk defendants released prior to trial, those held in jail before trial are four times more likely to receive a sentence of imprisonment and three times more likely to be given a longer prison sentence.[4]

Other consequences of being held in jail pretrial aren't always so visible, but researchers and others have noticed them.[5] A person who is in pretrial detention cannot dress as well as someone who comes to trial from home. Jurors who see defendants in shackles and jail uniforms may equate those

Visit https://www.youtube.com/watch?v=IS5mwymTIJU or scan this code with the QR app on your smartphone or digital device and listen to talk-show host John Oliver (*The Crime Report*'s "2015 Person of the Year") use humor to get at the heart of bail reform. How does this information relate to ideas discussed in this chapter?

outward features as signs of dangerousness. Pretrial detention limits a person's ability to work with his or her attorney to prepare a defense, contact witnesses, and help with other activities due to limited telephone use. Pretrial detention may disrupt a medical routine. Children whose parents are held in jail pretrial may have to move and disrupt their education. For these and other reasons, many argue today that the ability to maintain one's job, housing, caregiver responsibilities, and other matters should be available to all people awaiting their court date within the parameters of safety but not requiring they have financial resources to do so.

Whether monetary bail increases community safety is also an issue. Some have said that there is no empirical evidence to support this idea.[6] They argue that although a judge may have reason to detain a person out of concern for community safety and thus set a high monetary bail amount, the system allows defendants with money to go free even if they are dangerous, while keeping low-risk, poor people in jail unnecessarily and at great cost to taxpayers. The thinking also goes that a for-profit bonding company may recognize that a 10 percent fee from a high bail amount will result in a hefty profit and decide to post the bond to make a profit. On the other hand, bail bondspersons almost never write bail bonds for $1,000 or less because there is only a small profit to be made. They are far more likely to underwrite high bail amounts, which means that defendants charged with serious offenses are more likely to obtain bail than those accused of minor crimes.[7] This also means that bail bondspersons, not prosecutors or judges, are making critical decisions affecting the freedom of those accused of crime.

Effective Alternatives to Monetary Bail

There are a number of other effective alternatives to monetary bail. The use of evidence-based risk assessment can provide insight into the need to detain persons who may pose a risk to public safety or not appear for court. These tools usually classify persons as low risk, moderate risk, or high risk based on a review of their criminal history, education, employment, substance abuse, social networks, cognitions (thinking patterns), housing, finances, and recreation. The level of risk can then set into action the appropriate release option and match the offender with services (responsivity) that increase his or her appearance at court and reduce the threat to public safety. The use of valid risk assessment tools is still in its infancy across the United States, but more jurisdictions are beginning to implement them. Recently, the Laura and John Arnold Foundation, a private foundation addressing the use of fines and fees in the criminal justice system, developed the Public Safety Assessment (PSA).[8] The PSA is a scientifically validated risk assessment tool. The foundation spent $1.2 million in developing the tool in order to help jurisdictions use science in making the bail decision and combat the invisible set of assumptions based on race, class, and other factors that can come into play. Foundation researchers found that fewer than 10 objective factors—such as age, criminal record, and previous failures to appear in court, with more recent offenses given greater weight—were the best predictors of a defendant's behavior. Factoring in other considerations such as drug abuse and a face-to-face interview with the defendant did not improve accuracy.

Another effective alternative to monetary bail is the increased use of citations instead of arrest and booking. Connecticut, the District of Columbia, Maryland, North Carolina, and Wisconsin are part of a growing number of states that have passed laws to replace the cash bail system with risk assessment and risk-based supervision and expand the use of citation releases by law enforcement in lieu of custodial arrests for nonviolent

Visit https://www.vera.org/research/ bail-fines-and-fees or scan this code with the QR app on your smartphone or digital device and watch this podcast from the Vera Institute of Justice on how bail, fines, and fees in the criminal justice system impact poor communities in New Orleans. How does this information relate to ideas discussed in this chapter?

Visit http://www.npr.org/templates/story/ story.php?storyId=122725849 or scan this code with the QR app on your smartphone or digital device and listen to the podcast of the problems of the American money bail system and how the powerful commercial bail bonding lobby blocks pretrial services programs. How does this information relate to ideas discussed in this chapter?

offenses. Custodial arrests are enormously expensive and too often result in the unnecessary detention of low-risk individuals. There is public support for citations in lieu of arrest and booking for possession of small amounts of marijuana, driving with no operator's license, reckless driving, driving while license is revoked, and disorderly conduct.[9]

Another option to monetary bail is the use of release on recognizance for low-risk defendants. Low-risk defendants generally appear in court and are not rearrested because they are generally responsible in other areas of their lives. However, as you read in this chapter's opening story, the judge "took a chance" and believed that Earl Simmons (aka DMX) would appear in court as ordered. Whether Simmons actually believed the date was changed so he could perform in Las Vegas and earn money to pay child support or whether the judge's thinking was flawed because there was little science behind his bail decision remains unknown.

Technology in the form of automated phone calls, text messages, and e-mails can remind individuals of court dates and reduce failure to appear rates, thereby decreasing reliance on monetary bail after individuals fail to appear in court. These notification programs are used in the Miami County (Ohio) Municipal Court, Los Angeles County Traffic Court, and Multnomah County (Oregon) Circuit Court. All three jurisdictions have seen a reduction in failure to appear rates: 83 percent reduction in Miami County, 20 percent in Los Angeles County, and almost 45 percent in Multnomah County. Multnomah County launched its court notification program in 2005. In 2007, it reported a saving of $1.6 million for the county. Other counties are reaching out more aggressively to pretrial defendants with mailed post cards and personal telephone calls answering defendants' questions.

A final release option is to implement a deposit bond with the court and eliminate the need for commercial bail bonding. Illinois adopted this approach in 1963. Although it still uses monetary bail, the defendant pays 10 percent of her or his bond directly to the court. If she or he appears for all court dates and is not rearrested during the pretrial and trial process, all but a 3 percent administrative fee is returned. Failure to appear results in rearrest and liability for the full bond amount. The National Association of Pretrial Services Agencies (NAPSA), a professional association dedicated to promoting pretrial justice and public safety through rational pretrial decision making and practices informed by science, supports the professionalization of its members. NAPSA's Code of Ethics is shown in Exhibit 6-1.

Jails

CO6-2 # PURPOSE OF JAILS

jails

Locally operated correctional facilities that confine people before or after conviction.

total admission

The total number of people admitted to jail each year.

Except for six states that run combined jail/prison systems (Alaska, Connecticut, Delaware, Hawaii, Rhode Island, and Vermont), **jails** are locally operated correctional facilities that confine people before or after conviction. Jails are different from prisons (the subject of Chapter 7) in a number of ways that you will learn about as you read. The fundamental difference between jail and prison is the nature of their populations.[10]

Total admission is the total number of persons admitted to jail each year, which falls between 10 million and 13 million. That translates into about 34,000 people released from jails each day and about 238,000 released each week. The Vera Institute of Justice, an independent, nonprofit center for justice policy and practice in New York City, tells us that a *small minority of individuals is responsible for at least one-half of all admissions to jail,* people who return to jail over and over, what some refer to as frequent fliers.[11] In Chicago, for example, 21 percent of the individuals admitted to jail between 2007 and 2011 accounted for 50 percent of all admissions. In New York City, the situation is similar. From 2008 through midyear 2013, almost 500

EXHIBIT 6-1	National Association of Pretrial Services Agencies (NAPSA) Code of Ethics

As a pretrial services professional I will:

- Assist the criminal justice system in its dealings with pretrial defendants to the best of my ability and will conduct myself as a professional at all times;
- Respect the dignity of the individual, be they defendants, victims, or fellow criminal justice professionals;
- Respect the dignity and integrity of the court;
- Respect the presumption of innocence of all defendants, until proven guilty beyond a reasonable doubt, and to uphold the fundamental right of every accused person who has been arrested and is facing prosecution under the U.S. criminal justice system;
- Pledge that the information I provide to the court and the decisions I make are as accurate and objective as possible;
- Treat all people equally regardless of race, national origin, disability, age, gender, sexual orientation or religion;
- Protect the confidentiality of all information obtained, except when necessary to prevent serious, foreseeable, and/or imminent harm to a defendant or other identifiable person(s);
- Avoid impropriety or the appearance of impropriety;
- Avoid any conflicts of interest and will not evaluate, supervise and/or provide services to anyone I have an existing relationship with, nor enter into a personal or business relationship with anyone I evaluate, supervise or provide services to;
- Continue to pursue my own professional development and education to further my expertise in the field;
- Promote the growth of pretrial services, as well as encourage and cooperate with research and development in advancing the field;
- Respect and promote the fundamental principles and professional standards which guide pretrial services and will implement these best practices to the extent I am able;
- Refrain from providing legal advice to any pretrial defendants; and lastly,
- Promise to conduct myself as an individual of good character who will act in good faith in making reliable ethical judgments.

people were admitted to jail 18 times or more, accounting for more than 10,000 jail admissions and 300,00 days in jail.

The **average daily population (ADP)**, on the other hand, is the sum of the number of inmates in a jail or prison each day for a year divided by the total number of days in the year. Jail ADP at midyear 2014 was 744,592. Prison total admission is estimated at 626,644 a year, and prison ADP at year-end 2014, was 1,561,500 adults (see Chapter 7). The *daily* population of jails is lower than that of prisons, but the *annual* total of people incarcerated in jails is higher. Put another way, although prisons hold about twice the number of people on any given day than jails do, jails have almost 19 times the number of annual admissions. The jail population is, thus, dynamic, and the prison population is static. The changing nature of jail populations raises significant issues and problems that form the core of this chapter.

At midyear 2014, local jail authorities held or supervised 808,070 offenders.[12] Jail authorities supervised almost 8.0 percent of these offenders (63,478) in alternative programs outside jail facilities (see Exhibit 6–7 later in the chapter). A total of 744,592 were housed in local jails.

Inmates sentenced to jail usually have a sentence of 1 year or less. Seventy percent are released within 3 days; however, an estimated 20 percent will spend at least 1 month, 12 percent at least 2 months, and 4 percent will spend more than 6 months.[13]

At midyear 2014, the majority of the nation's jail population (almost 63 percent) were pretrial detainees.

average daily population (ADP)

Sum of the number of inmates in a jail or prison each day for a year, divided by the total number of days in the year.

EXHIBIT 6-2 | **American Jail Association**

Mission Statement

To band together all those concerned with or interested in the custody and care of persons awaiting trial, serving sentences, or otherwise locally confined; to improve the conditions and systems under which such persons are detained.

To advance professionalism through training, information exchange, technical assistance, publications, and conferences.

To provide leadership in the development of professional standards, pertinent legislation, management practices, programs, and services.

To present and advance the interests, needs, concerns, and proficiency of the profession as deemed appropriate by the membership and their representatives.

Source: Copyright © American Jail Association. Reprinted with permission.

CO6-3 Jails also incarcerate persons in a wide variety of other categories. Jails are used to do the following:

- Receive persons awaiting court action on their current charge.
- Readmit probation and parole violators and bail-bond absconders.
- Detain juveniles until custody is transferred to juvenile authorities.
- Hold persons with mental illness until they are moved to appropriate health facilities.
- Hold individuals for the military.
- Provide protective custody.
- Confine persons found in contempt.

- Hold witnesses for the courts.
- Hold inmates about to be released after completing a prison sentence.
- Transfer inmates to federal, state, or other authorities.
- House inmates for federal, state, or other authorities because of crowding of their facilities.
- Operate some community-based programs as alternatives to incarceration.
- Hold inmates sentenced to short terms (generally under one year) of incarceration.
- Hold persons for U.S. Immigration and Customs Enforcement.

The AJA mission statement is shown in Exhibit 6–2. This chapter will explore the problems of jails of the past and present and discuss direction for the 21st century.

Almost 40 percent of the nation's jails like the one pictured are small (less than 50 cells), holding only 3 percent of the jail population. Most small jails were built in the early part of the 20th century. What management style does this jail suggest?

© Photocyclops.com/SuperStock

JAILS IN HISTORY

CO6-4

It is believed that King Henry II of England ordered the first jail built in 1166. The purpose of that jail was to detain offenders until they could be brought before a court, tried, and sentenced. From that beginning, jails spread throughout Europe but changed in scope and size over time.

The Walnut Street Jail, started in Philadelphia in 1773, originally housed offenders without regard to sex, age, or offense. Following its redesignation as a penitentiary in 1790, it housed only convicted felons. Which religious group's principles influenced correctional institutions in Pennsylvania?
© Photo by Encyclopedia Britannica/UIG Via Getty Images

First Jail in the United States

The first jail in the United States was the Walnut Street Jail in Philadelphia, built in 1773. The jail housed offenders without regard to sex, age, or offense. Following the jail's opening, conditions quickly deteriorated. According to some, the jail became a "promiscuous scene of unrestricted intercourse, universal riot, and debauchery."[14] The Philadelphia Quakers had wanted the Walnut Street Jail to be a place where inmates reformed themselves through reflection and remorse.

In 1798 a fire destroyed the workshops at Walnut Street. The destruction brought about disillusionment and idleness. Rising costs crippled the jail's budget. Disciplinary problems rose with overcrowding, and escape and violence increased. The number of inmates who were destitute vagrants or debtors soared as did the incidence of disease. There were political conflicts between the religious Quakers and the non-Quaker prison board members. Prisoners rioted on March 27, 1820, and on October 5, 1835, the Walnut Street Jail closed. State prisoners were transferred to the new Eastern State Penitentiary in Philadelphia, the first institution of its kind in the world (see Chapter 7). County inmates and those awaiting trial were transferred to a new county jail.

By the close of the 19th century, most cities across the United States had jails to hold persons awaiting trial and to punish convicted felons. The sheriff became the person in charge of the jail. As crime increased and urban centers expanded, jails grew in importance, as did the sheriffs' control over jails.

Architecture and Inmate Management   CO6-5

In an attempt to better manage and control inmate behavior, jails have progressed through three phases of architectural design. Each design is based on a particular philosophy of inmate management and control.

First-Generation Jails First-generation jails were built in a linear design that dates back to the 18th century, when prison and jail design was shifting from single-cell and religious emphasis to congregate housing and secular administration.

In a typical **first-generation jail**, inmates live in multiple-occupancy cells or dormitories. The cells line corridors that are arranged like spokes. Inmate supervision is sporadic or intermittent; staff must patrol the corridors to observe inmates in their cells. Contact between jailers and inmates is minimal unless there is an incident to which jailers must react (see Exhibit 6–3).

The design of such linear jails reflects the assumption that inmates are violent and destructive and will assault staff, destroy jail property, and try to escape. The facility is designed to prevent these behaviors. Heavy metal bars separate staff from inmates. Reinforced metal beds, sinks, and toilets are bolted to the ground or wall. Reinforced concrete and razor wire surround the facility.

The biggest problem with first-generation jails is the inability of an officer to see what is going on in more than one or two cells at a time. That limitation gave rise to the second-generation jails of the 1960s.

Second-Generation Jails Second-generation jails emerged in the 1960s to replace old, run-down linear jails and provide officers the opportunity to observe as much of the housing area as possible from a single vantage point.

Second-generation jails adopted a different philosophical approach to construction and inmate management. In a **second-generation jail**, staff remain in a secure control booth overlooking inmate housing areas, called *pods* (see Exhibit 6–4). Although visual surveillance increases in such jails, surveillance is remote, and verbal interaction with inmates is even less frequent than in first-generation jails. Property destruction is minimized because steel and cement continue to define the living areas. Second-generation jails have been termed *podular remote-supervision facilities.*

Although staff can observe activity in common areas, or *dayrooms,* they are unable to respond quickly to problems or even to interact effectively with inmates because of the intervening security control booth. In both the first- and second-generation jails, the biggest problem is that staff and

first-generation jail

Jail with multiple-occupancy cells or dormitories that line corridors arranged like spokes. Inmate supervision is intermittent; staff must patrol the corridors to observe inmates in their cells.

second-generation jail

Jail where staff remain in a secure control booth surrounded by inmate housing areas called *pods* and surveillance is remote.

EXHIBIT 6–3   First-Generation Jail—Intermittent Surveillance

 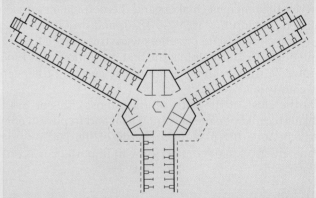

Cells line corridors in first-generation jails. Unable to observe all inmate housing areas from one location, prison and jail staff must patrol inmates' living areas to provide surveillance. What are the consequences of first-generation jails?
© Ingram Publishing RF

EXHIBIT 6–4 Second-Generation Jail—Remote Surveillance

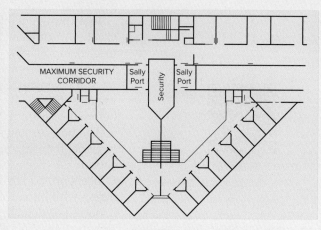

MAXIMUM SECURITY CORRIDOR | Sally Port | Security | Sally Port

Inmate living areas are divided into pods, or modules, in which cells are clustered around dayrooms that are under remote observation by staff in a secure control room. What are the consequences of second-generation jails?
© AP Photo/Charlie Riedel

inmates are separated. As David Parrish, former detention commander for the Hillsborough County Sheriff's Department (Tampa, Florida) put it, "Staff managed the hallways and control rooms, generally about 10 percent of the facility, while inmates ran the housing areas, roughly 90 percent."[15]

Third-Generation Jails **Third-generation jails**, also known as **direct-supervision jails**, emerged in 1974 when the Federal Bureau of Prisons opened three Metropolitan Correctional Centers (MCCs) in three cities: New York, Chicago, and San Diego. These three federal facilities were the first jails planned and designed to be operated under the principles of unit management, which later became known as *direct supervision* (see Exhibit 6–5 for a list of the nine principles of direct supervision). The housing unit design of such jails is podular. Inmates' cells are arranged around a common area, or dayroom. There is no secure control booth for the supervising officer, and there are no physical barriers between the officer and the

third-generation jail (also *direct-supervision jail*)

A jail where inmates are housed in small groups, or pods, staffed 24 hours a day by specially trained officers. Officers interact with inmates to help change behavior. Bars and metal doors are absent, reducing noise and dehumanization.

EXHIBIT 6-5 Nine Principles of Direct Supervision

1. **Effective control.** Staff firmly establish their authority over all space and activities in the unit.
2. **Effective supervision.** Continuous supervision is maintained by the unit officers.
3. **Competent staff.** Correctional standards guide recruitment.
4. **Staff and inmate safety.** Performance-based data are collected.
5. **Manageable and cost-effective operations.** There are more architectural choices, commercial-grade furnishings, and equipment options.
6. **Effective communication.** Direct communication exists between inmates and officers, officers and supervisors.
7. **Classification and orientation.** Know with whom you are dealing; intense supervision is maintained for the first 12 to 72 hours.
8. **Justice and fairness.** Unit officers exercise primary informal discipline.
9. **Ownership of operations.** Inmate policy decisions are guided by a team approach.

Visit http://www.youtube.com/ watch?v=f44GSsIWbJw or scan this code with the QR app on your smartphone or digital device and watch a podcast on the philosophy of direct supervision. How does this information relate to ideas discussed in this chapter?

inmates. Direct supervision places a single deputy directly in a "housing pod" with between 32 and 64 inmates. The officer may have a desk or table for paperwork, but it is in the open dayroom area.

In a third-generation jail, the inmate management style is direct supervision. An officer is stationed in the pod with the inmates, much like a teacher in a classroom. The officer moves about the pod and interacts with the inmates to manage their behavior. Advocates of direct supervision tell us that when correctional officers are in constant and direct contact with inmates, they get to know them and can recognize and respond to trouble before it escalates into violence.

The pod contains sleeping areas, dayroom space, all necessary personal hygiene fixtures, and sufficient tables and seats to accommodate unit capacity. Officers are not separated from inmates by a physical barrier. Officers provide frequent, nonscheduled observation of and personal interaction with inmates (see Exhibit 6–6). Due to the close contact, officers are expected to detect signs of tension between inmates and defuse the situation by either talking with inmates or by restricting privileges. They do this by using their communication skills training to maintain a nonviolent environment. Furnishings are used to reduce inmate stress caused by crowding, excessive noise, lack of privacy, and isolation from the outside world. Bars and metal doors are absent, reducing noise and the dehumanization common in first- and second-generation jails.

Direct-supervision jails facilitate staff movement, interaction with inmates, and control and leadership over pods. By supervising inmate activities directly, the staff can help change inmate behavior patterns rather than simply react to them. Staff control inmate behavior through the enforcement of boundaries of acceptable behavior and the administration of consequences for violating the boundaries. Observing unacceptable behavior and administering consequences is less likely to occur in first- and second-generation jails where staff supervision is sporadic and remote.

Some researchers tell us that pods and direct supervision provide a safer and more positive environment for inmates and staff than do first- and second-generation jails.[16] But other researchers have found few differences between the perceptions of officers in new generation versus traditional facilities.[17] In one study, new generation officers were no more satisfied

EXHIBIT 6–6   Third-Generation Jail—Direct Supervision

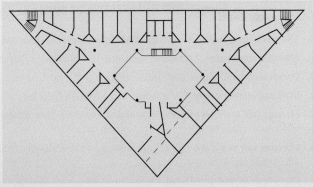

Cells are grouped in housing units, or pods. Each pod has a central dayroom. Prison staff are stationed inside the housing unit to encourage direct interaction between inmates and staff. What are the consequences of direct-supervision jails?
Courtesy of the Federal Bureau of Prisons

with their jobs, did not feel more connected to their coworkers, did not believe communication was improved, did not feel any greater sense of personal involvement in their work, and were just as likely to see their jobs as monotonous and routine as officers working in the more traditional facility. Possible reasons for the lack of difference include the short history of direct supervision, little supporting data, and the belief among sheriffs and jail administrators that direct-supervision facilities are not as "safe" or "strong" as remote-supervision facilities because of distance and physical separation from inmates.[18] Simply put, many agencies are not comfortable removing the "barriers" between "us and them."

Today, an estimated 349 of the 3,283 local jails use direct supervision, but as one researcher has asked, "Are they really direct-supervision jails?"[19] After receiving surveys from half of the direct–supervision jails, Christine Tartaro, professor of criminal justice at the Richard Stockton College of New Jersey, found that although many jails are being called direct supervision, few of them truly are. Only 40 percent said their facilities operate under a unit management structure, and few offered any inmate services other than recreation on the pod. The majority operated under traditional centralized management and a few used elements of both. Tartaro also found that half of the direct-supervision jails offered correctional officers no more than two days of communication skills training even though the training requirements for learning to communicate with a diverse group of inmates are difficult and need more than one or two days of instruction. The majority of Professor Tartaro's sample (70 percent) also identified their jail's furnishings and fixtures as vandalism resistant and half bolted their furniture to the floor, conveying the message that inmates are expected to misbehave. Furthermore, because of jail crowding, the majority of the inmates in direct–supervision facilities are no longer housed in single cells. Tartaro believes that jails that are only partially implementing the direct-supervision model are not secure or well-run facilities. This may explain why there are few differences between the perceptions of officers in new generation versus traditional facilities.

CHARACTERISTICS OF JAIL INMATES AND FACILITIES

CO6-6

Who is in jail? Why are they there? What do we know about the operation and administration of jail facilities? To these and related questions we now turn our attention.

Jail Inmates

The characteristics of jail inmates have changed little over the past decade. Since 2000, almost 9 of 10 jail inmates have been male; 4 of 10 have been white; 4 of 10 have been black; and 1 percent or less have been juveniles.

In June 2014, local jail authorities held or supervised 808,070 offenders, which was significantly lower than the peak of 858,385 inmates at midyear 2008. Almost 8.0 percent of these offenders (63,478) were supervised outside jail facilities (see Exhibit 6–7). A total of 744,592 were housed in local jails.

Another way to look at the nation's jail population is to consider the rate of incarceration. Confined jail populations give us a count of the total number held in jail (e.g., 744,592 offenders confined in local jails at midyear 2014). Because of differences in total population, however, such counts do not allow for accurate comparison of jurisdictions. Rates of jail

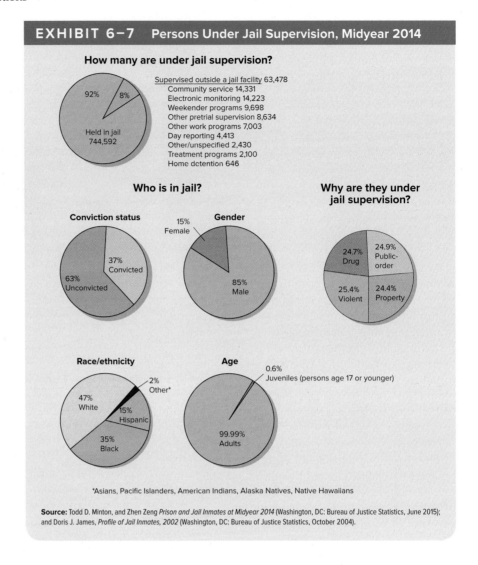

EXHIBIT 6–7 Persons Under Jail Supervision, Midyear 2014

How many are under jail supervision?

92% / 8%

Held in jail 744,592

Supervised outside a jail facility 63,478
Community service 14,331
Electronic monitoring 14,223
Weekender programs 9,698
Other pretrial supervision 8,634
Other work programs 7,003
Day reporting 4,413
Other/unspecified 2,430
Treatment programs 2,100
Home detention 646

Who is in jail?

Conviction status
37% Convicted
63% Unconvicted

Gender
15% Female
85% Male

Why are they under jail supervision?
24.7% Drug
24.9% Public-order
25.4% Violent
24.4% Property

Race/ethnicity
47% White
2% Other*
15% Hispanic
35% Black

Age
0.6% Juveniles (persons age 17 or younger)
99.99% Adults

*Asians, Pacific Islanders, American Indians, Alaska Natives, Native Hawaiians

Source: Todd D. Minton, and Zhen Zeng *Prison and Jail Inmates at Midyear 2014* (Washington, DC: Bureau of Justice Statistics, June 2015); and Doris J. James, *Profile of Jail Inmates, 2002* (Washington, DC: Bureau of Justice Statistics, October 2004).

incarceration, expressed as the number of jail inmates per 100,000 residents age 18 and older, provide for a more meaningful and useful analysis of trends in incarceration. With rate data, we can compare changes over time and jurisdictions with different populations. Exhibit 6–8 shows changes in the jail incarceration rate from 2000 through 2014. Note that the adult and juvenile incarceration rate increased from 220 inmates per 100,000 in 2000 to 259 inmates per 100,000 in 2007, and then declined to 234 in 2014. The adult only jail incarceration rate also declined from a high of 340 inmates per 100,000 at midyear 2007 to 302 per 100,000 at midyear 2014.

Several aspects of the nation's jail population are under scrutiny by politicians and policymakers. Much of the increase in the number of jail inmates is the result of drug crime enforcement. Persons who were jailed as a result of the 1980s war on drugs grew from around 9 percent in 1983 to 23 percent in 1989 and has remained there ever since. Today, practically every state, the federal government, and county municipalities are looking into ways to move low-level drug offenders out of jail. Many have either moved to legalize marijuana or decriminalize it, meaning no arrest, jail time, or criminal record for the first-time possession of a small amount of marijuana for personal consumption. The offense is treated like a minor traffic violation. As long as law enforcement agencies and politicians don't

EXHIBIT 6-8   Jail Incarceration Rate, 2000–2014

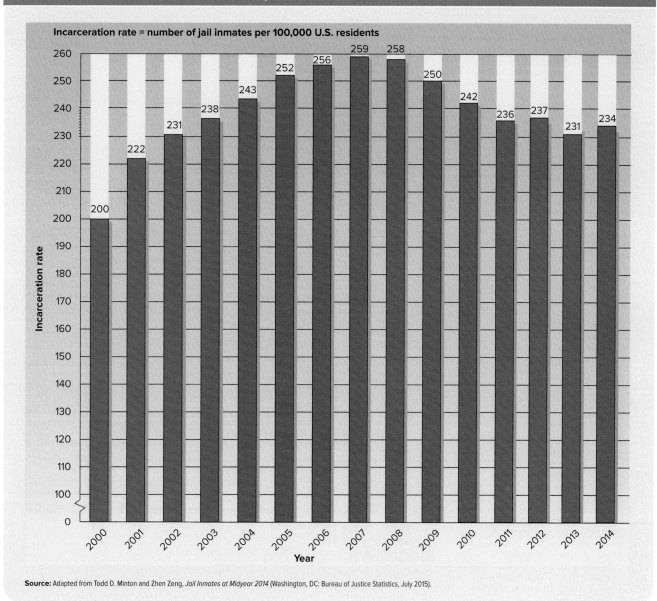

Incarceration rate = number of jail inmates per 100,000 U.S. residents

Source: Adapted from Todd D. Minton and Zhen Zeng, *Jail Inmates at Midyear 2014* (Washington, DC: Bureau of Justice Statistics, July 2015).

criminalize something else in the place of drug crime enforcement, we should expect to see jail populations decrease.

Another problem is the steady increase in the number of jail inmates who are pretrial detainees (63 percent in 2014, up from 56 percent in 2000). At a time when, by most common measures of public safety (FBI crime statistics), crime is down, we find the jail population increasing, leading one of the country's most respected voices in jail issues, Dr. Ken Kerle, to write that "this is another unhappy sign that inmate processing is slowing down."[20] If more jail inmates are not being tried, convicted, or sentenced, jail resources become overburdened, crowding results, and the conditions of confinement worsen. And later in this chapter, we present a discussion of another jail problem—jail inmates who suffer from mental illness, what the nation's sheriffs and jail administrators say is one of the most important problems jails are facing today.

Despite this gloomy picture, jails are in a unique position to help persons leaving jail and resuming life in the community. Today more and more policymakers are recognizing that because jail inmates usually have shorter lengths of stay than state or federal inmates, the community location of most jail facilities means less time away from family, friends, treatment providers, faith institutions, and other social supports. They also realize that jails have opportunities to develop strategies to reduce the criminalization of persons with mental illness and combat this list of problems with interventions and reentry programs prior to release.

Gender and Jail Populations   There has been an upsurge in the number of women incarcerated in the United States, explained, in part, by guideline sentencing under which gender is not regarded as an appropriate consideration. Although females have historically been treated more leniently than men at sentencing, guideline sentencing has tended to limit or end this practice.

The number of women in jail has more than quintupled over the past 30 years, from 19,000 in 1985, to 70,400 in 2000, to 108,800 in midyear 2014. The absolute number of women in jail is much smaller than the absolute number of men. However, their impact on jail operations is significant, raising concerns about the adequacy of jail facilities and the services provided.

The typical female jail inmate is poor, is a high school dropout with low skills, has held mainly low-wage jobs, is young (25 to 29), is unmarried with one to three children, and belongs to a racial minority.

Almost one-half of women and one-third of men in jail are first-time offenders (49 versus 37 percent).[21] Almost half of the women and men in jail were under the influence of alcohol or drugs at the time of the offense. Forty-six percent had members of their immediate families sentenced to prison. Two of every 10 grew up in a home where one or both parents abused drugs, alcohol, or both. And more than one-half of the women (55 percent) and 13 percent of the men had been physically or sexually abused before age 18. Women in jail need targeted interventions that address these issues. Other facts about women in jails is shown in Exhibit 6-9.

This profile also raises troubling concerns about the children of jailed mothers. Two-thirds of women in jail are mothers with children under age

---

EXHIBIT 6–9   **Ten Facts About Women in Jails**

1. Women are a lower public safety risk than men.
2. Women's pathways to crime are different than men's.
3. Women's participation in crime is related to their connections with others.
4. Women have histories of victimization and trauma.
5. Women's programs have been developed through the lens of managing men.
6. Classification systems have not been validated for women.
7. Women need gender-informed risk assessment tools that more accurately identify women's risks and needs.
8. Women respond more favorably when staff adhere to evidence-based, gender-responsive principles.
9. Women's transition and reentry from jail to the community is challenging because of their overwhelming needs as mothers, less evidence of employment history, and greater levels of poverty.
10. Women's technical violations (60% rearrested and nearly 33% returned to incarceration) stem from unmet survival needs such as meeting financial obligations, finding gainful employment, and finding safe housing.

18 who were living with them prior to detention. When mothers go to jail, children become silent victims. The children may already have been victims if their mothers used drugs during pregnancy. Young children, not yet capable of understanding why their mother is gone, where she has gone, and if or when she will return, may develop depression and feelings of abandonment. Even children who are fortunate enough to be placed with emotionally supportive caregivers must cope with seeing their mother only through a glass barrier and hearing her voice only over the phone. Studies have shown that children of incarcerated mothers have more behavioral problems at home and in school and are four times as likely to become juvenile delinquents as children from similar socioeconomic backgrounds with parents at home. Maintaining bonding with children and family is the most difficult female inmate experience.[22] Recognizing that children should not be made to suffer for the poor choices of their parents and recognizing that support for family maintenance is a societal value, some jails are establishing visitation and parenting programs that accommodate this need. Through such programs, jail administrators have the opportunity to become leaders in preserving families and reducing crime.

Some scholars believe that many women in jail do not pose a threat to public safety but are jailed because they do not have the financial resources to make bail, which makes our discussion of the problems with monetary bail at the beginning of this chapter even more salient for this group of offenders. Over 80 percent are charged with nonviolent traffic, property, drug, or public-order offenses.[23]

The increase in the number of women in jail has required that local officials identify and try to meet the needs of female inmates, yet severe limitations in resources often impede the provision of programs and services for women in jail. Jails are not prepared to house and treat rapidly rising female populations. They have difficulty providing appropriate housing, bed space, programs, jobs, mental health care, and other services. Women in jail have high needs for education, job training, health care, mental health care, alcohol and drug abuse counseling, and parenting skills development. Properly classifying women according to their risks and needs is beyond the scope of most jails in the United States.[24] The National Institute of Justice surveyed 54 jails and found that the same classification instrument was used for both male and female inmates in 50 jails. The survey found no effort to gauge women inmates' different needs, circumstances, and risk profiles.[25]

Ignoring problems relating to women in jail increases a jail's exposure to litigation and liability. The National Institute of Corrections argues against doing nothing: "The 'get tough on inmates' mood, combined with decreasing levels of accountability for maintaining some level of minimum standards, raises the specter of decreased funding for jails, corresponding cutbacks in staff and training, and the rebirth of the sorts of very brutal, barbaric, and often dangerous conditions that led to the initial wave of court intervention in the early 1970s."[26]

Women are normally housed in a "women's unit," often an afterthought built inside facilities designed for men or simply a replica of the men's facility design. Such design fails to take into account the different needs of women. For example, the traditional jail bunks and fixed-seating arrangements in the jail's dayroom or at dining room tables may present safety and comfort issues for women who are pregnant in jail. In Pennsylvania alone, 6 percent of the women who enter jail are pregnant. A related issue is whether women in jail should be allowed to use contraceptives. Interruptions in birth control use could increase the possibility that they might have unintended pregnancies shortly after release.[27]

Another deficiency affecting women in jail is staffing. Either there are no female correctional officers or there are too few to ensure around-the-clock supervision of women in jail. In the United States, nearly 7 in 10 jail officers were male in both in 2000 and at the beginning of 2014.[28] The result too often is that women inmates are exploited and abused by male staff. Ken Kerle, former managing editor of *American Jails,* argues that the best defense for a jail against female inmates' allegations of sexual harassment by male staff is to have a female officer present at all times.[29]

There are many issues to be resolved when developing a gender-responsive program for women in an environment that traditionally serves the needs of men. Recently the National Institute of Corrections released a report to help jail and prison administrators more effectively manage the women in their care.[30] According to the researchers, four factors influence women offenders' behavior. Understanding these factors in combination with each other will help jail administrators consider how to adjust policies and procedures and how to assess and improve services to women in their care. They are:

1. **Pathways perspective.** Women in jail often have histories of sexual and/or physical abuse and substance abuse and are clients of mental health services. These women typically are unskilled, earn low incomes, have sporadic work histories, and are single parents. Thus, understanding how women enter the criminal justice system helps jails improve their responses.

2. **Relational theory and female development.** Relational theory describes the different ways women and men develop. An important difference suggested by the research is that women develop a sense of self and self-worth when their actions arise out of, and lead back into, connections with others even if this means establishing dysfunctional relationships. Many women offenders are drawn into criminal activity because of their relationships with others. Knowing this explains why jail staff often perceive that communicating with female offenders is more difficult and time-consuming than communicating with male inmates.

3. **Trauma theory.** Trauma is the injury done by violence and abuse and it is largely unrecognized by the women offenders themselves. Mental health services that understand past trauma and its effect on current behavior are needed to respond to trauma.

4. **Addiction theory.** When substance abuse treatment programs for women are combined with additional pathway factors (mental illness, trauma, abuse), jail-based treatment is successful.

Stevyn Fogg, researcher with the Center for Effective Public Policy, tells us that there are three things that sheriffs and jail administrators can do to address the critical issues that women face in jail:[31]

1. Provide jail staff with training to understand the differences between female and male inmates, the implications of gender-responsive research, and information on trauma-informed care.

2. Provide jail staff with access to current studies of effective jail programs for female inmates and promising approaches to achieving successful outcome with female inmates.

3. Provide jail staff with skill-based training focused on effective communication, motivational interviewing, case management, and coaching—all concentrated on working with female inmates.

Visit www.brennancenter.org/sites/default/ files/publications/Racial%20Disparities%20 Report%2006252515.pd for scan this code with the QR app on your smartphone or digital device and read eight recommendations (pp. 27–43) that experts in law enforcement, corrections, judges, practitioners, researchers, and advocates believe are needed to reduce jail incarceration and racial disparities. How does this information relate to ideas discussed in this chapter?

Ethnicity and Jail Populations Whites comprise nearly 70 percent of the U.S. population but only 47 percent of the jail population. In the general population, Hispanics make up almost 16 percent, and blacks make up 12.7 percent. In jail, their populations are 15 percent and 35 percent, respectively.

Explanations for the overrepresentation of minorities in jail abound. One explanation has to do with the function of jails as pretrial detention centers. The jail population is heavily influenced by bail decisions as we pointed out at the beginning of this chapter. A number of researchers have found that judges impose higher bail—or are more likely to deny bail altogether—if the defendant is a racial minority.[32] Still another reason is the impact of the war on drugs and on law enforcement strategies of racial profiling. Other researchers have argued that the war on drugs has had a particularly detrimental effect on black males.[33] Across the past two decades, more black males than white males have been detained for drug offenses. Researchers at the University of Nebraska argue that police are *reactive* in responding to crimes against persons and property but are *proactive* in dealing with drug offenses. "There is evidence," they write, "to suggest that they [police] target minority communities—where drug dealing is more visible and where it is thus easier to make an arrest—and tend to give less attention to drug activities in other neighborhoods."[34]

Mental Illness and Jail Populations Among the many disadvantaged people in jail, the largest group is people with mental illness. Almost two-thirds (64 percent) of all jail inmates have a mental health problem compared to about 11 percent of the general adult population.[35] When researchers investigated the prevalence of "serious" mental illnesses defined as major depressive disorders, bipolar disorders, schizophrenia, and delusional disorders using structured clinical interviews with 20,000 adults entering five jails, they found that almost 15 percent of the men and 31 percent of the women had a serious mental illness.[36] Furthermore, according to the latest available data, 83 percent of jail inmates with mental illness did not receive mental health care after admission.[37] Persons living with mental

Sixty-four percent of jail inmates have mental health problems compared with about 11 percent of the general population. Women inmates at the Pinellas County facility (Clearwater, Florida) struggling with PTSD, loss of their children, and other problems meet with a clinical counselor every Thursday to talk while they make gifts for their children. Why are mentally ill inmates not fit individuals for retribution and punishment?

© Tampa Bay Times/Cherie Diez/The Image Works

illness are swept into the criminal justice system because of the failures of the public mental health system and the lack of adequate treatment in most poor communities. Today there may be as many as eight times more people with mental illness in the nation's jails (over 478,000) than there are in mental health hospitals (60,000).[38] The Los Angeles County Jail is the largest psychiatric inpatient facility in the United States with more than 3,400 prisoners suffering with mental health problems.[39] New York's Rikers Island is second with 3,000, and Chicago's Cook County Jail is third with more than 1,500.

Despite the large number of jail inmates with mental illness, these individuals are not often fit subjects for retribution or punishment. Because of the constant noise, bright lights, and an ever-changing population, jails do not offer rest or relief for people with mental illness, often meaning further deterioration in their illness. James Gondles, executive director of the American Correctional Association, said, "The notion that the prospect of incarceration will deter an individual with a mental illness from committing a crime does not apply to a population that cannot fully comprehend the consequences of its actions, especially in cases where crime is a direct result of illness."[40] Other experts tell us that the criminal justice system is ill-equipped to meet the special needs of persons with mental illness who are incarcerated or on supervised release in the community. They wind up in jail as a result of behavior linked to their illnesses. And once in jail, mentally ill inmates are more prone to act out in a way that could lead jail officers to use force. In fact, the Los Angeles County Sheriff's Office published a report showing that mentally ill inmates are involved in about one-third of use-of-force incidents by jail officers.[41]

Over the years, the nation's sheriffs have also said that jails are not equipped to meet the complex needs of persons living with mental illness and asked county and general hospitals to accept them as patients. The sheriffs spelled out six factors as to why jails should not be used for such people:

1. The mentally ill person has usually committed no crime.
2. County jails are overcrowded.
3. Small county sheriffs' officers are not specially trained for the proper handling and care of a mental patient.

4. Many jails do not have proper or adequate detention rooms for the mentally ill.

5. Detention in the county jail is unfair to the patient as well as to the corrections officers.

6. Psychiatrists agree that a patient originally detained in a jail is much more difficult to treat and readjust, and incarceration can contribute to the further decompensation of many people with mental illness.[42]

Throughout the United States and other nations worldwide, a well-known strategy to reduce the number of persons with mental illness from going to jail is the adoption of Crisis Intervention Teams (CIT).[43] CIT is a police-based first responder program that has become nationally known as the "Memphis Model" of pre-arrest jail diversion for those in a mental illness crisis. CIT is a community-based partnership that teams behavioral health and human service providers with community volunteers working together with law enforcement. The goal is to help persons in mental health crisis access medical treatment rather than place them in jail due to illness-related disorders. The benefits of CIT are shown in Exhibit 6–10. While CIT has not undergone enough research to be deemed an evidence-based practice, it has been successfully utilized in many law enforcement agencies worldwide and is considered a "best practice" model in law enforcement.[44]

Suicide, Homicide, Sexual Victimization, and Jail Populations

The problems of suicide, homicide, and sexual victimization are challenging ones for jail administrators. In 2013, (the last year for which data are available), a total of 967 jail inmates died while in the custody of local jails—almost 25 percent occurred in California and Texas.[45] The number of deaths increased from 958 deaths in 2012 to 967 in 2013, while the jail population decreased 4 percent. Suicide and heart disease have been the top two causes of death in local jails since 2000. Suicide has been the leading cause of death in jails every year since 2000. In 2013, one-third of jail inmate deaths were due to suicide. The jail suicide rate increased 14 percent, from 40 suicides per 100,000 jail inmates in 2012 to 46 per 100,000 in 2013. In the wake of the hanging death of Sandra Bland (arrested in a traffic stop) in a jail cell in Hempstead, Texas, in July 2015, a number of jails are making

Dr. Nneka Jones Tapia is the first clinical psychologist appointed to run a jail—the Cook County (Chicago, Illinois) Jail, which is the nation's second largest. How would you advise Dr. Tapia to reduce the number of mentally ill jail inmates?

© Jacobs Productions

EXHIBIT 6–10 | **Benefits of CIT**

✓ Immediacy of response
✓ Increased officer safety
✓ Reduced officer/citizen injuries
✓ Increased jail diversion
✓ Increased chance for consumer to connect to mental health system
✓ Increased officer confidence in calls
✓ Reduced liability
✓ Reduced unnecessary arrests or use of force
✓ Avoidance of costs to criminal justice system
✓ Positive perception of program
✓ Linkages to long-term services promoting recovery for the individual

Visit http://www.nytimes.com/2015/07/31/us/a-psychologist-as-warden-jail-and-mental-illness-intersect-in-chicago.html or scan this code with the QR app on your smartphone or digital device and watch a podcast of Dr. Nneka Jones Tapia, the nation's first clinical psychologist appointed to run the Cook County (Chicago, Illinois) Jail, discuss ways to treat jail inmates' mental health. How does this information relate to ideas discussed in this chapter?

major changes to the way they address mental illness in jail. Cook County (Chicago, Illinois) Sheriff Tom Dart appointed Dr. Nneka Jones Tapia, a clinical psychologist, to run the second-largest jail in the country, where more than one-fourth of the inmates suffer from a mental illness, which costs Illinois taxpayers more than $400 a day compared to less than $100 a day in the community.[46] The Texas Commission on Jail Standards is changing the jail intake form.[47] For instance, to indicate if military veterans in custody might have mental health issues, the form replaces the question "Do you have any previous military service?" with "Do you have nightmares, flashbacks, or repeated thoughts or feelings related to PTSD or something terrible from your past?" If an inmate answers "yes," the employee immediately notifies the supervisor, a magistrate, and a mental health official. Seemingly steps in the right direction, what impact these and other changes will remain an open question for now.

Kentucky is one state that successfully reduced its jail suicides from 17 to 4 per year by cross-training jail personnel and mental health providers, developing new screening instruments for arresting and booking officers, establishing a telephonic service that allows jail staff to call a licensed mental health professional for risk management consultation 24 hours a day, and establishing a statewide data collection and analysis system.[48]

The majority of jail inmate suicides typically occur within the first week of incarceration with nearly a quarter occurring within the first two days of admission (time of day is not a factor), are mostly violent offenders (violent offenders who commit suicide outnumber nonviolent offenders by a margin of 3 to 1), and are typically committed by hanging. The majority of inmates who commit suicide have a high school education, are unmarried, white, male, and between the ages of 25 and 44. More than one-third have a history of serious mental illness, and 8 of 10 had not yet been convicted but were awaiting trial.

The consequences of inmate suicide are lost lives, devastation to families, short- and long-term psychological effects on other inmates and correctional staff, expensive investigations and litigation, and medical care costs.

Homicide in jail is another concern of jail administrators, and here the news is not good. In 2000, 17 jail inmates were murdered. In 2006, the number peaked at 36; decreased to 16 in 2008; and continued to increase every year since, reaching 28 homicides in 2013. The literature on jail homicides offers very few insights other than revealing that kidnapping offenders are the most likely victims of jail homicides, followed by violent offenders, property offenders, and then public-order offenders. Drug offenders have the lowest homicide victimization rate. The majority of jail homicide victims are male, mostly between the ages of 18 and 54, and evenly split between white and black.

In 2003, Congress passed and President Bush signed the Prison Rape Elimination Act. It requires the U.S. Department of Justice to report on the incidence of rape and other forms of sexual victimization in correctional facilities. The Justice Department defines *sexual victimization* as all types of sexual activity, for example, oral, anal, or vaginal penetration; handjobs; touching of the inmate's buttocks, thighs, penis, breasts, or vagina in a sexual way; abusive sexual contacts (unwanted contacts with another inmate or any contacts with staff that involved touching of the inmate's buttocks, thigh, penis, breasts, or vagina, in a sexual way); and both willing and unwilling sexual contact. The Justice Department reported that 3.2 percent, approximately 24,000 of all jail inmates nationwide, experienced one or more incidents of sexual victimization by another inmate or facility staff in 2011–2012.[49] The rate of sexual victimization has not changed since 2007.

About 1.6 percent of jail inmates (11,900) reported an incident with another inmate, 1.8 percent (13,200) reported an incident with staff, and 0.2 percent (2,400) reported both an incident by another inmate and staff.

After conducting a series of public hearings, reviewing the data, conducting site visits, and speaking with correctional staff and inmates, the Prison Rape Elimination Act's review panel concluded that sexual assaults can be reduced by changing attitudes toward potentially vulnerable populations, including female, lesbian, gay, bisexual, transgender, queer (LGBTQ), and physically frail inmates; paying close attention to institutional design and surveillance; providing offender education and staff training; improving operational policies and post orders; and monitoring adherence to established policies. In addition, a reliable inmate-classification system; improved efforts on the part of first responders, investigators, and prosecutors; and timely victim assistance and health care services can help an agency reduce, if not eliminate, inmate sexual victimization.[50]

Juveniles and Jail Populations Over the past 25 years, there has been a dramatic reversal in the theory and practice of punishing juveniles. In the mid-1970s, juvenile offenders were deemed to have special needs, so Congress passed the Juvenile Justice and Delinquency Prevention Act of 1974. It contains four core requirements that participating states must address to receive federal juvenile justice grants:

1. Status offenders may not be held in secure confinement.
2. Juveniles generally may not be held in jails and lockups in which adults are confined.
3. When juveniles are temporarily detained in the same facilities as adults, they must have no "sight or sound" contact with adult inmates.
4. States are required to demonstrate efforts to reduce the disproportionate number of minority youth who come into contact with the juvenile justice system.

By 1996, however, in the face of pressure to increase punishment for juvenile offenders, new legislation allowed cities and states to detain juvenile offenders for up to 12 hours in an adult jail before a court appearance and made it easier to house juveniles in separate wings of adult jails. That shift in philosophy and policy has kept the percentage of juveniles held as adults at about 80 to 85 percent for the past decade. The juvenile population (persons age 17 or younger) held in adult jail facilities at midyear 2014 (4,200) decreased by more than half from its peak in 1999 (9,458). Most juveniles were male and held as adults (84 percent).

The incarceration of juveniles in adult jails is criticized for a number of reasons. Holding juveniles in adult jails places young people at greater risk of being physically, sexually, and mentally abused by adult offenders. Juvenile girls are especially vulnerable to sexual assault. Juveniles in adult jail are almost eight times more likely to commit suicide than are those in juvenile detention centers. One explanation is that juveniles are held in isolated parts of adult jails where they receive less staff support and supervision. Another is that jail staff are not trained to recognize depression in juveniles.

The U.S. Congress has discussed bills that would bar most juveniles charged as adults from being detained in adult jails unless a court finds, after a hearing, that it is in the interest of justice to do so. However, to date the Congress has not acted on any of the proposals.

JAIL ISSUES

All jail managers agreed that inmates are arriving in jail with more serious and costly mental health problems that they (the jail managers) are responsible for treating. Sheriffs and jail managers from across the United States met in 2007 and again in 2012 to make recommendations to the Justice Department.[58] They said they need other agencies and resources in the community to help share the burden of the treatment. Jails may be able to do a relatively good job of stabilizing a mentally ill person while he or she is in jail but are incapable of dealing with long-term needs. As a result, once released, the inmates reoffend and come back to jail.

We conclude this chapter by elaborating on other concerns of jail managers: privatization, reentry, accreditation, and evidence-based practices.

Privatization

CO6-7

privatization

A contract process that shifts public functions, responsibilities, and capital assets, in whole or in part, from the public sector to the private sector.

Jail Privatization

Privatization is defined as a contract process that shifts public functions, responsibilities, and capital assets, in whole or in part, from the public sector to the private sector.

Jails can be privatized in one of three ways: through private management, private sector development, or private services provision. With private management, private firms have total responsibility for the operation of a facility. This is the most common application of the term *privatization* and the most controversial aspect of the private sector's involvement in corrections.

With private sector development, the private sector develops, designs, and finances or arranges for the financing of jails. This often involves owning the jail and leasing it back to the jurisdiction through a lease/purchase contract, which serves as an alternative to a public bond issue or tax increase.

For private services provision, jails contract with private vendors to run services such as health and dental care, alcohol and drug treatment, mental health services, food service, training, and programming. This is the most familiar privatization model and the least controversial.

The debate between proponents and opponents of jail privatization surfaced early and continues today. Pressures for privatization come from escalating costs and crowded jails as well as from general dissatisfaction with county government. Jail privatization is sometimes seen as a practical option when a jurisdiction needs to update facilities quickly in response to a court order for additional capacity. Advocates of privatization claim that private organizations can operate facilities more efficiently and cost-effectively.

Opponents of jail privatization dispute cost comparisons or dismiss them altogether. Some insist that the fundamental point is that it is the responsibility of local governments to operate jails, not to delegate power and liability. Opponents believe that the administration of justice is a basic function of government and a symbol of state authority and should not be delegated. From this perspective, jails are, as John J. DiIulio Jr., University of Pennsylvania professor of politics, religion, and civil society, once put it, "a public trust to be administered on behalf of the community and in the name of civility and justice."[59]

Opponents also fear that if we privatize jails, we risk enabling private corporations to use their political influence to continue programs not in the public interest. For example, would private contractors keep jail occupancy rates high to maintain profit? Might private contractors accept only the best inmates, leaving the most troublesome for public facilities to handle?

© Jill Fuller

Jill M. Fuller

Case Manager, Post-Release Services—The GEO Group, Inc., Boca Raton, Florida

Jill M. Fuller is a case manager for The GEO Group's Post Release Services department in the Continuum of Care division. She works closely with returning citizens shortly before their release date and throughout their initial year of reentry to overcome obstacles and promote a successful transition back into society. The ultimate goals of her position are to establish a smooth transition from incarceration to the community, support returning citizens in their reentry efforts, decrease recidivism, and create safer communities.

Jill attended Florida Atlantic University for her undergraduate work and earned a bachelor's degree in criminology and criminal justice. She furthered her education through FAU with a master's of science in criminology and criminal justice, with a concentration in crime and criminal behavior. During her graduate career, she was selected for an internship with The GEO Group Inc. in its Research department. This provided her the opportunity to gain knowledge and experience in the field, while establishing herself in the company.

Jill possesses excellent communication and organizational skills, which have translated to success in developing key community resource relationships and providing a high level of case management with the returning citizens. She aspires to continue growing reentry initiatives and introducing positive and rehabilitative programs to those both currently and formerly incarcerated. Accordingly, Jill completed her master's degree capstone requirement on the topic of correctional facility dog training programs, detailing their positive effects on criminal attitudes and behaviors and their ability to address key issues in reentry and desistance.

> *"My advice for anyone interested in a career in reentry is to participate in an internship, advocate for returning citizens, and encourage community understanding in the importance of reentry services."*

Turning a jail over to a private corporation also raises questions about accountability. Who is responsible for monitoring the performance of the private contractor? Who will see that local laws and regulations are followed? As jail incarceration rates continue to rise, the debate over privatizing jails and the competition for new contracts will continue.

Jail Reentry (Begins at Entry)

Another solution to jail crowding is jail **reentry**, the process of transition that offenders make from prison or jail to the community. (We return to a discussion of reentry in Chapter 8.) It seems only natural to add jail reentry to the list of strategies so that fewer people, once released, return to jail.

Evidence suggests that improving inmate job skills, helping inmates find jobs upon release, and increasing inmate wage potential all have a significant impact on recidivism.[60] We find success stories in small rural jails and in large urban jails. Jim Parsons, director of the Vera Institute of Justice Substance Use and Mental Health Programs, describes three promising approaches to reentry that are particularly well suited to jail settings: (1) the use of administrative records as a way to target scarce resources to what we referred to earlier as "frequent fliers," those who are likely to benefit the most from receiving reentry services, (2) the Assess, Plan, Identify and Coordinate (APIC) model, and (3) strengths-based approaches to jail reentry programming.[61]

reentry

The transition offenders make from prison or jail to the community.

Using Jail Data to Target Frequent Fliers Cities in Connecticut and New York have created the Frequent Users Service Enhancement (FUSE) initiative to provide housing services for chronic users of both jail and shelter systems. FUSE providers in New York City conduct a quarterly data match between the city's jail and shelter records to identify people who meet the program's criteria of at least four jail and four shelter stays during the preceding five-year period. Preliminary results from an evaluation of the FUSE model in Connecticut found that the first 30 recruits to the program had incurred an estimated $12 million in lifetime jail and shelter system costs.

Once the list of the names has been produced, service providers match them against jail and shelter rosters to identify those who are eligible for FUSE's targeted housing supports.

Another approach to targeting reentry services is the Vera Institute of Justice's Service Priority Indicator (SPI). It uses four pieces of data that predict readmission to jail custody within one year of release: people who (1) were younger than 20 at admission, (2) had a current charge for either a property or drug offense, (3) had a specified number of prior jail admissions, and (4) had a jail admission within the previous eight weeks.

Based on these factors, the SPI classifies people as having "low," "medium," "high," or "very high" risk of recidivism. The SPI differentiates between the four groups and has found that 24 percent of the "low"-risk group readmitted to jail custody within one year of release compared with 84 percent of the "very high"-risk group.

The SPI addresses the limited resources available to conduct lengthy risk assessment interviews by providing an instrument for recidivism risk that can be automatically generated for every person as part of the standard jail intake system. Although the SPI is not designed to replace more detailed, in-person risk and needs assessments, it provides a method for directing available resources to individuals with an elevated risk of recidivism who may benefit from a more in-depth assessment.

APIC The APIC acronym summarizes the four essential stages of reentry service provision: *a*ssessing risks and needs, *p*lanning for treatment based on the assessment, *i*dentifying appropriate providers in the jail and in the community to address the inmate's needs, and *c*oordinating the transition back to the community and ensuring continuity of care. The APIC model also identifies a variety of commonly occurring reentry service needs, including housing, inpatient and outpatient treatment for mental health and substance abuse disorders, medication, counseling and other behavioral health services, medical care, income support and benefits, food and clothing, child care, and transportation.

Family and Peer Networks Families are often the primary source of financial and emotional support when people return from jail or prison. In addition, family contacts can be instrumental in helping former inmates identify employment opportunities and find housing. Helping people maintain contact with their families and intimate partners while they are incarcerated has been shown to improve both short- and long-term outcomes, buffering returning inmates from the damaging effects of incarceration.

Reentry strategies that support families are also important for the children and partners of people who were formerly incarcerated. The Bureau of Justice Statistics estimates that approximately 1.7 million children under the age of 18 in the United States have at least one parent in state or federal prison. An equivalent national figure is not available for jails,

In partnership with Shawsheen Valley Technical High School, the Culinary Arts Program at the Middlesex Jail and House of Correction (Billerica, Massachusetts) prepares inmates for careers in food service. At the end of the 12-week course, inmates receive a five-year ServSave National Restaurant Association certificate and 12 credits in culinary arts from Middlesex Community College. What are the pros and cons of teaching jail inmates new vocational skills?

© Photo by Pat Greenhouse/The Boston Globe via Getty Images

but estimates based on prison parenthood data suggest that there are between 700,000 and 800,000 children with at least one parent in jail on any given day.

Services that build on peer and family support networks are particularly suited to jails where families often live close by and tend to have relatively easy access to their incarcerated relatives. The Family Justice Program of the Vera Institute of Justice develops correctional interventions designed to capitalize on the existing strengths and supports found within families. One such program is the Children of Incarcerated Parents Program (CHIPP), a partnership between the New York City Administration for Children's Service (ACS) and the jail. The program's goal is to maintain and strengthen bonds between children in foster care and their incarcerated parents. One component of CHIPP, the Rikers Island Family Visitation Program, provides dedicated visiting days when children who are in foster care custody can visit their incarcerated parents. On these designated days, ACS transports children to the jail for extended two-hour visits, provides children's toys and games in the jail visiting area, and relaxes the usual rules limiting physical contact between inmates and their visiting relatives.

Educational, Vocational, and Inmate Work Programs

CO6-8

Many jail inmates have poor reading skills. National studies show that more than 40 percent of all jail inmates have less than a ninth-grade education.[62] They also have substance abuse problems and few job skills. They frequently cannot find jobs after they are released or can find only low-paid or temporary work. As a result, they often return to a life of crime.

Studies show that inmates who earn their GEDs while incarcerated are far less likely to return to crime. Educational and vocational programs help offenders help themselves, they boost self-esteem, and they encourage legitimate occupations upon release. Overall, it costs less to educate offenders and teach them job skills than to do nothing to change their attitudes, abilities, and outlooks. Ignoring an offender's educational and vocational

Visit abc13.com/news/jail-inmates-given-second-chance-by-learning-new-skills/1098390/ or scan this code with the QR app on your smartphone or digital device and watch the ABC podcast of Fort Bend County (Houston, Texas) jail inmates given a second chance by learning HVAC job skills. How does this information relate to ideas discussed in this chapter?

deficiencies leaves the offender with fewer marketable skills or qualifications when released, increasing the chance of a return to crime.

On an average day, nearly 20 percent of all jail inmates work at least six hours a day. Some jails go further, creating opportunities for inmates to learn work habits and skills that are in demand in the community, earn wages that apply to their fines, court costs, and family obligations, provide quality goods to consumers, and reduce inmate idleness. Jail industries making headlines include:[63]

- **Lewis County Jail, Chehalis, Washington.** Inmates who meet certain criteria are able to obtain certification in commercial baking and basic kitchen safety for employment in restaurants, cafes, hotels, cafeterias, delis, catering, and institutional operations.
- **Lafayette Parish, Louisiana.** Inmates manufacture and deliver can liners for trash and garbage use to government or nonprofit agencies in the state of Louisiana.
- **Two Bridges Regional Jail, Maine.** Inmates in one of the newest jail industries programs in the country design and fabricate wood items.
- **Franklin County Jail, Pennsylvania.** Inmates produce the newsletter for the Council for the Arts and wash, dry, and deliver uniforms for the Chambersburg Cardinals, a minor league football team.
- **Los Angeles Sheriff's Department Jail Enterprise Unit, California.** Inmates produce lunch and trash bags for the sheriff's food service unit, saving the sheriff's office over $100,000 annually instead of purchasing the bags.
- **Hampden County Jail, Massachusetts.** Inmates enroll in a Culinary Arts Program at Springfield Technical Community College and operate the Olde Armory Grille.

Elsewhere across the country, jail inmates are involved in animal grooming, auto repair, body work and detailing, events setup and breakdown, computer data entry, digital imaging, furniture assembly and repair, graphics, laundry, silk-screening, telephone marketing, and welding.

CO6-9 Jail Standards, Inspection, and Accreditation

Dr. Ken Kerle, probably the most known advocate today for improving our nation's jails, wrote recently, ". . . jail inspection is about as popular in many places as a skunk in the living room and many county officials, including sheriffs, would just as soon avoid it altogether. It is no accident that 12 states today have no jail inspections and 8 states with inspection standards have no enforcement agency to compel compliance."[64]

On the other hand, other states such as Illinois, New York, Pennsylvania, Ohio, and Texas mandate state oversight of county jails. Texas, for example, has the Commission on Jail Standards, an independent state agency with the authority to develop standards, conduct inspections, and fine or close jails if they fail to comply. New York state statute allows the Commission of Corrections' jail investigators to visit any of the state's prisons or county jails at any time and may view any records they deem necessary to complete their duties. The Commission has a $3 million budget and a full-time nine-member board appointed by the governor. They may close any correctional facility if it is unsafe, unsanitary, or inadequate. Any person who does not obey its orders is guilty of a misdemeanor. The American

Code of Ethics for Jail Officers

As an officer employed in a detention/correctional capacity, I swear (or affirm) to be a good citizen and a credit to my community, state, and nation at all times. I will abstain from questionable behavior which might bring disrepute to the agency for which I work, my family, my community, and my associates. My lifestyle will be above and beyond reproach, and I will constantly strive to set an example of a professional who performs his/her duties according to the laws of our country, state, and community and the policies, procedures, written and verbal orders, and regulations of the agency for which I work.

On the job I promise to

KEEP the institution secure so as to safeguard my community and the lives of the staff, inmates, and visitors on the premises.

WORK with each individual firmly and fairly without regard to rank, status, or condition.

MAINTAIN a positive demeanor when confronted with stressful situations of scorn, ridicule, danger, and/or chaos.

REPORT either in writing or by word of mouth to the proper authorities those things which should be reported and keep silent about matters which are to remain confidential according to the laws and rules of the agency and government.

MANAGE and supervise the inmates in an evenhanded and courteous manner.

REFRAIN at all times from becoming personally involved in the lives of the inmates and their families.

TREAT all visitors to the jail with politeness and respect and do my utmost to ensure that they observe the jail regulations.

TAKE advantage of all education and training opportunities designed to assist me to become a more competent officer.

COMMUNICATE with people in or outside of the jail, whether by phone, written word, or word of mouth, in such a way so as not to reflect in a negative manner upon my agency.

CONTRIBUTE to a jail environment which will keep the inmate involved in activities designed to improve his/her attitude and character.

SUPPORT all activities of a professional nature through membership and participation that will continue to elevate the status of those who operate our nation's jails. Do my best through word and deed to present an image to the public at large of a jail professional, committed to progress for an improved and enlightened criminal justice system.

Adopted by the American Jail Association Board of Directors on November 10, 1991, Revised May 19, 1993.

Ethical Dilemma 6–1: Female offenders have an average of 2.5 children. Increasing numbers of incarcerated, pregnant, and/or parenting women being sentenced to jail have resulted in many more children being separated from their mothers. Should jail administrators concern themselves with providing services for families of jail inmates? For more information, go to Ethical Dilemma 6–1 at www.justicestudies.com/ethics08.

Ethical Dilemma 6–2: Sometimes administrators must make hard decisions when faced with budget cuts. As a jail administrator, you must cut one position, either a correctional officer or a teacher. Which position will you cut? Why? For more information, go to Ethical Dilemma 6–2 at www.justicestudies.com/ethics08.

Ethical Dilemmas for every chapter are available online.

Source: Copyright © American Jail Association. Reprinted with permission.

Bar Association agrees with independent oversight and authority to act. It recommends that all federal, state, tribal, and territorial governments create independent bodies with broad authority and access to corrections facilities.[65] The American Jail Association's Code of Ethics for Jail Officers is shown in the Ethics and Professionalism box.

Jail accreditation is a process through which correctional facilities and agencies can measure themselves against nationally adopted standards and through which they can receive formal recognition and accredited status. Although jails were slow to respond to the standards movement, their

jail accreditation

Process through which correctional facilities and agencies can measure themselves against nationally adopted standards and through which they can receive formal recognition and accredited status.

response has increased in recent years. More than 130 adult local detention facilities have been accredited by ACA.

There are several reasons jails have been slow to adopt national standards or seek national accreditation. First, accreditation is expensive and time-consuming. Many jails do not have the resources to commit to it. This is especially true of small jails that are already overburdened. Second, jails hold relatively few long-term inmates. Few inmates are in a jail long enough to file a successful legal action regarding poor conditions in the jail. Knowing this, some jail administrators may not be willing to undergo the expense and burden of seeking accreditation. Third, some states have their own standards that jails must meet.

There are, however, at least five reasons for jails to have national accreditation:

1. Accreditation by the ACA indicates that a jail adheres to strict standards to protect the health and safety of staff and inmates.

2. Being accredited may help a jail defend itself against lawsuits over conditions of incarceration.

3. In preparing for the accreditation review, the sheriff's office may evaluate all operations, procedures, and policies, leading to better management practices.

4. With accreditation come professional recognition and status, greater appreciation by the community, and a sense of pride in the achievement and in the hard work that went into it.

5. And recently, ACA in conjunction with the American Jail Association, National Sheriff's Association, National Institute of Corrections, and the Federal Bureau of Prisons developed a set of core jail standards to establish minimum practices for small- and medium-size facilities. This new option makes certification easier now for small- and medium-size jails.

CO6-10   Evidence-Based Practices

The final priority identified by the group of sheriffs and jail administrators in 2007 and reiterated in 2012 relates to evidence-based practices. The body of jail-related research is very small compared to what is known about prisons, yet the sheriffs and jail administrators agreed that if more was known about what works in jails, they would be able to improve everything from efficiency and cost-effectiveness to public safety, agency accountability, and proactive planning.

Recognizing the role that drug abuse plays in criminal behavior, researchers asked sheriffs and jail administrators which of the 13 evidence-based practices recommended by the National Institute on Drug Abuse they implemented in their jails to treat substance abuse. The researchers found that jail administrators reported implementing an average of only 1.6 (see Exhibit 6–13).[66] Only four best practices are used in more than half of all jails: (1) comprehensive treatment methods to address offenders' multiple needs, (2) engagement with community agencies to provide services for drug-involved offenders, (3) use of positive incentives to encourage inmate behavior, and (4) use of standardized substance abuse assessment tools to understand the extent and impact of drug usage.

In spite of the fact that half of the jails use these four evidence-based practices, however, the jails have not conducted the rigorous evaluations that are necessary to show the impact the practices have on reduced criminal activity.

EXHIBIT 6–13   Percentage of Jails That Use Evidence-Based Practices to Treat Substance Abuse

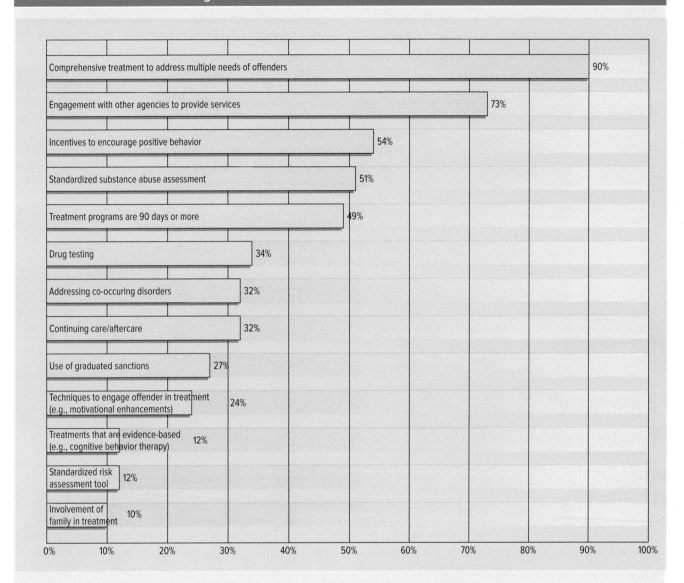

Comprehensive treatment to address multiple needs of offenders — 90%

Engagement with other agencies to provide services — 73%

Incentives to encourage positive behavior — 54%

Standardized substance abuse assessment — 51%

Treatment programs are 90 days or more — 49%

Drug testing — 34%

Addressing co-occuring disorders — 32%

Continuing care/aftercare — 32%

Use of graduated sanctions — 27%

Techniques to engage offender in treatment (e.g., motivational enhancements) — 24%

Treatments that are evidence-based (e.g., cognitive behavior therapy) — 12%

Standardized risk assessment tool — 12%

Involvement of family in treatment — 10%

Source: Adapted from Peter D. Friedman, Faye S. Taxman, and Craig E. Henderson, "Evidence-Based Treatment Practices for Drug-Involved Adults in the Criminal Justice System," *Journal of Substance Abuse Treatment,* vol. 32, no. 3 (2007), pp. 267–277.

PRISONERS CONFINED IN JAIL AND CALIFORNIA'S REALIGNMENT

CO6-11

In 2011, the U.S. Supreme Court ordered California to reduce prison over-crowding by 113,700 people by June 2013. To reduce the state prison population and minimize recidivism, California implemented Public Safety Realignment ("Realignment") under Assembly Bill (AB) 109 in October 2011. This policy redirected people convicted of nonserious, nonviolent, and nonsexual offenses from state to county jurisdiction. Most people convicted of these low-level offenses now serve their sentences in county jails rather than state prison and are supervised by county probation rather than state parole. Realignment also required most people who violate parole and return to custody to be incarcerated in county jail rather than state prison. When Realignment was implemented, concerns emerged that the new policy would increase crime. However, after Realignment, both violent crime and property crime rates generally declined, continuing the trends of the last two decades.[67]

Contrary to alarms raised about potential increases in crime, consistent reports examining offenses at the county level over time show Realignment and crime do not have a causal relationship. Vehicle theft, and theft in general, also do not appear to be worsening in counties with lower rates of nonviolent crime compared to those with the highest rates.

During the first three years of Realignment, the number of inmates counties had to release early from local jails because of space constraints increased by 37 percent across the state. However, in 2014, California voters approved Proposition 47, which reduced six different felonies—among them drug possession—to misdemeanors. The new law helped the state reach its court-ordered prison population goal and has acted as a release valve for counties, which are reporting a drop in jail populations. Many of the felonies covered by Realignment—those low-level crimes that no longer warrant state prison—are now misdemeanors that may not even require county jail.

REVIEW AND APPLICATIONS

SUMMARY

1 Some bail release options require money or property while others do not. Concerns over money bail have given rise to new alternatives.

2 The *daily* population of jails is lower than that of prisons, but the *annual* total of people incarcerated in jails is higher.

3 There are 3,283 locally operated jails in the United States. Besides incarcerating people who have sentences of a year or less, jails serve a number of purposes. They hold people awaiting trial, probation and parole violators, adults and juveniles awaiting transfer, and prison inmates about to be released. Sometimes they operate community-based programs. The jail population is different from the prison population in terms of total admissions and average daily population.

4 Jails emerged in Europe in the 12th century to detain offenders for trial. In the 15th and 16th centuries, the poor and unemployed were detained alongside criminals. The first jail in America was the Walnut Street Jail. Quakers designed it according to their principles of religious reflection and penance. It fell short of reaching its goals and closed in 1835.

5 American jails have progressed through three phases of architecture and inmate management: first-generation jails (linear design and sporadic supervision), second-generation jails (pod design and remote supervision), and third-generation jails (pod design and direct supervision).

6 By mid-2011, jails held or supervised 808,070 offenders, which was significantly lower than the peak of 858,385 inmates at midyear 2008. An estimated 37 percent of jail inmates are convicted offenders. Women represent 15 percent of the jail population; nonwhites, 53 percent; and juveniles, 0.6 percent. Almost two-thirds of all jail inmates have a mental health problem, and there are more people with mental illness in jail than there are in mental health hospitals. Suicide is the leading cause of death in jails, jail homicides are up, and 3.2 percent of all jail inmates experienced one or more incidents of sexual victimization involving another inmate or staff. By mid-2014, 84 percent of jail capacity was occupied. Thirty-seven jails are privatized. The most (eight) are in Texas.

7 Advocates of privatization claim they can build and operate jails more efficiently than can government. Opponents argue they cannot, or they dismiss the cost issues altogether. For them, operating a jail is a basic function of government and a symbol of state authority and should not be delegated.

8 Jail vocational and educational programs are important avenues for managing inmates, reducing recidivism, and successful reentry. They keep inmates occupied, boost self-esteem, and help inmates find jobs after release.

9 Jail standards, inspection, and accreditation are important for five reasons. First, inspection and accreditation indicate that a jail adheres to strict standards. Second, accreditation may help a jail defend itself against lawsuits over conditions of incarceration. Third, through inspection and accreditation, the sheriff's office may evaluate all jail operations, procedures, and policies, leading to better management practices. Fourth, accreditation generates professional recognition and status, greater appreciation by the community, and a sense of pride. And fifth, the ACA in conjunction with the American Jail Association, National Sheriff's Association, National Institute of Corrections, and the Federal Bureau of Prisons now has a set of core jail standards to establish minimum practices for small- and medium-size facilities. This new option makes certification easier for small- and medium-size jails.

10 The National Institute on Drug Abuse recommends 13 key evidence-based practices to treat substance abuse. However, jails implement an average of only 1.6. Four evidence-based practices are used in more than one-half of all jails. However, jails have not conducted scientific evaluations to show the impact the practices have on reduced criminal activity.

11 California's realignment act is the shift of responsibility for adult offenders and parolees from the state to the counties. The new law mandates that individuals sentenced for nonserious, nonviolent, or nonsex offenses will serve their sentences in county jails instead of state prison and will be supervised by county probation departments rather than state parole officers.

KEY TERMS

bail, p. 127	second-generation jail, p. 134	privatization, p. 152
pretrial detainee, p. 127	third-generation jail, p. 135	reentry, p. 153
jails, p. 130	direct-supervision jail, p. 135	jail accreditation, p. 157
total admission, p. 130	rated capacity, p. 148	
average daily population (ADP), p. 130	pay-to-stay jail, p. 150	
first-generation jail, p. 134	self-pay jails, p. 150	

QUESTIONS FOR REVIEW

1 What is the purpose of bail? Discuss bail release options and the concerns over money bail.

2 Describe how jail populations are different from prison populations.

3 Jails serve a number of purposes. Which do you believe is the most important and why?

4 Summarize the history of jails.

5 Explain how first-, second-, and third-generation jails differ.

6 What can you infer from the characteristics of jail inmates, facilities, and staff?

7 What ideas can you add to the arguments for and against jail privatization?

8 How do jail vocational and educational programs affect inmate behavior, recidivism, and reentry?

9 What ideas can you add to the arguments for and against jail standards, inspection, and accreditation?

10 Explain how jails could do more to implement evidence-based practices to treat substance abuse and demonstrate their impact on reduced criminal activity.

11 Explain the impact of California's realignment act on local jails and probation departments.

THINKING CRITICALLY ABOUT CORRECTIONS

Mentally Ill Inmates

Explain why mentally ill jail inmates should not be subjects for incarceration as some suggest, and why jails are ill-equipped to meet their needs.

Evidence-Based Practices

Why are evidence-based practices necessary for jails?

ON-THE-JOB DECISION MAKING

Promoting Direct Supervision

You are the administrator of a new county jail with the architecture and philosophy of direct supervision. The new jail replaced a jail built in 1912. Some of the senior staff have begun complaining to you about direct supervision. They say they don't like to interact with inmates. They talk about "the good old days" when inmates were "on the other side" of the reinforced glass and steel bars. There's even been a letter to the editor in the local newspaper complaining that the new jail doesn't "look like a jail."

1. What could you tell the senior staff about direct-supervision philosophy that might ease their concerns?
2. What strategies might you use to educate the public about the benefits of direct supervision?

Jail Tips for Justice Involved Women

The National Resource Center for Justice Involved Women and the American Jail Association developed a series of eight jail tip sheets to facilitate the implementation of gender-informed approaches with women in jail. Each tip sheet includes a brief overview of the topic, selected evidence-based research findings, and brief action steps that jail leadership and staff can take to enhance gender responsive practices. Locate the tip sheets at cjinvolvedwomen.org/jail-tip-sheets. After reviewing the tip sheets, assume you are a jail administrator. How would you encourage "buy-in" from your jail staff to follow research-based guidelines and change your facility's culture or norms that are based almost exclusively on gender neutral operational practices?

PRISONS TODAY

Change Stations or Warehouses?

© American Correctional Association.

CHAPTER OBJECTIVES

After completing this chapter you should be able to do the following:

1 Explain the differences between the Pennsylvania and Auburn prison systems.

2 Outline the nine eras of prison development.

3 Describe the characteristics of today's prisoners and discuss reasons for the incarceration of women and minority prisoners.

4 Explain what the evidence-based literature says about prison industries.

5 Report on the availability of education programs for prisoners.

6 Compare state and federal prison organization and administration.

7 Discuss the reasons prisons are overcrowded and the methods for controlling prison overcrowding.

8 Outline the emergence of supermax housing and its impact on prisoners and staff.

9 Discuss the impact of technology on corrections.

Without education, job skills, and other basic services, offenders are likely to repeat the same steps that brought them to prison in the first place. . . . This is a problem that needs to be addressed head-on. We cannot say we are doing everything we can to keep our communities and our families safe if we are not addressing the high rate at which offenders are becoming repeat criminals.

—Louisiana Governor Bobby Jindal (R), March 18, 2011

Jared Fogle, once the poster child for Subway after eating 700 sub sandwiches in a little less than one year and losing 245 pounds, went from a food addiction to a sex addiction. On November 19, 2015, Fogle was sentenced to 15 years and 8 months in federal prison after pleading guilty to child pornography and sex charges. U.S. District Court Judge Tanya Walton Pratt said Fogle must serve a minimum of 13 years before becoming eligible for time off with good behavior. After serving his sentence at the Federal Correctional Institution in Englewood, Colorado (a low-security federal prison with a program for sex offenders), Fogle will be on supervised release for the rest of his life. Judge Pratt also fined Fogle $175,000 and ordered him to forfeit $50,000 in assets and pay $1.4 million in restitution to 14 victims who are minors. Fogle's Federal Bureau of Prison inmate number is 12919-028. His earliest possible release date is July 11, 2029. What is a low-security prison, what types of offenders are confined there, and do you believe a low-security facility is appropriate for Fogle?

© AP Photo/Michael Conroy

From 2000 to 2015, Jared Fogle was the spokesperson for Subway's advertising campaign. He made more than 300 commercials attributing his weight loss of 245 pounds to eating turkey and veggie subs and exercising. But in 2015, the FBI and Indiana State Police seized Fogle's computers and other electronic equipment. Fogle pleaded guilty to distribution and receipt of child pornography and traveling from Indiana to New York City to engage in sexual acts with a 17-year-old girl. In November 2015, Fogle was sentenced to 15 years and 8 months in federal prison. He must serve a minimum of 13 years before becoming eligible for time off with good behavior, and he will be on supervised release for the rest of his life. Three days after his sentence, Fogle's wife, Kathleen McLaughlin, divorced him and said in court papers that Fogle was a deadbeat dad who spent too much time traveling and not enough time with his four-year-old son and two-year-old daughter.[1]

Later in this chapter, you will learn more about state and federal prison systems. We begin the chapter with a brief look at the history of American prisons. Then we discuss the composition of the prison population, programs for prisoners, the way America's prisons are organized and administered, why prisons are overcrowded, what can be done to reduce overcrowding, the issues surrounding supermax prisons, and how technology is shaping corrections.

Visit http://www.youtube.com/watch?v=0ikUWU3cbq8 or scan this code with the QR app on your smartphone or digital device and watch the podcast of Philadelphia's Eastern State Penitentiary illustrated with period lithographs, engravings, and photographs and understand the history of the prison from its initial practice of total solitary confinement through its transformation into an overcrowded "big house" to its replacement with a modern facility in 1970. How does this information relate to ideas discussed in this chapter?

CO7-1 HISTORY OF PRISONS IN AMERICA

Prisons are relatively modern social institutions, and their development is distinctly American. Until the mid-18th century, fines, banishment from the community, corporal punishment, and execution were the primary forms of punishing offenders. By the latter part of the century, incarceration was championed as a more humane form of punishment. It reflected and fueled a shift from the assumption that offenders were inherently criminal to a belief that they were simply not properly trained to resist temptation and corruption. The two prison systems that emerged in the United States—the Pennsylvania system and the Auburn system—were copied throughout the world.

The Pennsylvania and Auburn prison systems developed in the United States at the turn of the 19th century. Pennsylvania Quakers advocated a method of punishment more humane than the public corporal punishment used at the time. The Quakers shifted the emphasis from punishing the body to reforming the mind and soul. Together with an elite group of 18th-century Philadelphians, they ushered in the first **penitentiary,** a place for reform of offenders through repentance and rehabilitation. They believed prisoners needed to be isolated from each other in silence to repent, to accept God's guidance, and to avoid having a harmful influence on each other. Known as the **Pennsylvania system** or the **separate system,** the Eastern State Penitentiary, was designed for solitary confinement and labor with instruction in labor, morals, and religion.

The solitary confinement of the Pennsylvania system was expensive, and it reportedly drove prisoners insane and further hardened criminal tendencies. Reformers responded with what has been termed the **Auburn system:** regimentation, military-style drill, silence unless conversation was required in workshops, congregate working and eating, separation of prisoners into small individual cells at night, harsh discipline, shaved heads, black-and-white striped uniforms, and industrial workshops that contracted with private businesses to help pay for the institution. Prison factories in the 19th century produced shoes, barrels, carpets, engines, boilers, harnesses, clothing, and furniture—goods that could not be produced under the "solitary" system of Pennsylvania or not in quantities sufficient to make a profit. The first prison to use this system opened in Auburn, New York, in 1819. The Auburn system, congregate by day and separate by night, eventually gave way to congregate cells at night and removal of the restrictions against talking.

In the United States, the two competing philosophies of prison life clashed, and the debate over which system was superior raged on for decades. In the end, the Auburn system won out, but not because of any sympathy for the mental health of the prisoners. Pure and simple, the Auburn model was less expensive to build, and its congregate labor system

Interior view of a cellblock at Eastern State Penitentiary. Linear design and sporadic inmate supervision characterized Eastern State. What problems emerged at Eastern State that caused the demise of the Pennsylvania system?

© Frank Schmalleger

penitentiary

The earliest form of large-scale incarceration. It punished criminals by isolating them so that they could reflect on their misdeeds, repent, and reform.

Pennsylvania system (also *separate system*)

The first historical phase of prison discipline, involving solitary confinement in silence instead of corporal punishment; conceived by the American Quakers in 1790 and implemented at the Walnut Street Jail.

Auburn system

The second historical phase of prison discipline, implemented at New York's Auburn prison in 1815. It followed the Pennsylvania system and allowed inmates to work silently together during the day, but they were isolated at night. Eventually sleeping cells became congregate and restrictions against talking were removed.

The Eastern State Penitentiary, completed in 1829, was designed on the Quakers' principle of solitary confinement in silence with instruction in labor, morals, and religion. What name was given to this separate system of prisoner management?

© Paul Marotta/Getty Images

EXHIBIT 7-1	Stages of Prison History in the United States			
Stage	**Penitentiary Era**	**Mass Prison Era**	**Reformatory Era**	**Industrial Era**
Years	1790–1825	1825–1876	1876–1890	1890–1935
Goal	Rehabilitation and deterrence	Incapacitation and deterrence	Rehabilitation	Incapacitation
Characteristics	Separate and silent Congregate and silent	Congregate labor and living spaces without silence Contract prison labor	Indeterminate sentencing Parole	Public accounts industries Contract labor State-use labor Convict lease Public works labor
Examples of Institutions	Walnut Street Penitentiary, Philadelphia, PA Eastern State Penitentiary, Cherry Hill, PA Auburn Prison, Auburn, NY	Sing Sing Prison, Ossining, NY San Quentin State Prison, San Quentin, CA	Elmira, NY Indiana Reformatory for Women and Girls, Indianapolis, IN	Most major prisons
Related Events	1819 Auburn Penitentiary, New York, implements congregate, silent system. 1829 Eastern State Penitentiary opens under the Pennsylvania prison model.	1841 John Augustus begins the practice of probation in Massachusetts. 1871 *Ruffin* v. *Commonwealth* establishes that convicted felons not only forfeit liberty but also are slaves of the state; this provides the legal justification for courts to maintain a "hands-off doctrine." 1913 Eastern State Penitentiary converts to the Auburn prison model.	1876 The first women's prison, the Indiana Reformatory for Women and Girls, opens. 1876 Zebulon Brockway is appointed warden at Elmira Reformatory and initiates first parole system in the United States. 1878 First probation law is passed in Massachusetts.	1891 Federal prison system established. 1899 First juvenile court established in Cook County (Chicago), Illinois. 1914–1918 World War. 1929 Hawes-Cooper Act is passed to regulate interstate sale of prison-made goods. 1929 Great Depression begins. 1930 Federal Bureau of Prisons is established.

CO7-2 and factories resulted in higher productivity in the prison and higher profits for the state. The Pennsylvania system limited the type of work an inmate could do; hence, the costs of imprisonment were too high for the state to bear. In 1913, Eastern State Penitentiary, the epitome of the Pennsylvania system, converted to the Auburn system, ending the great debate. Congregate prisons have been the mode ever since. Today, however, new voices are calling for a return to long-term solitary confinement in supermax prisons (something we will discuss later in this chapter). Prisons in the United States have progressed through nine stages of development (see Exhibit 7–1).

EXHIBIT 7-1	Stages of Prison History in the United States *(continued)*

Punitive Era	Treatment Era	Community-Based Era	Warehousing Era	Just Deserts Era
1935–1945	1945–1967	1967–1980	1980–1995	1985–Present
Retribution	Rehabilitation	Reintegration	Incapacitation	Retribution
Strict punishment and custody	Medical model Emerging prisoner unrest	Intermediate sanction: halfway houses, work release centers, group homes, fines, restitution, community service	Sentencing guidelines End of discretionary parole release Serious crowding More prison riots	Just deserts Determinate sentencing Truth in sentencing Three-strikes law Serious crowding
U.S. Penitentiary, Alcatraz, CA	Patuxent Institution, Jessup, MD	Major prison riots (Attica, NY; Santa Fe, NM)	Most major prisons	Spreading through the United States
1934 Alcatraz ("Hellcatraz") opens. 1939 Great Depression ends. 1939–1945 World War II begins and ends. 1942–1945 Japanese and Japanese American relocation centers open and close.	1950 Federal Youth Corrections Act is passed to create treatment for offenders under the age of 22 in the federal system. 1964 *Cooper* v. *Pate* formally recognizes the constitutional rights of prisoners. 1967 *In re Gault,* U.S. Supreme Court rules that juvenile offenders are entitled to state-provided counsel and due process guarantees. 1967 President Johnson's Commission on Law Enforcement and Administration of Justice recommends changing the criminal justice system.	1970 Massachusetts becomes first state to close all of its juvenile reform schools. 1974 Robert Martinson's "What Works" is published and is used by politicians as reason to pull resources from prisons. 1976 Maine is first state to abolish discretionary parole board release. 1979 Prison Industry Enhancement (PIE) certification program repeals limitations on interstate commerce in prison-made goods.	1980s President Reagan declares "war on drugs." 1984 Federal Sentencing Reform Act imposes mandatory sentences for specific crimes. 1993 Three-strikes-and-you're-out laws spread across the United States. 1994 Congress passes the Violent Crime Control and Law Enforcement Act, which increases financial incentives for states to put more violent criminals in prison.	1994 Federal Bureau of Prisons opens its super-max prison. 1995 Eight states reinstate chain gangs. 1999 Number of people incarcerated in the United States exceeds 2 million for the first time. 2004 Abuse of prisoners at Abu Ghraib prison in Baghdad, Iraq, by U.S. military personnel becomes public. 2005 U.S. Supreme Court's *Booker* decision ruled it is in violation of the Sixth Amendment right to a trial by jury to enhance a sentence using facts not reviewed by the jury. 2007 Evidence-based research and economic recession shape correctional practice. 2008 President Bush signs Second Chance Act authorizing federal funds for state and federal reentry programs. 2010 Federal Fair Sentencing Act reduces disparity in sentencing between crack and powder cocaine offenses. 2011 California's Public Safety Realignment shifts states prisoners to county jails. 2014 U.S. Sentencing Commission voted unanimously to reduce sentencing guidelines for most federal drug trafficking offenders.

© Bettmann/Corbis

Visit https://www.youtube.com/ watch?v=FKiQi90U2AU or scan this code with the QR app on your smartphone or digital device and watch the podcast of prison history. How does this information relate to ideas discussed in this chapter?

Visit http://www.sentencingproject.org/. Click "Facts" and then "State-by-State Data" or scan this code with the QR app on your smartphone or digital device andview and compare key state criminal justice data. How does this information relate to ideas discussed in this chapter?

WHO IS IN PRISON TODAY?

The United States is the world's leader in incarceration. Holding only 5 percent of the world's population, the United States holds 25 percent of the world's prisoners and 30 percent of the world's incarcerated women. And the trend does not seem to be changing. From 1999 until 2015, the number of people in U.S. prisons has stabilized. On January 1, 2015, 1,561,500 prisoners were held in state and federal prisons, a decrease of only 1 percent from one year earlier.[2]

Today, 1 in every 143 U.S. persons is under the jurisdiction of a state or federal prison. If we include all correctional populations (probation, parole, jail, and prison), 1 in every 32 adults is under correctional control. Twenty-five years ago it was 1 in every 77. Most of this increase is a result of changes in sentencing, law and policy, not changes in crime rates. This explosion in the correctional population presents enormous challenges for public safety and public spending as this and other chapters explain.

The imprisonment rate—the number of sentenced prisoners per 100,000 U.S. residents—declined for the fourth straight year, falling to 471 from 492 in 2011. The rate of imprisoned people per 100,000 ranged from 60 in the federal prison system (the lowest) to 816 in Louisiana (the highest). Prison statistics among the states and the federal government are shown in Exhibit 7–2.

When prison and jail incarceration rates are combined, the United States imprisons 705 people per 100,000 population, up from 684 in 2000 and 601 in 1995. In terms of prisoners per 100,000 people, that's more than any other country in the world. Russia is second with 629, followed by Rwanda (604), St. Kitts and Nevis (588), and Cuba (531).[3] Almost three-fifths of countries (59 percent) have rates below 150 per 100,000.

States with almost identical populations and crime rates have widely different rates of incarceration. For example, in 2014 Wisconsin had a population of 5.7 million residents, a crime rate per 100,000 population of 2,378 offenses, and an incarceration rate of 371.[4] Minnesota had 5.4 million

EXHIBIT 7-2	Prison Statistics Among the States and the Federal Government, January 1, 2015				
Number of Prisoners Under Jurisdiction		**Incarceration Rate per 100,000 Population of Sentenced Prisoners**		**Number of Female Prisoners Under Jurisdiction**	
5 Highest					
Federal	191,374	Louisiana	816	Texas	12,690
Texas	158,589	Oklahoma	700	Federal	12,560
California	136,088	Alaska	633	Florida	7,303
Florida	102,870	Arkansas	599	California	6,382
Georgia	52,485	Mississippi	597	Ohio	4,208
5 Lowest					
Vermont	1,508	Federal	60	Rhode Island	68
North Dakota	1,603	Maine	153	Vermont	105
Rhode Island	1,880	Rhode Island	178	Maine	142
Maine	2,030	Massachusetts	188	North Dakota	187
Wyoming	2,383	Minnesota	194	Delaware	214

Source: Adapted from E. Ann Carson, *Prisoners in 2014* (Washington, DC: U.S. Department of Justice, Bureau of Justice Statistics, September 2015).

residents, a crime rate of 2,526 offenses, and an incarceration rate of only 194. With similar population and crime rates, Wisconsin's incarceration rate is almost twice as much as Minnesota's.

What causes these disparities among states and their prison use? An interesting answer to this question was provided by Bowers and Waltman. Their investigation of felony sentencing in the United States found that the preferences of the public weigh heavily on the sentencing of violent offenders. More recently, world leaders of the prison administrations of the 45 member countries of the Council of Europe concluded that levels of imprisonment are usually influenced more by political decisions than by levels of crime or rates of detection of crime. They also concluded that jurisdictions can choose to have high or low rates of imprisonment, and this choice is reflected in the sentencing patterns adopted by legislatures.[5] Today, as states grapple with the economic realities of imprisonment, we can see how political decisions about what constitutes dangerousness or seriousness impact prison populations. A decade ago, nonviolent offenders and parole violators would have been incarcerated. Today's economic problems find legislators and policymakers reducing prison time for drug offenders and nonviolent offenders and establishing programs like California's nonrevocable parole (see Chapter 6).

Privately Operated Prisons

The issue of correctional privatization was discussed in Chapter 6. The focus here is on the current use of privately operated prison facilities.

On January 1, 2015, private prisons held 8 percent of state and federal prisoners (40,017 federal and 91,244 state) in 107 privately operated prisons, up from 77,854 inmates in 101 private prisons in 2000.[6] Besides the federal system, 52 percent of the nation's prisoner population is held in nine states: Arizona, Florida, Georgia, Indiana, Mississippi, Ohio, Oklahoma, Tennessee, and Texas.

On August 18, 2016, the BOP delivered a blow to the private prison industry when it announced that it would either not renew contracts for

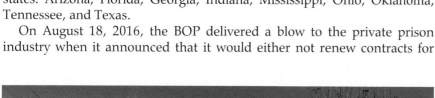

The GEO Group, Inc. is the world's leading provider of correctional, detention, and community reentry services with 104 facilities, approximately 87,000 beds, and 20,500 employees around the world. GEO's Graceville facility (Graceville, Florida) offers in-prison rehabilitation programs with the provision of postrelease and community reentry services through GEO's "Continuum of Care," which is rooted in evidence-based principles known to change criminal behavior. What are evidence-based principles?
© The GEO Group, Inc.

private prison operators when they expire or they will substantially reduce the contracts' scope. The BOP analyzed data from 14 private prisons and 14 BOP prisons with comparable inmate populations to evaluate how the private prisons performed relative to public prisons. The BOP reported that private prisons had more incidents of contraband, assaults (including sexual) by inmates on inmates, inmate fights, disruptive behavior by inmates, staff use of force on inmates, lockdowns, inmate discipline, telephone monitoring, and selected grievances per capita than the BOP facilities. To ensure that contract prisons are, and remain, a safe and secure place for housing federal inmates, the BOP recommended convening a working group of subject experts to evaluate why private prisons had more safety and security incidents than BOP institutions, and identify appropriate action to remedy the situation.

In order to improve monitoring and oversight of federally contracted prisons, the BOP made three recommendations:

1. Verify on a more frequent basis that inmates receive basic medical services.
2. Ensure that private prisons address vital functions related to their contracts, such as periodic validation of officer staffing levels.
3. Reevaluate the Large Secure Adult Contract Oversight Checklist of steps related to important operational areas on a regular basis with input from subject experts to ensure that the operational areas reflect the most important activities for contract compliance and that monitoring and documentation requirements and expectations are clear.

CO7-3 Gender

Women have historically represented a modest share of the prison population. However, since 1980, the number of women in prison has been increasing at a rate 50 percent higher than men. In 1980, 13,300 women were in prison. Today, almost 113,000 women are in state and federal prisons (the largest number since 2009), representing 7 percent of the U.S. prison population (see Exhibit 7–3). If current trends continue, 1 of every 18 black

On January 1, 2015, almost 113,000 women were under state or federal prison jurisdiction, almost 34 percent of them in California, Florida, Texas, and federal prisons. Why are women in prison, and what will it take to reduce their incarceration?

© Nicholas Asfouri/AFP/Getty Images

EXHIBIT 7–3 Persons Under the Jurisdiction of State or Federal Prisons, January 1, 2015

How many persons are under the jurisdiction of state and federal correctional authorities?

14% Federal prisoners

86% State prisoners

1,350,958	State prisoners
210,567	Federal prisoners
1,561,525	Total

Who is in prison?

Gender

7% Women

93% Men

Race/ethnicity*

33% White

22% Hispanic

36% Black

9% Others

*Hispanics may be of any race

Age

10% 55 or older

12% 18–24

19% 45–54

33% 25–34

26% 35–44

Why are they in prison?

State prisoners

53% Violent offenses[a]

1% Unspecified

16% Drug offenses

11% Public order offense[c]

19% Property offenses[b]

a. Violent offenses include murder, rape, assault, and robbery.
b. Property offenses include burglary, larceny/theft, motor vehicle theft, and fraud and other property.
c. Public order offenses include weapons, drunk driving, vice, morals and decency offenses, liquor law violations, and other public order offenses.

Federal prisoners

1% Unspecified

50% Drug offenses

6% Property offenses

7% Violent offenses

36% Public order offenses

Sources: E. Ann Carson, *Prisoner in 2014* (U.S. Department of Justice, Bureau of Justice Statistics, September 2015) and *Fact Sheet: U.S. Prison Population Trends* (Washington, DC: The Sentencing Project, August 2015).

females, 1 of every 45 Hispanic females, and 1 of every 111 white females can expect to spend time in prison.[7] In fact, when we look at women's incarceration in a global context, we find that nearly 30 percent of the world's incarcerated women are in the United States, twice the percentage as in China and four times as much as in Russia.[8] With the exception of Thailand and the United States itself, the top 44 jurisdictions throughout the world with the highest rate of incarcerating women are individual U.S. states.

On January 1, 2015, the federal prison system, along with California, Florida, and Texas, held 34 percent of all female inmates. See Exhibit 7–2 for the jurisdictions with the highest and lowest female prison populations.

The number of state, federal, and private confinement correctional facilities in the United States is 1,292. Minorities make up more than two-thirds of the prison population. Why is that so?

© A. Ramey/Photo Edit

Beth Richie, a professor of African American Studies and criminology, law and justice at the University of Illinois at Chicago, and Elaine Lord, former superintendent of the Bedford Hills Correctional Facility (New York's maximum-security prison for women), describe the racial/ethnic profile of women in prison as one of the most vivid examples of racial disparity in the United States and prison as the worst environment possible for mothers and women with mental illness.[9] Lord quit her job after 20 years because she stopped believing in the confinement of mentally ill women.

The majority of women in prison are women of color. Two-thirds are black, Hispanic, or of other nonwhite ethnic groups. They are also young and poor. Only one-third graduated from high school or earned a GED. Two-thirds have a history of physical or sexual abuse, and 3.5 percent are HIV positive. Three-fourths suffer from major depression and manic psychotic disorders. Sadly, the corrections literature suggests that, despite the fact that some women do quite well putting their lives back together when they are released from prison, most are likely to return to the same disenfranchised neighborhoods and difficult situations without having received any services to address their underlying problems. If it is true, as the corrections literature suggests, that prior arrest history predicts postprison recidivism, then the outlook for women prisoners is bleak: 65 percent of women in prison have a history of prior convictions. One-half have three or more convictions.

Scholars debate the reasons for the increase in women's incarceration over men's. Some suggest that as women moved into jobs from which they were formerly excluded, they gained the opportunities and skills to commit criminal acts for which incarceration was appropriate punishment. Others disagree, saying that poverty of young, female, single heads of households has contributed to the increase in women's crime and incarceration, particularly for property and drug offenses. One scholar put it this way: "The war on drugs has translated into a war on women."[10] Others think the criminal justice system is becoming more "gender blind" due to the emergence of "get-tough" attitudes and sentencing policies. Instead of seeing women offenders as weaker and giving them differential, if not preferential, treatment, judges and juries now sentence women more harshly whether they are first-time drug offenders or they have committed crimes against persons or property. The combined effects of harsh drug laws, changing patterns of drug use, and mandatory sentencing policies have lead to a significant increase in women's incarceration. Almost 25 percent of women in state prisons and almost 60 percent of women in federal prisons are serving time for nonviolent, drug-related offenses. Quite likely, the reason for the increase in women's incarceration is a product of all these theories. To reduce women's incarceration is to understand and implement programs about women's development, trauma, and addiction discussed in Chapter 6.

Race

The primary observation to be made about the prison population in the United States is that minorities are strikingly overrepresented. Although minorities comprise only 20 percent of the U.S. population, they make up more than two-thirds of all incarcerated offenders. Conversely, whites are underrepresented: more than 80 percent of the general population but only 33 percent of the prison population.

If current trends continue, 1 of every 3 black males born today can expect to go to prison in his lifetime as can 1 of every 6 Latino males compared to 1 in 17 white males.[11]

As is the case with so many other criminological controversies, there is a debate over the relationship between race and crime. Official prison data suggest that the reason more minorities are disproportionately in prison, and for longer terms, is differential crime offending. Almost 58 percent of the persons in prison for violent offenses on January 1, 2015, were minority. Recently, two Washington State Supreme Court justices stunned audiences when they said they didn't believe that anyone was in prison because of age, race, disability, and other factors. One of the Justices referred to those who represent the poor as "poverty pimps" and used the words "you people" when stating that black people commit crimes in their own communities.[12]

Others argue that the higher arrest rates, convictions, and sentences to prison of blacks are a function of racial profiling and racism in the criminal justice system. After reviewing 32 state-level studies of the decision to incarcerate and length of sentence imposed, Cassia Spohn, professor of criminology and criminal justice at Arizona State University, concluded there is ample evidence among these studies that, controlling for other relevant factors, blacks and Hispanics are more likely to be incarcerated than whites and, in some jurisdictions, receive longer sentences. And others have found gross racial disparities when arrest and incarceration for drug dependence and abuse are examined at the city and county levels.[13]

Still others argue that although discriminatory practices exist, it is improbable that criminal justice bias alone could account for the disproportionate arrest rates of blacks. They suggest the social problems of unemployment, economic deprivation, social disorganization, and social isolation of the nation's inner cities as additional causes. The inner city, the residence of most of the nation's poor, experiences by far the highest violence rates. Middle-class communities have more resources to deal with offenders, especially drug offenders, and get them into treatment. In low-income communities, those resources are not available, so a drug problem is more likely to develop into a criminal justice problem.

These levels of racial disparity are causing some states to implement racial impact statements. Policymakers routinely require analysis of the fiscal or environmental impact of proposed new laws, and it has been proposed that legislators do the same before implementing new sentencing laws. Iowa and Connecticut (two states with some of the highest black-to-white ratios of incarceration) took the lead among the states and enacted racial impact statements.

Visit https://www.youtube.com/ watch?v=IkFNDIzL9k or scan this code with the QR app on your smartphone or digital device and watch the podcast from the National Research Council that urges policymakers to reconsider sentencing policies and to seek crime-control strategies that are more effective, with better public safety benefits and fewer unwanted consequences. How does this information relate to ideas discussed in this chapter?

Age

The nation's population is aging, and this is reflected in the prison population. Middle-aged and older inmates make up a growing portion of the prison population. In 2000, 56 percent of the nation's prisoners were between 18 and 34 years old, 40 percent were between 35 and 54, and 4 percent were over 55. Today, for the sixth straight year, the representation of 18- to 34-year-olds had decreased to 45 percent, the presence of 35- to 54-year-olds had increased to 45 percent, and the presence of inmates 55 and older had increased to 10 percent (see Exhibit 7–3). In Chapter 12, we'll discuss the issues surrounding older prisoners in more detail.

Most Serious Offense

Another characteristic to compare is the most serious offense of which a prisoner was convicted. On January 1, 2015, 53 percent of state prisoners were held for violent offenses, up from 46 percent in 1995. The percentage of state prisoners held for property offenses dropped from 23 percent in 1995 to 19, and the percentage held for drug offenses dropped from 22 to 16 percent across the same time period. Convictions for public order offenses stayed the same at about 11 percent.

Among federal inmates, persons sentenced for drug offenses constituted the largest group (50 percent), similar to what it was in 1995. Immigration, weapon, and other public order offenders made up approximately 36 percent of the federal prison population up from 18 percent in 1995. The percentage of violent offenders in federal prison was 7 percent, similar to what it was in 1995. And property offenders constituted 6 percent, paralleling what it was in 1995 (see Exhibit 7–3).

Prison Industries

INMATE WORK AND EDUCATION

Among the most important elements of an inmate's institutional experience are the programs and services available. Today there is evidence-based research supporting the success rates against recidivism for correctional work and education programs and services.

But what does success mean? According to one of the best reviews of the current evidence of the effectiveness of adult correctional programming by Aos and his colleagues at the Washington State Institute for Public Policy, it means reducing recidivism by 5 to 15 percent.[14]

CO7-4

Work Assignments

Work is a very important part of institutional management and offender programs. Meaningful work programs are the most powerful tool prison administrators have in managing crowding and idleness, which can lead to disorder and violence. And now the news on prisoner work assignments is even better. The evidence-based reviews mentioned throughout the text show that the average prison work program reduces the recidivism rate of participants by almost 6 percent. Some prison work programs achieve better results, some worse. On average, however, researchers find that the typical prison work program can be expected to reduce recidivism by 6 percent.[15]

Prison work is generally of one of three types: operational assignments within the institution, community projects, or prison industry.

Operational Assignments In operational assignments within the institution, inmates perform tasks necessary to the functioning of the facility or larger corrections system. Institutional maintenance assignments including farm and other agricultural activities are the largest single option for inmate work. Forty-five states, the District of Columbia, and the Bureau of Prisons (BOP) pay inmates a wage for services rendered to the institution. The average wage range for institutional maintenance work is $0.99 to $3.98 per day. Inmates working in institutional maintenance perform the following types of work: laundry, heating and air conditioning repair, building maintenance and custodial service, landscaping and grounds maintenance, and food preparation and service.

Community Projects Many correctional institutions allow inmates to gain work experience through community projects. Offenders contribute their labor to benefit the community while developing job skills in a practical,

Inmates at Folsom State Prison in California learn to inspect, maintain, and repair cars and light trucks and pursue postincarceration employment as automotive service technicians and mechanics. The auto mechanics industry provides mechanical and electrical repair and maintenance work for cars, trucks, vans, and trailers. According to the U.S. Department of Labor, Bureau of Labor Statistics, the employment outlook for automotive service technicians and mechanics is projected to grow 5 percent from 2014 to 2024. What are the benefits of prison industries for inmates, their families, and victims while in prison and after release; for the institution; for the business community; and for taxpayers?
© Hector Amezcua/Sacramento Bee/MCT via Getty Images

nonprison setting. Construction/repair of public property and parks development and maintenance are by far the most common types of community work activities. Examples of other community projects include building houses for low-income persons, painting municipal swimming pools, providing snow removal services, providing backup firefighting services, and delivering antidrug programs in schools. In South Carolina, inmates who meet the criteria for community work build playground equipment, pick up trash on state highways, maintain and clean up state parks, aid flood victims, clean up debris after storm damage, and provide skilled labor for Habitat for Humanity. Inmate work organizations also raise money for the Special Olympics and other charities.

Prison Industry Enhancement Certification Program (PIECP) In 1979, Congress created the Prison Industry Enhancement Certification Program (PIECP) to encourage states and local correctional agencies to form partnerships with private companies to give inmates real work opportunities.

PIECP has two primary objectives: First, to generate products and services that enable prisoners to make a contribution to society, help offset the cost of their incarceration, compensate crime victims, and provide inmate family support. And second, to provide a means of reducing prison idleness, increasing inmate job skills, and improving the prospects for successful inmate transition to the community upon release.

Currently, PIECP operates in 37 states and four counties in the United States. These programs manage more than 175 business partnerships with private industry.[16] Offender salaries generate millions of dollars for victims' programs, inmate family support, for correctional institution room and board costs, state and federal taxes, and mandatory inmate savings.

In addition to PIECP, there are hundreds of innovative prison work programs across the United States. Inmates in many states train guide dogs to aid visually impaired persons, hearing dogs to assist those who are deaf and hearing impaired, and service dogs to assist individuals suffering from various physical needs. Some Colorado inmates construct fish tanks and then raise tilapia that are sold to vendors such as Whole Foods. Women inmates at the Belfair Mission Creek Corrections Center in Washington are taken to the rivers and canals around

Many state correctional systems channel prison labor into industrial and commercial programs. One such program is the Prison Blues® brand of jeans, T-shirts, work shirts, and yard coats manufactured by Oregon Corrections Enterprises, a division of the Oregon Department of Corrections. What benefits to inmates do such work programs provide?

© Oregon Corrections Enterprises

Federal Prison Industries (FPI)

A federal, paid inmate work program and self-supporting corporation.

UNICOR

The trade name of Federal Prison Industries. UNICOR provides such products as U.S. military uniforms, electronic cable assemblies, and modular furniture.

Hood Canal and are paid $1 an hour to spray pesticides in order to save salmon habitats. Inmates at the Washington State Penitentiary in Walla Walla work as research assistants for a professor of entomology at Washington State University to raise and tag Monarch butterflies to track their migratory path. They earn 42 cents an hour. At the Louisiana State Penitentiary in Angola, a maximum-security prison, inmates built Prison View, a nine-hole golf course that is on prison property and open to the public. Although inmates cannot play, they learned landscape design, horticulture, and groundskeeping. Inmates in Nebraska and 34 other states volunteer for a one-year-long rigorous Braille translation program certified by the Library of Congress. They earn between 38 cents and $1.08 an hour with at least half making 54 cents or less.

One of the best-known prison work programs operates at the Eastern Oregon Correctional Institution in Pendleton, Oregon, the famous mill town known for Pendleton fabrics. There, prisoners make a line of T-shirts, jackets, and jeans known as Prison Blues®. All 50 inmates working in the factory are paid prevailing industry wages, which range from a base of $7.80 to $9.58 per hour. They can also earn bonus incentives for quality and productivity. In an evaluation of 30 prison work programs examined by the Washington State Institute for Public Policy, an agency created by the state legislature to conduct research on policy issues, the studies showed an average 6 percent reduction in recidivism due to prison industry.

Federal Prison Industries and UNICOR On June 23, 1934, President Roosevelt signed the law that authorized the establishment of **Federal Prison Industries (FPI)**. FPI is a federal work program in which inmates are paid. Better known by its trade name, **UNICOR**, FPI is a self-supporting corporation owned by the federal government and overseen by a governing board appointed by the president.

The mission of FPI is to employ and provide job skills training to the greatest practical number of inmates confined within the Federal BOP; contribute to the safety and security of federal correctional facilities by keeping inmates constructively occupied; produce market-priced quality goods for sale to the federal government; operate in a self-sustaining manner; and minimize FPI's impact on private business and labor. FPI has traditionally relied on manufacturing office furniture, electronics, and clothing for the bulk of its business, but it has begun to enter new industries such as renewable energy (making solar panels, energy-efficient lighting, and small wind turbines). Federal agencies are required to purchase items when possible from UNICOR. This chapter's Economic Realities and Corrections: Prisons discusses the controversy surrounding UNICOR: Is it siphoning jobs at much lower wages that could be filled by those who need them?

What Impact Does UNICOR Have? There is very little independent research on whether UNICOR reduces criminal activity. More than 10 years ago, the federal BOP released a study that compared the postrelease activities of a group of inmates who had participated in UNICOR programs with those of another group of inmates who had not. The study found that inmates employed by UNICOR were 24 percent more likely, upon release, to become employed and remain crime free for as long as 12 years after release than those who were not involved in UNICOR programs. Another study showed that inmates employed in federal prison industries had survival times (measured by the number of days before recommitment) that were 20 percent longer than those of the comparison group.[17] However, independent evaluations have concluded that the results are not conclusive. Without independent evaluations, we do not know whether, and how much, UNICOR reduces criminal activity.

Education Programs

CO7-5

The majority of prisoners cannot read or write well enough to function in society. Among federal and state inmates, about 37 percent do not have a high school diploma or a GED compared to 19 percent of the general population.[18]

A survey of inmate education programs conducted by the American Correctional Association found that only 283,000 were participating in educational programs.[19] This may be due in part to the higher rate of learning disabilities found among inmates.[20] An estimated 30 to 50 percent of inmates have a learning disability compared with 5 to 15 percent of the general adult population.

However, can prison education programs rehabilitate prisoners so that they eventually contribute constructively to society upon reentry and cost less than incarceration? The answer is a resounding, "Yes, they can."

Research analysts with the Fortune Society, a prisoner reform advocacy group, found that it cost $44,000 per year to incarcerate one prisoner in New Jersey, whereas the cost to attend Princeton University is $37,000 per year.[21] A report by the Correctional Association of New York found lopsided spending on prison versus college education. Specifically, it cost $44,000 per year to house a prisoner in New York versus $7,645 tuition per year for a full-time in-state student within the State University of New York system.[22]

In 2013, the Rand Corporation published the results of the largest study to date measuring the effectiveness of correctional education on recidivism and employment.[23] It found that inmates who participated in correctional education programs—remedial education to develop reading and math skills, GED preparation, postsecondary education or vocational training—were 43 percent less likely to return to prison within three years of release in comparison to those who did not participate. The researchers also found that prisoners who participated in academic, or vocational education programs had a 13 percent better chance of finding employment than those who did not. And prisoners who participated specifically in vocational training programs (including welding, computing, culinary arts, construction trades, and auto mechanics) were 28 percent more likely to be employed after release from prison than those who did not participate. Attending education classes in prison has also been associated with improved social climate and communication and reduced problems with disciplinary infractions.

Education is also an opportunity for prisoners to earn good time credits (also called *earned time*). In at least 21 states, inmates can earn time off their sentences by participating in or completing educational courses. In Nevada, for example, an inmate can earn 10 days per month for participation in an education program, and an additional 60, 90, or 120 days for obtaining a certificate, diploma, or degree, respectively. Inmates in Arkansas earn 90 days off their sentence for completing either their GED or a vocational certificate.

So if corrections-based educational programs are effective in reducing recidivism, why are only 283,000 inmates enrolled? There are a number of reasons. First, correctional educators face substantial hurdles in delivering effective instruction. Inmates do not enter prison or jail to attend classes. They often do not see the importance of gaining an education, and many have a history of educational failure. They do not enroll in programs or

Visit http://www.youtube.com/ watch?v=KJYGvxiiCrk or scan this code with the QR app on your smartphone or digital device and watch the podcast of Jody Lewen, winner of the University of California at Berkley 2006 Peter E. Haas Public Service Award and director of the Patten University extension site, discuss her experiences teaching at San Quentin State Prison, and the inmates' reactions to the program. How does this information relate to ideas discussed in this chapter?

UNICOR, the trade name for Federal Prison Industries, Inc. (FPI), has not been immune to the nation's economic pinch. Since 2007, a tight economy, dwindling agency budgets, and Congressional moves to weaken its preferential status as the supplier of manufactured goods for federal agencies (UNICOR isn't allowed to sell to the private sector) have reduced the company's size.

The sluggish economy and tight budgets have reduced government orders, forcing the Bureau of Prisons to close or downsize 43 UNICOR factories; only 66 remain today. They manufacture clothing and textiles, electronics, fleet management and vehicular components, industrial products, office furniture, recycling activities, and data entry and encoding services. Under current practice—governed by intricate laws, regulations, and policies—federal agencies must buy prisoner-made goods if they are comparable in price, quality, and time of delivery to private sector goods with certain exceptions.

UNICOR's overall sales of approximately $885 million in 2009 fell to $772 million in 2010, $745 million in 2011, and $472 million in 2015.. UNICOR uses the revenue it generates to purchase raw materials and equipment (approximately 80 percent), to pay staff salaries (17 percent), and to pay inmate salaries (4 percent).

Under current law, all physically able federal inmates who are not a security risk are required to work. Inmates who are not employed by FPI have other labor assignments in prison. FPI work assignments are usually considered more desirable because their wages are higher (23 cents to $1.15 an hour) and allow inmates to learn a trade.

However, the economic recession caused layoffs in the number of FPI employees. From a high of approximately 23,200 inmates in 2007, the number of inmates employed by FPI dropped to approximately 12,300 in 2015. Federal corrections officials worry that FPI workforce cuts could spark unrest in already overcrowded federal facilities where industry jobs have kept prisoners occupied and out of recreation yards and housing units.

But it is not only the economic recession that is impacting FPI. Private industry and Congress want FPI to scale back. They use arguments similar to the ones they used in 1934 when the FPI was first introduced: With much lower wages, FPI is taking away jobs from law-abiding citizens who need them during the nation's toughest period of unemployment in decades.

Private manufacturers in rural Alabama, Mississippi, and Tennessee have had to lay off employees after losing clothing contracts for the Defense Department to UNICOR. Its lower operating costs and laws that require federal agencies to use inmate-made products when available enables UNICOR to undercut private manufacturers.

After losing a $45 million contract to UNICOR, Steven Eisen, CEO of Tennier Industries, a military clothing manufacturer in rural Tennessee, told reporters, "Our government screams, howls and yells how the rest of the world is using prisoners or slave labor to manufacture items, and here we take the items right out of the mouths of people who need it."[*] Representative Bill Huizenga, a Michigan Republican agreed, saying "If China did this—having their prisoners work at subpar wages in prisons—we would be screaming bloody murder."[†]

UNICOR supporters say it has not taken large numbers of jobs away from private industry. They documented only 300 layoffs directly linked to private companies losing work to federal prisoners at four textile plants in Alabama and Tennessee. Advocates also say that UNICOR faces challenges that private industry does not: Many convicted felons don't know how to work.

In recent years, support for Congressional critics of UNICOR has increased as jobs, competition, and the role of government have become potent political issues. Several members of the U.S. House of Representatives proposed overhaul legislation to limit UNICOR's preferential status as the supplier of manufactured goods to federal agencies by putting a limit on FPI's sales to the federal government. This would open more product areas to private companies and strengthen requirements that prices for prisoner-made products be competitive. Some proposed legislation would impose federal work-safety standards and higher wages, starting at $2.50 an hour. However, the bills have always stalled in the Senate.

Under current practice—governed by intricate laws, regulations, and policies—a federal agency must buy prisoner-made goods if FPI offers an item that is comparable in price, quality, and time of delivery to that of the private sector, with certain exceptions. The company's prices are not always the lowest, but it frequently has been able to underbid private companies, Congressional aides say.

FPI supporters argue that there is a high correlation between prisoners who work in prison industries and a higher-than-average success rate of not being rearrested, not being reconvicted, and not returning to prison. However, as we pointed out in this chapter and as stated by an analyst in crime policy with the Congressional Research Service,[‡] the limited number of rigorous evaluations of correctional industry programs makes it impossible to draw any definitive conclusions about the programs' ability to reduce recidivism. Another analysis that summarized the results of four evaluations of correctional industry programs also found that inmates who participated in correctional industry programs were less likely to recidivate. However, the researchers reported that they could not rule out sampling error as a possible explanation for the positive effect. The researchers also reported that many of the studies included in the analysis lacked stringent methodological rigor, thereby preventing the researchers from concluding that the programs lead directly to less reoffending. One wonders whether the economic recession that started in 2007 will produce any changes in the FPI program.

[*] As quoted in Diane Cardwell, "Private Businesses Fight Federal Prisons for Contracts," *The New York Times,* March 4, 2012, www.nytimes.com (accessed March 15, 2012).
[†] Ibid., and updates by the authors.
[‡] Nathan James, *Federal Prison Industries* (Washington, DC: Congressional Research Service, December, 2011), pp. 4–5.

Inmates at the Fremont Correctional Facility in Cañon City, Colorado, learn new career skills in renewable energy fields. They attend class five hours a day and do homework from a textbook in their cells. Inmates who pass the program earn certificates and 20 college credits. What is the illiteracy rate among prisoners compared to that of the general population? Why are there so few prisoners enrolled in education classes?

© Andy Cross/The Denver Post via Getty Images

participate in classes with the same enthusiasm as the noninstitutionalized population. Even negative peer pressure can discourage inmates from joining programs. Correctional educators face the challenge of motivating inmates to involve themselves in educational programming because they know that programming inside correctional facilities greatly influences what happens once inmates are released. Emphasizing the relevance of education to inmates, helping inmates experience success in learning, and developing an institutional culture that endorses the importance of education are vital components as correctional facilities work to achieve rehabilitation through education. Second, educational programming has not been a high priority in correctional budgeting, particularly because the beginning of the warehousing era. The bulk of correctional spending has been on security. Third, educational programming cannot be delivered when prisons are overcrowded.

However, today there is a new push for education in prison, especially college education. Private foundations such as Ford, Kresge, and Mellon have awarded grants for college education in prison. Their interest in prison education mirrors the shift we see in criminal justice discussed earlier in this text, motivated by a desire to make tax dollars work more efficiently. California governor Jerry Brown signed legislation in June 2015 that will fund four prisons to offer college

Twenty-eight inmates of the Mississippi State Penitentiary receive their Associate and Bachelor of Arts degrees from the New Orleans Baptist Theological Seminary's Christian Ministry program. Why are prisoner education and vocational training programs important?

© AP Photo/Rogelio V. Solis

classes. The legislation will pay for two to three classes each semester with up to 25 students in each class. Curriculum will focus on business and entrepreneurship with the chance to earn an associate's degree in liberal arts. Also in 2015, the federal government launched a limited pilot program to help prisoners pay for college. Incarcerated federal prisoners can apply for grants up to $5,775 to pay for tuition and related expenses in college-level programs offered in federal prison facilities across the nation.

PRISON ORGANIZATION AND ADMINISTRATION

All 50 states and the BOP operate prisons. In addition, four local jurisdictions in the United States operate prison systems: Cook County (Chicago), Illinois; Philadelphia; New York City; and Washington, DC. It is estimated that there are 1,292 state, federal, and private confinement facilities: 102 federal and 1,190 state.[24] (Private confinement facilities operate under contract to state or federal correctional authorities and are included in those counts.)

Jurisdictions use a variety of capacity measures to reflect both the space available to house inmates and the ability to staff and operate an institution. Some use rated capacity (first introduced in Chapter 6), which is the number of beds or inmates a state official assigns to an institution. Some use **operational capacity,** the number of inmates that a facility's staff, existing programs, and services can accommodate. Others use **design capacity,** the number of inmates that planners or architects intend for the facility. For instance, an architect might design a prison for 1,100 inmates. Administrators might add more staff, programs, and services to be able to confine 1,300 in the same space. The design capacity was 1,100, but the operational and rated capacities are 1,300. The institution is operating 18 percent above design capacity. Overall, state prisons are operating between 50 percent below capacity (Mississippi and New Mexico) and almost 50 percent over capacity (Illinois). See Exhibit 7–4 for the top 10

operational capacity

The number of inmates that a facility's staff, existing programs, and services can accommodate.

design capacity

The number of inmates that planners or architects intend for the facility.

| EXHIBIT 7-4 | Top Ten States with the Longest Prison Sentences |

State	Average Time Served 1990	Average Time Served 2009	Cost to State for Keeping Prisoners Longer	Quick Facts
1. Michigan	2.4 years	4.3 years	$471.9 million	$53,247 per prisoner per year kept 4.3 years instead of 2.4 years.
2. Pennsylvania	2.9 years	3.8 years	$316.6 million	Increase in time served a result of changes in how prisoners received parole. In 1994 required one out of five votes to grant parole. By 1996, changed to five out of nine.
3. New York	3.5 years	3.6 years	$65.6 million	$60,072 per prisoner per year kept 3.6 years instead of 3.5 years.
4. Virginia	1.7 years	3.3 years	$518.8 million	Second-highest percentage increase in the U.S.
5. Georgia	1.8 years	3.2 years	$536.1 million	$28,563 per prisoner per year kept 3.8 years instead of 1.8 years.
6. Arkansas	1.9 years	3.2 years	$305.1 million	Toughest sentences for drug offenders; average prisoner serves 3 years.
7. Oregon	2.4 years	3.2 years	$121.5 million	Lowest recidivism rate in U.S.—22 percent compared to 43 percent nationally.
8. Oklahoma	1.7 years	3.1 years	$203.9 million	$25,636 per prisoner per year kept 3.1 years instead of 1.7 years.
9. West Virginia	2.1 years	3.1 years	$74.8 million	$27,708 per prisoner per year kept 3.1 years instead of 2.1 years.
10. New Hampshire	2.4 years	3.1 years	$14.5 million	Tenth highest recidivism rate in the U.S. (44.2 percent).

Source: Adapted from Pew Center on the States, *Time Served: The High Cost, Low Return of Longer Prison Terms* (Washington, DC: The Pew Charitable Trusts, 2012).

states with the longest prison sentences and some quick facts about each one of them.

State Prison Systems

Organization The administration of state prisons is a function of the executive branch of government. The governor appoints the director of corrections, who in turn appoints the wardens of the state prisons. A change in governors often means a change in state prison leadership and administration.

The organization of most state prison systems involves a central authority, based in the state capital. Local communities, private contractors, or the state itself may provide prison services (from treatment and education to maintenance and repair). Still, for legal control and for maintaining an equitable distribution of resources, a centralized model has been maintained while in other areas of corrections (e.g., community corrections and probation), services are often decentralized.

Size and Costs State departments of corrections vary in size. The smallest is South Dakota's with more than 900 employees working in juvenile and adult institutions and community services and an annual operating budget of almost $110 million. The largest is California's with 60,000 authorized positions and an annual operating budget of $9 billion.[25]

An estimated 455,000 people work in adult correctional facilities: 66 percent are correctional officers; 12 percent are clerical, maintenance, and food service workers; 10 percent are professional/technical staff; 3 percent are educators; 2 percent are administrator; and 7 percent are other.[26] Male employees outnumber female employees by a ratio of 2 to 1. Nineteen percent of all correctional facility staff are black, and 7 percent are Hispanic. In the summer of 2010, a survey conducted by the American Correctional Association reported on correctional officer wages while in training, entry level after training, and after the first year of employment. The highest wages for training are $45,166 in Massachusetts, $40,000 in New Jersey, and $36,600 in California. For entry level after training, highest wages are $45,288 in California, $45,166 in Massachusetts, and $40,000 in New Jersey. After one year of employment, highest wages are $60,660 in California, $53,674 in New Jersey, and $48,653 in Massachusetts.[27]

Twenty years ago, the United States spent about $7 billion on corrections. Today, our prison system costs taxpayers anywhere between $60 to $80 billion a year.[28] Corrections is the fourth-largest category of states' spending following education, Medicaid, and transportation. The vast majority of funds that go to state corrections systems—9 of every 10 dollars—goes to prisons.[29] Some ask if the money spent on state corrections encroaches on funds for higher education because the money has to come from somewhere. Is there discussion about this kind of trade-off? Jennifer Gonnerman, a staff writer for the New Yorker, wrote, "When parents get a tuition bill for their kids' college education, I always think they should get a little note that says tuition went up $200 last year because we decided to build two new prisons. Then we can all decide whether we think that's a good use of our money or not."[30] Others have said, "Every additional dollar spent on prisons, of course is one dollar less that can go to preparing for the next Hurricane Katrina, educating young people, providing health care to the elderly, or repairing roads and bridges."[31] Exhibit 7–5 shows the ratio of corrections to higher education spending in 2007. Vermont, Michigan, Oregon, Connecticut, and Delaware spend as much money or more on corrections as they do on higher education.

Visit http://www.cbsnews.com/8301-3445_162-57418495/the-cost-of-a-nation-of-incarceration/ or scan this code with the QR app on your smartphone or digital device and watch the CBS NEWS Sunday Morning podcast detailing cost and other problems with the U.S. epidemic of incarceration. How does this information relate to ideas discussed in this chapter?

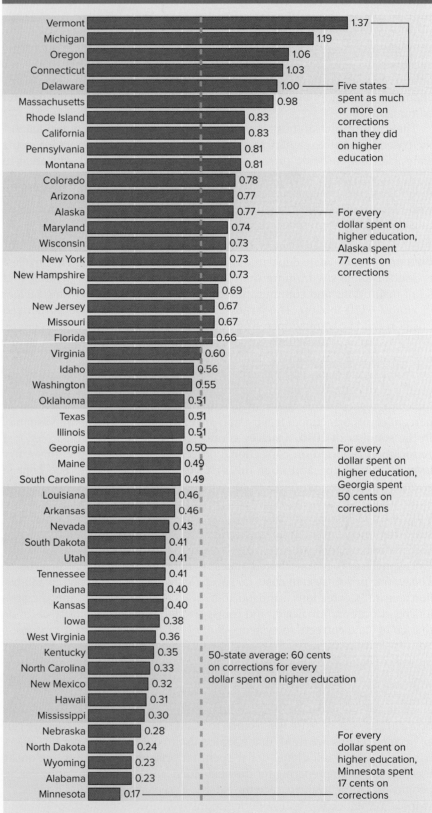

EXHIBIT 7–5 Ratio of Corrections Spending to Higher Education Spending, 2007

Vermont	1.37
Michigan	1.19
Oregon	1.06
Connecticut	1.03
Delaware	1.00
Massachusetts	0.98
Rhode Island	0.83
California	0.83
Pennsylvania	0.81
Montana	0.81
Colorado	0.78
Arizona	0.77
Alaska	0.77
Maryland	0.74
Wisconsin	0.73
New York	0.73
New Hampshire	0.73
Ohio	0.69
New Jersey	0.67
Missouri	0.67
Florida	0.66
Virginia	0.60
Idaho	0.56
Washington	0.55
Oklahoma	0.51
Texas	0.51
Illinois	0.51
Georgia	0.50
Maine	0.49
South Carolina	0.49
Louisiana	0.46
Arkansas	0.46
Nevada	0.43
South Dakota	0.41
Utah	0.41
Tennessee	0.41
Indiana	0.40
Kansas	0.40
Iowa	0.38
West Virginia	0.36
Kentucky	0.35
North Carolina	0.33
New Mexico	0.32
Hawaii	0.31
Mississippi	0.30
Nebraska	0.28
North Dakota	0.24
Wyoming	0.23
Alabama	0.23
Minnesota	0.17

Five states spent as much or more on corrections than they did on higher education

For every dollar spent on higher education, Alaska spent 77 cents on corrections

For every dollar spent on higher education, Georgia spent 50 cents on corrections

50-state average: 60 cents on corrections for every dollar spent on higher education

For every dollar spent on higher education, Minnesota spent 17 cents on corrections

Source: Jennifer Warren, *One in 100: Behind Bars in America 2008*. Published by The Pew Charitable Trusts, 2009. Reprinted with permission of The Pew Charitable Trusts.

States spend, on average, approximately $27,180 a year to incarcerate one offender.[32] "In states like Connecticut, Maine, Massachusetts, and Rhode Island, it's anywhere from $46,000 to $51,000." And depending on the prison security level, the capital costs of building one prison cell can be as much as $100,000. Five states with the most expensive prisoners are shown in Exhibit 7–6.

However, amounts that states are spending today on corrections have been significantly reduced. A combination of falling crime rates; a policy shift from lock-'em-up justice to rehabilitation and community sanctions for nonviolent, nonserious, and nonsex offenders; and a dwindling appetite for hefty prison budgets has lowered the number of people behind bars.

At least 17 states closed some of their prisons and invested a portion of the estimated $337 million in savings in infrastructure and civic institutions such as substance abuse treatment, housing, education, and jobs located in high-risk neighborhoods, a practice known as **justice reinvestment**.[33] Justice reinvestment is a data-driven approach that ensures that policymaking is based on a comprehensive analysis of criminal justice data and the latest research about what works to reduce crime, and is tailored to the needs of the local jurisdiction. Justice reinvestment in Texas alone resulted in $1.5 billion in construction savings and $340 million in averted annual construction costs.[34]

justice reinvestment

The practice of reducing spending on prisons and investing a portion of the savings into infrastructure and civic institutions located in high-risk neighborhoods.

Federal Bureau of Prisons

The Federal BOP is an entirely separate system from state and local prison systems. Before the 1890s, the federal government did not operate its own prisons. Instead, the Department of Justice paid state prisons and county jails to house people convicted of committing federal crimes. The public outcry over the convict lease system, however, motivated the passage of a federal law prohibiting the leasing of federal offenders. Many state prisons and county jails subsequently became reluctant to house federal offenders because it was not economically advantageous to incarcerate inmates they could not lease. Moreover, the expansion of federal law enforcement activities and the enactment of new federal laws in the late 19th century led to an increase in the prosecution of federal lawbreakers and to overcrowding in the prisons where they were held. With a growing population of federal prisoners and the growing reluctance of nonfederal prisons to house them, the federal government had no choice but to build prisons of its own. Congress authorized the establishment of three federal penitentiaries in 1891: at Atlanta (Georgia), Leavenworth (Kansas), and McNeil Island (Washington). The BOP was formally established in 1930. Today the BOP houses more than 191,000 inmates in 117 federal institutions, 15 privately managed prisons, 185 residential reentry centers, and home detention.

EXHIBIT 7-6	Five States with the Most Expensive Prisoners

Average Annual	Cost Per Prisoner
New York	$60,076
New Jersey	$54,865
Connecticut	$50,262
Vermont	$49,502
Rhode Island	$49,133

Source: Erika Rawes, "5 States with the Most Expensive Prisoners," Cheatsheet.com, March 27, 2015, www.cheatsheet.com/business/5-states-with-the-most-expensive-prisoners.html/?a=viewall (accessed January 10, 2016).

Today, almost 192,000 inmates are under the jurisdiction of the BOP (82 percent are in federal prison, 6 percent are in community-based facilities, and 12 percent are held in privately operated prisons under contract with the BOP). Of the almost 40,000 persons employed by the BOP, almost 30 percent are female and one-third are nonwhite. Career opportunities with the BOP range from inmate custody and programming positions, health services, operational readiness (vocational education), and support staff and administration. Consult the Federal BOP website for career opportunities (www.bop.gov).[35]

However, as discussed elsewhere in this chapter, all prisons, including the BOP, are under fire for incarcerating too many persons, bloated budgets, and recidivism topping 50 percent. On Monday, April 25, 2016, U.S. Attorney General Loretta Lynch launched a major effort to support and strengthen reentry programs and resources at the BOP and turn the tide on mass incarceration, federal spending, and recidivism. Known as the **Roadmap to Reentry,** the plan lays out a commitment to provide a reentry plan for every single federal inmate, taking into account factors such as past drug abuse, criminal history, and education. The roadmap also includes a plan to develop education, job training, substance-abuse programs, and life skills courses for all federal inmates in order to improve their chances of success upon release.

The Roadmap to Reentry identifies five evidence-based principles to improve the correctional practices and programs that govern the lives of those who will reenter society after incarceration. The five principles (shown in Exhibit 7–7) span the cycle of custody and beyond: from intake to incarceration through to release. They are designed to help formerly incarcerated federal inmates who have served their time (1) receive opportunities after leaving prison, (2) promote family unity, (3) contribute to the health of the nation's economy, (4) advance public safety, and (5) sustain the strength of the nation's communities.

In addition to the roadmap, the U.S. Department of Justice announced a series of family-friendly initiatives for inmates in federal prison, recognizing that research has shown that inmates who maintain supportive relationships with family members have far better outcomes when they leave prison. The U.S. government plans to:

- extend videoconferencing facilities to all female facilities by June 2016 to help female inmates stay connected with their families;
- pilot family-friendly programs that engage children of federal inmates in a variety of youth development activities—from academic support to mentoring—to try to stop the cycle of incarceration in four federal facilities in Connecticut, New York, Pennsylvania, and West Virginia; and
- establish a toll-free hotline to help formerly incarcerated federal inmates with community reentry issues such as how to obtain a copy of a birth certificate, apply for a license and other documents, and obtain information on job services.

We return to the topic of offender reentry in Chapter 8.

Prison Security Levels

Prisons are classified by the level of security they provide. Most local, state, and federal jurisdictions use maximum-, medium-, and minimum-security classifications. A **maximum- or close/high-security prison** is designed, organized, and staffed to confine the most violent and dangerous offenders for long periods. It imposes strict controls on the movement of inmates and their visitors, and custody and security are constant concerns. The prison has a highly secure perimeter with watchtowers and high walls. Inmates

Roadmap to Reentry

Principles of correctional reform to reduce recidivism by supporting and strengthening reentry programs and resources at the Federal Bureau of Prisons.

maximum- or close/high-security prison

A prison designed, organized, and staffed to confine the most dangerous offenders for long periods. It has a highly secure perimeter, barred cells, and a high staff-to-inmate ratio. It imposes strict controls on the movement of inmates and visitors, and it offers few programs, amenities, or privileges.

EXHIBIT 7−7 Federal Roadmap to Reentry

 U.S. DEPARTMENT OF JUSTICE

ROADMAP TO REENTRY

REDUCING RECIDIVISM THROUGH REENTRY REFORMS AT THE FEDERAL BUREAU OF PRISONS

PRINCIPLES FOR IMPROVED BOP REENTRY PRACTICES

The Roadmap to Reentry identifies five evidence-based principles guiding federal efforts to improve the correctional practices and programs that govern the lives of those who will seek to reenter society after incarceration. The Department of Justice takes the view that "reentry begins Day One." And, just as important, the Department's involvement does not end at the prison gates. As such, these corrections principles span the cycle of custody and beyond: from intake, to incarceration, through to release. The principles are as follows:

PRINCIPLE I

 Upon incarceration, every inmate should be provided an individualized reentry plan tailored to his or her risk of recidivism and programmatic needs.

DOJ ACTIONS:

The Department is enhancing the BOP's risk and needs assessment tools to inform development of reentry plans tailored to specific criminogenic needs of each incarcerated individual.

PRINCIPLE II

 While incarcerated, each inmate should be provided education, employment training, life skills, substance abuse, mental health, and other programs that target their criminogenic needs and maximize their likelihood of success upon release.

DOJ ACTIONS:

The Department, through BOP, has launched an effort to assess its education programs, life-skills programs and job-skills programs to ensure that those programs are evidence-based and targeted to the criminogenic needs of inmates.

PRINCIPLE III

 While incarcerated, each inmate should be provided the resources and opportunity to build and maintain family relationships, strengthening the support system available to them upon release.

DOJ ACTIONS:

The Department is enhancing the number and types of opportunities available for people in federal prisons to strengthen family relationships during their terms of incarceration.

PRINCIPLE IV

 During transition back to the community, halfway houses and supervised release programs should ensure individualized continuity of care for returning citizens.

DOJ ACTIONS:

To ensure that RRCs fulfill their vital role in the reentry process, the Department is assessing and evaluating the RRC model to develop improvements that provide residents enhanced reentry support.

PRINCIPLE V

 Before leaving custody, every person should be provided comprehensive reentry-related information and access to resources necessary to succeed in the community.

DOJ ACTIONS:

The Department is developing reentry-specific tools and support services to help returning citizens succeed after leaving federal custody.

Justice.gov/reentry

Source: United States Department of Justice, 2016.

EVIDENCE-BASED CORRECTIONS
Seeking Safety for Incarcerated Women

Seeking Safety is a manualized, cognitive–behavioral intervention for individuals with co-occurring post-traumatic stress disorder (PTSD) and substance-use disorders. The intervention targets many of the unique needs of incarcerated women with PTSD and substance-use disorders, which could interfere with their recovery and thus place them at risk for reoffending. The overall goal of Seeking Safety is to improve PTSD, depression, interpersonal skills, and coping strategies of incarcerated women.

Seeking Safety is a 12-week intervention, during which groups meet twice a week for two hours each time. As part of the treatment, Seeking Safety provides psychoeducation, which seeks to educate participants about the consequences of trauma and the links between trauma and substance use. Seeking Safety also integrates cognitive, behavioral, and interpersonal topics and teaches specific coping skills. The treatment consists of 25 topics (such as asking for help and coping with triggers) that address the cognitive, behavioral, interpersonal, and case management needs of persons with both substance-use disorders and PTSD. The intervention emphasizes the importance of stabilization, coping skills, and the reduction of self-destructive behavior.

Seeking Safety therapy draws upon cognitive–behavioral therapy (CBT). CBT holds that individuals' perceptions and thoughts about a situation will influence their emotional and behavioral reactions. Further, the cognitive model argues that individuals' perceptions and thoughts are often distorted when they are distressed. It is through cognitive therapy that individuals can learn to correct this negative thinking; identify and modify distorted beliefs about themselves, the world, and others; and learn to accept their difficulties

The program is rated Promising. Evaluation of Seeking Safety showed that at the 12-week follow-up interview, women in the treatment condition showed significantly greater decreases in their PTSD scores and their depression scores compared with women in the wait-list control condition.

Source: Adapted from https://www.crimesolutions.gov/ProgramDetails.aspx?ID=424.

Maximum-security prisons confine the most violent and dangerous offenders for long periods. They are surrounded by high walls and gun towers. The Polunsky Unit in Livingston, Texas, is also surrounded by a stun fence that delivers a nonlethal shock to inmates who try to escape. On average, how much does it cost to incarcerate one offender per year in a maximum-security prison?

© AP Photo/Brett Coomer

Medium-security prisons incarcerate less dangerous inmates than maximum-security prisons. They impose fewer controls on inmates' freedom of movement and place more emphasis on treatment and work programs. On average, how much does it cost to incarcerate one offender per year in a medium-security prison?

live in single- or multiple-occupancy barred cells. The staff-to-inmate ratio is high, routines are highly regimented, and prisoner counts are frequent. Programs, amenities, and privileges are few. The cost to incarcerate an inmate in maximum-security prison averages more than $34,000 per year.[36]

Inmates in a **medium-security prison** are considered less dangerous than those in maximum-security prisons and may serve short or long sentences. Medium-security prisons impose fewer controls on inmates' and visitors' freedom of movement than do maximum-security facilities. Outwardly, medium-security prisons often resemble maximum-security institutions, and they, too, have barred cells. The staff-to-inmate ratio is generally lower than in a maximum-security facility. Medium-security prisons place more emphasis on treatment and work programs than do maximum-security prisons, and the level of amenities and privileges is slightly higher. The cost to incarcerate an inmate in medium-security averages more than $26,000 per year.

medium-security prison

A prison that confines offenders considered less dangerous than those in maximum security, for both short and long periods. It places fewer controls on inmates' and visitors' freedom of movement than does a maximum-security facility. It, too, has barred cells and a fortified perimeter. The staff-to-inmate ratio is generally lower than that in a maximum-security facility, and the level of amenities and privileges is slightly higher.

Minimum-security prisons confine the least dangerous offenders. They are sometimes referred to as open institutions because they have no fences or walls surrounding them. On average, how much does it cost to incarcerate one offender per year in a minimum-security prison?

minimum-security prison

A prison that confines the least dangerous offenders for both short and long periods. It allows as much freedom of movement and as many privileges and amenities as are consistent with the goals of the facility. It may have dormitory housing, and the staff-to-inmate ratio is relatively low.

open institution

A minimum-security facility that has no fences or walls surrounding it.

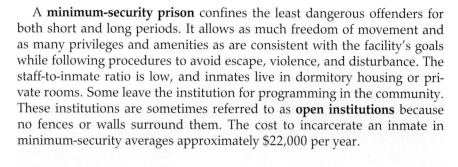

CO7-7

A **minimum-security prison** confines the least dangerous offenders for both short and long periods. It allows as much freedom of movement and as many privileges and amenities as are consistent with the facility's goals while following procedures to avoid escape, violence, and disturbance. The staff-to-inmate ratio is low, and inmates live in dormitory housing or private rooms. Some leave the institution for programming in the community. These institutions are sometimes referred to as **open institutions** because no fences or walls surround them. The cost to incarcerate an inmate in minimum-security averages approximately $22,000 per year.

OVERCROWDING

In the past, a prison was often referred to as "the big house." Today, however, a more appropriate description is "the full house." Over the past 25 years, the prison population has increased sixfold—from 240,000 to almost 1.6 million. Some say that prisons are "capacity driven"; that is, if you cut the ribbon, they are full. Saying exactly how full, though, is difficult because each state has its own method for measuring prison capacity.

Reasons for Prison Overcrowding

Prisons are overcrowded for at least three reasons. The first is a continuous increase in the number of people sent to prison. In 2000, almost 1.4 million persons were in state and federal prisons. On January 1, 2016, that number had increased to almost 1.6 million, an average annual increase of 1.8 percent.

The second reason is that offenders now serve a larger portion of their sentences because of mandatory minimum laws, the elimination of parole (see Chapter 8), and other policy choices. The average length of time served by federal inmates more than doubled from 1988 to 2012, rising from 18 months to almost 38 months.

The third reason prisons are overcrowded is that many incoming prisoners are drug users, not the drug dealers the tougher drug laws were designed to capture. The goal of tougher drug laws was to arrest and convict drug dealers, thereby reducing drug use and the drug-related crime rate. This goal has not been achieved. The majority of persons sentenced to prison for drug offenses are low-level, nonviolent offenders—primarily street-level dealers and couriers, not the kingpins or major traffickers the laws were written for.

A number of criminal justice scholars, policymakers, and reform organizations believe that we can eliminate prison overcrowding by cutting the prison population by 50 percent within the next 10 to 15 years.[37] The strategies are to release more inmates, reduce admissions and lengths of stay, make it easier to win parole, decide that community sanctions (Chapters 4 and 5) are more appropriate consequences than prison time, divert more individuals to mental health and addiction treatments, and redefine what offenses are considered violent in the first place. (Crimes such as petty theft, writing a bad check, receiving stolen property, and drug possessions are referred to as "wobblers" in many jurisdictions because they can be prosecuted as either a felony or misdemeanor.)

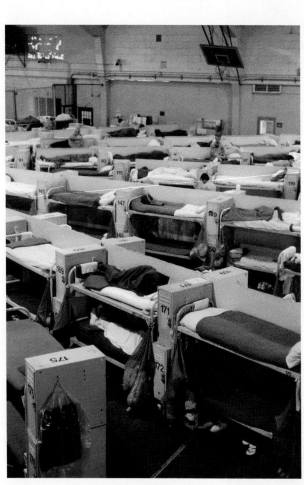

Although new prison facilities are being built, overcrowding continues to be an issue in many places. The auditorium of the Deuel Vocational Institution in Tracy, California, is converted into a dormitory to house prisoners. The prison has a design capacity of 1,681 but an operating capacity of 3,748. What are the consequences of prison overcrowding and what are the methods to reduce it?

© Frank Pedrick/The Image Works

If 100 percent of drug, public order, and property offenders in state prisons were given shorter sentences, paroled, sentenced to community sanctions, and/or diverted to mental health and treatment programs, the state prison population would be cut almost in half, from 1,350,000 to 686,000 prisoners. Would the reduction increase crime? Evidence from California, New Jersey, and New York suggests *no.* New Jersey and New York led the nation by *reducing* their prison population by 26 percent between 1999 and 2012, a period in which the nationwide state prison population rose by 10 percent. California experienced a 23 percent reduction in its prison population between 2006 and 2012, in contrast to a 1 percent reduction nationally. In all three states, while downsizing their prison populations, violent crime rates fell *at a faster pace* than they did in the country as a whole. Property crime rates also decreased in New Jersey and New York more than they did nationwide, while the reduction in California was slightly lower than the national average. The point to remember is that criminal justice policy decisions, and not crime rates, can increase prison populations or decrease them. Research tells us that substantial reductions in prison populations can be achieved without adverse effects on public policy.

Prison Overcrowding

Visit http://video.pbs.org/video/1945093979 or scan this code with the QR app on your smartphone or digital device and watch the PBS documentary discuss the U.S. Supreme Court's decision that ordered California to reduce its overcrowded prisons. How does this information relate to ideas discussed in this chapter?

SUPERMAX HOUSING

Prison systems have always needed a way to deal with inmates whose violent behavior makes it impossible for them to live with the general prison population. Generally such measures involve separating such inmates and are called *segregation* or *solitary confinement.* Prisoners who are dangerous or chronically violent, have escaped or attempted to escape from a high-security correctional facility, have incited or attempted to incite disruption in a correctional facility, or who have preyed on weaker inmates are removed from the general population. Earlier in this chapter, you learned that, in 1829, the Eastern State Penitentiary in Cherry Hill, Pennsylvania, was built on the principle of solitary confinement. However, in 1913 the Pennsylvania legislature dropped "solitary" from sentencing statutes, and housing arrangements at Eastern State became congregate. From that point forward, specialized housing units were developed for management and control of troublesome inmates.

The Federal BOP returned to the idea of controlling the most violent and disruptive inmates in indefinite solitary confinement when it opened Alcatraz in 1934. Alcatraz, which had a capacity of 275, did not offer any treatment program; its sole purpose was to incarcerate and punish the federal prison system's most desperate criminals and worst troublemakers. By 1963, Alcatraz was judged an expensive failure and was closed. For the next 10 years, prison officials used the *dispersal model*—problem prisoners were distributed to a number of prisons. Prison officials hoped that dispersal among populations of generally law-abiding inmates would dilute the influence of problem prisoners, but they soon learned that dispersing problem inmates across dozens of prisons led to having dozens of problem facilities.

CO7-8

At the federal supermax prison in Florence, Colorado, three mirrored-glass gun towers define the maximum-security level of heightened confinement. Officially known as the United States Penitentiary Florence Administrative Maximum (ADMAX), 25 percent of the 400 prisoners there will remain in confinement for the rest of their lives. What are the pros and cons of such facilities?
© AP Photo/Pueblo Chieftain, Chris McLean

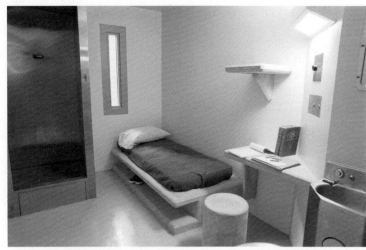

© Lizzie Himmel/Sygma/Corbis

SUPERMAX INMATE CELL DIAGRAM

Steel Shower (On Timer)

Window (4 Inch x 4 foot)

Television Lighting Radio

Desk

Steel Sink (w/Trapless Drain)

Concrete Bed

Steel Toilet (w/Automatic Shut-Off)

Concrete Stool

*Artist Rendering of General Cell In Facility Based on Photograph and Written Descriptions.

© Jonathon Ortiz-Smykla -www.LuckyBandanaDesign.com;

Each prisoner's bed, desk, stool, and bookcase at the federal supermax prison in Florence, Colorado, are made of reinforced concrete and anchored in place. Each 7 by 12-foot cell has a shower stall with flood-proof plumbing. Cells are staggered so that inmates cannot make eye contact with other inmates. Each cell has a double-entry door: an interior barred cage door backed up by a windowed steel door that prevents voice contact among prisoners. What kind of inmates should/should not be held in such facilities?

supermax housing

A freestanding facility, or a distinct unit within a facility, that provides for management and secure control of inmates who have been officially designated as exhibiting violent or serious and disruptive behavior while incarcerated.

The BOP reverted to the *concentration model*—all problem prisoners would be housed together in a separate facility. In 1994, the BOP opened its first **supermax housing** facility at Florence, Colorado. Officially known as United States Penitentiary Florence Administrative Maximum (ADMAX), the prison houses the 450 most dangerous, violent, escape prone, and security threat group STG federal inmate leaders. More than 25 percent will never be released from federal custody and will remain in confinement for the rest of their lives. Among the prisoners at ADMAX are Zacarias Moussaoui, confessed 9/11 conspirator; Olympic Park bomber Eric Rudolph; "Unabomber" Ted Kaczynski; Robert Hanssen, American FBI agent-turned Soviet spy; Oklahoma City bombing conspirator Terry Nichols; would-be "shoe bomber" Richard Reid; and 1993 World Trade Center bombing conspirator Ramzi Yousef. Today, 44 states, the District of Columbia, and the BOP now operate one or more supermax prisons that collectively house more than 80,000 inmates.

In 1994, construction cost for the federal supermax prison in Florence, Colorado, totaled $60 million ($150,000 per cell). Annual operating cost per cell per year is another $40,000, or $19.2 million total annually.

Supermax prisons are significantly more expensive to build than traditional prisons due in part to the enhanced and extensive high-security features on locks, doors, and perimeters; heavily reinforced concrete walls, ceilings, and floors; and incorporation of advanced electronic systems and technology. Providing meals and other services at individual cell fronts, having multiple-officer escorts, and maintaining elaborate electronic systems contribute to the high cost.

To date, research on super-maximum-security prisons is minimal despite the rapid increase in and costs of such facilities nationally. Criminologists, psychiatrists, lawyers, and the courts who have studied the effects of long-term solitary confinement report evidence of acute sensory deprivation, paranoid delusion belief systems, irrational fears of violence, resentment, little ability to control rage, and mental breakdowns. Forty-five percent of prisoners in Washington's supermax units were diagnosed as seriously mentally ill.[38]

The vast majority of inmates in long-term solitary confinement remain anxious, angry, depressed, insecure, and confused. Some commit suicide. For example, although isolated prisoners make up less than 2 percent of the total inmate population in California, they accounted for 42 percent of the suicides from 2006 to 2010.[39] The situation in federal prison is the same. U.S. Senator Richard Durbin (D-IL) held the first-ever congressional hearing on the use of solitary confinement in the federal prison system and learned that one-half of all prison suicides are committed by prisoners held in supermax prisons. The federal BOP agreed to a comprehensive review of the use of solitary confinement by an independent analyst.[40]

Among the most disturbing findings were:

- A large number of inmates in solitary confinement need mental health treatment, but aren't receiving it.
- No protocol exists to identify inmates with mental illness who should be kept out of solitary confinement.
- Inmates often receive a mental health diagnosis by medical students or interns who are not trained in psychiatry.
- No reentry programs or means of tracking for inmates coming out of segregation exist.

The impact of supermax facilities on staff is also a subject of much discussion. Having to deal on a daily basis with inmates who have proven to be the most troublesome—in an environment that prioritizes human control and isolation—presents staff with extraordinary challenges. When there is little interaction except in control situations, the adversarial nature of the relationships tends to be one of dominance and, in return, resistance on both sides. Stuart Grassian, a physician and expert on prison control units, believes that people who work in supermax facilities lose their capacity to be shocked by the kinds of things they see. "It may put money in your pocket," Dr. Grassian notes, "but over time it destroys you psychologically and brings out rage and sadism and violence and brutality."[41]

So far, only one study used a powerful type of research design to assess whether supermax prisons contribute to a decrease in prison violence, and the results are at best mixed. The study focused on four states, three of which had supermax prisons (Arizona, Illinois, and Minnesota) and one that did not (Utah). Researchers studied inmate-on-inmate and inmate-on-staff assaults and found that the opening of a supermax prison did not reduce the level of inmate-on-inmate violence although in Illinois there was a reduction in assaults on staff. The finding in Illinois suggested support for supermax prisons, but it raised this question: Why would a supermax prison reduce inmate-on-staff assaults but not inmate-on-inmate assaults?[42]

In 1995, inmates at California's Pelican Bay supermax unit challenged the constitutionality of extreme isolation and environmental deprivation. They claimed that the degree of segregation was so extreme and the restrictions so severe that the inmates confined there were psychologically traumatized and, in some cases, deprived of sanity. The federal court agreed. The court ruled in *Madrid* v. *Gomez* (1995) that "conditions in security housing unit did impose cruel and unusual punishment on mentally ill prisoners" and "those who were at particularly high risk for suffering very serious or severe injury to their mental health."[43] The court declared that the state of California could not continue to confine inmates who were already mentally ill or those who were at an unreasonably high risk of suffering serious mental illness in the supermax unit. The court also appointed a **special master** (a person appointed to act as the representative of the court) to work with the state of California to develop a satisfactory remedial plan and provide a progress report to the court.

However, not everyone agrees that the conditions of supermax confinement exacerbate symptoms of mental illness and create mental illness where none previously existed, and these findings may impact future court decisions. In January 2011, the U.S. Department of Justice released the results of a one-year longitudinal study of the psychological effects of supermax confinement conducted by the Colorado Department of Corrections.[44] The researchers found that psychological disturbances were not unique to prisoners in supermax confinement. Elevated psychological disturbances were present among prisoners in the general population as well. The researchers

Visit www.npr.org/sections/the two-way/2014/02/25/282672593/ solitary-confinement-costs-78k-per-inmate-and-should-be-curbed-critics-say or scan this code with the QR app on your smartphone or digital device and listen to former prisoners speak about the effects of solitary confinement at a congressional hearing. How does this information relate to ideas discussed in this chapter?

special master

A person appointed by the court to act as its representative to oversee remedy of a violation and provide regular progress reports.

also noted that there was initial improvement in psychological well-being for both groups at the first two testing sessions followed by relative stability for the remainder of the year. They also reported that contrary to expected findings, offenders with mental illness did not deteriorate over time in supermax confinement at a rate more rapid and more extreme than those without mental illness. They conclude that although inmates in supermax confinement possessed traits believed to be associated with long-term segregation, those features could not be attributed to supermax confinement alone because they were present at the time of placement and occurred in the comparison study group.

As you can imagine, however, the study has its critics. Among them is Dr. Stuart Grassian, Boston psychiatrist who is internationally recognized for describing the crippling effects of supermax confinement. Dr. Grassian described the report as "garbage in, garbage out. Their approach and methodology are fatally flawed."[45] Grassian and others argue that the research was flawed from the start because the researchers started with inmates experiencing mental health crises at the beginning of their study. Hence, their baseline data were slanted. They also question the truthfulness of the inmates' responses. Will inmates, they ask, admit to mental health problems if they are trying to earn their way out of supermax confinement? They also question the results of the study by raising the issue of the so-called Hawthorne Effect, a form of reactivity whereby subjects improve or modify an aspect of their behavior being experimentally measured simply in response to the fact that they are being studied, not in response to any particular experimental manipulation. The critics point out that two inmates were thrown out of the study because they made sexual advances to one of the female graduate students conducting the interviews.

Corrections professionals believe that there has to be a place in prisons and jails for different types of restrictive housing. However, how do we use restrictive housing to help manage inmate populations without causing the unintended mental and physical health problems noted earlier? The answer may be in the Solitary Confinement Study and Reform Act of 2015.

On July 30, 2015, two Democrats and two Republicans introduced a bill into the U.S. House of Representatives to dramatically reform the practice of solitary confinement in the U.S. federal prison system. The Solitary Confinement Study and Reform Act of 2015 would:

- establish the National Solitary Confinement Study and Reform Commission to study the practice of solitary confinement and recommend best practices for reform to Congress and the administration;
- require the Department of Justice to issue regulations on best practices that would bind federal prisons and incentivize changes in behavior in state and local prison systems;
- bring about significant changes to the way mentally ill prisoners are designated for solitary confinement;
- ensure that the duration of solitary confinement is limited to fewer than 30 days in any 45-day period;
- ensure that prisoners are placed in solitary confinement only when the safety or security of the facility or another person is at imminent risk or to punish an adult prisoner for an extremely serious disciplinary infraction;
- ensure that, prior to being subject to long-term solitary confinement, a prisoner is entitled to a meaningful hearing on the reason for and

duration of confinement and have access to legal counsel for such hearings;

- ensure that indefinite sentencing of a prisoner to long-term solitary confinement will not be allowed and that the prisoner will be afforded a meaningful review of the confinement at least once every 30 days and that prison officials record and provide a transcript of the review proceedings for the prisoner;

- ensure that prison officials design and implement programming that allows prisoners in solitary confinement to earn placement in less restrictive housing through positive behavior;

- limit the use of involuntary solitary confinement for the purpose of protective custody;

- ensure that prison officials improve access to mental health treatment for prisoners in solitary confinement; and

- ensure that prisoners with a serious mental illness are not held in long-term solitary confinement.

The bipartisan committee believes that the act will start a national conversation on the use of solitary confinement and move toward a more rational and fiscally responsible approach to incarceration. Recognizing that state and local prison systems use solitary confinement more than the federal system, how do you believe the Solitary Confinement Study and Reform Act can incentivize state and local prison systems to change?

TECHNOCORRECTIONS

CO7-9

The technological forces that made the use of cell phones commonplace is converging with corrections to create "technocorrections." Technological changes have impacted communication, offender and officer tracking and recognition, and detection.

Communication

Several years ago, the Federal BOP set up e-mail programs that allow inmates to send and receive e-mails.[46] According to the BOP, the program cuts down on the amount of paper mail (which can conceal drugs and other contraband), helps prisoners connect regularly with their families, and helps inmates build computer skills they can use when they return to the community. Messages are screened for key words, are read by correctional officers before they are sent, and can be sent only to contacts who agree beforehand to receive e-mail from specific inmates.

Technology has also produced the newest prison **contraband**—cell phones.[47] We used to think of prison contraband as a file inside a cake. Now it's a smartphone hidden under a mattress. Visitors smuggle them in. Drones drop them off. Inmates returning from work release smuggle them in. And staff sell them to inmates for as much as $1,000. The number of cell phones confiscated in California prisons increased from 261 in 2006 to more than 15,000 in 2011.[48] Cellphone confiscations by the Texas Department of Criminal Justice staff fell to 594 in 2013—a five-year low—from 738 the previous year.[49] California prison authorities twice found an LG flip phone under Charles Manson's mattress.

The solution may be a new system called *managed access.* Cell towers at each prison accept communication only from approved phones that prison officials control. The cost to install the system at all 33 California prisons

contraband

Any item that represents a serious threat to the safety and security of the institution.

Videoconferencing is estimated to have saved thousands of dollars in transporting defendants to and from jail or prison to a courtroom. Here, Dylann Roof appears via a video uplink from jail for his bond hearing in North Charleston, South Carolina. In federal court, Roof is charged with nine counts of using a firearm to commit murder, 12 hate crime charges, and 12 counts of violating a person's freedom of religion in the shooting deaths at Emanuel African Methodist Church in Charleston on June 17, 2015. Eighteen of the counts carry the federal death penalty. How does courtroom videoconferencing serve the interests of the defendant, courtroom personnel, and the community?

© Photo by Grace Beahm-Pool/Getty Images

Visit www.govtech.com/public-safety/Video-Visitation-Bus-Connects-Jail-Inmates.html or scan this code with the QR app on your smartphone or digital device and watch the podcast of Pinellas County (Florida) Sheriff Jim Coats talking about the video visitation bus, which travels to four cities in Pinellas County to facilitate communication between inmates and their families. How does this information relate to ideas discussed in this chapter?

was between $16 million and $33 million. A one-day test at a single California prison intercepted more than 4,000 attempts to place calls, send text messages, or access the Internet.[50] The payoff for the company installing the towers comes from inmates' use of prison pay phones. Their use at the test site went up by 64 percent in the days after the test. Other states would like the Federal Communications Commission to grant them authority to overpower the signal with a stronger one (called *jamming*) or "trick" the cell phone to react as if a "no service" signal is received (called *spoofing*). However, the Communications Act of 1934 prohibits the manufacture, importation, marketing, sale, or operation of jamming or spoofing devices because they would "bleed" over into the public broadcast area.

Videoconferencing Prison systems across the country are using videoconferencing for arraignments, interrogations, and visitation. Until Connecticut installed videoconferencing in all of its 18 prisons and Illinois installed them in all 25 state prisons, it sometimes cost as much as $1,800 to transport an inmate from prison to a courtroom. Connecticut and other states report using videoconferencing between judges and inmates to improve public safety and save money.[51]

The advantages of videoconferencing include:

- increasing the number of visitations conducted each day;
- reducing staff time in checking in visitors;
- reducing the staff time previously needed to escort inmates to a centralized visitation area or courtroom for arraignments and other preliminary proceedings;
- reducing inmate movement, thereby increasing safety for staff and inmates;
- reducing space requirements and construction and operating costs on visitation areas; and
- eliminating contraband that was formerly passed by visitors in face-to-face contact.

Videoconferencing can also be especially helpful in high-profile cases for which security is tighter and exposure to the public needs to be minimized.

Virtual visiting has become the latest trend in prisons; at least 20 states now have some type of videoconferencing system in place.[52] Because most prisoners are housed in facilities far removed from their homes, frequent visits sometimes are impossible, and video calls offer the opportunity for virtual face time.

However, we are beginning to see virtual visiting replacing face-to-face visiting altogether even when it is not necessary. In July 2012, the District of Columbia eliminated all face-to-face visitation and switched completely to video visiting.[53] Even a prisoner's family who lives nearby must go to a videoconference center to chat with the inmate. Although the District of Columbia Department of Corrections will save money by avoiding the costs and problems of escorting inmates and their families and friends to the visiting room, prisoners who now get no face time with families and friends are not enthusiastic about the change and see them as impersonal. Although the District of Columbia does not charge families and friends, other jurisdictions see virtual visiting as a cash cow and charge widely varying fees.

Jails in Washington and in Idaho allow inmates and visitors to register for one or two free 25-minute video visits per week. Thereafter, video calls average about $15 for 30 minutes.

The Virtual Visitation Program in Pennsylvania allows one 55-minute virtual visit a month for $15. Virginia's Department of Corrections charges $15 for 30 minutes and $30 for 60 minutes.[54]

However, not all agencies charge. The Pinellas County, Florida, Sheriff's Office outfitted a handicapped accessible bus with video visitation equipment, which travels to four cities.[55]

Telemedicine Telemedicine, one of the newest advances in medicine, is providing prisoners cost-effective health care. Taking a prisoner to a specialist outside the prison poses a danger to correctional officers and the community by giving the prisoner an opportunity to escape or to have contact with other people in a less-controlled environment. Telemedicine allows physicians to consult with on-site medical personnel through videoconferencing and compatible medical devices, such as medical microcameras. Health care in correctional settings is improved, and the substantial savings on in-prison consultations and on trips to local providers can offset the costs of introducing this technology. Arizona, for example, saved $237,000 by using telemedicine in nine correctional facilities.[56] Those states that have implemented telemedicine use it for medical and mental health services as well as for staff training and education.[57] However, some critics question the quality of medicine inmates receive via telemedicine, and point out that inmates need practice interacting effectively with people outside of prison.

Offender and Officer Tracking and Recognition

Automated kiosks, also discussed in Chapter 5, are on the way to replacing routine visits to probation and parole officers. Offenders are instructed to report to a kiosk at a specified location. There they are electronically interviewed and in some cases tested for alcohol by means of a breath analysis attachment. Using the kiosks, offenders can also e-mail their parole officers to schedule personal meetings. The system identifies the offender by reading a magnetic card and using a biometric fingerprint scanner. **Biometrics** is the automated identification or verification of human identity through measurable physiological and behavioral traits such as iris, retinal, and facial recognition; hand and finger geometry; fingerprint and voice

biometrics

The automated identification or verification of human identity through measurable physiological and behavioral traits.

Prison medical staff videoconference with an offsite physician about a prisoner's physical health. Advances in technology have helped make prisons and jails safer and more secure, while facilitating innovations such as telemedicine. What promises might tomorrow's technologies hold for correctional institutions?

© F. Carter Smith/Sygma/Corbis

identification; and dynamic signature. The biometrics of the future are body odor, ear shape, facial thermography, and thermal imagery.

Remote-location monitoring of offenders, also discussed in Chapter 5, is steadily improving and is likely to be used far more in the future. However, remote-location monitoring is not just for inmates. Correctional officers can also wear personal alarm and location units that allow a computer to track their locations and respond to distress signals by sending the closest officers to the site of the emergency.

Fairly new in the field of corrections is the global positioning system (GPS). Already used in airplanes, automobiles, and smartphones, GPS is now also used for monitoring offenders under community supervision. The GPS tracking unit worn by an offender allows computers to pinpoint the offender's location at any time to the precise street address. The device can be programmed to send a signal if an offender enters a forbidden zone or even a spoken warning emanating from the device itself instructing the offender to leave the area or face the consequences. In the field of inmate monitoring, there is also some discussion about implanting chips in offenders' bodies that would alert officials to unacceptable behavior. In some cases, when criminal activity was detected, the chip might give an electric shock that would temporarily shut down the offender's central nervous system.

A new technological tool designed to track an offender's alcohol consumption is the continuous transdermal alcohol monitoring device. An electrostatic pad presses against the offender's upper arm, chemically "tasting" sweat for signs of alcohol. A continuous transdermal alcohol monitor was used on Lindsay Lohan after she violated her probation stemming from DUI charges.[58]

Administrators are also relying on new telecommunications technology to help track inmates and former inmates. Speaker ID technology identifies a speaker even if he or she has a cold, just woke from a deep sleep, or has a poor telephone connection. Systems using speaker ID can be used to keep track of who calls inmates in prison and to monitor criminal activity such as escape plans, gang activity, and smuggling contraband. Speaker ID can also be used for low-risk offenders granted early parole as an alternative to incarceration. The system can make random calls and positively identify the speaker from his or her response. The offenders never know when or how they will receive calls. When no one answers the phone or the speaker is not identified, the system alerts authorities to a possible violation.

The use of facial recognition technology is also on the increase in corrections. All 300 employees of the Prince George County Correctional Center in Upper Marlboro, Maryland, swipe picture-image ID cards across a scanner. The swipe alerts the system that an employee is entering the facility. The system verifies the image from a database and using the biometrics of the employee's face, compares it to the one captured by the camera. Eventually, Prince George County will use biometric-based access control technology to screen visitors to determine whether they are ex-inmates.

The principles of geographic information systems (GISs) are also changing corrections.[59] GIS links graphics with tabular information to produce a graphical, layered, spatial interface or map that can help prison management in many ways.

Proponents foresee a time when corrections mapping can be used to do the following:

1. track and display inmate location and movement;
2. indicate whether a housing unit is balanced with regard to religion, group affiliation, age, race, and ethnicity;
3. pinpoint the locations of gang members and link them to each inmate's behavioral and criminal history as well as the inmate's rank in the hierarchy of the group;
4. pinpoint areas in a prison that are potentially dangerous such as hallways or blind corners where a number of assaults may have occurred;
5. incorporate aerial photos of a facility to check for possible security breaches and potential escape routes;
6. provide a basis for proactive investigation and enforcement, for example, mapping the flow of money in and out of prison and then linking it to data about visitation, telephone calls, and correspondence addresses to show a potential drug problem; and
7. link inmate data to the names, telephone numbers, and addresses of all the people the inmate had contact with during incarceration, in case of an escape.

Detection

To maintain prison security, researchers have developed new detection technologies. One is ground-penetrating radar (GPR), which can be used to locate underground escape tunnels. Another is heartbeat monitoring. Using the same technology employed by geologists to detect earthquakes, geophone machines can detect the heartbeat of an inmate trying to escape in a laundry or trash truck leaving the prison. In 1999, heartbeat monitoring prevented the escape of a prisoner in Tennessee. X-rays and magnetic resonance imaging scan the body for concealed weapons, eliminating the necessity for a physical search. Noninvasive drug detection technology places a swab or patch on the skin, which absorbs perspiration and signals the presence of illegal drugs. Pupillometry (a binocular-like device that flashes a light to stimulate pupil contraction) can also measure drug or alcohol use. Another technological tool for drug testing has inmates look through a viewfinder. Ion scans can also detect drug particles on visitors to correctional facilities. In addition, correctional officers can now control prison riots and disturbances using a joystick and monitor that directs an "assault intervention device," a 6-foot robot to blast millimeter waves that simulate intense heat under the skin where pain receptacles are located.

Implementation

Despite the increase in such technology, obstacles must still be overcome. Corrections personnel have been slow to embrace new technology, in part because new systems can be unreliable and difficult to maintain and have high life cycle costs. Ethical concerns about the rights of offenders might be another barrier to implementing new technology. Through a program sponsored by the Department of Justice—Staff and Inmate Monitoring (SAINT)—the Navy's Space and Naval Warfare System Center in Charleston, South Carolina, is systematically addressing biometric and smart card technology through development, testing, and evaluation of a prototype system in the Navy Consolidated Brig in Charleston.[60] There is no question, however, that new technologies are playing an increasingly important role in correctional institutions as a means to address critical health, safety, and security issues.

REVIEW AND APPLICATIONS

SUMMARY

1 The Pennsylvania and Auburn prison systems emerged in the United States at the turn of the 19th century. The Pennsylvania system isolated prisoners from each other to avoid harmful influences and to give prisoners reflection time so they might repent. The Auburn system allowed inmates to work together during the day under strict silence. At night, however, prisoners were isolated in small sleeping cells. With time, sleeping cells became congregate and restrictions against talking were removed.

2 There have been nine eras in U.S. prison history:
- Penitentiary era (1790–1825)
- Mass prison era (1825–1876)
- Reformatory era (1876–1890)
- Industrial era (1890–1935)
- Punitive era (1935–1945)
- Treatment era (1945–1967)
- Community-based era (1967–1980)
- Warehousing era (1980–1995)
- Just deserts era (1985–present)

3 On January 1, 2015, 1,350,958 people were under the jurisdiction of state correctional authorities, and 210,567 people were under the jurisdiction of the federal prison system. Of these state and federal inmates, 7 percent were female, 33 percent were white, 36 percent were black, and 22 percent were Hispanic. Reasons for the increase in women prisoners include women's presence in the U.S. labor market, which has brought about increased opportunities for crime; the increased poverty of young, female, single heads of households, which means that more women are turning to crime to support themselves and their families; changes in the criminal justice system, which no longer affords women differential treatment; and the combined effects of harsh drug laws, changing patterns of drug use, and mandatory sentencing policies. Reasons for the increase in minority prisoners include an increase in serious criminal activity that results in incarceration; racial profiling and racism by the criminal justice system; and the prevalence of social conditions that exist in the nation's inner cities, which is where most minorities in the United States regardless of race live, and the fact that large urban areas have the highest violence rates.

4 The evidence-based literature on prison industries shows that the average prison industry program reduces the recidivism rate of participants by almost 6 percent.

5 Among federal and state inmates, about 37 percent do not have a high school diploma or a GED compared to 19 percent of the general population. Only 283,000 inmates participate in educational programs. Evidence-based literature shows that corrections-based educational programs are effective in reducing crime.

6 All 50 states, the Federal Bureau of Prisons (BOP), and four local jurisdictions operate correctional institutions. State prison administration, a function of the executive branch of government, is most often organized around a central authority operating from the state capital. There are three levels of state prison security: maximum, for the most dangerous offenders serving long sentences; medium, for less dangerous offenders serving long or short sentences; and minimum, for the least dangerous offenders.

7 Prisons are overcrowded for at least three reasons. First, over the past decade, there has been an increase in imprisonment. Second, changes in federal and state sentencing laws require more offenders to serve longer periods. And third, there has been an increase in imprisonment for drug and violent offenses. Methods to control prison overcrowding include release more inmates, reduce admissions and lengths of stay, make it easier to win parole, decide that community sanctions are more appropriate consequences than prison time, divert more individuals to mental health and addiction treatments, and redefine what offenses are considered violent in the first place.

8 A supermax housing facility is a method for managing and controlling inmates who have been officially designated as violent or who exhibit serious and disruptive behavior while incarcerated. Some experts who have studied the effects of long-term solitary confinement report evidence of acute sensory deprivation, paranoid delusion belief systems, irrational fears of violence, resentment, little ability to control rage, and mental breakdowns. Others believe the conditions of supermax confinement do not exacerbate symptoms of mental illness or create mental illness where none previously existed. They tell us that psychological disturbances are present among prisoners in the general population as well. Supermax prisons also present extraordinary challenges for staff.

9 Technology has affected corrections in the areas of communication, offender and officer tracking and recognition, and detection.

KEY TERMS

penitentiary, p. 165

Pennsylvania system, p. 165

Auburn system, p. 165

Federal Prison Industries (FPI), p. 176

UNICOR, p. 176

operational capacity, p. 180

design capacity, p. 180

justice reinvestment, p. 183

Roadmap to Reentry, p. 184

maximum- or close/high-security prison, p. 184

medium-security prison, p. 187

minimum-security prison, p. 188

open institution, p. 188

supermax housing, p. 190

special master, p. 191

contraband, p. 193

biometrics. p. 195

QUESTIONS FOR REVIEW

1 Explain the differences between the Pennsylvania and Auburn prison systems.

2 Summarize the eras of prison development.

3 What can you infer from the characteristics of today's prisoners and the reasons for the incarceration of women and minority inmates?

4 Discuss the impact of the evidence-based literature on prison industries.

5 What ideas can you add to the reasons for including education for prisoners?

6 Compare and contrast how state and federal prisons are organized and administered.

7 Debate the reasons prisons are overcrowded and the methods to control it.

8 Summarize the emergence of supermax housing and its impact on prisoners and staff.

9 Debate the pros and cons of using technology in corrections.

THINKING CRITICALLY ABOUT CORRECTIONS

The Federal Roadmap to Reentry

Review the federal Roadmap to Reentry in Exhibit 7–7. Why does the U.S. Department of Justice refer to these reforms as evidence-based principles?

Solitary Confinement: Misconceptions and Safe Alternatives

In May 2015, the Vera Institute of Justice published a document spelling out 10 misconceptions about solitary confinement.

Download the document *Solitary Confinement: Common Misconceptions and Emerging Safe Alternatives* at https://www.vera.org/publications/solitary-confinement-common-misconceptions-and-emerging-safe-alternatives. For each misconception, outline the alternatives.

ON-THE-JOB DECISION MAKING

Technocorrections

Technology has affected corrections in the areas of communication, offender and officer tracking and recognition, and detection. If you were a warden making your first investment into using technology in your prison, where would you use technology?

Advancing Prison Education Programming

As the newly appointed director of prison education programming, you remember two things from your undergraduate corrections course: first, few inmates participate in prison education programs; second, while literacy alone will not prevent crime, it is one of the many skills needed to function well as a responsible and law-abiding adult in our society.

Your warden would like to create a model prison education program and asks you (1) what can be done with little or no budget increase to encourage more inmates to participate in prison education and (2) how will you know whether your strategies have been effective? What will you tell the warden?

PAROLE

Early Release and Reentry

© David R. Frazier/Science Source

[8]

CHAPTER OBJECTIVES

After completing this chapter you should be able to do the following:

1 Present a brief history of American parole development.

2 Understand the function of parole in the criminal justice system.

3 Define *parole* and explain the parole decision-making process.

4 Describe the characteristics of the parole population.

5 Explain what works in parole supervision.

6 Summarize current issues in parole.

> *We must create a pathway for people coming out of prison to get the jobs, skills, and education they need to leave a life of crime. That means supporting effective training and mentoring programs to help people transition into jobs. That means reevaluating the laws against hiring people with a criminal record so that we don't foreclose legal and effective ways out of poverty and crime. That also means giving former prisoners parenting skills so they can give their children the sense of hope and opportunity that so many of them were denied.*
>
> —Statement of Senator Barack Obama on the president signing the Second Chance Act into law, April 9, 2008

The U.S. Parole Commission (USPC) was established in May 1976 by the Parole Commission and Reorganization Act. The USPC is a semi-autonomous agency within the U.S. Department of Justice and decides parole cases involving federal and District of Columbia (DC) prisoners, military offenders who are in Bureau of Prisons (BOP) custody, transfer treaty cases (U.S. citizens transferred from foreign custody to the United States pursuant to a prisoner transfer treaty), and state probationers and parolees in the Federal Witness Protection Program.

At one time, the USPC was a much larger commission than it is today; it was scaled back in the 1980s following landmark changes in sentencing laws after Congress passed the Comprehensive Crime Control Act, which made major changes to federal sentencing and parole policies by replacing indeterminate sentences with determinate sentencing guidelines and abolishing parole and replacing it with "supervised release."

Today, the chairwoman of the USPC is J. Patricia Wilson Smoot. Ms. Smoot was nominated to the U.S. Parole Commission by President Barack Obama and confirmed by the U.S. Senate on September 16, 2010. On January 29, 2015, Commissioner Smoot became vice chair of the agency. She was designated as chairwoman on May 29, 2015.

Today, the major functions of the USPC are to:

- Manage the offender's risk in the community.
- Prescribe, modify, and monitor compliance with the terms and conditions governing offenders' behavior while on parole or on mandatory or supervised release.
- Issue warrants for violation of supervision.
- Determine probable cause for the revocation process.
- Revoke parole or mandatory or supervised release.
- Make parole release decisions.
- Authorize methods of release and conditions under which release occurs.
- Release from supervision those offenders who no longer pose a risk to public safety.
- Promulgate rules, regulations, and guidelines for the exercise of the USPC's authority and the implementation of a national parole policy.

Ms. J. Patricia Wilson Smoot was appointed chairwoman of the U.S. Parole Commission (USPC) in 2015. She is the first African American female chair of the commission. What sentencing laws changed in the 1980s that reversed the scope and function of the USPC?

© Lisa Helfert Photography

PAROLE AS PART OF THE CRIMINAL JUSTICE SYSTEM

parole

The conditional release of a prisoner, prior to completion of the imposed sentence, under the supervision of a parole officer.

discretionary release

Early release based on the paroling authority's assessment of eligibility.

Parole is the conditional release of a prisoner prior to completion of the imposed sentence under the supervision of a supervision officer (responsibility for offenders passes from the courts to the corrections system upon imprisonment). Parole is usually granted by authorities in the correctional system.

Release on parole may be mandatory or discretionary. **Discretionary release** is at the paroling authority's discretion within boundaries established by the sentence and the law. **Mandatory release** is early release after a specific period of time as specified by law. In those states that permit discretionary release, state laws give correctional officials the authority to change, within certain limits, the *length* of a sentence. Correctional officials may also change the *conditions* under which convicted offenders are supervised—for example, they may release offenders from prison to supervision in the community or to an outside facility. The American Probation and Parole Association (APPA), the nation's largest association of probation and parole professionals, supports discretionary parole (see Exhibit 8–1).

Historical Overview

The parole concept has its roots in an 18th-century English penal practice—indentured servitude. Judges transferred custody of physically fit condemned

mandatory release

Early release after a time period specified by law.

Parole and Reentry

CO8-1

Visit http://video.pbs.org/video/1290027448/ or scan this code with the QR app on your smartphone or digital device and watch the PBS podcast of transporting female convicts to Australia in 1789. How does this information relate to ideas discussed in this chapter?

felons to independent contractors, paying those contractors a fee to transport the prisoners to the American colonies and sell their services for the duration of their sentences to the highest bidder. This practice was similar to today's parole in that the indentured servant had to comply with certain conditions to remain in supervised "freedom." This practice was discontinued with the beginning of the American Revolutionary War in 1775 because English offenders were joining colonial forces against England.

From 1775 through 1856, English offenders were sent to Australia as punishment. Those who committed more felonies in Australia were transported to England's most punitive prison on Norfolk Island, 1,000 miles off the east coast of Australia. In 1840, British Navy Captain Alexander Maconochie was appointed superintendent of the penal colony. Maconochie favored indeterminate sentences rather than fixed sentences. He recommended and in part implemented a marks system to measure the prisoner's progress toward release from prison, and he urged a system of graduated release and aftercare of prisoners to resettle them in the community. He developed a "ticket of leave" system, which moved inmates through stages: imprisonment, conditional release, and complete restoration of liberty. Inmates moved from one stage to the next by earning "marks" for improved conduct, frugality, and good work habits. Although Maconochie had control over island tickets of leave, he could not control a graduated return to society in England. Maconochie's ideas did not blend well with the official English position on punishment, which was rooted in deterrence and relied on the infliction of suffering. He was removed in 1844 and the penal colony at Norfolk Island lapsed into a period of extraordinary brutality before it closed in 1856. Maconochie is referred to as the founder of parole.

In 1854, Sir Walter Crofton, director of the Irish prison system, implemented a system that was based on Maconochie's ticket of leave system. Crofton's version required that upon conditional release, a former inmate do the following:

1. Report immediately to the constabulary on arrival and once a week thereafter.
2. Abstain from any violation of the law.
3. Refrain from habitually associating with notoriously bad characters.
4. Refrain from leading an idle and dissolute life without means of obtaining an honest living.
5. Produce the ticket of leave when asked to do so by a magistrate or police officer.
6. Not change locality without reporting to the constabulary.[1]

The former inmate who did not comply with the conditions of release was reimprisoned. Crofton's system of conditional release is considered the forerunner of modern American parole.

Early American Parole Development The first legislation authorizing parole in the United States was enacted in Massachusetts in 1837. The Elmira Reformatory in New York, which opened in 1876, was the first U.S. correctional institution to implement an extensive parole program.

By 1889, 12 states had implemented parole programs; by 1944, all 48 states had enacted parole legislation.

Parole Development in the Early 20th Century The 1920s and early 1930s were a turbulent period in the United States. During Prohibition, organized crime increased, street gang warfare escalated, and the media provided obsessive coverage of criminals and their activities. Prison riots

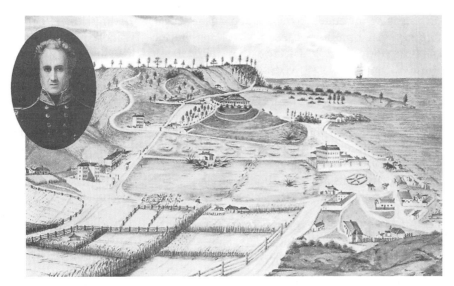

Captain Alexander Maconochie, who became superintendent of the British penal colony on Norfolk Island, Australia, in 1840, implemented a "ticket of leave" system to ease inmate transition from custody to freedom. Later, Sir Walter Crofton, director of the Irish prison system, implemented a system based on Maconochie's ideas. How did their systems influence current parole procedures?

Courtesy K. J. Maconochie, Esq., London. By E. V. Rippingille, 1836

Background: By Thomas Seller, 1835, by permission of The National Library of Australia

erupted in response to prisoner idleness and arbitrary rules and punishment. Prisons and the parole system failed to rehabilitate offenders.

The Wickersham Commission, a commission on law enforcement and observance appointed by President Herbert Hoover, issued a report in 1931 that advocated uniformity in state parole practices by recommending that states establish centralized policymaking boards to write standards and guidelines for parole practices.[2] This report included a list of the "essential elements" of a good parole system:

1. indeterminate sentence law permitting the offender to be released (conditionally) at the time when he or she is most likely to make a successful transition back to society;

2. provision of quality release preparation—in the institution—for the offender who is reentering the community;

3. familiarity by the parole officer with the home and environmental conditions of the offender before he or she leaves the institution; and

4. sufficient staffing levels to ensure an adequate number of parole officers to supervise parolees.[3]

The Wickersham Commission reported that parole was logical because it was an inexpensive way to supervise offenders. Moreover, the commission reported, the **parolee** earns money whereas the prisoner cannot support himself or herself and cannot contribute financially to his or her family. By 1944, all of the states had passed parole legislation.

Despite the fact that all states had enacted parole legislation, by the mid-1940s, opposition to it was strong. The attitude that parole boards were turning hardened criminals loose on society sparked a series of angry attacks through national and state commissions, investigatory hearings, editorials and cartoons, press releases, and books.[4] Opponents claimed that parole had a dismal performance record, its goals were never realized, parole board members and parole officers were poorly trained, and parole hearings were little more than hastily conducted, almost unthinking interviews.

In spite of the gap between its goals and reality, parole fulfilled important functions for officials in the criminal justice system. Wardens supported parole because the possibility of earning parole served as an incentive for offenders, making it easier to keep peace. Wardens also used parole to control prison overcrowding by keeping the number of people being released

parolee (aka formerly incarcerated)

A person who is conditionally released from prison to community supervision.

on parole about equal to the number of new prisoner admissions. Legislators supported parole because it cost less than incarceration. District attorneys supported parole because they felt it helped with plea bargaining. Without parole, district attorneys argued, there was little motivation for defendants, particularly those facing long prison sentences, to plead guilty to lesser crimes. District attorneys also supported parole because parolees could be returned to prison without new trial proceedings.

Together, these groups made a claim to the public that parole actually extended state control over offenders because the formerly incarcerated were supervised. Eventually, the public accepted the claim that parole was tough on criminals and that abolishing parole would end state control over dangerous persons.

Parole Development in the Late 20th Century Opposition to parole resurfaced in the 1960s and 1970s, this time as part of a larger political debate about crime, the purposes of sanctioning, and the appropriateness of the unlimited discretion afforded various sectors of the criminal justice system (paroling authorities in particular). During this period, the debate on correctional policy addressed both the assumptions of the rehabilitative ideal and the results of indeterminate sentencing and parole.

In the 1970s, research indicated that prison rehabilitation programs had few positive benefits. The formerly incarcerated were not rehabilitated, as parole advocates had claimed.[5] This position was supported on all sides of the political spectrum, including by those who believed that prisons "coddled" dangerous criminals and by those who questioned the ethics of coercing offenders into submitting to unwanted treatment as a condition of release.[6] These research findings led to many of the sentencing reforms of the 1970s and 1980s and helped usher in the warehousing and just deserts eras shown in Chapter 7. During a time when supporting parole represented a "soft" stance on crime and when crime rates and recidivism were up, the public did not want prisoners released on parole.

In 1987, the APPA voiced its support of parole and objected to efforts to abolish it. Nevertheless, in that same year, six states abolished discretionary parole board release. By the year 2000, 16 states and the federal government had abolished it, and another four states had abolished discretionary parole release for certain violent offenses or other crimes against a person, a topic we return to later in this chapter. The APPA position statement on parole is presented in Exhibit 8–2.

EXHIBIT 8-2 | American Probation and Parole Association

Position Statement on Parole

The mission of parole is to prepare, select, and assist offenders who, after a reasonable period of incarceration, could benefit from an early release while, at the same time, ensuring an appropriate level of public protection through conditions of parole and provision of supervision services. This is accomplished by:

- assisting the parole authority in decision making and the enforcement of parole conditions;
- providing prerelease and postrelease services and programs that will support offenders in successfully reintegrating into the community; and
- working cooperatively with all sectors of the criminal justice system to ensure the development and attainment of mutual objectives.

Source: Reprinted with permission of American Probation and Parole Association.

Reentry

Reentry is the use of programs targeted at promoting the effective reintegration of offenders back to communities upon release from prison and jail. Reentry has occurred since the Walnut Street Jail opened in 1773. However, the scale of offender reentry is larger today than ever before, and we face enormous challenges in managing the reentry of persons leaving prison and jail. Ninety-five percent of all prisoners will be released prior to the expiration of their sentences. In just 20 years, the number of inmates being released from prison has quadrupled. Almost 2,000 offenders leave state and federal prison every day and almost one-half are reincarcerated within three years for either committing a new crime or for violating conditions governing their release.[7]

Why is corrections not correcting? There are many reasons. Among them are the following:

- **Parole supervision:** Most parole officers manage large caseloads and typically meet with offenders for about 15 minutes once or twice a month. Why should we expect such a small amount of contact to make a large difference?

- **Shift in parole function:** Parole has shifted from a service orientation to a surveillance-oriented, control-based strategy centered on monitoring behavior, detecting violations, and enforcing rules. Surveillance technologies such as the global positioning system, remote-control monitoring, and drug testing make it easier to monitor behavior and detect violations. However, what academics and practitioners have been telling us for years—*that surveillance alone does not change criminal behavior*—is in fact a reality. To reduce a formerly incarcerated person's criminal activity, parole agencies and officers must employ evidence-based practices that focus on individual-level change and are shown to work such as academic and vocational education, cognitive-behavioral treatment, and drug courts.

- **Responses to technical violations:** Violators of probation and parole represent the fastest-growing category of admissions to jail and prison, a point we return to later in this chapter. One-third nationally, and 60 to 70 percent in some states such as California.[8] Wisconsin alone returned 4,000 formerly incarcerated persons to prison in 2013 for violating the technical terms of their release, such as traveling out of state, associating with felons and substance users, using a cell phone, or missing meetings with their supervision officers. In 2013, Wisconsin spent $140 million on returning persons to prison who did not commit new crimes.[9]

Recognizing the enormous cost of reincarcerating the formerly convicted for noncriminal offenses, some states have changed the way they respond to probation and parole violators. Kansas allows probation and parole officers to decide whether those who violate early release conditions for nonviolent offenses should go back to prison. Tennessee accelerates prison releases for probation and parole violators who are sent back to prison and complete drug abuse and other counseling programs. Arizona lets probation and parole violators end their community supervision early by applying "good time" (time that is subtracted from a person's sentence for positive behavior, program completion, etc.) against their sentences, thereby reducing the chances they could be sent back to prison for condition violations. Other changes are taking place across the country.

Offender Problems Research shows that when people are released from jail and prison, their job prospects are dim, their chances of finding a place to live are bleak, and their health is poor. Fewer than half have a job lined up before leaving prison. Three-fourths still have a substance abuse problem. More than one-third have a physical or mental disability. Almost one in five has hepatitis C. More than half have dependent children who rely on these reentering adults for financial support. Only one-third participated in educational programs while incarcerated, and even fewer participated in vocational training.[10] (See Exhibit 8–3.) These former inmates will work fewer weeks each year and earn less money as well as have limited upward mobility than if they had never been incarcerated. Research also shows that returning prisoners are increasingly concentrated in communities that are often crime ridden and lack services and support systems.[11] For example, in Illinois, 51 percent of prisoners released from state correctional institutions in 2001 returned to Chicago, and 34 percent of them returned to just 6 of Chicago's 77 neighborhoods. And, no services were located in two of those six neighborhoods. Regrettably, parole violations and new crimes are often committed because offenders reentering the community lack the skills and support to adapt to community life. But as we will discuss later, now that we know that there are geographic concentrations of returning prisoners to a handful of neighborhoods in most large cities, we have an opportunity to place our reentry efforts in those areas.

Prisoner reentry problems are magnified for women leaving prison, especially minority women. Nearly two-thirds of the women confined in jails and state and federal prisons are black, Hispanic, or of other nonwhite ethnic groups. Women in prison have a high rate of prior sexual or physical abuse, high rates of positive-HIV status and other sexually transmitted diseases, and high alcohol, drug use, and addiction rates at the time of arrest. "In most of their communities," writes Beth Richie of the University of Illinois at Chicago, "there are few services and very limited resources available to assist women in the process of reentry."[12]

The situation is even more grim when we look at the reentry problems for black women.[13] These women leaving prison have unique needs in the areas of family and health care that current reentry systems do not consider. Black children are more likely than white or Hispanic children to have a parent who is incarcerated. They are also more likely to be in foster care and remain there longer than white or Hispanic children. Due to their time in poverty, jail, and prison, black women are more vulnerable to becoming HIV positive. Compounding the problem is a generation of black men who are not present in the community to assist with childcare and provide an income for the home. Reentry services have not accounted for the additional

EXHIBIT 8–3	Service Needs of State and Federal Prisoners

Area of Need	Prevalence (Percentage of All Prisoners)
Substance abuse	75
Physical or mental disability	83
No high school diploma	86
No diploma or GED	40
Earned less than $600/month prior to incarceration	50
Homeless before or after incarceration	10

Source: The Council of State Governments, *The Report of the Re-Entry Policy Council: Charting the Safe and Successful Return of Prisoners to the Community* (Lexington, KY: The Council of State Governments, 2005), p. 49.

challenges that black women face but that white and Hispanic women do not. Although the challenges facing black women leaving prison are daunting, in recent years the United States has witnessed a surge of policy interest and innovation in response to these realities that we point out shortly.

Reentry Programs to Help the Formerly Incarcerated With so many problems and such high rearrest rates, it has become clear to many that simply placing an offender in prison does not deter future criminal behavior. The U.S. prison and parole systems have become a revolving door that cities and towns across the nation were not prepared to handle.

Researchers have found that individuals returning home from prison or jail have complex needs and must address a number of issues, which may include:[14]

- **Mental health.** The incidence of serious mental illnesses is two to four times higher among prisoners than it is among the general population.
- **Substance abuse.** Three-quarters of those returning from prison have a history of substance use. More than 70 percent of prisoners with serious mental illnesses also have a substance use disorder.
- **Housing and homlessness.** On average, about 10 percent of formerly incarcerated persons are homeless immediately following their release from prison.
- **Education and employment.** Two of every five prisoners and jail inmates lack a high school diploma or its equivalent. Employment rates and earnings histories of people in prisons and jails are often low before incarceration as a result of limited education experiences, low skill levels, and the prevalence of physical and mental health problems. Incarceration only exacerbates these challenges.
- **Children and families.** Approximately 2 million children in the United States have parents who are currently incarcerated, and more than 10 million minor children have parents who at some point have been under some form of criminal justice supervision.
- **Women.** Women parolees on reentry have gender-specific needs with respect to child care, protection from sexual harassment and abusive relationships, reproductive health problems, few job-related skills or experiences to support themselves or their children, and housing that is safe, secure, and affordable.

Recently, the Legal Action Center (LAC) published the results of an exhaustive two-year study of legal obstacles that people with criminal records face when they attempt to reenter society and become productive, law-abiding citizens. LAC developed a report card to "grade" how states deal with seven roadblocks that criminals face upon reentry: employment, public assistance and food stamps, housing benefits, voting, access to criminal records, parenting, and driving. States were graded from 1 (being the best) to 10 (the worst). Scores ranged from 10 to 48. States with the lowest overall scores have the fewest barriers to reentry. State scores are shown in Exhibit 8–4.

In response to the roadblocks, we see policymakers at all levels of government showing unprecedented interest in the record number of people coming out of prisons and jails.

The national Second Chance Act (SCA) was signed into law on April 9, 2008. It had received bipartisan support in both houses of Congress and from a broad spectrum of leaders representing state and local government, law enforcement, corrections, courts, service providers, and community organizations. This first-of-its-kind federal legislation authorizes making grants to government agencies and nonprofit organizations to provide

EXHIBIT 8–4 Report Card on How States Deal with the Legal Obstacles Prisoners Face on Reentry

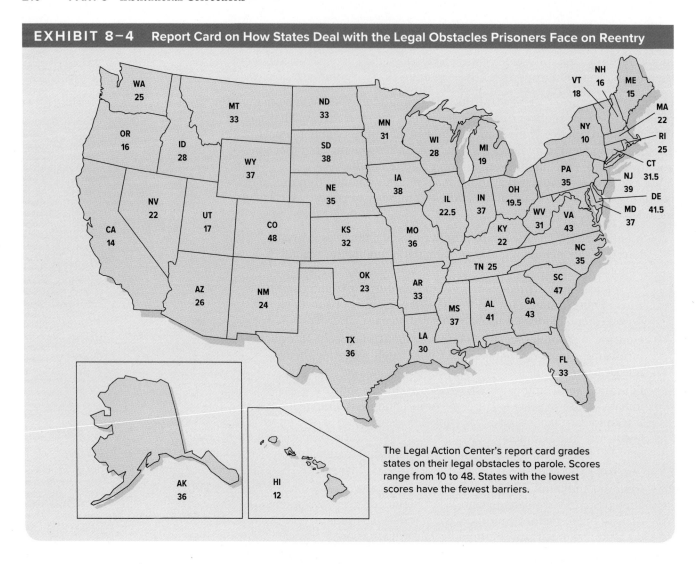

The Legal Action Center's report card grades states on their legal obstacles to parole. Scores range from 10 to 48. States with the lowest scores have the fewest barriers.

employment assistance, substance abuse treatment, housing, family programming, mentoring, victim support, and other services that can make a person's transition from prison or jail safer and more successful. Since 2009, more than 300 local, state, and tribal governments and nonprofit organizations have received SCA grants for reentry programs serving juveniles and adults. Examples of recent SCA awards are shown in Exhibit 8–5.

Before leaving this section on reentry programs to help the formerly incarcerated, let us share what several noted scholars and practitioners believe the corrections system should do while a person is incarcerated, is about to be incarcerated, and after incarceration to improve the chances for a successful return to the community. It is important to remember that there is no one-size-fits-all model to serve the formerly incarcerated, their families, and communities. If there were and were it known, the problems we face would not exist. Thus, while each of the three scholars and practitioners noted here offers evidence-based practices that are known to reduce crime, an integrated model of evidence-based practice to the issue of reentry is still on the horizon.

Jeremy Travis, former director of the National Institute of Justice, and now president of John Jay College of Criminal Justice and a reentry spokesperson, cites five principles for successful reentry.[15]

1. *Prepare for reentry.* Focus on real-world work opportunities that translate into work options on release, health care, community resources, and personal goals.

EXHIBIT 8-5	Summary of Second Chance Act Adult Offender Reentry Demonstration Projects

Grantee	Target Population	Basic Program Components
California: Solano County	Medium- or high-risk female offenders currently or recently incarcerated in the Soiano County jail	Intensive pre- and postrelease case management, **gender-specific cognitive-based therapies, peer mentoring,** transitional housing, employment assistance, parenting, and assistance with basic needs
Connecticut: Department of Corrections	Medium- or high-risk male and female offenders in four Connecticut DOC facilities and who are returning to the target area	A "reentry workbook" program; referrals to the facilities' job centers; prerelease reentry planning with community case managers; a **furlough component** for male offenders; **dual supervision** with parole officer/case manager and community advocate; and **120 days postrelease services**
Florida: Palm Beach County	Moderate- to high-risk male and female offenders who are returning to Palm Beach County from one Florida DOC correctional facility	**Prerelease services at the reentry center provided by counselors, followed by postrelease continued support and services provided by community case managers.** Services include education; employment assistance; transitional housing; parenting, life skills, cognitive behavioral change, victim impact; substance abuse and mental health; family reunification; and assistance with basic needs
Massachusetts: Boston	Male inmates at the Suffolk County House of Correction aged 18–30 with histories of violent or firearm offenses and gang associations who will return to one of Boston's high-crime hotspot areas	**Panel meeting** to introduce the program to and invite eligible offenders; **case management support and advocacy** (throughout incarceration, transition to the community, and after release); a two-week **job skills** course (before release); assistance with employment, education, basic needs, and health care; and referrals to community services
Minnesota: Department of Corrections	Male release violators who are returning to the Minneapolis-St. Paul metro area, and have at least 150 days of supervised release in the community	Individualized transition planning and prerelease case management from a **reentry coordinator,** handoff from pre- to postrelease case management through a **reentry team meeting;** postrelease case management and services **offered at a community hub**
New Jersey: Hudson County	Male and female offenders in the Hudson County House of Corrections who have diagnosed mental health, substance use, or co-occurring disorders	90-day in-jail substance abuse treatment in a gender-specific **therapeutic community** with focus on **cognitive behavioral programming;** prerelease, case management and transition planning postrelease case management, linkage to public benefits, and services delivered by **intensive outpatient/day treatment and supported housing providers**
Pennsylvania: Beaver County	Male and female offenders sentenced to the Beaver County Jail who have medium or high need for mental health or co-occurring services	Cognitive-based treatment groups, **highly structured vocational/educational services, transition planning, and case management and reentry sponsorship (mentoring) that begins in jail** and continues in the community

Note: DOC = department of correction
Source: Christine Lindquist, Janeen Buck Willison, Shelli Rossman, Jennifer Hardison Walters, and Pamela K. Lattimore, *Second Chance Act Adult Offender Reentry Demonstration Programs: Implementation Challenges and Lessons Learned* (Washington, DC: U.S. Department of Justice, September 2015).

2. *Build bridges.* Build bridges between prisons and communities to lessen the isolation of incarceration. Prisons in particular should take a proactive approach and reach out directly to the community to create partnerships (bridges) that provide resources and services for offenders.

3. *Seize the moment of release.* The formerly incarcerated and community partners should seize the moment of release as an opportunity for offenders to serve the community. Transitional housing, health care, and community ties should be available to offenders to provide alternatives to homeless shelters and crime.

4. *Strengthen concentric circles of support.* Family, peer groups, community institutions, social service agencies, and criminal justice agencies are closest to the offender upon release. Together, they have sustainable capital that is likely to be more available than state agencies alone.

5. *Successful reintegration.* Positive rewards go further in changing behavior than negative sanctions. Successful reintegration means recognizing the successes of a formerly incarcerated person and celebrating milestones.

Ed Latessa at the University of Cincinnati recommends three proven approaches for achieving successful reentry into the community.[16]

1. *Target high-risk offenders for greater success.* Studies indicate that low-risk offenders do not need programming because they tend to be more ready for change. Instead, resources should be focused on high-risk offenders who need it more.

2. *Focus on factors that correlate with crime.* Target risk factors that are known to be associated with crime and relapse such as antisocial attitudes, antisocial peers, substance abuse, and lack of problem solving and self-control.

3. *Cognitive behavioral treatment.* Successful cognitive behavioral treatment programs focus on the present and are action oriented. Without changing the ways the formerly incarcerated think and how they process information, housing, employment, and educational assistance alone will not reduce recidivism.

Elizabeth Gaynes, executive director of the Osborne Association (a 75-year-old nonprofit organization dedicated to serving those affected by incarceration), offers a practical prescription for persons who are or have been incarcerated. The suggested services are divided into three phases: incarcerated, about to be released, and formerly incarcerated.[17]

1. *Incarcerated.* Provide needed services and supports related to family, employment, mental and physical health, and spirituality, starting at the point of incarceration to begin planning for release.

2. *Those about to be released.* Prepare a comprehensive discharge plan that includes living arrangements, medications, identification, transportation, emergency funds, escorts, and linkage to community and/or faith-based organizations and mentors.

3. *Formerly incarcerated.* Make sure the formerly incarcerated have access to support and mentoring related to housing, substance abuse treatment, medicine and health care, education job training, employment, child care, identification, transportation, and emergency funds.

Ban the Box Research affirms that a conviction record reduces the likelihood of a job callback or offer by nearly 50 percent.[18] In response,

Visit http://www.youtube.com/watch?v=Xm8 XoWwkfHA or scan this code with the QR app on your smartphone or digital device and watch the podcast of "Boxed Out: Criminal Records & the 'Ban the Box' movement in Philadelphia." In 2011, Philadelphia passed an ordinance that bars employers from inquiring about the criminal histories or doing background checks of job applicants until after the initial interview. How does this information relate to ideas discussed in this chapter?

governments at all levels and private corporations have been equally busy in addressing reentry issues. Recognizing that 77 million Americans—or one in four adults—have a criminal record that can limit their job opportunities or shut them out of work altogether, at least 21 states; more than 100 cities and counties; the federal government; and private employers like Home Depot, Walmart, Target, Koch Industries, Facebook, Starbucks, and Bed Bath and Beyond have removed conviction questions from job applications—a reform commonly known as "ban the box." (See Exhibit 8–6.)[19] The new law allows employers to judge applicants on their qualifications first, without the stigma of a record. The law removes barriers to employment of people with criminal records by prohibiting employers from requiring disclosure of past convictions on

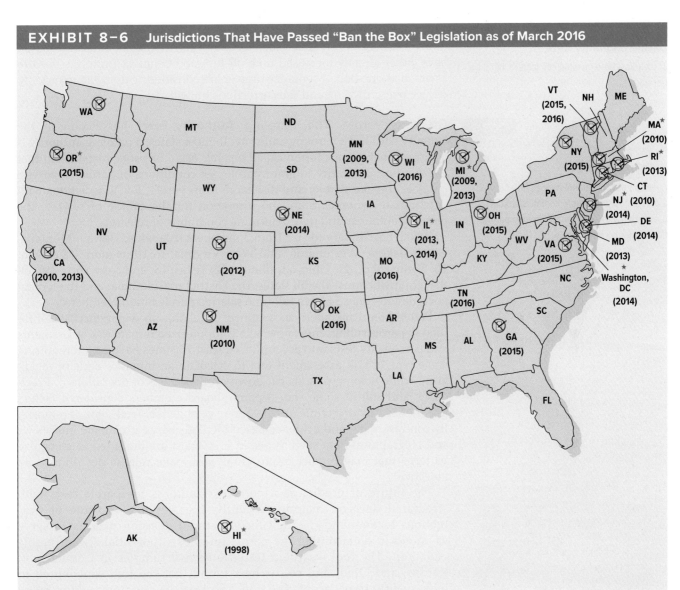

EXHIBIT 8–6 Jurisdictions That Have Passed "Ban the Box" Legislation as of March 2016

⋆ Removed the conviction history question on job applications for all employers.

Source: Adapted from Michelle Natividad Rodriguez, "Ban the Box" Is a Fair Chance for Workers with Records," National Employment Law Project, March 1, 2016, http://www.nelp.org/content/uploads/Ban-the-Box-Fair-Chance-Fact-Sheet.pdf (accessed March 13, 2016).

Visit http://www.nelp.org/publication/
unlicensed-untapped-removing-barriers-state-
occupational-licenses/ or scan this code with
the QR app on your smartphone or digital
device and learn more about the states that
restrict occupational licensing boards' consideration of criminal records. How does this
information relate to ideas discussed in this
chapter?

parole eligibility date

The earliest date on which an inmate might be
paroled.

paroling authority

A person or correctional agency (often called
a *parole board* or *parole commission*) that has
the authority to grant parole, revoke parole,
and discharge from parole.

initial applications, information that often ends any realistic job prospects for ex-offenders. Employers are asked to make individualized assessments instead of blanket exclusions and consider the age of the offense and its relevance to the job. Employers can ask about criminal backgrounds and run background checks after determining that an applicant meets minimum job qualifications. However the new reforms do not apply to police, schoolteachers or other government jobs working with children, the elderly, or the disabled.

Eligibility for Reentry An inmate's eligibility for parole is determined by the sentence received from the court as set by law. The **parole eligibility date** is the earliest date on which an inmate might be released. State statutes usually dictate parole eligibility dates and specify what portion of a sentence an offender must serve before being considered for release.

An offender's parole eligibility date is also affected by good time credit. At least 31 states and the federal government provide some type of good time incentives. Many states such as California, Michigan, and Washington have either already increased time off for good behavior from one-third to as much as one-half of sentence time or are considering doing so in order to reduce overcrowding and the corrections budget.[20]

Granting Parole—The Paroling Authority Every jurisdiction in the United States has a paroling authority. In most states, a **paroling authority** is a correctional agency (often called a *parole board* or *parole commission*) that has statutory authority to grant parole, set conditions of parole, supervise parolees, revoke parole, and discharge from parole. For jurisdictions with determinate sentencing and no discretion for the timing of release, the paroling authority still may determine conditions of release.

Parole boards vary in size from 3 members (Alabama, Hawaii, Montana, North Dakota, Washington, and West Virginia) to 10 or more (Michigan, 10; Connecticut, 11; Ohio, 11; Illinois, 12; Texas, 18; and New York, 19). Of the 52 jurisdictions—the 50 states, the District of Columbia, and the federal government—only 34 have full-time salaried parole board members.

Parole board members accustomed to relying on experience and intuition in parole rulings must now take computerized inmate risk assessments and personality tests into account.[21] At least 15 states have begun requiring some type of risk assessment tool to calculate an inmate's odds of recidivism, while helping prisons cut down on their costs of operations.[22] Previously (and still in some states) parole board members considered factors like the severity of a crime or whether an offender showed signs of remorse. By contrast, data- and evidence-based methods based on inmate interviews and biographical data such as age at first arrest are designed to recognize patterns that may predict future crime and make release decisions more objective.

The future of predicting a person's readiness for parole rests with structured decision making. Recently, the National Institute of Corrections recommended a tool for structured decision making to serve as an aid in determining the parole prognosis (potential risk of parole violation). The tool was field tested on small samples in Connecticut, Kansas, and Ohio, and researchers found that the tool contributed to high-quality, transparent, and consistent parole decision making by all three parole boards. Researchers are now expanding the sample size and inviting other states to join another round of evaluation. The new tool addresses the past criticisms regarding inconsistency and arbitrariness

A parole board meets to consider a release candidate. While discretionary release by parole boards was at one time very common, it has been eliminated in many jurisdictions. Does parole provide offenders with an effective opportunity to reintegrate into society?

© AFP/Getty Images

in parole decision making, draws on the body of evidence-based practices on recidivism and parole outcomes by ensuring that only relevant factors are considered in reaching parole decisions, and increases the transparency and defensibility of individual decisions.[23] The tool focuses on the following seven domains:

1. the offender's history of interaction with the criminal justice system prior to the current sentence;
2. the offender's behavior during the current sentence, both while incarcerated and during previous periods of community supervision on the current sentence;
3. factors that may influence an offender's ability to regulate his or her behavior, such as the presence of antisocial peers, substance use, impulsivity, and affective states such as jealousy and rejection;
4. the extent to which specific offender characteristics (e.g., gender, culture, language, age, program dosage, and targets) are incorporated and considered in the delivery of correctional programs and other interventions;
5. any evidence that an offender has benefited from his or her participation in correctional programming or otherwise changed during her or his sentence;
6. plans for postrelease, including housing, employment, community-based programs or interventions, and available support from family, partners, and peers; and
7. And any unique case factors relevant to an offenders' release outcome or to a parole decision (e.g., a medical condition or disability resulting in mobility issues).

There is a strong likelihood that as more mandatory minimum sentences and three-strikes laws are rolled back, parole boards will reemerge with more power than they have today. Structured decision making can result in better parole decisions, fewer victims, better management of prison resources, and justice reinvestment.

CO8-3 **Granting Parole—The Hearing** In general, parole hearings are attended by victims, the applicant, the institutional representative, and hearing examiners or parole board members. A two-year study of 5,000 parole hearings in Colorado found that the parole board heard too many cases to allow for individualized treatment.[24] The time for a typical parole hearing was 10 to 15 minutes. Unusual cases take longer.

In today's high-tech environment, a number of states are experimenting with video conferencing. The surge in virtual hearings is also a way for cash-strapped communities to boost efficiency and cut costs. So far, reported annual savings are $600,000 in Georgia, $30 million in Pennsylvania, and $50,000 in transportation costs in Ohio.[25]

The final decision to grant or deny parole is based on both eligibility guidelines and the interview. If parole is granted, a contract that defines the release plan is executed and the inmate is given a release date. The inmate who is conditionally released to community supervision is called a parolee.

The trend among parole authorities is to grant or deny parole on the basis of risk to the community. If parole is denied, the common reasons are "not enough time served," "poor disciplinary record," "need to see movement to lower security and success there," and "lack of satisfactory parole program" (proposed home, work, or treatment in the community). In that case, the inmate remains in prison, and a date is set for the next review. The waiting period between hearings depends on the jurisdiction and the inmate's offense.

For example, on Monday, August 29, 2016, the New York State Parole Board interviewed Mark David Chapman, the man who shot and killed John Lennon in 1980. Chapman was sentenced to 20 years to life in 1980 and became eligible for parole on December 4, 2000. For the ninth time, the parole board denied parole and wrote to Chapman:[26]

> "In spite of many favorable factors, we find all to be outweighed by the premeditated and celebrity seeking nature of the crime . . . From our interview and review of your records, we find that your release would be incompatible with the welfare of society and would so deprecate the seriousness of the crime as to undermine respect for the law." The transcript of Chapman's latest hearing was not immediately released. Chapman will next appear for a parole hearing in August 2018. Under New York law, Chapman is entitled to a parole hearing every other year.

Conditions of Parole Paroling authorities set specific conditions for parole on a case-by-case basis (see Exhibit 8–7). Parolees must comply with these conditions, averaging three years, which may include restitution, substance abuse aftercare, remote-electronic monitoring, and/or house arrest, among others.

Parolees are technically in state or federal custody; they have merely been granted the privilege of living in the community instead of prison. Parole officers, who work closely with the parolee and the paroling authority, carry out the supervision of parolees. They can initiate parole revocation hearings and return parolees to prison if they threaten community safety or otherwise violate the conditions of release. Depending on the severity of the crime and the risk presented by the offender, parole supervision can incorporate several types of contact with and "examination" of the parolee, including drug testing, setting of a curfew, remote-location monitoring, and employment verification.

The conditions under which parolees must live are very similar in form and structure to those for probationers. Sometimes the rules are

| EXHIBIT 8-7 | Sample State Conditions of Parole |

State of Alaska

Standard Conditions of Parole

The following standard conditions of parole apply to all prisoners released on mandatory or discretionary parole, in accordance with AS 33.16.150(a).

1. REPORT UPON RELEASE: I will report in person no later than the next working day after my release to the parole officer located at the PAROLE OFFICE and receive further reporting instructions. I will reside at _____.

2. MAINTAIN EMPLOYMENT/TRAINING/TREATMENT: I will make a diligent effort to maintain steady employment and support my legal dependents. I will not voluntarily change or terminate employment without receiving permission from my parole officer to do so. If discharged or if employment is terminated (temporarily or permanently) for any reason, I will notify my parole officer the next working day. If I am involved in an education, training, or treatment program, I will continue active participation in the program unless I receive permission from my parole officer to quit. If I am released, removed, or terminated from the program for any reason, I will notify my parole officer the next working day.

3. REPORT MONTHLY: I will report to my parole officer at least monthly in the manner prescribed by my parole officer. I will follow any other reporting instructions established by my parole officer.

4. OBEY LAWS/ORDERS: I will obey all state, federal, and local laws, ordinances, orders, and court orders.

5. PERMISSION BEFORE CHANGING RESIDENCE: I will obtain permission from my parole officer before changing my residence. Remaining away from my approved residence for 24 hours or more constitutes a change in residence for the purpose of this condition.

6. TRAVEL PERMIT BEFORE TRAVEL OUTSIDE ALASKA: I will obtain the prior written permission of my parole officer in the form of an interstate travel agreement before leaving the state of Alaska. Failure to abide by the conditions of the travel agreement is a violation of my order of parole.

7. NO FIREARMS/WEAPONS: I will not own, possess, have in my custody, handle, purchase, or transport any firearm, ammunition, or explosives. I may not carry any deadly weapon on my person except a pocket knife with a 3" or shorter blade. Carrying any other weapon on my person such as a hunting knife, axe, club, etc., is a violation of my order of parole. I will contact the Alaska Board of Parole if I have any questions about the use of firearms, ammunition, or weapons.

8. NO DRUGS: I will not use, possess, handle, purchase, give, or administer any narcotic, hallucinogenic (including marijuana/THC), stimulant, depressant, amphetamine, barbiturate, or prescription drug not specifically prescribed by a licensed medical person.

9. REPORT POLICE CONTACT: I will report to my parole officer, no later than the next working day, any contact with a law enforcement officer.

10. DO NOT WORK AS AN INFORMANT: I will not enter into any agreement or other arrangement with any law enforcement agency which will place me in the position of violating any law or any condition of my parole. I understand the Department of Corrections and Parole Board policy prohibits me from working as an informant.

11. NO CONTACT WITH PRISONERS OR FELONS: I may not telephone, correspond with, or visit any person confined in a prison, penitentiary, correctional institution or camp, jail, halfway house, work release center, community residential center, restitution center, juvenile correctional center, etc. Contact with a felon during the course of employment or during corrections-related treatment is not prohibited if approved by my parole officer. Any other knowing contact with a felon is prohibited unless approved by my parole officer. I will notify my parole officer the next working day if I have contact with a prisoner or felon.

12. CANNOT LEAVE AREA: I will receive permission from my parole officer before leaving the area of the state to which my case is assigned. My parole officer will advise me in writing of limits of the area to which I have been assigned.

13. OBEY ALL ORDERS/SPECIAL CONDITIONS: I will obey any special instructions, rules, or order given to me by the Alaska Board of Parole or by my parole officer. I will follow any special conditions imposed by the Alaska Board of Parole or my parole officer.

Source: State of Alaska Board of Parole, *Parole Handbook, Appendix II: Conditions of Parole*, June 1998.

established by law, but more often they are established by the paroling authority. The paroling authority can require any of the following forms of release: standard parole supervision, parole with enhanced treatment and programming conditions, halfway house placement, intensive supervision, parole with remote-electronic monitoring or voice and location tracking, or release with follow-up drug testing and payment of supervision fees and restitution.

RELIABLE RESEARCH. REAL RESULTS.

Enter your keyword(s) | Search Site | Advanced Search

EVIDENCE-BASED CORRECTIONS
New Jersey Halfway Back Program

During the 1980s and 1990s, New Jersey saw a dramatic rise in its state prison population. At the same time, the number of parole revocations that resulted in a return to prison for parolees also increased. This growth of admissions to prison for technical parole violators placed pressure on the state correctional budget. In 2001, the New Jersey State Parole Board (NJSPB) responded to this issue by developing Halfway Back, a new approach to manage parole violators, especially technical violators, emphasizing the use of intermediate sanctions and evidence-based practices.

Intermediate sanctions provide an alternative for technical parole violators who have violated the conditions of their parole but have not committed a new felony offense. Halfway Back combines therapeutic elements with confinement. The program is designed to keep technical parole violators out of incarceration—thereby not contributing to the prison population—while providing appropriate treatment services that will reduce the chances of recidivism or parole violation.

Halfway Back is a highly structured program that serves as an alternative to incarceration for technical parole violators or as a special condition of parole on release from prison in New Jersey. Halfway Back programs are run at nine different secure residential facilities in the state and provide parolees with an environment that is halfway between prison and ordinary parole release. The program is run by the NJSPB and targets technical parole violators who have failed to meet supervision conditions, relapsed, or demonstrated some other form of poor behavior (excluding new criminal charges). Halfway Back participants spend several months at a residential facility, receiving necessary treatment services, and are released back to their communities to finish the remainder of their sentence under parole supervision once they complete the program.

The program is rated Promising. Data on re-arrest found 59 percent of Halfway Back program participants were rearrested following release from prison, compared with 58 percent of parolees released to a Day Reporting Center (DRC), 62 percent of parolees who did not participate in a community program, and 79 percent of parolees who maxed out their prison sentence and received no community supervision.

Fifty-nine percent of Halfway Back participants were reconvicted for one of their charges. Participants in DRCs had the lowest reconviction rates; 32 percent were reconvicted for one of their charges. Sixty-two percent of parolees who did not participate in a community program were reconvicted, and 61 percent of parolees who maxed out their sentence were reconvicted.

Halfway Back participants had the lowest rate of reincarceration (17 percent), compared with 20 percent of DRC participants, 39 percent of parolees with no community programming, and 46 percent of max-outs.

Source: Adapted from https://www.crimesolutions.gov/ProgramDetails.aspx?ID=111.

Types of Parole Release on parole may be mandatory or discretionary. Discretionary parole decisions are made by a paroling authority such as a parole board or parole commission after its members review a case to determine whether they believe the prisoner is ready to be returned to the community. The criteria used to reach the decision vary from state to state, as discussed earlier. Discretionary parole decisions occur in jurisdictions using indeterminate sentencing.

Mandatory parole release is set by law and occurs in jurisdictions using determinate sentencing. It requires the correctional authority to grant parole after the inmate serves a specific period of time as required by law. Exhibit 8–8 compares discretionary and mandatory parole release.

Historically, most states have used discretionary parole release. But over the past few decades, the balance between the two methods of parole release shifted. In 1977, 69 percent of parolees received discretionary parole board release. States began moving away from discretionary prison release policies in the 1980s in favor of determinate sentences and mandatory prison release. However, as we suggested earlier, we may

EXHIBIT 8-8	Comparing Discretionary Release and Mandatory Release	
	Discretionary Release	**Mandatory Release**
Release date	Decided by parole board	Determined by law
Criteria	Based on parole board guidelines	None*
Postrelease supervision	Yes	Maybe

*Corrections authorities may have discretion to grant or deny good-time credits in mandatory release cases.

Source: Jeremy Travis and Sarah Lawrence, *Beyond the Prison Gates: The State of Parole in America* (Washington, DC: Urban Institute, 2002). Copyright © 2002 The Urban Institute.

be seeing signs that as mandatory minimum sentences and three-strikes laws are rolled back, parole boards will reemerge with more power. Notice in Exhibit 8–9 that 48 percent more persons entered parole due to a parole board decision in 2014 than in 2011, suggesting that the use of discretionary parole is on the rise.

Proponents of discretionary parole board release argue that parole boards serve a salutary function by requiring inmates to focus their efforts on successful reentry from prison to the community. Without the prospect of discretionary release, inmates have fewer incentives for engaging in good

EXHIBIT 8–9 Percentage of All Prison Releases, 1977, 2011, and 2014

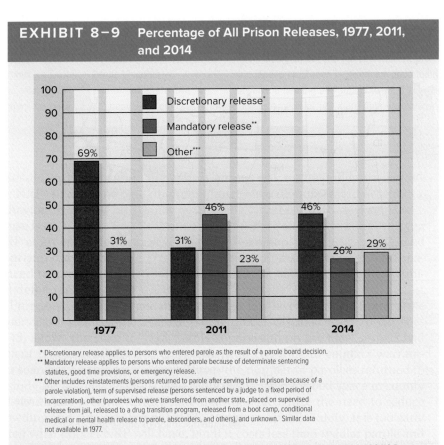

* Discretionary release applies to persons who entered parole as the result of a parole board decision.
** Mandatory release applies to persons who entered parole because of determinate sentencing statutes, good time provisions, or emergency release.
*** Other includes reinstatements (persons returned to parole after serving time in prison because of a parole violation), term of supervised release (persons sentenced by a judge to a fixed period of incarceration), other (parolees who were transferred from another state, placed on supervised release from jail, released to a drug transition program, released from a boot camp, conditional medical or mental health release to parole, absconders, and others), and unknown. Similar data not available in 1977.

Source: Adapted from Laura M. Maruschak and Erika Parks, *Probation and Parole in the United States, 2011* (Washington, DC: U.S. Department of Justice, Bureau of Justice Statistics, November 2012), pp. 7–8; and Danielle Kaeble, Laura M. Maruschak, and Thomas P. Bonczar, *Probation and Parole in the United States, 2014* (Washington, DC: U.S. Department of Justice, Bureau of Justice Statistics, November 2015), p. 19.

CO8-4 CHARACTERISTICS OF PAROLEES

The incarceration of more than 1.5 million adults in state and federal prisons has given many people a sense of safety and security. However, the majority of the population is also unconcerned—or unaware—that at least 95 percent of those who enter prisons eventually return to the community, and most do so in about two and one-half years. Some have put it this way: More prisoners in results in more prisoners out!

Almost 2,000 prisoners each day leave prison. About one in five leaves prison with no postrelease supervision because of changes in sentencing legislation that allow some prisoners to "max out" (serve their full sentences) and leave prison with no postcustody supervision as discussed previously.

The number of people leaving prison is expected to swell even more in the next few years as a result of the U.S. Sentencing Commission's 2014 Reduction of Drug Sentences Act, which aimed to reduce disparities in sentencing for like crimes. An estimated 30,000 federal inmates are expected to qualify for reductions of about two years, on average, as the new guidelines are applied retroactively. In November 2015 alone, almost 6,000 federal drug offenders nationwide were released. Each prisoner had to apply to his or her original sentencing judge, and local prosecutors and supervision officers also weighed in on those petitions. Preference was given to inmates who had participated in evidence-based programming—prison work, job training, or education. Inmates also had to show that they had no disciplinary infractions while incarcerated. Some will go directly into society, but most will transfer to either a halfway house for five or six months, to the custody of another state or county, or to home supervision.

According to the most recent data released by the Bureau of Justice Statistics, the U.S. parole population has changed little over the past few years.[28] On January 1, 2012, 854,600 offenders were on parole. Three years later the number was 856,900. Eighty-nine percent of the adults entering parole on January 1, 2015, were state parolees; the rest were federal. In midyear 2006, the Bureau of Justice Statistics estimated that 14,000 full-time parole officers were supervising the nation's parole population, each with a caseload of about 38 active parolees.[29] (Some agencies supervise both parolees and probationers.) Men and women made up nearly equal percentages of full-time employees.

The basic demographics of parolees have not changed much over the past 20 years. The typical adult parolee is a white, non-Hispanic male on mandatory parole and under active parole supervision for more than one year. The median age is 34, with an 11th-grade education. Women make up 11 percent of the parole population (see Exhibit 8–11). The region with the highest number of parolees is the South, followed by the West, Northeast, and Midwest.

Not all who are sent to prison are released on parole. Those who are the most serious offenders (those who have life sentences or who face the death penalty) or who have disciplinary problems while incarcerated generally are not paroled. Instead, they live out their lives in prison or are released when they have served their entire sentences.

Exhibit 8–12 defines parole populations among the states on January 1, 2015. Texas had the largest number of adults on parole, followed by Pennsylvania and California. The District of Columbia and Pennsylvania also had the highest rates of parole supervision, which means they used parole more than any other jurisdiction. Maine used parole the least.

EXHIBIT 8–11   Selected Characteristics of Adults on Parole

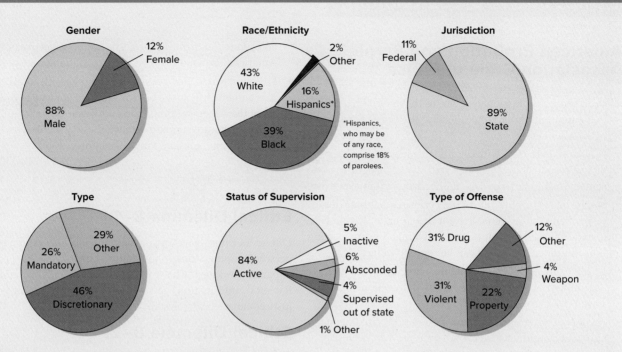

Source: Adapted from Danielle Kaeble, Laura M. Maruschak, and Thomas P. Bonczar, *Probation and Parole in the United States, 2014* (Washington, DC: U.S. Department of Justice, Bureau of Justice Statistics, November 2015).

EXHIBIT 8–12   Selected Parole Populations Among the States, January 1, 2015

Five Jurisdictions with the Largest Parole Populations	Number Supervised	Five Jurisdictions with the Highest Rates of Supervision	People Supervised per 100,000 Adult U.S. Residents	Five Jurisdictions with the Lowest Rates of Supervision	People Supervised per 100,000 Adult U.S. Residents
Texas	111,412	Pennsylvania	1,035	Maine	2
Pennsylvania	102,629	District of Columbia	965	Virginia	27
California	87,104	Arkansas	959	Florida	28
New York	44,889	Louisiana	835	Massachusetts	36
Illinois	29,644	Oregon	766	Rhode Island	55

Source: Adapted from Danielle Kaeble, Laura M. Maruschak, and Thomas P. Bonczar, *Probation and Parole in the United States, 2014* (Washington, DC: U.S. Department of Justice, Bureau of Justice Statistics, November 2015).

Parole Supervision: What Works?   CO8-5

In 2012, researchers at the Urban Institute, the Council of State Governments, and the John Jay College of Criminal Justice Prisoner Reentry Institute launched a clearinghouse to identify and analyze all research on the subject of prisoner reentry. Its purpose is to provide government agencies and criminal justice practitioners a scientifically solid basis for deciding which reentry programs work for the more than 700,000 people released from prison each year.

American Probation and Parole Association Code of Ethics

- I will render professional service to the justice system and the community at large in effecting the social adjustment of the offender.
- I will uphold the law with dignity, displaying an awareness of my responsibility to offenders while recognizing the right of the public to be safeguarded from criminal activity.
- I will strive to be objective in the performance of my duties, recognizing the inalienable right of all persons, appreciating the inherent worth of the individual, and respecting those confidences, which can be reposed in me.
- I will conduct my personal life with decorum, neither accepting nor granting favors in connection with my office.
- I will cooperate with my coworkers and related agencies and will continually strive to improve my professional competence through the seeking and sharing of knowledge and understanding.
- I will distinguish clearly, in public, between my statements and actions as an individual and as a representative of my profession.
- I will encourage policy, procedures, and personnel practices, which will enable others to conduct themselves in accordance with the values, goals, and objectives of the American Probation and Parole Association.
- I recognize my office as a symbol of public faith and I accept it as a public trust to be held as long as I am true to the ethics of the American Probation and Parole Association.
- I will constantly strive to achieve these objectives and ideals, dedicating myself to my chosen profession.

Source: Reprinted with permission of American Probation and Parole Association.

Ethical Dilemma 8–1:

Offenders often leave prison without job skills, money, or personal coping skills. Should they be released on parole? Is parole working? What can agencies do to assist parolees? For more information, go to Ethical Dilemma 8–1 at www.justicestudies.com/ethics08.

Ethical Dilemma 8–2:

A woman with young children is a repeat offender who has again violated her parole. Should she remain in the community, or should she return to prison? What are the issues? Should a parolee's gender make a difference in treatment? For more information, go to Ethical Dilemma 8–2 at www.justicestudies.com/ethics08.

Ethical Dilemmas for every chapter are available online.

Visit https://whatworks.csgjusticecenter.org/what_works or scan this code with the QR app on your smartphone or digital device and read what works on the effectiveness of a wide variety of reentry programs and practices. How does this information relate to ideas discussed in this chapter?

Approximately 1,000 studies have been identified as potentially being worth listing on the website, but to date only about 300 have been processed. Programs are characterized by whether they have strong or modest beneficial effects, no effect, or strong or modest harmful effects. The researchers also assessed each study's "rigor," which they translate as "how much can we trust the findings."

To date, preliminary findings have been compiled in four areas including brand name programs (those employing a variety of treatment options from mental health treatment to employment assistance to address returning prisoners' needs), employment, housing, and mental health. Examples include:

- comprehensive "aftercare" programs were found to be effective,
- employment programs for ex-offenders had mixed results,
- one-half of prison industry programs were rated as being effective, and
- only three analyses on housing issues were available.

CO8-6

ISSUES IN PAROLE

Over the past few decades, the face of parole has changed. This chapter concludes with a discussion of several important issues in parole, including voting rights, reentry courts, successful reintegration programs involving victims, the abolition of discretionary parole board release, prisoner reentry and community policing, and community-focused parole.

Can Parolees Vote?

Currently, an estimated 5.9 million people in the United States cannot vote because they have a felony conviction on their record.[30]

Parole: The Good and the Bad

Racial disparities in the criminal justice system also translate into diversities in the disenfranchised population as well—meaning that felons are restricted from voting. An estimated 38 percent (roughly 2 million persons) of the total disenfranchised population is black, far more than their percent in the general population. This suggests to some that racial disparities in disenfranchisement reflects not only increased involvement in criminal behavior but also biased policy and decision making.[31]

The U.S. Constitution, Article 1, Section 2, gives the matter of voting rights to the states. Only two states—Maine and Vermont—do not deny persons the right to vote based on a criminal conviction; even prisoners may vote by absentee ballot. People with felony convictions in Florida, Iowa, Kentucky, and Virginia are disenfranchised for life, unless they are granted clemency by the governor. The rest of the country falls somewhere in between. In some cities there are efforts to register jail inmates who have not yet been convicted and do not have a past felony conviction. Jails in the District of Columbia, Los Angeles, San Francisco, and elsewhere help inmates vote by absentee ballot. However most counties do not actively help jail inmates vote.

We present the arguments for and against felon disenfranchisement next. As you read them, remember that they have not been scientifically proven. They sound rational on the surface, but social science research has yet to validate them.

There are at least four arguments in support of felon disenfranchisement. First, inmates should be denied the right to vote as a matter of principle because they committed a felony. Second, states have the right to deny felons the right to vote as added punishment, just as they have the right to restrict felons from certain occupations. Third, denying felons the right to vote sends a message about respect for the law and acts as a deterrent to crime. And fourth, felons should be denied the right to vote because they cannot be trusted to make politically informed decisions.

Only Maine and Vermont do not place any restrictions on the right to vote for people with felony convictions. Missy Shea of the Vermont Secretary of State's office helps at Marble Valley Regional Correctional Facility in Rutland with the voter registration process. An estimated 5.9 million people in the United States have lost their voting rights as a result of a felony conviction. What are the arguments for and against felon disenfranchisement?
© AP Photo/Toby Talbot

On the other hand, there are five arguments against felon disenfranchisement. First, voting is not a privilege but a right guaranteed by the Constitution, and states don't have the right to take it away. Second, felon disenfranchisement laws are unfair to minorities who are treated unfairly by the criminal justice system—one of every eight adult black males is ineligible to vote. Third, felon disenfranchisement laws are not an effective form of punishment because most ex-felons did not vote before incarceration. Fourth, removal of an inmate's right to vote is inconsistent with reentry. Offenders should be encouraged to accept more responsibility for their future roles in the community, not less. John Timoney, former Miami police chief and commissioner of the Philadelphia police department, put it this way: "I do not

The Honorable M. Casey Rodgers, Chief Judge, U.S. District Court, Northern District of Florida, congratulates graduates of the Robert A. Dennis Jr. Reentry Court. Reentry courts manage the return to the community of individuals released from prison. What are the core elements of reentry court that facilitate an individual's successful return to the community?

© M. Casey Rodgers, Chief Judge, Northern District of Florida

reentry court

A court that manages the return to the community of individuals released from prison.

think we should give criminals an excuse for not reforming themselves because they are bitter about having had one of their most important rights—the right to vote—taken away. I think it is better to remove any obstacles that stand in the way of offenders resuming a healthy, full, productive life . . . my sense is, once you've cleared the four walls of the jail, your right to vote should be restored."[32] And fifth, once we open the door by declaring that a certain group of people does not deserve the basic right to vote, then which group of people might be the next we attempt to restrict?

Reentry Courts

It is incumbent on criminal justice policymakers who are interested in greater public safety and more efficient use of public tax dollars to consider how we might better handle the challenges of the almost 2,000 offenders who leave prison each day. Because of the potential threats that parolees pose to victims, families, children, and communities, investing in effective parole programs may be one of the best investments we make.

One of the latest innovations in helping offenders released from prison make a successful adjustment to the community is the reentry court. A **reentry court** manages the return to the community of individuals released from prison, using the authority of the court to apply graduated sanctions and positive reinforcement and to marshal resources to support the prisoner's reintegration.

The U.S. Department of Justice proposes that a reentry court have six core elements:

- **Assessment and planning.** Correctional administrators and the reentry judge meet with inmates who are near release to explain the reentry process, assess inmates' needs, and begin building links to a range of social services, family counseling, health and mental health services, housing, job training, and work opportunities that support reintegration.

- **Active judicial oversight.** The reentry court sees all prisoners released into the community with a high degree of frequency, maybe once or twice a month. Also involved are the parole officer and others responsible for assessing the parolee's progress. In court, offender progress is praised, and offender setbacks are discussed.

- **Case management of support services.** The reentry court acts as a service broker and advocates on behalf of parolees for "wraparound services" such as substance abuse treatment, job training, employment, faith instruction, family member support, housing, and community services.

- **Accountability to the community.** Reentry courts appoint broadbased community advisory boards to develop and maintain accountability to the community. Advisory boards also help courts negotiate the sometimes difficult task of brokering services for parolees and advocate on their behalf.

- **Graduated sanctions.** Reentry courts establish a predetermined range of graduated sanctions for violations of the conditions of release that do not automatically require return to prison.
- **Rewarding success.** Reentry courts incorporate positive judicial reinforcement actions after goals are achieved. Examples include negotiating early release from parole or conducting graduation ceremonies similar to those used in drug courts.

According to the U.S. Department of Justice, "The successful completion of parole should be seen as an important life event for an offender, and the court can help acknowledge that accomplishment. Courts provide powerful public forums for encouraging positive behavior and for acknowledging the individual effort in achieving reentry goals."[33] The U.S. Department of Justice is promoting the idea and asking communities to experiment with it, depending upon statutory framework, caseload considerations, administrative flexibility, and levels of collaboration among the judiciary, corrections officers, parole officers, police, business community, religious institutions, community organizations, and the like. Whichever form a reentry court takes, developing new ways that communities can manage and support offenders after release from prison with assistance in securing employment, housing, substance abuse treatment, family counseling, and other services is essential to our ability to reduce crime and keep communities safe.

The Robert A. Dennis Jr. (RAD) Reentry Court program in the U.S. District Court of Northern District of Florida has embarked on what may be the nation's only court evaluating reentry programs that randomly assign offenders to reentry and nonreentry programs. Beginning in 2012, every six months, eligible offenders are randomly assigned to either reentry court or supervision as usual. Eligibility criteria for the RAD reentry court include medium- to high-risk individuals (as measured by the federal postconviction risk assessment) and a minimum of 24 months remaining on supervision; no sex offenders are allowed. Participants progress through four phases, each of which lasts a minimum of 12 weeks (see Exhibit 8–13). Once participants complete the reentry court program, their term of supervision is reduced by 12 months. The impact evaluation will track all offenders for 36 months following release from prison. Evaluation results are expected in 2017.

Reintegration Involving Victims

Successful reintegration programs also involve victims.[34] Victims and victim organizations can assist in the reintegration of parolees by providing parole board members and parole officers with relevant information, offering their experience and expertise, and encouraging offender accountability.

Each year, about 30 million people in America become victims of crime. Most states give victims the right to (1) be notified about parole proceedings, (2) be heard on matters relating to the offender's parole, (3) be present at parole proceedings, and (4) receive restitution as a condition of parole.

Graduates of the Robert A. Dennis Jr. Reentry Court, U.S. District Court, Northern District of Florida. What are the criteria for participating in the Robert A. Dennis Jr. federal reentry court?

© Larry Mainer

EXHIBIT 8-13 | Robert A. Dennis Jr. Reentry Court Phases

PHASE 1 (Minimum of 12 Weeks)

Program Components of Phase 1

- Attend a cognitive behavioral treatment (CBT) program as directed
- Attend monthly reentry court sessions
- Submit to random urinalysis through code-a-phone or as directed
- Maintain crime-free lifestyle
- Comply with all supervision conditions, including but not limited to substance and mental health treatment as ordered
- Be current with any court-ordered financial obligations or must be abiding by a payment plan that addresses the obligation
- Participate in outreach project, as directed

Additional Phase 1 Components

- Meet with vocational rehabilitation, complete preliminary assessment report, and maintain follow-up
- Begin an educational program as directed (GED, college, adult literacy, technical)
- Begin employment program or secure and maintain employment, and submit verification
- Begin developing relapse prevention plan
- Meet and establish relationship with mentor

Criteria for Advancing

- No unexcused absences from scheduled services (vocational rehabilitation; mental health services; educational program; drug treatment; etc.) for 60 days prior to advancing
- No positive drug/alcohol tests for 60 days prior to advancing
- Have made progress toward employment as determined by the Reentry Court team *or*
- Have made progress toward enrollment in educational program (GED, college, adult literacy, technical)
- Have no new arrests or technical violations for duration of phase (arrest or violation results in sanctions imposed by Reentry Court; if allowed to return to Reentry Court following sanctions, participant must begin Phase 1 from start)
- Be current with any court-ordered financial obligations or must be abiding by a payment plan that addresses the obligation
- Approval to advance by Reentry Court team

PHASE 2 (Minimum of 12 Weeks after Completing Phase 1)

Program Components of Phase 2

- Attend a cognitive behavioral treatment (CBT) program as directed
- Attend monthly Reentry Court sessions
- Submit to random urinalysis through code-a-phone or as directed
- Maintain crime-free lifestyle
- Comply with all supervision conditions, including but not limited to substance and mental health treatment as ordered
- Be current with any court-ordered financial obligations or must be abiding by a payment plan that addresses the obligation
- Participate in outreach project, as directed

Additional Phase 2 Components

- Maintain/progress in educational program, as directed
- Maintain employment
- Continue developing relapse prevention plan
- Maintain relationship with mentor

Criteria for Advancing

- No unexcused absences from scheduled services for 75 days prior to advancing
- No positive drug/alcohol tests for 75 days prior to advancing.
- Consistent gainful employment as verified and approved by the Reentry Court team *or*
- Consistent full-time enrollment in educational program
- Obtain GED certification if applicable
- No new arrests or technical violations for duration of phase (arrest or violation results in sanctions imposed by Reentry Court; if participant allowed to return to Reentry Court following sanctions, return to Phase 1)
- Be current with any court-ordered financial obligations or must be abiding by a payment plan that addresses the obligation
- Approval to advance by Reentry Court team

PHASE 3 (Minimum of 12 Weeks after Completing Phase 2)

Program Components of Phase 3

- Attend a cognitive behavioral treatment (CBT) program as directed
- Attend monthly Reentry Court sessions
- Submit to random urinalysis through code-a-phone or as directed
- Maintain crime-free lifestyle
- Comply with all supervision conditions, including but not limited to substance and mental health treatment as ordered
- Be current with any court-ordered financial obligations or must be abiding by a payment plan that addresses the obligation
- Participate in outreach project, as directed

Additional Phase 3 Components

- Maintain/progress in educational program, as directed
- Maintain employment
- Continue developing relapse prevention plan
- Maintain relationship with mentor
- Fully integrated into and contributing to Reentry Court program

Criteria for Advancing

- No unexcused absences from scheduled services for 90 days prior to advancing
- No positive drug/alcohol tests for 90 days prior to advancing.
- Consistent employment with no disciplinary write-ups at work *or*
- Consistent full-time enrollment with satisfactory progress in educational program
- No new arrests or technical violations for duration of phase (arrest or violation results in sanctions imposed by Reentry Court; if participant allowed to return to Reentry Court following sanctions, return to Phase 1 or Phase 2 as determined by Reentry Court team)

EXHIBIT 8-13 Robert A. Dennis Jr. Reentry Court Reentry Court Phases *(continued)*

- Be current with any court-ordered financial obligations or must be abiding by a payment plan that addresses the obligation
- Actively participate in Reentry Court sessions
- Approval to advance by Reentry Court team

PHASE 4 (Minimum of 4 Weeks after Completing Phase 3)

Program Components of Phase 4

- Attend a cognitive behavioral treatment (CBT) program as directed
- Attend monthly Reentry Court sessions
- Submit to random urinalysis through code-a-phone or as directed
- Maintain crime-free lifestyle
- Comply with all supervision conditions, including but not limited to substance and mental health treatment as ordered
- Be current with any court-ordered financial obligations or must be abiding by a payment plan that addresses the obligation
- Participate in outreach project, as directed

Additional Phase 4 Components

- Maintain/progress in educational program, as directed
- Maintain employment
- Complete an approved, written relapse prevention plan and present relapse prevention plan to group
- Maintain relationship with mentor
- Actively facilitating positive and negative reinforcement in Reentry Court sessions

Criteria for Graduation

- Completion of CBT
- No positive drug/alcohol tests for duration of phase
- Consistent employment; OR
- Consistent full-time enrollment in educational program
- No new arrests or technical violations for duration of phase (arrest or violation results in sanctions imposed by Reentry Court; if participant allowed to return to Reentry Court following sanctions, return to Phase 1, Phase 2, or Phase 3 as determined by Reentry Court team)
- Present relapse prevention plan to group
- Demonstrate leadership in group
- Approval to graduate by Reentry Court team

POSTREENTRY COURT PHASE (24 weeks)

Components of Postreentry Court Phase

- Return to traditional supervision
- Maintain crime-free lifestyle
- Comply with all supervision conditions, including but not limited to substance and mental health treatment as ordered

Criteria for Early Termination (up to one year prior to the original expiration date) from the Term of Supervision

- No violations for duration of phase
- No arrests for duration of phase

These rights are designed to ensure that the views of victims are taken into account before decisions about parole are made and to help victims prepare themselves for the offender's release. Victim input can highlight the need for strict supervision or special conditions such as restitution orders, order of protection, or mandated treatment in order to discourage reoffending and encourage reintegration.

Programs involving victims operate in a number of ways. Some encourage victims to volunteer relevant information to parole officers. For example, in stalking cases, victims can tell parole officers whether offenders are in areas where they are not supposed to be. Other programs encourage victim–offender communication. In these programs, victims educate offenders about the impact of the crime and generate remorse in the hope that they can change offender behavior in the future. Whether the program features one-on-one conversation or a victim talking to an audience of imprisoned or paroled offenders, the aim is to convey to offenders the consequences of their actions in terms of the victims' pain and suffering.

Abolition of Discretionary Parole Board Release

Earlier in this chapter, we discussed the strong opposition to parole in the 1930s and that opponents wanted to abolish it. They argued that parole boards were turning hardened criminals loose on society, parole had a dismal performance record, its goals were never realized, parole board members and parole officers were poorly trained, and parole hearings were

REVIEW AND APPLICATIONS

SUMMARY

1 Early English judges spared the lives of condemned felons by exiling them first to the American Colonies and then to Australia as indentured servants. Captain Alexander Maconochie, superintendent of the British penal colony on Norfolk Island, devised a "ticket of leave" system that moved inmates through stages. Sir Walter Crofton used some of Maconochie's ideas for his early release system in Ireland. In the United States, Zebulon Brockway implemented a system of upward classification.

2 Paroling authorities play powerful roles in the criminal justice system. They determine the length of incarceration for many offenders and can revoke parole. The paroling authority's policies have a direct impact on an institution's population. Paroling authorities use state laws and information from courts and other criminal justice agencies to make release decisions.

3 *Parole* is the conditional release of a prison inmate prior to sentence expiration with supervision in the community. The parole process of release begins in the courtroom when the judge sentences an offender to either a determinate or an indeterminate sentence. After serving a certain portion of his or her sentence, an offender is eligible for parole release. That aspect varies from state to state. If an inmate maintains good conduct for a certain amount of time preceding the parole hearing and is granted parole, he or she must live in accordance with specified rules and regulations in the community. If a parolee either violates the technical conditions of parole or commits a new crime, he or she may have parole revoked.

4 The U.S. parole population changed little since 2011. On January 1, 2015, an estimated 856,900 offenders were on parole. One in every 280 U.S. adults is on parole. Eighty-nine percent are state parolees. The typical adult parolee is a white, non-Hispanic male, on mandatory parole and under active parole supervision for more than one year. His median age is 34, and he has an 11th-grade education. Women make up 11 percent of the parole population. The region with the highest number of parolees is the South, followed by the West, Northeast, and Midwest.

5 Researchers at the Urban Institute, the Council of State Governments, and the John Jay College of Criminal Justice Prisoner Reentry Institute launched a clearinghouse to identify and analyze all research done on the subject of prisoner reentry. It found that comprehensive "aftercare" programs were found to be effective, employment programs for ex-offenders had mixed results, and one-half of prison industries programs were rated as effective.

6 This chapter discussed six current issues in parole: inmate voting, reentry court, reintegration involving victims, abolition of parole, community policing and reentry, and community-focused parole. Only Maine and Vermont do not place any restrictions on the right to vote for people with felony convictions. Reentry court requires the parolee make regular court appearances for progress assessment. Reintegration involving victims encourages victims to educate offenders about the impact of the crime and generate remorse in the hope that they can change offender behavior in the future. Today, 16 states and the federal government have abolished discretionary release from prison by a parole board for all offenders. Another four states have abolished discretionary parole release for certain violent offenses or other crimes against a person. In community policing and reentry we find joint supervision of parolees by teams of police and parole officers. The goal of community-focused parole is to engage the community so the community engages parole.

KEY TERMS

parole, p. 202
discretionary release, p. 202
mandatory release, p. 203

parolee (aka formerly incarcerated),
p. 205
parole eligibility date, p. 214

paroling authority, p. 214
nonrevocable parole (NRP), p. 220
reentry court, p. 226

QUESTIONS FOR REVIEW

1 Explain the history of parole development in the United States.

2 Outline how parole functions in the criminal justice system.

3 Describe parole and the parole decision-making process.

4 What can you infer from the characteristics of the parole population?

5 What do you think about what works in parole supervision?

6 Critique the current issues in parole.

THINKING CRITICALLY ABOUT CORRECTIONS

Reentry and Cognitive Transformation

Individual-level change is required before opportunities for work, reuniting families, and providing housing make a difference in a parolee's life. Others refer to this change as cognitive transformation. How can parole agencies help offenders achieve cognitive transformation and successful reentry?

Abolish Parole?

Sixteen states and the federal government have abolished discretionary parole board release from prison in favor of mandatory release. Another four states abolished it for certain violent offenses or other crimes against a person. Proponents of discretionary prison release argue that abandonment of discretionary release has a detrimental effect. They believe that parole boards serve a salutary function by requiring inmates to focus their efforts on successful reentry from prison to the community. They argue that without the prospect of discretionary prison release, inmates have fewer incentives for cognitive transformation and opportunities for work, reuniting with families, and housing. Critically examine the issues of this debate.

ON-THE-JOB DECISION MAKING

Nonrevocable Parole

To help your state reduce prison crowding and the money it spends on prisons, your parole agency decides it is going to study California's nonrevocable parole law and urge your state legislature to adopt something similar. Go to the California Department of Corrections and Rehabilitation website http://www.cdcr.ca.gov/. Click first Parole and then Non-Revocable Parole tabs. Study the eligibility criteria. Are there criteria you believe should be added to the list or possibly deleted? Defend your position to a legislative subcommittee on criminal justice.

Mentors and Offender Reentry

As chief parole officer in your area, write a two-page proposal recommending the involvement of mentors in offender reentry. Include what you believe are the advantages of mentoring for offender reentry and strategies for recruiting, training, and matching mentors with parolees.

The Prison World

Part Four explores life inside prison for inmates and staff; the legal challenges surrounding their roles and responsibilities; and the special needs of inmates who are elderly, infected with HIV or AIDS, or mentally or physically challenged.

Custodial staff are most directly involved in the daily work of managing the inmate population. The extent to which correctional officers share beliefs, values, and behaviors is largely a function of the correctional officer subculture and each individual's personality.

Prisoners, too, develop a subculture that helps them adjust to the self-doubt, reduced self-esteem, and deprivations they experience as a result of confinement. Inmate subculture is also based on the life experiences that prisoners bring with them when they enter confinement. One question that we try to answer concerns why men's prisoner subculture encourages isolation but women's prisoner subculture encourages relationships.

For a century, prisoners were considered civilly dead, and prisons operated entirely without court intervention. However, in 1970, the U.S. Supreme Court declared that if states were going to operate prisons, they would have to do so according to the dictates of the Constitution. Since then, prisoners have reclaimed many of their conditional rights under the U.S. Constitution. But today, changes in state and federal statutes have slowed the pace of prisoners' rights cases, and the U.S. Supreme Court seems to have become less sympathetic to prisoners' civil rights claims.

Inmates with special needs—those who are elderly; suffer from HIV, AIDS, or other chronic diseases; or are mentally or physically challenged—present significant problems for correctional managers. Special needs inmates may be more prone to violence and disruption. They frequently require close monitoring to reduce the risk of suicide, and they may tax scarce medical resources and become targets of abuse by other inmates.

The preprison drug use and sexual activity of many prisoners has brought HIV, AIDS, and tuberculosis into jails and prisons. Managing these problems requires training in early detection, treatment, classification, staff education, and adequate funding. These problems are compounded by the fact that many prisoners have co-occurring physical and mental health problems.

[9] THE STAFF WORLD
Managing the Prison Population

CHAPTER OBJECTIVES

After completing this chapter you should be able to do the following:

1 List the staff roles within the organizational hierarchy of correctional institutions.

2 Identify the types of power available to correctional officers, and list and describe the most common correctional officer personality types.

3 List and describe the seven correctional officer job assignments.

4 Identify five significant correctional staff issues.

5 Detail the nature of workplace corruption among correctional personnel, and explain its causes.

6 Explain the impact that terrorism is having on prisons and on the operation of correctional institutions today.

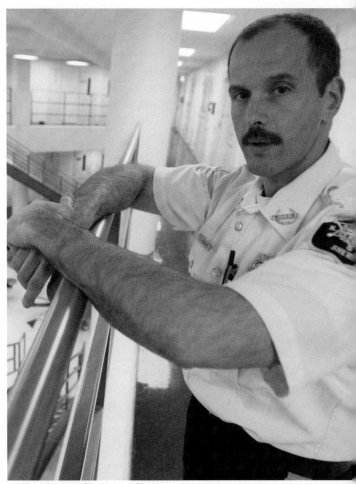

© Robert Sciarrino/Star Ledger/Corbis

Corrections is not a business where only one sex, race, religion, or type of person can succeed. It takes men and women of all races, religions, and color to create a dynamic and effective workforce to manage diverse inmates and solve the problems we face.

—Dora Schriro, former Missouri director of corrections

In 2016, the Pew Charitable Trusts, a highly regarded nonprofit organization that researches American social issues, sounded a warning saying that "many states face a dire shortage" of correctional officers.[1] The Trust cited New Mexico as "one of several states . . . trying to solve a dire shortage and high turnover in state correctional officers this year by proposing pay increases or starting new training academies." It found that many other states—including Michigan, Kansas, Nebraska, Missouri, West Virginia, North Carolina, Texas, and Oklahoma—are working hard to hire and retain more correctional officers. It is important to find a solution because, as the Trust notes, "Understaffed prisons result in long hours, fatigue and stress for guards, and canceled recreational and social programs for inmates, such as family visits—all of which can lead to potentially dangerous situations.[2]

A state correctional officer at work. Why is there a shortage of correctional staff in many states? What can be done to address the issue?
© Gordon Chibroski/Portland Press Herald via Getty Images.

THE STAFF HIERARCHY

CO9-1

Practically speaking, a prison of any size has a number of different staff roles—each with its own unique set of tasks. **Roles** are the normal patterns of behavior expected of those holding particular social positions. **Staff roles** are the patterns of behavior expected of correctional staff members in particular jobs. Eventually, many people internalize the expectations others have of them, and such expectations can play an important part in their self-perceptions.

Ideally, today's correctional staff members have four main goals:

1. to provide for the security of the community by incarcerating those who break the law;
2. to promote the smooth and effective functioning of the institution;
3. to ensure that incarceration is secure but humane; and
4. to give inmates the opportunity to develop a positive lifestyle while incarcerated and to gain the personal and employment skills they need for a positive lifestyle after release.[3]

Prison staff are organized into a hierarchy, or multilevel categorization, according to responsibilities. An institution's hierarchy generally has a warden or superintendent at the top and correctional officers at a lower level. A typical correctional staff hierarchy includes the following:

- administrative staff (wardens, superintendents, assistant superintendents, and others charged with operating the institution and its programs and with setting policy);
- clerical personnel (record keepers and administrative assistants);

roles

The normal patterns of behavior expected of those holding particular social positions.

staff roles

The patterns of behavior expected of correctional staff members in particular jobs.

- program staff (psychologists, psychiatrists, medical doctors, nurses, medical aides, teachers, counselors, caseworkers, and ministers—many of whom contract with the institution to provide services);
- custodial staff (majors, captains, lieutenants, sergeants, and correctional officers charged primarily with maintaining order and security);
- service and maintenance staff (kitchen supervisors, physical plant personnel, and many outside contractors); and
- volunteers (prison ministry, speakers, and other volunteers in corrections).

custodial staff

Those staff members most directly involved in managing the inmate population.

program staff

Those staff members concerned with encouraging prisoners to participate in educational, vocational, and treatment programs.

Organizational charts graphically represent the staff structure and the chain of command within an institution. An organizational chart for a typical medium-to-large correctional institution is shown in Exhibit 9–1. **Custodial staff** are most directly involved in managing the inmate population through daily contact with inmates. Their role is to control prisoners within the institution. **Program staff,** on the other hand, are concerned with encouraging prisoners to participate in educational, vocational, and treatment programs. Custodial staff, who make up more than 60 percent

EXHIBIT 9–1   Organizational Chart of a Typical Midsize or Large Correctional Institution

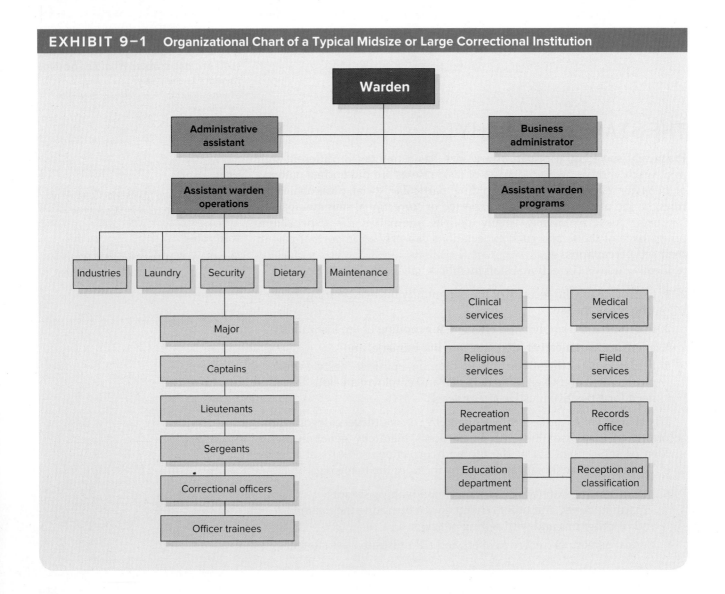

of prison personnel, are generally organized in a military-style hierarchy, from assistant or deputy warden down to correctional officer. Program staff generally operate through a separate organizational structure and have little in common with custodial staff.

To a great extent, prison management involves managing relationships—among employees, between employees and inmates, and among inmates. Prisons are unique in that most of the people in them (the inmates) are forced to live there according to the terms of their sentence; they really do not want to be there. Such a situation presents tremendous challenges. The people on the front lines dealing around the clock with such challenges are the correctional officers.

THE CORRECTIONAL OFFICER—
THE CRUCIAL PROFESSIONAL

Although security is still the major concern, correctional officers today are expected to perform a variety of other tasks. As one commentator has said,

> Correctional officers have more responsibilities [now] than in the past and their duty is no longer to merely watch over the prisoners. They now have to play several roles in keeping prisoners in line. They have to be "psychiatrists" when prisoners come to them with their problems, and they have to be "arbitrators and protectors" when inmates have complaints or problems with each other, while still watching out for their own safety. In these situations, the wrong decision could offend someone and start a riot. This makes correctional officers "prisoners" of the daily emotional and physical moods of the inmates.[4]

Don Josi and Dale Sechrest explain it this way: "Correctional officers today must find a balance between their security role and their responsibility to use relationships with inmates to change their behavior constructively. They routinely assume numerous essential yet sometimes contradictory roles (e.g., counselor, diplomat, caretaker, disciplinarian, supervisor, crisis manager), often under stressful and dangerous conditions."[5]

Josi and Sechrest then go on to say, "These divergent and often incompatible goals can prove problematic; role conflict, role diffusion, and role ambiguity may be difficult if not impossible to avoid."[6]

Bases of Power

`CO9-2`

Correctional officers rely on a variety of strategies to manage inmate behavior. After surveying correctional officers in five prisons, John Hepburn identified five types of officers' power, according to the bases on which they rest: legitimate power, coercive power, reward power, expert power, and referent power.

Legitimate Power Correctional officers have power by virtue of their positions within the organization. That is, they have formal authority to command. As Hepburn says, "The prison guard has the right to exercise control over prisoners by virtue of the structural relationship between the position of the guard and the position of the prisoner."[7]

Coercive Power Inmates' beliefs that a correctional officer can and will punish disobedience give the officer coercive power. Many correctional officers use coercive power as a primary method of control.

Securing an inmate in preparation for a trip back to his cell. Correctional officers need to elicit inmates' cooperation to effectively carry out their custodial duties. What are some techniques officers might use?
© Andrew Lichtenstein/ Sygma/Corbis

gain time

Time taken off an inmate's sentence for participating in certain positive activities such as going to school, learning a trade, and working in prison.

Reward Power Correctional officers dispense both formal and informal rewards to induce cooperation among inmates. Formal rewards include assignment of desirable jobs, housing, and other inmate privileges. Correctional officers are also in a position to influence parole decisions and to assign good-time credit and **gain time** to inmates. Informal rewards correctional officers use include granting special favors and overlooking minor infractions of rules.

Expert Power Expert power results from inmates' perceptions that certain correctional officers have valuable skills. For example, inmates seeking treatment may value treatment-oriented officers. Inmates who need help with ongoing interpersonal conflicts may value officers who have conflict-resolution skills. Such officers may be able to exert influence on inmates who want their help.

Referent Power Referent power flows from "persuasive diplomacy." Officers who win the respect and admiration of prisoners—officers who are fair and not abusive—may achieve a kind of natural leadership position over inmates.

Some years before Hepburn's study, Gresham Sykes wrote that correctional officers' power can be corrupted through inappropriate relationships with inmates.[8] Friendships with prisoners as well as indebtedness to them can corrupt. According to Sykes, staff members who get too close to inmates and establish friendships are likely to find their "friends" asking for special favors. Similarly, officers who accept help from inmates may one day find that it is "payback time." In difficult or dangerous situations, help may be difficult to decline. In such cases, staff members must be careful not to let any perceived indebtedness to inmates influence their future behavior.

The Staff Subculture

Staff Subculture

Prison life is characterized by duality. An enormous gap separates those who work in prisons from those who live in them. This gap has a number of dimensions. One is that staff members officially control the

A correctional officer talks with an inmate. Effective communication is one way of overcoming the differences in beliefs, values, and behaviors between inmates and prison staff. What barriers to communication might such differences create?
© Fat Chance Production/agefotostock

institution and enforce the rules by which inmates live. Other formal and informal differences exist, including differences in background, values, and culture. Primarily, however, the relationship between correctional officers and inmates can be described as one of structured conflict.[9]

Structured conflict is a term that highlights the tensions between prison staff members and inmates that arise out of the correctional setting. In one sense, the prison is one large society in which the worlds of inmates and staff bump up against one another. In another sense, however, the two groups keep their distance from each other—a distance imposed by both formal and informal rules. Conflict arises because staff members have control over the lives of inmates, and inmates often have little say over important aspects of their own lives. The conflict is structured because it occurs within the confines of an organized institution and because, to some extent, it follows the rules—formal and informal—that govern institutional life.

Both worlds—inmate and staff—have their own cultures. Those cultures are generally called *subcultures* to indicate that both are contained within and surrounded by a larger culture. One writer has defined **subculture** as the beliefs, values, behavior, and material objects shared by a particular group of people within a larger society.[10] That is the definition we will use. The subcultures of inmates and correctional officers exist simultaneously in any prison institution. The beliefs, values, and behavior that make up the **staff subculture** differ greatly from those of the inmate subculture. Additionally, staff members possess material objects of control, such as keys, vehicles, weapons, and security systems.

Kauffman has identified a distinct correctional officer subculture within prisons.[11] Those beliefs, values, and behaviors set correctional officers apart from other prison staff and from inmates. Their beliefs and values form an "officer code," which includes the following:

- Always go to the aid of an officer in distress.
- Do not "lug" (bring in for inmate use) drugs or other contraband.
- Do not rat on other officers.
- Never make a fellow officer look bad in front of inmates.

structured conflict

The tensions between prison staff members and inmates that arise out of the correctional setting.

subculture

The beliefs, values, behavior, and material objects shared by a particular group of people within a larger society.

staff subculture

The beliefs, values, and behavior of staff. They differ greatly from those of the inmate subculture.

- Always support an officer in a dispute with an inmate.
- Always support officer sanctions against inmates.
- Do not be a "white hat" or a "goody two-shoes."
- Maintain officer solidarity in dealings with all outside groups.
- Show positive concern for fellow officers.

Correctional Officers' Characteristics and Pay

Many people believe that working in corrections is not financially rewarding unless an employee can rise to supervisory positions. In an example to the contrary, the highest paid employee at the State Correctional Institution in Pittsburgh, Pennsylvania, in 2011 was a corrections officer (CO) who earned $139,000.[12] The officer held the lowest rank in the institution—just above trainee—but earned more than the prison's superintendent because of the amount of overtime he worked. According to published reports, many correctional officers earn six-figure incomes because of the number of hours they work. Exhibit 9–2 shows what correctional officers and supervisors earned in 2016 in various locales. The exhibit shows, for example, that the median annual correctional officer's salary in New York is about $49,000. The pay for correctional officers may vary depending on things like location; years of experience; level of education; and whether the correctional employer is state, federal, local, or private. As the exhibit indicates, supervisory personnel can earn far more than line officers, while those who receive overtime pay can more than double their base salary. When considering a job in corrections, it is important to realize that most employers offer significant benefits, including medical, dental, and vision insurance; sick and vacation leave; paid holidays; recruitment incentives; retention pay differentials; bilingual pay; education incentives; physical fitness incentive pay; and various employer/employee-funded retirement plans.

In terms of ethnicity, the American Correctional Association (ACA) says that most correctional personnel at state and local levels are white males. Two-thirds of female custodial and administrative staff members are white. Thirty-two percent of corrections personnel at the state level are members of minority groups.[13] Of these, most are black. See Exhibit 9–3 for the demographic characteristics of staff members working for the federal BOP in 2016.

| EXHIBIT 9–2 | Correctional Officer Pay in 2016, by Selected Jurisdictions |

	National		New York State[2]		Federal (BOP)[3]	
	Average Pay	Maximum Pay with Overtime[1]	Average Pay	Maximum Pay with Overtime*	Average Pay	Highest Paid
Captain	$59,000	N/A	$68,110	N/A	$81,823	$106,369
Lieutenant	$51,000	N/A	$61,215	N/A	$62,000	$83,010
Sergeant	$43,510	$78,010	$54,510	$89,000	$55,666	$67,354
Corrections Officer	$41,568	$89,110	$49,013	$141,000	$52,230	$122,000[4]
Officer Trainee	$31,500	N/A	$33,000	N/A	$39,400	N/A

Notes:

1. Estimated.

2. Amounts are for White Plains, NY.

3. From 2016-GS Salary Table.

4. Includes overtime.

* Supervisory personnel, including captains and lieutenants, are generally not eligible for overtime pay. Amounts shown do not include recruitment incentives, retirement, medical, or other benefits.

Source: Some data derived from simplyhired.com; salary.com; and USAjobs.com.

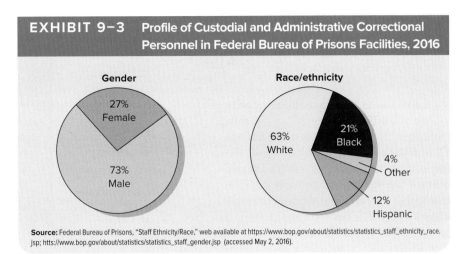

EXHIBIT 9-3 Profile of Custodial and Administrative Correctional Personnel in Federal Bureau of Prisons Facilities, 2016

Gender

27% Female

73% Male

Race/ethnicity

63% White

21% Black

4% Other

12% Hispanic

Source: Federal Bureau of Prisons, "Staff Ethnicity/Race," web available at https://www.bop.gov/about/statistics/statistics_staff_ethnicity_race.jsp; htts://www.bop.gov/about/statistics/statistics_staff_gender.jsp (accessed May 2, 2016).

Although blacks comprise only 12.6 percent of the U.S. population, they account for 21 percent of the correctional workforce. Hispanics are underrepresented (accounting for 16.3 percent of the country's population and just 12 percent of the correctional workforce), as are other minorities (5 percent of the population, 4 percent of correctional staff). Whites, who comprise 66% of the population are slightly underrepresented.

The federal BOP employs approximately 39,770 personnel in its prisons, and about 27 percent of them are women.[14] About 21 percent of correctional staff members in federal institutions are black. In juvenile facilities, females make up slightly more than 42 percent of the correctional workforce.

The ACA also says that approximately 13 percent of all correctional staff positions are supervisory (i.e., above the level of sergeant). Females hold 16 percent of all supervisory positions but fewer positions at the level of warden or superintendent.[15] Consult the Appendix: Careers in Corrections at the Online Learning Center website for the steps involved in career planning, developing employability and job readiness, and finding a job in corrections.

Correctional Officer Personalities

The staff subculture contributes to the development of **correctional officer personalities.** Those personalities reflect the personal characteristics of the officers as well as their modes of adaptation to their jobs and institutional conditions, the requirements of staff subculture, and institutional expectations.[16] We will next explore the common personality types that have been identified.[17]

The Dictator The dictator likes to give orders and seems to enjoy the feeling of power that comes from ordering inmates around. Correctional officers with dictator personalities are often strongly disliked by prisoners and may face special difficulties if taken hostage during a prison uprising. Some dictator officers cross the line by personally degrading inmates under their charge through the use of profanity or racist language or by displays of religious and ethnic intolerance. Certain aspects of the dictator personality may lead to illicit and illegal activities by forcing inmates to provide sexual and other favors.

The Friend The correctional officer who tries to befriend inmates is often a quiet, retiring, but kind individual who believes that close friendships

correctional officer personalities

The distinctive personal characteristics of correctional officers, including behavioral, emotional, and social traits.

Courtesy of Gary Cornelius

First Lieutenant Gary F. Cornelius

Programs Director, Fairfax County Adult Detention Center,
Fairfax County Office of the Sheriff, Fairfax, Virginia

First Lieutenant Gary Cornelius is programs director with the Fairfax County Adult Detention Center in Fairfax, Virginia. He has held this position since October 1995 but has been with the sheriff's department since 1978.

He earned his bachelor of arts and social sciences with a focus in criminal justice from Edinboro State College in Pennsylvania in 1974. He later completed specialized police courses at the Northern Virginia Criminal Justice Academy Basic Police School as well as the U.S. Secret Service. He is a former officer of the Uniformed Division of the Secret Service.

Lieutenant Cornelius is also the author of five books, including *The Twenty Minute Trainer, The Correctional Officer: A Practical Guide,* and *The Art of the Con: Avoiding Offender Manipulation.* "Writing gives me a chance to share what I have learned and to learn new concepts through research," he says.

His duties include the development and oversight of inmate programs, ranging from recreation to rehabilitation and substance abuse. He oversees inmate education, manages volunteers and college interns, and supervises other staff members in charge of inmate recreation.

Cornelius says he enjoys watching his efforts—and the efforts of his teammates—result in positive changes. "Probably the best thing about my job is working with good people who care about both jail security and making programs work for the betterment of inmates," he says. "The most difficult aspect is convincing staff of the need for programs, rehabilitative efforts, and volunteers. And trying to get through the old-fashioned 'jailhouse mentality.'"

What are the skills that serve him best in his day-to-day affairs? "Tolerance for others' points of view, patience, not giving up, and diplomatic people skills when dealing with both civilians and sworn staff," he says.

> *"Having staff work together on an idea and watching operations improve is one of the best parts of this job."*

with inmates will make it easier to control the inmates and the work environment. Inmates, however, usually try to capitalize on friendships by asking for special treatment, contraband, and the like.

The Merchant Merchant-personality correctional officers (also called *rogue officers* or *rotten apples*) set themselves up as commodity providers to the inmate population. If an inmate needs something not easily obtained in prison, the merchant will usually procure it—at a cost. Often such behavior is a violation of institutional rules, and it can lead to serious violations of the law as the merchant correctional officer smuggles contraband into the institution for the "right price." We will discuss correctional officer corruption in more detail later in this chapter.

The Turnkey Turnkey officers do little beyond the basic requirements of their position. A turnkey usually interacts little with other officers and does the minimum necessary to get through the workday. Unmotivated and bored, the turnkey may be seeking other employment. Some turnkey officers have become disillusioned with their jobs. Others are close to retirement.

The Climber The correctional officer who is a climber is set on advancement. He or she may want to be warden or superintendent one day and is probably seeking rapid promotion. Climbers are often diligent officers who perform their jobs well and respect the corrections profession. Climbers who look down on other officers, however, or attempt to look good by making coworkers look bad, can cause many problems within the institution.

The Reformer The reformer constantly finds problems with the way the institution is run or with existing policies and rules. He or she always seems to know better than anyone else and frequently complains about working conditions or supervisors.

The Do-Gooder The do-gooder is another type of reformer—one with a personal agenda. A devoutly religious do-gooder may try to convert other correctional officers and inmates to his or her faith. Other do-gooders actively seek to counsel inmates, using personal techniques and philosophies that are not integrated into the prison's official treatment program.

Although the personalities described here may be exaggerated, their variety suggests that correctional officer personalities result from many influences, including the following:

Tom Hanks as a correctional officer in The Green Mile. This chapter describes a variety of correctional officer personality types. Which do you think is the most common? The least?
© Ralph Nelson/KRT/Newscom

- general life experiences;
- biological propensities;
- upbringing;
- staff subculture;
- working conditions; and
- institutional expectations and rules.

CORRECTIONAL OFFICER JOB ASSIGNMENTS CO9-3

Seven different correctional officer roles or job assignments have been identified.[18] They are classified by their location within the institution, the duties required, and the nature of the contact with inmates. The seven types are as follows:

1. **Block officers** are responsible for supervising inmates in housing areas. Housing areas include dormitories, cell blocks, modular living units, and even tents in some overcrowded prisons. Safety and security are the primary concerns of block officers. Conducting counts, ensuring the orderly movement of prisoners, inspecting personal property, overseeing inmate activity, and searching prisoners are all part of the block officer's job. Block officers also lock and unlock cells and handle problems that arise within the living area. Block officers are greatly outnumbered by the inmates they supervise. Hence, if disturbances occur, block officers usually withdraw quickly to defensible positions within the institution.

2. **Work detail supervisors** oversee the work of individual inmates and inmate work crews assigned to jobs within the institution or outside it. Jobs assigned to inmates may include laundry, kitchen, and farm duties as well as yard work and building maintenance. Work detail supervisors must also keep track of supplies and tools and maintain

block officers

Those responsible for supervising inmates in housing areas.

work detail supervisors

Those who oversee the work of individual inmates and inmate work crews.

inventories of materials. Prison buildings are sometimes constructed almost exclusively with the use of inmate labor—creating the need for large inmate work details. On such large projects, supervising officers usually work in conjunction with outside contractors.

industrial shop and school officers

Those who ensure efficient use of training and educational resources within the prison.

3. **Industrial shop and school officers** work to ensure efficient use of training and educational resources within the prison. Such resources include workshops, schools, classroom facilities, and associated equipment and tools. These officers oversee inmates who are learning trades, such as welding, woodworking, or automobile mechanics or who are attending academic classes. Ensuring that students are present and on time for classes to begin, protecting the school and vocational instructors, and securing the tools and facilities used in instruction are all part of the job of these officers. The officers work with civilian instructors, teachers, and counselors.

yard officers

Those who supervise inmates in the prison yard.

4. **Yard officers** supervise inmates in the prison yard. They also take charge of inmates who are (a) moving from place to place, (b) eating, or (c) involved in recreational activities. Like other officers, yard officers are primarily concerned with security and order maintenance.

administrative officers

Those who control keys and weapons and sometimes oversee visitation.

5. **Administrative officers** are assigned to staff activities within the institution's management center. They control keys and weapons. Some administrative officers oversee visitation. As a result, they have more contact with the public than other officers do. Many administrative officers have little, if any, contact with inmates.

perimeter security officers

Those assigned to security (or gun) towers, wall posts, and perimeter patrols. These officers are charged with preventing escapes and detecting and preventing intrusions.

6. **Perimeter security officers** (also called *wall post officers*) are assigned to security (or gun) towers, wall posts, and perimeter patrols. They are charged with preventing escapes and detecting and preventing intrusions (such as packages of drugs or weapons thrown over fences or walls from outside). Perimeter security can become a routine job because it involves little interaction with other officers or inmates and because relatively few escape attempts occur. Newer institutions depend more heavily on technological innovations to maintain secure perimeters, requiring fewer officers for day-long perimeter observation.

relief officers

Experienced correctional officers who know and can perform almost any custody role within the institution, used to temporarily replace officers who are sick or on vacation or to meet staffing shortages.

7. **Relief officers** are experienced correctional officers who know and can perform almost any custody role in the institution. They are used to temporarily replace officers who are sick or on vacation or to meet staffing shortages.

CO9-4 # CORRECTIONAL STAFF ISSUES

Gender and Staffing

On a pleasant Sunday morning a few years ago, a high-custody female inmate at the Chillicothe (Missouri) Correctional Center was sitting in a dormitory, drinking her morning coffee. Having a good time, surrounded by friends, the inmate began laughing. Soon, however, the laughter turned to choking. Unable to breathe, she turned blue. Correctional officer Lisa Albin rushed to her side and found her hanging onto her bed, unable to speak. Albin remained calm as she applied the Heimlich maneuver to the inmate. After three attempts, the trapped coffee cleared the inmate's windpipe and she began breathing again. After the incident, the inmate wrote a letter of thanks to the superintendent, saying, "If it had not been for Mrs. Albin I could have very well died in that room. She literally saved my life and I will be forever grateful to her and for the training she received."[19]

Literature and films almost invariably portray correctional officers as "tobacco-chewin', reflective sunglasses-wearin', chain-gang-runnin',

---

EXHIBIT 9-4 | **American Correctional Association**

Public Correctional Policy on Employment of Women in Corrections

The American Correctional Association affirms the value of women employees and supports equal employment opportunities for women in adult and juvenile correctional agencies. To encourage the employment of women in corrections, correctional agencies should:

- ensure that recruitment, selection, and promotional opportunities for women are open and fair;
- assign female employees duties and responsibilities that provide career development and promotional opportunities equivalent to those provided to other employees;
- provide all levels of staff with appropriate training on developing effective and cooperative working relationships between male and female correctional personnel;
- provide all levels of staff with appropriate education and training in cross-gender supervision; and
- conduct regular monitoring and evaluation of affirmative action practices and be proactive in achieving corrective actions.

Source: Copyright © American Correctional Association. Reprinted with permission.

---

good ol' boys."[20] Today's officer generally defies this stereotype, and women working in corrections have helped erode this otherwise persistent myth. See Exhibit 9–4 for the ACA policy on women in corrections and Exhibit 9–5 for a map of the percentage of women working in adult correctional facilities throughout the United States in 2007.

Like most women working in male-dominated professions, female correctional officers face special problems and barriers—many of which are rooted in sexism. Prisons are nontraditional workplaces for women. As a consequence, female correctional officers—especially those working in men's prisons—often find themselves in a confusing situation. As one author explains it, "On the one hand, to be female is to be different, an outsider. On the other hand, female guards have much in common with and are sympathetic to their male peers as a result of their shared job experience."[21]

According to studies, female correctional officers typically say that they perform their job with a less aggressive style than men.[22] This difference in style seems due mostly to differences in life experiences and to physical limitations associated with women's size and strength. Life experiences prepare most women for helping roles rather than aggressive ones. As a consequence, women are more likely to rely heavily on verbal skills and intuition. Female correctional officers use communication rather than threats or force to gain inmate cooperation. They tend to talk out problems. Studies have also found that female correctional officers rely more heavily than male correctional officers on established disciplinary rules when problems arise. Male staff members, on the other hand, are more likely to bully or threaten inmates to resolve problems.

According to research, 55 percent of female officers indicate that their primary reason for taking a job in corrections is an interest in human service work or in inmate rehabilitation.[23] In striking contrast, only 20 percent of male officers give this as their primary reason for working in corrections.

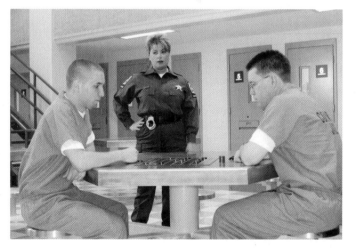

A female CO watches inmates playing a game of checkers. Female correctional officers competently perform day-to-day custodial tasks. Are there any areas of a male prison that female correctional officers should be barred from supervising?

© Thinkstock Images/Getty RF

EXHIBIT 9–5 Percentage of Women Working in Adult Correctional Facilities

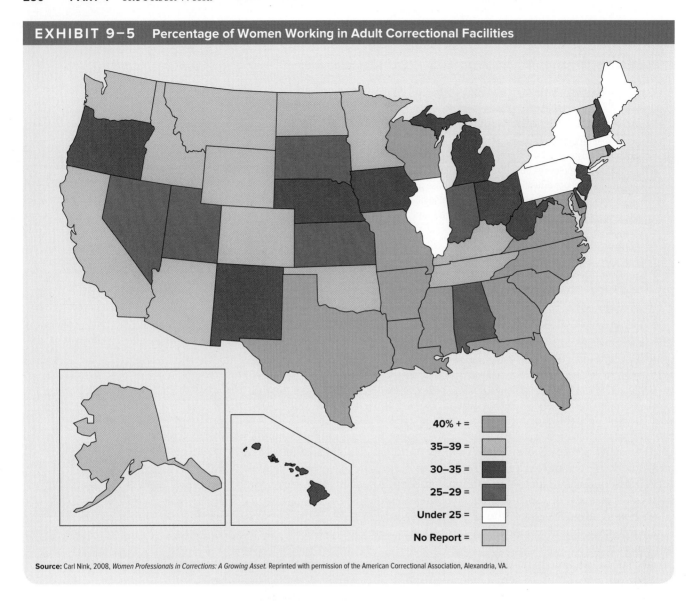

40% + =

35–39 =

30–35 =

25–29 =

Under 25 =

No Report =

Source: Carl Nink, 2008, *Women Professionals in Corrections: A Growing Asset.* Reprinted with permission of the American Correctional Association, Alexandria, VA.

Perhaps as a result of such attitudes, gender makes a dramatic difference in the number of assaults on correctional officers. One national survey of maximum-security prisons in 48 states, the District of Columbia, and the federal BOP showed that female officers were assaulted only about one-fourth as often as male officers.[24]

Although female correctional officers may take a different approach to their work, the skills they use complement those of male staff members. As one expert writes, "Women may humanize the workplace in small ways by establishing less aggressive relationships with inmates."[25]

Studies also show that male officers, by and large, believe that female officers competently perform day-to-day custodial tasks. Most male staff members are "pro-woman," meaning that they applaud the entry of women into the corrections profession.[26] Many male correctional officers do express concerns about women's ability to provide adequate backup in a crisis, however. It is important to note that the need to use force in prison is relatively rare and that officers generally do not respond to dangerous situations alone. Nonetheless, some female correctional officers report that in emergencies, some male officers adopt a protective, chivalrous attitude toward them. Women generally report that they resent such "special treatment" because it makes them feel more like a liability than an asset in an emergency.

Another issue concerning women in today's workplace is personal and sexual harassment. Studies show that few female correctional officers personally experience unwanted touching or other forms of sexual harassment. The forms of harassment women most commonly experience are physical (nonsexual) assaults, threats, unfounded graphic sexual rumors about them, and demeaning remarks from peers, inmates, and supervisors.[27]

A fair amount of harassment is tolerated in the correctional officer subculture. It is viewed as customary and is often accorded little significance. The response to any form of harassment, however, is determined by the officer experiencing it. He or she can tolerate it, resist it, or report it. Female correctional officers, however, express fear of being ostracized if they complain.

One writer has made the following recommendations for improving the acceptance of women as correctional officers:[28]

1. Require managers and guards to undergo training to sensitize them to the concerns of women working in prisons.
2. Establish a strong policy prohibiting sexual and personal harassment with significant consequences for harassers.
3. Screen male job candidates for their ability and willingness to develop relationships of mutual respect with female colleagues.

Stress

In all occupational categories, employers estimate that more than 25 percent of all reported sick time is due to stress.[29] **Stress**—tension in a person's body or mind resulting from physical, chemical, or emotional factors—appears to be more commonplace in prison work than in many other jobs. Nonetheless, it is often denied. As one writer on correctional officers' stress observed, "Most officers . . . try to disguise the toll taken by the job and make the best of what is often a frustrating situation. Though not immune to the pressures of the workplace, these officers project a tough, steady image that precludes sharing frustrations with other coworkers or family members. Some of these officers may be particularly vulnerable to stress."[30]

Correctional officers frequently deny that they are under stress, fearing that admitting to feelings of stress might be interpreted unfavorably. One correctional lieutenant, an 11-year veteran, reported repeatedly observing new correctional employees succumbing to the effects of stress by becoming depressed or turning to alcohol for relief. Although she wanted to intervene, she said she "couldn't" because "no one in law enforcement is allowed to show any emotion or signs of weakness."[31]

This kind of attitude is consistent with prevailing correctional culture, which has traditionally supported dysfunctional behaviors to the point where they have become self-sustaining and self-reinforcing. New recruits are especially vulnerable through unhealthy indoctrination into the negative aspects of correctional staff culture as they assimilate into the affected workplace.[32]

In misguided attempts to deal with the effects of stress, many COs resort to self-medication or other tactics to deal with feelings that they may not readily admit, even to themselves. Unfortunately, such ineffective methods do not alleviate the pressure and may instead make it worse.

Stress among correctional officers has a number of sources. Feelings of powerlessness, meaninglessness, social isolation, and self-estrangement

stress

Tension in a person's body or mind, resulting from physical, chemical, or emotional factors.

all contribute to stress. Some authors have identified job alienation as the major source of stress among COs.[33] Correctional officers rarely participate in setting the rules they work under and the policies they enforce; as a result, they may feel alienated from those policies and rules and from those who create them.

One recent report found that the most significant stressors faced by correctional officers include (in order of declining significance):[34]

- job dangerousness,
- job pay,
- conflict with supervisors,
- conflict with peers,
- role conflict,
- job satisfaction, and
- pressure due to gender.

Exhibit 9–6 shows this list graphically.

Symptoms of stress can be psychological, behavioral, or physical. Psychological symptoms of stress include anxiety, irritability, mood swings, sadness or depression, low self-esteem, emotional withdrawal, and hypersensitivity (to others and to what others say). Behavioral symptoms of stress include an inability to make decisions, increased interpersonal conflict, blocked creativity and judgment, poor memory, lowered productivity, and difficulty concentrating. The physical symptoms of stress include insomnia, headaches, backaches, gastrointestinal disturbances, fatigue, high blood pressure, and frequent illnesses.

Poorer job performance and exhaustion are the results of stress. When stress reaches an unbearable level, burnout can occur. Burnout, a severe reaction to stress, is "a state of physical and emotional depletion that results from the conditions of one's occupation."[35]

Studies have shown that a person's ability to tolerate stress depends on the frequency, severity, and types of stressors confronted.[36] Stress tolerance

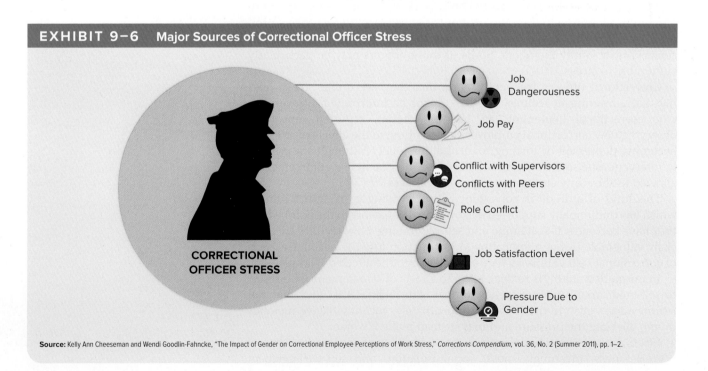

EXHIBIT 9–6   **Major Sources of Correctional Officer Stress**

CORRECTIONAL OFFICER STRESS

Job Dangerousness
Job Pay
Conflict with Supervisors
Conflicts with Peers
Role Conflict
Job Satisfaction Level
Pressure Due to Gender

Source: Kelly Ann Cheeseman and Wendi Goodlin-Fahncke, "The Impact of Gender on Correctional Employee Perceptions of Work Stress," *Corrections Compendium*, vol. 36, No. 2 (Summer 2011), pp. 1–2.

also depends on a number of personal aspects, including past experiences, personal values and attitudes, sense of control, personality, residual stress level, and general state of health.

Authorities suggest a number of techniques for avoiding or reducing job stress. Among them are the following:[37]

1. Communicate openly. Tell people how you feel.
2. Learn not to harbor resentment, not to gossip, and to complain less often.
3. Learn to feel confident in your skills, your values and beliefs, and yourself.
4. Develop a support system. Close friends, pets, social activities, and a happy extended family can all help alleviate stress.
5. Be a good and conscientious worker, but don't become a workaholic.
6. Learn to manage your time and do not procrastinate.
7. Make it a habit to get a good night's sleep.
8. Exercise regularly.
9. Watch your diet. Avoid excessive fat, sugars, salt, red meat, and caffeine.
10. Learn some relaxation exercises such as self-affirmation, mental imaging, deep breathing, stretching, massage, or yoga.
11. Try to have fun. Laughter can combat stress quite effectively.
12. Spend time cultivating self-understanding. Analyze your feelings and your problems—and recognize your accomplishments.
13. Set goals and make plans. Both bring order and direction to your life.

One especially effective strategy for coping with job stress is to develop clear and favorable role definitions. According to J. T. Dignam and colleagues, "Officers who have more opportunities for receiving assistance and goal clarification from supervisors and coworkers [are] less likely to experience role ambiguity than those for whom such support is not available or. Further, the risk of burnout or other deleterious consequences of occupational stress may be reduced for those who are 'insulated' by social support."[38]

Similarly, another group of researchers found that "support from colleagues or supervisors may be one of the most important factors ameliorating stress in the workplace."[39] The same researchers also found that when correctional officers felt "rewarding companionship" with fellow correctional officers, they reported fewer stressful events (even when objective measures showed an actual rise in such events). Most researchers agree that candidates need more extensive and thorough training to prepare them for the psychological and sociological consequences of becoming correctional officers.

Finally, the Desert Waters Correctional Outreach (DWCO—an organization that focuses on the occupational, personal, and family well-being of

Stress is an unhappy outcome of the correctional officer's job. How does on-the-job stress arise in the correctional officer's role? How might it be reduced?
© David Leeson/Dallas Morning News/The Image Works

staff of all disciplines within the corrections profession—has been working with the National Institute of Corrections to develop solutions to workplace stress. DWCO notes that successful "interventions involve gradually 'deprogramming' and 'reprogramming' staff's thinking, beliefs, and behaviors in response to challenging corrections workplace experiences, situations, and circumstances." DWCO says that "through an agency's efforts, current and future staff can learn to adapt successfully to occupational stressors" but notes that improvements in workplace culture can be "a slow and laborious—but deeply critical process."[40]

Staff Safety

Staff safety is a major stressor for individual correctional officers and a primary management concern for correctional administrators. Safety planning must include consideration of the following elements (adapted, in part, from studies of staff safety needs in both juvenile[41] and adult[42] institutions):

- a functionally designed physical plant that limits inmate movement and incorporates technologically advanced security systems, perimeter barriers, and rooms, doors, and locks;
- a behavior management system that establishes clear guidelines for acceptable behavior, reward systems to reinforce expected behavior, and disciplinary systems to discourage unacceptable behavior;
- appropriate staff and inmate relationships (in particular, staff must be aware of, and prepared to respond to, the dangers posed by prison gangs);
- policies and procedures, published in a manual and distributed to staff and supervisors, that support consistent implementation of rules and regulations and prevent the risk of staff letdowns resulting from excessive routine;
- shift scheduling that ensures a mutually supportive balance of senior and junior staff because a sound mix of age and experience facilitates the achievement of inmate control while providing opportunities for on-the-job development of junior officers by senior officers;
- effective supervision at every level;
- comprehensive staff training that ensures all correctional officers and their supervisors know every rule, regulation, policy, and procedure that affects their particular job (if, as the saying goes, knowledge is power, such training is key to empowering the staff to maintain a controlled, safe environment); and
- development of, and training for, a sound action plan that addresses all contingencies.

In addition to advocating thorough planning as just outlined, Stewart and Brown[43] urge continuing research to identify what works, what doesn't work, and emerging trends in staff safety. In particular, they recommend development of a safety program tailored to the needs of correctional officers nationwide. It should be modeled, they suggest, on safety programs designed for police officers, probation officers, and other officers in law enforcement.

Job Satisfaction

High levels of stress reduce the satisfaction correctional officers get from their jobs. In a sad indictment of the corrections field, a 1996 study found that correctional officers were significantly different from most other groups of correctional employees. "They showed the lowest levels of organizational commitment, possessed the highest levels of skepticism about organizational change, were the least positive about careers in corrections and the rehabilitation of offenders, possessed the lowest levels of job satisfaction, were the least involved in their jobs, and were described as having the poorest work habits and overall job performance."[44] In a separate study, correctional supervisors and managers were found to have much higher levels of job satisfaction and professionalism.[45]

One reason for the difference in job satisfaction between supervisory personnel and those on the front lines of corrections work is that correctional officers often feel alienated from policymaking.[46] As one writer puts it, "when looking at the atmosphere and environment of a state or federal prison, it would seem obvious what correction personnel like least about working there: surveys of personnel who resign or quit show that their biggest problems are with supervisory personnel rather than inmates."[47]

Correctional officers' job satisfaction appears to be tied to the amount of influence they feel they have over administrative decisions and policies. Officers who feel they have some control over the institution and over their jobs seem much more satisfied than officers who believe they have no control. Hence, it appears that correctional officers' job satisfaction can be greatly enhanced by caring administrators who involve the officers in policymaking.

For some correctional officers, the perception that their profession suffers a generally poor public image[48] further reduces their job satisfaction. Compared to local and state police officers and agents of the various federal law enforcement organizations, correctional officers may be viewed as the "poor relations" of the law enforcement family. As one researcher wrote, "Most people do not know of a child who says, I want to be a correctional officer when I grow up."[49]

Media portrayals of correctional officers exacerbate the situation. Movies and television often depict COs as lowly qualified "guards" (considered a derogatory title; "guards work at Macy's and banks")[50] whose primary function seems to be abusing prisoners. Correctional officers "believe they are seen as brutes, only a shade better than the people behind bars."[51] Consequently, COs have a difficult time overcoming these images as they attempt to convey the significance and professional demands of their positions to civic leaders and the public.[52]

There is evidence, however, that job satisfaction among correctional officers is rising. The rise may be partly due to increasing awareness of what correctional officers find most important in the work environment. Recent studies have identified the most important determinants of job satisfaction among correctional officers as (1) working conditions, (2) the level of work-related stress, (3) the quality of working relationships with fellow officers, and (4) length of service.[53]

In one of the most significant studies to date, treatment-oriented correctional staff reported far higher levels of job satisfaction than did custody-oriented staff.[54] The study was of survey data collected from 428 Arizona correctional service officers (CSOs) and 118 correctional program officers (CPOs). Job satisfaction was significantly greater among the human-services-oriented CPOs than among the traditional-custody-oriented CSOs. The findings suggest that additional attention should be given to enhancing and enriching the duties of correctional officers, extending their control over and involvement in prisoners' activities, and redefining their roles more as service workers than as control agents.

Determinants of job satisfaction appear to differ for male and female correctional officers. One study found that the quality of working relationships

Visit ccajob.com or scan this code with the QR app on your smartphone or digital device to watch two videos showing why a career in corrections can be enjoyable.

with other officers, the amount of stress experienced at work, the length of service as a correctional officer, and educational level were all positively related to job satisfaction for males.[55] Women officers, on the other hand, appeared to place more emphasis on the quality of working relationships with all other correctional officers (not just the ones with whom they worked) and tended to be happier in prisons at lower security levels. Other studies have related higher job satisfaction among white female officers to the officers' positive evaluation of the quality of supervision. In other words, white female correctional officers tend to be happier in prisons that they believe are well run.[56]

Professionalism

A common difference between a professional and a nonprofessional is that a professional learns every aspect of the job whereas a nonprofessional avoids the learning process and often considers it a waste of time. Professionals seek to prevent mistakes at all costs, but if they occur, the professional does not let them slide; nonprofessionals tend to ignore or hide them. A professional tries to be great, whereas a nonprofessional just tries to get by at what he or she does.

Professionalism is commitment to a set of agreed-upon values aimed at improving the organization while maintaining the highest standards of excellence and dissemination of knowledge.[57] In addition to having knowledge and skills, professionals must present humanistic qualities: selflessness, responsibility and accountability, leadership, excellence, integrity, honesty, empathy, and respect for coworkers and prisoners.

Professional correctional organizations that operate at the national level, such as the ACA (discussed in Chapter 1), have qualified and well-trained employees, well-run professional development departments, and well-developed standards of conduct. Such organizations provide the support needed for operating agencies and individual correctional facilities to achieve fairness in handling inmates and correctional personnel while documenting and addressing issues that may arise in inmate and employee conduct. These organizations also help to define common sets of values that establish the tone and climate for day-to-day operations in correctional facilities.

Visit www.youtube.com/watch?v=RTIm-Ham_es or scan this code with the QR app on your smartphone or digital device to watch a video showing a day in the life of a correctional officer.

Training can enhance professionalism. As more and more prison staff develop a professional perspective, the structural organization of prisons and interactions among staff and inmates may significantly change. What kinds of training may help correctional officers adjust to a changing environment?
Courtesy of Corrections Corporation of America

International Association of Correctional Officers: The Correctional Officer's Creed

To speak sparingly . . . to act, not argue . . . to be in authority through personal presence . . . to correct without nagging . . . to speak with the calm voice of certainty . . . to see everything and to know what is significant and what not to notice . . . to be neither insensitive to distress nor so distracted by pity as to miss what must elsewhere be seen. . . .

To do neither that which is unkind nor self-indulgent in its misplaced charity . . . never to obey the impulse to tongue lash that silent insolence which in time past could receive the lash . . . to be both firm and fair . . . to know I cannot be fair simply by being firm, nor firm simply by being fair. . . .

To support the reputations of associates and confront them without anger should they stand short of professional conduct . . . to reach for knowledge of the continuing mysteries of human motivation . . . to think; always to think . . . to be dependable . . . to be dependable first to my charges and associates and thereafter to my duty as employee and citizen . . . to keep fit . . . to keep forever alert . . . to listen to what is meant as well as what is said with words and with silences.

To expect respect from my charges and my superiors yet never to abuse the one for abuses from the other . . . for eight hours each working day to be an example of the person I could be at all times . . . to acquiesce in no dishonest act . . . to cultivate patience under boredom and calm during confusion . . . to understand the why of every order I take or give. . . .

To hold freedom among the highest values though I deny it to those I guard . . . to deny it with dignity that in my example they find no reason to lose their dignity . . . to be prompt . . . to be honest with all who practice deceit that they not find in me excuse for themselves . . . to privately face down my fear that I not signal it . . . to privately cool my anger that I not displace it on others . . . to hold in confidence what I see and hear, which by telling could harm or humiliate to no good purpose . . . to keep my outside problems outside . . . to leave inside that which should stay inside . . . to do my duty.

Source: Copyright © 2000 Bob Barrington. Used by permission of the International Association of Correctional Officers.

Ethical Dilemma 9–1: There are reports that find sexual misconduct is a problem in prisons for women. These reports state that male staff victimize women inmates. Should only female staff work in prisons for women? What are the issues? For more information go to Ethical Dilemma 9–1 at www.justicestudies.com/ethics08.

Ethical Dilemma 9–2: Stress among correctional staff is widespread, and your facility has a stress-reduction program. You are feeling very stressed, but you are afraid to take advantage of the program, thinking it may reflect poorly on you at promotion time. Do you participate in the program anyway? For more information go to Ethical Dilemma 9–2 at www.justicestudies.com/ethics08.

Ethical Dilemmas for every chapter are available online.

The vision provided by professional organizations helps build confidence that employees will be professional and will have integrity, respect, the ability to engage in teamwork, the motivation for continued learning, and commitment to the profession.

According to William Sondervan, former commissioner of the Maryland Division of Corrections and previous director of professional development for the ACA, professionalism in corrections is vitally important to the integrity, safety, and security of correctional agencies and institutions.[58] Corrections professionalism, says Sondervan, requires that any correctional organization establish or clarify the following three elements:

- **purpose**—the reason for an organization's existence;
- **mission**—what is done to support the organization's purpose; and
- **vision**—the planned future direction of the organization.

Together, says Sondervan, purpose, mission, and vision provide a roadmap for the development of professionalism within an organization.

Exhibit 9–7 depicts the formal mission, vision, and goals of the federal Bureau of Prisons and Exhibit 9–8 lists the values and beliefs that support the Bureau's mission and vision statements.

purpose
The reason for an organization's existence.

mission
That which is done to support an organization's purpose.

vision
The planned future direction of an organization.

EXHIBIT 9-7	Federal Bureau of Prisons Mission and Vision Statement

Mission

It is the mission of the Federal Bureau of Prisons to protect society by confining offenders in the controlled environments of prisons and community-based facilities that are safe, humane, cost-efficient, and appropriately secure, and that provide work and other self-improvement opportunities to assist offenders in becoming law-abiding citizens.

Vision

The Federal Bureau of Prisons, judged by any standard, is widely and consistently regarded as a model of outstanding public administration, and as the best value provider of efficient, safe and humane correctional services and programs in America.

This vision will be realized when the public is safe; prisons are safe; inmates successfully reenter society; we are a good steward of public funds; our staff are exceptional; our staff are treated equally; our staff are respected; our staff are safe; our staff have superior judgment; [and] our staff are happy.

Source: Federal Bureau of Prisons, https://www.bop.gov/about/agency/agency_pillars.jsp.

EXHIBIT 9-8	Federal Bureau of Prisons Core Values

Correctional Excellence	We are correctional workers first, committed to the highest level of performance.
Respect	We embrace diversity and recognize the value and dignity of staff, inmates and the general public.
Integrity	We demonstrate uncompromising ethical conduct in all our actions.
	We excel at our mission because we have a strong value system at our core. Combined with a comprehensive strategic plan, our agency has a clear vision of how to accomplish the correctional goals and operational objectives we have set out to achieve.

Source: Federal Bureau of Prisons, https://www.bop.gov/about/agency/agency_pillars.jsp.

Although the development of an appropriate mission statement is vital at the organizational level, the development of a sense of personal ethics is crucial to daily on-the-job success. In support of personal ethics, the International Association of Correctional Officers has published a Correctional Officer's Creed (see the Ethics and Professionalism box), which summarizes the duties and responsibilities of a correctional officer.

 ## Officer Corruption

A few years ago, 24 members of the violent Black Guerrilla Family prison gang were arrested in Maryland following a seven-month long investigation into the smuggling of contraband into Baltimore-area prisons.[59] Four of those arrested were state correctional officers. Using bribes, threats, and promised favors, leaders of the gang were able to coerce the officers into smuggling contraband to imprisoned associates and extorting money from other inmates. The favored prisoners feasted on salmon, shrimp, and other delicacies while smoking expensive cigars and drinking premium vodka. Using smuggled cell phones, they were able to arrange for attacks on witnesses and rival gang members living outside the prison. One of the corrupt officers, a woman who played a central role in facilitating the gang's illegal activities, is reported to have provided sexual favors for inmates in return for money.

In another incident that apparently stemmed from correctional officer corruption, 76-year-old convicted mass murderer Charles Manson was caught with a mobile phone in his prison cell at California's Corcoran State Prison in February 2011. It was the second time in two years that officers had confiscated a phone from Manson during a cell search. Manson, who is serving a life sentence, was convicted in the 1969 murders of seven people, including pregnant actress Sharon Tate.

Legislative analysts for the state of California estimate that more than 10,000 cell phones made their way into California prisons in 2010.[60] According to those same analysts, prison employees are the main source of smuggled phones that end up in the hands of prisoners. A recent California state inspector general's report detailed the story of how a single CO made $150,000 a year smuggling phones to inmates. Although his activities were eventually discovered and he was fired, he was not criminally prosecuted because it is not against the law in California to take cell phones into prisons—even though it is a violation of prison rules for inmates to possess them. Following the incident involving Manson, state senator Alex Padilla called on California Governor Jerry Brown to mandate the periodic searching of correctional officers reporting for work.

Other forms of correctional officer corruption and job malfeasance include the misuse of confidential information, drinking and abusing drugs while on duty, sleeping on duty, unnecessary roughness or brutality against inmates, racism, and filing false disciplinary reports on inmates. A small number of sadistic people may even be attracted to working in corrections because they think it will provide them the opportunity to physically abuse others. Preemployment personality inventories, background checks, and face-to-face preemployment interviews are all crucial in preventing such people from obtaining positions of authority in correctional facilities.

Contributing to the problem of corruption among correctional staff is low pay—especially in some jurisdictions. "If someone is desperate to make ends meet and someone offers them $2,100 to smuggle in a cell phone, it's a hell of a temptation," says Brian Olsen, executive director of a Texas labor union that represents Texas correctional officers.[61]

While all examples used in this chapter come from state correctional agencies, a look at statistics seems to show that corruption among federal correctional personnel is relatively rare. A recent Congressional report by the U.S. Department of Justice's (DOJ) Office of the Inspector General (OIG), for example, found only 238 likely cases of criminal misconduct by BOP employees.[62] Given that the number of persons employed by the BOP is approximately 39,000 BOP misconduct levels appear to be among the lowest in government.

Joyce Mitchell, 51, a former supervisor in the tailor shop at Clinton Correctional Facility in Dannemora, N.Y., stands alongside her attorney before a judge in the Plattsburgh City Court in New York in 2015. Mitchell was sentenced to more than two years in prison for helping two convicted murderers escape the facility where she worked. How can inmate manipulation of correctional workers be prevented?

© G. N. Miller-Pool/Getty Images

Fraternization with Inmates

On September 28, 2015, former prison employee Joyce E. Mitchell was sentenced to spend at least two years and four months in prison.[63] Mitchell, 51, had made national headlines following the escape of two convicted killers from a maximum-security prison in northern New York. The escape had been facilitated by Mitchell, who had apparently become romantically involved with one of the men and used her position as a supervisor in the prison's tailor shop to provide the escapees with hacksaws, replacement blades, and screwdrivers. In her defense, Mitchell argued that the convicts had exploited her emotional instability and that she feared for the safety of her family if she didn't help the men escape.

Some specialists in inmate psychology point out that "inmates have lived a lifestyle of lying, and using people and manipulating others is a way of life" for them. Not only do inmates attempt to manipulate staff members, but they also work at controlling and deceiving fellow inmates. While it is important for correctional officers to always be aware of the potential for inmate manipulation, it helps to know that some manipulation schemes are short term (like the effort to move a contraband cell phone from one inmate to another), and some are long term (like the escape that involved Joyce Mitchell) and take a long time to come to completion.[64]

One long-time correctional officer says that COs must always remember that "no inmate is your friend" and offers these guidelines to help others falling prey to inmate manipulation:[65]

1. Be an active part of your correctional team.
2. Be suspicious, question, and verify every inmate action or request.
3. Follow institutional rules, policies, and procedures.
4. Monitor and document inmate remarks, gestures, and actions.
5. Communicate openly and often with supervisors and other employees.
6. Know your job and get further education.
7. Learn to say "No."

CO9-6 THE IMPACT OF TERRORISM ON CORRECTIONS

Prisoner Radicalization

In 2009, convicted terrorist Kevin James, 32, was sentenced in federal court in Santa Ana, California, to 16 years in prison. James had pleaded guilty in 2007 to conspiracy to wage war against the United States[66] and had been accused of plotting terrorist attacks on Jewish and military targets throughout California. Among those targets were Los Angeles International Airport, the Israeli Consulate, and Army recruiting centers.

Those who investigated James's background found that he had formed an Islamic terrorist group in California's Tehachapi Prison in 1997. While serving a 10-year sentence for robbery, James joined the Nation of Islam—a traditional American Islamic faith. Soon, however, he became engaged with a fringe group of Sunni Muslims at Tehachapi. The group, known as *Jamiyyat Ui Islam Is Saheeh* (the Assembly of Authentic Islam, or JIS), operates today throughout prisons in California where it is known as a radical Islamist prison gang, or STG. JIS advocates attacks on enemies of the Islamic faith, the U.S. government, Jews, "infidels," and supporters of Israel.

Eventually, James took control of JIS and began distributing a handwritten manifesto known as the JIS Protocol in which he justified the killing of infidels. Following transfer to the maximum-security California State Prison in Sacramento, James recruited more inmates to join JIS and used soon-to-be paroled inmates to recruit additional members outside of prison. Using smuggled letters and phone calls, James communicated his plans for terrorist attacks to recruits on the outside.

Mark Hamm, a criminal justice professor who studied the case of Kevin James, notes that "prisoner radicalization grows in the secretive underground of inmate subcultures through prison gangs and extremist interpretations of religious doctrines that inspire ideologies of intolerance, hatred and violence."[67] Hamm also learned that "prisoners are radicalized through a process of one-on-one proselytizing by charismatic leaders." Especially vulnerable, says Hamm, are those inmates who no longer have contact with their families and are angry and embittered by their circumstances. "I discovered," says Hamm, "that charismatic leadership was more important than other commonly cited factors associated with prisoner radicalization."[68]

Because of their marginal social status, inmates may be particularly vulnerable to recruitment by terrorist organizations. According to Chip Ellis, research and program coordinator for the National Memorial Institute for the Prevention of Terrorism, "Prisoners are a captive audience, and they usually have a diminished sense of self or a need for identity and protection. They're usually a disenchanted or disenfranchised group of people, [and] terrorists can sometimes capitalize on that situation."[69] Ellis points out that inmates can be radicalized in a variety of ways, including exposure to extremist literature and other radical inmates as well as through anti-U.S. sermons delivered during religious services.

The FBI says that al-Qaeda continues to actively recruit followers inside American correctional institutions. Islamic terrorists are keenly aware of the 9,600 Muslims held in the federal prison system and see them as potential converts. "These terrorists seek to exploit our freedom to exercise religion to their advantage by using radical forms of Islam to recruit operatives," says FBI counterterrorism chief John Pistole.[70] "Unfortunately," notes Pistole, "U.S. correctional institutions are a valuable venue for such radicalization and recruitment."

Convicted terrorist Kevin James answers questions put to him during an exclusive TV interview with producer and investigative journalist Eric Longabardi. James is the founder of Jami-yyat Ui Islam Is Saheeh (the Assembly of Authentic Islam). Does terrorist recruiting take place in prison?
© Eric Longabardi

Anti-Terrorism Planning

Not only must today's prison administrators be concerned about inmate involvement in terrorist activities, they must also think about and plan for the impact of the terrorism event within their facilities and within the communities in which their facilities are located. Moreover, incarcerating those who have been convicted of acts of terrorism presents new challenges for correctional administrators. For example, Sheik Omar Abdel-Rahman, spiritual leader for many terrorists, including Osama bin Laden, is now serving a life sentence in a U.S. federal penitentiary for conspiring to assassinate former Egyptian president Hosni Mubarak and blow up five New York City landmarks in the 1990s. Speculation that the sheik continues to motivate terrorist acts against the United States gained credibility when his attorney was sentenced to 28 months in prison in 2006 for passing illegal communications between Abdel-Rahman and an Egyptian-based terrorist

Muslim prisoners at prayer in a Virginia correctional facility. Radicalized inmates of any faith can represent a threat to facility security. What connection might exist between radicalized inmates and criminals or terrorist groups on the outside?

© Andrew Lichtenstein/Corbis

organization known as the Islamic Group.[71] Another convicted terrorist, September 11 conspirator Zacarias Moussaoui, also known as the 20th hijacker, is serving a life sentence at the federal administrative maximum facility in Florence, Colorado. Moussaoui's fellow prisoners, housed on what has come to be known as "Bomber's Row," include al-Qaeda shoe bomber Richard Reid; Ramzi Yousef, mastermind of the 1993 World Trade Center bombing; seven of Yousef's accomplices; Ahmed Ressam, who was arrested at the Canadian border with explosives he intended to use to bomb Los Angeles International Airport; four men convicted in the 1998 bombing of U.S. embassies in Africa; and Abdul Hakim Murad, convicted in a 1995 al-Qaeda plan to bomb 12 airplanes during a two-day period.

Jess Maghan, former training director for the New York City Department of Corrections and now the director of the Forum for Comparative Corrections and professor of criminal justice at the University of Illinois at Chicago, points out that "the interaction of all people in a prison (staff, officers, and inmates) can become important intelligence sources."[72] Moreover, says Maghan, the flow of information between inmates and the outside world needs to be monitored in order to detect attack plans—especially when prisons house known terrorist leaders or group members. Covert information, says Maghan, can be passed through legal visits (where people conveying information may have no idea of its significance), sub rosa communications networks in prisons that can support communications between inmates and the outside world, and prison transportation systems.

A few years ago, the Institute for the Study of Violent Groups at Sam Houston State University charged that Wahhabism—the most radical form of Islam—was being spread in American prisons by clerics approved by the Islamic Society of North America (ISNA). ISNA is one of two organizations that the federal BOP uses to select prison chaplains to serve inmates in its facilities.[73] "Proselytizing in prisons," said the institute, "can produce new recruits with American citizenship." An example might be Chicago thug Jose Padilla, aka Abdulla al-Mujahir, who converted to Islam after exposure to Wahhabism while serving time in a Florida jail. Authorities claim Padilla intended to contaminate a U.S. city with a radiological dirty bomb. In 2007, Padilla was convicted of federal terrorism charges. Similarly, convicted shoe bomber Richard Reid converted to radical Islam while in an English prison before planning his attack on an American Airlines flight from Paris to Miami.[74]

A few years after the attacks of 9/11, the Office of the Inspector General of the U.S. Department of Justice released a review of the practices used by the federal BOP in selecting Muslim clergy to minister to inmates in the bureau's facilities. The report concluded that the primary threat of radicalization came not from chaplains, contractors, or volunteers but from inmates. According to the report, "Inmates from foreign countries politicize Islam and radicalize inmates, who in turn radicalize more inmates when they transfer to other prisons."[75] The report also identified a form of Islam unique to the prison environment called "Prison Islam."[76] The report said that Prison Islam is a form of Islam that is used by gangs and radical inmates to further unlawful goals. It adapts itself easily to prison values and promotes the interests of the incarcerated. Prison Islam was found to be especially common in institutions where religious services are led by lay *Mullahs* (spiritual leaders, who are often inmates)—a practice made necessary by a lack of Muslim chaplains. The report recommended that "the BOP can and should improve its process for selecting, screening, and supervising Muslim religious services providers. We recommend," said the report, that "the BOP take steps to examine all chaplains', religious contractors', and religious volunteers' doctrinal beliefs to screen out anyone who poses a threat to security." Echoing those sentiments is Mark Hamm, who says that the most significant thing that prison administrators can do to undercut terrorist recruitment in prison is to hire chaplains who have been properly vetted. "Without them," says Hamm, "radicalized prisoners are free to operate on their own, independent of religious authority to ensure moderation and tolerance."[77]

Indonesian terrorist Imam Samudra in prison in Bali awaiting execution. Samudra was convicted of masterminding terrorist bombings that killed 202 people in 2002 and was sentenced to death by firing squad. While imprisoned, Samudra wrote a jailhouse manifesto on the funding of terrorism through cyberfraud. He was executed in 2008. How might incarcerated terrorists constitute a threat to the facilities in which they are housed? To the rest of society?
© AP Photo/Ali Kurdi

In 2006, the U.S. Justice Department's OIG released another report—this one critical of BOP inmate mail monitoring procedures, saying that "the threat remains that terrorist and other high-risk inmates can use mail and verbal communications to conduct terrorist or criminal activities while incarcerated." The report was based on findings that three convicted terrorists had been able to send 90 letters to Islamic extremists in the Middle East in 2005, praising Osama bin Laden. The report noted the fact that the BOP does not have the needed number of translators proficient in Arabic who are able to read inmate mail and said that budget restrictions do not allow for the reading of all incoming and outgoing mail.[78]

The threat of a terrorist act being carried out by inmates within a prison or jail can be an important consideration in facility planning and management. Of particular concern is the possibility of bioterrorism. A concentrated population such as exists within a prison or jail would be highly susceptible to rapid transmission of the ill effects from such an attack.[79]

Significant recommendations for addressing the terrorist threat within correctional institutions come from Y. N. Baykan, a management specialist with the Maryland Division of Correction. Baykan says that no successful strategies are being used today to control radical Islamist influences in American prisons and suggests the following:[80]

- Prison administrators must realize that the threat of transnational terrorism in American facilities is real.
- Radical Islamic groups should be seen as sophisticated social networks rather than gangs.
- Prison authorities must evaluate existing policies and strategies, looking closely at the roles and backgrounds of chaplains and volunteers and the rules governing religious conversions.
- Meetings of radicals should be closely monitored as should incoming propaganda.
- Prison staff should be taught to understand political Islam and should use information-management solutions that involve cutting-edge collection, storage, and analysis of data.

- Prison authorities must follow what is happening in other countries and learn from it.
- Threat information should be shared by all stakeholders, including state and federal systems and other law enforcement agencies.

As the United States faces more and more threats of terrorism, it is likely that the issues identified here will take on greater significance for correctional facilities throughout the nation and around the world.

REVIEW AND APPLICATIONS

SUMMARY

1 There is a hierarchy of staff positions from warden (or superintendent) at the top down to correctional officer and correctional officer trainee. A typical correctional staff includes (1) administrative staff, (2) clerical personnel, (3) program staff, (4) custodial staff, (5) service and maintenance staff, and (6) volunteers.

2 The types of power available to correctional officers are legitimate power, coercive power, reward power, expert power, and referent power. Correctional officer personality types discussed in this chapter are (1) the dictator, (2) the friend, (3) the merchant, (4) the turnkey, (5) the climber, (6) the reformer, and (7) the do-gooder.

3 The seven correctional officer assignments are (1) block officers, (2) work detail supervisors, (3) industrial shop and school officers, (4) yard officers, (5) administrative officers, (6) perimeter security officers (also called *wall post officers*), and (7) relief officers.

4 The five significant correctional staff issues discussed in this chapter are (1) gender-related concerns, (2) correctional officer stress, (3) staff safety, (4) job satisfaction among those working in corrections, and (5) professionalism.

5 Some correctional officers become corrupt, and serious corruption can threaten the security of the institution. Greed, the desire for sexual gratification, and a lack of professionalism can all contribute to corruption among corrections personnel.

6 Today's prison administrators and corrections personnel must be vigilant against the threat of terrorism and must guard against terrorist activities from within the institution and from outside.

KEY TERMS

roles, p. 239

staff roles, p. 239

custodial staff, p. 240

program staff, p. 240

gain time, p. 242

structured conflict, p. 243

subculture, p. 243

staff subculture, p. 243

correctional officer personalities, p. 245

block officers, p. 247

work detail supervisors, p. 247

industrial shop and school officers, p. 248

yard officers, p. 248

administrative officers, p. 248

perimeter security officers, p. 248

relief officers, p. 248

stress, p. 251

purpose, p. 257

mission, p. 257

vision, p. 257

QUESTIONS FOR REVIEW

1 What staff roles does the hierarchy of a typical correctional institution include?

2 According to John Hepburn, what are five bases of the power that correctional officers use to gain inmate compliance?

3 What are the seven correctional officer job assignments?

4 What are the five significant correctional staff issues discussed in this chapter?

5 How might correctional officers become corrupt? What kinds of activities might corrupt officers engage in?

6 Briefly explain the impact that terrorism is having on prisons and prison administration.

THINKING CRITICALLY ABOUT CORRECTIONS

Prison Rape

James Gilligan, MD, contends that rape in prisons is "an intrinsic and universal part of the punishments that our government metes out to those whom it labels as 'criminal.'"[81] In essence, Gilligan suggests, prison administrators passively employ inmate-on-inmate rape as a management tool to control the prisoner population.

Dr. Gilligan bases his charge on three contentions:

First, the relevant legal authorities, from judges to prosecutors who send people to prison, to the prison officials who administer them, are all aware of the existence, the reality, and the near-universality of rape in the prisons. Indeed, this is one reason that many conscientious judges are extremely reluctant to send anyone to prison except when they feel compelled to, either by the violence of the crime or, as is increasingly true, by laws mandating prison sentences even for nonviolent crimes, such as drug offenses.

Second, the conditions that stimulate such rapes (the enforced deprivation of other sources of self-esteem, respect, power, and sexual gratification) are consciously and deliberately imposed upon the prison population by the legal authorities.

Third, all these authorities tacitly and knowingly tolerate this form of sexual violence, passively delegating to the dominant and most violent inmates the power and authority to deliver this form of punishment to the more submissive and nonviolent ones, so that the rapists in this situation are acting as the vicarious enforcers of a form of punishment that the legal system does not itself enforce formally or directly.

Given that rape is universally acknowledged as a crime, Dr. Gilligan's charge is tantamount to an accusation of criminal conspiracy of monumental proportions.

1. Do you believe there is merit to Gilligan's claims?

2. If so, how would you propose addressing this issue?

The Staff Subculture

The staff culture is generally instilled in correctional officer trainees by more experienced officers and by work experiences. Socialization into the staff subculture begins on the first day of academy training or the first day of work (whichever comes first). One of the most important beliefs of the staff subculture is that officers should support one another.

Some people argue that the staff subculture is dangerous because it can sustain improper and even illegal behavior while forcing correctional officers to keep to themselves what they know about such behavior. Others, however, suggest that the staff subculture is a positive element in the correctional world. It is important to correctional officer morale, they claim. They also suggest that it "fills the gaps" in formal training by establishing informal rules to guide staff behavior and decision making in difficult situations. The staff subculture can provide informal "workarounds" when the formal requirements of a correctional officer's position seem unrealistic.

1. Do you think the staff subculture contributes to or detracts from meeting the goals of institutional corrections? Why?

2. Do you think the staff subculture benefits or harms the lives and working environment of correctional officers? Explain.

3. What functions of the staff subculture can you identify? Rate each of those functions as positive or negative for its role in meeting the goals of institutional corrections.

ON-THE-JOB DECISION MAKING

Use of Force

You are an experienced correctional officer assigned to yard duty. As you patrol the prison yard, watching inmates milling around and talking, a fellow officer named Renée approaches you. Renée was hired only a week ago, and she has gained a reputation for being inquisitive—asking experienced correctional officers about prison work. Renée walks up and says, "You know, I'm wondering what I should do. Yesterday I saw an officer push an inmate around because the guy didn't do what he asked. I don't know if the inmate didn't hear what was being said, or if he was just ignoring the officer." Renée looks at the ground. "What am I supposed to do in a situation like that? Should I have said something right then? Should I talk to the officer privately? Should I suggest to the officer that maybe the inmate didn't hear him? He knows we aren't supposed to use force on inmates unless it's really necessary. If I see him do this kind of thing again, should I report him?" Looking up, Renée says, "I know we're supposed to support each other in here. But what would you do?" How would you respond to Renée's questions?

Former CO Inmate

For about four years, Alex Kaminsky was one of your fellow correctional officers at the McClellan Correctional Facility. During your service together, you developed a friendship close enough to include social occasions outside the job, and your wives became good friends.

Two years ago, Kaminsky was convicted of dealing controlled substances to inmates and received a 12- to 20-year sentence. Upon your recent transfer to the Brownley Correctional Facility, you discover that Kaminsky is one of the inmates incarcerated there. He resides in one of the cell blocks that falls in your area of responsibility and works on the maintenance crew that you supervise.

1. Should you seek assignment to another area of the prison or seek to have Kaminsky transferred out, to prevent the necessity of having contact with him? Explain.
2. If Kaminsky approaches you, should you permit the reestablishment of a relationship that might (or might not) prove beneficial to his rehabilitation?

THE INMATE WORLD

Living Behind Bars

© Scott Houston/Corbis

CHAPTER OBJECTIVES

After completing this chapter you should be able to do the following:

1 Explain what *inmate subculture* is, and explain how it forms.

2 Know what is meant by the *prison code,* and be able to list some elements of it.

3 Explain what is meant by *prison argot.*

4 List some common roles that male inmates assume.

5 Describe some major differences between women's and men's prisons.

6 Compare some of the characteristics of female inmates with those of male inmates.

7 Explain how the social structure in women's prisons differs from that in men's prisons.

> *In prison, those things withheld from and denied to the prisoner become precisely what he wants most of all.*
>
> —Eldridge Cleaver, African American author and activist

Laura Kaeppeler, Miss America 2012. Kaeppeler dedicated the year of her reign to the support of children of incarcerated parents. Today, she is married, living in California, and the proud mother of a new baby boy. What other issues do inmates face?

© A RD/Kabik/Retna Ltd./Corbis

In Laura Kaeppeler-Fleiss's life, things have been happening fast. The Malibu, California, housewife had her first child in 2015, following her marriage to television producer, Mike Fleiss in 2014. Not long before becoming a mom, however, Kaeppeler-Fleiss was crowned Miss America in 2012. She delighted corrections professionals when she dedicated the year of her reign to the theme "Circles of Support: Mentoring Children of Incarcerated Parents."[1] At the time, Kaeppeler-Fleiss said, "It's everyday life for millions of children, and it allows me to connect with people on a level they don't expect a pageant contestant to connect with them. This is a real problem people can relate to." Kaeppeler's father had been imprisoned when she was 17 for a white-collar crime.

This chapter will examine prison life, the inmate subculture, and the prison experience in general by looking first at men in prison and then at imprisoned women.

MEN IN PRISON

As we have already seen, most state inmates are male, belong to racial or ethnic minority groups, are relatively young, and have been incarcerated for a violent offense. A recent Bureau of Justice Statistics (BJS) study examined social, economic, and other characteristics of state inmates nationwide.[2] Highlights of that study are shown in Exhibit 10–1.

Prisons and other total institutions are small, self-contained societies with their own social structures, norms, and rules. Although not entirely isolated, prison inmates are physically, emotionally, and socially restricted from anything more than minor participation in the surrounding society. As a consequence, they develop their own distinctive lifestyles, roles, and behavioral norms.

In his classic work *Asylums,* Erving Goffman used the phrase **total institution** to describe a place where the same people work, eat, sleep, and engage in recreation together day after day.[3] Life within total institutions is closely planned by those in control, and activities are strictly scheduled. Prisons, concentration camps, mental hospitals, and seminaries are all total institutions, said Goffman. They share many of the same characteristics—even though they exist for different purposes and house different kinds of populations. His words were echoed years later by Hans Toch, who noted that "prisons are 24-hour-a-day, year-in-and-year-out environments in which people are sequestered with little outside contact."[4]

Goffman also identified a number of modes of adaptation to prison life by which inmates attempt to adjust to the conditions around them. Some inmates, said Goffman, *convert* to life within institutions, taking on the staff's view of themselves and of institutional society. Others *withdraw.* Still others make attempts at *colonization*—meaning that they strike a balance between values and habits brought from home and those dictated by the social environment of the prison. Finally, some inmates *rebel,* rejecting the demands of their surroundings and often ending up in trouble with authorities.

total institution

A place where the same people work, play, eat, sleep, and recreate together on a continuous basis. The term was developed by the sociologist Erving Goffman to describe prisons and other similar facilities.

EXHIBIT 10–1 National Profile of State Prison Inmates

57%
had a high school diploma or its equivalent

55%
had never married

43%
had lived with both parents most of the time while growing up

67%
were employed during the month before their arrest for their current crime

37%
had an immediate family member who had served time

38%
had not been incarcerated before

32%
committed their offense under the influence of alcohol

32%
committed their offense under the influence of drugs

96%
were U.S. citizens

Sources: E. Ann Carson, *Prisoners in 2014* (Washington, DC: Bureau of Justice Statistics, 2015); Bureau of Justice Statistics, *Characteristics of State Prison Inmates*, retrieved February 27, 2013 from www.ojp.usdoj.gov/bjs/crimoff.htm#inmates; Allen Beck et al., *Survey of State Prison Inmates, 1991* (Washington, DC: U.S. Department of Justice, March 1993); Christopher J. Mumola and Jennifer C. Karberg, "Drug Use and Dependence, State and Federal Prisoners, 2004" (Washington, DC: Bureau of Justice Statistics, 2006).

As Victoria R. Derosia of Castleton State College points out in her book *Living Inside Prison Walls,* some people "will make it through incarceration relatively unscathed and move on to a better life as a rehabilitated (or habilitated) citizen, while others will repeatedly fail at life outside prison. Offenders will successfully or poorly adjust to prison because of, or in spite of, who they were before incarceration, who they were while in prison, what they chose to do or not to do in prison, and who they want to become once released."[5]

What Is the Inmate Subculture?

Although any prison has its own unique way of life or culture, it is possible to describe a general inmate subculture that characterizes the lives of inmates in correctional institutions nationwide. The **inmate subculture**

inmate subculture (also *prisoner subculture*)

The habits, customs, mores, values, beliefs, or superstitions of the body of inmates incarcerated in correctional institutions; also, the inmate social world.

prisonization

The process by which inmates adapt to prison society; the taking on of the ways, mores, customs, and general culture of the penitentiary.

Inmate Subculture

pains of imprisonment

Major problems that inmates face, such as loss of liberty and personal autonomy, lack of material possessions, loss of heterosexual relationships, and reduced personal security.

CO10-1

deprivation theory

The belief that inmate subcultures develop in response to the deprivations in prison life.

importation theory

The belief that inmate subcultures are brought into prisons from the outside world.

integration model

A combination of importation theory and deprivation theory. The belief that, in childhood, some inmates acquired, usually from peers, values that support law-violating behavior but that the norms and standards in prison also affect inmates.

(also called the *prisoner subculture*) can be defined as "the habits, customs, mores, values, beliefs, or superstitions of the body of inmates incarcerated in correctional institutions."[6]

Prisoners are socialized into the inmate subculture through a process known as *prisonization*. The concept of **prisonization** was identified by Donald Clemmer in his book *The Prison Community*.[7] Clemmer defined *prisonization* as the process by which inmates adapt to prison society, and he described it as "the taking on of the ways, mores, customs, and general culture of the penitentiary." When the process of prisonization is complete, Clemmer noted, prisoners have become "cons."

In a further study of prisonization, Stanton Wheeler examined how prisoners adapted to life at the Washington State Reformatory.[8] Wheeler found that prisonization has greater impact with the passage of time. The prisonization of inmates, said Wheeler, can be described by a *U*-shaped curve. When an inmate first enters prison, the conventional values of the outside society still hold sway in his life. As time passes, however, he increasingly adopts the prison lifestyle. Wheeler also found that within the half-year before release, most inmates begin to demonstrate a renewed appreciation for conventional values.

In *The Society of Captives*,[9] Gresham Sykes described what he called the **pains of imprisonment**. According to Sykes, new inmates face major problems including the loss of liberty, a lack of material possessions, deprivation of goods and services, the loss of heterosexual relationships, the loss of personal autonomy, and a reduction in personal security. These deficits, Sykes noted, lead to self-doubts and reduced self-esteem. Prison society compensates for such feelings and reduces the pains of imprisonment for the prison population as a whole. It also meets the personal and social needs induced in inmates by the pains of imprisonment. In short, said Sykes, inmate society compensates for the losses caused by imprisonment, and it offers varying degrees of comfort to those who successfully adjust to it.

The inmate subculture can vary from one institution to another. Variations are due to differences in the organizational structure of prisons. Maximum-security institutions, for example, are decidedly more painful for inmates because security considerations require greater restriction of inmate freedoms and access to material items. As a result, the subcultures in maximum-security institutions may be much more rigid in their demands on prisoners than those in less secure institutions.

How Does an Inmate Subculture Form?

Early students of inmate subcultures, particularly Clemmer and Sykes, believed that such subcultures developed in response to the deprivations in prison life. This perspective is called **deprivation theory.** Shared deprivation gives inmates a basis for solidarity.[10]

A more recent perspective is that an inmate subculture does not develop in prison but is brought into prison from the outside world. Known as **importation theory,** this point of view was popularized by John Irwin and Donald R. Cressey.[11] It was further supported by the work of James Jacobs.[12] Importation theory holds that inmate society is shaped by factors outside prison—specifically, preprison life experiences and socialization patterns. Inmates who lived violent lives outside tend to associate with other violent inmates and often engage in similar behavior in prison.[13]

More realistic is the **integration model,** which acknowledges that both theories have some validity. According to the integration model, people undergo early socialization experiences. In childhood, some people

In some prisons, inmate subculture is fragmented as inmates form competing gangs and other groups along ethnic, racial, and geographic lines. How could the differences among such groups affect the order and stability of a prison?

© A. Ramey/Photo Edit

develop leanings toward delinquent and criminal activity, acquiring—from peer groups, parents and other significant adults, television, movies, other mass media, and even computer and video games—values that support law–violating behavior. Those who become inmates are also likely to have experienced juvenile court proceedings and may have been institutionalized as juveniles. As a consequence, such people are likely to have acquired many of the values, much of the language, and the general behavioral patterns of deviant or criminal subcultures before entering adult prison.

The integration model also recognizes, however, the effects that the norms and behavioral standards of inmates in a particular prison have on those who are imprisoned. If a new inmate has already been socialized into a criminal lifestyle, the transition into the inmate subculture is likely to be easy. For some people, however—especially white-collar offenders with little previous exposure to criminal subcultures—the transition can be very difficult. The language, social expectations, and norms of prison society are likely to be foreign to them.

Norms and Values of Prison Society

Central to prison society is a code of behavior for all inmates. The **prison code** is a set of inmate rules antagonistic to the official administration and rehabilitation programs.[14] Violations of the code result in inmate-imposed sanctions, ranging from ostracism to homicide. Sykes and Messinger have identified five main elements of the prison code:[15]

1. Don't interfere with the interests of other inmates. Never rat on a con. Don't have loose lips.
2. Don't lose your head. Don't quarrel with other inmates. Play it cool. Do your own time.
3. Don't exploit other inmates. Don't steal. Don't break your word. Pay your debts.
4. Don't whine. Be tough. Be a man.
5. Don't be a sucker. Don't trust the guards or staff. Remember that prison officials are wrong and inmates are right.

CO10-2

prison code

A set of norms and values among prison inmates. It is generally antagonistic to the official administration and rehabilitation programs of the prison.

Inmate Roles

prison argot

The special language of the inmate subculture.

inmate roles

Prison lifestyles; also, forms of ongoing social accommodation to prison life.

CO10-3

Prison Argot—The Language of Confinement

Prison argot is the special language of the inmate subculture. *Argot* is a French word meaning "slang." Prison society has always had its own unique language illustrated by the following argot-laden paragraph:

> The new con, considered fresh meat by the screws and other prisoners, was sent to the cross-bar hotel to do his bit. He soon picked up the reputation through the yard grapevine as a canary-bird. While he was at the big house, the goon squad put him in the freezer for his protection. Eventually, he was released from the ice-box and ordered to make little ones out of big ones until he was released to the free world. Upon release he received $100 in gate money, vowing never to be thrown in the hole or be thought of as a stool-pigeon again.[16]

Prison argot originated partly as a form of secret communication. Gresham Sykes, however, believed that it serves primarily as "an illustrative symbol of the prison community"—or as a way for inmates to mark themselves as outlaws and social outcasts.[17] Sykes's work brought prison argot to the attention of sociologists and criminologists. Since Sykes's time other authors have identified a number of words, terms, and acronyms in prison argot. Some of these terms are presented in Exhibit 10–2. Interestingly, rap musicians, many of whom have spent time in prison or deal with prison-related themes, have brought prison argot to a wider audience.

Social Structure in Men's Prisons

Inmate societies, like other societies, have a hierarchy of positions. Inmates assume or are forced into specific social roles, and some inmates—by virtue of the roles they assume—have more status and power than others.

Early writers often classified prisoners by the crimes they had committed or their criminal histories. Irwin, for example, divided prisoners into such categories as thieves (those with a culture of criminal values), convicts (time doers), square johns (inmates unfamiliar with criminal subcultures), and dope fiends (drug-involved inmates).[18]

Other writers have identified **inmate roles,** defining them as prison lifestyles or as forms of ongoing social accommodation to prison life. Each role has a position in the pecking order, indicating its status in the prison society.

About a decade ago, Frank Schmalleger developed a typology of male inmate roles.[19] It is based on actual social roles found among inmates in prison, and it uses the prison argot in existence when it was created to name or describe each type. Each type can be viewed as a prison lifestyle either chosen by inmates or forced on them. Some of the types were previously identified by other writers. Although the terminology used in the typology sounds dated, the types of inmates it identifies are still characteristic of prison populations today. The 13 inmate types are discussed in the following paragraphs.

CO10-4

The Real Man Real men do their own time, do not complain, and do not cause problems for other inmates. They see confinement as a natural consequence of criminal activity and view time spent in prison as an unfortunate cost of doing business. Real men know the inmate code and abide by it. They are well regarded within the institution and rarely run into problems with other inmates. If they do, they solve their problems on their own. They never seek the help of correctional officers or the prison administration. Although they generally avoid trouble within the institution, they usually continue a life of crime once released.

EXHIBIT 10-2   Prison Argot: The Language of Confinement

Argot in Men's Prisons

ace duce: best friend

back door parole: to die in prison

badge (or bull, hack, "the man," or screw): a correctional officer

ball busters: violent inmates

banger (or burner, shank, sticker): a knife

billys: white men

boneyard: conjugal visiting area

booty bandit: an imprisoned sexual predator who preys on weaker inmates

bug juice: antidepressant or antipsychotic medications provided by the medical staff

cantones: gang term for prisons

catch cold: to be killed

cat-J (or J-cat): a prisoner in need of psychological or psychiatric therapy or medication

cellie: cell mate

center men: inmates who are close to the staff

chester: child molester

chota: a correctional officer

croaker: a physician or a doctor

dancing on the blacktop: being stabbed

diaper sniper: child molester

diddler: a child molester or pedophile

dog: homeboy or friend

fag: a male inmate believed to be a natural (preprison) homosexual

fish: a newly arrived inmate

gorilla: an inmate who uses force to take what he wants from others

got stretched: became angry

grandma's: gang headquarters

hacks: correctional officers

hipsters: young, drug-involved inmates

homeboy: a prisoner from one's hometown or neighborhood

in the car: circle of friends

ink: tattoos

jointman: a prison inmate who behaves like a correctional officer

kite: a contraband letter

lemon squeezer: an inmate who has an unattractive "girlfriend"

lugger: an inmate who smuggles contraband into the facility

man walking: phrase used to signal that a guard is coming

merchant (or peddler): one who sells when he should give; or one who sells goods and services to other inmates illegally

nimby: not in my back yard

ninja turtles: correctional officers dressed in riot gear

punk: a male inmate who is forced into a submissive role during homosexual relations

rat (or snitch): an inmate who squeals (provides information about other inmates to the prison administration)

real men: inmates respected by other inmates

seed: the inmate's child

shank: a knife

schooled: knowledgeable in the ways of prison life

shakedown: search of a cell or a work area

shu (pronounced *shoe*): special housing unit

sleeved: covered with tatoos

slinging rock: selling crack

soda: cocaine

stainless-steel ride: lethal injection

toughs: those with a preprison history of violent crimes

tree jumper: rapist

turn out: to rape or make into a punk

veterano: a long-time gang member

wolf: a male inmate who assumes an aggressive role during homosexual relations

Argot in Women's Prisons

cherry (or cherrie): an inmate not yet introduced to lesbian activities

fay broad: a white inmate

femme (or mommy): an inmate who plays a female role during a lesbian relationship

lark: a woman who talks with the staff

safe: the vagina, especially when used for hiding contraband

stud broad (or daddy): an inmate who assumes a male role in a lesbian relationship

Sources: Gresham Sykes, *The Society of Captives* (Princeton, NJ; Princeton University Press, 1958); Rose Giallombardo, *Society of Women: A Study of Women's Prison* (New York: John Wiley, 1966); Richard A. Cloward et al., *Theoretical Studies in Social Organization of the Prison* (New York: Social Science Research Council, 1960). For a more contemporary listing of prison slang terms, see Reinhold Aman, *Hillary Clinton's Pen Pal: A Guide to Life and Lingo in Federal Prison* (Santa Rosa, CA: Maledicta Press, 1996); Jerome Washington, *Iron House: Stories from the Yard* (Ann Arbor, MI: QED Press, 1994); Morrie Camhi, *The Prison Experience* (Boston: Charles Tuttle, 1989); Harold Long, *Survival in Prison* (Port Townsend, WA: Loompanics Unlimited, 1990); insideprison.com (accessed March 24, 2009); Mother Jones, "A Glossary of Prison Slang" (July/August 2008), http://motherjones.com/politics/2008/07/glossary-prison-slang (accessed March 10, 2011).

The Mean Dude   Some inmates are notorious for resorting quickly to physical power. They are quick to fight and, when fighting, give no quarter. They are callous, cold, and uncaring. Mean dudes control those around them through force or the threat of force. The fear they inspire usually gives them a great deal of power in inmate society. At the very least, other inmates are likely to leave the mean dude alone.

The Bully   A variation of the mean dude is the bully. Bullies use intimidation to get what they want. Unlike mean dudes, they are far more likely to use threats than to use actual physical force. A bully may make his threats in public so that others see the victim's compliance.

The Agitator   The agitator, sometimes called a *wise guy,* is constantly trying to stir things up. He responds to the boredom of prison life by causing problems for others. An agitator may point out, for example, how a powerful inmate has been wronged by another inmate or that an inmate seen talking to a "rat" must be a snitch himself.

The Hedonist   The hedonist adapts to prison by exploiting the minimal pleasures it offers. Hedonists always seek the easy path, and they plot to win the "cushiest" jobs. They may also stockpile goods to barter for services of various kinds. Hedonists live only in the now with little concern for the future. Their lives revolve around such activities as gambling, drug running, smuggling contraband, and exploiting homosexual opportunities.

The Opportunist   The opportunist sees prison as an opportunity for personal advancement. He takes advantage of the formal self-improvement opportunities of the prison, such as schooling, trade training, and counseling. Other inmates generally dislike opportunists, seeing them as selfish *do-gooders.* Staff members, however, often see opportunists as model prisoners.

The Retreatist   Some inmates, unable to cope with the realities of prison life, withdraw psychologically from the world around them. Depression, neurosis, and even psychosis may result. Some retreatists attempt to lose themselves in drugs or alcohol. Others attempt suicide. Isolation from the general prison population combined with counseling or psychiatric treatment may offer the best hope for retreatists to survive the prison experience.

The Legalist   Legalists are known as *jailhouse lawyers,* or simply *lawyers,* in prison argot. They are usually among the better-educated prisoners, although some legalists have little formal education. Legalists fight confinement through the system of laws, rules, and court precedent. Legalists file writs with the courts, seeking hearings on a wide variety of issues. Although many legalists work to better the conditions of their own confinement or to achieve early release, most also file pleas on behalf of other prisoners.

The Radical   Radicals see themselves as political prisoners of an unfair society. They believe that a discriminatory world has denied them the education and skills needed to succeed in a socially acceptable way. Most of the beliefs held by radical inmates are rationalizations that shift the blame for personal failure onto society. The radical inmate is likely to be familiar with contemporary countercultural figures.

Visit http://www.youtube.com/watch?v= Y8NMLu5oNLo or scan this QR code with the QR app on your smartphone or digital device to view a video on women inmates in Maryland.

The Colonist Colonists, also referred to as *convicts*, turn prison into home. Colonists know the ropes of prison, have many "friends" on the inside, and often feel more comfortable in prison than outside it. They may not look forward to leaving prison. Some may even commit additional offenses to extend their stay. Colonists are generally well regarded by other prisoners. Many are old-timers. Colonists have learned to take advantage of the informal opportunity structure in prisons, and they are well versed in the inmate code.

The Religious Inmate Religious inmates profess a strong religious faith and may attempt to convert both inmates and staff. Religious inmates frequently form prayer groups, request special meeting facilities and special diets, and may ask for frequent visits from religious leaders. Religious inmates are often under a great deal of suspicion from inmates and staff, who tend to think they are faking religious commitment to gain special treatment. Those judged sincere in their faith may win early release, removal from death row, or any number of other special considerations.

The Punk The punk is a young inmate, often small, who has been forced into a sexual relationship with an aggressive, well-respected prisoner. Punks are generally "turned out" through homosexual rape. A punk usually finds a protector among the more powerful inmates. Punks keep their protectors happy by providing them with sexual services.

The Gang-Banger Gang-bangers, or those affiliated with prison gangs, know that there is power in numbers. They depend upon the gang for defense and protection as well as for the procurement of desired goods and services. Gang-bangers are known by their tattoos and hand signs, which indicate gang affiliation and can be read by anyone familiar with prison society. Prison gangs often have links outside prison—leading to continued involvement in crime by those directing them from inside prison and to the creation of channels for the importation of banned items into correctional facilities.

Inmates at a prayer service at Men's Central Jail in Los Angeles. How does this chapter describe a "religious" type of inmate?
© Carolyn Cole/Getty Images

The typical incident of sexual aggression, Lockwood found, is carried out by a group. About half the incidents Lockwood identified included physical violence, and another third involved threats. The incidents studied showed patterns of escalation from verbal abuse to physical violence.

Lockwood also found that prison rapes generally occur when gangs of aggressors circumvent security arrangements to physically control their victims. Fear, anxiety, suicidal thoughts, social disruption, and attitude changes develop in many victims of homosexual rape.

In 2003, in an effort to learn more about prison rape, Congress mandated the collection of prison rape statistics under the Prison Rape Elimination Act (PREA).[27] The PREA, which also established the federal Prison Rape Commission, calls for an evaluation of issues related to prison rape as well as for the development of national standards to help prevent prison rape.

Tasked by the PREA to gather data on prison rape, the BJS completed the first-ever national Survey of Sexual Victimization (SSV) based on reports of former state prison inmates in 2012. The survey, which has been conducted annually ever since, included information from completed interviews with 18,526 former inmates who were still under parole supervision. Recent survey results show:

- Administrators of adult correctional facilities report close to 9,000 allegations of sexual victimization annually.
- An estimated 9.6 percent of former state prisoners reported one or more incidents of sexual victimization during their most recent period of incarceration.
- Among all former state prisoners, 1.8 percent reported experiencing one or more incidents while in a local jail, 7.5 percent while in a state prison, and 0.1 percent while in a postrelease community treatment facility.
- About 52 percent of substantiated incidents of sexual victimization involved only inmates, while 48 percent of substantiated incidents involved staff with inmates.
- Females committed more than half of all substantiated incidents of staff sexual misconduct and a quarter of all incidents of staff sexual harassment.
- Injuries were reported in about 18 percent of incidents of inmate-on-inmate sexual victimization and in less than 1 percent of incidents of staff sexual victimizations.
- An estimated 35 percent of transgender inmates held in prisons and 34 percent held in local jails reported experiencing one or more incidents of sexual victimization by another inmate or facility staff in the past 12 months or since admission, if less than 12 months.
- When asked about the experiences surrounding their victimization by other inmates, 72 percent of transgender inmates said they experienced force or threat of force, and 29 percent said they were physically injured.[28]

Official reports by correctional administrators are unlikely to reflect the true incident of sexual violence. As BJS notes, "due to fear of reprisal from perpetrators, a code of silence among inmates, personal embarrassment, and lack of trust in staff, victims are often reluctant to report incidents to correctional authorities."[29] To circumvent such issues and to gather more reliable information, BJS has implemented a system of self-reports in which data are collected from incarcerated individuals as well as those recently released.

EVIDENCE-BASED CORRECTIONS
The "Moving On" Program

"Moving On" is a curriculum-based, gender-responsive intervention program created to address the different cognitive–behavioral needs of incarcerated women. Moving On is delivered in 26 sessions over the course of 12 weeks, with each session lasting 1.5 to 2 hours. Class sizes tend to be small, ranging from 5 to 10 participants (there is a maximum of 10 participants per facilitator). Sessions consist of both group and one-on-one discussions. Program activities include self-assessments, writing exercises, role-playing, and modeling activities. Participation in Moving On is voluntary. The program is offered on a quarterly basis to incarcerated women who are serving the last half of their confinement period.

The program is rated Promising. Participants in Moving On were significantly less likely to be rearrested or reconvicted, compared with the control group. Participating in Moving On lowered the risk of reoffending by 33 percent. It did not, however, not have a significant impact on reincarcerations for a new offense and technical violation revocations.

Source: Adapted from https://www.crimesolutions.gov/ProgramDetails.aspx?ID=476.

Under pressure from a federal judge, the state reduced the population at Tutwiler, sending hundreds of women to prisons out of state through contracts for prison space. By 2015, the Tutwiler prison was expanded to a design capacity of 417 inmates but contained 743 beds.[34] A year earlier, the U.S. Department of Justice had issued a findings letter concluding that Tutwiler subjects its women prisoners to a pattern and practice of sexual abuse in violation of the Eighth Amendment of the U.S. Constitution. The findings identified several systemic failures that led to patterns of abuse, including ineffective reporting and investigations and no grievance policy. Tutwiler, said the Justice Department, also failed to hold culpable staff accountable for abuses. One and a half years later, the allegations were dismissed after an agreement was reached to protect the women.[35]

Characteristics of Women Inmates

`CO10-6`

Many of our conceptions of female inmates derive more from myth than reality. Recent BJS surveys provide a more realistic picture of female inmates.[36] At the start of 2015, women comprised 7.0 percent of sentenced prisoners in the nation. Since 2000, the female prison population has grown almost 30 percent,[37] a noticeably higher rate of growth than experienced in the male prison population, which had a 20 percent increase during the same period. As of January 1, 2015, there were 112,961 women under the jurisdiction of state and federal prison authorities.[38]

Female prisoners largely resemble male prisoners in race, ethnic background, and age. However, they are substantially more likely to be serving time for a drug offense and less likely to have been sentenced for a violent crime. Women are also more likely than men to be serving time for larceny or fraud.

Female inmates have shorter criminal records than male inmates. They generally have shorter maximum sentences than men. Half of all women receive a maximum sentence of 60 months or less, and half of all men are sentenced to 120 months or less.

An imprisoned woman. How do men's and women's prisons differ?
© Robin Nelson/Zuma/Corbis

Significantly, more than 4 in 10 of the women prisoners responding to BJS surveys reported prior physical or sexual abuse. One of the major factors distinguishing male inmates from female inmates is that the women have experienced far more sexual and physical abuse than had the men. Interviews with incarcerated women have found that 70 percent of them report the occurrence of sexual molestation or severe physical abuse in childhood at the hands of parents or adolescent caregivers.[39] Fifty-nine percent report some form of sexual abuse in childhood or adolescence, and 75 percent of those interviewed report having been severely abused by an intimate partner as adults.

A report by the National Institute of Corrections (NIC) found that women enter correctional institutions through different "pathways" than men. According to the report, most women offenders are typically nonviolent and their crimes are less threatening to community safety than those committed by male offenders. "Women's most common pathways to crime," said the report, "result from abuse, poverty, and substance abuse"—all of which, according to the report, are interconnected.[40] Exhibit 10–5 is a comparison of selected characteristics of female and male state prisoners.

Offenses of Incarcerated Women

Drug offenses account for the incarceration of a high percentage of the women behind bars. Twenty-four percent of all women in state prisons are serving time on drug charges.[41] Some sources estimate that drug crimes and other crimes indirectly related to drug activities together account for the imprisonment of around 95 percent of today's women inmates. In short, drug use and abuse, or crimes stimulated by the desire for drugs and drug money, are what send most women to prison. This has been true for more than a decade. According to an ACA report, the primary reasons incarcerated women most frequently give for their arrest are (1) trying to pay for drugs, (2) attempts to relieve economic pressures, and (3) poor judgment.[42]

According to the BJS, before arrest, women in prison use more drugs than men and use those drugs more frequently.[43] About 59 percent of imprisoned women used drugs daily in the month before the offense for which they were arrested compared with 56 percent of the men. Female inmates are also more likely than male inmates to have used drugs regularly (65 percent vs. 62 percent), and to have been under the influence at the time of the offense (36 percent vs. 31 percent). Nearly one in four female inmates surveyed reported committing the offense to get money to buy drugs compared with one in six males.

Female inmates who used drugs differed from those who did not in the types of crimes they committed. Regardless of the amount of drug use, users were less likely than nonusers to be serving a sentence for a violent offense.

| EXHIBIT 10-5 | Characteristics of Women and Men in State Prisons |

Women in Prison

Criminal Offense

37% are in prison for violent offenses

25% are in prison for drug offenses

29% are in prison for property offenses

8% are in prison for public-order offenses

1% or less are in prison for other offenses

Criminal History

46% are nonviolent recidivists

28% have no previous sentence

26% are violent recidivists

Family Characteristics

78% have children

42% lived with both parents most of time growing up

33% had a parent/guardian who abused alcohol or drugs

17% were married at the time they committed the offense for which they were incarcerated

45% have never married

47% have a family member who had been incarcerated

Drug and Alcohol Use

59% used drugs daily in the month before the current offense

36% were under the influence of drugs at the time of the offense

12% were under the influence of alcohol at the time of the offense

Men in Prison

Criminal Offense

54% are in prison for violent offenses

18% are in prison for property offenses

17% are in prison for drug offenses

11% are in prison for public-order offenses

1% or less are in prison for other offenses

Criminal History

50% are violent recidivists

31% are nonviolent recidivists

19% have no previous sentence

Family Characteristics

64% have children

43% lived with both parents most of time growing up

26% had a parent/guardian who abused alcohol or drugs

18% were married at the time they committed the offense for which they were incarcerated

56% have never married

37% have a family member who had been incarcerated

Drug and Alcohol Use

56% used drugs daily in the month before the current offense

31% were under the influence of drugs at the time of the offense

18% were under the influence of alcohol at the time of the offense

Sources: E. Ann Carson, *Prisoners in 2014* (Washington, DC: U.S. Department of Justice, 2015); Allen Beck et al., *Survey of State Prison Inmates, 1991* (Washington, DC: U.S. Department of Justice, March 1993); Christopher J. Mumola and Jennifer C. Karberg, "Drug Use and Dependence, State and Federal Prisoners, 2004" (Washington, DC: Bureau of Justice Statistics, 2006).

Social Structure in Women's Prisons   `CO10-7`

As might be expected, the social structure and the subcultural norms and expectations in women's prisons are quite different from those in men's prisons. Unfortunately, however, relatively few studies of inmate life have been conducted in institutions for women.

One early study of women at the Federal Reformatory for Women in Alderson, West Virginia, was an effort to compare subcultural aspects of women's prisons with those of men's. Rose Giallombardo reached the conclusion that "many of the subcultural features of the institution are imported from the larger society."[44] Giallombardo believed that male and female inmate subcultures are actually quite similar except that women's prisons develop "a substitute universe," a world "in which inmates may preserve an identity, which is relevant to life outside the prison."

Giallombardo was unable to find in the women's prison some of the values inherent in a male inmate subculture, such as "Do your own time." The inmate subculture in a women's prison, she said, tends to encourage relationships rather than isolation. Hence, women are expected to share their problems with other inmates and to offer at least some support and encouragement to others. On the other hand, she observed, women prisoners tend to see each other as conniving, self-centered, and scheming. Hence, a basic tenet of the inmate subculture in a women's prison is "You can't trust other women." As Giallombardo put it, women prisoners tend to believe that "every woman is a sneaking, lying bitch."

Giallombardo concluded that the social structure of women's prisons and the social role assumed by each inmate are based on three elements:

1. the individual woman's level of personal dependence and her status needs (which are said to be based upon cultural expectations of the female role);
2. the individual's needs arising from incarceration combined with the institution's inability to meet female inmates' emotional needs; and
3. needs related to the individual's personality.

A more recent study was of inmates in the District of Columbia Women's Reformatory at Occoquan, Virginia.[45] Esther Heffernan identified three roles that women commonly adopt when adjusting to prison. According to Heffernan, women's roles evolve partly from the characteristics the women bring with them to prison and depend partly on the ways the women choose to adapt to prison life. The roles she described are discussed in the following paragraphs.

The Cool Inmate Cool women usually have previous records, are in the know, are streetwise, and do not cause trouble for other inmates while in prison. Cool women are seen as professional or semiprofessional criminals who work to win the maximum number of prison amenities without endangering their parole or release dates.

The Square Inmate Square women are not familiar with criminal lifestyles and have few, if any, criminal experiences other than the one for which they were imprisoned. They tend to hold the values and roles of conventional society.

The Life Inmate Life inmates are habitual or career offenders and are generally well socialized into lives of crime. They support inmate values and subculture. Life inmates typically have been in and out of prison from an early age and have developed criminal lifestyles dedicated to meeting their political, economic, familial, and social needs outside conventional society.

Recently, California State University (Fresno) criminologist Barbara Owens studied the culture of imprisoned women at Central California Women's Facility in Chowchilla, California, and found a "prison culture that is itself complex and diverse across numerous dimensions."[46] Owens identified a central component of that culture that she refers to as "the mix."

The mix, according to Owens, "is any behavior that can bring trouble and conflict with staff and other prisoners." It consists of fighting, doing drugs, prison-based lesbian activity ("homo-secting," in Owens's terms), and making trouble for the staff. It also involves continuing the kinds of behaviors that brought women to prison. Consequently, the mix is to be avoided by those who want to leave prison and not return. New women coming into the institution, Owens found, were advised to "stay out of the mix." The mix, says Owens, is also a state of mind, a way of thinking like a troublemaker.

One writer, summarizing the results of studies such as those discussed here, found that two primary features distinguish women's prisons from men's prisons:[47]

1. The social roles in women's prisons place greater emphasis on homosexual relations as a mode of adaptation to prison life.
2. The mode of adaptation a female inmate selects is best assessed by studying the inmate's preinstitutional experiences.

Pseudofamilies and Sexual Liaisons

A unique feature of women's prisons is pseudofamilies. **Pseudofamilies** are family-like structures, common in women's prisons, in which inmates assume roles similar to those of family members in free society. Pseudofamilies appear to provide emotional and social support for the women who belong to them. Courtship, marriage, and kinship ties formed with other women inmates provide a means of coping with the rigors of imprisonment. One inmate has explained pseudofamilies this way: "It just happens. Just like on the outside, you get close to certain people. It's the same in here—but we probably get even closer than a lot of families because of how lonely it is otherwise."[48]

Some authors suggest that pseudofamilies are to women's prisons what gangs are to men's.[49] Men establish social relationships largely through power, and gang structure effectively expresses such relationships. Women relate to one another more expressively and emotionally. Hence, family structures are one of the most effective reflections of women's relationships in prison, just as they are in the wider society. At least one study of prison coping behavior found that new female inmates, especially those most in need of support, advice, and assistance in adjusting to the conditions of incarceration, are the women most likely to become members of prison pseudofamilies.[50]

To a large extent, the social and behavioral patterns of family relationships in prison mirror their traditional counterparts in the community. Families in women's prisons come in all sizes and colors. They can be virtual melting pots of ethnicity and age. A member of a family may be young or old and may be black, white, or Hispanic. As in families in free society, there are roles for husbands and wives, sisters, brothers, grandmothers, and children. Roles for aunts and uncles do not exist, however.

"Stud broads," in prison argot, assume any male role, including that of husband and brother. Other inmates think of them as men. "Men" often assume traditional roles in women's prisons, ordering women around, demanding to be waited on, expecting to have their rooms cleaned and their laundry done, and so forth. Most women who assume masculine roles within prison are said to be "playing" and are sometimes called *players.* Once they leave, they usually revert to female roles. A "femme" or "mommy" is a woman who assumes a female role in a family and during homosexual activity.

Most women in prison, including those playing masculine roles, were generally not lesbians before entering prison. They resort to lesbian relations within prison because relationships with men are unavailable.

Although gender roles and family relationships within women's prisons appear to have an enduring quality, women can and sometimes do change

pseudofamilies

Family-like structures, common in women's prisons, in which inmates assume roles similar to those of family members in free society.

The kinship of substitute families plays a major role in the lives of many female inmates, who take the relationships very seriously. How might these relationships supplant values such as "do your own time" commonly found in the subculture of men's prisons?
© imageBROKER/imageBROKER/SuperStock

role genders. When a woman playing a male role, for example, reverts to a female one, she is said to have "dropped her belt." A stud broad who drops her belt may wreak havoc on relationships within her own family and in families related to it.

Special Needs of Female Inmates

Rarely are the special needs of imprisoned women fully recognized—and even less frequently are they addressed. Many of today's prison administrators and correctional officers still treat women as if they were men. Nicole Hahn Rafter, for example, says that many prisons have an attitude akin to "just add women and stir."[51]

A recent report by the NIC called for criminal justice agencies to acknowledge the "many differences between male and female offenders," and for the implementation of gender–responsive programming for treating the problems of imprisoned women.[52] **Gender-responsiveness** can be defined as "creating an environment . . . that reflects an understanding of the realities of women's lives and addresses the issues of the women."[53] Gender-responsive programming might, for example, strengthen policies against staff sexual misconduct in institutions that house women; provide more "safe and nurturing" drug treatment programs; and help inmate mothers to maintain strong relationships with their children. The NIC report concluded that " gender-responsive practice can improve outcomes for women offenders by considering their histories, behaviors, and life circumstances."[54]

Susan Cranford is division director of the Community Justice Assistance Division of the Texas Department of Criminal Justice. Rose Williams is warden of Pulaski State Prison in Hawkinsville, Georgia. Recently, Cranford and Williams suggested that "correctional staff should keep the unique needs of women offenders in mind."[55] They say that the effective running of a women's prison requires consideration of those needs.

A critical difference between male and female prisoners, say Cranford and Williams, is "the manner in which they communicate." Female offenders, they note, are usually much more open, more verbal, more emotional, and more willing to share the intimacies of their lives than men are. Male prisoners, like most men in free society, are guarded about the information they share and the manner in which they share it. "For men, information is power. For women, talking helps establish a common ground, a way to relate to others."

Gender-specific training is vital for corrections officers (COs) who work in women's prisons, say Cranford and Williams. Proper training, they write, can head off the development of inappropriate relationships (especially initiated by male staff members), which could lead to sexual misconduct. Moreover, staff members who work with women should receive additional training in negotiating and listening skills.

An example of effective gender-specific training is the task-oriented curriculum titled *Working with the Female Offender* developed by Florida's Department of Corrections.[56] The program addresses unique aspects of managing female inmates and provides correctional staff training in the behaviors, actions, needs, and backgrounds presented by female offenders. A special segment examines how female offenders relate to supervision in various institutional or community corrections settings.

Moreover, say Cranford and Williams, it is important to realize that a woman's children are usually very important to her and that many imprisoned women have children on the outside. Hence, parenting skills should

gender-responsiveness

The intentional creation of an environment that reflects an understanding of the realities of women's lives and addresses the special issues of women in correctional settings.

be taught to imprisoned mothers because most will rejoin and be with their children during critical stages in the children's development.

There are, however, those who feel that gender-responsive strategies won't work. The reason, they say, is because more and more women are being "convicted of crimes for which they would not previously have received a custodial sentence," and are being sent to prison "not because of the seriousness of their crimes, but mainly to receive psychological programming and reintegration training when, in fact, their main problems have stemmed from inadequate housing, poverty, and abusive men."[57] In other words, gender-responsive strategies assume that imprisonment can make a positive difference in women's lives, something that may not be true because such strategies often do little to address the problems women will again face upon release.

Mothers in Prison

According to one BJS study,[58] an estimated 6.7 percent of black women, 5.9 percent of Hispanic women, and 5.2 percent of white women are pregnant at the time of incarceration.

An estimated 4,000 women prisoners give birth each year, even though most women's prisons have no special facilities for pregnant inmates.[59] Some experts recommend that women's prisons should routinely make counseling available to pregnant inmates and that they should fully inform these women of the options available to them, including abortion and adoption.[60]

The ACA[61] recommends that institutions provide counseling for pregnant inmates, that "prenatal care" should be offered, and that deliveries should be made at community hospitals.[62] Similarly, the American Public Health Association's standards for health services in correctional institutions say that pregnant inmates should be provided with prenatal care, including medical exams and treatment, and that pregnant prisoners should be allowed a special program of housing, diet, vitamin supplements, and exercise.

Once inmates give birth, other problems arise—including the critical issue of child placement. Some states still have partial civil death statutes, which mean that prisoners lose many of their civil rights upon incarceration. In such states, women may lose legal custody of their children. Children either become wards of the state or are placed for adoption.

Although there is some historical precedent for allowing women inmates to keep newborns with them in the institutional setting, very few women's prisons permit this practice. Overcrowded prisons lack space for children, and the prison environment is a decidedly undesirable environment for children. A few women's prisons allow women to keep newborns for a brief period. Most, however, arrange for foster care until the mother is able to find relatives to care for the child or is released. Others work with services that put prison-born infants up for adoption. Some facilities make a special effort to keep mother and child together. Even relatively progressive prisons that allow mother–child contact usually do so only for the first year.

Many women are already mothers when they come to prison. BJS statistics[63] show that more than three-quarters of all women in prison in the United States have young children (i.e., under the age of 18). Black (69 percent) and Hispanic (72 percent) female inmates are more likely than white (62 percent) female inmates to have young children. Also, black women are more likely than other women to have lived with their young children before being imprisoned.

Incarcerated fathers and their daughters at the Richmond City Jail during a "Date with Dad Night" in 2013. Officials say that the dance offers a rare chance for fathers and daughters to bond. What are the problems faced by imprisoned parents? By their children?

© Marvin Joseph/The Washington Post via Getty

The children of 25 percent of women inmates with children under age 18 live with the other parent. More than a third of white female inmates report that their children are living with the children's fathers compared to a quarter of Hispanic women and less than a fifth of black women. Regardless of race, grandparents are the most common caregivers: 57 percent of imprisoned black mothers look to grandparents for child care as do 55 percent of imprisoned Hispanic mothers and 41 percent of imprisoned white mothers. Nearly 10 percent of the inmate mothers reported that their children are in a foster home, agency, or institution.

Worry about children affects female inmates' physical and emotional well-being. Although 78 percent of mothers (and 62 percent of fathers) report having at least monthly contact with their children, only 24 percent of mothers (and 21 percent of fathers) report personal visits from their children at least monthly.[64] A majority of both mothers (54 percent) and fathers (57 percent) report never having had a personal visit with their children since their imprisonment began.

According to BJS, nearly 90 percent of women with children under age 18 have had contact with their children since entering prison. Half of all women inmates surveyed have been visited by their children, four-fifths have corresponded by mail, and three-quarters have talked with children on the telephone. Female inmates with children under age 18 are more likely than those with adult children to make daily telephone calls to their children.

Understandably, inmate mothers frequently express concern about possible alienation from their children due to the passage of time associated with incarceration. They often worry that their children will develop strong bonds with new caretakers and be unwilling to return to them upon release.[65]

Finally, it is important to note that a number of women's prisons operate programs designed to develop parenting skills among inmates. Included are the Program for Caring Parents at the Louisiana Correctional Institute for Women; Project HIP (Helping Incarcerated Parents) at the Maine Correctional Center; and Neil J. Houston House, a program for nonviolent female offenders in Massachusetts.[66]

One recent study found that 1.7 million American children had a parent in prison.[67] Statistically speaking, 1 of every 43 American children has a parent in prison today, and ethnic variation in the numbers are striking. Although only 1 of every 111 white children has experienced the imprisonment of a parent, 1 of every 15 black children has had that experience. Moreover, between 1991 and 2007, the number of incarcerated fathers rose 76 percent while the number of incarcerated mothers increased by 122 percent.

The effects of parental incarceration on children can be significant. A number of studies show that the children of incarcerated mothers experience alienation, hostility, anger, significant feelings of abandonment, and overall dysfunction. They are much less likely to succeed in school than their peers and far more likely to involve themselves in gangs, sexual misconduct, sexual abuse, and overall delinquency.[68]

In the federal population, 63.4 percent of male prisoners and 58.8 percent of female prisoners have minor children. The state data reverse this distribution, with 65.3 percent of female inmates and 54.7 percent of male inmates having minor children.

It is noteworthy that male inmates are, for the most part, rarely provided any special assistance for maintaining contact with their children during their incarceration. During the past decade, however, administrators in women's institutions across the country have implemented measures to foster stronger bonds between incarcerated mothers and their children. Ranging from the establishment of prison nurseries to the development of special visitation areas, these measures seek to facilitate the continued family contact that appears to be so important to female offenders.[69]

With 1 in 12 inmates pregnant at the time of admission[70] and 22 percent of all minor children with a parent in prison being under 5 years old,[71] correctional administrators need to address the unique problems presented by pregnant offenders and those with very young children. Some institutions have opted to create nurseries on site. At Nebraska's Correctional Center for Women, for example, inmates due for release before their children are 18 months old may keep the children with them in a specially designated floor of a standard prison building. The mothers are provided parenting and child-care classes, and they work only part-time. While they work, other trained inmates provide child care.

Another example of programs designed to facilitate family bonding is the Ohio Reformatory for Women's annual three-day weekend camp, which brings children ages 6 to 12 from all over the state to spend days with their inmate mothers. Originally pioneered at Bedford Hills Correctional Facility, New York's maximum-security prison for women, such camping visits have become more common in other facilities as well. Some states even allow overnight camping trips, both on and off the prison grounds.

Inmates apply for the program in January each year. Local churches and other community service groups support the program.[72] Selection criteria include a review of inmates' disciplinary records during incarceration, and those whose crimes involved their children are prohibited from participating. During the weekend, activities such as storytelling, softball, crafts, and meals facilitate bonding between mother and child. The inmates return to the prison to sleep at night, but the children "camp out" in sleeping bags at a local church.

Another innovative effort is Florida's "Reading Family Ties: Face to Face" program.[73] Begun in February 2000, it uses high-speed videoconferencing technology to permit weekly family visits between incarcerated mothers in two rural institutions and their children in the Miami area. Inmate mothers may sit before an Internet-linked camera to read to their children. Logistical limitations, of course, are significant, but administrators plan to expand the program to other major cities in Florida.

Perhaps the most family-centered efforts are being tried in California and Illinois. Oakland's Project Pride[74] permits mothers convicted of nonviolent offenses to serve the last portion of their sentences in residential community settings with their preschool-age children. Under the Family Foundations Program in Santa Fe Springs (CA), sentencing of convicted mothers with substance abuse histories can include treatment in residential centers where they can live with their children. Similarly, at Illinois's Decatur Correctional Center, infants live in separate rooms with their mothers. Books and toys are plentiful in the unit, and large day rooms are decorated with colorful murals. The program is intended to serve women whose children will be two years old or younger by the time they are released from prison.[75]

Prison programs to help fathers learn better parenting are also on the increase. The National Fatherhood Initiative, for example, started Inside Out Dad in 2004, and it now operates in more than 400 prisons and jails nationwide. The program's goal is to reduce recidivism through better fathering.[76]

Some hard-liners might decry such programs as unjustified coddling of convicted offenders. Few, however, can argue the benefits such programs provide to the children of incarcerated parents. Meanwhile, it remains to be seen whether the programs will serve to sustain family relationships, ease prisoners' return to the family environment after release, and, ultimately, reduce recidivism rates.

Cocorrectional Facilities

In 1971, a disturbance at the federal women's prison at Alderson, West Virginia, led to calls for ways to expand incarceration options for women. The Federal BOP responded by moving low-security female prisoners from the crowded Alderson institution to a federal minimum-security prison at Morgantown, West Virginia. The Morgantown facility had been built for young men but had not reached its design capacity. With this move, the modern era of coed prisons, or cocorrections, was born.

A **coed prison** is a facility housing both men and women, and **cocorrections** is the incarceration and interaction of female and male offenders under a single institutional administration.[77] It is estimated that as many as 52 adult correctional institutions in the United States are coed and that they confine almost 23,000 men and 7,000 women.[78]

Since its inception, cocorrections has been cited as a potential solution to a wide variety of corrections problems. The rationales in support of cocorrections are that it:

1. reduces the dehumanizing and destructive aspects of incarceration by permitting heterosocial relationships;
2. reduces problems of institutional control;
3. creates a more "normal" atmosphere, reducing privation;
4. allows positive heterosocial skills to emerge;
5. cushions the shock of release;
6. increases the number of program offerings and improves program access for all prisoners; and
7. expands career opportunities for women.

An examination of the cocorrections literature from 1970 to 1990, however, found no evidence that cocorrections benefits female prisoners.[79] A former warden of a coed prison contends that "going coed" has often been done to appease male egos and smooth the running of men's prisons. Warden Jacqueline Crawford tells us that most women in prison have generally been exploited by the men in their lives. A coed prison, she says, furthers this experience because male prisoners continue the abuse women have come to expect from men.[80]

Others have found that some women's prisons have been turned into coed prisons, thus limiting correctional options for women. Overall, researchers have concluded, "Cocorrections offers women prisoners few, if any, economic, educational, vocational, and social advantages."[81] Whether prisoners released from coed prisons adjust better to the community or experience less recidivism has not been sufficiently studied.

Although literature related to single-sex prisons[82] has repeatedly shown poor overall performance in prisoner rehabilitation and public safety, correctional decision makers, policymakers, legislators, and the public are not calling for an end to one-sex imprisonment. If cocorrections is to become more than window dressing, however, it requires more attention to planning, implementation, and evaluation. Despite some early claims of success, coed prisons are not a quick fix for problems of prison administration.

coed prison

A prison housing both female and male offenders.

cocorrections

The incarceration and interaction of female and male offenders under a single institutional administration.

REVIEW AND APPLICATIONS

SUMMARY

1 Prison inmates live their daily lives in accordance with the dictates of the inmate subculture. The inmate subculture consists of the customs and beliefs of those incarcerated in correctional institutions. *Deprivation theory* holds that prisoner subcultures develop in response to the pains of imprisonment. *Importation theory* claims that inmate subcultures are brought into prisons from the outside world. The integration model uses both theories to explain prisoner subcultures.

2 An important aspect of the male inmate subculture is the prison code. The prison code is a set of norms for the behavior of inmates. Central elements of the code include notions of loyalty (to prison society), control of anger, toughness, and distrust of prison officials. Because the prison code is a part of the inmate subculture, it is mostly opposed to official policies.

3 The inmate subculture also has its own language, called *prison argot.* Examples of prison argot are "fish" (a new inmate), "cellie" (cell mate), and "homeboy" (a prisoner from one's hometown).

4 Inmate roles are different prison lifestyle choices. They include the real man, the mean dude, the bully, the agitator, the hedonist, the opportunist, the retreatist, the legalist, the radical, the colonist, the religious inmate, the punk, and the gang-banger.

5 There are far fewer women's prisons than men's in the United States. Women's prisons often have no gun towers or armed guards and no stone walls or fences topped by barbed wire. They tend to be more attractive and are often built on a cottage plan. Security in most women's prisons is more relaxed than in institutions for men, and female inmates may have more freedom within the institution than do their male counterparts in their institutions. Other gender-based disparities favoring male prisoners exist. A lack of funding and inadequate training have been cited to explain why programs available to women inmates are often not on a par with those available to male prisoners.

6 Female prisoners largely resemble male prisoners in race, ethnic background, and age. However, they are substantially more likely to be serving time for drug offenses and less likely to have been sentenced for violent crimes.

7 Although there are many similarities between men's and women's prisons, the social structure and the subcultural norms and expectations of women's prisons differ from those of men's prisons in a number of important ways. One important difference is that the prisoner subculture in a women's prison tends to encourage relationships rather than isolation. As a consequence, pseudofamilies arise, with fully developed familial relationships and roles.

KEY TERMS

total institution, p. 268	deprivation theory, p. 270	inmate roles, p. 272
inmate subculture, p. 269	importation theory, p. 270	pseudofamilies, p. 285
prisoner subculture, p. 269	integration model, p. 270	gender-responsiveness, p. 286
prisonization, p. 270	prison code, p. 271	coed prison, p. 290
pains of imprisonment, p. 270	prison argot, p. 272	cocorrections, p. 290

QUESTIONS FOR REVIEW

1 What is *inmate subculture,* and how is it central to understanding society in men's prisons?

2 What is the *prison code?* What are some of its key features? How does it influence behavior in men's prisons?

3 What is *prison argot?* Give some examples.

4 Explain what is meant by *inmate roles,* and give some examples.

5 In what ways do women's prisons differ from men's prisons?

6 Compare female and male inmates by their criminal histories, their family characteristics, and the offenses for which they are incarcerated.

7 How does the social structure of women's prisons differ from that in men's prisons? What are *pseudofamilies,* and why are they important to the society of women's prisons?

California's Folsom prison. In 2011, the U.S. Supreme Court ruled that California officials had to release as many as 58,000 inmates because of prison overcrowding. How did inmate rights figure into that decision?

© Janet Kopper/Getty Images RF

In 2011, the U.S. Supreme Court, in the case of *Brown* v. *Plata*, ordered the state of California to aggressively reduce its prison population by releasing as many as 58,000 inmates over the next two years.[1] The justices held that overcrowded conditions throughout the state's prisons had significantly deprived inmates of their right to adequate health care and thereby violated the Eighth Amendment's ban on cruel and unusual punishment. The high Court's ruling upheld an earlier order by a three-judge federal panel intended to reduce the number of inmates supervised by the California Department of Corrections and Rehabilitation (CDCR) to around 120,000. At the time of the ruling, the CDCR was supervising around 160,000 inmates in 33 facilities originally designed to hold only 84,000. The rest of the state's prisoners were housed under contract in correctional facilities outside of the state, but the Supreme Court determined that the policy of transferring inmates was inadequate to address California's overcrowding problem. In rendering the *Plata* ruling the justices were drawing upon a legal tradition recognizing the rights of inmates that began in the United States more than 40 years earlier.

CO11-1 THE HANDS-OFF DOCTRINE

In 1871, almost 140 years before the California order was issued, a Virginia judge declared the following: "A convicted felon . . . punished by confinement in the penitentiary instead of with death . . . is in a state of penal servitude to the State. He has, as a consequence of his crime, not only forfeited his liberty, but all his personal rights except those which the law in its humanity accords to him. He is for the time being the slave of the State. He is *civiliter mortuus;* and his estate, if he has any, is administered like that of a dead man. The Bill of Rights is a declaration of general principles to govern a society of freemen, and not of convicted felons and men civilly dead."[2]

In the case of *Ruffin* v. *Commonwealth,* the judge was voicing what had long been believed: that prisoners had no rights. It was this kind of thinking that long supported a "hands-off" approach to prisoners' rights. If inmates were really civilly dead, the federal government and the federal courts certainly had no cause to tell the states how to run their prisons.

Under the **hands-off doctrine,** U.S. courts for many decades avoided intervening in prison management. The doctrine was based on two rationales: (1) that under the *separation of powers* inherent in the U.S. Constitution,

hands-off doctrine

A historical policy of American courts not to intervene in prison management. Courts tended to follow the doctrine until the late 1960s.

the judicial branch of government should not interfere with the running of correctional facilities by the executive branch and (2) that judges should leave correctional administration to correctional experts. For a very long time in our nation's history, states ran their prisons as they saw fit. Prison inmates were thought of as "nonpersons," and rights pertained only to persons. Pleas from prisoners based on allegations of deprivations of their rights were ignored.

The hands-off doctrine and the philosophy of the prisoner as a slave of the state began to change in the mid-1900s. Public attitudes about punishment versus rehabilitation changed, and more and more people became aware that inmates had *no* rights. As a result, the courts began to scrutinize the correctional enterprise in America.

Decline of the Hands-Off Doctrine

The 1941 case of *Ex parte Hull* began a dismantling of the hands-off doctrine. Prior to *Hull,* it had been common for corrections personnel to screen inmate mail, including prisoner petitions for writs of *habeas corpus.* Corrections officials often confiscated the petitions, claiming they were improperly prepared and not fit to submit to court. In *Hull,* the Supreme Court ruled that no state or its officers may interfere with a prisoner's right to apply to a federal court for a writ of *habeas corpus.* Thus, court officials, not corrections officials, have the authority to decide whether such petitions are prepared correctly.

Although this seemed like a small step at the time, it would facilitate a major leap in prisoners' rights. Three years later, in *Coffin* v. *Reichard* (1944), the Sixth Circuit Court of Appeals extended *habeas corpus* hearings to consider the conditions of confinement. Even more important, the *Coffin* case was the first in which a federal appellate court ruled that prisoners do not automatically lose their civil rights when in prison.[3] In the words of the Court, a prisoner "retains all the rights of an ordinary citizen except those expressly, or by necessary implication, taken from him by law."

San Quentin State Prison in Marin County, California. Opened in 1852, it is one of the state's oldest and best-known correctional institutions. Under the hands-off doctrine, American courts long refused to intervene in prison management. When did the hands-off doctrine end?

© Justin Sullivan/Getty

Another important development occurred in 1961 with the Supreme Court's ruling in *Monroe* v. *Pape*. Prior to *Pape*, it was believed that the phrase "under color of state law" in the Civil Rights Act of 1871 meant that a Section 1983 suit (explained in more detail on page 358) could involve only actions authorized by state law. In *Pape*, however, the Court held that for activities to take place *under color* of state law, they did not have to be *authorized* by state law. The statute, said the Court, had been intended to protect against "misuse of power, possessed by virtue of state law and made possible only because the wrongdoer is clothed with the authority of state law."

Officials "clothed with the authority of state law" seemed to include state corrections officials. Thus, state corrections officials who violated an inmate's constitutional rights while performing their duties could be held liable for their actions in federal court regardless of whether state law or policy supported those actions.[4]

A third important case establishing inmates' rights to access the courts was *Cooper* v. *Pate* (1964). In *Cooper*, a federal circuit court clarified the *Pape* decision, indicating that prisoners could sue a warden or another correctional official under Title 42 of the U.S. Code, Section 1983, based on the protections of the Civil Rights Act of 1871.

Commenting on the importance of *Cooper*, one observer noted,

> Just by opening a forum in which prisoners' grievances could be heard, the federal courts destroyed the custodian's absolute power and the prisoners' isolation from the larger society. The litigation itself heightened prisoners' consciousness and politicized them.[5]

With prisoners' access to the courts now established, cases challenging nearly every aspect of corrections were soon filed. The courts, primarily the federal district courts, began to review prisoners' complaints and intervene on prisoners' behalf.

The hands-off era is said to have ended in 1970 when a federal district court declared in *Holt* v. *Sarver* the entire Arkansas prison system "so inhumane as to be a violation of the Eighth Amendment bar on cruel and unusual punishment."[6] Robert Sarver, the Arkansas commissioner of corrections, admitted that "the physical facilities at both [prison units named in the suit] were inadequate and in a total state of disrepair that could only be described as deplorable." Additionally, he testified that inmates with trustee status, some of them serving life or long-term sentences, constituted 99 percent of the security force of the state's prison system.

Commissioner Sarver continued, testifying that "trustees sell desirable jobs to prisoners and also traffic in food, liquor, and drugs. Prisoners frequently become intoxicated and unruly. The prisoners sleep in dormitories. Prisoners are frequently attacked and raped in the dormitories, and injuries and deaths have resulted. Sleep and rest are seriously disrupted. No adequate means exist to protect the prisoners from assaults. There is no satisfactory means of keeping guns, knives, and other weapons away from the prison population."[7]

The *Holt* court declared in 1970,

> The obligation . . . to eliminate existing unconstitutionalities does not depend upon what the Legislature may do or upon what the Governor may do. . . . If Arkansas is going to operate a Penitentiary System, it is going to have to be a system that is countenanced by the Constitution of the United States.[8]

The case of Holt v. Sarver *brought the hands-off era to a close and opened a new era of prisoners' rights. What were the issues involved in that case?*

© Comstock/Jupiterimages RF

Prisoner litigation had brought sad conditions to light, and the court had intervened to institute reforms for the prisoners in Arkansas.

PRISONERS' RIGHTS

Legal Foundations

Prisoners' rights have four legal foundations: the U.S. Constitution, federal statutes, state constitutions, and state statutes. Most court cases involving prisoners' rights have involved rights claimed under the U.S. Constitution, even though state constitutions generally parallel the U.S. Constitution and sometimes confer additional rights. State legislatures and Congress can also confer additional prisoners' rights.

The U.S. Constitution The U.S. Constitution is the supreme law of our land. At the heart of any discussion of prisoners' rights lies one question: What does the Constitution have to say? As scholars began to search the Constitution, they could find no requirement that prisoners give up all of their rights as U.S. citizens (and human beings) after conviction.

It is important to remember, however, that **constitutional rights** are not absolute. Does freedom of speech mean that you have a protected right to stand up in a crowded theater and yell "fire"? It does not (at least not unless there *is* a fire). That is because the panic that would follow such an exclamation would probably cause injuries and would needlessly put members of the public at risk of harm. Hence, the courts have held that, although freedom of speech is guaranteed by the Constitution, it is not an absolute right; in other words, there are limits to it (*Schenck* v. *United States,* 1919).

So, the central issue raised by those interested in prisoners' rights seems to be the degree to which a person retains constitutional rights when convicted of a criminal offense and sentenced to prison. Addressing that issue has become a job of the courts. The positions on it dependent upon the courts' interpretation of the U.S. Constitution, state constitutions, and federal and state laws. Generally speaking, the courts have recognized four legitimate **institutional needs** that justify some restrictions on the constitutional rights of prisoners:

1. maintenance of institutional *order;*
2. maintenance of institutional *security;*
3. *safety* of prison inmates and staff; and
4. *rehabilitation* of inmates.

According to the courts, *order* refers to calm and discipline within the institution, *security* is the control of individuals and objects entering or leaving the institution, *safety* means avoidance of physical harm, and *rehabilitation* refers to practices necessary for the health, well-being, and treatment of inmates.[9]

Federal Statutes Laws passed by Congress can confer certain rights on inmates in federal prisons. In addition, Congress has passed a number of laws that affect the running of state prisons. The Civil Rights Act of 1871, for example, was enacted after the Civil War to discourage lawless activities by state officials. Section 1983 reads as follows:

> Every person who, under color of any statute, ordinance, regulation, custom, or usage, of any State or Territory, subjects, or causes to be subjected, any citizen of the United States or other person within the jurisdiction thereof to the deprivation of any rights, privileges, or immunities secured by the Constitution and laws, shall be liable to the party injured in an action at law, suit in equity, or other proper proceeding for redress.

---

prisoners' rights

Constitutional guarantees of free speech, religious practice, due process, and other private and personal rights as well as constitutional protections against cruel and unusual punishments made applicable to prison inmates by the federal courts.

Prisoner Rights

constitutional rights

The personal and due process rights guaranteed to individuals by the U.S. Constitution and its amendments, especially the first 10 amendments, known as the *Bill of Rights.* Constitutional rights are the basis of most inmate rights.

institutional needs

Prison administration interests recognized by the courts as justifying some restrictions on the constitutional rights of prisoners. Those interests are maintenance of institutional *order,* maintenance of institutional *security, safety* of prison inmates and staff, and *rehabilitation* of inmates.

civil liability

A legal obligation to another person to do, pay, or make good something.

This section imposes **civil liability** (but not criminal blame) on any person who deprives another of rights guaranteed by the U.S. Constitution. The Civil Rights Act of 1871 allows state prisoners to challenge conditions of their imprisonment in federal court. Most prisoner suits brought under this act allege deprivation of constitutional rights. Another important piece of legislation is the Civil Rights of Institutionalized Persons Act (CRIPA),[10] which is discussed in more detail in Chapter 12.

State Constitutions Most state constitutions are patterned after the U.S. Constitution. However, state constitutions tend to be longer and more detailed than the U.S. Constitution and may contain specific provisions regarding corrections. State constitutions generally do not give prisoners more rights than are granted by the U.S. Constitution except in a few states such as California and Oregon. Inmates in such states may challenge the conditions of their confinement in state court under the state's constitutional provision.

CO11-3 **State Statutes** Unlike the federal government, state governments all have inherent police power, which allows them to pass laws to protect the health, safety, and welfare of their citizens. A state legislature can pass statutes to grant specific rights beyond those conferred by the state constitution. Often such legislation specifies duties of corrections officials or standards of treatment for prisoners. Prisoners who can show failure of officials to fulfill state statutory obligations may collect money damages or obtain a court order compelling officials to comply with the law.

A writ of habeas corpus is a court order requiring that a prisoner be brought before the court so that the court can determine whether the person is being legally detained. What is required of a state prisoner who wants to bring a habeas corpus action in federal court?

© Brand X Pictures RF

writ of *habeas corpus*

An order that directs the person detaining a prisoner to bring him or her before a judge, who will determine the lawfulness of the imprisonment.

Mechanisms for Securing Prisoners' Rights

Inmates today have five ways to challenge the legality of their confinement, associated prison conditions, and the practices of correctional officials: (1) a state *habeas corpus* action, (2) a federal *habeas corpus* action after state remedies have been exhausted, (3) a state tort lawsuit, (4) a federal civil rights lawsuit, and (5) a petition for injunctive relief.[11]

Writ of *Habeas Corpus* A **writ of *habeas corpus*** is an order from a court to produce a prisoner in court so that the court can determine whether the prisoner is being legally detained. *Habeas corpus* is Latin for "you have the body." A prisoner, or someone acting for a prisoner, files a *habeas corpus* petition asking a court to determine the lawfulness of the imprisonment. The petition for the writ is merely a procedural tool. If a writ is issued, it has no bearing on any issues to be reviewed. It guarantees only a hearing on those issues.

Federal and state prisoners may file *habeas corpus* petitions in federal courts. State prisoners must first, however, exhaust available state *habeas corpus* remedies. In 2000, of 11,880 petitions that inmates filed in *federal* courts, 3,870 (33 percent) were *habeas corpus* actions; of 46,371 petitions that inmates filed in *state* courts, 21,345 (46 percent) were *habeas corpus* actions.[12]

Tort Action in State Court State inmates can file a tort action in state court. A **tort** is a civil wrong, a wrongful act, or a wrongful breach of duty, other than a breach of contract, whether intentional or accidental, from which injury to another occurs. In tort actions, inmates commonly claim that a correctional employee, such as the warden or a correctional officer, or the correctional facility itself failed to perform a duty required by law regarding the inmate. Compensation for damages is the most common objective. Tort suits often allege such deficiencies as negligence, gross or wanton negligence, or intentional wrong.

tort

A civil wrong, a wrongful act, or a wrongful breach of duty, other than a breach of contract, whether intentional or accidental, from which injury to another occurs.

Federal Civil Rights Lawsuit Federal and state inmates can file suit in federal court alleging civil rights violations by corrections officials. Most of these suits challenge the conditions of confinement, under Section 1983 of the Civil Rights Act of 1871, which is now part of Title 42 of the U.S. Code. Lawsuits may claim that officials have deprived inmates of their constitutional rights, such as adequate medical treatment, protection against excessive force by correctional officers or violence from other inmates, due process in disciplinary hearings, and access to law libraries. According to the Bureau of Justice Statistics, 1 of 10 civil cases filed in U.S. district courts is *Section 1983 litigation* as it is commonly called.

When such suits seek monetary damages from federal agents for violation of constitutional rights, they are often referred to as *Bivens* actions, recalling the 1971 case in which the U.S. Supreme Court articulated inmates' entitlement to sue. In subsequent rulings (e.g., *FDIC* v. *Meyer*, 1994), the Court specified that "a *Bivens* action may only be maintained against an individual," not the federal agency by which he or she is employed, and it declined to extend the damage action authority of *Bivens* to permit suits against private entities operating correctional facilities under federal contract (*Correctional Services Corporation, Petitioner* v. *John E. Malesko*, 2001).

If inmates are successful in their civil suits, in state or federal courts, the courts can award three types of damages. **Nominal damages** are small amounts of money that may be awarded when inmates have sustained no actual damages, but there is clear evidence that their rights have been violated.

Compensatory damages are payments for actual losses, which may include out-of-pocket expenses the inmate incurred in filing the suit, other forms of monetary or material loss, and pain, suffering, and mental anguish. Some years ago, for example, a federal appeals court sustained an award of $9,300 against a warden and a correctional commissioner. The amount was calculated by awarding each inmate $25 for each day he had spent in solitary confinement (a total of 372 days for all the inmates) under conditions the court found cruel and unusual (*Sostre* v. *McGinnis*, 1971).

Punitive damages are awarded to punish the wrongdoer when the wrongful act was intentional and malicious or was done with reckless disregard for the rights of the inmate.

nominal damages

Small amounts of money a court may award when inmates have sustained no actual damages, but there is clear evidence that their rights have been violated.

compensatory damages

Money a court may award as payment for actual losses suffered by a plaintiff, including out-of-pocket expenses incurred in filing the suit, other forms of monetary or material loss, and pain, suffering, and mental anguish.

punitive damages

Money a court may award to punish a wrongdoer when a wrongful act was intentional and malicious or was done with reckless disregard for the rights of the victim.

Request for Injunctive Relief An **injunction** is a judicial order to do or refrain from doing a particular act. A request for an injunction might claim adverse effects of a health, safety, or sanitation procedure and might involve the entire correctional facility. It is important for anyone working in corrections to realize that a lack of funds cannot justify failure to comply with an injunction (*Smith* v. *Sullivan*, 1977).

injunction

A judicial order to do or refrain from doing a particular act.

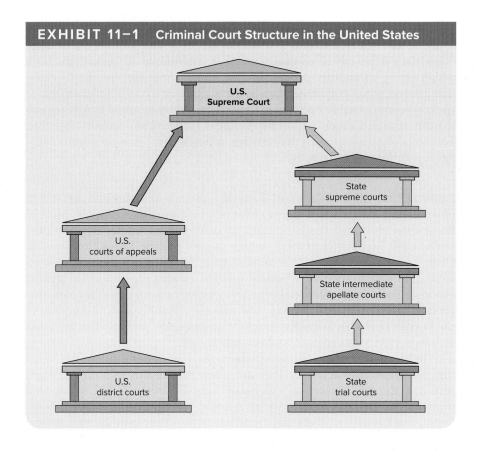

EXHIBIT 11–1 Criminal Court Structure in the United States

U.S. Supreme Court

State supreme courts

U.S. courts of appeals

State intermediate apellate courts

U.S. district courts

State trial courts

jurisdiction

The power, right, or authority of a court to interpret and apply the law.

The Criminal Court System There is a dual court system in the United States; the federal and state court systems coexist (see Exhibit 11–1). The federal court system is nationwide with one or more federal courts in each state. These courts coexist with state court systems. Whether a defendant is tried in a federal court or a state court depends on which court has jurisdiction over the particular case.

The **jurisdiction** of a court is the power or authority of the court to act with respect to a case before it. The acts involved in the case must have taken place or had an effect in the geographic territory of the court, or a statute must give the court jurisdiction.

District courts are the trial courts of the federal system. They have original jurisdiction over cases charging defendants with violations of federal criminal laws. Each state has at least one U.S. district court, and some, like New York and California, have as many as four. There are also federal district courts in Puerto Rico, the District of Columbia, and the U.S. territories. There are currently 11 U.S. courts of appeals arranged by circuit, a District of Columbia circuit, and one federal circuit (see Exhibit 11–2).

Each state has its own court system. Most state court structures are similar to the federal court structure—with trial courts, intermediate appellate courts, and a top appellate court. In most states, the trial courts are organized by county.

Although federal offenses are prosecuted in federal court and state offenses are prosecuted in state courts, the federal courts have supervisory jurisdiction over the administration of criminal justice in the state courts. The U.S. Supreme Court has ruled that constitutional requirements for criminal procedure in federal courts also apply to the states. Violation of

EXHIBIT 11–2 Geographic Boundaries of the U.S. Courts of Appeals and U.S. District Courts

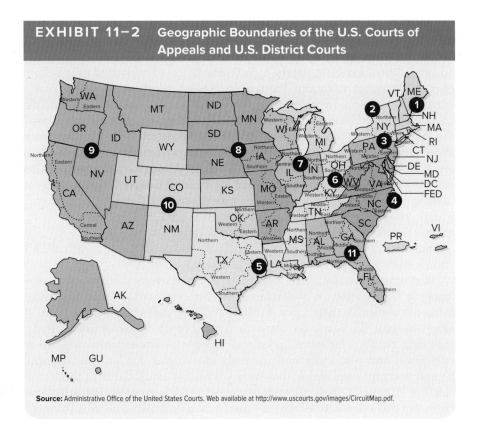

Source: Administrative Office of the United States Courts. Web available at http://www.uscourts.gov/images/CircuitMap.pdf.

these constitutional requirements can be the subject of both state appeals and federal suits by prisoners.

Inmate Grievance Procedures

Inmate grievance procedures are formal institutional processes for hearing inmate complaints. Grievance procedures, which typically employ internal hearing boards, are the method most frequently used by inmates to enforce the protections afforded to them by law.[13] Most inmate grievances concern discipline, program assignments, medical issues, personal property, and complaints against staff members. Only about 1 in 12 inmate grievances is approved or results in some action being taken by prison administrators to correct the problem.

The creation of formal mechanisms for the hearing of inmate grievances was encouraged by the comptroller general of the United States following the riot at New York's Attica Prison. The comptroller's report published in 1977[14] listed a number of reasons for establishing grievance mechanisms, including (1) promoting justice and fairness, (2) providing opportunities for inmates to voice complaints, (3) reducing the number of court cases filed by inmates, (4) assisting correctional administrators in the identification of institutional problems, and (5) reducing violence.

Today most correctional systems use a three-step process for resolving grievances. First, a staff member or committee in each institution receives complaints, investigates them, and makes decisions. Second, if a prisoner is dissatisfied with that decision, the case may be appealed to the warden. Third, if the prisoner is still dissatisfied, the complaint may be given to the state's commissioner of corrections or the state's corrections board. This three-step procedure satisfies the requirements for U.S. Department of Justice certification.

CO11-4 # THE PRISONERS' RIGHTS ERA (1970-1991)

Before the 1960s, the constitutional rights of prisoners were rarely acknowledged. In 1964, for example, the U.S. Supreme Court refused to hear a claim of religious rights violations brought by a Muslim prisoner in New York's correctional system. In that case, *Sostre* v. *McGinnis,* the inmate, Martin Sostre, a Nation of Islam member, filed a lawsuit claiming that he was denied the opportunity to practice his religion and that prison officials placed him in solitary confinement as a result of his requests to do so. Prior to the case reaching the Supreme Court, the U.S. Court of Appeals for the Second Circuit held that "It is not the business of the Federal Courts to work out a set of rules and regulations to govern the practices of religion in state prisons." Shortly thereafter, the U.S. Supreme Court voiced its agreement, refusing to hear Sostre's petition.

Soon things started to change, however, and what some have called a "prisoners' rights era" began to emerge around 1970.

As one writer notes, "The prisoners' rights movement must be understood in the context of a 'fundamental democratization' that has transformed American society since World War II, and particularly since 1960."[15] Over the past 55 years, an increasing number of once-marginal groups, including blacks, Hispanics, gays, and those who are economically disenfranchised and physically and mentally challenged, have acquired social recognition and legal rights that were previously unavailable to those outside the American social mainstream. Seen in this context, the prisoners' rights era was but a natural outgrowth of an encompassing social movement that recognized the existence and potential legitimacy of a wide number of group grievances.

Although the phrase *prisoners' rights era* might give the impression that prisoners won virtually every case brought during that period, such is not the case. Although prisoners did win some significant court battles, it was the turnaround in legal attitudes toward prisoners that was most remarkable. As we shall see, courts went from practically ignoring prison systems to practically running those systems. It might be more appropriate to refer to the period as the "court involvement era." We will now review some of the most important cases won *and* lost by inmates, presented in order of the constitutional amendments on which they were based.

CO11-5 When we speak of prisoners' rights, we are generally speaking of the rights found in four of the amendments to the U.S. Constitution. Three of these—the First (free expression), Fourth (privacy), and Eighth Amendments (cruel and unusual punishment)—are part of the Bill of Rights (the first 10 amendments to the Constitution). The fourth is the Fourteenth Amendment (deprivation of life, liberty, and property). Keep in mind that what we call *inmates' rights* today are largely the result of federal court decisions that have interpreted constitutional guarantees and applied them to prisons and prison conditions. Often such a case sets a **precedent,** serving as an example or authority for future cases. Rulings in cases that find violations of inmates' rights must be implemented by the administrators of affected correctional systems and institutions. (See Exhibit 11–3 for more U.S. Supreme Court cases involving prisoners' rights.)

precedent

A previous judicial decision that judges should consider in deciding future cases.

First Amendment

Congress shall make no law respecting an establishment of religion, or prohibiting the free exercise thereof; or abridging the freedom of speech, or of the press; or the right of the people peaceably to assemble, and to petition the government for a redress of grievances.

EXHIBIT 11-3	Selected U.S. Supreme Court Cases Involving Prisoners' Rights

Case Name	Year	Decision
Holt v. *Hobbs*	2015	Permitted prisoners to grow half-inch beards in accordance with religious beliefs.
Millbrook v. *U.S.*	2013	Federal correctional agencies are generally shielded against civil lawsuits seeking monetary damages for the acts or omissions of their employees.
Florence v. *Burlington County*	2012	Officials may strip-search persons who have been arrested and taken to a detention facility even though the arrest is for a minor offense, in order to insure the safety and security of the jail or detention.
Howes v. *Fields*	2012	Inmates who are facing questioning by law enforcement officers while incarcerated need not be advised of their *Miranda* rights.
Brown v. *Plata* (Eighth Amendment)	2011	Found that seriously overcrowded conditions in California prisons are a violation of the Eighth Amendment's ban on cruel and unusual punishment.
U.S. v. *Georgia*	2006	Under the Americans with Disabilities Act, a state may be liable for rights deprivations suffered by inmates held in its prisons who are disabled.
Johnson v. *California*	2005	The decision invalidated the California Department of Corrections and Rehabilitation's unwritten policy of racially segregating prisoners in double cells each time they entered a new correctional facility.
Wilkinson v. *Austin*	2005	The Court upheld an Ohio policy allowing the most dangerous offenders to be held in "supermax" cells following several levels of review prior to transfer.
Overton v. *Bazzetta*	2003	The decision upheld the Michigan Department of Corrections' visitation regulation that denies most visits to prisoners who commit two substance abuse violations while incarcerated.
Porter v. *Nussle* (Eighth Amendment)	2002	The "exhaustion requirement" of the Prison Litigation Reform Act of 1995 (PLRA) applies to all inmate suits about prison life, whether they involve general circumstances or particular episodes and whether they allege excessive force or some other wrong.
Hope v. *Pelzer* (Eighth Amendment)	2002	The Court found an Eighth Amendment violation in the case of a prisoner who was subjected to unnecessary pain, humiliation, and risk of physical harm.
Booth v. *Churner* (Eighth Amendment)	2001	The decision upheld a requirement under the PLRA that state inmates must "exhaust such administrative remedies as are available" before filing a suit over prison conditions.
Lewis v. *Casey*	1996	Earlier cases do not guarantee inmates the wherewithal to file any and every type of legal claim. All that is required is "that they be provided with the tools to attack their sentences."
Sandin v. *Conner* (Fourteenth Amendment)	1995	Perhaps signaling an end to the prisoners' rights era, this case rejected the argument that disciplining inmates is a deprivation of constitutional due process rights.
Wilson v. *Seiter* (Eighth Amendment)	1991	The case clarified the totality of conditions notion, saying that some conditions of confinement "in combination" may violate prisoners' rights when each would not do so alone.
Washington v. *Harper* (Eighth Amendment)	1990	An inmate who is a danger to self or others as a result of mental illness may be treated with psychoactive drugs against his or her will.

EXHIBIT 11-3 Selected U.S. Supreme Court Cases Involving Prisoners' Rights *(continued)*

Case Name	Year	Decision
Turner v. Safley (First Amendment)	1987	A Missouri ban on correspondence between inmates was upheld as "reasonably related to legitimate penological interests."
O'Lone v. Estate of Shabazz (First Amendment)	1987	An inmate's right to practice religion was not violated by prison officials who refused to alter his work schedule so that he could attend Friday afternoon services.
Whitley v. Albers (Eighth Amendment)	1986	The shooting and wounding of an inmate was not a violation of that inmate's rights, because "the shooting was part and parcel of a good-faith effort to restore prison security."
Ponte v. Real	1985	Inmates have certain rights in disciplinary hearings.
Hudson v. Palmer (Fourth Amendment)	1984	A prisoner has no reasonable expectation of privacy in his prison cell that entitles him to protections against "unreasonable searches."
Block v. Rutherford (First Amendment)	1984	State regulations may prohibit inmate union meetings and use of mail to deliver union information within the prison. Prisoners do not have a right to be present during searches of cells.
Rhodes v. Chapman (Eighth Amendment)	1981	Double-celling of inmates is not cruel and unusual punishment unless it involves the wanton and unnecessary infliction of pain or conditions grossly disproportionate to the severity of the crime committed.
Ruiz v. Estelle (Eighth Amendment)	1980	The Court found unconstitutional conditions in the Texas prison system—including overcrowding, understaffing, brutality, and substandard medical care.
Cooper v. Morin	1980	Neither inconvenience nor cost is an acceptable excuse for treating female inmates differently from male inmates.
Jones v. North Carolina Prisoners' Labor Union, Inc. (First Amendment)	1977	Inmates have no inherent right to publish newspapers or newsletters for use by other inmates.
Bounds v. Smith	1977	The case resulted in the creation of law libraries in many prisons.
Estelle v. Gamble (Eighth Amendment)	1976	Prison officials have a duty to provide proper inmate medical care.
Wolff v. McDonnell (Fourteenth Amendment)	1974	Sanctions cannot be levied against inmates without appropriate due process.
Procunier v. Martinez (First Amendment)	1974	Censorship of inmate mail is acceptable only when necessary to protect legitimate governmental interests.
Pell v. Procunier (First Amendment)	1974	Inmates retain First Amendment rights that are not inconsistent with their status as prisoners or with the legitimate penological objectives of the corrections system.
Cruz v. Beto (First Amendment)	1972	Inmates have to be given a "reasonable opportunity" to pursue their religious faiths. Also, visits can be banned if such visits constitute threats to security.
Johnson v. Avery	1968	Inmates have a right to consult "jailhouse lawyers" when trained legal assistance is not available.
Sostre v. McGinnis	1964	The Court refused to hear a Muslim inmate's petition concerning religious rights in New York prisons, thereby declining to impose any broad-based federal constitutional limits on prisoners' confinement.
Monroe v. Pape	1961	Individuals deprived of their rights by state officers acting under color of state law have a right to bring action in federal court.

RELIABLE RESEARCH. REAL RESULTS.

Enter your keyword(s)   Search Site   Advanced Search

EVIDENCE-BASED CORRECTIONS
Targeted Interventions for Corrections (TIC)

Targeted Interventions for Corrections (TIC) consists of six brief life-skill interventions to be used in a variety of correctional-based settings. The interventions address the core aspects of addiction treatment and recovery. They focus on what incarcerated individuals need to work on to improve their potential for early engagement in treatment and early recovery, including motivation for treatment, controlling anger, opening lines of communication, correcting criminal thinking errors, and improving social networks. The overall goal of TIC is to provide interventions that address drug-related problems and treatment needs in correctional populations. To be eligible to participate in a treatment program, inmates must have received a referral from a correctional authority, have enough time remaining on their sentence to complete the intervention, and provide consent to participate in treatment.

The program is rated Promising. TIC participants were found to significantly change their attitudes more favorably than control participants did. The treatment group average change was 4.0 percent, compared with 1.5 percent for the control group. TIC was found to make a statistically significant impact on psychosocial functioning of treatment participants compared with control-group participants. Psychological functioning included measures of decision making, self-esteem, depression, anxiety, and efficacy.

Source: Adapted from https://www.crimesolutions.gov/ProgramDetails.aspx?ID=369.

First Amendment guarantees are important to members of a free society. It is no surprise, then, that some of the early prisoners' rights cases concerned those rights. For example, in 1974, in *Pell* v. *Procunier,* four California prison inmates and three journalists challenged the constitutionality of regulation 415.071 of the California Department of Corrections and Rehabilitation (CDCR). That regulation specified that "press and other media interviews with specific individual inmates will not be permitted." The rule had been imposed after a violent prison episode that corrections authorities attributed at least in part to a former policy of free face-to-face prisoner–press interviews. Such interviews had apparently resulted in a relatively small number of inmates gaining disproportionate notoriety and influence with other prisoners.

The U.S. Supreme Court held that "in light of the alternative channels of communication that are open to the inmate appellees, [regulation] 415.071 does not constitute a violation of their rights of free speech." Significantly, the Court went on to say, "A prison inmate retains those first amendment rights that are not inconsistent with his status as prisoner or with the *legitimate penological objectives* of the corrections system" (emphasis added). **Legitimate penological objectives** are the permissible aims of a correctional institution. They include the realistic concerns that correctional officers and administrators have for the integrity and security of the correctional institution and the safety of staff and inmates. The *Pell* ruling established a **balancing test** that the Supreme Court would continue to use, weighing the rights claimed by inmates against the legitimate needs of prisons.

Freedom of Speech and Expression Visits to inmates by friends and loved ones are forms of expression. But prison visits are not an absolute right. In *Cruz* v. *Beto* (1972), the Supreme Court ruled that all visits can be banned if they threaten security. Although *Cruz* involved short-term confinement facilities, the ruling has also been applied to prisons.

Another form of expression is correspondence. As a result of various court cases, prison officials can (and generally do) impose restrictions on

legitimate penological objectives

The realistic concerns that correctional officers and administrators have for the integrity and security of the correctional institution and the safety of staff and inmates.

balancing test

A method the U.S. Supreme Court uses to decide prisoners' rights cases, weighing the rights claimed by inmates against the legitimate needs of prisons.

inmate mail. Inmates receive mail not directly from the hands of postal carriers but from correctional officers. They place their outgoing mail not in U.S. Postal Service mailboxes but in containers provided by the correctional institution.

Corrections officials often read inmate mail—both incoming and outgoing—in an effort to uncover escape plans. Reading inmate mail, however, is different from censoring it. In 1974, in *Procunier* v. *Martinez*, the U.S. Supreme Court held that the censoring of inmate mail is acceptable only when necessary to protect legitimate government interests. The case turned upon First Amendment guarantees of free speech.

Under a 1979 federal appeals court decision, in *McNamara* v. *Moody*, prison officials may not prohibit inmates from writing vulgar letters or those that make disparaging remarks about the prison staff. Similarly, although correctional administrators have a legitimate interest in curbing inmates' deviant sexual behavior, courts have held that viewing nudity is not deviant sexual behavior. Hence, prison officials may not ban mailed nude pictures of inmates' wives or girlfriends (*Peppering* v. *Crist,* 1981) although restrictions against posting them on cell walls have generally been upheld. Similarly, officials may not prevent inmates from receiving, by mail direct from publishers, publications depicting nudity unless those publications depict deviant sexual behavior (*Mallery* v. *Lewis,* 1983).

In 1989, in the case of *Thornburgh* v. *Abbott,* in an effort to clear up questions raised by lower court rulings concerning mailed publications, the U.S. Supreme Court ruled as follows:

> Publications which may be rejected by a warden include but are not limited to publications which meet one of the following criteria: (1) it depicts or describes procedures for the construction or use of weapons, ammunition, bombs, or incendiary devices; (2) it depicts, encourages, or describes methods of escape from correctional facilities or contains blueprints, drawings, or similar descriptions of Bureau of Prisons institutions; (3) it depicts or describes procedures for the brewing of alcoholic beverages or the manufacture of drugs; (4) it is written in code; (5) it depicts, describes, or encourages activities which may lead to the use of physical violence or group disruption; (6) it encourages or instructs in the commission of criminal activities; (7) it is sexually explicit material which by its nature or content poses a threat to the security, good order, or discipline of the institution or facilitates criminal activity.

Unless at least one of these standards is met, restrictions on the receipt of published materials—especially magazines and newspapers that do not threaten prison security—are generally not allowed. In the 2006 U.S. Supreme Court case of *Beard* v. *Banks,* however, the justices held that Pennsylvania prison officials could legitimately prohibit the state's most violent inmates from having access to newspapers, magazines, and photographs. Prison officials had argued that the policy helped motivate better behavior on the part of particularly difficult prisoners. The Court agreed, noting that "prison officials have imposed the deprivation only upon those with serious prison-behavior problems; and those officials, relying on their professional judgment, reached an experience-based conclusion that the policies help to further legitimate prison objectives."

Similarly, in the case of *Turner* v. *Safley* (1987), the Supreme Court upheld a Missouri ban on correspondence among inmates. Such a regulation is valid, the Court said, if it is "reasonably related to legitimate penological interests." *Turner* established that officials had to show only that a regulation was reasonably *related* to a legitimate penological interest. No clear-cut damage to legitimate penological interests had to be shown.

Inmate rights are not absolute but are limited by legitimate penological objectives. What does the phrase "legitimate penological objectives" mean?
© Andy Atchison/Corbis

The U.S. Supreme Court sided with corrections officials in its 1977 decision in *Jones* v. *North Carolina Prisoners' Labor Union, Inc.* In *Jones,* the Court upheld regulations established by the North Carolina Department of Correction that prohibited prisoners from soliciting other inmates to join the union and barred union meetings and bulk mailings concerning the union from outside sources. Citing *Pell* v. *Procunier,* the Court went on to say, "The prohibition on inmate-to-inmate solicitation does not unduly abridge inmates' free speech rights. If the prison officials are otherwise entitled to control organized union activity within the confines of a prison, the solicitation ban is not impermissible under the First Amendment, for such a prohibition is both reasonable and necessary."

Freedom of Religion Lawsuits involving religious practices in prison have been numerous for at least 40 years. In 1962, for example, in *Fulwood* v. *Clemmer,* the court of appeals for the District of Columbia ruled that the Black Muslim faith must be recognized as a religion and held that officials may not restrict members of that faith from holding services.

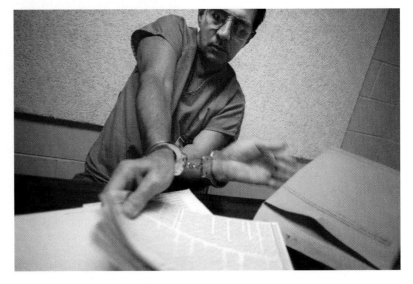

Inmates have limited rights to send and receive mail. Restrictions on inmates' mail focus on maintaining institutional security. Judicial interpretations of which constitutional amendment have led to inmates' rights to send and receive mail?
© David Leeson/Dallas Morning News/ The Image Works

In 1970, the U.S. Supreme Court refused to hear an appeal from inmate Jack Gittlemacker, who wanted the state of Pennsylvania to provide him with a clergyman of his faith. The Court held that although states must give inmates the opportunity to practice their religions, they are not required to provide clergy for that purpose.

In *Cruz* v. *Beto* (mentioned earlier), the Supreme Court also decided that inmates had to be given a "reasonable opportunity" to pursue their religious faiths. Later federal court decisions expanded this decision, requiring officials to provide such a "reasonable opportunity" even to inmates whose religious faiths were not traditional.

In 1975, the U.S. Court of Appeals for the Second Circuit ruled in *Kahane* v. *Carlson* that an Orthodox Jewish inmate has the right to a kosher diet unless the government can show good cause for not providing it. Similarly, the courts have held that "Muslims' request for one full-course pork-free meal once a day and coffee three times daily is essentially a plea for a modest degree of official deference to their religious obligations" (*Barnett* v. *Rodgers,* 1969).

On the other hand, courts have determined that some inmate religious demands need not be met. In the 1986 Fifth Circuit Court of Appeals case of *Udey* v. *Kastner,* for example, Muslim prisoners had requested raw milk, distilled water, and organic fruits, juices, vegetables, and meats. The special diet was so costly that a federal court allowed the prison to deny the inmates' request.

In 2000, the Religious Land Use and Institutionalized Persons Act (RLUIPA) became law. RLUIPA says, "No government shall impose a substantial burden on the religious exercise of a person residing in or confined to an institution even if the burden results from a rule of general applicability unless the government demonstrates that imposition of the burden on that person (1) is in furtherance of a compelling governmental interest; and (2) is the least restrictive means of furthering that compelling governmental interest." Because RLUIPA is a federal law, it is especially relevant to prison programs and activities that are at least partially supported with federal monies. In 2005, in the case of *Benning* v. *State,* the Eleventh Circuit Court of Appeals found in favor of a Georgia state prison inmate who claimed that RLUIPA supported his right as a "Torah observant Jew" to eat only kosher food and wear a yarmulke (or skullcap) at all times. Also in 2005, in the case of *Cutter* v. *Wilkinson,* the U.S. Supreme Court ruled in favor of past and present Ohio inmates who claimed that the state's correctional system failed to accommodate their nonmainstream religious practices. Finally, in 2015, again citing RLUIPA, the Court found in favor of a Muslim Arkansas inmate who wanted to grow a half-inch beard in accordance with his religious beliefs. The Court was not persuaded by arguments made by the Arkansas Department of Correction that beards could be used to conceal contraband. In that case, *Holt* v. *Hobbs* (2015), the justices wrote that the argument made by the department of correction was not compelling, "especially given the difficulty of hiding contraband in such a short beard."

Fourth Amendment

> The right of the people to be secure in their persons, houses, papers, and effects, against unreasonable searches and seizures, shall not be violated, and no Warrants shall issue, but upon probable cause, supported by Oath or affirmation, and particularly describing the place to be searched, and the persons or things to be seized.

The right to privacy is at the heart of the Fourth Amendment. Clearly, unreasonable searches without warrants are unconstitutional. Does this mean that an inmate has a right to privacy in his or her cell? When is it reasonable to search a cell without a warrant? Some suggest that the needs of institutional security prohibit privacy for inmates. Others argue that a prison cell is the equivalent of an inmate's house. Over the years, the courts have been fairly consistent in deciding that the privacy rights implied in this amendment must be greatly reduced in prisons to maintain institutional security.

Correctional officers searching a cell. Prisoners do not retain the right to privacy in their cells or possessions because institutional interests of safety and security supersede constitutional guarantees of privacy. Under which amendment to the Constitution does the right to be free from unreasonable searches and seizures fall?
© Photo by Gordon Chibroski/Portland Press/ Getty Images

In *United States* v. *Hitchcock* (1972), an inmate claimed that his Fourth Amendment rights had been violated by a warrantless search and seizure of documents in his prison cell. Previously, courts had generally held that "constitutionally protected" places—such as homes, motel rooms, safe-deposit boxes, and certain places of business—could not be searched without a warrant. In *Hitchcock,* however, the U.S. Court of Appeals for the Ninth Circuit created a new standard: "first, that a person have exhibited an actual (subjective) expectation of privacy and second, that the expectation be one that society is prepared to recognize as reasonable." The court concluded that, although Hitchcock plainly expected to keep his documents private, his expectation was not reasonable. In the words of the court,

> It is obvious that a jail shares none of the attributes of privacy of a home, an automobile, an office, or a hotel room. In prison, official surveillance has traditionally been the order of the day. . . . [Hence], we do not feel that it is reasonable for a prisoner to consider his cell private.

In *Hudson* v. *Palmer* (1984), a Virginia inmate claimed a correctional officer had unreasonably destroyed some of his permitted personal property during a search of his cell. The inmate also claimed that under the Fourth Amendment, the cell search was illegal. Echoing *Hitchcock,* the U.S. Supreme Court ruled that "a prisoner has no reasonable expectation of privacy in his prison cell entitling him to the protection of the Fourth Amendment against unreasonable searches." Similarly, in *Block* v. *Rutherford* (1984), the Court ruled that prisoners do not have the right to be present during searches of their cells.

In 1985, the Ninth Circuit Court of Appeals decided a case involving inmates at San Quentin State Prison (*Grummett* v. *Rushen*). The inmates had brought a class action lawsuit against prison administrators, objecting to the policy of allowing female correctional officers to view nude or partly clothed male inmates. Women officers, complained the inmates, could see male inmates while they were dressing, showering, being strip-searched, or using toilet facilities. Such viewing, said the inmates, violated privacy rights guaranteed by the U.S. Constitution.

At the time of the suit, approximately 113 of the 720 correctional officers at San Quentin were female. Both female and male correctional officers were assigned to patrol the cell block tiers and gun rails. Both were also assigned to supervise showering from the tiers and from the gun rails, but only male officers were permitted to accompany inmates to the shower cells and lock them inside to disrobe and shower. Female officers were allowed to conduct pat-down searches that included the groin area.

The court found that prison officials had "struck an acceptable balance among the inmates' privacy interests, the institution's security requirements, and the female guards' employment rights." According to the court,

> The female guards are restricted in their contact with the inmates, and the record clearly demonstrates that at all times they have conducted themselves in a professional manner, and have treated the inmates with respect and dignity. . . . Routine pat-down searches, which include the groin area, and which are otherwise justified by security needs, do not violate the Fourteenth Amendment because a correctional officer of the opposite gender conducts such a search.

Eighth Amendment

> Excessive bail shall not be required, nor excessive fines imposed, nor cruel and unusual punishments inflicted.

cruel and unusual punishment

A penalty that is grossly disproportionate to the offense or that violates today's broad and idealistic concepts of dignity, civilized standards, humanity, and decency (*Estelle* v. *Gamble*, 1976, and *Hutto* v. *Finney*, 1978). In the area of capital punishment, cruel and unusual punishments are those that involve torture, a lingering death, or unnecessary pain.

Many prisoners' rights cases turn upon the issue of **cruel and unusual punishment.** Defining such punishment is not easy. A working definition, however, might be "punishments that are grossly disproportionate to the offense as well as those that transgress today's broad and idealistic concepts of dignity, civilized standards, humanity, and decency."[16] Cases concerning constitutional prohibition of cruel and unusual punishment have centered on prisoners' need for decent conditions of confinement. In the case that began this chapter, *Brown* v. *Plata* (2011), for example, overcrowded conditions in California prisons were found to have violated the Eighth Amendment by making it impossible for adequate health care to be delivered to most inmates. Inmates' rights cases involving the Eighth Amendment cover areas as diverse as medical care, prison conditions, physical insecurity, psychological stress, and capital punishment. (See Chapter 3 for a discussion of capital punishment and related court cases.)

Medical Care In 2012, federal Judge Mark Wolf of the District of Massachusetts ordered the Massachusetts Department of Correction to provide a male inmate, Michelle Kosilek, with sex change surgery.[17] Kosilek, the judge noted, had twice tried to kill himself and even attempted to castrate himself—proving, in the judge's opinion, a need for immediate medical intervention. Kosilek is serving a life sentence for the murder of his wife.

The history of inmates' rights in the health care area can be traced to the 1970 case of *Holt* v. *Sarver* in which a federal district court declared the entire Arkansas prison system inhumane and found that it was in violation of the Constitution's Eighth Amendment's ban on cruel and unusual punishment.

In a related case, medical personnel in state prisons had given inmates injections of apomorphine without their consent in a program of "aversive stimuli." The drug caused vomiting, which lasted from 15 minutes to an hour. The state justified it as "Pavlovian conditioning." The federal courts, however, soon prohibited the practice (*Knecht* v. *Gillman*, 1973).

Another decision, that of *Estelle* v. *Gamble* (1976), spelled out the duty of prison officials to provide inmates with medical care. The Court held that prison officials could not lawfully demonstrate **deliberate indifference** to the medical needs of prisoners. In the words of the Court, "Deliberate indifference to serious medical needs of prisoners constitutes the 'unnecessary and wanton infliction of pain' proscribed by the Eighth Amendment." A serious medical condition is one that "causes pain, discomfort, or threat to good health" (*Rufo* v. *Inmates of Suffolk County Jail*, 1992). The mental health needs of prisoners are governed by the same constitutional standard of deliberate indifference as those described in court -opinions dealing with the physical health of inmates.[18]

deliberate indifference

Intentional and willful indifference. Within the field of correctional practice, the term refers to calculated inattention to unconstitutional conditions of confinement.

Prison Conditions The 1976 federal court case of *Pugh* v. *Locke* introduced the **totality of conditions** standard. That standard, said the court, is to be used in evaluating whether prison conditions are cruel and unusual. The *Pugh* court held that "prison conditions [in Alabama] are so debilitating that they necessarily deprive inmates of any opportunity to rehabilitate themselves or even maintain skills already possessed." The totality of conditions approach was also applied in a 1977 federal case, *Battle* v. *Anderson*, in which officials in overcrowded Oklahoma prisons had forced inmates to sleep in garages, barbershops, libraries, and stairwells. Oklahoma prison administrators were found to be in violation of the cruel and unusual punishment clause of the U.S. Constitution.

The U.S. Supreme Court ruled on the use of solitary confinement in *Hutto* v. *Finney* (1978). The Court held that confinement in Arkansas's segregation (solitary confinement) cells for more than 30 days was cruel and unusual punishment. It then went on to exhort lower courts to consider the totality

totality of conditions

A standard to be used in evaluating whether prison conditions are cruel and unusual.

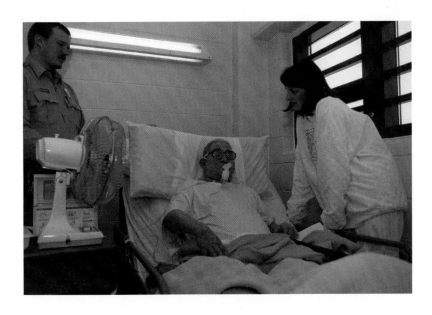

An inmate in the Nebraska State Penitentiary at Lincoln receives health care. A number of Eighth Amendment cases have established that prison officials have a duty to provide adequate medical care to inmates in their charge. How does the concept of "deliberate indifference" relate to that requirement?

© Mikael Karlsson/Alamy

of the conditions of confinement in future Eighth Amendment cases. Where appropriate, it said, a court should specify the changes needed to remedy the constitutional violation.

In the 1991 case of *Wilson* v. *Seiter,* the U.S. Supreme Court clarified the totality of conditions standard. The Court noted,

> Some conditions of confinement may establish an Eighth Amendment violation "in combination" when each would not do so alone, but only when they have a mutually enforcing effect that produces the deprivation of a single, identifiable human need such as food, warmth, or exercise—for example, a low cell temperature at night combined with a failure to issue blankets. . . . To say that some prison conditions may interact in this fashion is a far cry from saying that all prison conditions are a seamless web for Eighth Amendment purposes. Nothing so [shapeless] as "overall conditions" can rise to the level of cruel and unusual punishment when no specific deprivation of a single human need exists.

Several rulings have addressed inmate claims that overcrowding was cruel and unusual punishment. A U.S. Supreme Court case, *Rhodes* v. *Chapman* (1981), decided the issue of double-celling (housing two inmates in a cell designed for one) in long-term correctional facilities. In response to rising prison populations, Ohio authorities had begun double-celling. There was no evidence that Ohio authorities had wantonly inflicted pain through the practice, and double-celling had not resulted in food deprivation, a lower quality of medical care, or a decrease in sanitation standards. For those reasons, the Court denied the inmates' claims.

In *Rhodes,* the Court also emphasized that the Eighth Amendment prohibition of cruel and unusual punishment is a fluid concept that "must draw its meaning from the evolving standards of decency that mark the progress of a maturing society." In other words, what is considered cruel and unusual changes as society evolves.

In 1982, the U.S. Court of Appeals for the Seventh Circuit ruled, in *Smith* v. *Fairman,* that double-celling in a short-term facility (a jail) was not cruel and unusual punishment. The court said that government officials did not intend to punish inmates by double-celling. The double-celling was innocent overcrowding required by circumstances.

Many conditions of confinement that violate prisoners' Eighth Amendment rights can be remedied by changes in prison rules, by special training for correctional personnel, or by educational programs for prisoners. The remedies can be implemented through everyday administrative policies in the prison once prisoners' court petitions have brought violations to light. Relief of overcrowding, however, is not always within the power of prison administrators. Prison officials have little control over the sizes of their prisons or the numbers of inmates the courts assign to them. New prison facilities are expensive and take time to build.

The Eighth Amendment's prohibition of cruel and unusual punishment has been tied to prisoners' need for decent conditions of confinement. In determining whether conditions such as overcrowding and inadequate diet constitute a denial of such protection, courts have used the concept of totality of conditions. What is meant by the totality of conditions?

Fourteenth Amendment

> No State shall make or enforce any law which shall abridge the privileges or immunities of citizens of the United States; nor shall any State deprive any person of life, liberty, or property, without due process of law; nor deny to any person within its jurisdiction the equal protection of the laws.

When the Constitution and the Bill of Rights became law, the people of many states thought the document applied only to federal courts and to federal law. This attitude prevailed at least until the end of the Civil War. After the war, to clarify the status of the newly freed slaves and to apply the Bill of Rights to state actions, the Fourteenth Amendment was passed. The just-quoted portion of the Fourteenth Amendment is relevant to our discussion.

Most cases involving prisoners' rights and the Fourteenth Amendment deal with issues of **due process.** Due process requires that laws and legal procedures be reasonable and that they be applied fairly and equally. The right to due process is a right to be fairly heard before being deprived of life or liberty.

By 1987, long after the hands-off doctrine had eroded, U.S. Supreme Court justice Sandra Day O'Connor summarized the thrust of earlier opinions, holding that "prison walls do not form a barrier separating prison inmates from the protections of the Constitution" (*Turner* v. *Safley*). Without access to the courts, O'Connor said, inmates have no due process opportunities.

To bring their cases to court, however, prisoners need access to legal materials, and many of them need legal assistance. What if one inmate understands how to file cases with the court, but a second inmate does not? Does the second inmate have a right to enlist the aid of the first? "Yes," said the U.S. Supreme Court in *Johnson* v. *Avery* (1968). Inmates have a right to consult "jailhouse lawyers" (other inmates knowledgeable in the law) when trained legal advisers are not available.

The case of *Wolff* v. *McDonnell* (1974) expanded the concept of due process by applying it to disciplinary actions within prisons. Prior to *Wolff,* prison administrators had the discretion to discipline inmates who broke prison rules. Disciplinary procedures were often tied to vague or nonexistent rules of conduct and were exercised without challenge. A prisoner might be assigned to solitary confinement or might have good-time credits reduced because of misconduct. Because the prisoner was physically confined and lacked outside communication, there was no opportunity for the prisoner to challenge the charge. The *Wolff* Court concluded that sanctions (disciplinary actions) could not be levied against inmates without appropriate due process, saying,

> [The state of Nebraska] asserts that the procedure for disciplining prison inmates for serious misconduct is a matter of policy raising no constitutional issue. If the position implies that prisoners in state institutions are wholly without the protection of the Constitution and the Due Process Clause, it is plainly untenable. Lawful imprisonment necessarily makes unavailable many rights and privileges of the ordinary citizen, a retraction justified by the consideration underlying our penal system. . . . But though his rights may be diminished by the needs and exigencies of the institutional environment, a prisoner is not wholly stripped of constitutional protections when he is imprisoned for a crime.

The *Wolff* Court imposed minimal due process requirements on prison disciplinary proceedings that could lead to solitary confinement or reduction of good-time credits. The requirements included (1) advance notice by means of a written statement of the claimed violation, (2) a written statement by an impartial fact finder of the evidence relied on and the reasons for imposing punishment, and (3) an opportunity to testify and call witnesses unless the fact finder concluded such proceedings would undermine institutional security.

In 1976, inmates lost three due process appeals. First, in *Baxter* v. *Palmigiano,* the Supreme Court decided that due process for an inmate in a disciplinary hearing does not include a right to counsel even when the consequences are potentially "serious." In a second opinion issued that year (*Meacham* v. *Fano*),

due process

A right guaranteed by the Fifth, Sixth, and Fourteenth Amendments to the U.S. Constitution and generally understood, in legal contexts, to mean the expected course of legal proceedings according to the rules and forms established for the protection of persons' rights.

Inmates must be allowed access to the courts and assistance in preparing their cases. To meet that requirement, most states stock law libraries in each correctional institution. Under which clause of the Fourteenth Amendment does inmates' access to the courts fall?

© Shepard Sherbell/Corbis

the Court held that prisoners have no right to be in any particular prison and therefore have no due process protections before being transferred from one prison to another. A third case (*Stone* v. *Powell*) denied prisoners the right in most instances to seek federal review of state court Fourth Amendment search-and-seizure decisions.

Inmates' right to legal materials was formally recognized in 1977 in the U.S. Supreme Court decision in *Bounds* v. *Smith.* In *Bounds,* the Court held,

The fundamental constitutional right of access to the courts requires prison authorities to assist inmates in the preparation and filing of meaningful legal papers by providing prisoners with adequate law libraries or adequate assistance from persons trained in the law.

As a result of the *Bounds* decision, law libraries were created in prisons across the nation.

As we saw in Chapter 9, one challenge facing corrections personnel is to find safe, humane ways to manage inmate populations. Inmates often have grievances regarding conditions of confinement or disciplinary actions for infractions. Those grievances must be dealt with to maintain the safety and security of the institution. The Supreme Court's decision in *Jones* v. *North Carolina Prisoners' Labor Union, Inc.* (1977) required prisons to establish and maintain formal opportunities for the airing of inmate grievances. *Ponte* v. *Real* (1985) required prison officials to explain to inmates why their requests to have witnesses appear on their behalf at disciplinary hearings were denied.

The due process clause protects against unlawful deprivation of life or liberty. When a prisoner sued for damages for injuries (*Daniels* v. *Williams,* 1986), the Supreme Court ruled that prisoners could sue for damages in federal court only if officials had inflicted injury intentionally. According to the Court, "The due process clause is simply not implicated by a negligent act of an official causing unintended loss or injury to life, liberty, or property."

A 2001 ruling by a panel of federal judges in the case of *Gerber* v. *Hickman* addressed a unique claim of unlawful deprivation of life. Gerber wanted to impregnate his wife. He was, however, serving a life sentence in a California Department of Corrections and Rehabilitation (CDCR) prison, and CDCR regulations prohibit conjugal visits for life-term prisoners. Consequently, the Gerbers could not employ the usual method for creating the child they desired.

Undeterred, Gerber sought permission to artificially inseminate his wife. CDCR officials denied his request, citing the facts that (1) impregnating his wife was not medically necessary for Gerber's physical well-being and (2) Gerber had failed to show that denial of the request would violate his constitutional rights.

In a civil suit, however, Gerber alleged that the CDCR regulation violated the due process clause by denying him his constitutional right to procreate. On a defendant's motion, the suit was dismissed in federal district court. Gerber appealed to the U.S. Court of Appeals for the Ninth Circuit where a three-judge panel initially held "that the right to procreate survives incarceration." The panel reversed the district court's dismissal and reinstated

Gerber's claim, mandating further review of the case. Upon review, however, the full Ninth Circuit Court of Appeals ruled that prison inmates do not have a constitutional right to fatherhood. The appellate court's majority opinion cited the 1984 U.S. Supreme Court case of *Hudson* v. *Palmer* (mentioned earlier in this chapter), which held that "while persons imprisoned . . . enjoy many protections of the Constitution, it is also clear that imprisonment carries with it the . . . loss of many significant rights."

As we have seen, federal and state inmates can file suits in federal court alleging civil rights violations by corrections officials. In 1988, the U.S. Supreme Court (in *West* v. *Atkins*) decided that private citizens who contracted to do work for prisons could be sued for civil rights violations against inmates. The Court found that such contractors were acting "under color of state law," as required by Section 1983 of the Civil Rights Act of 1871.

As a result of Supreme Court decisions, most prisons now have rules that provide for necessary due process when prisoners appear before disciplinary committees. The makeup of disciplinary committees varies among institutions. The committees may include both inmates and free citizens.

End of the Prisoners' Rights Era

By the late 1980s, the prisoners' rights era was drawing to a close. Following a change in the composition of the Supreme Court, the justices sitting on the Court had become less sympathetic to prisoners' civil rights claims. As discussed earlier, the 1986 case of *Daniels* v. *Williams* helped establish the notion that due process requirements were intended to prevent abuses of power by correctional officials, not to protect against mere carelessness. Furthermore, judicial and legislative officials began to realize that inmates frequently abused what had previously been seen as their right of access to the courts. As state costs of defending against **frivolous lawsuits** by inmates began to grow, federal courts began to take a new look at prisoners' rights.

frivolous lawsuits
Lawsuits with no foundation in fact. They are generally brought for publicity, political, or other reasons not related to law.

Examples of abuse of the court system by prison inmates abound. One inmate sued the state of Florida because he got only one bread roll with dinner. He sued two more times because he did not get a salad with lunch and because prison-provided TV dinners did not come with drinks. He sued yet again because his cell was not equipped with a television. Another inmate claimed prison officials were denying him freedom of religion. His religion, he said, required him to attend prison chapel services in the nude. Still another inmate, afraid that he could get pregnant through homosexual relations, sued because prison officials would not give him birth control pills.

As early as 1977, the U.S. Supreme Court refused to hear an appeal from Henry William Theriault, founder of the Church of the New Song (or CONS).[19] Theriault, an inmate at the federal penitentiary in Atlanta, had a mail-order divinity degree. Members of CONS celebrated communion every Friday night. They claimed that prison officials must supply them with steak and Harvey's Bristol Cream sherry for the practice. Although "Bishop Theriault" admitted that he had originally created CONS to mock other religions, he claimed that he became a serious believer as the religion developed and acquired more followers. The U.S. Supreme Court dismissed that argument and held that the First Amendment does not protect so-called religions that are obvious shams.

The Cases   One of the important cases setting the stage for a review of prisoners' claimed rights was that of *Turner* v. *Safley*, decided in 1987.

In *Turner,* the U.S. Supreme Court established a four-pronged test for determining the reasonableness of prison regulations. In order for a prison regulation to be acceptable, said the Court, there must first be a "valid, rational connection" between the prison regulation and the "legitimate governmental interest" offered to justify it. A second factor relevant in determining the reasonableness of a prison restriction, especially one that limits otherwise established rights, is whether alternative means of exercising that right remain available to prison inmates. If they do, then the restriction is more acceptable. A third consideration is the impact that accommodating an asserted constitutional right would have on officers and other inmates and on the allocation of scarce prison resources. If accommodation makes the job of correctional officers more dangerous or if it is unduly expensive, then it need not be granted. Finally, the fourth prong holds that prisoners have no recourse if there are no readily available alternatives that might permit exercise of claimed rights without compromising penological goals. In other words, if inmates or their attorneys cannot suggest a workable alternative to meet an asserted right, then accommodations need not be made.

In *Wilson* v. *Seiter* (1991), the U.S. Supreme Court sided with prison officials in a way uncharacteristic of the previous two decades. In *Wilson,* the Court found that overcrowding, excessive noise, insufficient locker space, and similar conditions did not violate the Constitution if the intent of prison officials was not malicious. The Court ruled that the actions of officials did not meet the "deliberate indifference" standard defined in *Estelle* v. *Gamble* (1976).

After *Wilson,* inmates won very few new precedent-setting cases. The courts either reversed themselves or tightened the conditions under which inmates could win favorable decisions. Decisions supporting freedom of religion had been among the earliest and most complete victories during the prisoners' rights era. Even in that area, however, things began to change. The courts held that crucifixes and rosaries could legally be denied to inmates because of their possible use as weapons (*Mark* v. *Nix,* 1993, and *Escobar* v. *Landwehr,* 1993). Although some jurisdictions had previously allowed certain Native American religious items within prisons (*Sample* v. *Borg,* 1987), the courts now ruled that prohibiting ceremonial pipes, medicine bags, and eagle claws did *not* violate the First Amendment rights of Native American inmates (*Bettis* v. *Delo,* 1994).

In the 1992 Supreme Court case of *Hudson* v. *McMillan,* the "deliberate indifference" standard was interpreted as requiring both actual knowledge *and* disregard of the risk of harm to inmates or others. This tighter definition allowed federal courts to side more easily with state prison officials in cases in which prisoners claimed there was deliberate indifference. In 1994, in the case of *Farmer* v. *Brennan,* the Supreme Court ruled that even when a prisoner is harmed and even when prison officials knew that the risk of harm existed, officials cannot be held liable if they took appropriate steps to mitigate that risk.

If there was any question that the prisoners' rights era had ended, that question was settled in 1995 by the case of *Sandin* v. *Conner.* In *Sandin,* the Supreme Court rejected the argument that, by disciplining inmates, a state deprived prisoners of their constitutional right not to be deprived of liberty without due process. "The time has come to return to those due process principles that were correctly established and applied in earlier times," said the Court. A year later, the decision in *Lewis* v. *Casey* overturned portions of *Bounds* v. *Smith.* The *Bounds* case had been instrumental in establishing law libraries in prisons. The Court in *Lewis* held, however, that "*Bounds* does not guarantee inmates the wherewithal to file any and every type of legal claim but requires only that they be provided with the tools to attack their sentences."

In *Edwards* v. *Balisok* (1997), the Supreme Court made it even harder to successfully challenge prison disciplinary convictions. The Court held that prisoners cannot sue for monetary damages under Section 1983 of the U.S. Code for loss of good-time credits until they are able to sue successfully in state court to have their disciplinary conviction set aside.

In 2003, in the case of *Overton* v. *Bazzetta,* the Court upheld visitation regulations established by the Michigan Department of Corrections that denied most visits to prisoners who had committed two substance abuse violations while incarcerated. In its ruling, the Court said that "the regulations bear a rational relation to legitimate penological interests [sufficient] to sustain them." Wording taken directly from the Court's opinion is shown in Exhibit 11–4. It provides a summary of the factors used by the courts to decide whether prison regulations meet constitutional requirements.

In a somewhat different kind of case, the U.S. Supreme Court found that federal correctional officers are "law enforcement officers" within the meaning of federal law—and that they are therefore immune from claims alleging injury or loss of property "caused by negligence or a wrongful act or omission" when acting within their scope of employment. The case, *Ali* v. *Federal Bureau*

EXHIBIT 11-4 | *Overton v. Bazzetta* (2003)

Responding to concerns about prison security problems caused by the increasing number of visitors to Michigan's prisons and about substance abuse among inmates, the Michigan Department of Corrections (MDOC) promulgated new regulations limiting prison visitation. . . .

The fact that the regulations bear a rational relation to legitimate penological interests suffices to sustain them regardless of whether respondents have a constitutional right of association that has survived incarceration. This Court accords substantial deference to the professional judgment of prison administrators, who bear a significant responsibility for defining a corrections system's legitimate goals and determining the most appropriate means to accomplish them. The regulations satisfy each of four factors used to decide whether a prison regulation affecting a constitutional right that survives incarceration withstands constitutional challenge.

First, the regulations bear a rational relationship to a legitimate penological interest. The restrictions on children's visitation are related to MDOC's valid interests in maintaining internal security and protecting child visitors from exposure to sexual or other misconduct or from accidental injury. They promote internal security, perhaps the most legitimate penological goal, by reducing the total number of visitors and by limiting disruption caused by children. It is also reasonable to ensure that the visiting child is accompanied and supervised by adults charged with protecting the child's best interests. Prohibiting visitation by former inmates bears a self-evident connection to the State's interest in maintaining prison security and preventing future crime. Restricting visitation for inmates with two substance-abuse violations serves the legitimate goal of deterring drug and alcohol use within prison.

Second, respondents have alternative means of exercising their asserted right of association with those prohibited from visiting. They can send messages through those who are permitted to visit, and can communicate by letter and telephone. Visitation alternatives need not be ideal; they need only be available.

Third, accommodating the associational right would have a considerable impact on guards, other inmates, the allocation of prison resources, and the safety of visitors by causing a significant reallocation of the prison system's financial resources and by impairing corrections officers ability to protect all those inside a prison's walls.

Finally, [complainants] have suggested no alternatives that fully accommodate the asserted right while not imposing more than a [minimum] cost to the valid penological goals.

Source: *Overton v. Bazzetta*, 539 U.S. 126 (2003), Syllabus.

of Prisons,[20] involved a federal prisoner who claimed that some of his personal belongings had disappeared when he was transferred between prisons.

Finally, in two cases from 2012, the Supreme Court sided with correctional officials in limiting the rights of inmates. In the first case, *Howes* v. *Fields* (2012), the Court found that inmates who face questioning by law enforcement officers while they are incarcerated need not be advised of their *Miranda* rights prior to the start of interrogation. In the second case, *Florence* v. *Burlington County* (2012), the Court ruled that officials had the power to strip-search persons who had been arrested prior to admission to a jail or other detention facility even if the offense for which they were arrested was a minor one. In that case, Justice Kennedy, writing for the majority, noted that "maintaining safety and order at detention centers requires the expertise of correctional officials, who must have substantial discretion to devise reasonable solutions to problems." He went on to write that "the term 'jail' is used here in a broad sense to include prisons and other detention facilities."

The Legal Mechanisms Changes in state and federal statutes have also slowed the pace of prisoners' rights cases. In 1980, Congress modified the Civil Rights of Institutionalized Persons Act.[21] It now requires a state inmate to exhaust all state remedies before filing a petition for a writ of *habeas corpus* in federal court. In effect, a state prisoner must give the state an opportunity to correct alleged violations of its prisoners' federal rights (*Duncan* v. *Henry,* 1995). Inmates in federal prisons may still file *habeas corpus* petitions directly in federal court. In their petitions, federal inmates are now required to show (1) that they were deprived of some right to which they were entitled despite the confinement and (2) that the deprivation of this right made the imprisonment more burdensome.

The Prison Litigation Reform Act of 1995[22] (PLRA) was another legislative response to the ballooning number of civil rights lawsuits filed by prisoners. It restricts the filing of lawsuits in federal courts by:

1. requiring state prisoners to exhaust all local administrative remedies prior to filing suit in federal court;
2. requiring inmates to pay federal filing fees unless they can claim pauper status;[23]
3. limiting awards of attorneys' fees in successful lawsuits;
4. requiring judges to screen all inmate lawsuits and immediately dismiss those they find frivolous;
5. revoking good-time credit toward early release if inmates file malicious lawsuits;
6. barring prisoners from suing the federal government for mental or emotional injury unless there is an accompanying physical injury;
7. allowing court orders to go no further than necessary to correct the particular inmate's civil rights problem;
8. requiring some court orders to be renewed every two years or be lifted; and
9. ensuring that no single judge can order the release of federal inmates for overcrowding.

In May 2001, the U.S. Supreme Court further restricted inmate options under the PLRA. The ruling mandates that inmates must complete prison administrative processes that could provide some relief before suing over prison conditions even if that relief would *not include a monetary payment* (*Booth* v. *Churner,* 2001).

A 2005 study of the PLRA's effectiveness conducted by the National Council for State Courts (NCSC), found that the PLRA "achieved its intended effects" and significantly lowered the number of frivolous filings by inmates in federal courts.[24]

FEMALE INMATES AND THE COURTS

CO11-6

The prisoners' rights movement has been largely a male phenomenon. While male inmates were petitioning the courts for expansion of their rights, female inmates frequently had to resort to the courts simply to gain rights that male inmates already had.

The Cases

One early state case, *Barefield* v. *Leach* (1974), demonstrated that the opportunities and programs for female inmates were clearly inferior to those for male inmates. In that case, a court in New Mexico spelled out one standard for equal treatment of male and female inmates. The court said that the equal-protection clause of the Constitution requires equal treatment of male and female inmates but not identical treatment. *Barefield*, however, was a state case—not binding on other states or the federal government.

In 1977, in *State, ex rel. Olson* v. *Maxwell,* the Supreme Court of North Dakota ruled that a lack of funds was not an acceptable justification for unequal treatment of male and female prisoners. Although this decision also came in a state court case, it would later be cited as a legal authority in a similar federal court case.

In *Glover* v. *Johnson* (1979), a U.S. district court case, a group of female prisoners in the Michigan system filed a class action lawsuit claiming that they were denied access to the courts and constitutional rights to equal protection. The prisoners demanded educational and vocational opportunities comparable to those for male inmates. At trial, a prison teacher testified that, although men were allowed to take shop courses, women were taught remedial courses at a junior high school level because the attitude of those in charge was "Keep it simple, these are only women." The court

Inmates dressed in cap and gown are honored at a GED graduation ceremony in a California prison. Many claims of female inmates have focused on the failure of correctional institutions to provide them with educational opportunities and medical care comparable to those provided to male inmates. The equal-protection clause of which amendment guarantees female inmates conditions of confinement comparable to those of male inmates?
© Marmaduke St. John/Alamy

found that "the educational opportunities available to women prisoners in Michigan were substantially inferior to those available to male prisoners." Consequently, the court ordered a plan to provide higher education and vocational training for female prisoners in the Michigan prison system. *Glover* was a turning point in equal treatment for imprisoned women. Since 1979, female inmates have continued to win the majority of cases seeking equal treatment and the elimination of gender bias.

In the 1980 case of *Cooper* v. *Morin,* the U.S. Supreme Court accepted neither inconvenience nor cost as an excuse for treating female jail inmates differently from male inmates. Female inmates at a county jail in New York had alleged that inadequate medical attention in jail violated their civil rights. Later that same year, a federal district court rejected Virginia's claims that services for female prison inmates could not be provided at the same level as those for male inmates because of cost-effectiveness issues (*Bukhari* v. *Hutto,* 1980). Virginia authorities said that the much smaller number of women in prison raised the cost of providing each woman with services. The appellate court ordered the state of Virginia to provide equitable services for inmates, regardless of gender.

An action challenging the denial of equal protection and the conditions of confinement in the Kentucky Correctional Institution for Women was the basis of *Canterino* v. *Wilson,* decided in U.S. district court in 1982. The district court held that the "levels system" used to allocate privileges to female prisoners, a system not applied to male prisoners, violated both the equal-protection rights and the due process rights of female inmates. The court also held that female inmates in Kentucky's prisons must have the same opportunities as men for vocational education, training, recreation, and outdoor activity.

In 1982, in *McMurray* v. *Phelps,* a district court in Louisiana ordered an end to the unequal treatment of female inmates in that state's jails. (Recall that the federal courts have supervisory jurisdiction over state courts.) The next year, the Seventh Circuit Court of Appeals found that strip searches of female misdemeanor offenders awaiting bond in a Chicago lockup were unreasonable under the Fourth Amendment (*Mary Beth G.* v. *City of Chicago,* 1983). In addition, the court found that a policy of subjecting female arrestees to strip searches while subjecting similarly situated males only to hand searches violated the equal-protection clause of the Constitution.

In 1994, in a class action suit by female inmates, a federal district court held the District of Columbia Department of Corrections liable under the Eighth Amendment for inadequate gynecological examinations and testing, inadequate testing for sexually transmitted diseases, inadequate health education, inadequate prenatal care, and an inadequate overall prenatal protocol (*Women Prisoners of the District of Columbia Department of Corrections* v. *District of Columbia,* 1994).

Court oversight of OB-GYN services at the District of Columbia Department of Corrections ended in 2004, following an agreement in which the department promised to continue to provide adequate services for women inmates. The agreement ended 33 years of court oversight of the DC department—involving a total of 15 class action lawsuits filed by inmate groups or their representatives during that time.[25]

Also in 2004, U.S. district judge Myron Thompson approved a settlement in a class action lawsuit centered on concerns about medical care and general conditions at three Alabama women's prisons. Thompson said that the settlement, which required lowering the number of prisoners held at three locations, would not make the facilities "comfortable or pleasant" but would "afford class members the basic necessities mandated by the United States Constitution."[26] Affected were the Julia Tutwiler Prison for Women, the Tutwiler Annex, and the Birmingham Work Release Facility—all operated by the Alabama Department of Corrections. The lawsuit, filed by the Southern Center for Human Rights, had complained of "intensely overcrowded" and "unbearably hot and poorly ventilated dormitories." Tutwiler Prison had been built in the 1940s to hold no more than 364 inmates but was filled with more than 1,000 inmates at the time of the lawsuit. Under the agreement, the population was lowered to 700 by sending some inmates to prisons in Louisiana and by releasing others under community supervision.

CORRECTIONAL OFFICER CIVIL LIABILITY AND INMATE LAWSUITS

Until recently, the **doctrine of sovereign immunity** barred legal actions against state and local governments. The doctrine of sovereign immunity held that a governing body or its representatives could not be sued because it made the law and therefore could not be bound by it. Consequently, federal and state correctional facilities and their officers, acting in their official capacity, were generally held to be immune from lawsuits.

doctrine of sovereign immunity
A historical legal doctrine that held that a governing body or its representatives could not be sued because it made the law and therefore could not be bound by it.

Today, however, immunity is a much more complex issue. Some states have officially abandoned any claims of immunity through legislative action. New York State, for example, has declared that public agencies are equally as liable as private agencies for violations of constitutional rights. Other states, such as California, have enacted statutory provisions that define and limit governmental liability.[27] A number of state immunity statutes have been struck down by court decision. In general, states are moving in the direction of setting dollar limits on liability and adopting federal immunity principles, including "good faith" and "reasonable belief" rules, to protect individual officers.

At the federal level, the concept of sovereign immunity is embodied in the Federal Tort Claims Act (FTCA),[28] which grants broad immunity to certain federal government agencies—especially law enforcement agencies—when their employees act negligently within the scope of their employment. In the 2008 U.S. Supreme Court case of *Ali* v. *Federal Bureau of Prisons,* the Court held that federal correctional officers are law enforcement officers for purposes of civil litigation and found that the BOP was immune to the type of suit that had been brought against it. In *Ali,* a federal prison inmate filed suit against the BOP under the FTCA,[29] which authorizes "claims against the United States for money damages . . . for injury or loss of property . . . caused by the negligent or wrongful act or omission of any employee in the government while acting within the scope of his office or employment." In denying Ali's claim, the Court found that the law specifically provides immunity for federal law enforcement officers and determined that federal corrections personnel are "law enforcement officers" within the meaning of the law. In the 2013 case of *Millbrook* v. *U.S.,*[30] the Court reaffirmed its earlier finding that federal correctional officers are law enforcement officers whose agencies are protected against suits under the FTCA for acts or omissions that arise within the scope of their employment.

Individual officers (as opposed to the agencies for which they work), however, are not necessarily protected under federal or state law. Nonetheless, federal courts have generally shielded correctional officers from "constitutional lawsuits if reasonable officers believe their actions to be lawful in light of clearly established law and the information the officers possess." In doing so, the Court has recognized a form of qualified immunity as a defense, "which shields public officials from actions for damages unless their conduct was unreasonable in light of clearly established law."[31] According to the Court, "[T]he qualified immunity doctrine's central objective is to protect public officials from undue interference with their duties and from potentially disabling threats of liability."[32]

REVIEW AND APPLICATIONS

SUMMARY

1 The hands-off doctrine was a working philosophy of the courts in this country until 1970. It allowed corrections officials to run prisons without court intervention. The hands-off doctrine existed because courts were reluctant to interfere with activities of the executive branch and because judges realized that they were not experts in corrections.

2 The key legal sources of prisoners' rights are the U.S. Constitution, federal statutes, state constitutions, and state statutes.

3 Inmates can challenge the legality of their confinement, associated prison conditions, and the practices of correctional officials through (1) a state *habeas corpus* action, (2) a federal *habeas corpus* action, (3) a state tort lawsuit, (4) a federal civil rights lawsuit, and (5) an injunction to obtain relief.

4 During the prisoners' rights era (1970–1991), inmates won many court cases based on claims that conditions of their confinement violated their constitutional rights. Court decisions affected inmate rights to freedom of expression, including free speech; personal communications; access to the courts and legal services; religion; assembly and association; the voicing of grievances about disciplinary procedures; protection from personal and cell searches; health care, including diet and exercise; protection from violence; adequate physical conditions of confinement; and rehabilitation.

5 Most prisoners' claims focus on denial of constitutional rights guaranteed by the First (freedom of expression and religion), Fourth (freedom from unlawful search and seizure), Eighth (freedom from cruel and unusual punishment), and Fourteenth (due process and equal protection of the law) Amendments.

6 The prisoners' rights movement has been largely a male phenomenon. More recently, female inmates have had to petition the courts to gain rights that male inmates already had.

7 In times past, the doctrine of sovereign immunity shielded federal, state, and local governments from lawsuits. More recently, however, correctional agencies—at least on the federal level—have been protected by federal law from certain civil suits stemming from the negligent actions of their employees. Individual officers are also shielded by court precedent to the extent that their actions are reasonable in light of clearly established law.

KEY TERMS

hands-off doctrine, p. 294
prisoners' rights, p. 297
constitutional rights, p. 297
institutional needs, p. 297
civil liability, p. 298
writ of *habeas corpus,* p. 298
tort, p. 299

nominal damages, p. 299
compensatory damages, p. 299
punitive damages, p. 299
injunction, p. 299
jurisdiction, p. 300
precedent, p. 302
legitimate penological objectives, p. 305

balancing test, p. 305
cruel and unusual punishment, p. 310
deliberate indifference, p. 311
totality of conditions, p. 311
due process, p. 313
frivolous lawsuits, p. 315
doctrine of sovereign immunity, p. 321

QUESTIONS FOR REVIEW

1 Why was the hands-off doctrine so named? What was the basis for the doctrine?

2 What are the key legal sources of prisoners' rights?

3 What are the legal mechanisms through which inmates can challenge the legality of their confinement and associated prison conditions?

4 What rights were won by inmates during what the book calls the *prisoners' rights era?*

5 What constitutional amendments are most often cited by prisoners claiming rights? What claimed rights are associated with each of these amendments?

6 Do the rights accorded male inmates correspond to the rights of female inmates? Why or why not?

7 What is the doctrine of sovereign immunity? To what extent are today's correctional officers shielded from civil lawsuits brought by inmates?

THINKING CRITICALLY ABOUT CORRECTIONS

Freedom of Nonverbal Expression

The right to freedom of nonverbal expression is said to be implied in the First Amendment. Hence, how people wear their hair and how they dress are expressions that some believe are protected by the First Amendment.

1. Might there be modes of dress that interfere with a correctional institution's legitimate goals?
2. If so, what might they be?

Checks and Balance

On January 11, 2003, in a dramatic legal move shortly before leaving office, former Illinois governor George Ryan commuted the sentences of every one of the state's 167 death row inmates. Four of the sentences were reduced to 40-year terms; the remaining 163 sentences were commuted to life in prison. Governor Ryan based his action on his determination

of inherent arbitrariness and unfairness in the application of capital punishment and on the high risk of executing an innocent person.

Although the scope of his action is unusual, the commutations typify the power placed in the hands of each state's chief executive. Essentially, this means that, within the respective states and based solely on personal opinion, a single individual is empowered to overturn sentencing decisions and attendant legal rulings on those decisions made at any level up to and including the nation's most powerful court, the U.S. Supreme Court.

1. Should this be the case?
2. Does the lack of a legal mechanism to counter a governor's decision regarding a pardon or a commutation violate the principle of checks and balances so intricately woven into America's state and federal governmental structures?

ON-THE-JOB DECISION MAKING

Inmate Communications

You are a prison administrator. The prison where you work has a rule that inmates may write letters in English only. This rule seems sensible. After all, if inmates could write in languages not understood by correctional officers, they could discuss plans to escape, riot, or smuggle drugs or weapons into the prison. The courts allow the censoring of outgoing inmate mail; what good is that power if corrections personnel cannot read the mail?

You realize, however, that inmates who cannot write in English will have difficulty communicating with the outside world and with their families. Inmates unable to write in English will not even be able to write to their attorneys. You also wonder what might happen if an inmate can write in English but his parents can read only a foreign language. If the inmate and his parents cannot afford long-distance phone

calls, they will not be able to communicate with each other at all. You begin to consider how the English-only rule might be changed to facilitate wholesome communications while still preventing communications that might endanger the safety of the institution and the inmate population.

1. Can the English-only rule be amended to meet the inmate needs discussed here while still being consistent with legitimate institutional concerns? If so, how?
2. Does an inmate have a constitutionally protected right to communicate with his or her parents?
3. What if that right conflicts with prison policy?

Law Libraries

The Supreme Court's ruling in *Bounds* v. *Smith* (1977) led to the establishment of law libraries for prisoner use in correctional facilities throughout the nation. Numerous subsequent prisoner civil suits resulted in follow-on rulings mandating the need to maintain these libraries with up-to-date reference materials in serviceable condition.

You are an advisor on correctional issues on the staff of your state's attorney general. In the past few weeks, she has repeatedly complained that these rulings impose excessive financial demands on the state's already nearly impoverished correctional system. In particular, she says, routine vandalism by inmates who tear pages from law books and take the pages back to their cells—or simply discard them—is especially costly. It also creates a circumstance in which another inmate could threaten another civil suit upon finding a book to be "unserviceable" when attempting to use it, a threat to which the system can respond only by immediately purchasing a replacement book.

This, the attorney general says, typifies a cycle that causes an extraordinary drain on limited financial resources. She rants about the "ludicrous" fact that the reference material in her own office is so out of date as to be virtually unusable, but she cannot fix the problem because she spends that portion of her budget on repeatedly restoring the prisoners' law libraries in the various institutions throughout the state.

The attorney general has tasked you to resolve this issue.

1. What will you do?
2. Might advances in information technology be the key to a solution?

SPECIAL PRISON POPULATIONS

Prisoners Who Are Substance Abusers, Who Have HIV/AIDS, Who Are Mentally Challenged, and Who Are Elderly

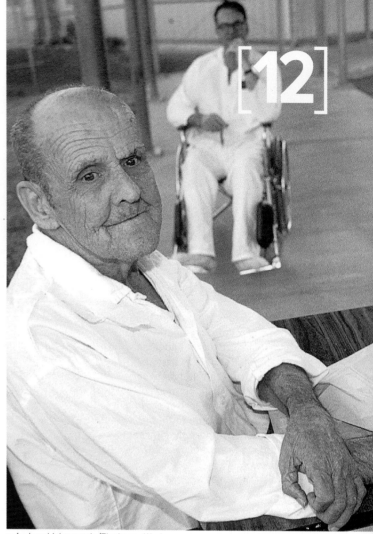

© Andrew Lichtenstein/The Image Works

CHAPTER OBJECTIVES

After completing this chapter you should be able to do the following:

1 Define the term *inmate with special needs.*

2 Report on the management needs of special population inmates.

3 Report on the impact of substance abusers on the corrections system.

4 Discuss why treating HIV in prison is difficult.

5 Discuss the five essential elements of cost-effective management of HIV/AIDS inmates.

6 Explain why so many inmates have mental illnesses.

7 Describe ways to divert persons with mental illness from the criminal justice system.

8 List the cost, recidivism, and health issues associated with older inmates.

9 Review the legal issues surrounding special population inmates.

> *I cannot think of a more challenging or needful segment of our work than our involvement with special populations.*
>
> —Thomas Patterson (former Utah director of corrections), 'Addressing Special Populations in Corrections,' *Corrections Today,* vol. 74, no. 4, August–September 2012.

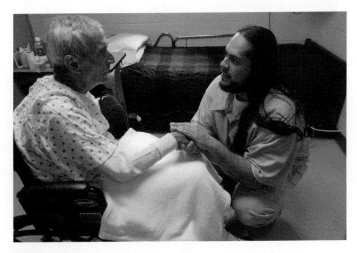

Increasingly, prisons and jails are dealing with a growing population of inmates with special needs. **Inmates with special needs** are prisoners who exhibit unique physical, mental, social, and programmatic needs that distinguish them from other prisoners and for whom jail and prison management and staff have to respond to in nontraditional and innovative ways. These special populations suffer from mental illness; chemical dependency (drug or alcohol); communicable diseases (especially HIV/AIDS and tuberculosis); chronic diseases (e.g., diabetes, heart disease, seizures, and detoxification); the general problems of people who are elderly; the special concern of managing young female offenders in correctional settings; the problems that arise when youthful offenders are housed in adult institutions; and the issues arising from sexual identity, prisoner victimization, transgender prisoners, and the management of sex offenders within correctional settings. Space does not allow us to discuss all of these populations. The ones that garner the most attention are prisoners who are substance abusers, those who suffer from HIV/AIDS, those who are mentally challenged, and the elderly.

Forty years ago, there were almost 9,000 state and federal prisoners age 55 and older. Today, that number stands at almost 250,000. Experts project that by 2030 this number will be more than 400,000, amounting to more than one-third of all prisoners in the United States—enough to fill the Louisiana Superdome more than three times. What are the special needs of elderly inmates?

© Sharon Gekoski-Kimmel/KRT/Newscom

inmates with special needs
Prisoners who exhibit unique physical, mental, social, and programmatic needs that distinguish them from other prisoners and to whom jail and prison management and staff have to respond in nontraditional and innovative ways.

INMATES WITH SPECIAL NEEDS

CO12-1

Special-needs inmates present operational and administrative problems for correctional staff—it is often difficult for the staff to know what they are observing or, once they recognize an inmate's special needs, how to address the situation. Thomas Patterson, former executive director of the Utah Department of Corrections, once said that more and more special populations are the norm rather than the exception.[1] He went on to say that if we add sex offenders and substance abusers to the mix of special populations, upward of 80 percent of offenders would require attention to the challenges they present inside prisons and jails.[2] "To turn a blind eye on special populations is to neglect ethical and humane obligations and more rapidly spin the turnstile of recidivism."[3]

CO12-2

A statewide research study on jail management in New Mexico found that inmates with special needs require extra attention from jail staff.[4] For example, they must be watched closely for possible suicide. Almost 9 of 10 such inmates disrupt normal jail activities; 7 of 10 require an excess of scarce medical resources; 4 of 10 engage in acts of violence; and almost 3 of 10 are abused by other inmates. The characteristics of inmates with special needs, the treatment programs offered, and the policies for dealing with those inmates depend on the type of special need.

The American Correctional Association (ACA) urges correctional agencies to develop and adopt procedures for the early identification of inmates with special needs, to provide the services that respond to those needs, and to monitor and evaluate the delivery of services in both community and institutional settings (see Exhibit 12–1). This chapter reviews the management and treatment of the five largest groups of inmates with special needs: substance-abusing inmates, HIV-positive and AIDS inmates, inmates with mental illness, inmates with tuberculosis, and older inmates.

Substance-Abusing Inmates

Alcohol and other drug problems are the common denominator for most offenders in the criminal justice system, and untreated substance-abusing offenders are more likely to relapse to drug abuse and return to criminal behavior. A **substance-abusing inmate** is an incarcerated person suffering from dependency on one or more substances including alcohol and a wide range of drugs.

substance-abusing inmate

An incarcerated individual suffering from dependency on one or more substances including alcohol and a wide range of drugs.

EXHIBIT 12–1 | **American Correctional Association**

Public Correctional Policy on Offenders with Special Needs

Introduction:

The provision of humane and gender-responsive programs and services for the accused and adjudicated requires addressing the special needs of juvenile, youthful and adult offenders. To meet this goal, correctional agencies should develop and adopt procedures for the early identification of offenders with special needs. Agencies should provide the services that respond to these needs and monitor and evaluate the delivery of services in both confined and community settings.

Policy Statement:

Correctional systems must assure provision of specialized services, programs and conditions of confinement to meet the special needs of offenders. To achieve this, correctional systems should:

A. Identify the juvenile, youthful and adult offenders who require special care or programs including:

- Offenders with psychological needs, developmental disabilities, psychiatric disorders, behavioral disorders, disabling conditions, neurological impairments, and substance abuse disorders;
- Offenders who have acute or chronic medical conditions, are physically disabled or terminally ill;
- Older offenders;
- Offenders with social and/or educational deficiencies, learning disabilities, or language barriers;
- Offenders with special security or supervision needs;
- Sex offenders; and
- Female offenders.

B. Provide services and programs in a manner consistent with professional standards and nationally accepted exemplary practices. Such services and programs may be provided within the correctional agency itself, by referral to another agency that has the necessary specialized resources, or by contracting with private or volunteer agencies or individuals that meet professional standards;

C. Provide appropriately trained, licensed and/or certified, staff, contractors and volunteers for the delivery of, care, programs, and services and provide incentives to attend the continuing education and training necessary to maintain credentials and state-of-the-art, knowledge and mastery-level skills;

D. Maintain professionally appropriate records of all delivered services and programs;

E. Conduct evaluations of service delivery adherence to program standards, while also evaluating the effectiveness of the services, with regular feedback to administrators and service providers for continuous quality improvement; and

F. Provide leadership and advocacy for legislative and public support to obtain the resources needed to meet these special needs.

Source: Copyright © American Correctional Association. Reprinted with permission.

Substance abuse takes a toll on users, the community, and the criminal justice system. Today, between 60 and 80 percent of individuals under supervision of the criminal justice system have a substance use-related issue. This includes individuals who committed a crime to support a substance use disorder, those charged with a drug-related crime, and others who simply use drugs illegally or abuse alcohol regularly. However, only 11 percent receives any treatment while incarcerated.[5] Another 458,000, although not meeting the strict medical criteria for alcohol and drug abuse and addiction nevertheless were either under the influence of alcohol or other drugs at the time of their offense, stole money to buy drugs, are substance abusers, violated the alcohol or drug laws, or share some combination of these characteristics. Consider these startling statistics reported by the national Center on Addiction and Substance Abuse (CASA) at Columbia University. Alcohol and drugs are involved in

- 78 percent of violent crimes;
- 83 percent of property crimes; and
- 77 percent of public order, immigration or weapons offenses, and probation/parole violations.

As this chapter points out, we know how to reduce the costs of incarceration and the crimes committed by substance-involved offenders. However, the barriers to action include the setting of mandatory sentences that eliminate the possibilities of alternative sentencing such as drug courts or parole, the lack of a clear mandate to provide treatment, the economic interests in prison expansion, politicians who are more concerned with being reelected and fear being labeled "soft on crime" by opponents, and the failure of public policy to reflect the science of addiction and changing public attitudes about addiction and justice. But there is good news as we pointed out in Chapters 3 and 7 on sentencing trends and reforms. A number of states (and the federal government) have either reversed mandatory sentencing or are considering doing so. There are more examples of evidence-based practices informing correctional policy today as evidenced across these chapters. And the public doesn't think treatment is bad. An ABC news poll found that two-thirds of Americans support state laws requiring treatment—not jail time for first- and second-time drug offenders.[6]

Drug Use and Dependence Policymakers and politicians on both sides of the aisle now agree that the war on drugs has not affected persons who commit prison-bound offenses. The U.S. Department of Justice tells us that nearly one-third of state inmates and one-fourth of federal inmates committed their offenses under the influence of drugs.[7] Drug use in the month before the offense by state prisoners remained unchanged from 1997 (stable at 56–57 percent), but drug use in the month before the offense by federal prisoners rose from 45 to 50 percent. You learned in Chapter 7 that 16 percent of state prisoners are incarcerated for drug offenses, down from 21 percent a decade ago. At the federal level, it's 50 percent, down from 56 percent a decade ago. Clearly, the number of state and federal inmates in prison for drug offenses is the reason California and other states are treating rather than incarcerating drug offenders and why some states and local jurisdictions have moved to legalize the recreational use of marijuana, decriminalize it, or reduce its penalty. If we are releasing inmates with as little as $50, no treatment (as documented by CASA), a bus ticket, and a "good luck" wish, why is it difficult to understand why they are committing new crimes and reentering the system?

Almost two-thirds of all U.S. jail and prison inmates (some 1.5 million) meet the medical criteria for substance abuse addiction but only 11 percent receive any treatment while incarcerated. What should jails and prisons do to control the revolving door of drug and alcohol abusers and addicts in and out of prison?

© Marvin Joseph/The Washington Post/Getty Images

Drug Treatment Programs Why should prisoners receive drug treatment? According to Jeremy Travis, president of John Jay College of Criminal Justice and former director of the National Institute of Justice (NIJ), there are two powerful reasons.[8]

First, drug offenders consume a staggering volume of illegal drugs, and any reduction in their drug use represents a significant reduction in the nation's demand for illegal drugs. About 60 percent of the cocaine and heroin consumed by the entire nation in a year is consumed by individuals arrested in that year. Drug treatment has the potential for significantly reducing the nation's demand for illegal drugs.

Second, we now know from the evidence-based literature that we can reduce drug use in the offender population. Drug abuse treatment improves outcomes for drug-abusing offenders and has beneficial effects for public health and safety. There is ample, consistent, and cumulative evidence that cognitive behavioral therapy (CBT) for incarcerated populations is an effective intervention for drug abusers even if the motivation for entering treatment is coerced.[9] The National Treatment Improvement Evaluation Study found that cognitive-based treatment programs in prison produced reductions in criminal behavior and in arrests.[10] Participation in correctional substance abuse treatment is also associated with enhanced mental health and physical health. Ideally, treatment programs should begin the moment a person enters prison. Research shows that CBT programs that start nine months to a year before prison release are offered when offenders are under community supervision along with community-based aftercare services (housing, education, employment, and health care), attract and retain staff who demonstrate concern for the offender's welfare, and give offenders a clear understanding of the program's rules and the penalties for breaking them provide the greatest chances for success.[11] Community aftercare services are particularly important for substance abusers because they tend to have medical problems such as cirrhosis of the liver, diabetes, and HIV/AIDS.

The criminal justice system has become the largest source of mandated, or coerced, drug treatment in the United States.[12] Contrary to what some believe, research consistently indicates that offenders' motivations for

Many inmates enter prison addicted to illegal drugs. Although there's evidence that cognitive-based drug and alcohol treatment in prison reduces recidivism, only 11 percent of inmates who need substance abuse treatment actually receive it. Should correctional facilities be required to provide cognitive-based substance abuse treatment? What are the benefits of cognitive-based substance abuse treatment?
© SuperStock RF

entering drug treatment (voluntary or coerced) are not as important in treatment outcome as their *ultimate length of stay* in treatment. The longer inmates participate in treatment, the more likely they are to adopt prosocial attitudes and overcome their initial resistance. (Generally, better outcomes are associated with treatment that lasts longer than 90 days with the greatest reductions in drug abuse and criminal behavior occurring to those who complete treatment.) This point is important because treatment in a prison always involves an element of coercion.

With almost 2,000 inmates returning to the general population every day, correctional health and public health are becoming increasingly intertwined. Health care and disease prevention in correctional facilities must become a top priority for correctional managers and all correctional personnel.

Findings from evidence-based research tell us that (1) rehabilitation is more likely to succeed for those offenders who complete drug treatment programs, and (2) reducing drug-seeking behavior aids in management of jail facilities. A NIJ-sponsored research study found that the greatest benefit of drug treatment programs in jails was that they provided a "behavioral management tool" that controlled inmates' behavior and helped lower the incidence of inmate violence.[13]

The study evaluated five drug treatment programs in California and New York. At all five sites, substance abuse inmates in drug treatment programs had lower rates of serious physical violence and other behavioral problems (e.g., insubordination and possession of nondrug contraband) than those not in the programs. During a one-year follow-up, 83 percent of the inmates in drug treatment and 77 percent of the control group were not convicted of another offense.

What Works? Principles of Drug Abuse Treatment for Criminal Justice Populations Controlling the revolving door of drug and alcohol abusers and addicts in the criminal justice population is an important aspect of management for corrections officials. The National Institute on Drug Abuse (NIDA) looked at all the research that had been published on drug abuse treatment for the last 40 years and discovered 13 principles that constitute effective drug treatment.[14] They are:

1. Drug addiction is a brain disease that affects behavior and the brain's anatomy and chemistry, and these changes can last for months or years after the individual has stopped using drugs.

2. Effective drug abuse treatment engages participants in a therapeutic process, retains them in treatment for an appropriate length of time, and helps them learn to maintain abstinence over time.

3. Effective drug abuse treatment must last long enough to produce stable behavioral changes.

4. A comprehensive assessment of the nature and extent of an individual's drug problems and mental health evaluation is the first step in effective drug abuse treatment.

5. Tailoring services to fit the needs of the individual is an important part of effective drug abuse treatment because individuals differ in terms of age, gender, ethnicity, problem severity, recovery stage, and level of supervision needed.

6. Effective drug abuse treatment programs carefully monitor drug use through urinalysis or other objective methods because individuals trying to recover from drug addiction may experience a relapse, or return, to drug use.

7. Effective drug abuse treatment programs target cognitions (thoughts and feelings that are associated with criminal behavior). These include believing that one is entitled to have things one's own way; feeling that one's criminal behavior is justified; failing to be responsible for one's actions; and constantly failing to anticipate or appreciate the consequences of one's behavior.

8. Effective drug abuse treatment programs incorporate treatment planning for drug-abusing offenders, and treatment providers are aware of correctional supervision requirements as treatment goals.

9. Effective drug abuse treatment programs recognize that continuity of care helps offenders deal with problems at reentry such as learning to handle situations that could lead to relapse, learning how to live drug free in the community, and developing a drug-free peer support network.

10. Effective drug abuse treatment programs recognize that a balance of rewards and sanctions encourages prosocial behavior and treatment participation.

11. Effective drug abuse treatment programs recognize that offenders with co-occurring drug abuse and mental health problems require an integrated approach that combines drug abuse treatment with psychiatric treatment, including the use of medication to address depression, anxiety, and other mental health problems.

12. Effective drug abuse treatment programs recognize that medications are an important part of treatment for many drug-abusing offenders and can be instrumental in enabling offenders with co-occurring mental health problems to function successfully in society.

13. Effective drug abuse treatment programs understand that rates of infectious diseases such as tuberculosis and HIV/AIDS are higher in drug abusers, incarcerated offenders, and those under community correctional supervision than in the general population.

HIV-Positive and AIDS Inmates

HIV/AIDS is the fourth leading cause of death worldwide. **HIV** is the acronym for **human immunodeficiency virus,** which is any of a group of retroviruses that infect and destroy T cells, which help the immune system fight off infections. When enough of a person's T cells have been destroyed by HIV, he or she is diagnosed with **AIDS,** or **acquired immunodeficiency syndrome**, the last stage of HIV infection. The AIDS virus attacks the body's natural immune system, making it unable to fight off diseases. In this state, a person is highly vulnerable to life-threatening conditions, which people with healthy immune systems can fight off easily.

Corrections professionals should be concerned with treating communicable diseases in the inmate population for at least four reasons:

1. Sexually transmitted diseases can be spread to other inmates.

2. Correctional employees and prison visitors are at risk of becoming infected from inmates with communicable diseases if appropriate precautions are not implemented.

3. Almost 2,000 prisoners are released every day from prison. Unless they are effectively treated, they may transmit their diseases into the community, threatening public health.

4. Unless prisoners are treated in prison, they become a financial burden on community health care systems.[15]

HIV (human immunodeficiency virus)

A group of retroviruses that infect and destroy helper T cells of the immune system, causing the marked reduction in their numbers that is diagnostic of AIDS.

AIDS (acquired immunodeficiency syndrome)

A disease of the human immune system that is characterized cytologically, especially by reduction in the numbers of CD4-bearing helper T cells to 20 percent or less of normal, rendering a person highly vulnerable to life-threatening conditions. The disease is caused by infection with HIV commonly transmitted in infected blood and bodily secretions (as semen), especially during sexual intercourse and intravenous drug use.

It is also likely that when laws regarding mandatory sentencing, three strikes, and truth in sentencing were enacted, legislatures ignored the evidence-based literature in two arenas. First, the data show that the increasing population of aging prisoners is not due to any "elderly crime wave" but to individuals entering prison at a younger age and staying there until they are old—often for not so serious crimes. These people are caught in the net of the newer habitual offender and mandatory minimum laws and are given punishments of 20 years or more for low-level and drug offenses. In Texas, 65 percent of prisoners age 50 and older are incarcerated for nonviolent drug, property, and other crimes.[46] In North Carolina, 26% of prisoners age 50 and older are in prison under habitual offender laws or for drug crimes. Another 14% are in prison for fraud, larceny, burglary, breaking and entering, and traffic and public order violations.

Second, recidivism drops dramatically with age. For example, in New York, only 7 percent of prisoners who were released from prison at ages 50 to 64 returned for new convictions within three years. That number drops to 4 percent for prisoners aged 65 and older. In Virginia, only 1.3 percent of prisoners age 55 and older returned to prison for a new conviction. The driver of reimprisonment for this older age group seems to be parole violations—which could result from missing a meeting with a parole officer, having a positive drug test, or having contact with a victim—and can return individuals to prison without a conviction for a new crime.

The ways corrections officials are reining in expenses for their aging prison populations without sacrificing the quality of care or public safety include using telehealth technologies (initially discussed in Chapter 7), outsourcing prison health care, enrolling prisoners in Medicaid, collaborating with outside partners, and paroling older and/or ill inmates.[47]

Telehealth (aka telemedicine) refers to the use of electronic information and telecommunications technologies to support, among other things, long-distance health care services, issues we discussed in Chapter 7. This strategy can help improve prisoners' access to primary care doctors and specialists while reducing transportation and security problems.

Many states are also looking to outside partners to provide all or part of their prison health care services at lower costs while maintaining or improving the quality of care. The fields of gerontology, social work, philanthropy, and health are uniquely positioned and qualified to inform and implement both short- and long-term solutions to the aging prisoner crisis. Interdisciplinary knowledge, investment from the philanthropic community, and collaborative partnerships possess opportunities to make lasting contributions to the policies and best practices affecting the aging prison population. Effective management and oversight—for example, attaching performance standards and tracking systems to contract or monitor the timeliness and effectiveness of prisoners' treatment—are critical to the success of these partnerships.

A number of states have also made a concerted effort to enroll eligible prisoners in Medicaid so that the program can be billed for qualifying health services, which are limited to the care delivered outside of prison, such as at an offsite hospital or nursing home, when the inmate has been admitted for more than 24 hours. States can obtain federal Medicaid reimbursement that covers at least 50 percent of enrolled prisoners' inpatient hospitalization costs. They may save additional dollars because Medicaid typically pays the lowest provider rates of any payor in a state. States expanding their Medicaid eligibility under the Affordable Care Act may reap the largest savings. States may also assist eligible inmates leaving prison with their enrollment in Medicaid or new health insurance marketplaces, helping to preserve the continuity of health care treatments between prison and the community.

And, as mentioned earlier, even though states have released relatively few older, terminally ill, or incapacitated inmates under medical or geriatric parole because of narrow eligibility criteria, complicated applications, lengthy review processes, difficulty in assessing medical suitability, and a shortage of nursing home spaces for such, granting medical or geriatric parole when appropriate can achieve notable savings, even if the state retains financial responsibility for parolees' health care costs outside prison.

SEXUALLY TRANSMITTED DISEASES IN JAIL

Most studies on infectious diseases in correctional facilities focus on prison. The problem of sexually transmitted diseases (STDs) in jail is addressed less frequently even though some believe that STDs are more common in jail than in prison.[48] However, rapid turnover and frequent movement of inmates make jails difficult settings in which to study the prevalence of various diseases. But recently, the Society of Correctional Physicians (SCP) published a report on the increase of STDs in jail and the difficulties diagnosing and treating four of the most common STDs found in jail today: **syphilis, gonorrhea, chlamydia,** and **genital herpes.** According to the SCP, after declining for many years, the rates of syphilis, gonorrhea, and chlamydia began increasing in jails and juvenile detention centers in 2000, especially among female prisoners.

The jail environment may be the key to controlling STDs, but less than half of the nation's jails have a policy of routine screening, and even in those jails with routine screening, less than half of the inmates were tested for syphilis, gonorrhea, or chlamydia. The SCP also found another problem: Approximately half of arrestees were released within 48 hours, but most jails received the inmates' test results more than 48 hours after admission.

The type of screening for STDs in jail should be based on the prevalence of STDs as measured by the population served. For example, gonorrhea and chlamydia are four times higher in northern Florida than they are in northern California. The key to controlling STDs is to continuously collect, monitor, and analyze information and then to discuss the results with public health officials. Diagnosis also requires a thorough nonjudgmental sexual history and a careful genital exam.

syphilis

A sexually transmitted disease caused by the bacteria *Treponema pallidum*. If left untreated, syphilis can cause serious heart abnormalities, mental disorders, blindness, other neurological problems, and death. Syphilis is transmitted when an infected lesion comes in contact with the soft skin of the mucous membrane.

gonorrhea

The second most common sexually transmitted disease. Often called *the clap*, gonorrhea is caused by the *Neisseria gonorrhea* bacteria found in moist areas of the body. Infection occurs with contact to any of these areas.

chlamydia

The most common sexually transmitted disease. Caused by the bacteria *Chlamydia trachomatis*, it can affect the eyes, lungs, or urogenital (urinary-genital) area, depending on the age of the person infected and how the infection is transmitted.

genital herpes

A sexually transmitted disease caused by the herpes simplex virus, or HSV. It is one of the most common STDs in the United States.

LEGAL ISSUES

CO12-9

Providing inmates adequate health care is of concern to the courts and professional associations. In 1976, the U.S. Supreme Court ruled in *Estelle v. Gamble*[49] that inmates have a constitutional right to reasonable, adequate health services for serious medical needs. However, the Court also made clear that such a right did not mean that prisoners have unqualified access to health care. Lower courts have held that the Constitution does not require that medical care provided to prisoners be perfect, the best obtainable, or even very good.[50] Nevertheless, health care professionals and inmate advocates—such as the American Medical Association, the American Correctional Health Services Association, and the National Commission on Correctional Health Care—insist on alleviating the pain and suffering of all persons, regardless of their status. They believe that no distinction should be made between inmates and free citizens.

Another important piece of legislation affecting inmate health care is the Civil Rights of Institutionalized Persons Act (CRIPA).[51] This law places prisoners in a class with others confined in government institutions, such as people with disabilities and elderly people in government-run nursing homes.

Inmates with Disabilities

Inmates with special needs face numerous difficulties. Consider the case of Ronald Yeskey. Yeskey was sentenced to 18 to 36 months in a Pennsylvania correctional facility. He was recommended for a motivational boot camp, which would have shortened his sentence to six months. He was, however, refused admission to the boot camp because of a physical disability—hypertension. He sued, claiming the ADA prohibits any "public entity" from discriminating against a "qualified individual with a disability" because of that disability.

In 1998 in a unanimous opinion, the U.S. Supreme Court held that state prisons fall squarely within the ADA's definition of a "public entity."[52] Reacting to the decision, Yeskey's attorney noted, "The court's ruling means that prison officials cannot discriminate against prisoners with disabilities and must make reasonable modifications to prison operations so that these prisoners will have reasonable access to most prison programs";[53] otherwise, prisoners can sue for monetary damages.

Inmates with HIV/AIDS

Most suits by prisoners with HIV/AIDS are claims that officials have violated a prisoner's rights by revealing the condition or by segregating the prisoner because of the condition. In 1988, officials in Erie County, New York, placed an HIV-positive female prisoner in a segregated prison wing reserved for inmates with mental illness. They also placed on her possessions red stickers revealing her HIV-positive status. The inmate sued, claiming denial of her rights to privacy and due process. The district court agreed (*Nolley* v. *County of Erie*, 1991). In the same year, however, the Eleventh Circuit Court of Appeals held that an Alabama policy of isolating all HIV-positive inmates did not violate the Fourth or Eighth Amendments (*Harris* v. *Thigpen* and *Austin* v. *Pennsylvania Dept. of Corr.*).

Other legal issues relate to the work assignments of HIV/AIDS inmates. In 1994 in *Gates* v. *Rowland*, the Ninth Circuit Court of Appeals ruled that California correctional officials could continue to bar HIV-positive inmates from working in prison kitchens. The court made it clear that its decision was based more on the anticipated reactions of prisoners receiving the food than on any actual risk of infection. The court agreed that food service "has often been the source of violence or riots" because inmates "are not necessarily motivated by rational thought and frequently have irrational suspicions or phobias that education will not modify" and because prisoners "have no choice of where they eat." Correctional officials had based their policy, the court said, on "legitimate penological concerns."

Inmates with Mental Illness

The federal courts have recognized the right of inmates who are mentally ill to treatment. According to a district court in Illinois, this right is triggered when it becomes reasonably certain that (1) the prisoner's symptoms demonstrate a serious mental disease or brain injury, (2) the disease or injury is curable or at least treatable, and (3) delaying or denying care would

Inmates with Mental Illness

Prisoners in wheelchairs and others with special needs place an extraordinary strain on prison resources. Inmates with disabilities are protected under the federal Americans with Disabilities Act (ADA) of 1990. What does the act require of correctional facilities? What are the alternatives to incarceration for inmates with disabilities?

© Mark Peterson/SABA/Corbis

cause substantially more harm to the inmate (*Parte* v. *Lane,* 1981). In 1990, in *Washington* v. *Harper,* the U.S. Supreme Court ruled that inmates who are dangerous to themselves or others as a result of mental illness may be treated with psychoactive drugs against their will. Such involuntary drug treatment, however, has to be in the best interest of the inmate's mental health, not just for the convenience of the correctional institution.

REVIEW AND APPLICATIONS

SUMMARY

1 Some inmates require special treatment or care because they suffer from mental illness, chemical dependency, a communicable disease, or typical problems associated with people who are elderly. These inmates present unique problems for correctional staff and administrators.

2 Inmates with special needs present significant management problems because they are typically more violent and prone to be disruptive, require close monitoring as suicide risks, tax scarce medical resources, and are often targets of abuse by other inmates.

3 A tenfold increase in prison populations over the past 25 years caused a commensurate increase in the number of inmates with substance abuse problems. These inmates tremendously drain finite resources, are disruptive to daily life within the walls, and create unique management problems in all areas of prison life.

4 Special difficulties related to HIV/AIDS among prison populations include privacy issues, disruption of the prison routine due to the frequency of taking medication, inmate distrust of the medical and legal systems, fear of side effects, and the legal dilemma embodied in the principle of least eligibility.

5 The five essential elements of cost-effective management of HIV/AIDS inmates are early detection and diagnosis, medical management and treatment, inmate classification and housing, education and training of staff and inmates, and funding.

6 The increase in the number of inmates with mental illness is attributable to several factors: the deinstitutionalization of persons who are mentally ill to nonsecure residential environments; stricter commitment laws; failure to know who should and should not be in jail; failure to treat them before they enter the criminal justice system; less stringent discharge criteria; reduction or elimination of public funding; lack of adequate insurance coverage; and three-strikes laws because those with mental illness may, when the illness is not effectively treated, be less able to follow the rule of law.

7 Ways to divert persons with mental illnesses from the criminal justice system include the creation of law enforcement–mental health liaison programs, increased training of law enforcement personnel, and a general improvement in the funding and effectiveness of community health services.

8 Estimates are that, on average, each older inmate is afflicted with three chronic illnesses that require ongoing and expensive medical treatment. Some question the equity of providing such free treatment to criminal offenders when the same free treatment is not provided to the public at large. The annual cost of incarcerating an inmate who is elderly is significantly higher than the average per inmate cost of incarceration.

9 In 1976, the U.S. Supreme Court ruled in *Estelle* v. *Gamble* that inmates have a constitutional right to reasonable, adequate health services for serious medical needs. However, the Court also made clear that such a right did not mean that prisoners have unqualified access to health care. The Civil Rights of Institutionalized Persons Act (CRIPA) places prisoners in a class with others confined in government institutions. In 1998, the U.S. Supreme Court held that state prisons fall squarely within the ADA's definition of a "public entity" and prohibits them from discriminating against a "qualified individual with a disability" because of that disability. Federal courts have ruled differently on whether segregation of inmates with HIV violates the inmate's rights to privacy and due process. A district court agreed, a circuit court of appeals disagreed. The federal courts have also recognized the right of inmates who are mentally ill to treatment.

KEY TERMS

inmates with special needs, p. 326

substance-abusing inmate, p. 327

HIV (human immunodeficiency virus), p. 331

AIDS (acquired immunodeficiency syndrome), p. 331

principle of least eligibility, p. 333

Americans with Disabilities Act (ADA), p. 339

hospice, p. 339

syphilis, p. 343

gonorrhea, p. 343

chlamydia, p. 343

genital herpes, p. 343

QUESTIONS FOR REVIEW

1 What defines an inmate with special needs?

2 Summarize the management problems that special-needs inmates pose for corrections officials.

3 What criteria would you use to assess the impact that substance abusers have on the corrections system?

4 How would you design a system that makes it easier to treat HIV in prison?

5 What ideas can you add to the five essential elements of providing cost-effective management of HIV/AIDS inmates?

6 What evidence explains why there are so many inmates with mental illness in prison?

7 Suggest additional strategies for diverting persons with mental illness from the criminal justice system.

8 What should corrections do about the cost and health issues associated with older inmates?

9 Why is it important to understand the legal issues surrounding special population inmates?

THINKING CRITICALLY ABOUT CORRECTIONS

Aging Prison Population and Costs

As the prison population ages, the costs of incarcerating large numbers of older inmates will skyrocket. This, in turn, will strain correctional budgets and adversely impact correctional administrators' ability to provide essential services to the general prisoner population. Should inmates who are elderly be released from incarceration? Could services provided by other public agencies be tapped to meet the needs of inmates who are elderly? If so, which services might be invoked?

The Principle of Least Eligibility

Discussions of the principle of least eligibility invariably fire emotions. Should inmates rate free medical care that is not available to law-abiding citizens? Why or why not? Would you support a ballot proposal to formalize the principle of least eligibility as law in your state? Why or why not? If such a law were adopted, do you think it would withstand challenge through the state and federal court systems? Why or why not?

ON-THE-JOB DECISION MAKING

How to Use Personal Experience to Advance Correctional Training in HIV/AIDS

You are the warden of a state prison and on record as a supporter of the principle of least eligibility. Walter Edmunds is one of your most dependable correctional officers. Mature, calm, and unfailingly professional, Edmunds can be counted on in every crisis. You have come to rely on his leadership as a positive element among the correctional staff. Unfortunately,

Edmunds has a young son dying of AIDS, which he contracted through a blood transfusion during an appendectomy.

Yesterday your medical staff conducted training for your correctional officers on procedures for handling inmates suffering from HIV and AIDS. About 10 minutes into the training session, Edmunds apologized for interrupting and then asked why the prisoners received top-notch medical treatment for free treatment that ordinary law-abiding citizens can't afford.

From that single question, things quickly deteriorated, and Edmunds became increasingly agitated. Before long, the training room was in turmoil as Edmunds's questions and angry comments whipped up the sympathy and anger of his fellow correctional officers.

Clearly out of his depth, the medical officer canceled the remainder of the training session and then bolted to your office. By the time he finished relating the incident, one of your correctional lieutenants appeared to report that the unionized correctional staff was in an uproar and threatening to walk off the job. What would you do to defuse this situation? Once you contained the crisis, how would you handle Edmunds?

Deciding Legitimate Penological Concerns

You are a correctional lieutenant at a state prison that has a conjugal visitation program. Carl Packard, one of your inmates, was recently diagnosed as HIV-positive. During an interview with a member of the medical staff, Packard acknowledged recent illicit drug use during which he shared a needle with other inmates. He and the medic believe this needle sharing to be the source of Packard's HIV infection.

Yesterday, Packard applied for a conjugal visit with his wife. You summoned him to your office and asked if he had advised his wife of his infection. Packard stated he had not and that he had no intention of "tellin' that bitch nothin'." This morning, you sought guidance from the prison's legal advisor and the warden. They informed you that infection with HIV did not prohibit an inmate's participation in the conjugal visitation program and that privacy policies prohibit you from informing Mrs. Packard of her husband's physical condition. You strongly believe that the threat to Mrs. Packard's health and safety outweighs what you consider to be ill-advised rules and policies.

1. What do you do?
2. What is your reasoning?

ENDNOTES

Chapter 1

1. "Drone's Heroin Delivery to Ohio Prison Yard Prompts Fight Among Inmates," *Associated Press,* August 4, 2015.
2. Stephen Ohlemacher, "2 Prison Inmates Claim $1.1 Billion in Tax Refunds; 173,000 Fraudulent Prison Tax Returns Uncovered," *Huffington Post,* January 17, 2013, www.huffingtonpost.com/2013/01/18/prison-tax-fraud-billion-refund-inmates_n_2502137.html (accessed January 30, 2013).
3. "The New Wolfhound-PRO Contraband Cell Phone Detector to be 'Unleashed' at the American Correctional Association Winter Conference," PRNewswire, January 25, 2011, www.prnewswire.com/news-releases/the-new-wolfhound-pro-contraband-cell-phone-detector-to-be-unleashed-at-the-american-correctional-association-winter-conference-114559409.html (accessed March 15, 2011).
4. The word *outlawed* is used loosely. Although some states have outlawed inmate possession of working cell phones and some others are moving in that direction, such possession is more often a violation of administrative regulations.
5. For an in-depth discussion of this issue, see Steven Raphael and Michael A. Stoll (eds.), *Do Prisons Make Us Safer? The Benefits and Costs of the Prison Boom* (New York: Russell Sage Foundation, 2010).
6. PEW Charitable Trusts, *Growth in Federal Prison System Exceeds States* (Washington, DC: PEW, 2015).
7. John F. Pfaff, "The Causes of Growth in Prison Admission and Populations," http://web.law.columbia.edu/sites/default/files/microsites/criminal-law-roundtable-2012/files/Pfaff_New_Admissions_to_Prison.pdf (accessed January 5, 2016).
8. Michael C. Campbell, Matt Vogel, and Joshua Williams, "Historical Contingencies and the Evolving Importance of Race, Violent Crime, and Region in Explaining Mass Incarceration in the United States," *Criminology,* 2015. doi: 10.1111/1745-9125.12065
9. *Charles Colson Task Force on Federal Corrections* (Washington, DC: Urban Institute, 2015).
10. Fox Butterfield, "Crime Keeps on Falling, but Prisons Keep on Filling," *New York Times* News Service, September 28, 1997.
11. See, for example, Jory Farr, "A Growth Enterprise," www.press-enterprise.com/focus/prison/html/agrowthindustry.html (accessed March 28, 2002).
12. Campbell, Vogel, and Williams, "Historical Contingencies and the Evolving Importance of Race, Violent Crime, and Region in Explaining Mass Incarceration in the United States."
13. Margaret Werner Cahalan, *Historical Corrections Statistics in the United States, 1850–1984* (Washington, DC: U.S. Department of Justice, 1986).
14. E. Ann Carson and Daniela Golinelli, *Prisoners in 2012* (Washington, DC: Bureau of Justice Statistics, 2013).
15. Laura M. Maruschak and Thomas P. Bonczar, *Probation and Parole in the United States, 2012* (Washington, DC: Bureau of Justice Statistics, 2013).
16. Melissa Hickman Barlow, "Sustainable Justice: 2012 Presidential Address to the Academy of Criminal Justice Sciences," *Justice Quarterly,* 2012, pp. 1–17, 1 First Article.
17. Texas Department of Criminal Justice, "$4,000 Recruiting Bonus for New Correctional Officers," http://www.tdcj.state.tx.us/divisions/hr/coinfo/bonus.html (accessed January 5, 2016).
18. Cahalan, *Historical Corrections Statistics.*
19. National Institute of Corrections, *Environmental Scan 2013* (Washington, DC: USDOJ, 2014).
20. Ibid.
21. The figure may be somewhat misleading, however, because an offender who commits a number of crimes may be prosecuted for only one.
22. Much of the following material is adapted from Bureau of Justice Statistics, *Report to the Nation on Crime and Justice,* 2nd ed. (Washington, DC: Bureau of Justice Statistics, 1988), pp. 56–58.
23. President's Commission on Law Enforcement and Administration of Justice, *The Challenge of Crime in a Free Society* (Washington, DC: U.S. Government Printing Office, 1967), p. 159.
24. National Advisory Commission on Criminal Justice Standards and Goals, *Corrections* (Washington, DC: U.S. Government Printing Office, 1975), p. 2.
25. Bureau of Justice Statistics, *Correctional Populations in the United States, 1995* (Washington, DC: U.S. Government Printing Office, 1997).
26. Dianne Carter, "The Status of Education and Training in Corrections," *Federal Probation,* vol. 55, no. 2 (June 1991), pp. 17–23.

Chapter 2

1. Eli Saslow, "In California, Prop 47 Has Turned Into a 'Virtual Get-Out-of-Jail Free Card,'" *The Washington Post,* October 10, 2015.
2. Martin Kaste, "California Cops Frustrated with 'Catch-and-Release' Crime-Fighting," *NPR,* January 22, 2016, http://www.npr.org/2016/01/22/463210910/california-cops-frustrated-with-catch-and-release-crime-fighting (accessed January 22, 2016).
3. National Institute of Corrections, *Implementing Evidence-Based Practice in Community Corrections: The Principles of Effective Intervention* (n.d.), http://www.nicic.org/pubs/2004/019342.pdf.
4. Justice Statistics Research Association, "An Introduction to Evidence-Based Practices," April 2014, http://www.jrsa.org/projects/ebp_briefing_paper1_summary.pdf (accessed February 16, 2016).
5. Lawrence W. Sherman et al., *Preventing Crime: What Works, What Doesn't, What's Promising* (Washington, DC: National Institute of Justice, 1997).
6. Center for Evidence-Based Corrections, University of California, Irvine, http://ucicorrections.seweb.uci.edu (accessed January 30, 2013).
7. National Criminal Justice Association, "How Three States Are Using Evidence to Build State Criminal Justice Policies," http://www.ncjp.org/content/how-three-states-are-using-evidence-build-state-criminal-justice-policies (accessed February 16, 2016).
8. Minnesota Department of Corrections. *The Effects of Prison Visitation on Offender Recidivism* (Rochester, MN: Minnesota DOC, 2011).
9. Cullen, Francis T., Cheryl Lero Jonson, and Daniel S. Nagin. "Prisons Do Not Reduce Recidivism: The High Cost of Ignoring Science," *The Prison Journal,* vol. 91, no. 3 (2011), pp. 48S–65S.
10. Bob Barrington, "Corrections: Defining the Profession and the Roles of Staff," *Corrections Today,* August 1987, pp. 116–120.
11. Arlin Adams, *The Legal Profession: A Critical Evaluation,* 93 Dick. L. Rev. 643 (1989).
12. Harold E. Williamson, *The Corrections Profession* (Newbury Park, CA: Sage, 1990), p. 79.
13. Adams, *The Legal Profession.*
14. Williamson, *The Corrections Profession,* p. 20.
15. P. P. Lejins, "ACA Education Council Proposes Correctional Officer Entry Tests," *Corrections Today,* vol. 52, no. 1 (February 1990), pp. 56, 58, 60.

16. Mark S. Fleisher, "Teaching Correctional Management to Criminal Justice Majors," *Journal of Criminal Justice Education,* vol. 8, no. 1 (Spring 1997), pp. 59–73.

17. See Robert B. Levinson, Jeanne B. Stinchcomb, and John J. Greene III, "Corrections Certification: First Steps Toward Professionalism," www.aca.org/development/doc_certification firststeps.pdf (accessed March 23, 2003).

18. See the ACA's Professional Certification Program Web page at www.corrections.com/aca/development/certification.htm (accessed September 10, 2013) for more information.

19. The AJA defines a jail manager as "a person (sworn or civilian) who directs, administers, and/or is in charge of the operations of an adult jail facility, division, bureau, department, program, and/or shift; and/or a person (sworn or civilian) who supervises the work and performance of an employee or employees in an adult jail facility." See AJA, *CJM: Handbook for Candidates,* www.corrections.com/aja/cjm_handbook.pdf (accessed March 25, 2007).

20. Omi and Howard Winant, *Racial Formation in the United States: From the 1960s to the 1980s* (New York: Routledge and Kegan Paul, 1986), p. 145.

21. National Center for Women and Policing, *Equality Denied: The Status of Women in Policing, 2001* (Beverly Hills, CA: NCWP, 2002), p. 11.

22. Williamson, *The Corrections Profession.*

Chapter 3

1. Shane Smith, "Fixing the System: An Interview with President Obama on Prison Reform," VICE Media LLC, October 5, 2015, http://www.vice.com/read/fixing-the-system-0000760-v22n10 (accessed December 10, 2015).

2. Andrew von Hirsch, *Doing Justice: The Choice of Punishments* (New York: Hill and Wang, 1976), pp. 48–49.

3. Francis T. Cullen and Paul Gendreau, "Assessing Correctional Rehabilitation: Policy, Practice, and Prospects," in Julie Horney (ed.), *Criminal Justice 2000,* Vol. 3 (Washington, DC: National Institute of Justice, 2000).

4. Robert Martinson, "What Works? Questions and Answers About Prison Reform," *Public Interest,* vol. 35 (Spring 1974), pp. 22–54.

5. Cullen and Gendreau, "Assessing Correctional Rehabilitation."

6. Edgardo Rotman, *Beyond Punishment: A New View on the Rehabilitation of Criminal Offenders* (Westport, CT: Greenwood, 1990), p. 11.

7. Marty Price, "Crime and Punishment: Can Mediation Produce Restorative Justice for Victims and Offenders?" www.vorp.com/articles/crime.html (accessed February 9, 1999).

8. E. Ann Carson, *Prisoners in 2014* (Washington, DC: U.S. Department of Justice, Bureau of Justice Statistics, September 2015), p. 13.

9. *Furman* v. *Georgia,* 408 U.S. 238 (1972).

10. Death Penalty Information Center, www.deathpenaltyinfo.org (accessed January 29, 2016).

11. Ibid.

12. Tracy L. Snell, *Capital Punishment, 2013—Statistical Tables* (Washington, DC: U.S. Department of Justice, Bureau of Justice Statistics, December 2014).

13. Robert M. Bohm, *Deathquest III: An Introduction to the Theory and Practice of Capital Punishment in the United States,* 3rd ed. (Cincinnati, OH: Anderson, 2007); Raymond Paternoster, Robert Brame, and Sarah Bacon, *The Death Penalty: America's Experience with Capital Punishment* (New York: Oxford University Press, 2008).

14. John Boger, "Landmark North Carolina Death Penalty Study Finds Dramatic Racial Bias," www.deathpenaltyinfo.org (accessed January 29, 2016).

15. A. Dugan, "Solid Majority Continue to Support Death Penalty," Gallup, October 15, 2015.

16. Damla Ergun, "New Low in Preference for the Death Penalty," ABC News, June 5, 2014, http://abcnews.go.com/blogs/politics/2014/06/ new-low-in-preference-for-the-death-penalty/ (accessed January 29, 2016).

17. *Ring* v. *Arizona,* 122 U.S. 2428 (2002).

18. James Liebman, Jeffrey Fagan, and Valerie West, *A Broken System: Error Rates in Capital Cases, 1973–1995* (New York: Columbia University School of Law, 2000), p. i; Barry Latzer and James N. G. Cauthen, *Justice Delayed? Time Consumption in Capital Appeals: A Multistate Study* (Washington, DC: U.S. Department of Justice, March 2007). The authors found a median of 966 days to complete direct appeals across 14 states from 1992 to 2002. Processing direct appeals was fastest in Virginia (295 days) and slowest in Ohio, Tennessee, and Kentucky (1,388, 1,350, and 1,309 days, respectively). See also Timothy G. Poveda, "Estimating Wrongful Convictions," *Justice Quarterly,* vol. 18, no. 3 (September 2001), pp. 689–708; Talia Roitberg Harmon, "Predictors of Miscarriages of Justice in Capital Cases," *Justice Quarterly,* vol. 18, no. 4 (December 2001), pp. 949–968.

19. Nancy Phillips, "In Life and Death Cases, Costly Mistakes," *The Inquirer,* October 23, 2011, www.philly.com (accessed January 29, 2016).

20. Liebman, Fagan, and West, *A Broken System,* p. 18.

21. Matt O'Connor, "Jury Believes Ex-Chicago Cop Framed by FBI," *Chicago Tribune,* January 25, 2005; Shaun Hittle, "10 Years Later, Eddie Lowery's Name Is Clear and the Man Accused of the Rape for Which Lowery Was Convicted Is Behind Bars," Channel 49 News, February 11, 2010, www.ktka.com (accessed January 29, 2016).

22. Mike Ward, "Tab for Wrongful Convictions in Texas: $65 Million and Counting," *Statesman,* February 10, 2013, www.statesman.com (accessed January 29, 2016).

23. Liebman, Fagan, and West, *A Broken System,* pp. 391–428.

24. Alan Johnson, "Leave Death Penalty Up to a Panel?" *The Columbus Dispatch,* January 13, 2013, www.dispatch.com (accessed January 29, 2016).

25. John Schwartz, "Confessing to Crime, But Innocent," *The New York Times,* September 13, 2010, www.nytimes.com (accessed January 29, 2016).

26. *Atkins* v. *Virginia,* 536 U.S. (2002).

27. *Roper* v. *Simmons,* 543 U.S. (2005).

28. *Transforming Prison, Restoring Lives: Final Recommendations of the Charles Colson Task Force on Federal Corrections* (Washington, DC: Urban Institute, January 2016).

29. Nicole D. Porter, *The State of Sentencing 2015: Developments in Policy and Practice* (New York: Vera Institute of Justice, 2016).

30. Cesare Beccaria, *On Crimes and Punishment.* Trans. Henry Paolucci (Englewood Cliffs, NJ: Prentice Hall, 1963 [1764]).

31. Edgardo Rotman, *Beyond Punishment: A New View on the Rehabilitation of Criminal Offenders* (Westport, CT: Greenwood Press, 1990), p. 3.

Chapter 4

1. James Fisher, "Ex-Ravens Cheerleader Sentenced for Rape of a 15-Year-Old Boy," *USA Today,* August 21, 2015, www.usatoday.com/story/sports/nfl/2015/08/21/molly-shattuck-ravens-cheerleader-sentenced-rape-boy/32108039/ (accessed November 27, 2015).

2. Robert Panzarella, "Theory and Practice of Probation on Bail in the Report of John Augustus," *Federal Probation,* vol. 66, no. 3 (December 2002), pp. 38–43.

3. Sanford Bates, "The Establishment and Early Years of the Federal Probation System," *Federal Probation,* vol. 14 (1950), pp. 16–21; Joel R. Moore, "Early Reminiscences," *Federal Probation,* vol. 14 (1950), pp. 21–29; Richard A. Chappell, "The Federal Probation System Today," *Federal Probation,* vol. 14 (1950), pp. 30–40.

4. Danielle Kaeble, Laura M. Maruschak, and Thomas P. Bonczar, *Probation and Parole in the United States, 2014* (Washington, DC: U.S. Department of Justice, Bureau of Justice Statistics, November 2015).

5. Ibid., p. 4.

6. Caroline Wolf Harlow, *Prior Abuse Reported by Inmates and Probationers* (Washington, DC: Department of Justice, Bureau of Justice Statistics, April 1999).

7. Matt Apuzzo and John Eligon, "Ferguson Police Tainted by Bias, Justice Department Says," *The New York Times,* March 4, 2015, www.nytimes.com/2015/03/05/us/us-calls-on-ferguson-to-overhaul-criminal-justice-system.html?_r=0 (accessed November 29, 2015).

8. Lauren-Brooke Eisen, *Charging Inmates Perpetuates Mass Incarceration* (New York: Brennan Center for Justice, New York University School of Law, 2015).

9. Joseph Shapiro, "As Court Fees Rise, the Poor Are Paying the Price," National Public Radio, May 23, 2014, www.npr.org/2014/05/19/312158516/increasing-court-fees-punish-the-poor (accessed November 29, 2015).

10. Barbara Krauth and Larry Link, *State Organizational Structures for Delivering Adult Probation Services* (Washington, DC: U.S. Department of Justice, National Institute of Corrections, June 1999), pp. 3–5.

11. David J. Krajicek, "Why 'Tough on Crime' Failed," *The Crime Report,* June 9, 2015, interview with University of Texas at Austin criminologist William R. Kelly, www.thecrimereport.org/news/inside-criminal-justice/2015-06-why-tough-on-crime-failed (accessed December 2, 2015).

12. Steve Aos, Marna Miller, and Elizabeth Drake, *Evidence-Based Adult Corrections Programs: What Works and What Does Not* (Olympia, WA: Washington State Institute for Public Policy, 2006); and Jennifer L. Sheem and Sarah Monchak, "Back to the Future: From Klocklar's Model of Effective Supervision to Evidence-Based Practice in Probation," *Journal of Offender Rehabilitation,* vol. 47, no. 3 (2008), pp. 220–247.

13. Mario Paparozzi and Matthew DeMichele, "Probation and Parole: Overworked, Misunderstood, and Under-Appreciated: But Why?" *The Howard Journal,* vol. 47, no. 3 (July 2008), pp. 275–296.

14. James A. Gondles Jr., "The Probation and Parole System Needs Our Help to Succeed," *Corrections Today,* vol. 65, no. 1 (February 2003), p. 8.

15. "Missouri Considers New Sentencing System," *Corrections Compendium,* vol. 29, no. 6 (November/December 2004), p. 39.

16. American Bar Association, *Standards Relating to Sentencing Alternatives and Procedures* (Chicago: American Bar Association, n.d.).

17. Mark Sanders, "Building Bridges Instead of Walls: Effective Cross-Cultural Counseling," *Corrections Today,* vol. 65, no. 1 (February 2003), pp. 58–59.

18. Peter Finn and Sarah Kuck, *Stress Among Probation and Parole Officers and What Can Be Done About It* (Washington, DC: U.S. Department of Justice, National Institute of Justice, 2005).

19. American Probation and Parole Association, *Caseload Standards for Probation and Parole* (Lexington, KY: APPA, September 2006), www.appa-net.org (accessed December 18, 2015).

20. Michelle Gaseau, *Mapping to Improve Supervision and Community Corrections,* October 23, 2000, www.corrections.com (accessed December 18, 2015); Jaishankar Karuppannan, "Mapping and Corrections: Management of Offenders with Geographic Information Systems," *Corrections Compendium,* vol. 30, no. 1 (January/February 2005), pp. 7–9, 31–33.

21. Peggy Burke, "Probation and Parole Violations: An Overview of Critical Issues," in Madeline M. Carter (ed.), *Responding to Probation and Parole Violators* (Washington, DC: National Institute of Corrections, April 2001), p. 6.

22. See, for example, Alex Piquero, "Cost-Benefit Analysis for Jail Alternatives and Jail," October 2010, criminology.fsu.edu/wp-content/uploads/Cost-Benefit-Analysis-for-Jail-Alternatives-and-Jail.pdf (accessed December 4, 2015); and Marc Santora, "City's Annual Cost Per Inmate Is $168,000, Study Finds," *The New York Times,* August 23, 2013, www.nytimes.com/2013/08/24/nyregion/citys-annual-cost-per-inmate-is-nearly-168000-study-says.html?_r=0 (accessed December 4, 2015).

23. Peter B. Wood and David C. May, "Prison, Reentry, and Offenders' Perceptions of Correctional Punishments," in Matthew S. Crow and John Ortiz Smykla (eds.), *Offender Reentry: Rethinking Criminology and Criminal Justice* (Boston: Jones & Bartlett, 2013), pp. 385–398.

24. Eric J. Wodahl, John H. Boman, and Brett E. Garland, "Responding to Probation and Parole Violations: Are Jail Sanctions More Effective Than Community-Based Graduated Sanctions?" *Journal of Criminal Justice,* vol. 43, no. 3 (May–June 2015), pp. 242–250.

25. *HOPE in Hawaii: Swift and Sure Changes in Probation* (Washington, DC: National Institute of Justice, June 2008); see also Angela Hawken and Mark Kleiman, *Managing Drug-Involved Probationers with Swift and Certain Sanctions: Evaluating Hawaii's HOPE* (Washington, DC: U.S. Department of Justice, National Institute of Justice, December 2009).

26. Mark Kleiman, "African Americans Suffer from High Rates of Incarceration and Crime: Here's How to Drastically Reduce Both," *Washington Monthly,* January/February 2013, www.washingtonmonthly.com (accessed January 19, 2013).

27. Burke, "Probation and Parole Violations," pp. 5–6.

28. Ibid., p. 5.

Chapter 5

1. Bonnie Malkin and Jessica Winch, "Oscar Pistorius Released from Prison in South Africa," October 20, 2015, www.telegraph.co.uk/ (accessed December 19, 2015).

2. See, for example, "Changing Public Attitudes Toward the Criminal Justice System," www.soros.org/initiatives/usprograms/focus/justice/articles_publications/publications/hartpoll_20020201 (accessed December 19, 2015); Marc Mauer, *Race to Incarcerate* (New York: Free Press, 2006), p. 13; Frank T. Cullen and Brenda A. Vose, "Public Support for Early Intervention: Is Child Saving a Habit of the Heart?" *Victims and Offenders,* vol. 2, no. 2 (2007), pp. 109–124; "The UConnPoll: Prison Crowding," University of Connecticut, Center for Survey Research and Analysis, March 8, 2004.

3. William H. DiMascio, *Seeking Justice: Crime and Punishment in America* (New York: Edna McConnell Clark Foundation, 1997), p. 43.

4. Pew Center on the States, "Public Attitudes on Crime and Punishment," www.pewcenteronthestates.org, September 2010 (accessed November 16, 2015); Pew Center on the States, "Public Opinion on Sentencing and Corrections Policy in America," www.pewcenteronthestates.org, March 2012 (accessed December 19, 2015).

5. Betsy A. Fulton, Susan Stone, and Paul Gendreau, *Restructuring Intensive Supervision Programs: Applying What Works* (Lexington, KY: American Probation and Parole Association, 1994).

6. Doris Layton MacKenzie, "Evidence-Based Corrections: Identifying What Works," *Crime & Delinquency,* vol. 46, no. 4 (October 2000), pp. 457–472.

7. Doris Layton MacKenzie, *What Works in Corrections: Reducing the Criminal Activities of Offenders and Delinquents* (New York: Cambridge University Press, 2006), p. 322; and Steve Aos, Marna Miller, and Elizabeth Drake, *Evidence-Based Public Policy Options to Reduce Future Prison Construction, Criminal Justice Costs, and Crime Rates* (Olympia, WA: State Institute for Public Policy, 2006), p. 6.

8. Joan Petersilia, Arthur J. Lurigio, and James M. Byrne, "Introduction," in James M. Byrne, Arthur J. Lurigio, and Joan Petersilia (eds.), *Smart Sentencing: The Emergence of Intermediate Sanctions* (Newbury Park, CA: Sage, 1992), pp. ix–x; Elizabeth Deschenes, Susan Turner, and Joan Petersilia, *Intensive Community Supervision in Minnesota: A Dual Experiment in Prison Diversion and Enhanced*

Supervised Release (Washington, DC: National Institute of Justice, 1995); Joan Petersilia and Susan Turner, *Evaluating Intensive Supervision Probation/Parole: Results of a Nationwide Experiment* (Washington, DC: National Institute of Justice, May 1993).

9. Aos, Miller, and Drake, *Evidence-Based Public Policy Options.*

10. "Washington State Researchers Rates What Works in Treatment," *Criminal Justice Newsletter,* September 1, 2006, p. 2.

11. See http://crimesolutions.gov (accessed December 19, 2015).

12. "Washington State Researchers Rates What Works in Treatment," *Criminal Justice Newsletter.*

13. National Association of Drug Court Professionals, www.nadcp.org/whatis/ (accessed December 19, 2015).

14. West Huddleston and Douglas B. Marlowe, *Painting the Current Picture: A National Report on Drug Courts and Other Problem-Solving Court Programs in the United States* (Alexandria, VA: National Drug Court Institute, 2011).

15. "Types of Drug Courts," National Association of Drug Court Professionals, www.nadcp.org (accessed December 19, 2015).

16. "New Data Shows Veterans Treatment Court Surge," Justice For Vets, www.justiceforvets.org (accessed December 19, 2015).

17. Aos, Miller, and Drake, *Evidence-Based Public Policy Options;* Christopher T. Lowenkamp, Alexander M. Holsinger, and Edward J. Latessa, "Are Drug Courts Effective: A Meta-Analytic Review," *Journal of Community Corrections,* vol. 28 (Fall 2005), pp. 5–10; Deborah Koetzle Shaffer, *Reconsidering Drug Court Effectiveness: A Meta-Analytic Review* (Las Vegas, NV: Department of Criminal Justice, University of Nevada, 2006); David B. Wilson, Ojmarrh Mitchell, and Doris Layton MacKenzie, "A Systematic Review of Drug Court Effects on Recidivism," *Journal of Experimental Criminology,* vol. 2, no. 4 (November 2006), pp. 459–487; Doris Layton MacKenzie, *What Works in Corrections: Reducing the Criminal Activities of Offenders and Delinquents,* pp. 221–240. M. Finigan, S. M. Carey, and A. Cox, *The Impact of a Mature Drug Court Over 10 Years of Operation* (Portland, OR: NPC Research, 2007); D. C. Gottfredson, B. W. Kearley, S. S. Najaka and C. M. Rocha, "The Baltimore City Drug Treatment Court: 3-Year Outcome Study," *Evaluation Review,* 29, pp. 42–64; D. C. Gottfredson, S. S. Najaka, B. W. Kearley, and C. M. Rocha, "Long-term Effects of Participation in the Baltimore City Drug Court Treatment Court: Results from an Experimental Study," *Journal of Experimental Criminology,* 2, pp. 67–98.

18. Aos, Miller, and Drake, *Evidence-Based Public Policy Options.*

19. "Drug Courts Unavailable to Most," *Corrections Today,* vol. 71, no. 6 (December 2009), p. 16; and Sam Hananel, "Drug Courts Successful for Few Who Get It," *The Washington Post,* November 30, 2009, www.washingtonpost.com (accessed December 19, 2015).

20. Bureau of Justice Assistance, *How to Use Structured Fines (Day Fines) as an Intermediate Sanction* (Washington, DC: Department of Justice, November 1996).

21. "Finn's Speed Fine Is a Bit Rich," MSNBC online, http://news.bbc.co.uk/2/hi/business/3477285.stm (accessed December 19, 2015); "Sentencing Law and Policy," May 12, 2009 and December 1, 2009, sentencing.typepad.com (accessed December 19, 2015).

22. Aos, Miller, and Drake, *Evidence-Based Public Policy Options,* p. 9.

23. Michael Tonry, "Parochialism in U.S. Sentencing Policy," *Crime & Delinquency,* vol. 45, no. 1 (1999), p. 58.

24. DiMascio, *Seeking Justice,* pp. 43–45.

25. Ibid., p. 37.

26. Dale G. Parent et al., *Day Reporting Centers* (Washington, DC: National Institute of Justice, 1995).

27. Michael Ostermann, "An Analysis of New Jersey's Day Reporting Center and Halfway Back Programs: Embracing the Rehabilitative Ideal Through Evidence-Based Practices," *Journal of Offender Rehabilitation,* vol. 48 (2009), pp. 139–153.

28. Douglas J. Boyle, Laura M. Ragusa-Salerno, Jennifer L. Lanterman, and Andrea Fleisch Marcus, "An Evaluation of Day Reporting

Centers for Parolees," *Criminology & Public Policy,* vol. 12, no. 1 (2013), pp. 119–143.

29. Pew Charitable Trusts, *Public Safety, Public Spending: Forecasting America's Prison Population 2007–2011* (Philadelphia, PA: Pew Charitable Trusts, 2007).

30. Robert S. Gable and Kirkland R. Gable, "The Practical Limitations and Positive Potential of Electronic Monitoring," *Corrections Compendium,* vol. 32, no. 5 (September/October 2007), pp. 6–8, 40–42.

31. Joseph Shapiro, "As Court Fees Rise, the Poor Are Paying the Price," National Public Radio, May 23, 2014, www.npr.org/2014/05/19/312516/increasing-court-fees-punish-the-poor (accessed December 22, 2015).

32. Todd D. Minton and Zhen Zeng, *Jail Inmates at Midyear 2014* (Washington, DC: U.S. Department of Justice, Bureau of Justice Statistics, June 2015).

33. Eric Markowitz, "Chain Gang 2.0: If You Can't Afford This GPS Ankle Bracelet, You Get Thrown in Jail," *International Business Times,* September 21, 2015, www.ibtimes.com/chain-gang-20-if-you-cant-afford-gps-ankle-bracelet-you-get-thrown-jail-2065283 (accessed December 22, 2015).

34. Darren Gowen, "Overview of the Federal Home Confinement Program, 1988–1996," *Federal Probation,* vol. 64, no. 2 (December 2000), pp. 11–18; see also Brian K. Payne and Randy R. Gainey, "The Electronic Monitoring of Offenders Released from Jail or Prison: Safety, Control, and Comparisons to the Incarceration Experience," *The Prison Journal,* vol. 84, no. 4 (December 2004), pp. 413–435.

35. William Bales, Karen Mann, Thomas Blomberg, Gerry Gaes, Kelle Barrick, Karla Dhungana, and Brian McManus, *A Quantitative and Qualitative Assessment of Electronic Monitoring* (Washington, DC: U.S. Department of Justice, National Institute of Justice, January 2011).

36. Layton MacKenzie, *What Works in Corrections,* p. 322.

37. Ibid., p. 335; see also William D. Burrell and Robert S. Gable, "From B. F. Skinner to Spiderman to Martha Stewart: The Past, Present and Future of Electronic Monitoring of Offenders," *Journal of Offender Rehabilitation,* vol. 46, no. 3/4 (2008), pp. 101–118.

38. "Nationwide RRC Contracts," https://www.bop.gov/about/facilities/residential_reentry_management_centers.jsp (accessed December 22, 2015).

39. Division of Criminal Justice, Office of Research and Statistics, *Executive Summary: 2000 Community Corrections Study Results* (Denver: State of Colorado, Division of Criminal Justice, Office of Research and Statistics, March 22, 2001), www.cdpsweb.state.co.us/ors/docs.htm (accessed December 22, 2015).

40. Christopher T. Lowenkamp and Edward J. Latessa, "Developing Successful Reentry Programs: Lessons Learned from the 'What Works' Research," *Corrections Today,* vol. 67, no. 2 (April 2005), pp. 72–77; and "Halfway Houses Seen as Way to Cut Prison Costs in Ohio," www.cleveland.com/metro (accessed December 22, 2015).

41. Aos, Miller, and Drake, *Evidence-Based Public Policy Options.*

42. Steve Schultze, "Clarke Drops Plan for Early Prisoner Release," *Journal Sentinel* (Milwaukee, WI), January 27, 2010, www.jsonline.com; and Steve Schultze, "Milwaukee County's Inmate Training Program Raising Concerns," *Journal Sentinel* (Milwaukee, WI), December 5, 2010, www.jsonline.com (accessed December 22, 2015).

43. Merry Morash and Lila Rucker, "Critical Look at the Idea of Boot Camp as Correctional Reform," *Crime & Delinquency,* vol. 36 (1990), pp. 204–222; DiMascio, *Seeking Justice,* p. 41.

44. Doris L. MacKenzie and J. W. Shaw, "The Impact of Shock Incarceration on Technical Violations and New Criminal Activities," *Justice Quarterly,* vol. 10, no. 3 (1993), pp. 463–486.

45. Dionne T. Wright and G. Larry Mays, "Correctional Boot Camps, Attitudes, and Recidivism: The Oklahoma Experience," *Journal of Offender Rehabilitation,* vol. 28, no. 1/2 (1998), pp. 71–87.

46. Jeanne B. Stinchcomb and W. Clinton Terry III, "Predicting the Likelihood of Rearrest Among Shock Incarceration Graduates: Moving Beyond Another Nail in the Boot Camp Coffin," *Crime & Delinquency,* vol. 47, no. 2 (April 2001), pp. 221–242.

47. See, for example, Cheryl L. Clark and David W. Aziz, "Shock Incarceration in New York State: Philosophy, Results, and Limitations," in Doris L. MacKenzie and Eugene E. Hebert (eds.), *Correctional Boot Camps: A Tough Intermediate Sanction* (Washington, DC: National Institute of Justice, 1996), pp. 38–68; MacKenzie and Hebert, *Correctional Boot Camps;* Parent, *Correctional Boot Camps.*

48. Dale Parent, "Boot Camps Failing to Achieve Goals," *Overcrowded Times,* vol. 5 (1994), pp. 8–11; Doris Layton MacKenzie, "Boot Camps: A National Assessment," *Overcrowded Times,* vol. 5 (1994), pp. 14–18; Philip A. Ethridge and Jonathan R. Sorensen, "An Analysis of Attitudinal Change and Community Adjustment Among Probationers in a County Boot Camp," *Journal of Contemporary Criminal Justice,* vol. 13, no. 2 (May 1992), pp. 139–154.

49. W. J. Dickey, *Evaluating Boot Camp Prisons* (Washington, DC: National Institute of Justice, 1994); Peter Katel and Melinda Liu, "The Bust in Boot Camps," *Newsweek,* February 21, 1994, p. 26; Parent, "Boot Camps Failing to Achieve Goals."

50. Doris L. MacKenzie and Claire Souryal, *Multi-Site Evaluation of Shock Incarceration: Executive Summary* (Washington, DC: National Institute of Justice, 1994); see also Doris L. MacKenzie and A. Piquero, "The Impact of Shock Incarceration Programs on Prison Crowding," *Crime & Delinquency,* vol. 40 (1994), pp. 222–249.

51. E. Ann Carson, *Prisoners in 2014* (Washington, DC: U.S. Department of Justice, Bureau of Justice Statistics, September 2015).

52. *Minnesota's Community Corrections Act Counties: Doing What Works to Keep Our Communities Safe,* www.maccac.org/WhatWorks Brochure.pdf (accessed November 27, 2015).

53. Christopher Hartney and Susan Marchionna, *Attitudes of U.S. Voters Toward Nonserious Offenders and Alternatives to Incarceration* (Oakland, CA: National Council on Crime and Delinquency, June 2009).

54. George F. Cole et al., *The Practice and Attitudes of Trial Court Judges Regarding Fines as a Criminal Sanction* (Washington, DC: National Institute of Justice, 1987).

Chapter 6

1. Matt Coyne and Michael D'Onofrio, "Rapper DMX Arrested for Failure to Pay Child Support," *USA Today,* October 28, 2015, www.usatoday.com/story/life/nation-now/2015/10/28/dmx-child-support-arrest/74768980/ (accessed December 22, 2015); Danielle Harling, "DMX Struck with Arrest Warrant: Rapper's Team Responds," *HipHopDX,* December 15, 2015, hiphopdx.com/news/id.36657/title.dmx-struck-with-arrest-warrant (accessed December 22, 2015).

2. Nick Wing, "Our Bail System Is Leaving Innocent People to Die in Jail Because They're Poor," *Huffington Post,* July 14, 2016, http://www.huffingtonpost.com/entry/cash-bail-jail-deaths_us_57851f50e4b0e05f052381cb?utm_content=buffer5da8e&utm_medium=social&utm_source=twitter.com&utm_campaign=buffer (accessed August 15, 2016).

3. Salvador Rizzo, "Chief Justice Rabner Pushes for Reforms to N.J. Courts," *The Star Ledger,* May 21, 2013, www.nj.com/politics/index.ssf/2013/05/chief_justice_rabner_pushes_fo.html#incart_m-rpt-2 (accessed December 23, 2015).

4. "Pretrial Criminal Justice Research," Laura and John Arnold Foundation, November 2013, http://www.arnoldfoundation.org/wp-content/uploads/2014/02/LJAF-Pretrial-CJ-Research-brief_FNL.pdf (accessed December 22, 2015).

5. Melissa Neal, *Bail Fail: Why the U.S. Should End the Practice of Using Money for Bail* (Washington, DC: Justice Policy Institute, 2012), p. 13.

6. Ibid., p. 21.

7. Jonathan Lippman, *2013 State of the Judiciary, Let Justice Be Done* (Albany, NY: Court of Appeals Hall, 2013), pp. 5–6.

8. Shaila Dewan, "Judges Replacing Conjecture with Formula for Bail," *The New York Times,* June 26, 2015, www.nytimes.com/2015/06/27/us/turning-the-granting-of-bail-into-a-science.html?_r50 (accessed December 23, 2015).

9. As cited in Melissa Neal, *Bail Fail,* p. 31.

10. Michael O'Toole, "Jails and Prisons: The Numbers Say They Are More Different Than Generally Assumed," *American Jails,* www.corrections.com/aja/mags/articles/toole.html (accessed March 7, 2013); see also Daron Hall, "Jails vs. Prisons," *Corrections Today,* vol. 68, no. 1 (February 2006) p. 8.

11. Ram Subramanian, Ruth Delaney, Stephen Roberts, Nancy Fishman, and Peggy McGarry, *Incarceration's Front Door: The Misuse of Jails in America* (New York: Vera Institute of Justice, February 2015); Marilyn Chandler Ford, "Frequent Fliers: The High Demand User in Local Corrections," *California Journal of Health Promotion,* vol. 3, no. 2 (2005), pp. 61–71.

12. Todd D. Minton and Zhen Zeng, *Jail Inmates at Midyear 2014* (Washington, DC: Bureau of Justice Statistics, June 2015).

13. Doris J. James, *Profile of Jail Inmates, 2002* (Washington, DC: U.S. Department of Justice, Bureau of Justice Statistics, July 2004); Allen J. Beck, "What Do We Know About Jails at the National Level?" Presentation at the Jail Reentry Roundtable, Urban Institute, Washington, DC, June 27, 2006.

14. Marilyn D. McShane and Frank P. Williams III (eds.), *Encyclopedia of American Prisons* (New York: Garland, 1996), p. 494.

15. David M. Parrish, "The Evolution of Direct Supervision in the Design and Operation of Jails," *Corrections Today,* www.corrections.com/aca/cortoday/october00/parrish.html (accessed December 23, 2015).

16. Linda Zupan, *Jails: Reform and the New Generation Philosophy* (Cincinnati, OH: Anderson, 1991); see also Richard Wener, "The Invention of Direct Supervision," *Corrections Compendium,* vol. 30, no. 2 (March/April, 2005), pp. 4–7, 32–34.

17. Brandon K. Applegate and Eugene A. Paoline III, "Jail Officers' Perceptions of the Work Environment in Traditional Versus New Generation Facilities," *American Journal of Criminal Justice,* vol. 31 (2007), pp. 64–80.

18. Dennis McCave, "Testing the Seams: When the Limits Are Pushed in Direct Supervision," *American Jails,* vol. 16, no. 1 (2002), pp. 51–56.

19. Peter Perroncello, "Direct Supervision: A 2001 Odyssey," *American Jails,* vol. 15, no. 6 (2001), p. 25. See also Constance Clem et al., *Direct Supervision Jails: 2006 Sourcebook* (Longmont, CO: National Institute of Corrections Information Center, September 2006); Christine Tartaro, "Are They Really Direct Supervision Jails? A National Study," *American Jails,* vol. 20, no. 5 (November/December 2006), pp. 9–17.

20. Ken Kerle, "Jail Statistics: The Need for Public Education," *American Jails* (September/October 2006), p. 5.

21. Doris J. James, *Profile of Jail Inmates, 2002* (Washington, DC: U.S. Department of Justice, Bureau of Justice Statistics, July 2004).

22. James Austin, Luiza Chan, and Williams Elms, *Women Classification Study—Indiana Department of Corrections* (San Francisco, CA: National Council on Crime and Delinquency, 1993).

23. James, *Profile of Jail Inmates, 2002;* see also Gail Elias and Kenneth Ricci, *Women in Jail: Facility Planning Issues* (Washington, DC: U.S. Department of Justice, National Institute of Corrections, March 1997).

24. Tim Brennan and James Austin, *Women in Jail: Classification Issues* (Washington, DC: U.S. Department of Justice, National Institute of Corrections, March 1997).

25. Merry Morash, Timothy S. Bynum, and Barbara A. Koons, *Women Offenders: Programming Needs and Promising Approaches* (Washington, DC: U.S. Department of Justice, National Institute of Justice, August 1998).

26. William C. Collins and Andrew W. Collins, *Women in Jail: Legal Issues* (Washington, DC: U.S. Department of Justice, National Institute of Corrections, December 1996).

27. Rich Lord, "ACLU Study Faults Jails on Women's Health Care," *Pittsburgh Post-Gazette*, February 16, 2012, www.post-gazette.com (accessed December 26, 2015).

28. Todd D. Minton, Scott Ginder, Susan M. Brumbaugh, Hope Smiley-McDonald, and Harley Rohloff, *Census of Jails: Population Changes, 1999–2013* (Washington, DC: Bureau of Justice Statistics, December 2015).

29. Kenneth Kerle, "Women in the American World of Jails: Inmates and Staff," *Margins: Maryland's Law Journal on Race, Religion, Gender, and Class*, vol. 2, no. 1 (Spring 2002), pp. 41–61.

30. Barbara Bloom, Barbara Owen, and Stephanie Covington, *Gender-Responsiveness Strategies Research, Practice, and Guiding Principles for Women Offenders* (Washington, DC: U.S. Department of Justice, National Institute of Corrections, June 2003); Tara Gray, G. Larry Mays, and Mary K. Stohr, "Inmate Needs and Programming in Exclusively Women's Jails," *Prison Journal*, vol. 75, no. 2 (1995), pp. 186–195.

31. Stevyn Fogg, "Female Inmates in Jail Settings: Identifying Challenges and Critical Issues," *American Jails*, vol. 26, no. 6 (January/February 2014), pp. 12–16.

32. Samuel Walker, Cassia Spohn, and Miriam DeLone, "Corrections: A Picture in Black and White," in Tara Gray (ed.), *Exploring Corrections* (Boston: Allyn & Bacon, 2002), pp. 13–24.

33. Michael Tonry, *Malign Neglect* (New York: Oxford University Press, 1995); *Targeting Blacks: Drug Law Enforcement and Race in the United States* (New York: Human Rights Watch, 2008); and Ryan S. King, *Disparity by Geography: The War on Drugs in America's Cities* (Washington, DC: The Sentencing Project, 2008).

34. Walker, Spohn, and DeLone, "Corrections," p. 16.

35. Doris J. James and Lauren E. Glaze, *Mental Health Problems of Prison and Jail Inmates* (Washington, DC: U.S. Department of Justice, Bureau of Justice Statistics, September 2006).

36. Henry J. Steadman, Fred C. Osher, Pamela Clark Robbins, Brian Case, and Steven Samuels, "Prevalence of Serious Mental Illness Among Jail Inmates," *Psychiatric Services*, vol. 60, no. 6 (June 2009), pp. 761–765.

37. Doris J. James and Lauren Glaze, *Mental Health Problems of Prison and Jail Inmates* (Washington, DC: Bureau of Justice Statistics, 2006).

38. Henry J. Steadman, Fred C. Osher, Pamela Clark Robbins, Brian Case, and Steven Samuels, "Prevalence of Serious Mental Illness Among Jail Inmates."

39. Sally Satel, "Out of the Asylum, Into the Cell," *The New York Times*, November 1, 2003, www.psychlaws.org/GeneralResources/article199.htm (accessed January 13, 2007); Bazelon Center for Mental Health Law, "Lawsuit Alleges Civil Rights Violations in Cook County Jail," August 12, 2003, www.bazelon.org/newsroom/archive/2003/8-12-03cookcounty (accessed December 27, 2015).

40. James A. Gondles, "The Mentally Ill Don't Belong in Jail," *Corrections Today*, vol. 67, no. 2 (April 2005), p. 6.

41. Lance Couturier, Frederick Maue, and Catherine McVey, "Releasing Inmates with Mental Illness and Co-occurring Disorders into the Community," *Corrections Today*, vol. 67, no. 2 (April 2005).

42. Kenneth E. Kerle, *Exploring Jail Operations* (Hagerstown, MD: American Jail Association, 2003), p. 31.

43. Ken Kerle, "The Mentally Ill and Crisis Intervention Teams: Reflections on Jails and the U.S. Mental Health Challenge," *The Prison Journal*, vol. 96 (January 2016), pp. 153–161.

44. Amy C. Watson and Anjali J. Fulambarker, "The Crisis Intervention Team Model of Police Response to Mental Health Crises: A Primer for Mental Health Practitioners," *Best Practices in Mental Health*, vol. 8, no. 2 (December 2012), pp. 1–8.

45. Margaret Noonan, Harley Rohloff, and Scott Ginder, *Mortality in Local Jails and State Prisons, 2000–2013—Statistical Tables* (Washington, DC: Bureau of Justice Statistics, August 2015).

46. Frank Main, "Psychologist Hired to Run Cook County Jail," *Chicago Sun-Times*, May 19, 2015, chicago.suntimes.com/news/7/71/618900/psychologist-hired-run-cook-county-jail (accessed May 21, 2015).

47. Johnathan Silver, "New Statewide Jail Form Aimed at Suicide Risks," *The Texas Tribune*, November 13, 2015, www.texastribune.org/2015/11/13/county-jails-adopt-revised-intake-form-next-month/ (accessed December 28, 2015).

48. Connie Milligan and Ray Sabbatine, "From Public Crisis to Innovation—The Mental Health Crisis Network," *American Jails*, vol. 21, no. 6 (January/February 2008), pp. 9–14.

49. *PREA Data Collection Activities, 2013* (Washington, DC: Bureau of Justice Statistics, June 2013).

50. G. J. Mazza, *Report on Sexual Victimization in Prisons and Jails: Review Panel on Prison Rape* (Washington, DC: Department of Justice, April 2012).

51. James J. Stephan and Georgette Walsh, *Census of Jails, 2006* (Washington, DC: U.S. Department of Justice, Bureau of Justice Statistics, December 2011).

52. Todd D. Minton and Zhen Zeng, *Jail Inmates at Midyear 2014*.

53. Christian Henrichson, Joshua Rinaldi, and Ruth Delaney, *The Price of Jails: Measuring the Taxpayer Cost of Local Incarceration* (New York: Vera Institute of Justice, May 2015).

54. American Correctional Association, Vital Statistics in Corrections (Lanham, MD: ACA, 2000), p. 26. See also Nicolas Median Mora, "New York Jails Cost Twice as Much as What the City Says They Cost," *BuzzFeed News*, May 21, 2015, www.buzzfeed.com/nicolasmedinamora/new-york-jails-cost-twice-as-much-as-what-the-city-says-they#.meLG722Wm (accessed December 29, 2015).

55. Lauren-Brooke Eisen, *Paying for Your Time: How Charging Inmate Fees Behind Bars May Violate the Excessive Fines Clause* (New York: Brennan Center for Justice, New York University School of Law, July 2014).

56. Jennifer Steinhauer, "For $82 a Day, Booking a Cell in a 5-Star Jail," *The New York Times*, April 29, 2007, www.nytimes.com (accessed December 29, 2015); Jennifer Steinhauer, "Some Jails Let Prisoners Pay to Stay in Nicer Surroundings," *The San Diego Union-Tribune*, April 29, 2007, www.signonsandiego.com (accessed December 29, 2015); Larry Welborn and Eric Carpenter, "Jaramillo Wants to Pay for Jail," *The Orange County Register*, March 3, 2007, www.ocregister.com (accessed December 29, 2015). See also the Web sites of the Huntington Beach (CA) police department, Torrence (CA) police department, and Santa Ana (CA) police department. Beverly Hills Police Department opened its pay-to-stay jail in late 2009.

57. Alex Doobuzinskis, "$85-a-Night Jail a Hit with L.A.'s Celebrity Convicts," www.prisonlegalnews.org (accessed December 29, 2015).

58. Jeanne B. Stinchcomb and Susan W. Campbell, *Jail Leaders Speak: Current and Future Challenges to Jail Operations and Administration* (Washington, DC: U.S. Department of Justice, Bureau of Justice Statistics, 2008). Susan W. McCampbell, "Priorities of the Day," *American Jails*, vol. 26, no. 6 (January/February 2013), pp. 15–19.

59. As cited in National Institute of Corrections, *Briefing Paper: Trends in Jail Privatization* (Boulder, CO: National Institute of Corrections Information Center, February 1992).

60. Christine Tartaro and Marissa P. Levy, "Factors Associated with Recidivism Among Reentry Program Participants in the Jail Setting: Results and Recommendations," in Matthew S. Crow and John Ortiz Smykla, *Offender Reentry: Rethinking Criminology and Criminal Justice* (Boston, MA: Jones & Bartlett, 2014), pp. 125–146.

61. James Parsons, "Addressing the Unique Challenges of Jail Reentry," in Matthew S. Crow and John Ortiz Smykla, *Offender Reentry: Rethinking Criminology and Criminal Justice* (Boston, MA: 2014), pp. 104–123.

62. Doris J. James, *Profile of Jail Inmates, 2002* (Washington, DC: Bureau of Justice Statistics, October 2004), p. 2.

63. Rod Miller, "When Jail Inmates Work Everyone Wins," *American Jails*, vol. 24, no 3 (July/August 2010), pp. 8–16.

64. Kenneth E. Kerle, *Exploring Jail Operations*, p. 128.

65. American Bar Association, Criminal Justice Section, Report to the House of Delegates, August 21, 2008, www.abanet.org/crimjust/policy/am08104b.pdf-2008-08-21 (accessed January 20, 2011).

66. Peter D. Friedman, Faye S. Taxman, and Craig E. Handerson, "Evidence-Based Treatment Practices for Drug-Involved Adults in the Criminal Justices System," *Journal of Substance Abuse Treatment,* vol. 32, no. 3 (April 2007), pp. 267–277.

67. Mike Males, *Realignment and Crime in 2014: California's Violent Crime in Decline* (San Francisco, CA: Center on Juvenile and Criminal Justice, August 2015).

Chapter 7

1. Bill Chappell, "Jared Fogle Sentenced to 15 Years in Prison for Sex with Minors, Child Pornography," *NPR,* November 19, 2015, www.npr.org/sections/thetwo-way/2015/11/19/456622271/jared-fogle-to-learn-sentence-for-sex-with-minors-child-pornography (accessed December 20, 2015); Yaron Steinbuch, "Jared Fogle Pleads Guilty, Blames Diet for His Sex Crimes," *New York Post,* November 19, 2015, nypost.com/2015/11/19/subways-jared-pleads-guilty-to-kiddie-porn-and-sex-crime-charges/ (accessed December 20, 2015); Meg Wagner, "Ex-Subway Pitchman Jared Fogle Was Absent Father, Skipped Time with Own Children to Travel: Divorce Records," *New York Daily News,* November 26, 2015, www.nydailynews.com/news/national/jared-fogle-skipped-time-kids-travel-divorce-record-article-1.2447569 (accessed December 20, 2015).

2. E. Ann Carson, *Prisoners in 2014* (Washington, DC: U.S. Department of Justice, Bureau of Justice Statistics, September 2015).

3. Roy Walmsley, *World Prison Population List,* 8th ed. (London: Kings College, University of London, January 2009), www.prisonstudies.org (accessed January 6, 2016).

4. Federal Bureau of Investigation, "Crime in the United States 2014," www.fbi.gov/about-us/cjis/ucr/crime-in-the-u.s/2014/crime-in-the-u.s.-2014/tables/table-5 (accessed January 6, 2016); Carson, *Prisoners in 2014.*

5. Andrew Coyle, "The Use and Abuse of Prison Around the World," *Corrections Today* (December 2004), pp. 64–67; see also David A. Bowers and Jerold L. Waltman, "Do More Conservative States Impose Harsher Felony Sentences? An Exploratory Analysis of 32 States," *Criminal Justice Review,* vol. 18, no. 1 (Spring 1993), pp. 61–70.

6. Danielle Kaeble, Lauren Glaze, Anastasios Tsoutis, and Todd Minton, *Correctional Populations in the United States, 2014* (Washington, DC: Bureau of Justice Statistics, December 2015); E. Ann Carson and William J. Sabol, *Prisoners in 2011* (Washington, DC: U.S. Department of Justice, Bureau of Justice Statistics, December 2012); James J. Stephan and Jennifer C. Karberg, *Census of State and Federal Facilities, 2000* (Washington, DC: U.S. Department of Justice, Bureau of Justice Statistics, October 2003); and James J. Stephen, *Census of State and Federal Correctional Facilities, 2005* (Washington, DC: U.S. Department of Justice, Bureau of Justice Statistics, October 2008).

7. Marc Mauer, "Addressing Racial Disparities in Incarceration," *The Prison Journal,* vol. 91, no. 3 (2011), pp. 87–101.

8. Aleks Kajstura and Russ Immarigeon, *States of Women's Incarceration: The Global Context* (Northampton, MA: Prison Policy Initiative, n.d.), www.prisonpolicy.org/ (accessed January 6, 2016).

9. Beth R. Richie, "Challenges Incarcerated Women Face as They Return to Their Communities: Findings from Life History Interviews," *Crime & Delinquency,* vol. 47, no. 3 (July 2001), pp. 368–389; and Elaine A. Lord, "The Challenges of Mentally Ill Offenders in Prison," *Criminal Justice and Behavior,* vol. 35, no. 8 (August 2008), pp. 928–942.

10. Meda Chesney-Lind, "Putting the Breaks on the Building Binge," *Corrections Today,* vol. 54, no. 6 (August 1992), p. 30.

11. Mauer, "Addressing Racial Disparities in Incarceration."

12. Steve Miletich, "Two State Supreme Court Justices Stun Some Listeners with Race Comments," *The Seattle Times,* October 22, 2010, seattletimes.nwsource.com (accessed January 6, 2016).

13. Cassia Spohn, *Thirty Years of Sentencing Reform: The Quest for a Racially Neutral Sentencing Process* (Washington, DC: U.S. Department of Justice, National Institute of Justice, 2000); Phillip Beatty, Amanda Petteruti, and Jason Ziedenberg, *The Vortex: The Concentrated Racial Impact of Drug Imprisonment and the Characteristics of Punitive Counties* (Washington, DC: Justice Policy Institute, 2007); Ryan S. King, *Disparity by Geography: The War on Drugs in America's Cities* (Washington, DC: The Sentencing Project, May 2008).

14. Steve Aos, Marna Miller, and Elizabeth Drake, *Evidence-Based Public Policy Options to Reduce Future Prison Construction, Criminal Justice Costs, and Crime Rates* (Olympia, WA: State Institute for Public Policy, 2006).

15. Aos, Miller, and Drake, *Evidence-Based Public Policy Options.*

16. Bureau of Justice Assistance, *Prison Industry Enhancement Certification Program,* www.bja.gov/ProgramDetails.aspx?Program_ID=73 (accessed January 8, 2016).

17. W. Saylor and G. Gaes, *Study of "Rehabilitating" Inmates Through Industrial Work Participation, and Vocational and Apprenticeship Training* (Washington, DC: Federal Bureau of Prisons, 1996); Joseph Summerill, "Congress Continues to Dismantle UNICOR," *Corrections Today,* vol. 67, no. 4 (July 2005) pp. 26–27, 30.

18. "Pathways from Prison to Postsecondary Education Project," A project announcement by the Vera Institute of Justice, New York, 2013.

19. "Inmate Education Programs," *Corrections Compendium,* vol. 33, no. 3 (May/June 2008), p. 9.

20. Anne F. Parkinson and Stephen J. Steurer, "Overcoming the Obstacles in Effective Correctional Instruction," *Corrections Today,* vol. 66, no. 2 (April 2004), pp. 88–91.

21. Jamaal Abdul-Alim, "Exploring the Use of Pell Grants to Go from Prison to College," *Juvenile Justice Information Exchange,* December 10, 2012, www.jjie.org (accessed January 9, 2016).

22. Ibid.

23. Lois M. Davis, Robert Bozick, Jennifer L. Steele, Jessica Saunders, and Jeremy N. V. Miles, *Evaluating the Effectiveness of Correctional Education* (Santa Monica, CA: Rand Corporation, 2013).

24. James J. Stephan, *Census of State and Federal Correctional Facilities, 2005* (Washington, DC: U.S. Department of Justice, Bureau of Justice Statistics, October 2008).

25. Excerpted from California and South Dakota's departments of corrections Web sites (accessed January 10, 2016).

26. Stephan, *Census of State and Federal Correctional Facilities 2005,* p. 12; Jon Ortiz, "Fiscal Changes Hit Prison Officers Union Hard," *The Sacramento Bee,* June 28, 2009, www.sacbee.com (accessed January 10, 2016).

27. American Correctional Association, "Correctional Officer Wages and Benefits," *Corrections Compendium,* vol. 35, no. 2 (Summer 2010), pp. 21–39.

28. "The Cost of a Nation of Incarceration," *CBS NEWS Sunday Morning,* www.cbsnews.com, April 22, 2012 (accessed January 10, 2016).

29. *The Continuing Fiscal Crisis in Corrections: Setting a New Course* (New York: Vera Institute of Justice, October 2010), p. 7.

30. Jennifer Gonnerman, "An Expert Analyzes the Prison Population Boom" *Village Voice,* February 22, 2000, p. 56; and Pew Center on the States, *One in 31: The Long Reach in American Corrections* (New York: Pew Charitable Trusts, March 2009), p. 20.

31. Pew Charitable Trusts, *Public Safety, Public Spending: Forecasting America's Prison Population 2007–2011* (Philadelphia: Pew Charitable Trusts, 2007).

32. Vera Institute of Justice, *The Potential of Community Corrections to Improve Safety and Reduce Incarceration* (New York: Vera Institute of Justice, July 2013).

33. Nicole D. Porter, *On the Chopping Block 2012: State Prison Closings* (Washington, DC: The Sentencing Project, December 2012) and The

Sentencing Project, *Life Goes On: The Historic Rise in Life Sentences in America* (Washington, DC: The Sentencing Project, September 2013).

34. Urban Institute, *The Justice Reinvestment Initiative: Experience from the States* (Washington, DC: Urban Institute, 2012).

35. Nathan James, *The Federal Prison Population Buildup: Overview, Policy Changes, Issues, and Options* (Washington, DC: Congressional Research Service, January 22, 2013), p. 15.

36. Annual incarceration costs vary by jurisdiction. Federal estimates are provided here. See Nathan James, *The Federal Prison Population Buildup: Overview, Policy Changes, Issues, and Options*, p. 15.

37. Dana Goldstein, "How to Cut the Prison Population by 50 Percent," The Marshall Project, www.themarshallproject.org/2015/03/04/how-to-cut-the-prison-population-by-50-percent#.0uU4zytKm (accessed January 11, 2016).

38. See, Hope Metcalf, Jamelia Morgan, Samuel Oliker-Friedland, Judith Resnik, Julia Spiegel, Haran Tae, Alyssa Roxanne Work, and Brian Holbrook, "Administrative Segregation, Degrees of Isolation, and Incarceration: A National Overview of State and Federal Correctional Policies," Yale Law School, Public Law Working Paper No. 301, for an overview of state and federal policies related to long-term isolation of inmates, the commonalities and variations among jurisdictions, comparisons across jurisdictions, and consideration of how and when administrative segregation is and should be used. See also, Richard H. McCleery, "Authoritarianism and the Belief System of Incorrigibles," in Donald R. Cressy (ed.), *The Prison: Studies in Institutional Organization and Change* (New York: Holt, Rinehart & Winston, 1961), pp. 260–306; *Wright* v. *Enomoto* (July 23, 1980), pp. 5, 15; *Madrid* v. *Gomez*, 889 F. Supp. 1146 (N.D. Cal. 1995); Craig Haney, "Infamous Punishment: The Psychological Consequences of Isolation," *National Prison Project Journal* (Spring 1993); Craig Haney, "A Culture of Harm: Taming the Dynamics of Cruelty in Supermax Prisons," *Criminal Justice and Behavior*, vol. 35, no. 8 (August 2008), pp. 956–984; David Lovell, "Patterns of Disturbed Behavior in a Supermax Population," *Criminal Justice and Behavior*, vol. 35, no. 8 (August 2008), pp. 985–1004.

39. Paige St. John, "Report Decries Suicides, Isolation Cells in California Prisons," *Los Angeles Times*, September 27, 2012, www.latimes.com (accessed January 11, 2016).

40. George F. Will, "When Solitude Is Torture," *The Washington Post*, February 20, 2013, www.washingtonpost.com (accessed January 11, 2016).

41. As quoted in Corey Weinstein, "Even Dogs Confined to Cages for Long Periods of Time Go Berserk," in John P. May and Khalid R. Pitts (eds.), *Building Violence: How America's Rush to Incarcerate Creates More Violence* (Thousand Oaks, CA: Sage, 1999), p. 122.

42. Chad S. Briggs, Jody L. Sundt, and Thomas C. Castellano, "The Effect of Supermaximum Security Prisons on Aggregate Levels of Institutional Violence," *Criminology*, vol. 41, no. 4 (March 2006), pp. 1341–1376.

43. *Madrid* v. *Gomez*, 889 F. Supp. 1146 (N.D. Cal. 1995).

44. Maureen L. O'Keefe, Kelli J. Klebe, Alysha Stucker, Kristin Sturm, and William Leggett, *One Year Longitudinal Study of the Psychological Effects of Administrative Segregation* (Washington, DC: U.S. Department of Justice, National Institute of Justice, October 2010).

45. Susan Greene, "Questioning Study that Showed Inmates in Solitary Get Better," *Denver Post*, November 7, 2010, www.denverpost.com (accessed January 11, 2016).

46. "Federal Prisons Set Up E-mail Programs," *Corrections Compendium*, vol. 33, no. 5 (September/October 2008), p. 35.

47. Sarah Wheaton, "Inmates in Georgia Prisons Use Contraband Phones to Protest," *The New York Times*, December 12, 2010, www.nytimes.com (accessed January 11, 2016); Kim Severson and Robbie Brown, "Outlawed, Cellphones Are Thriving in Prisons," *The New York Times*, January 2, 2011, www.nytimes.com (accessed January

11, 2016); Steve Kanigher, "Prisons Face Threat of Smuggled Cell Phones," *Las Vegas Sun*, December 17, 2010, www.lasvegassun.com (accessed January 11, 2016); Brian Haas, "Dogs To Help Sniff Out TN Inmates' Cell Phones," *The Tenneessean*, July 26, 2011, www.tennessean.com (accessed January 11, 2016); Jack Dolan, "Charles Manson Had a Cellphone? California Prisons Fight Inmate Cellphone Proliferation," *Los Angeles Times*, December 2, 2010, www.latimes.com (accessed January 11, 2016); Therese Apel, "State's Prisons Test Technology: Cell Phones Blocked Behind Bars," *The Clarion-Ledger* (Jackson, MS), September 9, 2010, www.clarionledger.com (accessed January 11, 2016).

48. Teresa Wiltz, *States Bedeviled by Contraband Cellphones in Prison* (Washington, DC: Pew Charitable Trusts, 2016); Kurt Erikson, "Officials Target Cellphones in Illinois Prisons," December 7, 2011, Pantagraph.com, www.pantagraph.com (accessed January 11, 2016); Jack Dolan, "Phone Smuggling Case Costs 20 California Prison Workers Their Jobs," *Los Angeles Times*, October 14, 2012, www.latimes.com (accessed January 11, 2016).

49. Jack Dolan, "Prisons to Block Use of Smuggled Phones," *Los Angeles Times*, April 17, 2012, www.latimes.com (accessed January 11, 2016).

50. Susan Haigh, "Prisons Beef Up Teleconferencing to Save Money," *USA Today*, November 23, 2008, www.usatoday.com (accessed January 11, 2016).

51. Sadhbh Walshe, "Prison Video Visits Threaten to Put Profit Before Public Safety," *The Guardian*, October 25, 2012, www.guardian.co.uk (accessed January 11, 2016).

52. Susan D. Phillips, *Video Visits for Children Whose Parents Are Incarcerated* (Washington, DC: The Sentencing Project, October 2012).

53. Ibid.

54. Ibid.

55. "Telemedicine Expanding in Ohio Prison System," TECHbeat, Spring 2002, p. 10; and "More States Turn to Videoconferencing," *Corrections Today*, vol. 71, no. 3 (June 2009), p. 14.

56. "Inmate Health Care and Communicable Diseases," *Corrections Compendium*, vol. 34, no. 4 (Winter 2009), pp. 13–35.

57. Graeme Wood, "Prison Without Walls," *The Atlantic*, September 2010, www.theatlantic.com (accessed January 11, 2016).

58. "CORMAP It," TECHbeat, Summer 2002, p. 5.

59. Christopher A. Miles and Jeffrey P. Cohn, "Tracking Prisoners in Jail with Biometrics: An Experiment in a Navy Brig," *NIJ Journal*, no. 253 (January 2006), pp. 6–9.

Chapter 8

1. Charles L. Newman, *Sourcebook on Probation, Parole and Pardons*, 3rd ed. (Springfield, IL: Charles C Thomas, 1970), pp. 30–31; see also Norval Morris, *Maconochie's Gentlemen: The Story of Norfolk Island and the Roots of Modern Prison Reform* (New York: Oxford University Press, 2002).

2. G. W. Wickersham, *Reports of the United States National Commission on Law Observance and Enforcement: Wickersham Commission, Report on Penal Institutions, Probation and Parole* (Washington, DC: U.S. Government Printing Office, 1930–1931), p. 324.

3. Ibid. p. 325.

4. David J. Rothman, *Conscience and Convenience: The Asylum and Its Alternatives in Progressive America* (Boston: Little Brown, 1980), pp. 159–161.

5. Douglas R. Lipton, Robert Martinson, and Judith Wilks, *The Effectiveness of Correctional Treatment: A Survey of Treatment Evaluation Studies* (New York: Praeger, 1975).

6. Peggy McGarry, *Handbook for New Parole Board Members* (Philadelphia: Center for Effective Public Policy, 1989), p. 4.

7. Patrick A. Langan and David J. Levin, *Recidivism of Prisoners Released in 1994* (Washington, DC: U.S. Department of Justice, Bureau of

Justice Statistics, July 2002); see also Pew Charitable Trusts, *Public Safety, Public Spending: Forecasting America's Prison Population 2007–2011* (Philadelphia: Pew Charitable Trusts, 2007); Pew Center on the States, *State of Recidivism: The Revolving Door of America's Prisons* (Washington, DC: The Pew Charitable Trusts, April 2011), p. 2.

8. Heather West and William J. Sabol, *Prisoners in 2007* (Washington, DC: U.S. Department of Justice, Bureau of Justice Statistics, December 2008), Appendix Table 5, p. 17.

9. Sarah Maslin, "Thousands Return to Prison Without Committing New Crimes," *McClatchy News,* August 21, 2014, http://www.governing.com/news/headlines/mct-wisconsin-parolees.html (accessed March 11, 2016).

10. The Council of State Governments, *The Report of the Re-Entry Policy Council: Charting the Safe and Successful Return of Prisoners to the Community* (Lexington, KY: The Council of State Governments, 2005).

11. Nancy G. La Vigne et al., *Prisoner Reentry and Community Policing Strategies for Enhancing Public Safety* (Washington, DC: Urban Institute, 2006); Marc Mauer and Meda Chesney-Lind (eds.), *Invisible Punishment: The Collateral Consequences of Mass Imprisonment* (New York: The New Press, 2002).

12. Beth E. Richie, "Challenges Incarcerated Women Face as They Return to Their Communities: Findings from Life History Interviews," *Crime & Delinquency,* vol. 47, no. 3 (July 2001), p. 370.

13. Geneva Brown, *The Intersectionality of Race, Gender, and Reentry: Challenges for African-American Women* (Washington, DC: American Constitution Society, November 2010).

14. Theodire M. Hammett, Cheryl Roberts, and Sofia Kennedy, "Health-Realted Issues in Prisoner Reentry," *Crime & Delinquency,* vol. 47, no. 3 (2001), pp. 390–409; U.S. Department of Justice, Office of Justice Programs, Bureau of Justice Statistics, and U.S. Department of Justice, Federal Bureau of Prisons, *Survey of Inmates in State and Federal Correctional Facilities, 1997* (Ann Arbor, MI: Inter-university Consortium for Political and Social Research, 2001), doi:10.3886/ICPSR02598.v1; Paula M. Ditton, *Mental Health and Treatment of Inmates and Probationers* (Washington, DC: U.S. Department of Justice, Bureau of Justice Statistics, 1999); Caroline Wolf Harlow, *Education and Correctional Populations* (Washington, DC: U.S. Department of Justice, Bureau of Justice Statistics, 2003); Harry J. Holzer, Steven Raphael, and Michael A. Stoll, *Employment Barriers Facing Ex-Offenders* (Washington, DC: The Urban Institute, 2003); *Children with Incarcerated Parents,* Annie E. Casey Foundation, www.aecf.org (accessed March 11, 2016); Cheryl G. Swanson, Courtney W. Schnippert, and Amanda L. Tryling, "Reentry and Employment: Employers' Willingness to Hire Formerly Convicted Felons in Northwest Florida," in Matthew S. Crow and John Ortiz Smykla (eds.), *Offender Reentry: Rethinking Criminology and Criminal Justice* (Boston, MA: Jones & Bartlett, 2014), pp. 203–224.

15. Jeremy Travis, *But They All Come Back: Facing the Challenges of Prisoner Reentry* (Washington, DC: Urban Institute, 2005).

16. Edward J. Latessa and Charles Lowenkamp, "What Works in Reducing Recidivism," *St. Thomas Law Journal,* vol. 3, no 3. (2006), pp. 521–535.

17. Elizabeth Gaynes, *Reentry: Helping Former Prisoners Return to Communities* (Baltimore: Annie E. Casey Foundation, 2005).

18. Devah Pager, "The Mark of a Criminal Record," *American Journal of Sociology,* vol. 108, no. 5 (March 2003), pp. 937–975, as cited in Michelle Natividad Rodriguez, "'Ban the Box' Is a Fair Chance for Workers with Records," National Employment Law Project, March 1, 2016, http://www.nelp.org/content/uploads/Ban-the-Box-Fair-Chance-Fact-Sheet.pdf (accessed March 13, 2016).

19. Ibid.

20. The Pew Charitable Trusts, *Collateral Costs: Incarceration's Effect on Economic Mobility* (Washington, DC: The Pew Charitable Trusts, 2010), p. 25; and Josh Farley, "Will the State Bring Back Half-Off Sentences for Good Behavior?" *Kitsap Sun* (Bremerton, WA), October 9, 2010, www.kitsapsun.com (accessed March 13, 2016).

21. "More States Use Risk-Assessment Software in Making Parole Decisions," *The Crime Report,* October 12, 2013, www.thecrimereport.org (accessed March 14, 2016).

22. Jacob Kastrenakes, "Prisons Turn to Computer Algorithms for Deciding Who to Parole," *The Verge,* October 14, 2013, www.theverge.com (accessed March 14, 2016).

23. Ralph Serin and Renee Gobeil, *Analysis of the Use of the Structured Decisionmaking Framework in Three States* (Washington, DC: U.S. Department of Justice, National Institute of Corrections, September 2014).

24. Mary West-Smith, Mark R. Pogrebin, and Eric D. Poole, "Denial of Parole: An Inmate Perspective," *Federal Probation,* vol. 63, no. 2 (December 2000).

25. Colleen Long, "Courts Nationwide Hold Hearings with Video," *The Denver Post,* May 8, 2011, www.denverpost.com (accesses March 14, 2016).

26. Parole Board Interview, In the Matter of Mark D. Chapman, Wednesday, August 20, 2014. http://www.scribd.com/doc/237904048/Mark-David-Chapman-81A3860-August-2014 (accessed March 14, 2016).

27. "Non-Revocable Parole," California Department of Corrections and Rehabilitation, www.cdcr.ca.gov/Parole/Non_Revocable_Parole/index.html (accessed March 14, 2016); Sam Stanton, "Critics Say New California Parole Policy Is Costly, Dangerous," *The Sacramento Bee,* April 12, 2010, www.sacbee.com (accessed May 8, 2013); and John Wilkens, "Inmates Released Under New Law," *The San Diego Union Tribune,* January 26, 2010, www.signonsandiego.com (accessed May 8, 2013).

28. Danielle Kaeble, Laura M. Maruschak, and Thomas P. Bonczar, *Probation and Parole in the United States, 2014* (Washington, DC: U.S. Department of Justice, Bureau of Justice Statistics, November 2015).

29. Thomas P. Bonczar, *Characteristics of State Parole Supervising Agencies, 2006* (Washington, DC: U.S. Department of Justice, Bureau of Justice Statistics, August 2008).

30. "Disenfranchisement News," *The Sentencing Project,* September 3, 2015, www.sentencingproject.org (accessed March 17, 2016).

31. Marc Mauer, "Voting Behind Bars: An Argument for Voting by Prisoners," *Howard Law Journal,* vol. 54, no. 3 (2011), pp. 549–566.

32. John F. Timoney, "Two More Issues for President Obama, with Implications for Justice and Race," *Subject to Debate: A Newsletter of the Police Executive Research Forum,* vol. 22, no. 11 (November 2008), p. 2.

33. *Reentry Courts: Managing the Transition from Prison to Community* (Washington, DC: Office of Justice Programs, September, 1999), p. 9.

34. Susan Herman and Cressida Wasserman, "A Role for Victims in Offender Reentry," *Crime & Delinquency,* vol. 47, no. 3 (July 2001), pp. 428–445.

35. Andrew von Hirsch, *Doing Justice: The Choice of Punishments, Report of the Committee for the Study of Incarceration* (New York: Hill and Wang, 1976).

36. Jessica Fargan, "Herald Eyes Parole Votes, Turns to Court for Records' Release," *Boston Herald,* November 13, 2008 www.bostonherald.com (accessed May 7, 2013).

37. La Vigne et al., *Prisoner Reentry and Community Policing, Strategies for Enhancing Public Safety,* p. 16.

38. Justin Jones and Edward Flynn, "Cops and Corrections: Reentry Collaborations for Public Safety," *Corrections Today,* vol. 70, no. 2 (April 2008), pp. 26–29; and Ashbel T. Wall II and Tracy Z. Poole, "Partnerships with Local Law Enforcement and Community Agencies: A Critical Component to Successful Prison Reentry Initiatives," *Corrections Today,* vol. 70, no. 2 (April 2008), pp. 30–37.

39. Donald G. Evans, "Community-Focused Parole," *Corrections Today,* vol. 68, no. 7 (December 2006), pp. 90–91.

Chapter 9

1. Jen Fifield, "Stateline: Many States Face Dire Shortage of Prison Guards," March 1, 2016, http://www.pewtrusts.org/en/research-and-analysis/blogs/stateline (accessed March 30, 2016).

2. Ibid.

3. See Sylvia G. McCollum, "Excellence or Mediocrity: Training Correctional Officers and Administrators," *The Keeper's Voice*, vol. 17, no. 4 (Fall 1996).

4. Anthony R. Martinez, "Corrections Officer: The 'Other' Prisoner," *The Keeper's Voice*, vol. 18, no. 1 (Spring 1997).

5. Don A. Josi and Dale K. Sechrest, *The Changing Career of the Correctional Officer: Policy Implications for the 21st Century* (Boston: Butterworth-Heinemann, 1998), p. 11.

6. Ibid., p. 12.

7. John Hepburn, "The Exercise of Power in Coercive Organizations: A Study of Prison Guards," *Criminology*, vol. 23, no. 1 (1985), pp. 145–164.

8. Gresham Sykes, *The Society of Captives* (Princeton, NJ: Princeton University Press, 1958).

9. See, for example, James B. Jacobs and Lawrence J. Kraft, "Integrating the Keepers: A Comparison of Black and White Prison Guards in Illinois," *Social Problems*, vol. 25, no. 3 (1978), pp. 304–318.

10. Adapted from John J. Macionis, *Society: The Basics*, 2nd ed. (Englewood Cliffs, NJ: Prentice Hall, 1994), p. 405.

11. Kelsey Kauffman, *Prison Officers and Their World* (Cambridge, MA: Harvard University Press, 1988), pp. 85–86.

12. Rich Lord, "It Doesn't Pay to Get Promoted in Pa. Prisons," *Pittsburgh Post-Gazette*, February 26, 2012.

13. American Correctional Association, *Vital Statistics in Corrections* (Lanham, MD: ACA, 2000), p. 143; James J. Stephan and Jennifer C. Karberg, *Census of State and Federal Correctional Facilities, 2000* (Washington, DC: Bureau of Justice Statistics, 2003).

14. Federal Bureau of Prisons, "About Our Agency," https://www.bop.gov/about/agency (accessed May 2, 2016).

15. ACA, *Vital Statistics in Corrections.*

16. See, for example, E. Poole and R. M. Regoli, "Work Relations and Cynicism Among Prison Guards," *Criminal Justice and Behavior*, vol. 7 (1980), pp. 303–314.

17. Adapted from Frank Schmalleger, *Criminal Justice Today: An Introductory Text for the 21st Century*, 9th ed. (Upper Saddle River, NJ: Prentice Hall, 2007).

18. Lucien X. Lombardo, *Guards Imprisoned: Correctional Officers at Work*, 2nd ed. (Cincinnati, OH: Anderson, 1989).

19. Adapted from Dora B. Schriro, "Women in Prison: Keeping the Peace," *The Keeper's Voice*, vol. 16, no. 2 (Spring 1995).

20. Ibid.

21. M. I. Cadwaladr, "Women Working in a Men's Jail," *FORUM*, vol. 6, no. 1 (1994).

22. Ibid.

23. N. C. Jurik and J. Halemba, "Gender, Working Conditions, and the Job Satisfaction of Women in a Non-Traditional Occupation: Female Correctional Officers in Men's Prisons," *Sociological Quarterly*, vol. 25 (1984), pp. 551–566.

24. Joseph R. Rowan, "Who Is Safer in Male Maximum Security Prisons?" *The Keeper's Voice*, vol. 17, no. 3 (Summer 1996).

25. Ibid.

26. See, for example, Stephen Walters, "Changing the Guard: Male Correctional Officers' Attitudes Toward Women as Co-workers," *Journal of Offender Rehabilitation*, vol. 20, no. 1 (1993), pp. 47–60.

27. Cadwaladr, "Women Working in a Men's Jail."

28. Ibid.

29. Public Service Commission (of Canada), "Stress and Executive Burnout," *FORUM*, vol. 4, no. 1 (1992). Much of the material in this section is taken from this work.

30. B. M. Crouch, "The Guard in a Changing Prison World," in B. M. Crouch (ed.), *The Keepers: Prison Guards and Contemporary Corrections* (Springfield, IL: Charles C. Thomas, 1980).

31. Shannon Black, "Correctional Employee Stress & Strain," *Corrections Today*, October 2001, p. 99.

32. Caterina Spinaris and Mike Denhof, "Countering Staff Stress—Why and How," *National Jail Exchange*, 2015.

33. Lombardo, *Guards Imprisoned.*

34. Kelly Ann Cheeseman and Wendi Goodin-Fahncke, "The Impact of Gender on Correctional Employee Perceptions of Work Stress," *Corrections Compendium*, vol. 36, no. 2 (Summer 2011), p. 1–2.

35. Public Service Commission, "Stress and Executive Burnout."

36. For an excellent overview of the literature on correctional officer stress, see Tammy L. Castle and Jamie S. Martin, "Occupational Hazard: Predictors of Stress Among Jail Correctional Officers," *American Journal of Criminal Justice*, vol. 31, no. 1 (Fall 2006), pp. 65–80.

37. "Not Stressed Enough?" *FORUM*, vol. 4, no. 1 (1992). Adapted from C. C. W. Hines and W. C. Wilson, "A No-Nonsense Guide to Being Stressed," *Management Solutions*, October 1986, pp. 27–29.

38. J. T. Dignam, M. Barrera, and S. G. West, "Occupational Stress, Social Support, and Burnout Among Correctional Officers," *American Journal of Community Psychology*, vol. 14, no. 2 (1986), pp. 177–193.

39. M. C. W. Peeters, B. P. Buunk, and W. B. Schaufeli, "Social Interactions and Feelings of Inferiority Among Correctional Officers: A Daily Event-Recording Approach," *Journal of Applied Social Psychology*, vol. 25, no. 12 (1995), pp. 1073–1089.

40. Spinaris and Denhof, "Countering Staff Stress—Why and How."

41. Jessie W. Doyle, "6 Elements That Form a Context for Staff Safety," *Corrections Today*, October 2001, pp. 101–104.

42. Terry L. Stewart and Donald W. Brown, "Focusing on Correctional Staff Safety," *Corrections Today*, October 2001, pp. 90–93.

43. Ibid.

44. David Robinson, Frank Porporino, and Linda Simourd, "Do Different Occupational Groups Vary on Attitudes and Work Adjustment in Corrections?" *Federal Probation*, vol. 60, no. 3 (1996), pp. 45–53. See also Francis T. Cullen et al., "How Satisfying Is Prison Work? A Comparative Occupational Approach," *Journal of Offender Counseling Services and Rehabilitation*, vol. 14, no. 2 (1989), pp. 89–108.

45. Timothy J. Flanagan, Wesley Johnson, and Katherine Bennett, "Job Satisfaction Among Correctional Executives: A Contemporary Portrait of Wardens of State Prisons for Adults," *Prison Journal*, vol. 76, no. 4 (1996), pp. 385–397.

46. Lombardo, *Guards Imprisoned.*

47. Martinez, "Corrections Officer."

48. Thomas Gillan, "The Correctional Officer: One of Law Enforcement's Toughest Positions," *Corrections Today*, October 2001, p. 113.

49. Black, "Correctional Employee Stress & Strain," p. 99.

50. Andrew Metz, "Life on the Inside: The Jailers," in Tara Gray (ed.), *Exploring Corrections* (Boston: Allyn & Bacon, 2002), p. 65.

51. Ibid., p. 64.

52. Black, "Correctional Employee Stress & Strain," p. 99.

53. Stephen Walters, "The Determinants of Job Satisfaction Among Canadian and American Correctional Officers," *Journal of Crime and Justice*, vol. 19, no. 2 (1996), pp. 145–158.

54. John R. Hepburn and Paul E. Knepper, "Correctional Officers as Human Services Workers: The Effect on Job Satisfaction," *Justice Quarterly*, vol. 10, no. 2 (1993), pp. 315–337.

55. Stephen Walters, "Gender, Job Satisfaction, and Correctional Officers: A Comparative Analysis," *The Justice Professional*, vol. 7, no. 2 (1993), pp. 23–33.

56. Dana M. Britton, "Perceptions of the Work Environment Among Correctional Officers: Do Race and Sex Matter?" *Criminology*, vol. 35, no. 1 (1997), pp. 85–105.

57. Adapted from William Sondervan, "Professionalism in Corrections," in Frank Schmalleger and John Smykla (eds.), *Corrections in the Twenty-First Century*, 5e (New York: McGraw-Hill, 2011), p. 572.

58. Ibid.

59. Justin Fenton, "Indictments Reveal Prison Crime World," *Baltimore Sun*, April 18, 2009.

60. Jack Dolan, "California Prison Guards Union Called Main Obstacle to Keeping Cell Phones Away from Inmate," *Los Angeles Times*, February 4, 2011. Web posted at http://www.latimes.com/news/local/la-me-prison-guards-20110204,0,2785860.story (accessed February 21, 2011).

61. Mike Ward, "Low Pay May Make Prison Guards Ripe for Smugglers," *American Statesman*, October 24, 2008.

62. U.S. Department of Justice, Office of the Inspector General, *Semiannual Report to Congress: April 1, 2008–September 30, 2008* (Washington, DC: USGPO, 2008).

63. Marc Santora, "Joyce Mitchell, Ex-Prison Employee, Is Sentenced," *The New York Times*, September 28, 2015; Gary F. Cornelius, "Avoiding Inmate Manipulation," Corrections.com, February 14, 2011, http://www.correctionsone.com/correctional-psychology/articles/3328579-Avoiding-inmate-manipulation (accessed March 30, 2016).

64. Ibid.

65. Tracy Barnhart, "Inmate Manipulations," Corrections.com, June 21, 2009, http://www.corrections.com/tracy_barnhart/?p=298 (accessed March 30, 2016).

66. International Herald Tribune, "Man Behind U.S. Terrorism Plot Gets 16 Years," March 6, 2009. Web posted at http://www.iht.com/articles/ap/2009/03/06/america/NA-US-Terrorism-Probe.php (accessed March 27, 2009).

67. Mark S. Hamm, "Prisoner Radicalization: Assessing the Threat in U.S. Correctional Institutions," *NIJ Journal* (No. 261), p. 17.

68. Ibid., p. 18.

69. Quoted in Meghan Mandeville, "Information Sharing Becomes Crucial to Battling Terrorism Behind Bars," Corrections.com, December 8, 2003, http://database.corrections.com/news/results2.asp?ID_8988 (accessed August 1, 2005).

70. "FBI: Al-Qaida Recruiting in U.S. Prisons," United Press International wire service, January 7, 2004, http://database.corrections.com/news/results2.asp?ID_9148 (accessed August 1, 2005).

71. "Lawyer Sentenced to 28 Months in Prison on Terrorism Charge," Court TV News, October 16, 2006, www.courttv.com/news/2006/1016/cynne_Stewart_ap.html.

72. Jess Maghan, *Intelligence-Led Penology: Management of Crime Information Obtained from Incarcerated Persons*, paper presented at the Investigation of Crime World Conference, 2001, p. 6.

73. Institute for the Study of Violent Groups, "Land of Wahhabism," *Crime and Justice International*, March/April 2005, p. 43.

74. Office of the Inspector General, *A Review of the Federal Bureau of Prisons' Selection of Muslim Religious Services Providers* (Washington, DC: U.S. Department of Justice, 2004).

75. Ibid., p. 8.

76. Ibid.

77. Mark S. Hamm, "Terrorist Recruitment in American Correctional Institutions: An Exploratory Study of Non-Traditional Faith Groups," nonpublished paper, December 2007.

78. U.S. Department of Justice, Office of the Inspector General, *The Federal Bureau of Prisons' Monitoring of Mail for High-Risk Inmates* (Washington, DC: U.S. Government Printing Office, 2006).

79. Keith Martin, "Corrections Prepares for Terrorism," Corrections Connection News Network, January 21, 2002, www.corrections.com (accessed July 10, 2005).

80. Y. N. Baykan, "The Emergence of Sunni Islam in America's Prisons," *Corrections Today*, February 2007, pp. 49–51.

81. James Gilligan, *Violence: Reflections on a National Epidemic* (New York: Vintage Books, 1997), p. 165.

Chapter 10

1. "Miss Wisconsin Makes Father's Prison Time a Miss America Platform," CBS News, January 15, 2012, www.cbsnews.com/8301-31749_162-57359505-10391698/miss-wisconsin-makes-fathers-prison-time-a-miss-america-platform (accessed May 18, 2012).

2. Allen Beck et al., *Survey of State Prison Inmates, 1991* (Washington, DC: U.S. Department of Justice, March 1993), www.ojp.usdoj.gov/bjs/pub/ascii/sospi91.txt.

3. Erving Goffman, *Asylums: Essays on the Social Situation of Mental Patients and Other Inmates* (Garden City, NY: Anchor Books, 1961).

4. Hans Toch, *Living in Prison: The Ecology of Survival*, reprinted. (Washington, DC: American Psychological Association, 1996), p. xv.

5. Victoria R. DeRosia, *Living Inside Prison Walls: Adjustment Behavior* (Westport, CT: Praeger, 1998).

6. "Inmate Subculture," in Virgil L. Williams (ed.), *Dictionary of American Penology: An Introductory Guide* (Westport, CT: Greenwood, 1979).

7. Donald Clemmer, *The Prison Community* (Boston: Holt, Rinehart & Winston, 1940).

8. Stanton Wheeler, "Socialization in Correctional Communities," *American Sociological Review*, vol. 26 (October 1961), pp. 697–712.

9. Gresham M. Sykes, *The Society of Captives: A Study of a Maximum Security Prison* (Princeton, NJ: Princeton University Press, 1958).

10. Stephen C. Light, *Inmate Assaults on Staff: Challenges to Authority in a Large State Prison System*, dissertation, State University of New York at Albany (Ann Arbor, MI: University Microfilms International, 1987).

11. John Irwin and Donald R. Cressey, "Thieves, Convicts and the Inmate Culture," *Social Problems*, vol. 10 (Fall 1962), pp. 142–155.

12. James Jacobs, *Stateville: The Penitentiary in Mass Society* (Chicago: University of Chicago Press, 1977).

13. Miles D. Harer and Darrell J. Steffensmeier, "Race and Prison Violence," *Criminology*, vol. 34, no. 3 (1996), pp. 323–355.

14. John M. Wilson and Jon D. Snodgrass, "The Prison Code in a Therapeutic Community," *Journal of Criminal Law, Criminology, and Police Science*, vol. 60, no. 4 (1969), pp. 472–478.

15. Gresham M. Sykes and Sheldon L. Messinger, "The Inmate Social System," in Richard A. Cloward et al. (eds.), *Theoretical Studies in Social Organization of the Prison* (New York: Social Science Research Council, 1960), pp. 5–19.

16. Peter M. Wittenberg, "Language and Communication in Prison," *Federal Probation*, vol. 60, no. 4 (1996), pp. 45–50.

17. Sykes, *The Society of Captives*.

18. John Irwin, *The Felon* (Englewood Cliffs, NJ: Prentice Hall, 1970).

19. Adapted from Frank Schmalleger, *Criminal Justice Today*, 7th ed. (Upper Saddle River, NJ: Prentice Hall, 2003).

20. Lindsay Leban, Stephanie M. Cardwell, Heith Copes, and Timothy Brezina, "Adapting to Prison Life: A Qualitative Examination of the Coping Process among Incarcerated Offenders," *Justice Quarterly*, 2015, http://dx.doi.org/10.1080/07418825.2015.1012096 (accessed May 20, 2016).

21. See, for example, Donald Tucker, *A Punk's Song: View from the Inside* (AMS Press, 1981), from which some of the information here is adapted.

22. Ibid.

23. Ibid.

24. Ibid.

25. Daniel Lockwood, *Sexual Aggression Among Male Prisoners*, dissertation, State University of New York at Albany (Ann Arbor, MI: University Microfilms International, 1978); Daniel Lockwood, "Issues in Prison Sexual Violence," *The Prison Journal*, vol. 58, no. 1 (1983), pp. 73–79.

26. Adapted from Toch, *Living in Prison*, p. 274.

27. Pub. L. No. 108–79.

28. Bureau of Justice Statistics, "PREA Data Collection Activities, 2015," http://www.bjs.gov/content/pub/pdf/pdca15.pdf (accessed May 20, 2016).

29. Allen J. Beck and Timothy A. Hughes, *Sexual Violence Reported by Correctional Authorities, 2004* (Washington, DC: Bureau of Justice Statistics, 2005).

30. E. Ann Carson, *Prisoners in 2014* (Washington, DC: U.S. Department of Justice, 2015).

31. Phyllis J. Baunach, "Critical Problems of Women in Prison," in Imogene L. Moyer (ed.), *The Changing Roles of Women in the Criminal Justice System* (Prospect Heights, IL: Waveland Press, 1985), pp. 95–110.

32. See John W. Palmer and Stephen E. Palmer, *Constitutional Rights of Prisoners*, 6th ed. (Cincinnati, OH: Anderson, 1999).

33. American Correctional Association, *Standards for Adult Correctional Institutions* (Lanham, MD: ACA, 1990).

34. Alabama Department of Corrections, *Monthly Statistical Report for November 2010* (Montgomery, AL: Alabama Department of Corrections, 2011), p. 3.

35. U.S. Department of Justice, Office of Public Affairs, "Justice Department Reaches Landmark Settlement with Alabama," May 28, 2015.

36. Lawrence A. Greenfeld and Tracy L. Snell, *Women Offenders*, Bureau of Justice Statistics Special Report (Washington, DC: Bureau of Justice Statistics, December 1999, revised October 3, 2000); Carson and Golinelli, *Prisoners in 2012*.

37. Carson, *Prisoners in 2014*.

38. Ibid.

39. Angela Browne, Brenda Miller, and Eugene Maguin, "Prevalence and Severity of Lifetime Physical and Sexual Victimization Among Incarcerated Women," *International Journal of Law and Psychiatry*, vol. 22, no. 3–4 (1999), pp. 301–322.

40. Bloom et al., *Gender-Responsive Strategies: Research, Practice, and Guiding Principles for Women Offenders* (Washington, DC: National Institute of Corrections, 2003).

41. Carson, *Prisoners in 2014*.

42. American Correctional Association, *Female Offenders: Meeting Needs of a Neglected Population* (Laurel, MD: ACA, 1993).

43. Tracy Snell, *Women in Prison* (Washington, DC: Bureau of Justice Statistics, 1994).

44. Rose Giallombardo, *Society of Women: A Study of a Women's Prison* (New York: John Wiley, 1966).

45. Esther Heffernan, *Making It in Prison: The Square, the Cool, and the Life* (New York: Wiley-Interscience, 1972).

46. Barbara Owens, "The Mix: The Culture of Imprisoned Women," in Mary K. Stohr and Craig Hemmens (eds.), *The Inmate Prison Experience* (Upper Saddle River, NJ: Prentice Hall, 2004), pp. 152–172.

47. Williams, "Inmate Subculture," p. 109.

48. Kathryn Watterson, *Women in Prison: Inside the Concrete Tomb*, 2nd ed. (Boston: Northeastern University Press, 1996), p. 291.

49. For example, see John Gagnon and William Simon, "The Social Meaning of Prison Homosexuality," in David M. Petersen and Charles W. Thomas (eds.), *Corrections: Problems and Prospects* (Englewood Cliffs, NJ: Prentice Hall, 1980).

50. Doris Layton MacKenzie, James Robinson, and Carol Campbell, "Long-Term Incarceration of Female Offenders: Prison Adjustment and Coping," *Criminal Justice and Behavior*, vol. 16, no. 2 (1989), pp. 223–238.

51. Nicole Hahn Rafter, *Partial Justice: Women, Prisons and Social Control* (New Brunswick, NJ: Transaction, 1990).

52. Bloom et al., *Gender-Responsive Strategies*.

53. Barbara Bloom and Stephanie Covington, *Gendered Justice: Programming for Women in Correctional Settings*, paper presented at the American Society of Criminology annual meeting, San Francisco, November 2000, p. 11.

54. Bloom et al., *Gender-Responsive Strategies*.

55. Susan Cranford and Rose Williams, "Critical Issues in Managing Female Offenders," *Corrections Today*, vol. 60, no. 7 (December 1998), pp. 130–135.

56. John DeBell, "The Female Offender: Different . . . Not Difficult," *Corrections Today*, vol. 63, no. 1 (February 2001), pp. 56–61.

57. Pat Carlen, "Analyzing Women's Imprisonment: Abolition and Its Enemies," *Women, Girls & Criminal Justice*, vol. 7, no. 6 (October/November 2006), p. 85.

58. Tracy L. Snell, "Women in Prison," *Bureau of Justice Statistics Bulletin* (Washington, DC: Bureau of Justice Statistics, March 1994).

59. As estimated by Vesna Markovic, "Pregnant Women in Prison: A Correctional Dilemma?" *The Keepers' Voice*, Summer 1995.

60. Ibid.

61. American Correctional Association, *Standards for Adult Correctional Institutions*, 3rd ed. (ACA, January 1990).

62. Gerald Austin McHugh, "Protection of the Rights of Pregnant Women in Prison and Detention Facilities," *New England Journal of Prison Law*, vol. 6, no. 2 (Summer 1980), pp. 231–263.

63. Snell, "Women in Prison."

64. National Institute of Corrections, *Services for Families of Prison Inmates* (Washington, DC: NIC, 2002), p. 3.

65. Phyllis Jo Baunach, "Critical Problems of Women in Prison," in Imogene L. Moyer (ed.), *The Changing Roles of Women in the Criminal Justice System* (Prospect Heights, IL: Waveland Press, 1985), p. 16.

66. John J. Sheridan, "Inmates May Be Parents, Too," *Corrections Today*, vol. 58, no. 5 (August 1996), p. 100.

67. Patricia Allard and Judith Greene, *Children on the Outside: Voicing the Pain and Human Costs of Parental Incarceration* (New York: Justice Strategies, 2011).

68. L. Wright and C. Seymour, *Working with Children and Families Separated by Incarceration: A Handbook for Child Welfare Agencies* (Washington, DC: Child Welfare League of America, 2000).

69. Kelsey Kauffman, "Mothers in Prison," *Corrections Today* (February 2001), pp. 62–65.

70. Harrison and Beck, *Prisoners in 2006*.

71. Christopher J. Mumola, *Incarcerated Parents and Their Children*, Bureau of Justice Statistics Special Report (Washington, DC: Bureau of Justice Statistics, August 2000), p. 1.

72. Suzanne Hoholik, "Weekend Camp Lets Mother, Kids Bond," *The Columbus Dispatch*, July 22, 2000, pp. A1–A2.

73. Rini Bartlett, "Helping Inmate Moms Keep in Touch," *Correctional Compass* (Tallahassee, FL: Department of Corrections, February 2001), www.dc.state.fl.us/pub/compass/0102/page07.html (accessed June 2, 2007).

74. Kauffman, "Mothers in Prison," p. 62.

75. Huey Freeman, "Illinois Prison Program Guides New Mothers," Pantagraph.com, www.pantagraph.com/news/state-and-regional/illinois/article_ab1d5106-4631-11df-97d4-001cc4c002e0.html (accessed March 12, 2011).

76. Rick Jervis, "Prison Dads Learn Meaning of 'Father,'" *USA Today*, June 18, 2010, www.usatoday.com/news/nation/2010-06-17-prison-dads_N.htm (accessed March 15, 2011).

77. John Ortiz Smykla, "Coed Prison: Should We Try It (Again)?" in Charles B. Fields (ed.), *Controversial Issues in Corrections* (Boston: Allyn & Bacon, 1999), pp. 203–218.

78. John Ortiz Smykla and Jimmy J. Williams, "Co-Corrections in the United States of America, 1970–1990: Two Decades of Disadvantages for Women Prisoners," *Women & Criminal Justice*, vol. 8, no. 1 (1996), pp. 61–76.

79. Ibid.

80. Jacqueline K. Crawford, "Two Losers Don't Make a Winner: The Case Against the Co-correctional Institution," in John Ortiz Smykla (ed.), *Coed Prison* (New York: Human Sciences Press, 1980), pp. 263–268.

81. Smykla and Williams, "Co-corrections in the United States," p. 61.

82. Lawrence W. Sherman et al., *Preventing Crime: What Works, What Doesn't, What's Promising* (Washington, DC: NIJ, 1997).

Chapter 11

1. Rich Pedroncelli, "Judges Back a One-Third Reduction in State Prison Population," *Los Angeles Times*, February 10, 2009.
2. *Ruffin v. Commonwealth*, 62, Va. 790, 1871.
3. Frances Cole, "The Impact of *Bell v. Wolfish* Upon Prisoners' Rights," *Journal of Crime and Justice*, vol. 10 (1987), pp. 47–70.
4. D. J. Gottlieb, "The Legacy of *Wolfish* and *Chapman*: Some Thoughts About 'Big Prison Case' Litigation in the 1980s," in I. D. Robbins (ed.), *Prisoners and the Law* (New York: Clark Boardman, 1985).
5. James B. Jacobs, *New Perspectives on Prisons and Imprisonment* (Ithaca, NY: Cornell University Press, 1983).
6. *Holt v. Sarver*, 442 F.2d 304 (1971).
7. Ibid.
8. *Holt v. Sarver*, 309 F.Supp. 362 (E.D.Ark.1970), aff'd, 442 F.2d 304 (8th Cir. 1971).
9. Todd Clear and George F. Cole, *American Corrections*, 4th ed. (New York: Wadsworth, 1997).
10. Civil Rights of Institutionalized Persons Act, 42 U.S.C. § 1997 et seq. (1976 ed., Supp. IV), as modified 1980. (Current through P.L. 104–150, approved June 3, 1996.)
11. R. Hawkins and G. P. Alpert, *American Prison Systems: Punishment and Justice* (Englewood Cliffs, NJ: Prentice Hall, 1989).
12. John Scalia, *Prisoner Petitions Filed in U.S. District Courts, 2000, with Trends 1980–2000* (Washington, DC: U.S. Department of Justice, December 2001).
13. Florida Department of Corrections, Office of the Inspector General, *Annual Report* 1994–1995, www.dc.state.fl.us/pub/IGannual/19941995/page6.html (accessed May 30, 2002).
14. *Report of the Comptroller General of the United States: Grievance Mechanisms in State Correctional Institutions and Large-City Jails* (Washington, DC: U.S. Government Printing Office, June 17, 1977), Appendix I.
15. James B. Jacobs, "The Prisoners' Rights Movement and Its Impacts," in Edward J. Latessa, Alexander Holsinger, James W. Marquart, and Jonathan R. Sorensen, *Correctional Contexts: Contemporary and Classical Readings*, 2nd ed. (Los Angeles: Roxbury, 2001), p. 211. Reprinted from James B. Jacobs, *Crime and Justice*, vol. II (Chicago: University of Chicago Press, 1980).
16. See *Estelle v. Gamble*, 429 U.S. 97 (1976), and *Hutto v. Finney*, 437 U.S. 678 (1978).
17. Sheri Qualters, "Federal Judge Orders Sex-Reassignment Surgery for Mass. Prisoner," *Law Journal*, September 4, 2012.
18. American Civil Liberties Union, *ACLU Position Paper: Prisoners' Rights* (Fall 1999), www.aclu.org/library/PrisonerRights.pdf (accessed March 2, 2011).
19. In 1977, Theriault's appeal to the U.S. Supreme Court was denied (see 434 U.S. 953, November 14, 1977).
20. *Ali v. Federal Bureau of Prisons*, 552 U.S. 214 (2008).
21. In Section 1997e, Congress created a specific, limited exhaustion requirement for adult prisoners bringing actions pursuant to section 1983.
22. Prison Litigation Reform Act, Pub. L. No. 104-134, § 801-10, 110 Stat. 1321 (1995).
23. If a prisoner wishes to proceed as an indigent on appeal, the prisoner must file in the district court, with the notice of appeal, a motion for leave to proceed as an indigent, a certified copy of a prison trust account statement, and Form 4 from the Appendix of Forms found in the *Federal Rules of Appellate Procedure*.
24. Fred L. Cheesman, Brian J. Ostrom, and Roger A. Hanson, *A Tale of Two Laws Revisited: Investigating the Impact of the Prison Litigation Reform Act and the Antiterrorism and Effective Death Penalty Act* (Williamsburg, VA: National Center for State Courts, 2005).
25. "Court Intervention Ends for D.C. DOC," *Corrections Today*, December 2004, p. 12.
26. "Judge Approves Settlement in Alabama Prison Lawsuit," *Corrections Journal*, August 9, 2004, p. 1.
27. California Government Code, Section 818.
28. Federal Tort Claims Act, U.S. Code, Title 28, Section 1346(b), 2671–2680.
29. U.S.C. Section 1346(b)(1).
30. *Milbrook v. U.S.*, U.S. Supreme Court, No. 11-10362 (decided March 27, 2013).
31. *Elder v. Holloway*, 114 S.Ct. 1019, 127 L.Ed.2d 344 (1994).
32. Ibid.

Chapter 12

1. Thomas E. Patterson, "Addressing Special Populations in Corrections," *Corrections Today*, vol. 74, no. 4 (August/September, 2012), p. 10.
2. Ibid., p. 10.
3. Ibid., p. 10.
4. G. Larry Mays and Daniel L. Judiscak, "Special Needs Inmates in New Mexico Jails," *American Jails*, vol. 10, no. 2 (1996), pp. 32–41.
5. National Center on Addiction and Substance Abuse, *Behind Bars II: Substance Abuse and America's Prison Population* (New York: National Center on Addiction and Substance Abuse, Columbia University, February 2010).
6. Kate Miltner, "Treatment over Jail Time Poll: Most Favor Efforts to Combat Addiction over Punishment," http://abcnews.go.com/sections/politics/dailynews/poll010606.html (accessed February 12, 2016).
7. Christopher J. Mumola and Jennifer C. Karberg, *Drug Use and Dependence, State and Federal Prisoners, 2004* (Washington, DC: U.S. Department of Justice, Bureau of Justice Statistics, October 2006).
8. Jeremy Travis, *Framing the National Agenda: A Research and Policy Perspective*. Speech to National Corrections Conference on Substance Abuse, April 23, 1997.
9. M. D. Anglin and Y. Haer, "Treatment of Drug Abuse," in Michael Tonry and James Q. Wilson (eds.), *Drugs and Crime: Crime and Justice: A Review of Research*, vol. 13 (Chicago: University of Chicago Press, 1990), pp. 393–460; D. N. Nurco, T. W. Kislock, and T. E. Hanlon, "The Nature and Status of Drug Abuse Treatment," *Maryland Medical Journal*, vol. 43 (January 1994), pp. 51–57; D. D. Simpson et al., "A National Evaluation of Treatment Outcomes for Cocaine Dependence," *Archives of General Psychiatry*, vol. 56, no. 6 (1999), pp. 507–514; Doris Layton MacKenzie, *What Works in Corrections: Reducing the Criminal Activities of Criminals and Delinquents* (New York: Cambridge University Press, 2006).
10. Center for Substance Abuse Treatment, *NTIES: The National Treatment Improvement Study—Final Report* (Rockville, MD: U.S. Department of Health and Human Services, Substance Abuse and Mental Health Services Administration, 1997).
11. Marcia R. Chaiken, *Prison Programs for Drug-Involved Offenders* (Washington, DC: National Institute of Justice, October 1989); D. A. Andrews et al., "Does Correctional Treatment Work? A Clinically Relevant and Psychologically Informed Meta-Analysis," *Criminology*, vol. 28, no. 3 (1990), pp. 369–404; Donald Lipton and Frank Pearson, *The CDATE Project: Reviewing Research on the Effectiveness of Treatment Programs for Adults and Juvenile Offenders*, paper presented at the annual meeting of the American Society of Criminology, Chicago, IL, 1996.
12. Lana D. Harrison, "The Revolving Prison Door for Drug-Involved Offenders: Challenges and Opportunities," *Crime & Delinquency*, vol. 47, no. 3 (July 2001), pp. 462–485.
13. Sandra Tunis et al., *Evaluation of Drug Treatment in Local Corrections* (Washington, DC: U.S. Department of Justice, 1997).
14. National Institute on Drug Abuse, *Principles of Drug Abuse Treatment for Criminal Justice Populations—A Research-Based Guide* (Washington, DC: U.S. Department of Health and Human Services, 2006).

15. National Commission on Correctional Health Care, *The Health Status of Soon-to-Be-Released Inmates: A Report to Congress,* Vol. I (Washington, DC: U.S. Department of Justice, September 2004), p. ix.

16. Laura M. Maruschak, *HIV in Prisons, 2001–2010* (Washington, DC: U.S. Department of Justice, Bureau of Justice Statistics, September 2012).

17. *Management of the HIV-Positive Prisoner* (New York: World Health CME, n.d.).

18. Michael S. Vaughn and Leo Carroll, "Separate and Unequal: Prison Versus Free-World Medical Care," *Justice Quarterly,* vol. 15, no. 1 (March 1998), pp. 3–40.

19. Laura M. Maruschak, Marcus Berzofsky, and Jennifer Unangst, *Medical Problems of State and Federal Prisoners and Jail Inmates, 20112* (Washington, DC: U.S. Department of Justice, Bureau of Justice Statistics, February 2015).

20. American Correctional Association, *Managing Special Needs Offenders* (Lanham, MD: American Correctional Association, 2004).

21. Jaime Shimkus, "Side by Side, Ministers and Detainees Test for HIV Infection," *CorrectCare,* Fall 2001, p. 16.

22. Stephanie Mencimer, "There Are 10 Times More Mentally Ill People Behind Bars Than in State Hospitals," *MotherJones,* April 8, 2014 (accessed February 14, 2016).

23. Ibid.

24. As quoted in Phillip Comey, "Health Care and Prisons: Considering the Connection," *On the Line* (Lanham: MD. American Correctional Association, November 2005), p. 1.

25. Risdon N. Slate et al., "Doing Justice for Mental Illness and Society: Federal Probation and Pretrial Service Officers as Mental Health Specialists," *Federal Probation,* vol. 67, no. 3 (December 2003).

26. Maloney, Ward, and Jackson, "Study Reveals."

27. The Bazelon Center for Mental Health Law, *Position Statement on Involuntary Commitment, 1999.* As cited in The Sentencing Project, *Mentally Ill Offenders in the Criminal Justice System: An Analysis and Prescription* (Washington, DC: The Sentencing Project, January 2002), p. 4.

28. Randy M. Bourn et al., "Police Perspectives on Responding to Mentally Ill People in Crisis: Perceptions of Program Effectiveness," *Behavioral Sciences and the Law,* vol. 16, no. 4 (1998), pp. 393–402.

29. "Mental Health Courts," Council of State Governments. https://csgjusticecenter.org/mental-health-court-project/ (accessed February 14, 2016).

30. Laura N. Honegger, "Does the Evidence Support the Case for Mental Health Courts? A Review of the Literature," *Law and Human Behavior,* vol. 39, no. 5 (October 2015), pp. 478–488.

31. See for example, http://store.samhsa.gov/list/series?name=Evidence-Based-Practices-KITs (accessed February 14, 2016); Kim T. Mueser, William C. Torrey, David Lynde, Patricia Singer, and Robert E. Drake, "Implementing Evidence-Based Practices for People with Severe Mental Illness," *Behavior Modification,* vol. 27, no. 3 (July 2003), pp. 387–411.

32. See, for example, http://akmhcweb.org/Articles/pact.htm (accessed February 14, 2016).

33. American Association for Community Psychiatrists, *Position Statement on Persons with Mental Illness Behind Bars, 1999,* www.wpic.pitt.edu/aacp/finds/mibb.html (accessed February 14, 2016). See also Arthur J. Lurigio, "Effective Services for Parolees with Mental Illnesses," *Crime & Delinquency,* vol. 47, no. 3 (July 2001), pp. 446–461;

other recommendations can be found in Elaine A. Lord, "The Challenges of Mentally Ill Female Offenders in Prison," *Criminal Justice and Behavior,* vol. 35, no. 8 (August 2008), pp. 928–942; Kenneth Adams and Joseph Ferrandino, "Managing Mentally Ill Inmates in Prison," *Criminal Justice and Behavior,* vol. 35, no. 8 (August 2008), pp. 913–927.

34. Joann B. Morton, *An Administrative Overview of the Older Inmate* (Washington, DC: National Institute of Corrections, August 1992), www.nicic.org.

35. Inimal M. Chettiar, W.C. Bunting, and Geoffrey Schotter, *At America's Expense: The Mass Incarceration of the Elderly* (New York: American Civil Liberties Union, June 2012).

36. Ibid.

37. Ibid.

38. Ryan S. King and Marc Mauer, *Aging Behind Bars: "Three Strikes" Seven Years Later* (Washington, DC: The Sentencing Project, August 2001).

39. Anne Seidlitz, "National Prison Hospice Association Facilities Deal with Inmate Deaths," *CorrectCare,* vol. 12, no. 1 (Spring 1998), p. 10; see "Appendix" in Statement of Professor Jonathan Turley before a Joint Hearing of the Senate Subcommittee on Aging and Long Term Care, Senate Committee on Public Safety, and Senate Select Committee on the California Correctional System, February 25, 2003.

40. Michael J. Osofeky, Philip J. Zimbardo, and Burl Cain, "Revolutionizing Prison Hospice: The Interdisciplinary Approach of the Louisiana State Penitentiary at Angola," *Corrections Compendium,* vol. 29, no. 4 (2004), pp. 5–7; Emma Quail, "Prisons Get Grayer, But Efforts to Release the Dying Lag," *City Limits,* August 6, 2013, www.citylimits.org (accessed February 29, 2016).

41. Osborne Association, *The High Costs of Low Risk: The Crisis of America's Aging Prison Population* (Bronx, NY: Osborne Association, July 2014).

42. As quoted in Mark Johnson, "No-Risk Inmates' Release Debated: Dying, Disabled, Aged Are Eligible," *The News and Observer,* January 22, 2009, www.newsobserver.com (accessed February 29, 2016).

43. Ronald H. Aday, "Golden Years Behind Bars: Special Programs and Facilities for Elderly Inmates," *Federal Probation,* vol. 58, no. 2 (June 1994), pp. 47–54; Brie A. Williams et al., "Being Old and Doing Time: Functional Impairment and Adverse Experiences of Geriatric Female Prisoners," *Journal of the American Geriatric Society,* vol. 54, no. 2 (April 2006), pp. 702–707.

44. *Goodman & United States* v. *Georgia,* 546 U.S. 126 (2006).

45. American Civil Liberties Union, *At America's Expense: The Mass Incarceration of the Elderly,* p. ii.

46. Ibid., p. ii.

47. Pew Charitable Trusts, *State Prison Health Care Spending* (Washington, DC: Pew Charitable Trusts, July 2014).

48. Karl Brown, "Managing Sexually Transmitted Diseases in Jails," *HEPP Report,* vol. 6, no. 9 (September 2003), pp. 1–3.

49. *Estelle* v. *Gamble,* 429 U.S. 97 (1976).

50. Vaughn and Carroll, "Separate and Unequal," pp. 3–40.

51. Civil Rights of Institutionalized Persons Act, 42 U.S.C. 1997 et seq. (1976 ed., Supp. IV), as modified 1980. (Current through P.L. 104–150, approved June 3, 1996.)

52. *Pennsylvania Department of Corrections* v. *Yeskey,* 524 U.S. 206 (1998).

53. Associated Press, "Supreme Court Upholds Rights of Disabled Inmates," June 15, 1998; *Goodman &United States* v. *Georgia.*

GLOSSARY

Numbers in parentheses indicate the pages on which the terms are defined.

A

absconding   Fleeing without permission of the jurisdiction in which the offender is required to stay. (92)

accreditation   The process through which correctional facilities and agencies can measure themselves against nationally adopted standards and through which they can receive formal recognition and accredited status.

adjudication   The process by which a court arrives at a final decision in a case; or the second stage of the juvenile justice process in which the court decides whether the offender is formally responsible for (guilty of) the alleged offense. (12)

administrative officers   Those who control keys and weapons and sometimes oversee visitation. (248)

aggravating circumstances   Factors that may increase the culpability of the offender. (52)

AIDS (acquired immunodeficiency syndrome)   A disease of the human immune system that is characterized cytologically, especially by reduction in the numbers of CD4-bearing helper T cells to 20 percent or less of normal, rendering a person highly vulnerable to life-threatening conditions. The disease is caused by infection with HIV commonly transmitted in infected blood and bodily secretions (as semen), especially during sexual intercourse and intravenous drug use. (331)

Americans with Disabilities Act (ADA)   Public Law 101-336, enacted July 26, 1990, which prohibits discrimination and ensures equal opportunity for people with disabilities in employment, state and local government services, public accommodations, commercial facilities, and transportation. It also mandates the establishment of TDD/telephone relay services. (339)

arraignment   An appearance in court prior to trial in a criminal proceeding. (13)

Auburn system   The second historical phase of prison discipline, implemented at New York's Auburn prison in 1815. It followed the Pennsylvania system and allowed inmates to work silently together during the day, but they were isolated at night. (165)

average daily population (ADP)   The sum of the number of inmates in a jail or prison each day for a year, divided by the total number of days in the year. (130)

B

bail   A written obligation with or without collateral security, given to a court to guarantee appearance before the court. (127)

balancing test   A method the U.S. Supreme Court uses to decide prisoners' rights cases, weighing the rights claimed by inmates against the legitimate needs of prisoners. (305)

bifurcated trial   Two separate hearings for different issues in a trial, one for guilt and the other for punishment. (52)

biometrics   The automated identification or verification of human identity through measurable physiological and behavioral traits. (195)

block officers   Those responsible for supervising inmates in housing areas. (247)

boot camp   A short institutional term of confinement that includes a physical regimen designed to develop self-discipline, respect for authority, responsibility, and a sense of accomplishment. (115)

C

capital crime   A crime for which the death penalty may but need not necessarily be imposed. (47)

capital punishment   Lawful imposition of the death penalty. (45)

case investigation   The first major role of probation officers, consisting of interviewing the defendant and preparing the presentence report (PSR). (82)

certification   A credentialing process, usually involving testing and career development assessment, through which the skills, knowledge, and abilities of correctional personnel can be formally recognized. (28)

chlamydia   The most common sexually transmitted disease. Caused by the bacteria *Chlamydia trachomatis,* it can affect the eyes, lungs, or urogenital (urinary-genital) area, depending on the age of the person infected and how the infection is transmitted. (343)

citation   A type of nonfinancial pretrial release similar to a traffic ticket. It binds the defendant to appear in court on a future date.

civil liability   A legal obligation to another person to do, pay, or make good something. (298)

clemency   Kindness, mercy, forgiveness, or leniency, usually relating to criminal acts.

cocorrections   The incarceration and interaction of female and male offenders under a single institutional administration. (290)

coed prison   A prison housing both female and male offenders. (290)

community corrections   A philosophy of correctional treatment that embraces (1) decentralization of authority, (2) citizen participation, (3) redefinition of the population of offenders for whom incarceration is most appropriate, and (4) emphasis on rehabilitation through community programs. (118)

community corrections acts (CCAs)   State laws that give economic grants to local communities to establish community corrections goals and policies and to develop and operate community corrections programs. (118)

community service   A sentence to serve a specified number of hours working in unpaid positions with nonprofit or tax-supported agencies. (106)

compensatory damages   Money a court may award as payment for actual losses suffered by a plaintiff, including out-of-pocket expenses incurred in filing the suit, other forms of monetary or material loss, and pain, suffering, and mental anguish. (299)

concurrent sentences   Sentences served together. (42)

conditional release   Pretrial release under minimum or moderately restrictive conditions with little monitoring or compliance. It includes ROR, supervised pretrial release, and third-party release.

consent decree   A written compact, sanctioned by a court, between parties in a civil case, specifying how disagreements between them are to be resolved.

constitutional rights   The personal and due process rights guaranteed to individuals by the U.S. Constitution and its amendments, especially the first 10 amendments, known as the Bill of Rights. Constitutional rights are the basis of most inmate rights. (297)

contraband   Any item that represents a serious threat to the safety and security of the institution. (193)

correctional clients   Prison inmates, probationers, parolees, offenders assigned to alternative sentencing programs, and those held in jails. (9)

correctional officer personalities   The distinctive personal characteristics of correctional officers, including behavioral, emotional, and social traits. (245)

corrections   All the various aspects of the pretrial and post conviction management of individuals accused or convicted of crimes. (15)

corrections professional   A dedicated person of high moral character and personal integrity who is employed in the field of corrections and takes professionalism to heart. (28)

cost-benefit analysis   A systematic process used to calculate the costs of a program relative to its benefits. Programs showing the largest benefit per unit of expenditure are seen as the most effective. (21)

crime   A violation of the criminal law. (4)

crime rate   The number of major crimes reported for each unit of population.

criminal justice   The process of achieving justice through the application of the criminal law and through the workings of the criminal justice system. Also, the study of the field of criminal justice. (10)

criminal justice system   The collection of all the agencies that perform criminal justice functions, whether these are operations or administration or technical support. The basic divisions of the criminal justice system are police, courts, and corrections. (11)

cruel and unusual punishment   A penalty that is grossly disproportionate to the offense or that violates today's broad and idealistic concepts of dignity, civilized standards, humanity, and decency (*Estelle* v. *Gamble,* 1976, and *Hutto* v. *Finney,* 1978). In the area of capital punishment, cruel and unusual punishments are those that involve torture, a lingering death, or unnecessary pain. (310)

custodial staff   Those staff members most directly involved in managing the inmate population. (240)

D

day fine   A financial penalty scaled both to the defendant's ability to pay and the seriousness of the crime. (103)

day reporting center (DRC)   A nonresidential facility to which an offender reports every day or several days a week for supervision and treatment. (108)

death penalty   The punishment of execution, imposed on a person who had been legally convicted of a capital crime.

death row   A prison area housing inmates who have been sentenced to death.

deliberate indifference   Intentional and willful indifference. Within the field of correctional practice, the term refers to calculated inattention to unconstitutional conditions of confinement. (311)

deprivation theory   The belief that inmate subcultures develop in response to the deprivations in prison life. (270)

deserts   See **just deserts.** (36)

design capacity   The number of inmates that planners or architects intend for the facility. (179)

deterrence   The discouragement or prevention of crimes through the fear of punishment. (37)

direct-supervision jail   See **third-generation jail.** (135)

discretionary release   Early release based on the paroling authority's assessment of eligibility. (202)

doctrine of sovereign immunity   A historical legal doctrine that held that a governing body or its representatives could not be sued because it made the law and therefore could not be bound by it. (321)

drug court   A special court that is given responsibility to treat, sanction, and reward drug offenders with punishment more restrictive than regular probation but less severe than incarceration. (100)

due process   A right guaranteed by the Fifth, Sixth, and Fourteenth Amendments to the U.S. Constitution and generally understood, in legal contexts, to mean the expected course of legal proceedings according to the rules and forms established for the protection of persons' rights. (313)

E

equity   The sentencing principle that similar crimes and similar criminals should be treated alike and sentences should be guided by established, regularly applied standards or guidelines. (65)

evidence-based corrections (EBC)   (also called *evidence-based penology*) The application of social scientific techniques to the study of everyday corrections procedures for the purpose of increasing effectiveness and enhancing the efficient use of available resources. (21)

evidence-based practice (EBP)   The implementation of programs that have been studied and found to be effective. (21)

exonerate   To clear of blame and release from death row. (489)

F

fair sentencing   Sentencing practices that incorporate fairness for both victims and offenders. *Fairness* is said to be achieved by implementing principles of proportionality, equity, social debt, and truth in sentencing. (64)

Federal Prison Industries (FPI)   A federal, paid inmate work program and self-supporting corporation. (176)

felony   A serious criminal offense; specifically, one punishable by death or by incarceration in a prison facility for more than a year. (8)

fine   A financial penalty used as a criminal sanction. (103)

first-generation jail   Jail with multiple-occupancy cells or dormitories that line corridors arranged like spokes. Inmate supervision is intermittent; staff must patrol the corridors to observe inmates in their cells. (134)

frivolous lawsuits   Lawsuits with no foundation in fact. They are generally brought for publicity, political, or other reasons not related to law. (315)

G

gain time   Time taken off an inmate's sentence for participating in certain positive activities such as going to school, learning a trade, and working in prison. (242)

gender-responsiveness   The intentional creation of an environment that reflects an understanding of the realities of women's lives and addresses the special issues of women in correctional settings. (286)

general deterrence   The use of the example of individual punishment to dissuade others from committing crimes. (38)

genital herpes   A sexually transmitted disease caused by the herpes simplex virus or HSV. It is one of the most common STDs in the United States. (343)

gonorrhea   The second most common sexually transmitted disease. Often called *the clap*, gonorrhea is caused by the *Neisseria gonorrhea* bacteria found in moist areas of the body. Infection occurs with contact to any of these areas. (343)

guided discretion   Decision making bounded by general guidelines, rules, or laws. (52)

H

hands-off doctrine   A historical policy of the American courts not to intervene in prison management. Courts tended to follow the doctrine until the late 1960s. (294)

HIV (human immunodeficiency virus)   A group of retroviruses that infect and destroy helper T cells of the immune system, causing the marked reduction in their numbers that is diagnostic of AIDS. (331)

hospice   An interdisciplinary, comfort-oriented care facility that helps seriously ill patients die with dignity and humanity in an environment that facilitates mental and spiritual preparation for the natural process of dying. (339)

I

importation theory   The belief that inmate subcultures are brought into prison from the outside world. (270)

incapacitation   The use of imprisonment or other means to reduce an offender's capability to commit future offenses. (38)

individualization   The sentencing principle that unique circumstances and attributes of each case and each person entering the criminal justice system should inform the sentence and the rehabilitation programs, treatment, and services provided. (65)

industrial shop and school officers   Those who ensure efficient use of training and educational resources within the prison. (248)

infraction   A minor violation of state statute or local ordinance punishable by a fine or other penalty, or by a specified, usually very short term of incarceration. (9)

injunction   A judicial order to do or refrain from doing a particular act. (299)

inmate roles   Prison lifestyles; also, forms of ongoing social accommodation to prison life. (272)

inmate subculture   (also called *prisoner subculture*) The habits, customs, mores, values, beliefs, or superstitions of the body of inmates incarcerated in correctional institutions; also, the inmate social world. (269)

inmates with special needs   Prisoners who exhibit unique physical, mental, social, and programmatic needs that distinguish them from other prisoners and to whom jail and prison management and staff have to respond in nontraditional and innovative. (326)

institutional corrections   That aspect of the correctional enterprise that "involves the incarceration and rehabilitation of adults and juveniles convicted of offenses against the law, and the confinement of persons suspected of a crime awaiting trial and adjudication." (14)

institutional needs   Prison administration interests recognized by the courts as justifying some restrictions on the constitutional rights of prisoners. Those interests are maintenance of institutional *order*, maintenance of institutional *security*, *safety* of prison inmates and staff, and *rehabilitation* of inmates. (297)

integration model   A combination of importation theory and deprivation theory. The belief that, in childhood, some inmates acquired, usually from peers, values that support law-violating behavior but that the norms and standards in prison also affect inmates. (270)

intensive supervision probation (ISP)   Control of offenders in the community under strict conditions, by means of frequent reporting to a probation officer whose caseload is generally limited to 30 offenders. (99)

intermediate sanctions   New punishment options developed to fill the gap between traditional probation and traditional jail or prison sentences and to better match the severity of punishment to the seriousness of the crime. (96)

J

jail accreditation   Process through which correctional facilities and agencies can measure themselves against nationally adopted standards and through which they can receive formal recognition and accredited status. (157)

jails   Locally operated correctional facilities that confine people before or after conviction. (130)

jurisdiction   The power, right, or authority of a court to interpret and apply the law. (300)

just deserts   Punishment deserved. A just deserts perspective on criminal sentencing holds that criminal offenders are morally blameworthy and are therefore *deserving* of punishment. (36)

justice reinvestment   The practice of reducing spending on prisons and investing a portion of the savings into infrastructure and civic institutions located in high-risk neighborhoods. (181)

L

legitimate penological objectives   The realistic concerns that correctional officers and administrators have for the integrity and security of the correctional institution and the safety of staff and inmates. (305)

M

mandatory death penalty   A death sentence that the legislature has required to be imposed upon people convicted of certain offenses. (52)

mandatory release   Early release after a time period specified by law. (203)

mass incarceration   The overuse of correctional facilities, particularly prisons, in the United States as determined by historical and cross-cultural standards. We live in an era of mass incarceration. (4)

maximum- or close/high-security prison   A prison designed, organized, and staffed to confine the most dangerous offenders for long periods. It has a highly secure perimeter, barred cells, and a high staff-to-inmate ratio. It imposes strict controls on the movement of inmates and visitors, and it offers few programs, amenities, or privileges. (186)

medium-security prison   A prison that confines offenders considered less dangerous than those in maximum security, for both short and long periods. It places fewer controls on inmates' and visitors' freedom of movement than does a maximum-security facility. It has barred cells and a fortified perimeter. The staff-to-inmate ratio is generally lower than that in a maximum-security facility, and the level of amenities and privileges is slightly higher. (187)

minimum-security prison   A prison that confines the least dangerous offenders for both short and long periods. It allows as much freedom of movement and as many privileges and amenities as are consistent with the goals of the facility. It may have dormitory housing, and the staff-to-inmate ratio is relatively low. (187)

misdemeanor   A relatively minor violation of the criminal law, such as petty theft or simple assault, punishable by confinement for one year or less. (8)

mission   That which is done to support an organization's purpose. (257)

mitigating circumstances   Factors that, although not justifying or excusing an action, may reduce the culpability of the offender. (52)

N

new offense violation   Arrest and prosecution for the commission of a new crime. (92)

nolo contendere   A plea of "no contest." A no-contest plea may be used by a defendant who does not wish to contest conviction. Because the plea does not admit guilt, however, it cannot provide the basis for later civil suits. (13)

nominal damages   Small amounts of money a court may award when inmates have sustained no actual damages, but there is clear evidence that their rights have been violated. (299)

noninstitutional corrections   (also called *community corrections*) That aspect of the correctional enterprise that includes "pardon, probation, and parole activities, correctional administration not directly connectable to institutions, and miscellaneous [activities] not directly related to institutional care." (14)

nonrevocable parole (NRP)   A type of unsupervised parole that cannot be revoked for technical violations; the person does not report to a parole officer. (220)

O

open institution   A minimum-security facility that has no fences or walls surrounding it. (187)

operational capacity   The number of inmates that a facility's staff, existing programs, and services can accommodate. (179)

P

pains of imprisonment   Major problems that inmates face, such as loss of liberty and personal autonomy, lack of material possessions, loss of heterosexual relationships, and reduced personal security. (270)

pardon   An executive act that removes both punishment and guilt.

parole   The conditional release of a prisoner, prior to completion of the imposed sentence, under the supervision of a parole officer. (202)

parole eligibility date   The earliest date on which an inmate might be paroled. (214)

parolee (aka formerly incarcerated)   A person who is conditionally released from prison to community supervision. (205)

paroling authority   A person or correctional agency (often called a *parole board* or *parole commission*) that has the authority to grant parole, revoke parole, and discharge from parole. (214)

parsimony   Sentences should be the least necessary in a given situation to attain its end. Imposition of a sentence more severe than is necessary is harmful. (65)

pay-to-stay jail   (also called *self-pay jails*) An alternative to serving time in a county jail. Offenders convicted of minor offenses are offered privileges for a fee from $85 to $255 per day. (150)

penitentiary   The earliest form of large-scale incarceration. It punished criminals by isolating them so that they could reflect on their misdeeds, repent, and reform. (165)

Pennsylvania system   (also called *separate system*) The first confinement in silence instead of corporal punishment; conceived by the American Quakers in 1790 and implemented at the Walnut Street Jail. (165)

perimeter security officers   Those assigned to security (or gun) towers, wall posts, and perimeter patrols. These officers are charged with preventing escapes and detecting and preventing intrusions. (248)

pleasure-pain principle   The idea that actions are motivated primarily by a desire to experience pleasure and avoid pain. (38)

precedent   A previous judicial decision that judges should consider in deciding future cases. (302)

pretrial detainee   A defendant who is held in jail prior to trial on criminal charges because no bail is posted or bail is denied. (127)

principle of least eligibility   The requirement that prison conditions—including the delivery of health care—must be a step below those of the working class and people on welfare. (333)

prison   A state or federal confinement facility that has custodial authority over adults sentenced to confinement. (4)

prison argot   The special language of the inmate subculture. (272)

prison code   A set of norms and values among prison inmates. It is generally antagonistic to the official administration and rehabilitation programs of the prison. (271)

prisoner subculture   See **inmate subculture**. (269)

prisoners' rights   Constitutional guarantees of free speech, religious practice, due process, and other private and personal rights as well as constitutional protections against cruel and unusual punishments made applicable to prison inmates by the federal courts. (297)

prisonization   The process by which inmates adapt to prison society; the taking on of the ways, mores, customs, and general culture of the penitentiary. (270)

privatization   A contract process that shifts public functions, responsibilities, and capital assets, in whole or in part, from the public sector to the private sector. (152)

probation   The conditional release of a convicted offender into the community, under the supervision of a probation officer. It is conditional because it can be revoked if certain conditions are not met. (71)

profession   An occupation granted high social status by virtue of the personal integrity of its members. (25)

professional associations   Organized groups of like-minded individuals who work to enhance the professional status of members of their occupational group. (28)

program staff   Those staff members concerned with encouraging prisoners to participate in educational, vocational, and treatment programs. (240)

property crime   Burglary, larceny-theft, motor vehicle theft, and arson as reported by the FBI's Uniform Crime Reporting Program.

proportionality   The sentencing principle that the severity of punishment should match the seriousness of the crime for which the sentence is imposed. (64)

pseudofamilies   Family-like structures, common in women's prisons, in which inmates assume roles similar to those of family members in free society. (285)

punitive damages   Money a court may award to punish a wrongdoer when a wrongful act was intentional and malicious or was done with reckless disregard for the rights of the victim. (299)

purpose   The reason for an organization's existence. (257)

R

racism   Social practices that explicitly or implicitly attribute merits or allocate value to individuals solely because of their race. (30)

rated capacity   The maximum number of beds or inmates allocated to each jail facility by a state or local rating official. (148)

recidivism   The repetition of criminal behavior; generally defined as *rearrest*. It is the primary outcome measure for probation as it is for all corrections programs. (80)

reentry   The transition offenders make from prison or jail to the community. (153)

reentry court   A court that manages the return to the community of individuals released from prison. (226)

rehabilitation   (also called *reformation*) The changing of criminal lifestyles into law-abiding ones by "correcting" the behavior of offenders through treatment, education, and training. (39)

reintegration   The process of making the offender a productive member of the community. (39)

release on bail   The release of a person upon that person's financial guarantee to appear in court.

release on recognizance (ROR)   Pretrial release on the defendant's promise to appear for trial. It requires no cash guarantee.

relief officers   Experienced correctional officers who know and can perform almost any custody role within the institution, used to temporarily replace officers who are sick or on vacation or to meet staffing shortages. (248)

remote-location monitoring   Technologies, including Global Positioning System (GPS) devices and electronic monitoring (EM), that probation and parole officers use to monitor remotely the physical location of an offender. (111)

reprieve   An executive act that reduces the severity of punishment (e.g., from death to life imprisonment) but the person remains guilty.

residential reentry center (RRC)   A medium-security correctional setting that resident offenders are permitted to leave regularly—unaccompanied by staff—for work, education or vocational programs, or treatment in the community but require them to return to a locked facility each evening. (113)

restoration   The process of returning to their previous condition all those involved in or affected by crime—including victims, offenders, and society. (40)

restorative justice   A systematic response to wrongdoing that emphasizes healing the wounds of victims, offenders, and communities caused or revealed by crime . (40)

retribution   A sentencing goal that involves retaliation against a criminal perpetrator. (36)

revenge   Punishment as vengeance; an emotional response to real or imagined injury or insult. (36)

revocation   The formal termination of an offender's conditional freedom. (90)

revocation hearing   A due process hearing that must be conducted to determine whether the conditions of probation have been violated before probation can be revoked and the offender removed from the community. (90)

roadmap to reentry   Principles of correctional reform to reduce recidivism by supporting and strengthening reentry programs and resources at the Federal Bureau of Prisons. (183)

roles   The normal patterns of behavior expected of those holding particular social positions. (239)

S

salient factor score (SFS)   A scale, developed from a risk-screening instrument, used to predict parole outcome.

second-generation jail   Jail where staff remain in a secure control booth surrounded by inmate housing areas called *pods* and surveillance is remote. (134)

self-pay-jails   See pay-to-stay jail.

sentence   The penalty a court imposes on a person convicted of a crime. (35)

sentencing   The imposition of a criminal sanction by a sentencing authority, such as a judge. (35)

serious error   Error that substantially undermines the reliability of the guilt finding or death sentence imposed at trial. (52)

social order   The smooth functioning of social institutions, the existence of positive and productive relations among individual members of society, and the orderly functioning of society as a whole. (35)

special master   A person appointed by the court to act as its representative to oversee remedy of a violation and provide regular progress reports. (191)

specific deterrence   The deterrence of the individual being punished from committing additional crimes. (37)

staff roles   The normal patterns of behavior expected of correctional staff members in particular jobs. (239)

staff subculture   The beliefs, values, and behavior of staff. They differ greatly from those of the inmate subculture. (243)

stress   Tension in a person's body or mind, resulting from physical, chemical, or emotional factors. (251)

structured conflict   The tensions between prison staff members and inmates that arise out of the correctional setting. (243)

subculture   The beliefs, values, behavior, and material objects shared by a particular group of people within a larger society. (243)

substance-abusing inmate   An incarcerated individual suffering from dependency on one or more substances including alcohol and a wide range of drugs. (327)

supermax housing   A freestanding facility, or a distinct unit within a facility, that provides for management and secure control of inmates who have been officially designated as exhibiting violent or serious and disruptive behavior while incarcerated. (189)

supervision   The second major role of probation officers, consisting of resource mediation, surveillance, and enforcement. (85)

sustainable justice   Criminal laws and criminal justice institutions, policies, and practices that achieve justice in the present without compromising the ability of future generations to have the benefits of a just society. (7)

syphilis   A sexually transmitted disease caused by the bacteria *Treponema pallidum*. If left untreated, syphilis can cause serious heart abnormalities, mental disorders, blindness, other neurological problems, and death. Syphilis is transmitted when infected lesions come in contact with the soft skin of the mucous membrane. (343)

T

technical violation   A failure to comply with the conditions of probation or parole. (92)

third-generation jail   (also called *direct-supervision jail*) A jail where inmates are housed in small groups, or pods, staffed 24 hours a day by specifically trained officers. Officers interact with inmates to help change behavior. Bars and metal doors are absent, reducing noise and dehumanization. (135)

three-strikes laws   Three-strikes laws impose mandatory prison sentences, generally a life sentence, on those convicted of an offense if they have been previously convicted of two prior serious criminal offenses. (38)

tort   A civil wrong, a wrongful act, or a wrongful breach of duty, other than a breach of contract, whether intentional or accidental, from which injury to another occurs. (299)

total admission   The total number of people admitted to jail each year. (130)

total institution   A place where the same people work, play, eat, sleep, and recreate together on a continuous basis. The term was developed by the sociologist Erving Goffman to describe prisons and other facilities. (268)

totality of conditions   A standard to be used in evaluating whether prison conditions are cruel and unusual. (311)

truth in sentencing (TIS)   The sentencing principle that requires an offender to serve a substantial portion of the sentence and reduces the discrepancy between the sentence imposed and actual time spent in prison. (38)

U

UNICOR   The trade name of Federal Prison Industries. UNICOR provides such products as U.S. military uniforms, electronic cable assemblies, and modular furniture. (176)

V

victim-impact statement   A description of the harm and suffering that a crime has caused victims and survivors. (41)

victims' rights   The fundamental rights of victims to be represented equitably throughout the criminal justice process. (461)

violent crime   Interpersonal crime that involves the use of force by offenders or results in injury or death to victims. In the FBI's Uniform Crime Reports, violent crimes are murder, forcible rape, robbery, and aggravated assault.

vision   The planned future direction of an organization. (257)

W

work detail supervisors   Those who oversee the work of individual inmates and inmate work crews. (247)

writ of *habeas corpus*   An order that directs the person detaining a prisoner to bring him or her before a judge, who will determine the lawfulness of the imprisonment. (298)

Y

yard officers   Those who supervise inmates in the prison yard. (248)

CASE INDEX

SUBJECT INDEX

A

Abdel-Rahman, Omar, 38, 261
absconding, 92
Abu Ghraib prison (Iraq), 167
accountability, 26
accreditation, 26, 157
acquired immunodeficiency syndrome (AIDS), 331
   See also AIDS/HIV
ACT (Assertive Community Treatment) Program, 336–337
addiction theory, for female offenders, 142
adjudication, 12
administrative officers, 248
advisory sentencing guidelines, 59
Affordable Care Act (ACA) of 2011, 342
African American people. *See* ethnicity/race
age. *See also* children
   older inmates, 338–343
   prison inmate, 173, 281, 338–343
aggravating circumstances, 52
agitator inmate role, 274
AIDS/HIV, 171, 208, 237, 326, 327, 329, 332–334
   dealing with inmates, 334
   definitions, 331
   education and prevention, 334
   legal issues, 344
   treatment, 332–334
Alabama
   correctional econometrics, 221
   female inmates, 280–281, 320–321
   jails/prisons, 280–281, 320–321
   parole and reentry, 214, 221
Ala-Pietila, Pekka, 104
Alaska
   jails/prisons, 130
   marijuana legalization, 61
   parole and reentry, 217
Albin, Lisa, 248–249
Alcatraz (California), 167, 189
alcohol. *See* substance-abusing inmates
Alexander, Travis, 14
al-Qaeda, 262
American Association for Community Psychiatrists, 337
American Bar Association (ABA)
   disclosure of presentencing report, 84
   jails, 156–157
   pretrial release standard, 131
American colonies, indentured servants, 203–204
American Correctional Association (ACA), 1, 25
   certification, 28–29
   community corrections, 119
   community service and restorative justice, 107, 108
   correctional officer characteristics, 244
   correctional officer wages, 181
   ethics, 26–28
   higher education policy, 29
   identifying inmates with special needs, 327

   inmate education programs, 177
   intermediate sanctions, 98, 108
   jail standards, 158
   mothers in prison, 287
   offenders with special needs, 327
   professional development, 28
   role of corrections, 15–16
   sentencing, 59–60
   standards and accreditation, 26
   universal precautions, 334
   women in corrections, 249
   women's prison guidelines, 280
American Correctional Health Services Association, 343
American Jail Association (AJA), 1, 28
   Code of Ethics for Jail Officers, 157
   intermediate sanctions, 97–99
   Jail Manager Certification Commission (JMCC), 29
   jail standards, 157
   mission statement, 132
American Medical Association (AMA), 343
American Probation and Parole Association (APPA), 1, 28, 73, 74, 80–81, 87–88, 98, 203, 206, 224
American Public Health Association, 287
American Revolution, 204
Americans with Disabilities Act (ADA) of 1990, 339, 344
Amnesty International, 46
Antiterrorism and Effective Death Penalty Act (AEDPA) of 1996, 54
Aos, Steve, 173
APIC, 154
APPA. *See* American Probation and Parole Association (APPA)
appellate review, 13
Aramark, 149
Arias, Jodi, 14
Arizona
   correctional officer job satisfaction, 255
   intermediate sanctions, 106
   jails/prisons, 149, 169, 191, 195
   parole and reentry, 207
   probation, 207
Arkansas
   intermediate sanctions, 61
   jails/prisons, 296, 311–312
   parole and reentry, 223
   sentencing, 180
arraignment, 12
arrest, 11, 129–130
Asian people. *See* ethnicity/race
Assertive Community Treatment (ACT) Program, 336–337
Asylums (Goffman), 268
Attica Correctional Facility (New York State), 167, 301
Auburn system, 165, 166
Augustus, John, 75–76, 166
Australia
   exile and transportation of prisoners, 203–205
   intermediate sanctions, 107
   parole, 203–204
average daily population (ADP), 130–131, 148

N